Reading Poetry

Teaching at university level which is not also in touch with research is not university teaching. (John Smith, late leader of the British Labour Party, 1993)

Reading Poetry
An Introduction

Second edition

Tom Furniss and Michael Bath

PEARSON
Longman

Harlow, England • London • New York • Boston • San Francisco • Toronto
Sydney • Tokyo • Singapore • Hong Kong • Seoul • Taipei • New Delhi
Cape Town • Madrid • Mexico City • Amsterdam • Munich • Paris • Milan

Pearson Education Limited

Edinburgh Gate
Harlow CM20 2JE
United Kingdom
Tel: +44 (0)1279 623623
Fax: +44 (0)1279 431059
Website: www.pearsoned.co.uk

First edition published in Great Britain in 1996
Second edition published 2007
© Pearson Education Limited 2007

The rights of Tom Furniss and Michael Bath to be
identified as authors of this work have been asserted
by them in accordance with the Copyright,
Designs and Patents Act 1988.

ISBN: 978-0-582-89420-4

British Library Cataloguing in Publication Data
A CIP catalogue record for this book can be obtained from the British Library

10   9   8   7   6   5   4   3   2
11   10   09   08   07

Set by 35 in 10.5/13pt Sabon
Printed in Malaysia (CTP-VVP)

The Publisher's policy is to use paper manufactured from sustainable forests.

Contents

Contents

To all our students and teachers,
past, present and future
and to Linda Glenn

Acknowledgements

We would like to thank a number of readers who have read parts of the manuscript at various stages in the composition and/or made helpful suggestions: Annabel Bath, Lowell Edmunds, Donald Fraser, Linda Glenn, David Goldie, Suzanne Hall, Kenneth McNeil, Martin Montgomery, Jonathan Sawday, Alison Thorne and Zoë Wicomb. Special thanks are due to Derek Attridge, who generously read and commented on most of the first draft of the first edition and was supportive throughout. Thanks are also due to the four anonymous readers for Harvester, who made useful and provocative suggestions at an early stage of the first edition, and to the reader who read the whole typescript of the first edition when it went to press. We would also like to acknowledge the generosity of colleagues in the Department of English Studies at the University of Strathclyde, who covered teaching and administrative duties during a period of sabbatical leave which enabled us to complete the first edition. For invaluable help on the second edition we would especially like to thank Donald Fraser, Linda Glenn, Zoë Wicomb, our editor Philip Langeskov, our copy-editor Helen MacFadyen, and the anonymous reader whose report included a number of suggestions for improvements.

We are grateful to the following for permission to reproduce copyright material:

Faber and Faber (World excluding USA) and Farrar, Strauss and Giroux, LLC (USA) for 'The Thought-Fox' from COLLECTED POEMS by Ted Hughes. Copyright © 2003 by The Estate of Ted Hughes; Carcanet Press Limited (UK/Commonwealth) and New Directions Publishing Corp. (USA/Canada) for William Carlos Williams, 'To a Poor Old Woman', 'Spring and All' and 'This is Just to Say', from COLLECTED POEMS: 1909–1939, vol. 1. Copyright © 1938 by New Directions Publishing Corp. Reprinted by permission of New Directions Publishing Corp.; for HD (Hilda Doolittle), 'Sea Rose', from COLLECTED POEMS, 1912–1944. Copyright © 1982 by The Estate of Hilda Doolittle. Reprinted by permission of New Directions Publishing Corp.; Carcanet Press Limited/Elizabeth Barrett for 'Spring' and Untitled Sonnet, from *Selected Poems* published by Carcanet Press Ltd. Reprinted by permission (UK/Commonwealth) or permission requested (USA/Canada); Carcanet Press for Hugh MacDiarmid, 'In the Children's Hospital', from *Complete Poems*, vol. 1; for Petrarch, 'Lord Love', from *Canzoniere*, tr. J.G. Nichols (2000); Faber and Faber (World excluding USA and Canada) and Farrar, Strauss and Giroux, LLC (USA and Canada) for 'Sonnet 23' from COLLECTED POEMS: 1937–1971 by John Berryman. Copyright © 1989 by Kate Donahue Berryman; for Edwin Morgan, 'Glasgow Sonnets, 10', from

Collected Poems 1949–87 (1990); and for Edmund Blunden, 'Vlamertinghe', from *Selected Poems* (1993); W.W. Norton & Company for E.E. Cummings, 'o sweet spontaneous', 'Me up at does' and 'somewhere i have never travelled, gladly beyond', from *Complete Poems 1904–1962*. 'O sweet spontaneous' , 'Me up at does' and 'somewhere i have never travelled, gladly beyond' are reprinted from COMPLETE POEMS 1904–1962, by E.E. Cummings, edited by George J. Firmage, by permission of W.W. Norton & Company. Copyright © 1991 by the Trustees for the E.E. Cummings Trust and George James Firmage; for A.R. Ammons, 'Pet Panther' from *Lake Effect Country*. Copyright © 1983 by A.R. Ammons. Used by permission of W.W. Norton & Company, Inc.; Bloodaxe Books for Eleanor Brown, 'The Lads', 'Waltz', 'Sonnet VIII' and 'What Song the Sirens Sang', from *Maiden Speech* (1996); Eleanor Brown: Maiden Speech (Bloodaxe Books, 1996) www.bloodaxebooks.com; for Jackie Kay, 'In My Country', from *Other Lovers* (1993). Jackie Kay: Other Lovers (Bloodaxe Books, 1993) www.bloodaxebooks.com; Faber and Faber (World excluding USA and Canada) and Farrar, Strauss and Giroux, LLC (USA and Canada) for excerpt from 'The Schooner Flight' and 'A Far Cry from Africa' from COLLECTED POEMS 1948–1984 by Derek Walcott. Copyright © 1986 by Derek Walcott; for Jean Binta Breeze, 'The Wife of Bath Speaks in Brixton Market', from *The Arrival of Brighteye* (2000). Jean Binta Breeze: The Arrival of Brighteye (Bloodaxe Books, 2000) www.bloodaxebooks.com; for Elizabeth Garret, 'By All Means Tell the Truth', from *A Two-Part Invention* (1998). Elizabeth Garrett: A Two-Part Invention (Bloodaxe Books, 1998) www.bloodaxebooks.com; Yale University Press for John Hollander, 'Swan and Shadow', from *Types of Shape*, copyright © 1991 by John Hollander; Scottish Academic Press for William Soutar, 'He Who Weeps', from *Poems in Scots and English* (1975); Polygon Books for Norman MacCaig, 'Fetching Cows', from *Collected Poems* (1985). 'Fetching Cows' by Norman MacCaig, from *Collected Poems* is reproduced by permission of Polygon, an imprint of Birlinn Ltd. (www.irlinn.co.uk); for Daniel O'Rourke, 'Great Western Road', from *Dream State: the New Scottish Poets*. 'Great Western Road' by Daniel O'Rourke, from *Dream State: the New Scottish Poets* is reproduced by permission of Polygon, an imprint of Birlinn Ltd. (www.birlinn.co.uk); Random House, Inc. (USA, its territories and possessions/Canada/P.I./Open Market/EU) and David Higham Associates for 'The Negro Speaks of Rivers', 'Theme for English B' and 'Harlem' from Langston Hughes, *The Collected Poems of Langston Hughes*. 'The Negro Speaks of Rivers', copyright © 1994 by the Estate of Langston Hughes, 'Harlem (2)', copyright 1951 by Langston Hughes, 'Theme for English B', copyright © 1994 by The Estate of Langston Hughes, from THE COLLECTED POEMS OF LANGSTON HUGHES by Langston Hughes, edited by Arnold Rampersad with David Roessel, Associate Editor. Used by permission of Alfred A. Knopf, a division of Random House, Inc.;

Profile Books Ltd for 'Serpent's Tail' from *Mangoes and Bullets* by John Agard; University of Illinois Press for Josephine Miles, 'Reason', from *Collected Poems, 1930–83*. Copyright 1983 by Josephine Miles. Used with permission of the Estate of Josephine Miles and the University of Illinois Press; Anvil Press Poetry for Carol Ann Duffy, 'Boy', from *The Other Country* (1990). 'Boy' is taken from 'The Other Country' by Carol Ann Duffy published by Anvil Press Poetry in 1990; BMG Music Publishing Ltd for Elvis Costello, 'Peace in Our Time'. Peace in Our Time, Words & Music by Elvis Costello © Copyright 1984 BMG Music Publishing Limited. Used by permission of Music Sales Limited. All Rights Reserved. International Copyright Secured; Faber and Faber (World excluding USA) and Oxford University Press, Inc (USA) for 'Childhood' from COLLECTED POEMS (1984) by Edwin Muir. By permission of Faber and Faber and Oxford University Press, Inc; Houghton Mifflin Company (USA) and Penguin Books for Geoffrey Hill, 'September Song', from *New & Collected Poems, 1952–1992* (1994). Reproduced by permission of Penguin Books Ltd. 'September Song' from NEW & COLLECTED POEMS, 1952–1992 by Geoffrey Hill. Copyright © 1994 by Geoffrey Hill. Reprinted by permission of Houghton Mifflin Company. All rights reserved. Faber and Faber (World excluding USA) and Farrar, Strauss and Giroux, LLC (USA) for 'Punishment' from OPENED GROUND: SELECTED POEMS 1966–1996 by Seamus Heaney. Copyright © 1998 by Seamus Heaney; Houghton Mifflin Company for Archibald MacLeish, 'Ars Poetica', from *Collected Poems, 1917–1982* (1985). 'Ars Poetica' from COLLECTED POEMS, 1917–1982 by Archibald MacLeish. Copyright © 1985 by The Estate of Archibald MacLeish. Reprinted by permission of Houghton Mifflin Company. All rights reserved. Houghton Mifflin Company (USA/Canada/Open Market) and Sterling Lord Literistic for Anne Sexton, 'Abortion', from *All My Pretty Ones* (1962). 'The Abortion' from ALL MY PRETTY ONES by Anne Sexton. Copyright © 1962 by Anne Sexton, renewed 1990 by Linda G. Sexton. Reprinted by permission of Houghton Mifflin Company and SLL/ Sterling Lord Literistic, Inc. All rights reserved; Oxford University Press for Dante, 'The Power of Love', from *Vita Nuova*, tr. Mark Musa (1992). By permission of Oxford University Press; University of Pittsburgh Press for Billy Collins, 'Taking Off Emily Dickinson's Clothes', from *Picnic, Lightning*, by Billy Collins, © 1998. Reprinted by permission of the University of Pittsburgh Press; Faber and Faber (British Commonwealth) and Random House, Inc (US, its territories and possessions, Canada, P.I, Open Market, E.U.) for 'September 1 1939' edited by Edward Mendelson, copyright 1940 and copyright renewed 1968 by W.H. Auden, from SELECTED POEMS, EXPANDED EDITION by W.H. Auden. Used by permission of Faber and Faber and Vintage Books, a division of Random House, Inc; Sangster's Book Stores Limited for 'Back to Africa' from *Jamaican Labrish* by Louise Bennett (1983); Peepal Tree Press for David Dabydeen,

'Slave Song', from *Slave Song* (Sydney: Dangroo Press, 1984; Leeds: Peepal Tree Press, 2005); Faber and Faber (World excluding US) and Farrar, Strauss and Giroux, LLC (USA) for excerpt from 'Talking in Bed' from THE WHITSUN WEDDINGS by Philip Larkin Copyright © 1988, 2003 by the Estate of Philip Larkin; Renaissance Press for George Bruce, 'What is a Haiku?', from *Through the Letterbox: Haikus by George Bruce*, illustrated by Elizabeth Blackadder, ed. Lucina Prestige, published by Renaissance Press 2003; ISBN: 0954396103; David Higham Associates and New Directions Publishing Corp. (USA/Canada) for Dylan Thomas, 'Do Not Go Gentle into That Good Night', from *Collected Poems*, published by Dent. By Dylan Thomas, from THE POEMS OF DYLAN THOMAS, copyright © 1952 by Dylan Thomas. Reprinted by permission of New Directions Publishing Corp. 'One Art' from 'THE COMPLETE POEMS 1927–1979' by Elizabeth Bishop. Copyright © 1979, 1983 by Alice Helen Methfessel. Reprinted by permission of Farrar, Straus and Giroux, LLC; Faber and Faber (British Commonwealth) and Random House, Inc (US, its territories and possessions, Canada, P.I, Open Market, E.U.) for 'Our Bias' by W.H. Auden, copyright 1940 & renewed 1968 by W.H. Auden, from COLLECTED POEMS by W.H. Auden. Used by permission of Faber and Faber and Random House, Inc; 'Song'. Copyright © 2002 by Adrienne Rich. Copyright © 1973 by W.W. Norton & Company, Inc., 'Orion'. Copyright © 2002 by Adrienne Rich. Copyright © 1969 by W.W. Norton & Company, Inc., from THE FACT OF A DOORFRAME: SELECTED POEMS 1950–2001 by Adrienne Rich. Used by permission of the author and W.W. Norton & Company, Inc.

Preface

This introduction to the study of poetry had its origins in a first-year undergraduate course taught by the authors at the University of Strathclyde in Glasgow in the early 1990s. Our decision to write the book arose from our feeling that there was no textbook available which discussed poetry in the ways in which we were trying to teach our students. Most introductions to poetry written for students seemed to us to be based on outmoded and problematic assumptions about poetry and the reading of poetry. Developments in criticism and theory over the previous twenty or thirty years had transformed academic writing about literature in general, but such research rarely filtered down into student guides to poetry. Thus a gap had opened up between academics' research interests and their teaching practices. This was largely a result of late-twentieth century developments in the discipline which could not be ignored in any teaching that accepted what we take to be a fundamental responsibility of any university course – that is, the education of students in ways that are informed by the best thinking and research. Today's students need to acquire an unprecedented range of technical, historical and theoretical skills – they have to be technically competent, theoretically literate and historically informed. In other words, students need to develop what has been called 'literary competence'. This book is designed to help students develop such competence.

It is now ten years (as we write this new preface) since the first edition of *Reading Poetry* appeared. In those ten years, the book has sold consistently well (about 10 000 copies in all) and we have received positive feedback from individual readers and students and from teachers and academics who use it for courses. In that time, some impressive textbooks on reading poetry have appeared, including John Strachan and Richard Terry's *Poetry* (2000), James Fenton's *An Introduction to English Poetry* (2003), Jeffrey Wainwright's *Poetry: The Basics* (2004), the second edition of John Lennard's *The Poetry Handbook* (2005) and no less than three new editions of X.J. Kennedy and Dana Gioia's *An Introduction to Poetry* (1998, 2002, 2004). The appearance of such books, each of which is of great interest in itself, is a hopeful sign that there might be a renewed interest in poetry in university departments of English. But none of these books tries to do what we tried to do in *Reading Poetry*, which covers a far greater range of issues and attends to them in greater theoretical and historical depth. In this way, *Reading Poetry* was and is an ambitious book, especially in terms of the way each chapter takes the reader on a journey from the basics of a topic to its sophisticated theoretical and historical implications and ends with practical exercises. Its unique approach encourages us to believe that there is scope for a second edition of *Reading Poetry*, especially because we have discovered new poets and poems since 1996 that we want to share with readers. The main differences from the first edition are the inclusion of a new chapter on Post-Colonial Poetry, a significant increase in the number of exercises at the end of chapters, a fuller discussion of 'rhyme' as an aspect of prosody, and a new Glossary of technical terms for describing poetry at the end.

One of the main problems that teachers and academics face is that it is no longer realistic – if it ever was – to assume that students come to university with any great familiarity with poetry and ways of reading it. This book is aimed at readers who have not read much poetry, and we have tried not to make too many assumptions about the kinds of knowledge which students currently bring to the texts they are required (or choose) to study at university. Many students nevertheless bring an implicit awareness of linguistic and cultural conventions and social and political issues to their reading, derived from their experience of popular cultural forms. The present book tries to make use of this knowledge, and to show how it can lead on to highly productive ways of reading poetry.

One of the traditional assumptions about reading poetry at university has been that it calls upon a range of specialised skills which demand particular kinds of instruction. Ever since English was instituted on the educational curriculum in the early-twentieth century, teachers have recognised that students find poetry particularly difficult. The growth of 'practical criticism' in the 1930s and 1940s can be seen, to a large extent, as a response to this recognition since, although 'practical criticism' was eventually applied to other genres and literary forms, it originated in the attempts of I.A. Richards and those who followed him to develop a methodical set of techniques for the close reading of poetry. More recent developments have called into question many of the theoretical assumptions and pedagogic principles on which 'practical criticism' based its analytic methods. Yet most teachers, including the authors of this book, still believe that particular kinds of close reading are fundamental to the study of literature at university. Much of what we do in this book can be seen as an attempt to introduce students to what seem to us to be the most important forms of those essential skills of close reading and analysis.

Unlike traditional exponents of 'practical criticism', however, we stress throughout this book that close reading cannot be divorced from literary theory or from history. Today's students need to recognise the theoretical basis of what they are doing when they are reading and writing about literary texts. Teachers demand increasingly sophisticated skills from students whose knowledge of the literary base is increasingly attenuated, so it is vital to work out ways of bridging this epistemological gap. Although literary theory is sometimes thought to have contributed to this problem, the best literary theory (as opposed to 'theory') is that which emerges out of insightful readings of literary texts and empowers students to examine basic principles and understand and articulate their own experience of literary texts. Our method throughout this book is continually to ask our readers to question for themselves what is going on in the process of reading, and thus to become more self-reflexive about the processes and assumptions involved in studying poetry.

In demanding greater self-awareness of our students, however, we can hardly not also require it of their teachers. Since writing the first edition of this book, more than ten years ago, we have become increasingly conscious of the extent to which the current teaching of literature (and especially poetry) in secondary schools is theoretically naïve and opaque (a situation that is partly driven by the kinds of questions that appear in public examinations at all levels). This seems rather surprising, given the fact that the academic study of literature has come through a phase of development, in the later twentieth century, that was dominated by 'theory'. The two authors of this book have no wish to impose a single theory of literature on readers or students, and do not – as it happens – share a common position on many theoretical issues. However we are firmly committed to the view that all reading habits are based on theoretical assumptions (however unformulated) and have theoretical implications (not all of which are untenable). Teaching practices and assessment criteria that are not based on explicit theoretical assumptions that would stand up to scrutiny are, we suggest, academically incompetent. In this second edition of *Reading Poetry* we have therefore challenged at least some of the prevalent assumptions that too often inflect the wording of examination questions and learning practices which many of our students will have experienced at school, because they seem to us to lack the kind of theoretical awareness that we now expect of our students. Indeed we find that we now have to put our first-year students at university through a process of un-learning before they can begin to think productively and self-reflectively about reading poetry. We placed a key statement by a British politician of the early 1990s as the epigraph to our first edition and, naturally, we considered updating it for the new edition. However, although most of our readers – even in Britain – are unlikely now to know who John Smith was, his statement that teaching that is not in touch with research is not university teaching remains as true today as it was in 1993. If it signals our continuing concern in this book to address the real issues involved in reading poetry, and to challenge the shallow, untheorised assumptions which they may have been encouraged to learn at school, then the epigraph will continue to earn its keep.

The fact that all reading is informed by theoretical assumptions means that all reading is also historical, since assumptions about what poetry is, and what reading it involves, change through history. History in this sense involves not only the historical context of poetic texts but also the history of literary forms, of writing practices and of ways of reading. We have tried to introduce students to each of these dimensions of literary history in the chapters that follow, even though we do not claim to have dealt with any of them comprehensively. We give the date of every poem cited or referred to because we believe it is important for readers to 'place' the poems we examine, even when historical issues are not under discussion. (The date is normally that of the poem's first publication; in some cases, however, if a poem was not printed until some time after it was written, the date is that of composition, where this is known.)

Although we do not assume readers' familiarity with 'major' texts and authors from the traditional canon, we have not attempted in this book either to reinstate or to replace that canon. Our choice of examples is usually determined by their intrinsic interest and their relevance to our argument, though we have also attempted to show that the skills and issues we attend to are applicable across a range of texts that are familiar and unfamiliar, canonical and marginal. One of the things we have tried to do is to read canonical and non-canonical poems alongside one another in order to see what differences each makes to the other. Our 'Key to Poems and Passages Discussed' at the end of the book is intended to offer course tutors a quick-reference guide to the primary reading which our book itself supplies; this may or may not be deemed sufficient for a particular academic course or teaching programme, though we are convinced that only wide reading of many different poems will build up the primary experience which any competent close reading requires; hence our discussions and exercises offer frequent suggestions for further reading of both primary and secondary sources in libraries or on the Internet, and one of the key skills we aim to develop is the ability to trawl such information sources. Our 'Key to Poems Discussed' will, we hope, quickly allow decisions to be made about any further reading or purchases that may be required of students when planning a teaching programme centred on *Reading Poetry*.

The book is intended for different kinds of uses and users. Teachers and university lecturers may wish to use it as a course text or as a resource for their own teaching. Students may be required to use it as a course text, but they may also find it useful for private study or as back-up reading for a poetry class in a college or university. It is hoped that non-academic readers – and even poets – may also find it stimulating and helpful. Each chapter is devoted to a particular set of skills, formal features and theoretical questions, and usually attempts to place them in a historical framework. To a certain extent, therefore, each chapter is a discrete, self-standing unit. The sequence of the chapters is carefully staged, however, so that each chapter builds on what has gone before and prepares readers for later chapters. These often return to poems or issues discussed earlier in order to develop a new point in the context of the new issue being discussed. Given that we argue, in 'Hearing Voices in Poetic Texts', that working out the speech situation is often the best way of making initial sense of a poem, we have sometimes introduced this topic much earlier in our own teaching than we do in the book, and we considered rearranging the sequence of chapters in the second edition to accommodate this. In the end, however, we decided to follow the same sequence as in the first edition, beginning with what we call a 'Formal Introduction' on the basis that we argue that the formal organisation of poetry into lines is the only consistent marker of poetry and the source of its difference from other forms of literature. Nevertheless, teachers and students may of course use the chapters in any sequence they please.

Part Three of this book contains chapters which will develop readers' confidence in researching historical, intertextual, literary and generic contexts, and not just the skills of close reading that we cover in Parts One and Two. The identification of most of these contexts requires sources of information to be found in libraries or on the Internet, and for that reason in this edition we have designed further exercises and interactive questions which develop these skills. However, it cannot be stressed too strongly that close reading is hardly ever separated from relevant research into contexts, and we make frequent cross reference in our later chapters to issues and examples which have already been discussed in earlier ones. Often the revisiting of earlier examples, once relevant contexts have been identified, can be seen to inform, or sometimes transform, our original questions and answers.

Each chapter ends with exercises which invite the reader to test out what has been learned in the course of the chapter. Some of the exercises have been changed because we have found better or more appropriate examples than those in our first edition, though we have not changed just for the sake of change. The present edition has significantly increased the number of these exercises in order to cover the ground more fully, test more of the skills and techniques that have been discussed, or sometimes to deal with aspects of a topic that have only been glanced at in the chapter. As a consequence, we believe that the second edition of *Reading Poetry* has more scope than the first edition for use as a self-sufficient set text for university level courses on poetry. Students and teachers will find that some of the questions are more leading than others, though the aim of the exercises is always to enable readers to work out their own readings and responses rather than to reach predetermined conclusions. Most of the exercises can be carried out by an individual reader, but all of them are also appropriate for collaborative discussion in a classroom or 'workshop' session. Some ask the reader to try out particular exercises with a friend or colleague – reading aloud, rewriting or reformatting a text – in order to check out the results. As well as rewriting poems into different forms, some exercises also involve readers attempting to write their own poems according to the formal or generic principles dealt with in particular chapters. In the present edition we have added to the number of such exercises in creative writing: students of music or the visual arts have always been required to do some creative work, but in literary studies 'creative writing' has traditionally had a much more uncertain status. It is nevertheless remarkable how much you can learn about poetry from trying to write it. Pedagogic models for such exercises probably still need to be designed and road-tested, however, before they can become at all widely accepted, though we would like to point out Stephen Fry's stimulating *The Ode Less Travelled: Unlocking the poet within* (London: Hutchinson, 2005) as a step in the right direction.

The discussion in the main text makes frequent reference to the published research of other scholars, and readers may wish to follow up some of those references by using the Bibliography at the end of the book. As John Smith implies in our epigraph, the study of poetry, like any other university discipline, has to be in touch with the best research. This is also why we have used on-page footnotes. Writing, teaching and studying at university level involve the acknowledgement that ideas and arguments arise out of the work of an intellectual community, not out of thin air. At the end of the book, there are two kinds of index: a general Index and a Key to all poems discussed in the book or used as exercises. In this second edition of *Reading Poetry* we have also added a Glossary of literary terms that are required for or commonly used in the discussion of poetry. Like the end-of-chapter exercises, the Glossary should be regarded not merely as an appendix or supplement to our main text, but rather as an integral part of the book.

How, then, might teachers or students read and use this book? Of course, like most authors, we dream of readers who start at page one and read the whole book right through to the end (with pauses for meals, sleep, or occasional comfort breaks). Indeed, we think we have written a book which could profitably be read from cover to cover; but we know that this is not the way most academic textbooks get read. We have therefore tried to create a book that can be used in a variety of ways to support the academic teaching and learning of students and general readers. Readers can dip into this book and structure its learning in many different ways: the new Glossary, we suggest, should be seen as a central tool in such structuring. Many of the technical terms included in the Glossary relate to issues examined at greater length in the main text. Readers who need to prepare for classroom discussion of particular topics, issues or examples might start by checking the Glossary for relevant entries. Each Glossary entry offers at least a definition of the term, often with an illustrative example. In many cases, however, we have written a longer entry to clarify some of the issues, problems and assumptions which, in our experience, students need to understand in the usage of poetic terms. Often a Glossary entry signals (in **bold**) related terms which can usefully be looked up elsewhere in the Glossary: thus under **register** readers will find cross-references to **field**, **pitch**, **tone** and **connotation**. Read all these and you will, we think, be quite adequately prepared to discuss and analyse such features of poetic texts in an essay, reading exercise or class discussion. If you then turn to our Index you will find further reference to the places in our main text where some or all these terms are used or discussed more fully. Such cross-referencing is much more methodically built into the second edition of this book than it was into the first; this is in response to comments made by academic users of the first edition in a survey carried out by our publishers, which suggested that the interactive aspects in the main text were one of the book's most user-friendly features. The new Glossary does not include only terms already discussed or used in the main text, however, since there are many terms in it which we do not discuss elsewhere. We have made a particular point of offering definitions and examples of terms and concepts which we do not use in the main part of the book but which students are likely to encounter when reading critical books and articles about poetry. These include the traditional terminology of classical metrical analysis, which we do not favour for the reasons given in Chapter Two. But if you still need to know what a 'trochee' is, this book will now tell you.

We have abbreviated the titles of a few works to which frequent reference is made. *Princeton* is Alex Preminger and T.V.F. Brogan, eds, *The New Princeton Encyclopedia of Poetry and Poetics* (1993); Abrams, *Glossary* is M.H. Abrams *A Glossary of Literary Terms*, 6th edn (1993). Full details of all works cited can be found in the Bibliography.

T.F., M.B.

Part One

FORMAL INTRODUCTION

Chapter 1

What Is Poetry? How Do We Read It?

■ Received Ideas and Common Assumptions

One of the concerns of this book will be repeatedly to ask questions about what poetry is and to question those things about poetry which we take for granted – including the category of poetry itself. This might seem a rather peculiar line of enquiry, since we tend to assume that we know what poetry is.[1] Our claim, however, is that reading poetry involves often unrecognised or unexamined assumptions about the nature of poetry. We want to show that it is important to become aware of these assumptions and to place them alongside other, quite different, assumptions because this will enhance or even transform our reading of poetry.

Attempts to answer the question 'What is poetry?' usually end up trying to define it against what it is not. There are perhaps three interrelated ways of doing this. Poetry can be defined as a **genre** by saying that it is different from the other main literary genres of narrative prose fiction and drama. A second definition – based on features of *language* – distinguishes between the way poetry uses language and so-called 'ordinary' uses of language. A third definition – this time on *formal* lines – would differentiate poetry from prose on the basis that it is arranged differently on the page.[2] We will examine each of these claims throughout the course of this book. What this examination will reveal is a set of common assumptions about poetry which are probably shared by a large proportion of readers in Britain and North America in the early

---

[1] It is revealing that M.H. Abrams does not provide an entry on 'poetry' in his *Glossary of Literary Terms* (he does give entries on 'novel' and 'drama').

[2] For a more elaborate exposition of the various ways of defining poetry against what it is not, see 'poetry' in *Princeton*.

twenty-first century (and perhaps in many other parts of the English-speaking world and beyond).

One of the arguments of this book will be to suggest that poetry is not one thing but many things. This is not only because we have different ways of describing poetry, or because there is a huge variety of language practices which are included under the umbrella term 'poetry', but also because what are assumed to be the defining characteristics of poetry change through history. These changing assumptions not only affect the practice of poets but also influence the kinds of poetry which are valued and the ways of reading which readers tend to adopt. The result of all this is that the category we call poetry is unstable and, possibly, that there may be no essential thing called 'poetry' at all.

Yet it would seem possible to challenge this line of argument by the commonsensical assertion that we know a poem when we see one. Even readers who have not read very much poetry seem to share certain conceptions about what poetry is, and about what constitutes 'good' poetry. It will therefore be useful at this point to examine a poem to which, experience tells us, most people will usually respond as 'good' or 'proper' poetry. In doing this we will try to identify those features which make it seem 'poetic' to such readers. For reasons which we will examine later, Keats seems to embody our collective idea of the quintessential poet, and his '**Ode** to a Nightingale' (1819) is often thought of as an exemplary poem. It is for these reasons that we will make this poem a test case in our attempt to make explicit our culture's implicit assumptions about what poetry is.

Ode to a Nightingale
1

My heart aches, and a drowsy numbness pains
    My sense, as though of hemlock I had drunk,
Or emptied some dull opiate to the drains
    One minute past, and Lethe-wards had sunk:
'Tis not through envy of thy happy lot,   5
    But being too happy in thine happiness –
        That thou, light-winged Dryad of the trees,
           In some melodious plot
Of beechen green, and shadows numberless,
    Singest of summer in full-throated ease.   10
2
O, for a draught of vintage! that hath been
    Cool'd a long age in the deep-delved earth,
Tasting of Flora and the country green,
    Dance, and Provençal song, and sunburnt mirth!
O for a beaker full of the warm South,   15

Full of the true, the blushful Hippocrene,
   With beaded bubbles winking at the brim,
     And purple-stained mouth,
   That I might drink, and leave the world unseen,
    And with thee fade away into the forest dim: 20
3
Fade far away, dissolve, and quite forget
   What thou among the leaves hast never known,
The weariness, the fever, and the fret
   Here, where men sit and hear each other groan;
Where palsy shakes a few, sad, last gray hairs,   25
   Where youth grows pale, and spectre-thin, and dies;
     Where but to think is to be full of sorrow
      And leaden-eyed despairs;
   Where Beauty cannot keep her lustrous eyes,
    Or new Love pine at them beyond tomorrow.   30
4
Away! away! for I will fly to thee,
   Not charioted by Bacchus and his pards,
But on the viewless wings of Poesy,
   Though the dull brain perplexes and retards.
Already with thee! tender is the night,   35
   And haply the Queen-Moon is on her throne,
     Cluster'd around by all her starry Fays;
      But here there is no light,
Save what from heaven is with the breezes blown
   Through verdurous glooms and winding mossy ways.   40
5
I cannot see what flowers are at my feet,
   Nor what soft incense hangs upon the boughs,
But, in embalmed darkness, guess each sweet
   Wherewith the seasonable month endows
The grass, the thicket, and the fruit tree wild;   45
   White hawthorn, and the pastoral eglantine;
     Fast-fading violets cover'd up in leaves;
      And mid-May's eldest child,
The coming musk-rose, full of dewy wine,
   The murmurous haunt of flies on summer eves.   50
6
Darkling I listen; and for many a time
   I have been half in love with easeful Death,
Call'd him soft names in many a mused rhyme,

To take into the air my quiet breath;
  Now more than ever seems it rich to die,   55
    To cease upon the midnight with no pain,
      While thou art pouring forth thy soul abroad
        In such an ecstasy!
    Still wouldst thou sing, and I have ears in vain –
      To thy high requiem become a sod.   60

7

Thou wast not born for death, immortal Bird!
  No hungry generations tread thee down;
The voice I hear this passing night was heard
  In ancient days by emperor and clown:
Perhaps the self-same song that found a path   65
    Through the sad heart of Ruth, when, sick for home,
      She stood in tears amid the alien corn;
        The same that oft-times hath
    Charm'd magic casements, opening on the foam
      Of perilous seas, in faery lands forlorn.   70

8

Forlorn! the very word is like a bell
  To toll me back from thee to my sole self!
Adieu! The fancy cannot cheat so well
  As she is fam'd to do, deceiving elf.
Adieu! adieu! thy plaintive anthem fades   75
    Past the near meadows, over the still stream,
      Up the hill-side; and now 'tis buried deep
        In the next valley-glades:
    Was it a vision, or a waking dream?
      Fled is that music: – Do I wake or sleep?   80

What we would like to do here is draw attention to various features of the poem which contribute to the feeling that this is 'authentic poetry'. This will entail examining how the poem uses certain poetic conventions which are themselves based on particular assumptions about what poetry is. It will also involve asking whether these assumptions and conventions require us to read poetry in ways which accord with them – that is, do particular kinds of poetry encourage or demand particular ways of reading? Our answers to both questions are deeply bound up with each other: our assumptions about what poetry is will shape our way of reading poetry, and our way of reading poetry will tend to influence which poems we regard as exemplary poetry. In other words, we want to suggest that poetry is as much a product of ways of reading as of ways of writing.

■ Poetry As Expression – the Experience of Its Speaker?

Some of the most deep-rooted preconceptions about poetry in our culture are that it records profound personal emotion and experience, that it is often about nature, and that it should be 'imaginative'. Keats's 'Ode' seems indeed to confirm these preconceptions. The very event itself – a poet listening in solitude to a nightingale, surrounded by woods and flowers – seems especially poetic. And this poet's imaginative response to the bird is presented as a powerful and deeply significant experience which we are invited to share. One of the questions that we will be asking is the extent to which the 'poetic' quality of this event is derived from the profundity of the experience itself, from the specific ways in which the poem articulates the experience, or from the fact that Keats has chosen a topic which certain cultural assumptions have attuned us to regard as already intrinsically poetic. As we shall see in Chapter 10, nightingales – as opposed to, say, starlings – are birds which come already invested with 'poetic value' from their frequent appearance in poetry.

Perhaps one of the reasons this pessimistic but deeply moving poem is so popular is the assumption that it gives us direct access to the profound inner experience of the poet himself. Many readers have sought to 'explain' the poem by referring to Keats's biography – especially to the fact that he had recently nursed his brother as he died of tuberculosis. The poem becomes additionally poignant when we remember that Keats himself died of the same disease only two years later at the age of twenty-five.[3] For these reasons, Keats's life and poetry have been fused in the imaginations of readers perhaps more than is the case with any other poet. This is a particularly telling instance of our claim that the assumptions we bring to a poem subtly shape our reading of it. For reasons that will emerge in the course of this book, we want to discourage you from reading poems for biographical meaning – which is why we ascribe the voice in this poem to a 'poetic **speaker**' rather than to Keats. However interesting Keats was as a human being, we want to encourage you to concentrate on reading his poetry rather than trying to recreate his thoughts and feelings. As T.S. Eliot puts it: 'Honest criticism and sensitive appreciation is directed not upon the poet but upon the poetry.'[4]

'Ode to a Nightingale' invites us to read it as an intense and sincere expression of experience – as the opening words of the poem ('My heart aches') attest. This is reinforced by the speaker's claim that his 'pain' arises not through 'envy' of the nightingale's 'happy lot' but through a profound empathy

---

[3] For an example of such a reading, see Brian Stone, *The Poetry of Keats* (Harmondsworth: Penguin, 1992).

[4] 'Tradition and the Individual Talent', in *Selected Prose of T.S. Eliot*, ed. Frank Kermode (London: Faber, 1975), p. 26.

which he feels with the nightingale. In fact, the whole poem is driven by the speaker's attempt to merge his consciousness with the nightingale. In the second stanza (poems are divided into 'stanzas' not 'verses') he longs for a glass of special wine, on the assumption that it will somehow enable him to escape the world and join the nightingale. We learn in the third stanza why the speaker wants to 'dissolve' and to merge his consciousness with the bird. The real world, he claims, is a place 'where men sit and hear each other groan' (24). In the fourth stanza, he abandons the idea of wine (represented figuratively by Bacchus, the god of wine) in favour of poetry as a means of escaping this world and flying to the nightingale on 'the viewless wings of Poesy'. For one brief moment, the speaker apparently feels that poetry has indeed transported him from the human world to the realm of the nightingale: 'Already with thee! tender is the night' (35). The speaker feels that this intense moment of poetic communication is a perfect moment to die, and so leave the world and its woes for ever: 'Now more than ever seems it rich to die'. Yet the last stanza brings the speaker back to earth when he realises that his union with the nightingale was simply an illusion; the bird's song fades away into the next valley and he is left alone, bewildered and 'forlorn'.

What we have achieved so far is a paraphrase of the poem's 'plot', and this has helped us begin to clarify what the poem is 'about'. This is quite an effective way of beginning to analyse any poem because it provides a provisional framework upon which we can build a more precise analysis of the poem's local details. What we have also achieved is confirmation of the fact that this poem does indeed conform with our expectation that poetry records intense personal experience – though we are suggesting that it is the experience of an invented speaker rather than that of the poet himself.

■ Poetry as a Response in the Reader?

The assumption that poetry is the expression of intense personal experience usually involves a related assumption about what we are supposed to do when we read such a poem. Victorian readers assumed that the proper response to such poetry was to be moved by it, and high-school students studying literature in the early twenty-first century are encouraged to believe that the most important factor in reading a poem is to have some kind of personal response to it. This emphasis on personal and emotional response at high-school level can be seen in the following exam question: 'Choose a poem which makes you feel happy or sad or angry. Say what the poem is about and why it makes you feel happy or sad or angry. What particular words or phrases in the poem make you feel that way?' Another question asks students to compare two poems in terms of 'the impact the poets' writing makes on you'. But to ask such questions is to invite students to report responses that may have less to do with the poems themselves and more to do with the student's own emotional life (when I read this poem I think of my grandmother . . .). What kind of personal response might be appropriate to 'Ode to a Nightingale'? What kind of response would reveal something about the poem rather than our own sensibility? Are we expected to experience a sympathetic response to the poet's (or the speaker's) intense feelings? In reading the first stanza, should we, too, try to experience happiness so intense that it is almost painful? Should we try to empathise with the nightingale in the way that the poetic speaker does? And are we expected to share the speaker's sense of loss in the last stanza when the vision has dissolved? Framing these questions in this way allows us to suggest that, although we want to encourage students to enjoy the imaginative pleasure of reading poetry, such responses in themselves can be pretty vacuous. More profound aesthetic pleasures, we want to argue, emerge from a more careful and sustained analysis that involves the intellect as well as the emotions and that tells us something about how the poem's language might produce emotional and aesthetic effects in readers.

■ Poetry and the World: The Poem as a Representation of Life?

Another way of approaching the poem would be to ask how accurately it represents the real world. Such an approach does not seem to get us very far with this poem, since it is not really a description of an action or an object at all. It is not really 'about' a nightingale, but about the *idea* of a nightingale and what it means for the speaker. This is shown by the way the speaker seems to believe that this particular bird is 'immortal' (61), and by the way he addresses it as if it could understand and respond to what he says. This latter feature is an example of a poetic convention called '**apostrophe**' – which can be defined as 'a figure of speech in which the speaker addresses an abstract or an absent thing as though it were living and present'. Yet even this extremely poetic convention does not entirely remove the poem from recognisable experience: we talk to pets and toy animals in this way, and even though not many of us yearn to pair up with a nightingale, most of us may have occasionally felt that the world is a pretty miserable place, and we may have tried to escape from it in some way or other. Thus, the driving force of the poem – the recognition of sorrow and despair, and the desire to escape them – seems to be in touch with more general human experience, as is the insight that our various means of escape bring only temporary relief.

■ Reading for the Message?

Thus we could say that the poem gives us a particular insight into 'the human condition'. Such a response alerts us to another way of reading which has been current in the history of literature and is still in circulation – that is, to assume that literature can offer us deep insights about life. Such an assumption encourages us to read literature for its 'moral message'. Keats's 'Ode' seems to be saying that the ecstasies offered us by nature, wine, poetry, love and beauty are transient illusions which provide only temporary respite from the permanence of human suffering (see lines 29–30). Yet reading this poem (or perhaps any poem) in order to discover its 'message' seems to lead to pretty banal conclusions that could be put more straightforwardly or more powerfully. Thus, although students are often encouraged to read poems for their 'message', we want to stress that this is an unproductive and misleading approach to poetry. As the Scottish poet Norman MacCaig once said in a TV interview, 'If you want messages, go to Safeway's'. (In the west of Scotland, 'messages' is a word for groceries; Safeway's was a supermarket chain.)

◼ Romantic Poetry

Many of the assumptions we have examined and questioned in the previous sections – that poetry records or represents the profound imaginative experience and moral insight of a creative genius – derive from ideas developed by Romantic writers in the period in which Keats lived. One of the characteristic assumptions of Romantic theory is Wordsworth's assertion that 'all good poetry is the spontaneous overflow of [the] powerful feelings' of a specially gifted individual – someone who 'being possessed of more than usual organic sensibility had also thought long and deeply'.[5] Romantic theory thus tends to stress that poetry is the direct product of the special imaginative capacity of the individual genius. The quality of a poem is a measure of the poet's sensibility, and the quality of a reader's response is in turn a measure of his or her sensibility.

Yet the fact that most readers tend to share these Romantic assumptions does not mean that this is the only way to read poetry in general, or even Romantic poetry in particular. This is only one of a number of possible ways of reading poetry; we do not have to read Romantic poetry on its own terms – that is, as if we were Romantics. The fact that so many people hold Romantic assumptions about art does not mean that they are true, or always insightful; it indicates, instead, how such assumptions continue to be reproduced in education and the media. In the twentieth century, literary theorists and critics of various persuasions resisted and criticised such Romantic readings and ways of 'explaining' poetry. One of the projects of this book, in fact, is to put you in

---

[5] 'Preface to *Lyrical Ballads*', in Wordsworth, *The Lyrical Ballads*, ed. R.L. Brett and A.R. Jones (London: Methuen, 1968), pp. 241–72, 246. 'Organic sensibility' refers to the responsiveness of the senses.

touch with some of these more recent assumptions about poetry, since we feel that they yield more insights into poetic texts than those produced by 'Romantic' ways of reading.

◼ Close Reading and the Language of Poetry

Romantic readings of literary texts tend to focus on questions about sincerity of feeling, emotional response and profundity of insight. More recent ways of reading poetry, however, beginning with New Criticism in the middle decades of the twentieth century, place more emphasis on the close reading of the actual language of the poetic text itself. One of the things we will be stressing in this book is that a particularly rewarding and challenging way of reading poetry is the careful analysis of the interplay between the language and form of individual poems. In fact, we will attempt to show that it is only through this process that the emotional power, mimetic possibilities and moral implications of a poetic text can be produced and experienced. The stress on 'close reading' will inevitably raise the question of whether the language of poetry differs from other discourses and uses of language. Although many readers say that a poem ought to be enjoyed for its own sake, the critical reading of poetry involves trying to understand how that pleasure is produced. What will emerge in this chapter is that poetry – or at least this particular poem – achieves its emotional power by working the resources of the language to the limit.

'Ode to a Nightingale' is particularly interesting in terms of the way it uses language to produce specific effects. One way in which its language announces itself as 'poetic' is through the employment of what is called '**poetic diction**' – words and phrases which we conventionally associate with poetry. The use of archaic second-person pronouns such as 'thou' and 'thy', of phrases like 'verdurous glooms', and **allusions** to classical mythology all conform to our received notions of poetic language. Poetic diction of this kind is sometimes called 'flowery', but this is not a very accurate or revealing term. Poets, critics and linguists have come up with a number of more suggestive ways of describing 'poetic' language, each of which involves differentiating between poetic and what is usually called 'non-poetic' or 'ordinary' language (we will see that such distinctions are not as stable as we might think). One way of describing the way Keats is using language is to call it a 'heightened' language. The nineteenth-century poet Gerard Manley Hopkins, for example, suggested that poetic language 'shd. be the current language heightened, to any degree heightened and unlike itself' (Letter to Robert Bridges, 14 August, 1879). Another way of describing poetic language is in terms of 'literariness' – that is, the sum of those qualities of the language which make it literary rather than non-literary. The most helpful descriptive term of all is '**register**', a term used by linguists to refer to the fact that language varies according to the context in which it is used.[6] The language appropriate to a scientific report is different from the language used in soap operas or in a letter to a friend, and each discourse, activity or context has its own appropriate register. The peculiar conventions of poetic language, therefore, mark it as the register appropriate to poetry. As we will see, this register changes through history (which is why some poems use a register which seems more archaic to us than others).

Another striking feature of Keats's language in this poem is the sustained use of sound-patterning, such as **rhyme** or **alliteration**. 'Ode to a Nightingale' can be said to be a melodious poem about a melodious bird since it plays upon the pleasure we often get from the sounds of language. In an unexpected way, however, the poem's denouement suggests that it is the sound of words which destroys the illusion which it had earlier created. In the very moment when the speaker claims that the song of the nightingale has had a magic charm throughout history, the chime of his own words breaks the spell:

> The voice I hear this passing night was heard
>   In ancient days by emperor and clown:
> Perhaps the self-same song that found a path
>   Through the sad **h**eart of Ruth, when, sick for home,
>   She stood in tears amid the alien corn;
>   The same that oft-times **h**ath
> Charm'd magic casements, opening on the foam
>   Of perilous seas, in **f**aery **l**ands **f**orlorn.
>
> Forlorn! the very word is like a **bell**
>   To **toll** me back from thee to my **sole** self!
> Adieu! the fancy cannot cheat so **well**
>   As she is fam'd to do, deceiving elf. (63–74)

The concentrated use of alliteration in the penultimate stanza (culminating in 'faery lands forlorn') could be said to present an equivalent to the charm of the nightingale's song. Yet the critical moment of this technique suddenly reverses its effect in that the word 'forlorn' brings the poetic speaker down to earth. This occurs as much through the sound of the word as through its meaning. We are told that the word 'forlorn' echoes 'like a bell' to 'toll' the speaker back to his 'sole self'. (In doing so, it changes its meaning: applied to the 'faery lands' it means lost or disappeared, but when the speaker applies it to himself

---

[6] For an introduction to the use and effects of register in literature, see 'Language and Context: Register', in M. Montgomery *et al.*, *Ways of Reading: Advanced reading skills for students of English literature*, 3rd Edn (London: Routledge, 2007), pp. 67–76; for a more extended discussion, see Lance St John Butler, *Registering the Difference: Reading Literature through Register* (Manchester and New York: Manchester University Press, 1999), especially chapters 5, 6, 9 and 10.

it means forsaken or wretched.) Such chiming effects resonate throughout the first four lines of the last stanza, through end-rhyme, **internal rhyme** and **assonance** ('bell', 'toll', 'sole self', 'well', 'elf'). In an interesting way, these conventional poetic devices work here to undo the poetic effects of the earlier part of the poem. The poem seems to get tangled up in the material nature of language itself, and can no longer produce transcendental illusions.

As well as emphasising or foregrounding the sounds of words, the poem seems to explore the possibilities and pleasures of **figurative** language. In the second stanza, for example, the speaker is literally asking for a glass of wine, but this is never explicitly mentioned. Instead, the poem presents us with figurative terms for wine, calling it 'a draught of *vintage*' (11) and 'a beaker full of *the warm South*' (15). These figures are effective in that they endow the wine with certain associations and connotations. The Oxford English Dictionary reminds us that 'vintage' means enriched through time, rare, mature, valuable, 'usually connoting [a wine] of good or outstanding quality'. The poem also endows the wine with the positive associations we have of nature: 'tasting of Flora and the country green' (13), this wine is the essence of flowers and the countryside ('Flora' here refers not to a modern brand of margarine but to the Roman goddess of springtime and flowers). Its association in the poem with dance, song and mirth also makes this wine celebratory. The second **metaphor** – wine as 'the warm South' – does not simply tell us that this wine comes from southern countries, but picks up on particular associations of southern Europe which are then developed in 'Provençal song' and 'sunburnt mirth'(14). In this way, Keats's figurative descriptions of the wine draw on some of the connotations of southern Europe that were prevalent in Britain in his time and are still used in holiday and wine advertisements on television. Keats's highly 'poetic' language turns out to employ techniques and devices which are now most often seen in advertising. This is appropriate because in a sense the speaker is trying to sell himself (and/or the reader) the idea that wine might offer a way out of the everyday suffering which is so vividly presented in the following stanza's account of 'leaden-eyed despairs' (28).

This brief example of 'close reading' (which could be extended throughout the poem) suggests that reading poetry involves a special way of attending to its language (a reading in slow motion) which appears different from the way we read 'everyday' language (though this way of reading also turns out to be appropriate for analysing other media – such as advertisements – which attempt to affect us in powerful and subtle ways). Close reading pays careful attention to the language of poetry and to how it works – how the poem achieves its effects through employing poetic conventions and techniques which exploit specific cultural connotations. We move away from the rather vague personal impressions which result from Romantic assumptions about poetry and arrive at a way of reading which talks about how the actual language of the poem generates effects and meanings. This attention to the conventions of poetic language is one of the ways of discussing poetry which will be encouraged throughout this book.

Yet the fact that such techniques of 'close reading' are useful in analysing other kinds of language as well as poetry indicates that the features they respond to cannot be defining features of poetry. All discourses employ figurative language (in varying degrees and for different purposes), and the sound effects of alliteration, rhyme, and so on can occur in any kind of language use (and they are not invariably present in poetry). This fact has led critics and theorists to attempt to distinguish poetic uses of such figurative and aural devices from their use in other kinds of discourse (sermons, political speeches and slogans, advertisements, catch phrases, jokes, novels, plays, songs). Some writers have suggested that these features are used for different purposes in poetry from those they have in other discourses (for aesthetic pleasure rather than, say, political persuasion). Others have said that, whereas such features are a kind of spurious decoration in most instances, in poetry they reveal a 'verbal art' whose carefully designed 'form' is as important as its 'content'. But all such arguments are problematic attempts to distinguish poetry from prose and other non-poetic discourses on the basis of features which are actually common to both.

■ The Lineation of Poetry

In fact, the only watertight distinction between poetry and most non-poetic discourses is that poetry is set out on the page in lines whose length is decided by the author, whereas lines of prose run from margin to margin and are governed by arbitrary factors such as page width and font size. (In other words, whereas the division of poetry into lines may be significant, the division of prose into lines is a meaningless feature: the meaningful divisions of prose are sentences and paragraphs, not lines.) Lines of poetry, then, are measured not by a ruler or by the width of the page but according to the poet's own design. We will see in later chapters that this is not a trivial fact but a distinguishing feature which has numerous consequences.

The lines of 'Ode to a Nightingale' are organised into equal groups ('stanzas') and are of equal length (with one exception per stanza). The line length is measured by the number of **syllables**: to keep it simple, for the moment, each of Keats's lines has ten syllables (except for the eighth line of each stanza, which has only six). The fact that the length of each line fits into a regular template (the number of stressed and unstressed syllables per line is kept constant) means that Keats's poem is an example of metrical **verse** ('**metre**' is etymologically related to 'measure'). The consequences of employing such a metrical form are manifold; here, we simply want to stress a couple of points. The poem's metrical regularity sets up a visual and aural framework or pattern within which all the other linguistic effects we have talked about take place. An instance of this is that rhyme words do not appear randomly, but usually at the end of lines (they are end-rhymes). The rhyme words thus contribute to the poem's overall pattern, reinforcing the metrical structure. At the same time, when Keats employs extra rhymes which are internal to the line (the 'internal rhymes' of 'toll' and 'sole', for instance) this draws extra attention to these important words and the relation between them. Every other sound effect and figurative device slots into and reinforces this pattern, and this becomes part of our experience of reading the poem. Indeed, it is a powerful means by which this poem becomes 'poetic'. Thus we would claim that it is the division into lines which is the basis of poetry and the origin of the poetic effect (rhyme, by contrast, is not a necessary feature of poetry).

Yet the highly regular pattern of lines in the 'Ode' does not produce a sense that the poem is rigidly structured. In fact, our own feeling about the poem is that it seems free-flowing and 'spontaneous'. We want to suggest that this effect is, paradoxically, a product of technique rather than chance or spontaneity. It is largely produced by the fact that, although Keats has set up a strict metrical template of equal line lengths, the structure of his sentences hardly ever coincides with the line structure. Thus, for example, the sentence beginning 'thy plaintive anthem' starts somewhere in the middle of the line and then spills over the ends of three lines before pausing at 'valley-glades' and finally ending at the end of a line with 'waking dream':

> Adieu! adieu! thy plaintive anthem fades
> Past the near meadows, over the still stream,
> Up the hill-side; and now 'tis buried deep
> In the next valley-glades:
> Was it a vision, or a waking dream?
> Fled is that music: – Do I wake or sleep? (75–80)

In dynamic contrast to the extended sentence that overruns several line endings, the last line is divided into two equal, self-contained phrases which fit neatly within the line structure. It is this unpredictable interplay between regular line and **stanza form** and irregular sentence structure which gives the language a sense of spontaneous energy. (You could test this by converting the poem into prose and seeing if the movement of the sentences produces the same effects.)

■ Poetry and Meaning

But, although such close attention to the local effects of linguistic detail is fascinating in itself, it becomes more interesting when we can relate it to larger questions – such as 'What does the poem mean?' We have already offered one kind of answer to this in suggesting that the poem can be read as a comment upon 'the human condition'. Yet recent theories of literature have taught us to be suspicious about such claims by stressing that all meaning is historically and culturally specific rather than universal. In our close reading of the 'Ode' we had to specify what 'the warm South' might mean in a poem written in Britain in the early nineteenth century. The Mediterranean countries of southern Europe have a significance in Britain which is historically and culturally specific to Britain (and to northern Europe in general). For an Australian or South American reader, by contrast, the 'south' may have very different connotations. In addition, the very question 'what does the poem mean?' – although it is often encountered in schools and universities – can be disastrously misleading since it can lure even experienced readers into trying to translate a subtle and complex poem like 'Ode to a Nightingale' into a 'meaning' that will often seem reductive or banal in comparison with the poem itself. Nonetheless, the question of meaning (or meanings) cannot be put to one side. But rather than reading a poem as if it were a message with a single meaning that has to be decoded, we suggest that you approach poetry in terms of the way it explores questions or issues in meaningful ways (in the course of the book we sometimes suggest that a poem has an 'argument'). In our experience, the most interesting poems remain meaningful no matter how many times we read them and new meanings emerge as we re-read them across the years. Thus we can never assume that we have 'got' a poem's meaning once and for all and no longer need to return to it.

Recent theories have also suggested that different ways of reading, informed by different assumptions about what poetry is and about the purpose of reading poetry, may well produce different versions of the 'same' poem (just as different directors will produce very different interpretations of the 'same' play) and thus, perhaps, different meanings. Yet all such readings or 'productions' have to prove themselves by close reference to the language of the poem itself. The idea that different readings or meanings may be equally valid does not mean that 'anything goes', nor does it mean that an interpretation cannot be wrong.

The complex language of Keats's 'Ode' yields different readings according to the assumptions we bring to it and the questions we ask of it. Our present concern in this chapter is to ask 'What is poetry?' This means that our approach to Keats's poem is not a disinterested one – we have a question in mind before we read it. Approaching Keats's poem with this question in mind produces a revealing result in that it allows us to suggest that the 'Ode' can be read as a poem about poetry itself. This can be seen in the way many of the **images** it uses, though they refer to various other things, turn out to have associations with poetry. Thus the speaker chooses wine as his first avenue of escape from the tribulations of mortal suffering, but its power derives from the way it is said to taste of 'Provençal song' (14) – which links it with the late-medieval troubadours, who were poet-musicians of Provence in the eleventh to thirteenth centuries. Much the same connection between wine and poetry is made when wine is described as 'the true, the blushful Hippocrene' (16); this suggests that this wine will induce poetic inspiration, since the Hippocrene was a fountain of the Muses who were thought to inspire classical poets in Ancient Greece.[7] However, having initially identified wine and the heightening of the senses (or intoxication) it provides with the effect of poetry in these images, the speaker goes on to affirm the superiority of poetry itself as a means of transcending his condition:

> Away! away! for I will fly to thee,
> Not charioted by Bacchus and his pards,
> But on the viewless wings of Poesy . . . (31–33)

It is poetry itself, then, which seems to offer the speaker the best chance of soaring up to the heightened world of the nightingale. By employing the 'wings of Poesy', the speaker will not only achieve poetic 'flight' – or a flight of the imagination – but will thereby become *like* the nightingale.

In this way, the poem emerges as a celebration or exploration of the power of poetry itself to help us escape a world of suffering. But the poetry being tested here is not poetry in general but a specifically Romantic kind of poetry. A key term for Romantic poetry is 'imagination' – though it is important to realise that this term has a history of changing uses, and that even the Romantic poets had different theories about what it is and how it works.[8] For Keats, the imagination was primarily a means of achieving a sympathetic oneness between the self and other things – between an observing human being and the person, creature or object being observed. In one of his letters, Keats claimed: 'if a Sparrow come before my Window I take part in its existence and pick about the Gravel'.[9] This is a specific instance of Keats's repeated suggestion in his letters that the poetic imagination is exhibited by the poet's capacity to dissolve his own identity in an act of empathy with something outside the self. The 'poetical Character', he writes, 'has no self – it is everything and nothing – It has no character. . . . A Poet is the most unpoetical of any thing in existence; because he has no Identity.' Instead, the poet is continually informing

---

[7] A good edition of the poem will present footnotes explaining such allusions, but you will be able to trace them for yourself by using reference books such as E.C. Brewer's *Dictionary of Phrase and Fable* (London, 1870, revised edition London: Cassell, 1981) or the Internet.

[8] For a succinct discussion of the imagination as a changing historical term, see 'imagination' in *Princeton*.

[9] Keats to Benjamin Bailey, 22 November 1817, in *Letters of John Keats, A Selection*, ed. Robert Gittings (Oxford: Oxford University Press, 1975), p. 38.

'and filling some other Body'.[10] Keats's account of the poetic imagination and the character of the poet lends further support to our claim that 'Ode to a Nightingale' is a poem about poetry since, as we have seen, its speaker strives to escape from suffering by losing his own identity and becoming one with the nightingale through an act of sympathetic identification. And it is the poetic imagination – the 'wings of Poesy' – which holds out the greatest promise for such a merging of speaker and bird.[11]

Yet, just as wine is rejected in favour of poetry, so poetry itself is found wanting at the end of the poem by failing to fulfil its promise:

> Forlorn! the very word is like a bell
> To toll me back from thee to my sole self!
> Adieu! the fancy cannot cheat so well
> As she is fam'd to do, deceiving elf. (71–74)

The poem ends, therefore, by recognising the limitations of the imagination: the 'fancy' has failed, and leaves the speaker alone with his 'sole self' (for Keats, the terms 'fancy' and 'imagination' were interchangeable).[12] However wonderful the sense of flight which the fancy or imagination can produce, it is revealed at the end as a kind of cheat whose limitation is either that it is not true or lasting or that it does not cheat effectively enough. The speaker's attempt to use the poetic imagination as a means of overcoming the difference between self and other fails, and the nightingale's 'plaintive anthem' vanishes into 'the next valley-glades'. It is therefore possible to suggest that this quintessential Romantic poem also investigates and criticises Romantic conceptions of poetry in so far as they claim that the poetic imagination can transcend 'the human condition' or overcome the difference between self and other, or self and nature. The 'Ode to a Nightingale', then, needs to be read not as a beautiful, escapist poem but as a poem which takes a hard, critical look at 'Romantic' assumptions about poetry – including Keats's own. (This reading depends entirely on the last stanza, and it would thus be an interesting experiment to

---

[10] Keats to Richard Woodhouse, 27 October 1818, in Keats, *Letters*, p. 157.

[11] In the letter to Benjamin Bailey referred to above, Keats talks of the 'Wings of imagination', Keats, *Letters*, p. 37.

[12] The terms 'fancy' and 'imagination' were used interchangeably in eighteenth-century poetry and by most Romantic poets in the early nineteenth century, despite the fact that critics and theorists in England and Germany had begun to distinguish the terms as referring to quite distinct creative processes. In this distinction, 'fancy' becomes downgraded as a mechanistic process of assembling ideas, while 'imagination' comes to refer to a natural, even semi-divine, creative faculty. The most well-known and eventually influential distinction between fancy and the imagination along these lines was made by Coleridge in his *Biographia Literaria* (1817). Keats's use of 'fancy' in 'Ode to a Nightingale' as a term to describe his version of the sympathetic imagination ignores this distinction. See 'Fancy' and 'Imagination' in *Princeton*.

read the poem without it.[13] Try it now, and try to articulate your sense of the difference between the complete and the shortened versions of the poem.)

▓ The Poet's Intention

We have acknowledged that our reading of Keats's poem depends, to some extent, on the assumptions we brought to it and the questions we asked of it. Our argument that it is a poem about poetry arose in the context of a discussion in which we were asking the question: 'What is poetry?' Critics often appear to be saying that poems 'really' mean something different from what they appear to mean, and students of literature are often led to assume that the interpretation of a text is a matter of finding its 'hidden message'. In this instance, Keats's 'Ode to a Nightingale', we seem to have suggested, is not 'really' about a nightingale, but about poetry.

A potential response to our interpretation would be to ask whether we are claiming that we now understand what Keats was 'really' trying to say in this poem. This raises the problem of the author's **intention**. It seems quite natural to assume that the purpose of reading poetry is to discover the poet's intention in writing it, and thus it may be surprising to learn that a great deal of controversy has arisen over this assumption. Eliot's insistence that criticism should be directed upon the poem rather than the poet led the so-called New Critics to claim that a poem should be read on its own terms rather than in terms of its author's statements about his or her intentions when writing it. A poet's intentions, they argued, are of interest only if they are fully realised in the poem itself. There would thus be no point in going to the author to seek confirmation of a particular interpretation.

It is possible to identify at least four interrelated problems with the notion of authorial intention. First, there is the problem of access. In many cases, as with Keats, the poet may be dead and may have left no record of his or her intentions concerning a particular poem; in such a case, to claim to know what the poet's intentions were would be tantamount to claiming to be able to read the minds of the dead – which is an art that we do not profess. Secondly, even when we have access to statements of intention which are independent of the poem, we should not necessarily be constrained by them since, after all, poets sometimes deliberately mislead readers, or forget what their original intentions were; their intentions may have changed in the course of writing, or in

---

[13] It is interesting that an early review of the collection of poems in which Keats first published 'Ode to a Nightingale' quoted the whole poem minus the first and last stanzas. The anonymous reviewer of 1820 found the 'Ode' the most delightful poem in the collection, claiming: 'The third and seventh stanzas have a charm for us which we find it difficult to explain' (quoted in G.M. Matthews, ed., *Keats: The critical heritage* (London: Routledge, 1971), pp. 214–15).

subsequent revisions, and a writer may have great difficulty summing up what he or she was trying to do at any particular stage of writing. Thirdly, people often say things which have meanings they did not consciously intend and were not aware of, and, particularly in poetry, those unintended meanings are often as interesting as intended meanings – it is difficult to assume, in the wake of Freud, that all human intentions can be consistent and unitary. Fourthly, in the light of these considerations, we need to ask why the author's intentions should be privileged over what the text itself seems to say, or what careful readers discover it to be saying.

We can apply some of these questions to our interpretation of Keats's 'Ode'. It will, we hope, be clear from our discussion that we were anxious to justify our reading by close reference to the poem itself, which is why we constantly quoted the evidence from the text which supported our interpretation. Clearly, we cannot ask Keats whether he knew that he was 'really' writing a poem about poetry but, even if we could, it is worth asking whether it would make any difference. Would it invalidate our interpretation if Keats (in a surviving letter, for instance) had described his intentions in quite different terms from our own claims about the poem? If Keats's conscious intentions were different from our interpretation of the poem's meaning, but nevertheless compatible with it, what would you conclude from this? And if Keats's declared intentions were wholly at odds with our interpretation, what would you conclude from that? Is an author always the best reader of his or her own writing? Even if the answer is no, does that mean that an author's intentions have *no* interest for us as readers? If we can find evidence of a writer's beliefs and preoccupations from his or her other actions and writings – as we did earlier when we documented Keats's ideas of the imagination and of the 'poetical Character' from his letters – is not such evidence valuable when it supports our reading? If so, why should we ignore it when it contradicts our interpretation? Does such 'external' evidence have the same value, however, as evidence drawn from the text of the poem itself?

The fact that we have not given categorical answers to these questions may suggest why the issue of authorial intention should have proved so problematic and controversial for modern criticism.[14] However, we would insist that our

---

[14] The anti-intentionalist case is forcibly argued by Wimsatt and Beardsley, 'The Intentional Fallacy', in W.K. Wimsatt, *The Verbal Icon: Studies in the meaning of poetry* (Kentucky: University of Kentucky Press, 1954), reprinted in David Lodge, ed., *Twentieth Century Literary Criticism: A reader* (London: Longman, 1972), pp. 334–44. The contrary view, that all valid meanings are intended meanings, is argued by E.D. Hirsch, *Validity in Interpretation* (New Haven, CT: Yale University Press, 1967). More recent theories have questioned the idea of intention more radically by problematising our idea of the author: see Roland Barthes, 'The Death of the Author' and Michel Foucault, 'What is an Author?', both in David Lodge, ed., *Modern Criticism and Theory: A reader* (London: Longman, 1988), pp. 167–72, 197–210.

particular interpretation of Keats's 'Ode to a Nightingale' does not need to support itself by claiming that what we have uncovered is Keats's intention in writing the poem. That is not what we are claiming for our reading. We do nevertheless believe that what we have identified is an important and interesting meaning of the poem, and not something we have arbitrarily invented or imagined. It is for these reasons that the ways of reading poems presented in this book will rarely worry about or make claims for the author's intentions. This is not to say that an author's intentions are irrelevant or uninteresting – they are not – but that we can never be certain what those intentions were, and that in any case such intentions are not the final arbiter of a poem's meaning. In fact in this book we are less concerned with *what* poems mean than with *how* they mean. As a consequence, our focus is on reading poetic texts themselves, not on reading the minds of poets.

■ And Now for Something Completely Different

We have claimed that Keats's 'Ode to a Nightingale' represents most readers' idea about what poetry is. To test this claim, we would like to compare Keats's poem with the poem below, published in 1974 by Charles Simic:

The Garden of Earthly Delights

Buck has a headache. Tony ate
a real hot pepper. Sylvia weighs
herself naked on the bathroom
scale. Gary owes $800 to the
Internal Revenue. Roger says   5
poetry is the manufacture of lightning rods.
José wants to punch his wife
in the mouth. Ted's afraid
of his own shadow. Ray talks
to his tomato plants. Paul   10
wants a job in the post office
selling stamps. Mary keeps
smiling at herself in the mirror.
And I,
I piss in the sink   15
with a feeling of
eternity.

Although it is true that in impromptu surveys some students say they prefer Simic's poem to Keats's (some even claim that it is more 'poetic'), nevertheless there is usually an overwhelming consensus that Keats's poem is both 'better' and more 'poetic' than Simic's. It might be said that this result is inevitable, since we have chosen a poem which seems as utterly unlike Keats's as could be imagined. But this is precisely why a comparison between the two poems will allow us to become more aware of those features of Keats's poem which make it sound and look more like 'real' poetry (or our received idea about what poetry is). Our method here will be, once more, to look closely at the poem's language to see how it achieves its effects.

In terms of poetic form, Keats's poem looks and sounds poetic through his use of formal features such as metre and rhyme, whereas Simic's reads more like a list of comments which have no relation to the fact that it is divided into lines (the fact that 'weighs' rhymes with 'says' in some accents seems entirely coincidental). A second apparent difference between the poems is in terms of their subject matter. Our received ideas about poetry suggest that flowers and birds are inherently more poetic subjects than bathroom scales or tax problems. This difference is related to a difference of diction or register (that is, the choice of words and phrases): compare 'some melodious plot / Of beechen green' with 'Gary owes $800 to the / Internal Revenue'. A further difference between the poems is in the different images we are given of the poetic speakers. Whereas Keats's speaker displays a 'poetic' sensibility (this is one of the main points of the poem), Simic's seems quite the reverse – as revealed in his admission 'I piss in the sink' (15). The impression that Keats's diction is more 'poetic' than Simic's is also produced by the former's use of cultural allusions (references to the myths and literature of earlier periods or cultures) – for example, in calling the nightingale a 'light-winged Dryad of the trees' (a Dryad was 'a tree-nymph' in classical mythology).

This comparison has revealed some of the features of what we usually think of as 'traditional' poetry, but it also indicates that there are radically different kinds of poetry (we will explore this further in later chapters). One of the things which seems clear enough is that Simic is not trying to write a poem like Keats's. This means that we ought to judge each poem in terms of what it achieves rather than what we think it ought to have achieved based on our conceptions of what poetry should be. There are reasons for enjoying Simic's poem, but they are different from the reasons why we might enjoy Keats's.

Rather than employing the kind of 'poetic' language found in Keats, Simic's poem seems more like a list of mundane observations about everyday urban life in the United States in the late twentieth century. The poem therefore raises interesting points in a discussion of what poetry is, since it plays upon our expectations about poetry. If we feel a sense of shock at encountering such 'ordinary' language in a poem, that is because we are expecting something else – probably something like Keats. This sense of shock is perhaps most acute when we encounter the word 'piss' in a poem. This is not because the word itself is so shocking – it is used quite casually in some contexts – but because it appears in a poem. Again, the effect of this depends upon its discrepancy with our expectations about poetry, and can therefore alert us to those expectations.

Part of the poem's impact, then, depends on its relationship to other poems. But there is also an internal tension at work in the poem itself. The use of mundane language acts as a setting against which sudden glimpses of more 'poetic' language seem all the more startling. This juxtaposition of vulgar and poetic registers is most stark in the last four lines:

> And I,
> I piss in the sink
> with a feeling of
> eternity.

The effect here depends precisely upon the clash between sacred and profane language – without this, the effect of either would be diluted. Perhaps, too, these lines, set apart as they are from the rest of the poem, make a kind of Romantic claim about the poem's speaker, foregrounding his 'poetic sensibility' in contrast to the other characters. These lines become still more intriguing if we think a little more about the poem's title, which alludes to a triptych of paintings by Hieronymus Bosch called 'Garden of Terrestrial Delights' (*c*.1510). The left wing of the triptych shows naked Adam and Eve in their *Earthly Paradise*, and the right wing shows *Hell*, where the damned are suffering all kinds of exotic torments. It is the central panel, however, which supplies the title under which the whole triptych is generally known: *Garden of Earthly Delights*, and the garden is full of naked figures engaged in all kinds of bizarre activities, sexual, procreative and (despite the word 'Earthly' in the title) out-of-this-world. It is hard for the viewer to decide whether this very strange 'Garden' is closer, in its evident 'delights', to the Garden of Eden, or whether, on the contrary, it represents the sinful pleasures that tempt human beings after mankind's Fall from paradise and which anticipate the equally bizarre and other-worldly torments of Hell that await us as depicted on the following panel. Simic's allusion to this painting invites us to look for parallels between poem and painting. Is Simic suggesting that the mundane chaos of modern life is like Bosch's vision of the Garden of Earthly Delights? And if so, is it more like his paradise, or more like his hell? And does the very banality and everyday familiarity of the world occupied by Simic's speaker not seem very different from the extraordinary fantasy world portrayed in all three panels of Bosch's painting? And does this allow us to reinterpret the poem's last lines as either a moment of transcendence or a moment of despair in which the speaker feels that, as in hell, his torments will go on for all eternity? Have we, then, unexpectedly arrived at the possibility that Keats's and Simic's poems are radically different versions of the same theme? Is Simic's speaker also seeking a way out of a world in which we 'sit and hear each other groan'?

It might even be that, as in Keats's poem, the vehicle of escape or transcendence in Simic's poem is poetry itself. Within the list of mundane observations which makes up the first part of the poem, there is an unexpected claim about the nature of poetry: 'Roger says / poetry is the manufacture of lightning rods' (5–6). The statement is quite surprising, since we are being invited to think of poetry as a manufacturing process. This is startling because it contradicts most of our received ideas about poetry. Keats himself asserted that 'if Poetry comes not as naturally as the Leaves to a tree it had better not come at all'.[15] Our idea that poetry comes 'naturally' to the poet, and that it should not involve labour or anything artificial or technical, is yet another assumption which we have inherited from Romanticism. Simic's metaphor is intriguing because there may not, at first sight, be any obvious similarity between poetry and the 'manufacture of lightning rods'. One way of interpreting this metaphor is to think about the function of lightning rods: to conduct electrical energy from storms to the earth. The metaphor might therefore be claiming that poetry creates some kind of medium which conducts energy from the 'heavens' to the earth. It would then be a very new metaphor for the very old concept that poetry is a vehicle for some kind of divine inspiration. In this reading the poem combines two previously incompatible ideas: although the writing of poetry might be a manufacturing activity, the product (a poem) works as a medium which will conduct inspiration, spark the reader's imagination, or even set up a channel through which a lightning-like imaginative impulse may pass from author to reader. In other words, there is a concept of imagination at work in this poem which is only partly dissimilar to Romantic ideas.

■ Readers' Assumptions and the Reading Experience

Our readings of Keats's and Simic's poems have demonstrated that we do not (perhaps cannot) approach any poem as 'innocent' readers free from preconceptions about poetry. Although Simic's poem is a remarkably 'individual' and 'modern' poem, our response to and understanding of it partly depend on our

---

[15] Keats to John Taylor, 27 February 1818, in Keats, *Letters*, p. 70.

knowledge of poems such as 'Ode to a Nightingale'. The impact of the poem relies precisely upon the disjunction between our preconceptions about poetry and the poem we actually read. What this means is that our original question – 'What is poetry?' – is not an irrelevant question even though we may not be able definitively to answer it. On the contrary, this is a question which influences our response to everything we take to be poetry, since we have a large number of internalised assumptions about what poetry is and what it does which we bring to bear on any poem we read.

Most of the features we have identified as being authentically 'poetic' in Keats's poem are actually characteristic of Romantic poetry rather than poetry in general. This fact reveals the way in which our assumptions are shaped by the history of culture. Although we may believe that our ideas are personal to us, attention to the history of culture (of which the history of poetry is a part) reveals that our assumptions are inherited from the past and from the way our present culture relates to the past. We should be wary of thinking that the continued existence of Romantic ideas about poetry means that they are more correct or better than other ideas. Periods prior to the Romantic period had very different ideas about poetry, ideas which shaped the ways in which poetry was written, read and valued. This means that one of the tasks that face us if we want to become better readers of poetry is to familiarise ourselves with these different conventions by reading more poetry from different periods.

Yet gaining a familiarity with the changing historical assumptions about poetry may lead us to question our own place within that history. Why is it, for example, that we continue to have and value Romantic conceptions about poetry more than 150 years after the 'official' end of the Romantic period'? One answer to this is the fact that Romantic conceptions continued to have force throughout the nineteenth century, and still influence popular ideas about literature and writers today. Some of these ideas were given new life in the theory and practice of the so-called New Criticism which shaped university teaching of literature in the United States and Britain in the middle decades of the twentieth century. A combination of popular ideas about poetry and a watered-down version of New Criticism continues to influence the way literature is taught in schools in Britain and the United States. The same assumptions underlie the way poetry is discussed on television, in book reviews in newspapers and magazines, and in popular films such as *Dead Poets Society* (Touchstone Pictures, 1989). This is one of the reasons why we continue to regard Keats's 'Ode' (written nearly two hundred years ago) as an exemplary poem.

The fact that different theories about poetry have been held at different historical moments indicates why it is impossible to give a definitive answer to the question 'What is poetry?' All answers to that question will inevitably be historically and theoretically contingent. And the fact that our assumptions about poetry are shaped by our own place in history, and by the unconscious theories about literature which our particular culture holds and disseminates, means that we ourselves cannot stand outside history and theory to see what poetry 'really is'.

The idea that we cannot step outside history or theory is a relatively recent one. Its consequence is that many literary critics have become quite self-conscious about their own 'position' as readers in relation to a text. This self-reflexivity has led to a proliferation of literary theories. Since New Criticism lost its dominant place in the study of literature in universities, no single literary theory has taken its place. Most literature departments in universities these days feel it necessary to teach classes on 'literary theory', and guides to literary theory have flooded the market. Such classes and books will typically discuss a range of theories, including Russian Formalism, Structuralism, Post-Structuralism, Psychoanalysis, Marxism, Feminism, Reader Response and New Historicism.[16] Each of these theoretical approaches to literature brings its own explicitly formulated assumptions and agenda to a literary text, and asks its own characteristic questions of it. There are incompatibilities between these theories, and some critics will adopt one at the expense of the others in order to be able to declare an identifiable 'position'.[17] More interesting interpretative work is done, however, by critics who explore the overlap between theories and are prepared to use whatever critical tools and theoretical assumptions particular passages in a literary text seem to call for. This is why we are not setting out to teach any particular literary theory so that you will be able to 'apply' it to the next poem you come across. Instead, we want to stimulate you to think about poetry in theoretically informed ways which will allow you to be attentive to the theoretical implications of the features of each particular poem you read.

[16] For good examples of such books, see Ann Jefferson and David Robey, *Modern Literary Theory: A comparative introduction*, 2nd edn (London: Batsford, 1986); Terry Eagleton, *Literary Theory: An introduction* (Oxford: Blackwell, 1983); Raman Selden, *A Reader's Guide to Contemporary Literary Theory* (Sussex: Harvester, 1985); Peter Collier and Helga Geyer-Ryan, *Literary Theory Today* (London: Polity Press, 1990). The best, and most comprehensive collection of literary theory is Vincent B. Leitch *et al.*, eds. *The Norton Anthology of Theory and Criticism* (New York and London: Norton, 2001). For a good, wide-ranging collection of twentieth-century theoretical reflections on poetry, see Jon Cook, *Poetry in Theory: An Anthology 1900–2000* (Oxford and Malden, MA: Blackwell, 2004).

[17] For an example of an approach which rigidly separates different theoretical approaches to poetry, see David Buchbinder, *Contemporary Literary Theory and the Reading of Poetry* (London: Macmillan, 1991).

Exercises

1 Read the following poem (by Ted Hughes, 1957) several times, and then answer the questions that follow:

The Thought-Fox

I imagine this midnight moment's forest:
Something else is alive
Beside the clock's loneliness
And this blank page where my fingers move.

Through the window I see no star: 5
Something more near
Though deeper within darkness
Is entering the loneliness:

Cold, delicately as the dark snow,
A fox's nose touches twig, leaf;   10
Two eyes serve a movement, that now
And again now, and now, and now

Sets neat prints into the snow
Between trees, and warily a lame
Shadow lags by stump and in hollow   15
Of a body that is bold to come

Across clearings, an eye,
A widening deepening greenness,
Brilliantly, concentratedly,
Coming about its own business   20

Till, with a sudden sharp hot stink of fox
It enters the dark hole of the head.
The window is starless still; the clock ticks,
The page is printed.

(a) Try to describe who (or what) the speaker of this poem is and the situation which the poem presents.

(b) Why does the poem begin with 'I imagine'? How much of what follows is imagined – is it just the 'midnight moment's forest', or everything in the poem?

(c) How does Hughes make the coming and movement of the fox seem vividly immediate in lines 9–21?

(d) Rewrite the whole poem: (i) without stanza divisions; (ii) in continuous prose. What differences are there between each version?

(e) In the chapter we discussed the effect in 'Ode to a Nightingale' of the dynamic and irregular interplay between line endings and sentence structure. Does Hughes use similar techniques to achieve appropriate effects in this poem? Begin by marking where each sentence in the poem begins and ends, and note what relationship there is between these sentences and the line and stanza structure. How does the relation between verse form and sentence structure work in the long second sentence which presents the movement of the fox?

(f) How do you interpret the fact that the fox 'enters the dark hole of the head' (22)? What *is* the dark hole of the head? Is there any relation between this dark hole into which the fox disappears and the earlier lines which tell us that 'Something more near / Though deeper within darkness/ Is entering the loneliness' (6–8)?

(g) What difference would it make if the poem began with the second stanza ('Through the window I see no star') and ended halfway through the last stanza with 'It enters the dark hole of the *night*'?

(h) Why is the poem called 'The Thought-Fox'?

(i) Why does the poem end with the line 'The page is printed'? What page is printed? And what is printed on it? What do you make of the echo between this line and the fact that we are told that the fox 'Sets neat prints into the snow'?

(j) What assumptions about poetry can you discover in the poem? Are they more like Keats's or more like Simic's?

2 Read the following poem – William Blake's 'The Tyger' – several times and then try to answer the questions that follow; 'The Tyger' appeared in Blake's *Songs of Innocence and of Experience* (1794) as a companion poem to 'The Lamb':

The Tyger

Tyger tyger, burning bright,
In the forests of the night:
What immortal hand or eye,
Could frame thy fearful symmetry?

In what distant deeps or skies   5
Burnt the fire of thy eyes!
On what wings dare he aspire?
What the hand, dare sieze the fire?

And what shoulder, & what art,
Could twist the sinews of thy heart?   10
And when thy heart began to beat,
What dread hand? & what dread feet?

What the hammer? what the chain,
In what furnace was thy brain?
What the anvil? what dread grasp,   15
Dare its deadly terrors clasp?

When the stars threw down their spears
And water'd heaven with their tears:
Did he smile his work to see?
Did he who made the Lamb make thee?   20

Tyger, Tyger burning bright,
In the forests of the night:
What immortal hand or eye,
Dare frame thy fearful symmetry?

(a) What image of the 'tyger' emerges in this poem?

(b) This poem consists of a series of questions – about who made the 'tyger' – that are never explicitly answered: is there an implicit answer in the questions themselves? Try to decide who or what made the 'tyger' by reading the questions very carefully.

(c) How does the poem suggest the 'tyger' was made? What kind of creative process is implied in the questions?

(d) What kind of creator is implied in the questions?

(e) What kind of relationship between creator and creation do the questions imply?

(f) Is there a general theory of creativity implicit in the poem? Could that general account of the creative process, and the relationship between creator and creation, be applied to the creation of the poem 'The Tyger'?

(g) Blake is normally thought of as a Romantic poet; is the theory of creativity in this poem a Romantic theory?

(h) The notebook that Blake used between about 1789 and 1818 to draft his poems has survived; it contains two drafts of 'The Tyger', including the following first draft (words in italics and brackets indicate deletions or alternatives):

Tyger Tyger burning bright
In the forests of the night
What immortal hand [&] or eye
[*Could/Dare*] frame thy fearful symmetry

[*In what/Burnt in*] distant deeps or skies
[*Burnt the/The cruel*] fire of thine eyes
On what wings dare he aspire
What the hand dare sieze the fire

And what shoulder & what art
Could twist the sinews of thy heart
And when thy heart began to beat
What dread hand & what dread feet

[*Could fetch it from the furnace deep*
And in (the) thy horrid ribs dare steep
In the well of sanguine woe
In what clay & in what mould
Were thy eyes of fury rolld]

[*What/Where*] the hammer [*what/where*] the chain
In what furnace was thy brain
What the anvil what [*the arm/arm/grasp/clasp*] dread grasp
[*Could*] Dare its deadly terrors [*clasp/grasp*] clasp

Tyger tyger burning bright
In the forests of the night
What immortal hand & eye
Dare [*form*] frame thy fearful symmetry

And [*did he laugh*] dare he [*smile/laugh*] his work to see
[*What the shoulder (ankle) what the knee*]
[*Did*] Dare he who made the lamb make thee
When the stars threw down their spears
And waterd heaven with their tears

(i) Compare and contrast the first draft with the version that Blake eventually printed, trying to follow the changes that Blake made. Would you say that Blake managed to improve the poem between its first draft and the final version?

(j) What does this exercise indicate about the creation of poetry?

(k) Blake sometimes claimed that his poems were inspired by or dictated to him by spiritual beings. On the evidence of the composition of 'The Tyger', what is your opinion of this claim?

(l) In a letter of 27 February 1818, Keats wrote one of the classic statements of the Romantic theory of creativity: 'if Poetry comes not as naturally as the Leaves to a tree it had better not come at all'. Nonetheless, the drafts of Keats's poetry show that he usually put a great deal of effort into writing and revising his poems (see Robert Gittings, ed., *The Odes of Keats and Their Earliest Known Manuscripts* [London: Heinemann, 1970] and Jack Stillinger, ed., *John Keats: Poetry Manuscripts at Harvard* [Cambridge, Mass. and London: Belknap Press of Harvard University Press, 1990]). How do you account for this discrepancy between theory and practice?

3 Here is a selection of the many poems about poetry that have been written in English in all periods. Read as many of them as you can (many of them can be found in the *Norton Anthology of Poetry*, 5th edn, ed. Ferguson, *et al.*): Shakespeare, 'Sonnet 55' (1609); Anne Bradstreet, 'The Author to Her Book' (1678); William Morris, 'The Earthly Paradise' (1868–70); A.E. Housman, 'Terence, This is Stupid Stuff . . .' (1896); Marianne Moore, 'Poetry' (1921); Archibald MacLeish, 'Ars Poetica' (1926); A.R. Ammons, 'Poetics' (1971); John Ashbery, 'Paradoxes and Oxymorons' (1981); Tom Wayman, 'What Good Poems Are For' (1980); Leslie Marmion Silko, 'How to Write a Poem about the Sky' (1981); Dana Gioia, 'The Next Poem' (1991); Billy Collins, 'The Trouble with Poetry' (2005).

Read each poem several times and try to articulate the theory of poetry it is promoting or the assumptions about poetry which it takes for granted. How do the assumptions in each poem compare with those of Keats and those of Simic?

Chapter 2

Rhythm and Metre

■ We've All Got Rhythm

In asking the question 'What is poetry?' in Chapter 1, we argued that the only sustainable difference between poetry and other language uses is that poetry is divided into lines. If this is the defining feature of poetry, from which all else follows, then this must be the first thing we attend to in this book. This means that we need to begin with an account of poetic **rhythm** and metre.

This is a necessary but risky way of beginning. Our experience of teaching poetry suggests that the aspect of studying poetry over which students experience most anxiety is the fact that they may be required to analyse a poem's rhythm or metre. One of the reasons for this anxiety is that the method of analysis which is usually taught in schools, universities and textbooks adopts a set of terms and assumptions which are, quite literally, alien to poetry in English. Students are required to cut up poetry into 'feet' which are given Greek names which have to be memorised. This artificial process seems to have little to do with the way we actually experience and derive pleasure from poetic rhythms. We believe that the approach we will use in this book is much more user-friendly and appropriate to our experience of poetry.[1] At the same time,

---

[1] The discussion of rhythm and metre which follows is based on principles of analysis developed by Derek Attridge, *The Rhythms of English Poetry* (London: Longman, 1982), and *Poetic Rhythm* (Cambridge: Cambridge University Press, 1995); also see Thomas Carper and Derek Attridge, *Meter and Meaning: An introduction to rhythm in poetry* (London: Routledge, 2003). For traditional methods of analysing metre, see Geoffrey Leech, *A Linguistic Guide to English Poetry* (London: Longman, 1969), pp. 103–30; Paul Fussell, *Poetic Meter and Poetic Form* (New York: Random House, 1979); John Hollander, *Rhyme's Reason: A guide to English verse* (New Haven, CT: Yale University Press, 1981); *Abrams*, pp. 112–17; and Jon Stallworthy, 'Versification', in Manganet Ferguson, *et al.*, *Norton Anthology of Poetry*, 5th edn (New York and London: Norton, 2004), pp. lxi–lxxx.

however, we recognise the fact that many teachers will expect students to know or use the 'standard' method of analysis. For this reason, we will indicate as we go along how the method we follow correlates with the more usual system. (This comparison is developed still further in the Glossary at the end of the book.)

It is curious that poetic rhythm should cause such unease. Rhythm is fundamental to our very existence and to the way we experience life in our bodies. Our bodies work in rhythmic ways: our heartbeat, our breathing, the way we walk, run, dance, swim. We experience time as rhythmical – the rhythms of darkness and light, of work and rest, the phases of the moon, the regular cycle of the seasons, and so on. Rhythm has physical and mental effects upon us which are deeply related to aesthetic experience. When we dance we move our bodies in rhythmic ways which coincide with the rhythms of music, and this can have a range of different pleasurable effects – from those of the waltz to those of a rave. Jogging, swimming and even walking become a pleasure only when and if we get into a rhythm.

If we are able to absorb and gain pleasures from the rhythms of physical movement, dance and music, we need to examine why it is that the question of rhythm in poetry causes so much anxiety. One of the answers to this is perhaps that students are not usually given credit for simply enjoying a poem's rhythm or metre but are asked to describe or analyse it in technical terms. Moreover, many people find it difficult to bring to conscious knowledge what they unconsciously 'know' and enjoy. Thus, for example, it is possible to experience the intoxicating, trance-like effect of dancing to house music without ever consciously recognising that it achieves this effect through an almost monotonous use of 4×4 rhythmic patterns (see below). In a similar way, readers may derive pleasure from a poem's use of rhythm without being able to analyse that rhythm. In fact, people find it hard at first even to 'hear' the rhythmic patterns of their everyday speech. The very attempt to become conscious of the way we pronounce a word or phrase can make us unable to hear how we say it, or even make us 'forget' how to say it!

The problem here is not restricted to the question of metre. Instead, this is one manifestation of a larger problem. Put simply, the issue at stake here is the apparent incompatibility between enjoyment and analysis. This apparent incompatibility – or the assumption that they are incompatible – involves fundamental theoretical questions. In fact the distinction made by Immanuel Kant (1724–1804) between *Kunst* (art) and *Wissenschaft* (science) has become a major distinction in Western culture (enshrined in different subjects at school and in different faculties in universities). The distinction and relation between art and science has been a major question in Western philosophy. Wordsworth's claim that 'we murder to dissect'[2] is a typically Romantic response to

---

[2] See 'The Tables Turned', in Wordsworth, *Lyrical Ballads*, pp. 105–6.

this question, suggesting that analysis somehow does violence to the artistic object which is analysed. Yet it is impossible to study literature at university without analysis. To study literature involves not just imaginatively responding to texts but becoming able to describe why and how a text induces particular kinds of effect and response. One of the aims of this book is to show that this process of analysis can in itself be a source of pleasure. In effect, then, we will be questioning the Romantic assumption that analysis 'murders' art. This assumption will be questioned in at least two ways: first, by asking whether any kind of reading could be completely free from analysis; secondly, by trying to give our readers the experience that analysis can enhance rather than destroy enjoyment – that, to rework Wordsworth's metaphor, analysis makes poetry more 'alive' or helps us to understand and appreciate its 'life'.

We cannot ignore the fact that poems are organised according to rhythmic and metrical principles. Such principles are the reason why poetry is laid out on the page in the way it is – that is, in lines whose length is governed not by the margins of the page (as in prose) but according to a design predetermined by the poet. This visual difference between poetry and prose is not simply a trivial fact which we can note and then ignore. Instead, it is the first signal that a reader is likely to register that he or she is confronted by a poem rather than some other kind of written language. The spatial layout of lines on a page says to the reader 'this is poetry', and is likely to affect the way he or she reads the words which are organised in this way.

A telling example of this fact occurred to one of the present writers as an undergraduate student in the late 1970s. In a first-year class called 'Practical Criticism', groups of students were presented each week with an anonymous poem to analyse in the course of the seminar through open discussion. Although such a class format was somewhat old-fashioned by then, some of the lecturers managed to use it in instructive ways. One week we were presented with a poem, as usual, and we spent about forty minutes analysing it as a group, finding all kinds of subtle and significant things in its figurative language and form. After we had done this, however, the tutor revealed that the 'poem' we had so carefully analysed was in fact a short item from a newspaper which had been rearranged into lines and presented to us as a poem. Rather than feeling that we had been cheated into making fools of ourselves, we realised that we had been coaxed into arriving at an important insight – that the layout on the page (together with the expectations set up by the institutional context) had stimulated us to read this news item as if it were poetry.[3] The general lesson of this is that the way poetry is laid out on the page acts as

---

[3] This exercise was modelled on an exercise carried out by Stanley Fish and reported in the essay 'How to Recognize a Poem when You See One', in Fish, *Is There a Text in this Class?* (Cambridge, MA: Harvard University Press, 1980).

a visual signal which causes us to alter the way in which we read. A second and related lesson is that the experience of poetry perhaps relies as much on *how* we read as on *what* we read.

■ Written Poetry and the Traces of Poetry's Oral Origins

At this point it is worth making some other apparently obvious remarks which nevertheless have more consequences than are initially apparent. When we think of poetry as being organised into lines on a page, we are thinking of written poetry. Our experience of poetry in contemporary Western culture is mostly through silent reading. Even when we do hear poetry being performed orally (on recordings, at poetry readings or 'performances') it is usually read or memorised from a written text. In the past, however, poetry was also, or even pre-eminently, an oral form (this is still the case in many contemporary cultures): bards and balladeers would entertain at court or act as circulators of news by moving from place to place. Such oral poetry was composed and transmitted mainly by and for people who could not read or write. Even after the development of the printing press in the fifteenth century, books remained rare and illiteracy was widespread. The oral bards did not necessarily compose their poetry but inherited and transmitted traditional poems which they would modify in performance or in response to events. Such poetry had to be memorised (though not necessarily word-for-word), and various mnemonic devices (aids to memory) were built into the poems themselves. These included ritualistic formulae and different kinds of sound **parallelism**, such as alliteration, rhyme and metre.

The oral (or aural) origins of poetry still persist in written poetry today. Many of the devices of written poems which we analyse in the classroom (alliteration, rhyme and metre) were originally devised in order to make poetry more memorable for both the bard and the listeners. It is even possible to suggest that without such oral/aural ghosts of the past, poetry would cease to be poetry. This is most clearly the case with rhythm and metre. Rhythm in language is, by definition, an aural effect – something we hear (whether in reading aloud or through sounding the words silently in our imagination). Metre is simply the organisation of the rhythms of the language into regular units. As we noted in the previous chapter, 'metre' is etymologically related to 'measure', and 'measure' has a couple of specialised meanings which it is revealing to note. According to the *Shorter Oxford English Dictionary*, 'measure' has a number of meanings, including the following: (a) a 'measured sound or movement'; (b) 'an air, tune, melody' and 'the time of a piece of music'; (c) 'rhythmical motion, especially as regulated by music'; and (d) 'a grave or stately dance'. These meanings of 'measure' indicate the close relationships between the aural and physical rhythms of poetry, music and dance, but they also suggest why written poetry is laid out on the page in measured lines. Poetic lines on the page are arranged in order to indicate in a spatial way the rhythms and measures of the poem as it is performed and experienced as sound in time.

Poetry is not, of course, the only kind of discourse which is written in lines. When songs of all kinds are written down, they are organised into lines. The length of the lines is not arbitrarily chosen but forms a regular pattern which indicates the linguistic and musical rhythms. This similarity between songs and poems offers one way of taking some of the mystery out of the question of metre in poetry. Although poetry is increasingly experienced through silent reading, we hear songs everywhere in our culture – as nursery rhymes, hymns and carols, football chants, jingles, pop songs, and so on. As children we seem to derive great pleasure from the rhythmic structures of the stories, rhymes, poems and songs which are read to us.[4] Yet as we grow older we seem to lose that immediate pleasure in the rhythms of the texts we read – perhaps because we are taught to get information, excitement or pleasure from the content rather than the form of what we read (though if we have to read regularly to young children, we can regain the skills and pleasures of reading rhythmically). With songs, however, the rhythmic performance of the words along with the music is at least as important as what the words say. Even if we are not musicians, by listening to a song several times we absorb and understand (if only in an unconscious way) its rhythmical form. This kind of knowledge can remain with us all our lives.

■ Have You Got Rhythm?

To test out our claim that we've all got rhythm, we would like you to try the following exercise. We have taken the first few lines of a traditional **ballad** and rearranged them as prose. What we'd like you to do is arrange them into what you take to be the original lines of the song. We anticipate that most of you will be able to do this – not because you will necessarily know this particular ballad, but because you will be able to 'hear' how it goes through an unconscious familiarity with the ballad structure. This tacit familiarity comes through exposure to other ballads and the many kinds of song whose forms are similar to the ballad. Of course, those readers who know the song which Bob Dylan based upon it – 'A Hard Rain's A–gonna Fall' – will have a head

---

[4] The verse stories of Dr Seuss, with their extraordinary rhythms and rhymes, are great favourites with children in many Anglophone countries. For collections of children's verse, see Iona and Peter Opie, eds, *The Oxford Book of Children's Verse* (Oxford and New York: Oxford University Press, 1973), Neil Philip, ed., *The New Oxford Book of Children's Verse* (Oxford and New York: Oxford University Press, 1996), and Elise Paschen, ed., *Poetry Speaks to Children* (Naperville, ILL: Sourcebooks, 2005).

start. In carrying out this exercise, you should read the words out loud – or, better still, try to 'hear' them in your mind as you read silently.

'O where ha' you been, Lord Randal, my son? And where ha' you been, my hand-some young man?' 'I ha' been at the greenwood; mother, mak my bed soon, for I'm wearied wi' huntin', and fain wad lie down.' 'And wha met ye there, Lord Randal, my son? And wha met you there, my handsome young man?' 'O I met wi' my true-love; mother, mak my bed soon, for I'm wearied wi' huntin', and fain wad lie down.'

When you have arranged this into lines, we believe that you will also be able to divide the lines up into stanzas. Try it now.

▧ What Is Rhythm?

We need to begin at the beginning by asking what rhythm is. The simple answer to this is that rhythm occurs whenever there is a regular repetition of similar events which are divided from each other by recognisably different events. A basic visual example of this would be a regularly flashing light (like that of a lighthouse). This can be said to develop a binary sequence which goes as follows: light–dark, light–dark, light–dark, and so on. An aural example would be the regular sound of a bleeper: bleep–quiet, bleep–quiet. Rhythms can occur not only as on–off sequences like these, but in a variety of different ways. The only requirement is that there is an alternation between similar but recognisably different events. Walking can become rhythmical because it involves moving alternate legs – in fact, the regularity of military marching is achieved through the regimental sergeant-major's rhythmical chanting of 'left–right, left–right, left–right'. (It would be interesting to know whether this makes marching a pleasurable activity; certainly, the use of marching songs helps endurance on long marches.)

The rhythms we have looked at so far involve the sequential alternation of two events – which we can call binary or 'duple' rhythms. (For purposes which will soon become clear, it will be helpful to think of duple rhythm in terms of numbers: 'one–two, one–two, one–two'.) Although there are more complex rhythms than duple rhythm, they are always composed out of sequences of 'beats' and 'offbeats'. A dance rhythm which may be familiar to some readers is that of the waltz. Beginners learning to dance the waltz have to programme their bodies to move according to the waltz rhythm, otherwise they risk the humiliation of continually treading on their partner's toes. The basic rhythm of the waltz is easy enough and is often counted out in the learning process: 'one–two–three, one–two–three.' This is called a triple rhythm, for obvious reasons. But the crucial question to the novice dancer is where the beats and offbeats fall. This is why a beginner is made to hear where the beat falls in the way the sequence of numbers is chanted: '**one**–two–three, **one**–two–three, one–two–three . . .'. In this rhythm, then, the beat is achieved by the 'one', while the offbeat is achieved by the 'two–three'. Because the strong beat comes before the weaker beat, the pattern 'beat–offbeat' is called a **falling rhythm**. Thus the waltz rhythm can be called a 'falling triple rhythm'. (If the **stress** had fallen on the third element rather than the first – 'one–two–**three**, one–two–**three**' – then this would be called a **rising rhythm**.) Indeed, the relationship between counting and rhythm is programmed into us from our early years in playground games and in the classroom, where multiplication tables are (or used to be) memorised through the rhythms of group chanting – a technique which was so effective that the present writers can still hear the tones of the way we chanted the tables (this is just one example of how rhythmic language can be memorable). The fact that group chanting is always rhythmical reveals the link between rhythm in language and rhythm in music (which is the basis of song). Indeed, the use of counting to establish rhythm is not restricted to learning to waltz: it is a feature of all music, and can be used to help co-ordinate different musicians in a band or orchestra, or to work out what 'time signature' a piece of music is in.

We have now gathered all the principles and terms we need in order to describe most rhythmic sequences. All we need to ask of any rhythm is whether it is (i) duple or triple, and (ii) rising or falling. Thus, in fact, there are four basic kinds of rhythm:

(a) rising duple: 'one–**two**, one–**two**';
(b) falling duple: '**one**–two, **one**–two';
(c) rising triple: 'one–two–**three**, one–two–**three**';
(d) falling triple: '**one**–two–three, **one**–two–three'.

The traditional mode of analysing poetic rhythm and metre also identifies these patterns but gives them different names derived from the analysis of poetic metre in the classical languages (Greek and Latin):

(a) rising duple = 'iambic' rhythm;
(b) falling duple = 'trochaic' rhythm;
(c) rising triple = 'anapaestic' rhythm;
(d) falling triple = 'dactylic' rhythm.

■ What Is Metre?

If we have now articulated the basic building blocks of rhythm, we only need to add that metrical form (metre) is achieved simply through measuring the way rhythmic units are combined together – that is, through arranging rhythmic units in groups which are regularly repeated. In poetry written in English there are two basic measures or numbers of rhythmic unit per line: four per line and five per line. (In traditional metrical analysis, the four-unit line is called a '**tetrameter**' (from the Greek for 'four') and the five-unit line is called a '**pentameter**' (from the Greek for 'five' – cf., pentagon, etc.).) The differences between these measures can be illustrated by adapting the counting principles used thus far. If we put an 'and' between numbers we can establish clearly where beats and offbeats occur, since the word 'and' is very rarely given stress in English speech: '**one** and **two** and **three**'. Thus a metre consisting of four-beat lines will look like this:

> and one and two and three and four
> and five and six and seven and eight
> and one and two and three and four
> and five and six and seven and eight.

In this example, we have used rising duple units (in which 'seven' is pro-nounced virtually as one syllable). A four-beat rising **triple metre** would look like this:

> and a one and a two and a three and a four
> and a five and a six and a seven and an eight
> and a one and a two and a three and a four
> and a five and a six and a seven and an eight.

If you read these metrical forms out loud (or sound them in your head as you read silently) you should discover that they both have a strongly insistent metrical pattern which almost coaxes you into a chant-like rendition. Furthermore, you will perhaps feel that a momentum emerges which seems to insist that all four lines have to be chanted in order to complete the pattern. This pattern of four four-beat lines is very common in poetry and in songs, so it is useful to have a way of describing it. Following Attridge, we will call it the 4 × 4 pattern (*Rhythms of English Poetry*, p. 83). The insistent momentum of this pattern is such that it can survive even if we mix up the kinds of unit which compose it. Thus the following lines employ a mixture of duple and triple units:

> and one and two and three and four
> and five and six and seven and eight
> and nine and ten and eleven and twelve
> and thirteen and fourteen and fifteen and sixteen.

In order to mark the beat pattern, we follow Attridge in using the following convention (with 'b' underneath the beats and 'o' underneath the offbeats):

```
and one and two and three and four
o    b   o b    o       b o   b
and five and six and seven and eight
o    b   o b   o   b    o     b
```

For the moment, we will postpone the analysis of the third and fourth lines.

The other major metrical form in poetry in English is the five-beat form, in which the lines are measured into rhythmic units of five:

```
and one and two and three and four and five
o    b   o   b o    b o   b o    b
and six and seven and eight and nine and ten
o    b o   b    o    b   o    b o   b
```

The distinctive feature of the five-beat metre is that it does not have the chant-like quality of the four-beat metre, nor does it have the latter's tendency to organise itself into groups of four lines. We will examine the consequences of these facts later.

We now have all the basic terms and principles needed for describing poetic metre: we are able to describe the rhythmic units (e.g., rising duple) and are able to say whether they are measured out in four-beat lines or five-beat lines. Thus we might describe a poem's metre as five-beat rising duple. In the traditional system, this would be '**iambic pentameter**'; a four-beat falling triple metre would be 'dactylic tetrameter', and so on (see Glossary).

▪ The Syllable as the Basic Unit of Rhythm in Language

The rhythmic units we have examined above consist of groups of two or three words: 'left–right', 'one–two–three', 'and one', and so on. But it is important to realise that the basic element of rhythm is not the word but the syllable. We have been able to clarify the principles of rhythmic and metrical form because we have, for the most part, been using one-syllable words (we compressed 'seven' into one syllable, and we introduced multisyllabic words such as 'eleven' or 'thirteen' without comment).

In the analysis of poetic rhythms and metre, it is important to understand what a syllable is and to be able to analyse a multisyllabic word into its component syllables. The *Shorter OED* tells us that a syllable is 'a vocal sound or set of sounds uttered with a single effort of articulation and forming a word or an element of a word'. This is a crucial definition for an understanding of rhythm in language, because it reminds us that speech is produced through muscular movements of the human body – this is why the rhythms of speech are fundamentally related to the other kinds of rhythms which we produce

41

with our bodies, such as drumming, running or dancing. Each 'effort of articu-
lation' is produced through the combined actions of the lungs, the vocal cords
and the mouth (teeth, tongue, lips). A syllable is the result of a '*single* effort of
articulation'. It is thus the basic element of rhythm in speech – in just the same
way, for example, that a step is the basic element of rhythm in walking, march-
ing or running. The fact that a syllable is produced by an effort of articulation
is precisely why we are suggesting that you read out loud the examples we are
looking at in this chapter (alternatively, you can try to hear them in your head
as you read silently).

But in order to be clear what a syllable actually sounds like (or looks like on
the page) it is worth quoting further from the *Shorter OED*'s definition. It goes on
to say that a syllable is an element of 'a spoken language comprising a . . .
vowel or vowel equivalent . . . with or without one or more . . . consonants or con-
sonant equivalents'. The vowels, you will remember, are the sounds repres-
ented by the letters *a*, *e*, *i*, *o*, *u*, or by combinations of those letters (*ou*, *ie*, etc.), or
by 'vowel equivalents' (*y*, for example). Thus a syllable can consist simply of one
vowel – as in one-syllable words such as 'a' and 'I'. More often, a syllable begins
or ends with a consonant – as in the following monosyllabic (single-syllable)
words: to, be, at, ill, by. More consonants can be added, as follows: sad, sound,
creeps, sprints. (In fact, linguists tell us that syllables in English can begin with
as many as three consonants and end with as many as four.[5]) But no matter how
many consonants are added, such syllables remain single syllables as long as
they (i) are 'uttered with a single effort', (ii) form 'a word or an element of a word',
and (iii) contain a single vowel sound. (Although the tongue moves in the
making of a diphthong sound, it can still be regarded as a single vowel sound.)

But the English language does not consist merely of single-syllable words.
Many words are made up of two or more syllables. Two-syllable words require
two distinct efforts of the vocal apparatus in order to pronounce them: words
like 'abstract' or 'holy' are made up of two separate syllables: ab-stract, ho-ly.
Syllables, then, are the basic building elements of words, and can be combined
to make multisyllabic words of varying numbers of syllables. Such words can,
in turn, be analysed into the separate syllables of which they are made: multi-
syllabic = mul-ti-syl-la-bic. Although the rhythmic units and metrical forms
analysed above consist of monosyllabic words, in most instances poetry will
contain a mixture of words of different numbers of syllables:

and five and fourteen and fifteen and six.

To be able to see how this works in practice, we need to understand a few
more basic facts about the English language.

[5] See Leech, *Linguistic Guide to English Poetry*, pp. 63, 89–90.

In the analyses of rhythmic units and lines thus far, it is clear where the beats occur in the lines. Most readers will give more emphasis to the numbers rather than the 'ands' in the following line:

one and **two** and **three** and **four**.

For the purpose of analysing poetic rhythm and metre, we say that the numbers in this line are 'stressed' while the 'ands' receive less stress (or are 'unstressed'). Stress occurs when we give slightly more 'weight' to one syllable than to another – through slightly increasing the duration and/or the loudness of the syllable, or through giving it a slightly higher **pitch**. The awkward thing is that we do this automatically – we don't have to think about it. But when we try to become conscious of this it sometimes happens that we cannot hear or reproduce consciously what we habitually do without thinking about it. It's a bit like trying to analyse what we do when we ride a bicycle or swim.

One of the most important things to realise is that rhythm is a fact of everyday language use; it is not some mysterious thing confined to poetry or invented by teachers in order to baffle students. If we adopt the convention of marking a stressed syllable with '/' above the vowel and an unstressed syllable with '-' above the vowel, we can begin by looking at the way we pronounce some multisyllabic words:

```
 - / -      / -      / -      - / - -
eleven   thirteen  fourteen  modernity
```

```
  / - / -      - /  - / -      / -  /
repetition   interpretation  fellowship
```

One important thing to note here is that we tend to pronounce multisyllabic words in ways which alternate the stresses and unstresses. This clearly conforms to our definition of rhythm above, where we suggested that it consists of regularly alternating events. One of the reasons for this is that speech production is a physical process and, as we have seen, the human body tends to move in rhythmic ways. Thus the successive individual efforts required to produce multisyllabic words tend to alternate in terms of the amount of energy expended.[6]

This rhythmic feature can also be seen when we combine words into sentences:

---

[6] For a discussion of this aspect of verbal rhythm, see Attridge, *Rhythms of English Poetry*, pp. 64–72.

/   -   - / -   -   / -   -   /   - / -
One of the reasons for this is that speech production
                     - -   / - -   / -
                   is a physical process.

Our analysis of this sentence demonstrates several further points. First, we automatically speak in regularly rhythmic ways. Secondly, rhythm seems to act as a 'carrier' of speech – in other words, the regular rhythm seems to help keep the speech moving. Thirdly, although the alternation of effort given to successive syllables is related to the way our bodies produce speech through muscular action, stress patterns in speech are also affected by how 'important' a word is in the sentence. Thus the 'less important' words – such as 'of', 'the', 'is' – are given less stress here than the 'more important' words such as 'speech' or the first syllable of 'reasons'. For the same reason, although the word 'this' in the above sentence is in a stress position, it is not likely to receive the same amount of stress as, say, 'speech'. In other words, in contrast to the counting models above, the amount of stress given to stressed syllables in actual sentences tends to vary. Fourthly, this example shows that the stressed syllables are produced at roughly regular intervals in time, and that the interval between stresses may be occupied by a varying number of unstressed syllables. This is why English is called a 'stress-timed' language. (All these features might become clearer to you if you try to imagine how a computer-generated version of the above sentence might sound: although computers can now be programmed to generate the phonetic sounds of spoken language with some accuracy, they do not reproduce the subtle modulations of stress which make up the rhythm of the language. This is why they talk like robots.)

In everyday speech we usually choose rhythmically regular rather than irregular ways of constructing phrases (without necessarily being conscious of the fact):

/   - - /   - -   / - -   /
English is marked by its strong use of stress.

This means that when we do say or hear irregularly stressed phrasing, we are more likely to take notice:

/   /   /   /   /
Its use of strong stress is what marks English.

In this example, the stresses, rather than being distributed evenly along the line, actually bunch together in the phrases 'strong stress' and 'marks English'. This is not an impossible sentence, of course, but its rhythmic irregularity does tend to draw attention to itself.

The fact that 'everyday' language is always rhythmic reveals that the difference between poetry and 'ordinary' language use is *not* that one is rhythmic while the other is unrhythmic. The difference, rather, is that poetry shapes the natural rhythms of the language in order to achieve certain effects. Poetry may, for example, make use of irregular stress patterns precisely because they draw attention to themselves. But the major way in which poetry shapes the rhythms of the language is by arranging rhythmic sequences of words into regular measured lines in order to form what we call metre.

We have suggested that there are two basic metrical forms in English poetry – the four-beat line and the five-beat line. This does not mean that you will only encounter four-stress or five-stress lines in the poems you read. In fact, you may often encounter poems written in three-stress lines, and you may sometimes come across six-stress lines. But, as Attridge suggests, when six-stress lines are read out loud they tend to resolve themselves into four-beat patterns (two six-stress lines can sound like three four-beat lines) because the four-beat pattern is so insistent. And, as we will see below, the insistence of the four-beat pattern means that three-stress lines tend to be experienced as incomplete realisations of an underlying four-beat metre (especially when three-stress lines alternate with four-stress lines). Five-stress lines are the only form that does not succumb to the powerful gravitational pull of the 4 × 4 pattern; this is why five-beat metre is the only real alternative to four-beat metre and why these two metres are the two basic metrical templates of English verse. What we would like to do now is explore actual examples of the four-beat and five-beat forms, together with their historical significance in the history of poetry in English.

■ Four-beat Metres

Four-beat metre is the dominant form in popular and oral poetry, although it is also found in the literary tradition. It appears in nursery rhymes, hymns, ballads, pop songs and other kinds of popular poetry and song. In the course of your reading you may well come across other line lengths (such as two-beat or six-beat lines), but most of them can be thought of as variants of the four-beat line – except, that is, for the five-beat line. It is thus worth examining four-beat metres at some length.

Some key insights about the four-beat form can be revealed by combining the method of marking stressed syllables with the method of marking beats and offbeats:

```
  -    /    -         /  -        /  -    /
and one and two and three and four
  o    b    o         b  o        b o    b
```

```
-   /   -   /   -   /   -   /
and five and six and seven and eight
o   b   o   b o   b   o   b

-   /   -   /   -   - / - -       /
and nine and ten and eleven and twelve
o   b   o   b o   b   o       b

-   /   - -   /   - -   /   - -   /   -
and thirteen and fourteen and fifteen and sixteen
o       b   o   b       o   b   o   b
```

There are some important things to notice here. First, the actual stress pattern of the words used coincides exactly with the pattern of beats: we can say that the rhythm matches the metre (we will see that this is not always the case). Secondly, although there are four stresses in each line, the number of unstressed syllables varies considerably. This can be seen simply by counting the number of syllables per line: while there are eight syllables in the first line, there are twelve in the fourth. Yet this variation in the number of unstressed syllables does not affect the momentum of the 4 × 4 pattern of beats. In other words, the important factor in this metrical form is the number of stresses per line, not the number of syllables. This is why this form is called 'strong-stress verse' – it is the stresses that count, while the number of unstressed syllables can vary considerably. As a consequence, although the beats coincide neatly with the stresses in a one-to-one relationship, the offbeats coincide with, or are 'realised' by, varying numbers of unstressed syllables: sometimes an offbeat is realised by a single unstressed syllable (as in the first line), sometimes by two unstressed syllables (as in the fourth line). The potential for such variation sometimes makes it difficult to attach a single descriptive label to the rhythmic form of a whole poem or stanza of 4 × 4 verse. In the above example, while the first line is clearly in rising duple rhythm, most of the last line is in rising triple rhythm. As we will see from actual examples, such variation often occurs in 4 × 4 verse. (This is one reason why the 'standard' method of analysing metre is not very useful.)

We said earlier that metre is etymologically related to measure. We can now see that we can begin our analysis of a poem's metre by two simple measurements: (i) count the total number of syllables per line; (ii) count the number of stresses per line (these will usually, but not always, indicate the beats). If there are four stresses per line, you are probably reading four-beat metre. If the number of syllables per line is constant, then you simply need to work out the ratio of stresses to syllables in order to have a good idea of whether it is duple (1 : 2) or triple (1 : 3) rhythm. If the number of syllables per line varies, then your poem is not falling neatly into duple or triple rhythm.

The 4 × 4 form is nearly always reinforced by end-rhymes (in various patterns) – as in the first stanza of the Scottish popular ballad 'The Twa Corbies':

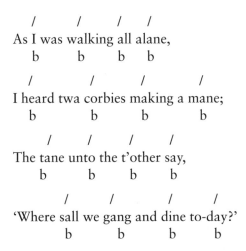

```
       /     /    /    /
As I was walking all alane,
   b      b     b    b

   /         /        /         /
I heard twa corbies making a mane;
   b         b        b         b

     /     /     /    /
The tane unto the t'other say,
   b       b     b     b

     /      /        /       /
'Where sall we gang and dine to-day?'
       b        b        b       b
```

A point to note here is the way stressed syllables often alliterate and hence reinforce the metrical structure: 'mak-' /'mane', 'tane'/'t'o-', 'dine'/'day'. The following stanza from Blake's 'Song' (1783) shows a literary poet using a similar form at least two hundred years after 'The Twa Corbies':

> How sweet I roam'd from field to field,
> And tasted all the summer's pride,
> 'Till I the prince of love beheld,
> Who in the sunny beams did glide!

The connection between 4 × 4 poetic form and popular nursery rhymes and songs can help those of our readers who find the analysis of poetic rhythms and metre difficult. The interplay between music and text not only indicates the profound relationship between songs and the 4 × 4 poetic form, but should help you to 'feel' the rhythms of the language and the ways in which they are shaped into metrical forms. In songs there are three rhythmic principles which interrelate with one another – the natural rhythmic phrasing of the words, the metre and the bar structure (or 'measure') of the music. When these coincide with and reinforce one another, the analysis of the poetic metre of the lyrics is made relatively easy. This is the case with nursery rhymes, as in 'Twinkle, Twinkle Little Star' (which combines the tune of the 1761 French melody '*Ah! vous dirai-je, Maman*' with Jane Taylor's 1806 poem 'The Star'). The song-text exhibits a fairly regular falling duple metre in 4 × 4 form (the repetition of the first two lines at the end of the stanza fits the tune and serves as a **refrain** throughout the song):

> Twinkle, twinkle, little star,
> How I wonder what you are!
> Up above the world so high,
> Like a diamond in the sky.
> Twinkle, twinkle, little star,
> How I wonder what you are!

The music of this song (which many of you will know from childhood) is in 4/4 time. This effectively means that it is in a falling duple rhythm that coincides exactly with the falling duple rhythm of the lyrics. (Musical metres are always falling – in other words, a bar of music always begins with a beat, not an offbeat.) In this song, then, the musical beats coincide with the metrical beats of the language – an effect that is brought out by group singing or chanting. Indeed, children readily demonstrate that they are able to feel where the beats come in a song like this, particularly when they sing it in unison with others. If you feel unable to feel or analyse the metrical pattern of the lyrics, we suggest that you either find a child to help you or try singing it out loud (either alone or with friends). As soon as you do so, you will hear where the metrical beats should fall.

While 'Twinkle, Twinkle Little Star' is in falling duple metre, the most common metrical form in English poetry is rising duple metre (as in 'The Twa Corbies' and Blake's 'Song'). Even poems that begin with a stress tend to settle into rising metres:

    /   - - /   - / - /
    Calm is the morn without a sound,
    /   - - / - /   -   /
    Calm as to suit a calmer grief,
    - / - /   - / - /
    And only through the faded leaf
      - / - / - - /   - /
    The chestnut pattering to the ground
       (Tennyson, *In Memoriam* (1833), section 11)

But Blake's 'The Tyger' (1794) establishes a falling pattern which adds to the sense of tension in the poem:

    / - / - / -   /
    Tyger! Tyger! burning bright
    / - / - / - /
    In the forests of the night.

Most poems in falling duple metre, as in this case, lack the final unstressed syllable.

Four-beat triple metre also comes in rising and falling forms. Triple metre is used frequently in popular verse and tends to have a light-hearted rocking effect:

> /   -   -   /   - /   - -   /
> Ride a cock-horse to Banbury Cross
>
>   -   / - -   / - - /   -   -   /
> To see a fine lady upon a white horse,
>
> /   -   - / - -   /   -   - /
> Rings on her fingers and bells on her toes,
>
>   /   -   -   / -   - / -   -   /
> She shall have music wherever she goes.

Yet this form is used for quite different effects in Thomas Hardy's 'The Voice' (1914):

> /   -   -   /   -   - / -   - /   -   -
> Woman much missed, how you call to me, call to me,
>
> /   -   - /   - -   / -   -   /
> Saying that now you are not as you were

The difference between these two examples of triple rhythm ought to forewarn readers against the assumption that certain rhythms 'mean' particular things or have predetermined effects.

The insistent momentum of the 4 × 4 metre allows for other interesting variations and effects. One of these occurs in the so-called 'ballad stanza' in which the stress pattern is 4-3-4-3 rather than 4-4-4-4. Because the 4 × 4 pattern seems to have an inevitable and deeply familiar momentum of its own, we seem predisposed to complete it mentally even when it is not fully realised in the poem itself:

> Mary had a little lamb
>   b   b   b   b
>
> Its fleece was white as snow;
>   b   b   b   (b)
>
> And everywhere that Mary went,
>   b   b   b   b
>
> Her lamb was sure to go.
>   b   b   b   (b)

The bracketed 'b' at the end of the second and fourth lines indicates what we call a 'virtual beat' – a beat which the 4 × 4 metrical pattern induces us to 'hear' even though it is not actually realised in the language.[7] Try chanting the rhyme out loud while tapping the beats with a pencil – we predict that you will find yourself wanting to tap a fourth beat at the ends of lines two and four. In songs, such as the carol 'O Little Town of Bethlehem' (Phillips Brooks, 1868), the unrealised fourth beat of the words is often realised by the music:

> O little town of Bethlehem
> How still we see thee lie!
> Above thy deep and dreamless sleep
> The silent stars go by.

In each verse of Robert Burns's song 'Green Grow the Rashes' (1784), the virtual beat of the second and fourth lines is filled in, as it were, with a meaningless syllable – presumably to fulfil the demands of the musical rhythm:

> There's nought but care on ev'ry han',
> In ev'ry hour that passes, O:
> What signifies the life o' man,
> An' 'twere na for the lasses, O? (5–8)

We are now in a position to examine the first stanza of 'Lord Randal' (another Scottish popular ballad) in order to give the 'solution' to the exercise we asked you to carry out earlier. This examination should reveal the metrical principles underlying your decision to arrange the words as you did (we are assuming that you got it right!):

```
  -   /   -   -   /   -   /   -   -  /
'O where ha' you been, Lord Randal, my son?
      b         b         b         b
  -      /   -   -  /   -  /  -   -      /
And where ha' you been, my handsome young man?'
      b         b       b           b
  - -  /  -   -  /  -      /  -  /   - -  /
'I ha' been at the greenwood; mother, mak my bed soon,
      b         b             b         b
  - -      /  -   - /  -  -   /  -   -  /
For I'm wearied wi' huntin', and fain wad lie down.'
          b        b         b        b
```

<hr/>

[7] Attridge uses the term 'unrealized beat' in *Rhythms of English Poetry*, but switches to the less clumsy 'virtual beat' in *Poetic Rhythm*.

'Lord Randal', then, is another example of the 4 × 4 form (even though it is a ballad it does not use the 'ballad stanza'). There are several different features here which reinforce this arrangement into lines: the division into sentences, the question-and-answer structure, the near-rhymes at the end of the lines (which were probably full rhymes in the Scots language in the sixteenth century). Yet although the above analysis of the rhythm and metre responds to its insistent 4 × 4 form, a closer look at the analysis reveals a number of interesting features. In contrast to the counting model of 4 × 4 metrical form that we began with, where the natural rhythm of the words exactly coincides with the underlying metrical form, in this actual example there is somewhat of a mismatch between natural rhythms and metrical beat. Instead of being a 'fault', however, this adds interest to the ballad.

In the first line, rhythm and metre match, and this serves to set up a pattern of expectation for the whole ballad:

```
 -    /   -  -   /   -    /   -  -  /
'O where ha' you been, Lord Randal, my son?
     b         b          b         b
```

In the third line, however, there are some revealing mismatches between metre and natural rhythm:

```
 -  -  /   -   -  /   -     /  -  /   -  -   /
'I ha' been at the greenwood; mother, mak my bed soon,
      b         b              b        b
```

Although the requirements of normal pronunciation lead us to stress the first syllable of 'mother', in the context of this line this stress does not realise a beat, since the metre does not require a beat (the four beats of the line are successfully realised by 'been', 'green-', 'mak', and 'soon'). This example reveals that stresses do not always have the function of realising beats. It shows that the 4 × 4 metre is so insistent that it can override the natural stress patterns of speech. As a consequence, there is often a tension between the demands of natural speech rhythms and the demands of metrical form. In this instance, we say that the first stressed syllable of 'mother' is 'demoted' into an offbeat position.

Although this might seem complicated on a first reading, we believe it does describe what we actually do or experience in reading such lines. This is why we asked you to carry out the exercise on 'Lord Randal' before we got into any consideration of metrical analysis. We believe (hope!) that you were able to arrange the poem into its ballad form simply by 'feeling' how its rhythms demand this particular line arrangement. Analysis is merely a way of accounting

51

for or describing what we feel. Trying to analyse the third line before you had an overall feel for the ballad's metrical movement might have led to all kinds of confusion and perplexity.

This example shows that there are two simultaneous principles at work in metrical poetry in English: the demands of natural speech rhythms and the demands of the underlying metrical pattern. Sometimes these harmoniously coincide; sometimes tensions of various kinds occur between them. It is this continually varying relation between natural speech rhythms and metrical form which makes this formal aspect of poetry so interesting in its own right, and which means that poetry generally avoids the kind of mechanical, metronomic effects produced by the counting models that we used to explain metrical form.

Before we move on to look at the way five-beat metres break with the 4 × 4 pattern, it should be stressed that a good deal of four-beat poetry, especially in the literary tradition, is not confined to four-line stanzas. Some four-beat poetry extends the stanza beyond four lines (or cuts it short), and some poems are not written in stanzas at all but in **verse paragraphs** like much five-beat poetry (see below). Yet the insistent pull of the 4 × 4 form can often be felt in such poems, especially when the **rhyme scheme** encourages it. This can be seen (or felt) in the opening lines of William Morris's 'The Haystack in the Floods' (1858), a 165-line poem written in paragraphs:

> Had she come all the way for this,
> To part at last without a kiss?
> Yea, had she borne the dirt and rain
> That her own eyes might see him slain
> Beside the haystack in the floods?
>
> Along the dripping leafless woods,
> The stirrup touching either shoe,
> She rode astride as troopers do;
> With kirtle kilted to her knee,
> To which the mud splashed wretchedly;
> And the wet dripped from every tree
> Upon her head and heavy hair,
> And on her eyelids broad and fair;
> The tears and rain ran down her face.

■ Five-Beat Metres

The other major metrical form in poetry in English is the five-beat form, in which the lines are measured into rhythmic units of five:

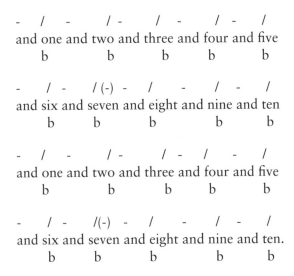

```
  -   /   -     / -     / -     / -     /
and one and two and three and four and five
    b         b        b       b       b

  -    /  -    / (-) -  /    -   /   -    /
and six and seven and eight and nine and ten
    b       b        b          b        b

  -   /   -     / -     / - /     -    /
and one and two and three and four and five
    b         b        b      b        b

  -    /  -    /(-)  -  /    -   /   -    /
and six and seven and eight and nine and ten.
    b       b        b          b        b
```

In these lines, the natural rhythms of the language fit neatly into the five-beat line. Yet even in this highly regular, mechanical model it will be apparent that the five-beat line does not have the inevitable, sing-song momentum of the four-beat line, and does not set up a pattern of expectation which requires a four-line stanza. We have presented four lines here to be consistent, but five-beat lines come in various stanza lengths and in what are called 'verse paragraphs' – whose name indicates that the number of lines in each paragraph varies according to the needs of the meaning, not according to some predetermined stanza pattern. Because the five-beat line escapes from the singsong chant effect of the 4 × 4 metre (with its associations with nursery rhymes, hymns, ballads, and so on), it can seem more faithful to natural speech rhythms, and can create the impression of an individual speaking voice.

Most five-beat verse is formed out of rising, duple rhythmic units. And whereas four-beat verse is flexible regarding the number of unstressed syllables which may appear between the stresses, five-beat verse is much more restrictive in this respect. Since a five-beat line is usually in duple rhythm, it follows that there will be ten syllables per line (which is why this verse form is sometimes called '**decasyllabic**'). Thus we can say that the typical five-beat line will be a ten-syllable, five-beat line in duple, rising metre. In the traditional terminology, such a line is called 'iambic pentameter'. Because this is such an important line, and because the term iambic pentameter is used so frequently in literary criticism, we feel that students ought to be familiar with this term from traditional analysis. Iambic pentameter is relatively easy to 'measure': if all the lines of a poem contain ten syllables and five stresses, then you have a five-beat metre which is almost certainly iambic pentameter. Because it controls the total number of syllables in a line, as well as the number of stresses, five-beat verse is called 'syllable-stress' verse – that is, as well as defining the number of stresses per line, it also defines the number of syllables.[8]

Iambic pentameter is a hugely important metrical line. It is found almost exclusively in 'literary' verse. A great deal of the major poetry and poetic drama of the literary 'canon' in English is written in iambic pentameter. Particularly in the form of **'blank verse'** (unrhymed iambic pentameter), this flexible metrical form can produce the effect of an individual speaking voice simultaneously with a sense of heightened dignity. This is because iambic pentameter is not a fixed grid which forces every syllable into its allotted place – it does not dominate natural speech rhythms in the way that the 4 × 4 line does. Instead, it shapes a whole range of natural speech rhythms into the line, and thus inevitably sets up all kinds of subtle tensions with the metrical pattern. No doubt this flexibility and subtlety is one reason why Shakespeare used it as the dominant form in his plays, as in the following lines from the well-known speech in *Hamlet* (III, i):

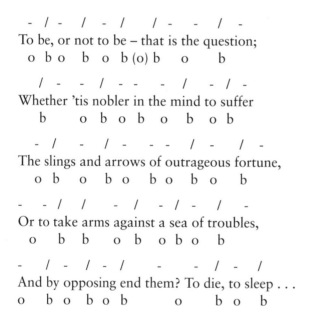

Perhaps the first thing to notice here is that these lines contain eleven rather than ten syllables. (Try counting them.) An eleven-syllable line will occasionally appear in iambic pentameter, but it is unusual to see a run of them like this. If we look through the lines in order to see how the natural speech

<hr>

[8] An alternative name is **'accentual-syllabic'** verse, on the basis that stress is sometimes called 'accent'; we have followed Attridge in *Poetic Rhythm* in deciding to avoid the confusion that could arise over 'accent' by using the term 'syllable-stress'.

rhythms (indicated above the line) are shaped to realise the offbeat–beat pattern of the iambic pentameter (indicated below the line), it is possible to see a number of moments where subtle tensions and ambiguities appear. In the first line, beats and stresses neatly coincide until we come to 'that is'; the iambic pentameter would seem to require a stress on 'is' ('that *is* the question'), but although natural speech rhythms would allow such an emphasis in certain contexts, the actual context of these lines suggests that 'that' needs to be stressed (emphasising that *that* is the question which has to be faced). But although this would seem to violate the iambic pentameter pattern, we do not actually feel any such violation in reading it. This is because a 'virtual offbeat' is realised between 'be' and 'that' by the syntactic pause (marked by the dash). And the flexibility of the metre then allows the next offbeat to be realised by two unstressed syllables ('is the'). The effect of this is that we have a perfect iambic pentameter line which has the rhythmic feel of spontaneous speech.

The second line begins with a beat because of the stress on the first syllable of 'whether'. In traditional methods of **scansion** this would be called a 'reversed **foot**', and we would be told that the metre had momentarily switched to a 'trochaic' pentameter. We feel that this tells us very little about how readers experience or perform the line – which is as a flexible five-beat line rather than as a line of iambic pentameter which starts off on the wrong foot. We do not hear or read lines of verse as being cut up into separate 'feet', but in terms of the subtle ways in which the actual language realises the metre. Our analysis suggests that the first beat is realised by the two syllables of 'whether' (alternatively, we could say that the first offbeat is realised by the two unstressed syllables '-er 'tis'). Later in the line there is another moment of subtle modification when the beat is realised by the unstressed word 'in'.

Similar modifications and complications appear throughout Hamlet's speech, and in most five-beat verse. In other words, the realisation of iambic pentameter in actual poetry is open to all kinds of subtle modifications which make it a dynamically flexible form (in marked contrast to the rather wooden rhythms of our counting models, in which stress and beat coincide in mechanical fashion). When the natural rhythms of the language are shaped into lines of iambic pentameter, all kinds of adjustments are made to both: not all stresses take beats, not all unstressed syllables are offbeats, and beats may be realised by pauses or by two syllables. Just as the music of live musicians never follows a strict metronomic beat, poetry rarely falls rigidly into mechanical metrical patterns.

The kind of mid-line break in the syntax which we noted in the first line of Hamlet's speech is called a '**caesura**' (from the Latin for cutting). There is an even stronger caesura in the fifth line when the first sentence of the speech ends mid-line with a question mark. The use of caesura, then, is one way in which the sense and syntax of what is being said can run against the grain, as it were,

of the iambic pentameter line. A second device which adds to this effect is
'**enjambment**' or the 'run-on line'. This occurs when the syntax and sense of
what is being said overflow the line ending, as occurs between the second and
third lines of Hamlet's speech:

> Whether 'tis nobler in the mind to suffer
> The slings and arrows of outrageous fortune

When the devices of caesura and run-on lines are added to the fact that iambic
pentameter is not a rigid template, and not so dominant as the 4 × 4 metre,
it becomes clear how unrhymed iambic pentameter can give the effect of pro-
ducing flexible and individual speech rhythms which are subtly 'dignified' or
'elevated' by the underlying metrical form.

Iambic pentameter may have been introduced into English verse through an
attempt to imitate the poetry of continental Europe. Chaucer used rhymed
iambic pentameter in the fourteenth century, but the form fell out of use, and
changes in the pronunciation of English meant that later readers were unable
to scan Chaucer's verse. Iambic pentameter was reintroduced in the Early-
Modern or 'Renaissance' period (the sixteenth and seventeenth centuries) by
poets such as Henry Howard, Earl of Surrey (1517–47). Surrey also invented
English blank verse, based on Italian models, in his translation of two books of
Virgil's *Aeneid* (1539–46). The flexibility of blank verse made it the staple met-
rical form of Renaissance verse drama, and writers such as Christopher
Marlowe paved the way for Shakespeare's use of it. Yet it is also notable that
many dramatists of the period (including Shakespeare) frequently shift
between prose and blank verse in their plays (and sometimes employ four-beat
rhymed verse and songs). Often, but not always, blank verse is assigned only
to the 'noble' characters, or used when a certain formality of utterance is
required. This suggests that, although blank verse gives a sense of the natural
rhythms of speech, its metrical form makes it more formal (in a double sense)
than prose or colloquial speech.

Although blank verse came to dominate English Renaissance drama, Surrey's
use of blank verse in poetry attracted few imitators. Renaissance poetry is
almost invariably rhymed in both four- and five-beat metres (Shakespeare's
poetry is always rhymed). The first major break with rhyme in poetry is
Milton's use of blank verse in his **epic** poem *Paradise Lost* in 1667 (Surrey's
pioneering example was also in the epic form). In a preface to the second edi-
tion of *Paradise Lost* (1674), Milton celebrated the 'liberty' of blank verse as
escaping from the 'bondage of rhyming', and hence posited a link between
poetic and political liberty. Milton's break with rhyme in *Paradise Lost*,
together with a full exploitation of the elasticity of the iambic pentameter form

and English syntax, set a precedent for the use of blank verse which eventually had enormous influence on the subsequent history of poetry in English (as we shall see in later chapters).

Yet, although *Paradise Lost* sought to liberate iambic pentameter from the 'bondage' of rhyme, other poets continued to make good use of rhymed iambic pentameter and sometimes did so by increasing its formal constraints. The use of iambic pentameter in rhyming **couplets** (aa, bb) was introduced into English poetry by Chaucer. In the sixteenth century, this form became fairly standard for long poems such as Shakespeare's *Venus and Adonis* (1593) or Marlowe's *Hero and Leander* (1598). In the seventeenth century, such rhyming couplets came to be called '**heroic couplets**' because of their frequent use in epic poems and plays. Despite Milton's example in *Paradise Lost*, the heroic couplet remained the dominant poetic form in all kinds of poetry from the mid-seventeenth to the mid-eighteenth century. In this so-called 'Neoclassic Period' the heroic couplet was often constrained even further in what are called '**closed couplets**'. Perhaps the most effective way of understanding the closed couplet is to look at some lines from Alexander Pope's *An Essay on Criticism* (1709):

> A little learning is a dangerous thing;
> Drink deep, or taste not the Pierian spring.
> There shallow draughts intoxicate the brain,
> And drinking largely sobers us again. (215–18)

In these lines the units of meaning (the phrases and sentences) coincide neatly with the metrical form (there is no use of run-on lines). Each sentence is bound up within a rhyming couplet, and the line breaks coincide with the division of each sentence into phrasal units of meaning. This does not mean, however, that Pope's verse is at all 'wooden'. Within the constraining template of the metrical and grammatical structure there is a degree of flexible interplay between speech rhythms and metrical form. In the first of these lines, the natural stresses of 'little learning' and 'dangerous thing' emphatically realise the iambic beat, while the unstressed 'is' in the position of the line's third beat is much less prominent. The second line has a more complex relation to iambic pentameter: although the caesura after 'deep' coincides with the metre, the line as a whole is difficult to scan. We would normally want to stress both words in 'drink deep', but this would break with the iambic pentameter pattern; 'taste not' is another difficult phrase in the context of this line, since the natural pronunciation (stressing 'taste'), though it realises the line's metrical requirements, does not match the emphasis of the line (where 'not' needs to be stressed); and at the end of the line, 'Pierian spring', with its stress–unstress–unstress–stress pronunciation, also creates tensions with the iambic pentameter. In contrast, the following couplet fits quite neatly into iambic pentameter. The overall effect, then, is a sense of measured liberty – of limited flexibility within a highly structured framework. We will see in Chapter 10 that this effect of the form coincides exactly with Pope's political ideology as well as exemplifying the constraints he is recommending to fellow poets in these lines (the Pierian spring in Greek mythology was one of the haunts of the Muses: this is another poem about poetry). But if the closed heroic couplet is therefore appropriate to the constraint of the 'conservative' thought of the Neoclassical period, Romanticism's emphasis on poetic and political liberty 'opened up' the couplet once more – as in the opening lines of Keats's *Endymion* (1818):

> A thing of beauty is a joy for ever:
> Its loveliness increases; it will never
> Pass into nothingness, but still will keep
> A bower quiet for us, and a sleep
> Full of sweet dreams . . .

This brief history of the iambic pentameter shows something of the range of ways in which this metrical form has been used (and continues to be used). We have seen that the most interesting poetry in iambic pentameter does not slavishly follow the metre's template but bends and shapes it to produce subtle rhythmic variations and effects. This is done mainly through introducing tensions between the expected metrical form and the actual rhythm of the language, and by varying the way the syntax and phrasing relate to the line – through the use of caesura and **end-stopped** and run-on lines. We have also seen that although rhythm and metre might initially appear to be merely matters of poetic form, they are actually intimately related to questions of meaning. And the history of the way iambic pentameter has been used in English poetry also indicates that questions of metrical form can open out to larger cultural and political questions.

■ Free Verse

Free verse is the name given to poetry which does not conform to any metrical pattern. (Although free verse often discards rhyme, the absence of rhyme in itself is not a sign of free verse.) But although free verse is not metrical, it nevertheless uses line divisions which shape the rhythms of the language for specific ends (otherwise it would not be poetry). Free verse is associated with the experimental poetry of the twentieth century, yet there are interesting precedents from earlier periods. Perhaps the most influential of all precedents is the translation of the poetry of the Old Testament in the so-called 'Authorised Version' of the Bible that first appeared in 1611. The 1611 translations of biblical texts such as the 'Song of Solomon' and 'The Book of Psalms' contain some of the most memorable free verse in the English language, as we can see in the opening lines of Psalm 23:

> The Lord is my shepherd; I shall not want.
> He maketh me to lie down in green pastures:
> He leadeth me beside the still waters.
> He restoreth my soul:
> He leadeth me in the paths of righteousness for his name's sake.

In translating biblical poetry as free verse the early seventeenth-century translators were quite faithful to the forms of ancient Hebrew poetry, whose structuring principle was neither rhyme nor metre but parallelism – as Bishop Robert Lowth later recognised in his *Lectures on the Sacred Poetry of the Hebrews* (1753).[9] In the opening lines of Psalm 23 quoted above, there is no regular metre and no rhyme (apart from the echo between 'pastures' and 'waters'). Instead, the lines are marked by the syntactic parallelism (i.e., repetition with difference) of phrases such as 'He maketh', 'He leadeth', etc. (In fact, as we will see in Chapter 4, parallelism can be seen as the underlying formal principle of all poetry.)

The English translation of the Bible authorised by King James in 1611 has undoubtedly done more to shape and influence English language poetry than any other text. It is perhaps no coincidence that Milton uses lines of varying lengths, irregularly rhymed, in *Samson Agonistes* (1671), a verse drama that retells one of the most well-known of biblical stories. William Blake's poetry is even more under the spell of the King James Bible. It uses a wide range of different poetic metres and sometimes experiments with forms which cannot be accommodated into any particular metre. In the preface 'To the Public' that introduces his massive poem *Jerusalem* (1804–1820), Blake echoes Milton's preface to *Paradise Lost* but strikes out for even more poetic freedom:

> When this Verse was first dictated to me I consider'd a Monotonous Cadence like that used by Milton & Shakespeare & all writers of English Blank verse, derived from the modern bondage of Rhyming; to be a necessary and indispensable part of Verse. But I soon found that in the mouth of a true Orator such monotony was not only awkward, but as much a bondage as rhyme itself. I therefore have produced a variety in every line, both of cadences & number of syllables. . . . Poetry Fetter'd, Fetters the Human Race!

In the nineteenth century, Matthew Arnold also wrote poetry which broke with regular metrical forms. But perhaps the most influential pioneer of free

---

[9] For a scholarly account of the Bible's poetry, see John B. Gabel, Charles B. Wheeler and Anthony D. York, *The Bible as Literature: An Introduction* (Oxford and New York: Oxford University Press, 2000), pp. 34–39.

verse in the nineteenth century was the American poet Walt Whitman, whose radical departures from regular metrical forms are often said to be an important aspect of his attempt to create a specifically American poetry liberated from the European tradition and based on an ideology of individual freedom. A particularly interesting example of Whitman's play with the poetic line is his 'When I Heard the Learn'd Astronomer' (1865):

> When I heard the learn'd astronomer,
> When the proofs, the figures, were ranged in columns before me,
> When I was shown the charts and diagrams, to add, divide,
>   and measure them,
> When I sitting heard the astronomer where he lectured with much
>   applause in the lecture room,
> How soon unaccountable I became tired and sick,
> Till rising and gliding out I wander'd off by myself,
> In the mystical moist night-air, and from time to time,
> Look'd up in perfect silence at the stars.

Try reading this poem a few times, concentrating on the rhythmic 'feel' of the lines. In doing this, you will perhaps notice that there is something different about the rhythmic form of the last line. It is easy enough to see that these lines vary considerably in length, and analysis confirms this. The eight lines contain 9, 12, 18, 22, 13, 14, 13 and 10 syllables respectively, while the stress pattern goes 4, 5, 6, 8, 5, 5, 5, 5. Yet this analysis also reveals that the last line is likely to be a standard five-beat line, since it contains ten syllables and five stresses. In fact, the line turns out to be a fairly regular iambic pentameter:

```
   -   /  -  /  -  /-  /   -  /
Look'd up in perfect silence at the stars
```

In this poem, then, the free verse is not used as a kind of analogue for American 'freedom', but in an almost opposite way. The long, sometimes ungainly lines in the bulk of the poem coincide with the speaker listening to the astronomer, and the implication is that the astronomer's lecture is long-winded and rather mechanical. When the speaker goes out to look at the stars themselves, however, he experiences a moment of silent harmony. The contrast between this and the experience of the lecture is emphasised by the perceptible difference between the harmonious line of iambic pentameter and the ungainly lines which have gone before. In this poem, then, natural harmony is experienced through conformity to a traditional metrical form rather than through breaking with it. This reveals that the analysis of rhythmic form in free verse cannot be done through importing any preconceptions about the meaning of form. Instead, the relationship between form and meaning always has to be read in the terms set up by the individual poem itself.

The term 'free verse' (or *vers libre*), however, is more properly reserved to describe the poetry of European modernism. The poets who are perhaps most associated with free verse in Anglo-American poetry are Ezra Pound, T.S. Eliot and William Carlos Williams. In his essay 'Reflections on *Vers Libre*' (1917), Eliot claimed that the term was something of a misnomer, since the individual lines of any 'free verse' can be scanned – that is, each line will fall into some kind of rhythmic pattern which could be described according to the number of stressed and unstressed syllables, and the pattern they form.[10] Eliot is right to say that individual lines of free verse can be scanned, but he is wrong to suggest that this makes them metrical. Any sample of the English language will approximate to rhythmic regularity because, as we have seen, rhythm is the fundamental carrier of the language itself, but that does not mean that we all speak or write in metrical verse. Metre does not consist simply in rhythmic lines but in a regular pattern of repeated line forms. Free verse does not develop such a pattern. In free verse the division into lines remains the important formal feature (otherwise it would be prose rather than poetry), but this division is not made according to a predetermined pattern. Contrapuntal tensions between line and meaning are set up, as in metrical poetry, but the poet creates these effects by manipulating line lengths rather than through playing off units of meaning against a regular metrical template.

Examples of such effects can be seen in the following poem by William Carlos Williams (1935):

To a Poor Old Woman

munching a plum on
the street a paper bag
of them in her hand

They taste good to her   5
They taste good
to her. They taste
good to her

You can see it by
the way she gives herself   10
to the one half
sucked out in her hand

Comforted
a solace of ripe plums

---

[10] Eliot, *Selected Prose of T.S. Eliot*, p. 316.

> seeming to fill the air   15
> They taste good to her

There are consistencies in this 'free' verse. If we take the title as the first line, the poem consists of four four-line stanzas. Yet our counting technique reveals the non-metrical nature of these lines: the syllable count varies from three to six and the stresses from one to three. The line divisions occur not according to a regular metrical unit but in ways which cut up and manipulate phrases in order to produce semantic hesitations and awkwardnesses which tease the reader (as in the first stanza). The virtual absence of punctuation means that the reader has to decide how to organise the relations between sense units; line breaks become ambiguous, since the reader often hesitates about whether or not a line ending should be treated as a division of sense (is each line end-stopped or run-on?). The second stanza is almost a demonstration piece which indicates the semantic possibilities which occur when the same sentence is placed in different relationships with the line breaks. Try reading this stanza for yourself and asking whether or not the emphasis of each repetition of the statement is subtly altered by the way it is broken up by the line divisions.

Eliot's claim that the individual lines of free verse can be scanned would be borne out by Williams's poem. But free verse allowed poets to take still more radical liberties with the line which would seem to preclude scansion altogether. E.E. Cummings's 'O sweet spontaneous . . .' (1923) is a case in point:

> O sweet spontaneous
> earth how often have
> the
> doting
>
>   fingers of   5
> prurient philosophers pinched
> and
> poked
>
> thee
> , has the naughty thumb   10
> of science prodded
> thy
>
>   beauty .   how
> often have religions taken
> thee upon their scraggy knees   15
> squeezing and
>
> buffeting thee that thou mightest conceive
> gods

> (but
>
> true   20
>
> to the incomparable
> couch of death thy
> rhythmic
> lover
>
>   thou answerest   25
>
> them only with
>
>   spring)

The line lengths in this poem are much more diverse than they are in Williams's poem, and single-syllable lines would seem beyond the need of scansion. Here Cummings is beginning to experiment with the possibility opened up by free verse of exploiting the shape the poem creates on the page and using space to suggest semantic or syntactic nuances (for example, in the last three lines). This is a first step towards 'visual poetry' and '**concrete poetry**' in which manipulating the shape of poems on the page was taken a lot further (as we shall see in Chapter 3).

Yet Eliot seems correct when he says in his essay on *vers libre* that artistic freedom can be perceived as such only against some kind of regularity (if there is no regularity of any kind in a poem, then it is simply chaotic). In metrical verse, metre itself can serve as a regular marker against which the free movement of syntax can be foregrounded (as in Milton or Keats). In the free verse of 'The Thought-Fox' the line and stanza structure sets up enough regularity for the precipitous movement of the syntax (and the fox) to be felt in the reading. In free verse, the syntax may be quite standard: 'The Thought-Fox' is divided into perfectly intelligible sentences, and 'O sweet spontaneous . . .' can be read as two quite conventional sentences divided up into four-line 'stanzas' (save for the last three lines). Some of Milton's sentences in *Paradise Lost* are far more disruptive of conventional syntax. It would seem that in the ongoing experimentation with the dynamic interplay between line structure and sentence structure, one of the elements is usually controlled to act as a foil against which the irregularity of the other element can be experienced. Cummings tends to experiment with only one of these dimensions of poetic language at any one time. The above example is genuinely free verse, yet the sentence structure is fairly conventional. The following poem by Cummings (1963) may look as if it is free verse, but is in fact highly regular:

> Me up at does
>
> out of the floor
> quietly Stare

a poisoned mouse

still who alive   5

is asking What
have i done that

You wouldn't have

Cummings takes great liberties with syntax and grammar here in order to pro-
duce an ambiguous poem which makes it impossible to decide whether the
poem is spoken by the poisoned mouse or by the human poisoner. But the
poem's form is highly regular, not only in the symmetry of the pattern of lines
on the page and in its use of half-rhyme (does/mouse, etc.), but also in the fact
that every line contains four syllables and two stresses.

▨ Prose Poems?

In the previous chapter, we argued that the only substantive difference between
poetry and prose is that poetry is organised into lines. In the present chapter,
we have examined the different kinds of line that poetry can employ – five-beat
metre, four-beat metre with variants, and free verse. And in the following two
chapters we will be examining the range of different poetic effects that arise
from poetic lineation. But our basic supposition would appear to be threatened
by the existence of a genre called the 'prose poem', which originated in
European Romanticism and French Symbolism and still has its practitioners
and champions (one of the milestones in the development of the prose poem
was the French poet Charles Baudelaire's *Petits Poèmes en prose* (1869); cele-
brated modern examples are Geoffrey Hill's *Mercian Hymns* (1971)). In a
useful discussion of the history and characteristic features of the prose poem,
Princeton claims that it is a 'controversially hybrid and (aesthetically and even
politically) revolutionary genre' that is 'suitable to an extraordinary range of
perception and expression' and features 'high patterning, rhythmic and figural
repetition, sustained intensity, and compactness' (*Prose Poem*). But such effects
and features can often be found in literary prose without there being any need
to call that piece of prose a prose poem (we could call it poetic prose). From
our point of view, the very notion of a 'prose poem' is **oxymoronic** and para-
doxical. Poetic devices and effects can be found in all kinds of language use
without requiring us to call such instances 'prose poems'. Hill's *Mercian
Hymns* use suggestive and complex poetic language, but they are not able to
make use of the subtle interplay between poetic language and the poetic line
that we claim is characteristic of poetry (to help you make up your own mind
on this issue we have included an exercise on a prose poem at the end of the
following chapter). At the same time, it has to be admitted that we do not feel
inclined to call every piece of language that is divided up into lines a poem (the

term 'verse' is sometimes used to refer to lineated language that doesn't seem good enough or poetic enough to be called 'poetry'). In the following two chapters we want to suggest that, although lineation is the only formal feature that differentiates poetry from prose, what is really interesting about poetry is the way a particular poem exploits the potential effects of lineation in combination with other formal and figurative devices.

Exercises

1 (a) Pronounce each of the following words in a natural way and try to listen to the stress patterns of your pronunciation. Then (i) work out how many syllables there are; and (ii) mark '/' above the stressed syllables and '-' above the unstressed syllables. Are there any ambiguities, or any words which might be stressed differently in different contexts or usages?

training   facility   fallibility   pronunciation
        protest   entering   unusual   natural   decision

(b) Now try marking the stress patterns of the following sentences (read them out loud or 'voice' them silently in your head):

The training facilities are very unusual.
I'll protest against this decision.
The protest march was ineffective.

2 Try to identify the metrical pattern of the following passages of poetry by reading them out loud and listening to the metrical beat which you feel as you do so. Then carry out the instructions that follow the passages.

It was not Death, for I stood up,
And all the Dead, lie down –
It was not Night, for all the Bells
Put out their Tongues, for Noon.
    (from Emily Dickinson, poem 510 [c.1862])

When the voices of children are heard on the green
And laughing is heard on the hill,
My heart is at rest within my breast
And everything else is still.
    (from William Blake, 'Nurse's Song', 1789)

Long neglect has worn away
Half the sweet enchanting smile;
Time has turned the bloom to gray;

Mold and damp the face defile.
(from Emile Brontë, 'Long neglect . . .', 1837)

In your next letter I wish you'd say
where you are going and what you are doing;
how are the plays, and after the plays
what other pleasures you're pursuing:
(from Elizabeth Bishop, 'Letter to N.Y.', 1955)

Now that I have your face by heart, I look
Less at its features than its darkening frame
Where quince and melon, yellow as young flame,
Lie with quilled dahlias and the shepherd's crook.
Beyond, a garden. There, in insolent ease
The lead and marble figures watch the show
Of yet another summer loath to go
Although the scythes hang in the apple trees.
(from Louise Bogan, 'Song for the Last Act', 1949)

(a) Now (i) count the syllables in each line; (ii) mark the stressed and unstressed syllables; (iii) count the number of stressed syllables per line; (iv) try to mark the underlying metrical pattern of beats and off-beats (using the symbols 'b' and 'o').

(b) Using the information gleaned in (a), try to say whether each poem's rhythmic pattern is:

> free verse?
> four-beat or five-beat verse?
> rising or falling metre?
> duple or triple metre (or a combination of both)?
> iambic pentameter?
> blank verse?

(c) Are there any places in the poems where the natural rhythms of words and phrases have been overridden or complicated by the needs of the metrical pattern? What effects (if any) does this have?

(d) Compare and contrast the different effects of the metre in each poem.

3 Read the following poem and then carry out the instructions that follow.

The Lads
The lads, the lads, away the lads;
we are the Boys, who make this Noise: hoo, ha; hoo-*ha*;
a-*way*, awayawayaway, a-*way*, away;
ere we go, ere we go, ere we go;

we are the Boys, who make this Noise:
hoo *ha*.

Away the lads. I love your poetry.
It strips the artform down to nakedness,
distilling it to spirituous drops
of utter purity.
I like the way you shout it all so loud,
revelling in the shamelessness
of its repetitiousness; the way it never stops
delighting
you. You've every right to be proud
of your few, brief, oral formulae –
any of which will do, for *Match of the Day*,
or Friday night, Lads' Night Out,
lagered up and fighting –
you are the lads. You've every right to shout.

Your poetry belligerently asserts
what nobody would trouble to deny:
that you are the lads; that there you go;
that yours will never be to reason why.
My unsingable songs cannot do more for me
than rid me of my epicene disgust,
after I've served you all ten pints and watched
you flushing up with random rage and lust.

You'll smack each other's heads tonight
and shag each other's birds;
you are the Boys, who make this Noise.
What need have you for words?

We will not argue, therefore, you and I.
Your poetry serves your purpose; mine serves mine.
You only tell me what I don't deny,
and I don't tell you anything. That's fine.

Away, the lads. Your deathless chants will be
heard in these bars and streets long after we
are dead (for lads are mortal too); your sons
will never feel the need for different ones.

(Eleanor Brown, 1996)

(a) Try to work out the metrical form or rhythmic pattern of the whole poem,
indicating whether each section is five-beat, four-beat or free verse and
marking the transitions between these different forms.

(b) We will be returning to this poem in later chapters and exercises, but for now try to develop a preliminary hypothesis about why this poem varies in its use of metre and lineation: is there any relationship between the subject matter and the variations in metre and lineation?

4 In this exercise we want you to try writing a poem for yourselves. A key decision for you in this, we suggest, will be what metrical form to use – and the decision to use free verse is still a decision. Maybe you have already tried writing some poetry, in which case you will know how difficult it sometimes is to find a subject for a poem. If you don't have any experience of writing verse, don't panic – you don't have to write an epic: six to ten lines will be enough. And for a subject, try writing a poem describing or reflecting on (or imagining) a person or event you might have come across in the street, or in a shopping mall, or in the pub (Williams's 'To a Poor Old Woman', or Brown's 'The Lads', might give you some ideas about how you could make a poem out of such apparently 'ordinary' observations and reflections).

(a) Once you have chosen your subject, start by trying to fit just one of the things you could say about it into a four-beat line. Then do the same for another line. Don't try, at this stage, to make it rhyme, and don't worry if the description is completely made up. It can be quite ordinary, as long as it fits with the metre. 'The woman wore a dark brown coat' is a four-beat line that got us started.

(b) Once you have three or four such lines where the sense is complete within each four-beat line, try making up a couple of lines where the sense runs on over the line ending, e.g. 'The woman wrapped the dark brown coat / Around her in the freezing rain'.

(c) When you have written eight to ten such lines of four-beat verse, re-write it as five-beat verse by adding words or phrases to amplify or modify your meaning: 'The lonely woman standing in the rain / Had such a worried look, I thought she'd cry'. And again, see if you can run on the sense (as we've done here) from one line to the next.

(d) When you've got eight to ten lines of five-beat verse, chop it up in order to make it into free verse: e.g., 'The lonely woman / Standing in the rain had / Such a worried / Look I thought she'd / Cry.

(e) You now have three different poems (or versions of a poem). Try marking the beats and stresses in each of your poems/versions to ensure that, for the four-beat and five-beat versions, you have the right number in each line.

(f) When you are happy with the three versions of your poem, in four-beat, five-beat and free verse, ask yourself what differences (if any) there are between them. Did the different rhythmic patterns ever lead you to change the meaning? Is one of your versions more lyrical or song-like than the others?

(g) Is there any version where you feel it would sound better if it rhymed? If so, try playing around with it now to see if you can find a rhyme word for one or two of your lines; don't worry if your rhyme word changes the sense: see where it leads you, and notice how difficult, or easy, it is to place your rhyme word at the end of a line which works grammatically and still has the beats in the right place. Then award yourself a prize and our hearty congratulations for effort. This exercise will be good practice for our next two chapters, in which questions of end-rhymes and line endings will be to the fore.

Chapter 3

Significant Form: Metre and Syntax

■ Form and Content

In discussions about texts of all kinds, we often differentiate between content and form. This generally refers to a distinction between *what* is said and the *way* it is said. If it is possible to make this distinction, it would seem to follow that the same thing could be said in a different way. Thus, if we do not understand what someone is saying, we often ask him or her to 'put it another way'. Writers of expository prose (as in the present book) sometimes use the formula 'in other words' as a prelude to explaining what they mean. Yet in some kinds of language use, form seems as important as content in producing the desired effect. Many politicians employ the simple but effective rhetorical device of enforcing the point they are making by repeating it three times with variations: 'Our policy is morally correct, extremely effective, and popular with the public' (invented example); 'Friends, Romans, countrymen, lend me your ears' (*Julius Caesar*, III. ii). A joke can be ruined by telling it in the wrong order or by bungling the punch line, and a paraphrase of a joke rarely gets a laugh. Such examples suggest that in language uses in which the effect is a crucial part of the purpose or meaning, the form plays an important role in producing that effect.

Poetic form is a general term for a range of features. As with the examples just discussed, it concerns the way a poem presents its material. Form may be taken as equivalent to 'structure' – the shaping of the poem's contents in order to generate specific effects (such as dramatic suspense, the exploration and resolution of conflict, the timing of a 'punch line'). But poetry has more kinds of formal feature than any other discourse. Poetic form may include the shape of the poem on the page – how many lines it has, how long or short they are, whether or not it is divided into stanzas. Form may also include the way a poem uses patterns of sound – metre, rhyme pattern, alliteration. The term may also be used to refer to what we can loosely call the poem's style – the kind of language it uses, its word-choice or diction, its syntax, its figurative devices, its mode of address. There is also some overlap or confusion between form and genre – a term used to identify what kind a poem belongs to (see Chapter 11); some genres are strongly marked by formal patterning (such as the **sonnet** and the **sestina**). More often, a poem's form is understood as the way it combines all these elements into an overall pattern in which each element contributes to (or sometimes conflicts with) the poem's purpose, effect or meaning.

Questions about the relationship between form and content in poetry have produced a good deal of controversy. The question is usually whether content and form can be separated from one another, or whether they are inseparable. There are a number of different answers to this question:

1 poetic form is a kind of aesthetic additive which makes poetry more pleasurable to read and its message more palatable;
2 poetic form is a kind of aesthetic container in which a poem's contents are delivered;
3 the form of a poem echoes or reflects its meaning;
4 there is an organic relationship between form and content which makes them inseparable;
5 poetic form resists and disrupts meaning;
6 poetic form needs to be understood in terms of the historical or ideological context in which the poem was written.

Some of these assumptions are quite clearly opposed to or incompatible with others: (1) and (2) imply that the form of a poem is purely aesthetic, whereas (3) and (4) seem to imply that it has some semantic function – reflecting or affecting the meaning. The idea that form might resist or disrupt meaning (5) is one which could arise whenever the formal features of a poem seem to assert themselves in ways which impede understanding of its 'message', so that the form seems to 'get in the way' of what the poem is saying. That is clearly incompatible with the idea that form and content are part of a larger 'organic' unity. But the idea that form needs to be understood in terms of a poem's historical or ideological context is not incompatible with any of these assumptions; indeed, some of these assumptions correspond to the dominant assumptions which poets and readers have held at different historical periods.

The idea that poetic form and content are inseparable – so that the form of a poem is itself, in some way, significant – has been one of the most influential of critical assumptions, and continues to affect the way students are taught to analyse poetic form. For this reason it makes sense to begin our examination of received ideas about the relationship between form and content in poetry by looking at some poetry where the formal properties of the language seem to reinforce the meaning. The example we have chosen is a passage from Milton's

Paradise Lost (1667), a poem which retells the biblical story of the book of Genesis. The following lines are part of a description of how Satan begins his difficult journey out of Hell through Chaos to Earth, where he has resolved to bring about the fall of humankind. Satan ('the warie Fiend') has alighted on the brink of an abyss before crossing the wide sea of Chaos:

> Into this wild abyss,   910
> The womb of Nature and perhaps her grave,
> Of neither sea, nor shore, nor air, nor fire,
> But all these in their pregnant causes mixt
> Confus'dly, and which thus must ever fight,
> Unless th'Almighty Maker them ordain   915
> His dark materials to create more worlds,
> Into this wild abyss the warie Fiend
> Stood on the brink of Hell and look'd a while,
> Pondering his voyage; for no narrow frith
> He had to cross. (II, 910–20)   920

These lines constitute a single sentence, beginning midway through line 910 and ending midway through line 920, and make use of enjambment (run-on lines) to produce a sense of dynamic interplay between line structure and syntax. But it is the syntax itself which may present you with the greatest initial difficulty. The simplest sentence structure in English is subject–verb–object (as in 'I love you' or 'She stood on the bank of the river'). Such structures can be elaborated by adding extra clauses – as in 'She stood on the bank of the river and peered into the murky water'. This sentence can be formed in a different way (its form can be changed): 'She peered into the murky water as she stood on the bank of the river'. One of the ways poetry imposes form onto the language is precisely by re-forming syntax in such ways. Thus a poem might rework this sentence as follows: 'Into the murky water, standing on the bank of the river, she peered'. In this example, 'standing on the bank of the river' has become a parenthesis in the main sentence: 'Into the murky water she peered'. This sentence can be described grammatically: 'Into [preposition] the murky water [object] she [subject/agent] peered [verb]'. In other words, the order of subject and object is reversed, and the verb is delayed until the end. Milton's sentence in the above passage is more complicated than this, but its structure is similar. What we now want to examine are some of the effects of Milton's deviation from normal sentence structure. We shall be suggesting that the syntax of these lines acts out what the sentence actually describes.

The idea that the form of the writing echoes or reflects the meaning in Milton's passage was posited by one of its eighteenth-century readers, Jonathan Richardson, who made the following comment in his *Explanatory Notes* on *Paradise Lost* in 1734:

'tis observable the poet himself seems to be doing what he describes, for the period [that is, the sentence] begins at [line] 910. Then he goes not on directly, but lingers; giving an idea of chaos before he enters into it.[1]

Richardson's comment appears to be recognising how, by beginning this sentence 'Into this wild abyss' and then delaying what Satan does 'into it' by interposing six lines of parenthesis, the passage creates what we can call 'suspended syntax'. This syntactic delay or suspension mimics Satan's pause on the brink of the abyss and keeps the reader in suspense while Milton elaborates on the description of chaos. Indeed, Satan pauses, and the reader is kept waiting so long that the opening phrase has to be repeated in line 917: 'Into this wild abyss the warie Fiend / Stood on the brink of Hell and look'd a while'.

The way this suspended syntax mimes the action at this point may also be reinforced by the line division. Although there is no punctuation after 'Fiend', and the syntax of line 917 runs on into line 918, the line divisions may induce readers to pause momentarily before reading on to find out what the 'Fiend' does. It would be worth re-reading these lines and asking yourself whether (particularly if you read the lines aloud) you are inclined to mark the end of line 917 by pausing, however momentarily, after the word 'Fiend'. It might be possible, then, to claim that a reader's uncertainty concerning any purely metrical pause after 'Fiend' reinforces the way the suspended syntax acts out the meaning of these lines – after all, the whole passage is describing Satan's hesitation. Both syntax and lineation, then, can be said to be miming or acting out that hesitation, so that the poetry would be doing what it is saying. Yet there is a further complication in these lines, since the delayed verb 'Stood', when it does eventually arrive, does not resolve the syntactical suspense at all clearly. Readers might well expect 'Into this wild abyss . . . the Fiend jumped' or 'plunged' or 'looked'. Instead, what we get is 'Into this wild abyss [he] / Stood'. That is, to say the least, unidiomatic – you don't 'stand into' anything in English. It is only with the second verb, 'look'd', that we (at last!) get a verb that can complete the grammar at all satisfactorily.

Some readers might be inclined, once they recognise the strange syntax in these lines, to criticise Milton's 'faulty' grammar. Indeed, one of Milton's earliest editors 'corrected' the grammar at many points in the poem, including this one.[2] But if the syntax and grammar of this passage were 'normalised' the effects we have just described, in which the syntax acts out what is being narrated and causes us to participate imaginatively in that action, would be lost.

---

[1] Cited in Christopher Ricks, *Milton's Grand Style* (Oxford: Oxford University Press, 1963), pp. 78–9.

[2] *Milton's Paradise Lost: A new edition*, ed. Richard Bentley (London: 1732).

These lines exhibit that close relationship between form and meaning which readers have often felt to be one of the desirable, if not definitive, character-istics of poetic language. By manipulating the form of the sentence and taking advantage of the effects made available by metrical form, Milton can be said to be making the form *significant*. In what follows we will be looking at various ways in which poetry uses 'significant form'.

■ Anglo-American New Criticism

The assumption that form and meaning should be closely related in poetry was most strongly affirmed by Coleridge in his *Biographia Literaria* (1817).[3] Coleridge argued that the form of a poem was something that developed from within the poem itself, like the organic growth of a plant. This Romantic theory of organic form was taken up and developed by the New Critics in the twentieth century as an all-embracing description of poetic form which included all the techniques of versification, word-choice, figurative devices, and so on. In this theoretical practice, which may well have influenced the way you have been taught to respond to poetry, the various formal features of the lan-guage of poetry are said to embody, rather than merely reflect, a poem's mean-ing. Readers are taught the difficult, but rewarding, techniques of discovering how a poem's entire formal system – its metre, line breaks, rhyme, assonance, **consonance**, alliteration – works together in complex ways to make the poem's message far more profoundly realised than it could have been in any non-poetic discourse.

The New Critical assumptions about the relationship of form and content are articulated most clearly in Cleanth Brooks's essay about what he calls 'The Heresy of Paraphrase'.[4] In this essay he celebrates 'the resistance which any good poem sets up against all attempts to paraphrase it' (p. 196). The idea that it is possible adequately to paraphrase a poem induces us to 'split the poem between its "form" and its "content"' (p. 201). Brooks rejects this 'dualism', quoting with approval W.M. Urban's *Language and Reality*: 'form and con-tent, or concept and medium, are inseparable' (p. 199). This is because, for Brooks, 'The relation between all the elements [in a poem] must surely be an organic one – there can be no question about that' (p. 200). The formal fea-tures of a poem do not merely echo or 'contain' the sense, but play an active part in shaping it:

---

[3] Coleridge, Samuel Taylor, *Biographia Literaria: Biographical sketches of my literary life and opinions*, eds James Engell and W. Jackson Bate (Princeton: Princeton University Press, 1983).

[4] Cleanth Brooks, *The Well Wrought Urn* (New York: Reynal & Hitchcock, 1947, repr. London: Methuen, 1968).

> The truth is that the apparent irrelevances which metrical pattern and metaphor introduce . . . become relevant when we realize that they function in a good poem to modify, qualify, and develop the total attitude. (p. 209)

In analysing poetry, then, we need to pay attention not only to *what* a poem says but also to *how* it says it (in fact, though we can make such distinctions intellectually, we cannot separate one from another in an actual poem). Such New Critical assumptions underlie the way students of literature are often asked not merely to analyse a poem's metre or identify its use of rhyme or alliteration, but also to describe how they 'modify, qualify and develop' the poem's meaning – which is essentially what we have done with the passage from *Paradise Lost* above.

Another classic work of New Criticism is W.K. Wimsatt's *The Verbal Icon* (1954). Wimsatt explains the title in a prefatory note: 'The term icon is used today by semiotic writers to refer to a verbal sign which somehow shares the properties of, or resembles, the objects which it denotes' (p. x). Wimsatt's notion of the icon is influenced by the philosopher C.S. Peirce's distinction between three different kinds of sign: the arbitrary sign, the index and the icon. In arbitrary signs (such as words) there is no natural or inevitable relationship between form and meaning. In an index, the relationship between sign and meaning is causal, as when one says that dark clouds are a 'sign' of rain. An icon, however, is the kind of sign that bears some inherent resemblance to the thing it signifies: a portrait resembles the person it depicts; a map actually resembles the countries it represents. Poetry, of course, like all verbal discourse, uses words – arbitrary signs which have no causal relationship with or resemblance to that which they signify or refer to. Wimsatt's purpose in *The Verbal Icon*, however, is to argue that poetry is unlike other forms of discourse in that it tries to make its language iconic. His claim is that poetry uses language in a range of ways which 'somehow' seem to make it resemble the thing which is being described or presented. At a general level, Wimsatt, like other New Critics, argues that a good poem's 'content' ought to deal with the full complexity and richness of human life, and that its form (the interplay of all its technical devices) ought to display a corresponding richness and complexity. As Wimsatt puts it, 'Complexity of form is sophistication of content. The unity and maturity of good poems are two sides of the same thing' (p. 82).

Both Brooks and Wimsatt stress that they are talking about the relationship between form and content in *good* poems, and this indicates that this principle of the inseparability of form and content is being proposed as a criterion of evaluation. That is certainly the way this principle had already been understood by many twentieth-century critics, particularly those who were preoccupied with the evaluation and revaluation of particular texts and authors. In 1936, for instance, F.R. Leavis condemned Milton's style on the grounds that it was uniformly heightened and inflated in ways which made it impossible for precise, local meanings to be fully realised in the verse: 'To say that Milton's verse is magniloquent is to say that it is not doing as much as its impressive pomp and volume seem to be asserting.'[5] Leavis goes on to argue that

> subtlety of movement in English verse depends on the play of the natural sense movement and intonation against the verse structure. . . . No such play is possible in a medium in which the life of idiom, the pressure of speech, is as completely absent as it is in Milton's Grand Style. (p. 51)

Leavis contrasts Milton's language with John Donne's in this respect; in Donne's poetry, he claims, 'The words seem to do what they say' (a formula which echoes Jonathan Richardson's comment on the lines from *Paradise Lost* which we analysed above). Although Leavis's essay anticipates American New Criticism by some years, the idea that 'good' poems somehow close the gap between doing and saying is wholly compatible with the New Critics' idea that form and content should be inseparable. In the criticism influenced by these assumptions, the belief that a good poem is one that somehow 'does' what it 'says' became axiomatic.

Leavis's objections to Milton's poetry were largely answered by Christopher Ricks in a book whose title, *Milton's Grand Style* (1963), alludes to the very passage, with its concluding claim about Milton's style, that we have quoted from F.R. Leavis above. Ricks shows how the language of *Paradise Lost* can be analysed in ways that reveal precisely that play of 'natural sense movement and intonation against the verse structure' which Leavis denies. In passage after passage (including the passage we have already analysed), this enables Ricks to suggest that Milton's words do indeed seem to 'do what they say'. In many instances it is a matter of the relationship between metre and syntax, in which the dynamics of the sentence structure, working across the line endings and setting up their own rhythms and grammatical suspensions, act out what is being described.

But though Ricks's defence of Milton's style questions the accuracy of Leavis's analysis, it clearly shares the evaluative criteria on which it was based. We would like to examine the possibilities opened up by such criteria by looking at another passage from *Paradise Lost* which responds to the same process of 'reading in slow motion' that we recommended at the beginning of this book. The following lines describe the creation of the world in such a way that the formal properties of the language give us an extremely vivid impression of the way the Creator imposes order on chaos – the same chaos which we have seen Satan teetering on the brink of in the passage we discussed earlier.

[5] 'Milton's Verse', in F.R. Leavis, *Revaluation: Tradition and development in English poetry* (London: Penguin, 1964), p. 45; the article first appeared in 1933 in the journal *Scrutiny*.

The point of view this time is that of the angels standing on the boundary of heaven, a viewpoint which the descriptive language encourages the reader to share:

> On heav'nly ground they stood, and from the shore
> They view'd the vast immeasurable abyss
> Outrageous as a sea, dark, wasteful, wild,
> Up from the bottom turn'd by furious winds
> And surging waves, as mountains to assault
> Heav'ns highth, and with the centre mix the pole.
>   Silence, ye troubl'd waves, and thou deep, peace,
> Said then th'Omnific Word, your discord end. (VII, 210–17)

Even before analysing the passage, it might be felt that this is a dynamic and energetic piece of description in which the language is somehow turbulent in describing turbulence, then calm and orderly when referring to God's imposition of order. Only careful analysis, however, will show what the metre and rhythm contribute to this effect. *Paradise Lost* is written in blank verse – unrhymed iambic pentameters – but simply to identify the metre does not take us very far towards showing how the sound of these lines appears to realise their meaning by making the turbulence of chaos more fully present in the description. We could get closer to such a demonstration by paying attention to those places where it seems difficult to place the regular duple rising stress on the syllables which an iambic pentameter metre normally requires. For instance, the word 'immeasurable', in line 211, seems itself to be immeasurable (remember that metre literally means 'measure'). How many syllables does it have? Where do the two beats required by the metre actually fall? The fourth of these lines (213) seems to require a stress on the first word, 'Up', even though the underlying metrical pattern would lead us to expect it to be unstressed. Traditional **prosody** would say that this line starts out on a 'reversed foot', which is simply a way of registering the way the opening of this five-beat line breaks with the iambic pentameter by beginning with a beat rather than an off-beat. In effect, the line starts with falling duple metre before reverting to rising duple metre. The important thing is to notice this modulation in the overall metrical pattern and to think about its effect in relation to the poem's meaning. The unexpected, and hence salient, stress on the preposition could be said to dramatise the very turbulence it describes. It is not just the literal meaning of the word that achieves this effect but its position in the line, separated from the verb that governs it: the normal word order would be 'Turned up from the bottom', so we could say that the disturbed syntax reflects the disturbance that is being described. This, together with the disturbance of the expected metre, would help us to account for the impression that the very turbulence of chaos is reproduced in the verse movement.

The extraordinary line in which God ('th'Omnific Word') imposes order on this chaos responds to a similar analysis. Our own analysis of the way the stresses fall in line 117 is as follows:

```
/ -   -  / -  /   -  /  /   /
Silence, ye troubl'd waves, and thou deep, peace,
 b       b      b           b      b
```

This rhythm disturbs the regular iambic pattern of the blank verse at the beginning and the end of the line. 'Silence' requires a stress on the first syllable and shifts the beat to the very beginning of the line. At the end of the line the two words 'deep, peace' seem to require equal weight or stress (the assonance of their identical vowel sound reinforces their need for equal emphasis), even though only one of them ('peace') realises the beat. These metrical irregularities produce effects which appear to emphasise and act out the meaning. The effect of beginning the line with an unexpected stress seems to add to the imperative force of God's command of 'Silence'. At the end of the line the double stress ('deep, peace') powerfully overrides the metre, while the assonance suggests through its very sound the calmness and order it is prescribing. Both 'Silence' and 'peace' are imperatives in this sentence, and could be seen as synonyms, yet their different relation to the metrical form of the line gives them a very different rhetorical force, so that we seem to hear the act of creation in the very sound of the line. It is as though the divine *fiat* is immediately carried out – as though God has only to order something and it immediately comes to pass.

A model for such a rhetorical effect could be found in the Bible's description of creation in Genesis 1: 3: 'And God said, Let there be light; and there was light'. This may be why Milton chooses to call God 'th'Omnific Word' ('Omnific' means 'maker of everything'). The key text for seeing God as 'Word' or *Logos* is John 1: 1, 'In the beginning was the Word, and the Word was with God, and the Word was God'. This text provided the traditional justification for identifying God as 'Word' when thinking of his powers as Creator, partly because these opening words are the same three words ('In the beginning') that open the Book of Genesis itself which, as its name implies, is about the creation of the world. Milton quotes the same three words very near the beginning (I, 9) of his own poem to signal his closeness to his biblical source. Although this research into the biblical subtext to Milton's text seems to have shifted from 'formal' analysis to analysis of allusions, influences and intertextuality – issues we shall examine in greater detail in Chapter 13 – it may suggest how careful Milton has been in giving substance in his own verse to his account of the creative power of the voice of God. In effect, both in the Bible and in Milton, God can be thought of as the most powerful and effective poet of all, since the universe really does *do* what he *says*. Yet it is Milton's own poetry which allows us to experience God's effective creative voice by re-creating its effects through the poem's own language. It is the interplay of form and content in Milton's own verse that allows us to 'hear' God's commands taking effect. Thus Milton as poet can be seen as imitating God's creativity. That may be because Milton shared something of Sir Philip Sidney's belief that the creativity of the poet ('maker') was the closest we could get on earth to the creativity of the Creator ('the Heavenly Maker of that maker').[6]

■ The Double Pattern

Our analysis of passages from *Paradise Lost* has paid particular attention to the interaction between syntax and verse line, and the way this forms a **double pattern** which allows the poem's form to appear to act out its content. 'Double pattern' is a term used by Richard Bradford to account for the relationship between metre and syntax in poetic texts of many different kinds. Bradford explains this 'double pattern' as 'the interrelationship between the structures of language as a whole and the specific details of what is variously known as metre, prosody or, in its broadest sense, versification'.[7] All speakers of English, he reminds us, have internalised the first pattern – the grammatical, syntactic and semantic structures of the language: 'We understand and create linguistic statements because we know that some words should and some words should not follow one another in order to create intelligible meaning' (Bradford, p. 3). These sequential structures, which allow us to create and understand meaning-ful sentences, are found in poetry as well as in all other uses of language (although, as we have seen, poetry often plays around with these sequences in order to produce specific effects). The first pattern, then, concerns the syntactic and grammatical rules which shape the meaning of sentences in language in general, and thus has to do with meaning. The second pattern is made by shap-ing the *sounds* of language, and is unique to poetry:

> Occasionally, and often by accident, this referential, syntactic pattern of discourse will create surface patterns of rhythm and sound which draw upon the materiality of language but which do not relate directly to its conventions of meaning and signification. The double pattern occurs when this secondary, surface pattern is deliberately deployed as a regular and persistent feature of the text. The unit by which we measure and classify this secondary pattern is the poetic line. (p. 3)

---

[6] Sidney, *The Prose Works of Sir Philip Sidney*, vol. III, ed. A. Feuillerat (Cambridge: Cambridge University Press, 1962), p. 8.

[7] Richard Bradford, *A Linguistic History of English Poetry* (London: Routledge, 1993), p. 3.

The second pattern, then, is a matter of poetic form, of prosody or versi-fication, and the poetic line. The 'double pattern' is the interplay between the semantic and syntactic pattern and the pattern of the poetic line. In exploring the relationship of these two patterns, we are thus attending to the relationship of form to meaning in poetry at its most fundamental level.

In our examination of the two passages from *Paradise Lost* we have, in fact, been attending to the effects of the double pattern. These passages 'do' what they 'say', we have argued, because of the combined effect of the way Milton manipulates sentence structure and plays it off against line endings. Milton himself seems to have recognised this interplay in the comment he makes on 'The Verse' of *Paradise Lost* in the note added to the second edition of his poem in 1674, which argues that the 'true musical delight' of poetry 'consists only in apt numbers, and the sense variously drawn out from one verse into another'. This description of the way 'sense' (syntax and meaning) is 'vari-ously' extended from one line ('verse') to the next is probably the best account of how syntax relates to metre in Milton's poem. This movement might equally well be described, in Leavis's terms, as a 'play of the natural sense movement and intonation against the verse structure', or in Bradford's terms as the 'double pattern'. The 'double pattern', in fact, is a useful term for describing the subtle interplay in iambic pentameter poetry between sentence structure and metrical form that we analysed in the previous chapter.

■ Double Syntax

The interplay between metre and syntax in poetry can be seen particularly clearly in the effect known as 'double syntax'. The term 'double syntax' des-cribes what happens when the reader is uncertain how to construe the sen-tence structure when it flows over a line ending. The syntax becomes 'double' when the word or phrase at the line ending can be taken as belonging grammat-ically either with what comes before or with what comes after it. The grammar becomes ambiguous in *Paradise Lost*, for example, when Milton describes how his own inspiration is turned into verse ('numbers') in the poem itself:

> Then feed on thoughts, that voluntarie move
> Harmonious numbers (III, 37–38)

Donald Davie, who seems to have been the first reader to identify this effect, makes the following comment on these lines:

At the line-ending 'move' seems intransitive, and as such wholly satisfying; until the swing on to the next line, 'Harmonious numbers', reveals it . . . as transitive. This flicker of hesitation about whether the thoughts move only themselves, or something

81

else, makes us see that the numbers aren't really 'something else' but are the very thoughts themselves, seen under a new aspect.[8]

An intransitive verb has no object, so if 'move' were intransitive the thoughts would 'move' nothing but themselves. A 'transitive' verb is one that takes a direct object, so 'move' would be transitive if it is 'Harmonious numbers' that are being moved. It will be apparent that the way a reader takes the grammar here will be largely affected by whether or not he or she inserts a metrical pause at the line ending – that is, by the extent to which the reader has internalised the convention which leads us to pause at line endings when we are reading verse. If we pause at the end of the line, we are likely to think of the thoughts as voluntarily moving themselves. But as soon as we read on into the next line, we have to revise our interpretation by understanding that what the thoughts 'move' are 'harmonious numbers'.

Double syntax may potentially be found in all poetry that uses run-on lines because it is an effect produced by the double pattern of syntax and metre (this is not to say that every run-on line will produce double syntax – the device is relatively rare).[9] Some of the tonal ambiguities in Eleanor Brown's 'The Lads' are achieved through the double syntax made possible by enjambment:

> Away the lads. I love your poetry.
> It strips the artform down to nakedness,
> distilling it to spirituous drops
> of utter purity.
> I like the way you shout it all so loud,
> revelling in the shamelessness
> of its repetitiousness; the way it never stops
> delighting
> you. You've every right to be proud
> of your few, brief, oral formulae –

Pause for a moment to examine the effects of the line endings in this passage. Identify all the uses of enjambment (run-on lines). Are there any moments where the enjambment works to produce double syntax or where the speaker's

---

[8] Davie, 'Syntax and Music in *Paradise Lost*', in Frank Kermode, ed., *The Living Milton: Essays by various hands* (London: Routledge & Kegan Paul, 1960), pp. 70–84, quoted in Ricks, *Milton's Grand Style*, p. 42; the useful expression 'double syntax' goes back to Ricks (e.g. p. 96).

[9] Curiously, in his lively and often illuminating *An Introduction to English Poetry* (London and New York: Penguin, 2003), James Fenton appears to rule out the possibility of double syntax by insisting that a reader should not pause at the end of any line where there is enjambment (pp. 30–31). This is curious, because it would suggest that lineation is entirely pointless and without effect.

apparent meaning or **tone** at the end of one line is significantly modified when you read on to the next line? (As we will suggest in Chapter 8, the speaker's tone is indicated by his or her attitude: in these lines, the question of tone relates to the speaker's attitude towards the lads she is addressing and/or towards their poetry.)

Double syntax can also be seen in the following lines from Book III of *Paradise Lost*, in which God argues that he was justified in allowing Adam and Eve the freedom to fall into sin:

> for so
> I formed them free, and free they must remain,
> Till they enthrall themselves: I else must change
> Their nature (III, 123–26)

The line break at the end of line 125 ('I else must change') momentarily encourages the reader to regard the syntax as complete, so that God seems to be arguing that he would have to change his own nature if he were to do things differently. It is only as we read on, over the line ending, that we are prompted to revise this provisional construction of the syntax, so that what would have to be changed is now seen as human nature rather than the unchanging attributes of the deity (the verb again becomes transitive rather than intransitive). Although it can be claimed that line 126 resolves the **ambiguity**, that flicker of hesitation over the line ending opens up the possibility that God himself is momentarily caught between the two possibilities. Pausing at the end of line 125, the reader is momentarily given the impression that God is considering changing his own nature. For God to change his own nature would be even more disturbing, and more theologically contentious, than to change his creatures. Reading on into the next line thus involves a semantic surprise, but it is less problematic than the impression produced at the end of the previous line.

■ Reader Response Theory and Poetic Form

Although double syntax was first identified by critics such as Donald Davie and Christopher Ricks, who have strong affinities with New Criticism and its assumptions about poetic form, its theoretical implications have been developed by more recent critics and theorists in ways which challenge the New Critical account of poetic form. These challenges go under the name of Reader Response Theory, and their major exponent is the American critic Stanley Fish, who developed his reading of Milton's syntax in a book on *Paradise Lost* called *Surprised by Sin* (1967). Some of the reasons why Fish thinks that double syntax challenges the formalist assumptions of New Criticism can be seen in a comment he makes in an article on Milton's sonnets:

formalist criticism, because it is spatial rather than temporal in its emphasis, either ignored or suppressed what is really happening in the act of reading. Thus, in the case of three sonnets by Milton, what is really happening depends upon a moment of hesitation or syntactic slide, when a reader is invited to make a certain kind of sense only to discover (at the beginning of the next line) that the sense he has made is either incomplete or simply wrong.[10]

Although this may look very close to Davies's and Ricks's accounts of the experiential effect of double syntax, it arises out of a theory which claims to challenge New Critical assumptions. The challenge depends to a large extent on the distinction Fish is making here between the 'spatial' and 'temporal' dimensions of poetic form. It is frequently asserted that the New Critics' stress on form and structure meant that they thought of poems as spatial objects. There is evidence to support this claim – as in the titles of the two books we have mentioned, *The Well Wrought Urn* and *The Verbal Icon*, which seem to imply that poems are beautifully shaped objects whose appeal is to the eye.[11] Reader Response Theory insists that literary texts are not static objects – like paintings or sculptures – but consist of sequential patterns that are experienced by a reader in a temporal fashion as he or she moves from word to word and sentence to sentence. Clearly, whether we think of a poem as a static object or a temporal process has consequences for the way we think about poetic form and its effects.

Reader Response Theory was first developed in Germany, where it is known as Reception Theory. Unlike New Criticism, which tended to think of a poem as 'the words on the page', and therefore assumed that form is intrinsically 'there' in the poem, German Reception Theory and American Reader Response criticism both argue that a text comes into being – is formed – only when it is being experienced by an actual reader. That process is, above all, a temporal one. Reception Theory is best known to English readers through the writings of Wolfgang Iser, whose essay 'The Reading Process: a Phenomenological Approach' signals in its title the emphasis this theory places on reading as

---

[10] Stanley Fish, *Surprised by Sin: The reader in Paradise Lost* (New York: St Martin's Press, 1967), p. 311.

[11] New Criticism was not as consistently committed to the view that poems are spatial 'icons' or 'urns' as its opponents sometimes allege. Brooks, for instance, develops an account of poetic structure which is responsive to the temporal nature of the reading experience: 'The essential structure of a poem . . . resembles that of architecture or painting: it is a pattern of resolved stresses. Or, to move closer still to poetry by considering the temporal arts, the structure of a poem resembles that of a ballet or musical composition. It is a pattern of resolutions and balances and harmonisations, developed through a temporal scheme. . . . The dynamic nature of drama, in short, allows us to regard it as an action rather than as a formula for action or as a statement about action' (*Well Wrought Urn*, pp. 203–4).

process and as an experience of consciousness.[12] Although most of Iser's examples are taken from prose narrative, they have a bearing on how we respond to poems. Iser argues that, although texts are made up of individual sentences, these sentences look backwards and forwards to each other in dynamic ways:

> Every sentence contains a preview of the next and forms a kind of viewfinder for what is to come; and this in turn changes the 'preview' and so becomes a 'viewfinder' for what has been read.
>
> (Iser, in Lodge, *Modern Criticism and Theory*, p. 215)

Sentences may confirm a reader's expectations, built up through reading previous sentences, but equally they may frustrate them, since 'literary texts are full of unexpected twists and turns, and frustration of expectations' (p. 216). Moreover, the range of potential expectations is greater than any single realisation can ever accommodate: 'With all literary texts, then, we may say that the reading process is selective, and the potential text is infinitely richer than any of its individual realizations' (p. 216).

Reception Theory's description of how a reader 'realises' a text is opposed to the 'objectivity' which New Criticism claimed for its description of poetic form. The New Critics attempted to show how the formal properties of a poem cohered into an overall unity which produced what we might call a 'closed' text. For Iser, such **closure** is not a feature of formal or semantic properties in the text itself but, rather, the result of a series of provisional and selective decisions in the mind of an active reader: closure (a concept we shall examine more fully in Chapter 16) is an experiential achievement of the reader, not a feature of the text's formal properties.

Our discussion of the effect of the double syntax of Book III, lines 123–26 of *Paradise Lost*, started out by arguing that this is a *formal* feature of the text itself. It is the way the lines are arranged on the page with a line break which divides the sentence at a crucial point ('I else must change / Their nature') which makes the effect possible. Yet the *experience* of hesitation, of choosing one meaning only to have to revise that meaning immediately afterwards, is one that only a reader can have. On the one hand, then, it is possible to identify the way formal features 'act out' what is being said. We have seen such examples of 'significant form' in, say, the way Milton's syntax mimes Satan's suspended pause on the edge of the abyss, or in the way the sound of his verse seems to mimic God's creative imperative. On the other hand, these formal features produce reading experiences which are dynamic and temporal. Milton's suspended syntax keeps the reader in suspense, and the semantic shock of God's apparently pondering whether to change his nature can be experienced

---

[12] Iser, 'The Reading Process: A phenomenological approach', *New Literary History* 3 (1972) reprinted in Lodge, *Modern Criticism and Theory*, pp. 211–28.

only temporally by a reader. In a sense, New Criticism is correct to stress the importance of objectively identifiable features of poetic form, but Reader Response Theory is equally correct in emphasising the dynamic and temporal effects of form in the reading experience.

■ Significant Form and the Temporal Nature of Reading

In the remainder of this chapter we want to explore some of the wider historical and theoretical implications of these issues for the way we respond to poetry of different periods and in a variety of different metres and forms. Our examples are all poems in which the form appears to have some meaningful relation to the content, where the sound might seem an echo to the sense. Such poems might thus be said to be 'doing' what they are 'saying'. It will be important with most of these examples to ask whether it makes any difference if the poem is read out loud, rather than seen as words on a page. It will also be interesting to ask whether the form of the poem is spatial and static or temporal and dynamic. We might assume, if we do not think about it too carefully, that a poem's form is static and spatial when it is printed on the page, but dynamic and temporal when it is read aloud. But, as we shall indicate when we try to read the poems that follow, silent reading is also a temporal process – and one which brings out some of the important differences between New Critical and Reader Response theories that we have already identified.

One way of separating out the variety of things that 'form' can refer to in poetry would be to distinguish between auditory and visual effects. One of the most obvious ways in which form reflects meaning in poetry is through **onomatopoeia,** an auditory effect in which the sound seems to imitate the sense. Although the notion of onomatopoeia can be limiting and misleading, it can be extended to include all the ways poems exploit the sounds of the language so that they seem to act out meaning. Most of the examples we have looked at thus far are onomatopoeic in this sense. But poems may also imitate what they are describing through their shape on the page. There are various types of poetry which, at different periods, have made the shape of the poem appear to have a significance quite separate from any metrical pattern which the line divisions might be signalling. Modern examples of this are called 'concrete poems', but the idea is not a new one. The Renaissance period produced a fair number of poems shaped like wings, altars, eggs or columns, since it found models for them in a collection of ancient **lyric** or **epigrammatic** poems known as *The Greek Anthology* (compiled in the fourteenth century from poems dating from 700 BCE to CE 1000). Such examples are usually known as 'figure poems'.

The most famous example of such figure poems in English is George Herbert's 'Easter Wings' (1633), a poem which imitates a wing-shaped poem from *The Greek Anthology* by the poet Simmias of Rhodes.

Easter Wings

Lord, who createdst man in wealth and store,
  Though foolishly he lost the same,
    Decaying more and more,
      Till he became
        Most poore: 5
        With thee
      O let me rise
    As larks, harmoniously,
  And sing this day thy victories:
Then shall the fall further the flight in me.   10

My tender age in sorrow did beginne:
  And still with sicknesses and shame
    Thou didst so punish sinne,
      That I became
        Most thinne.   15
        With thee
      Let me combine,
    And feel this day thy victorie:
  For, if I imp my wing on thine,
Affliction shall advance the flight in me.   20

This is a poem whose visual form (its shape) calls attention to itself by imitating the wings which it refers to. In early editions the poem was printed sideways on the page, and to see how it resembles wings you will have to turn our page round. You might ask what kind of wings this typographic arrangement suggests. Are they birds' or angels' wings? Sometimes this kind of visual trick can seem pretty trivial, and it certainly went radically out of fashion in the eighteenth century. Yet we want to show that it is worth paying close attention to 'Easter Wings'. If we are asked what the significance of the winged stanza shapes is, various answers might suggest themselves. They could certainly be related to the extended metaphor of flight in the poem, and a discussion of the way the poem uses this metaphor might be a rewarding exercise (you may recall our own examination in Chapter 1 of how Keats used the imagery of flight in his 'Ode to a Nightingale'). However, a different range of issues is raised if we ask whether the form of this poem is functioning as a visual icon or as a set of auditory signals. The assumption that the poem is making a wholly visual appeal has been made by many readers. Paul Fussell, for instance, in a book called *Poetic Meter and Poetic Form* (1979), claims that

> This of course is very witty, but like most shaped poems it incurs one important disadvantage: it makes an unbalanced appeal – its structure directs itself more to the eye than to the ear. . . . Our eyes admire, but we are left with the feeling that the

visual experience of the stanzas has triumphed inharmoniously over their auditory appeal. (p. 170)

Fussell's comment does not quite say that the poem has *no* 'auditory appeal'. Indeed, an analysis of its metre reveals that it has a duple rising (iambic) metre, and that each line either loses ('Decaying more and more') or regains two syllables (one foot). Clearly, if the poem were read aloud it would be impossible to suggest to a listener that such reduction and expansion resembled birds' (or angels') wings. However, it could be argued that such an oral performance would realise something equally important about the dynamics of the stanza shape which a merely visual response to their iconic pattern might miss.

In order to recognise what the auditory pattern suggests, we need to remind ourselves of what the poem is about. Easter is the Christian festival of resurrection, which is what the wings symbolise. But the shape of the stanzas is not just a **symbol** of Christ's death and resurrection; the diminution and extension of the lines also mime the fall and resurrection of humankind ('man'), and the spiritual death and rebirth of the individual believer – the speaker himself: 'My tender age in sorrow did beginne' (11). The resurrection and rebirth of the individual, and of humanity in general, are, of course, precisely what Christ's death and resurrection make possible in Christian belief: this is the meaning of the Easter festival. The poem can be read as a prayer in which the speaker calls on Christ to help him achieve his own resurrection: 'With thee / Let me combine . . . For, if I imp my wing on thine, / Affliction shall advance the flight in me' (16–20).

But if this is the meaning of the poem, we would argue that only a temporal reading of the poem's spatial form dynamically acts out this meaning. The dynamic movement of the stanzas can be realised only through reading them sequentially, one line after another. The loss of one metrical beat in each of the first five lines, and its restoration in each of the five succeeding ones, can be said to act out the feeling of loss and renewal dynamically in each of the stanzas. As the reader goes through the poem, there is a sense of narrowing down or dying, passing through the narrow straits ('Most thinne. / With thee'), and then a sense of release, expansion, flight, as each stanza opens out again. Such a process is temporal, not just visual, and is closely identified with the argument of the poem, creating a profound interrelationship between the poem's dynamic message and its dynamic form. Just as the poem's language identifies Christ's death and resurrection with those of humanity in general (in the first stanza) and the individual believer (in the second), so the poem's shape works to unite these three processes. It thus seems significant that the turning point of each stanza – the point where it begins to rise up or expand after fading into thinness, poverty, annihilation – is the moment where humankind and/or the speaker seeks to become unified with Christ: 'Most poor: / *With* thee'; 'Most thinne. / *With* thee' (emphasis added). It is as though the re-growth or flight is a direct result of the phrase 'With thee', and the shape of the stanza is making that very point. This is what the speaker means when he says that he must 'imp my wing on thine' if he is to fly – in falconry, to 'imp' is a verb meaning 'to engraft feathers in a damaged wing, so as to restore or improve [a bird's] powers of flight' (*Shorter OED*). Each stanza imps its wing on Christ at its turning point or centre, grafting extra syllables onto each line as it moves out of the crisis point of the middle lines. In doing so, the poem's form offers a dynamic reading experience which acts out the whole secret of Christian resurrection, the meaning of the Easter festival.

Moreover, there is something quite extraordinary going on with the syntax, enjambment and punctuation at the crucial turning point in each stanza. The 1633 punctuation, which we have followed here, puts a colon after 'Most poore' in the first stanza and a full stop after 'Most thinne' in the second. This suggests that 'Most poore' belongs syntactically with the previous line ('Till he became / Most poore') rather than with the following line. The next line starts what is effectively a new sentence: 'With thee / O let me rise'. This structural break certainly makes sense, for human poverty in Christian thinking results from separation from Christ, whereas salvation results from being reunited with him. Thus the two halves of each stanza enact this contrast between separation and salvation. But the fact that seventeenth-century punctuation often signalled pauses rather than logical relations in the syntax allows another kind of reading. If we override the punctuation we end up with another example of 'double syntax', where the reader experiences a flicker of hesitation over the line ending as to whether the sense is complete within the line or not – that is to say, an ambiguity about whether the line is end-stopped or not. Should we read 'Till he become most poor' or 'most poor with thee' (or somehow both at the same time)? Christ's poverty, his suffering – or what line 15 calls his 'thinne'-ness – are important articles of Christian doctrine: Christ became man and suffered on earth in the flesh in order to secure our redemption from sin. It was by sharing human deprivation, taking our sins upon himself, that he earned our atonement. He became most poor with us, and our salvation is supposed to depend on our becoming 'most poor' with him. Moreover, if we disregard the 1633 punctuation, we have a closer unification of the three levels of falling and resurrection that we have described as being identified in the dynamics of each stanza, since 'man' and Christ become more closely identified if there is no full stop or colon at these turning points in the stanzas.[13]

---

[13] We are not recommending that you should lightly disregard an author's punctuation but, as we have suggested, punctuation has not always functioned according to today's conventions. Herbert's poems survived only because on his deathbed he gave a manuscript of them to a visitor. An earlier manuscript survives which, though not in Herbert's handwriting, has corrections to the poems in his hand. It includes a version of 'Easter Wings' that is significantly different from the printed version, though it does have full stops after lines 5, 10, 15 and 20. The manuscript version may be found in Amy Charles, ed., *The Williams Manuscript of George Herbert's Poems* (Delmar, NY: Scholars' Facsimiles and Reprints, 1977), p. 28.

■ Concrete Poetry

Similarly productive uncertainties about the conventional distinction between spatial and temporal form, and about the status of the poetic line, can be observed in John Hollander's 'Swan and Shadow' (1967). This is an example of 'Concrete Poetry', a type of visual poetry pioneered by a number of avant-garde writers in the twentieth century which takes many different forms and has, at various times, been claimed to serve a variety of different ideological and aesthetic ends (see 'concrete poetry' in *Princeton*). Concrete poems tend to move words and letters about on the page, as we saw E.E. Cummings doing in Chapter 2, in unconventional ways which fracture the syntax and problematise conventional ways of reading – often challenging that unity of form and function which we have seen New Criticism demanding of poetry. Yet many concrete poems follow the example of Renaissance figure poems such as Herbert's 'Easter Wings' by arranging the words on the page to form a recognisable image whose shape echoes or mimes the subject matter of the poem. The form of such poems thus becomes a part of their meaning.

```
                        Dusk
                      Above the
                  water hang the
                        loud
                         flies
                        Here
                        O so
                        gray
                        then
                      What              A pale signal will appear
                      When          Soon before its shadow fades
                      Where          Here in this pool of opened eye
                      In us      No Upon us As at the very edges
                  of where we take shape in the dark air
                    this object bares its image awakening
                      ripples of recognition that will
                          brush darkness up into light
    even after this bird this hour both drift by atop the perfect sad instant now
                        already passing out of sight
                      toward yet-untroubled reflection
                    this image bears its object darkening
                    into memorial shades Scattered bits of
                    light      No of water Or something across
                    water          Breaking up No Being regathered
                    soon              Yet by then a swan will have
                      gone                Yes cut out of mind into what
                      vast
                      pale
                        hush
                        of a
                        place
                         past
                  sudden dark as
                      if a swan
                        sang
```

This poem's lines are organised on the page in order to create an image of the swan above its reflected image or shadow in the water, the longest middle line evidently representing the level surface of the water. Yet what seems to be going on in Hollander's poem is not only the mimesis of an object, but also the imitation of a process. As we read the poem, the image gradually coheres into a solid form and then disintegrates as the swan glides out of sight. Although the poem appears static on the page, our temporal experience of reading it imitates an experience which changes through time. Notice how the way the poet has exploited the separation of the neck from the breast and body of the swan registers the way the swan takes shape as a recognisable form after the initial sight of the flies. In the upper half the sequence of interrogatives – 'What', 'When', 'Where' (if they *are* interrogatives: there are no question marks) – captures this questioning of the experience. As each question is answered in the body of the swan, so the body itself takes shape. In the corresponding lines of the 'Shadow' the images – 'light', 'water' – are no sooner named than they are denied in the repeated 'No' as the image becomes unreal.

That the poem is about an experience in time is suggested by the fact that the central line which separates Swan from Shadow on the page is full of references to time, culminating as it does in the word 'now'. But that word 'now' is no sooner fixed in the central line than it passes into memory, over the enjambment, as the subsequent line qualifies it: 'already passing out of sight'. Thus we move from sight to 'yet-untroubled reflection' (in both senses of 'reflection'). The language and form of this poem are not just referential, they are emotive and, as we will suggest, self-referential. They are emotive in that they are attempting to imitate an experience: what it feels like to watch a swan come into sight and then glide out of sight. It is notable how often referential statements are revised or redefined as experiential ones in the poem. Thus, although we might try to read the line 'Here in this pool of opened eye' as a metaphorical description of the pool, round and clear like an open eye, it is more convincing if we read it as a metaphor for the eye itself. The pool is identified with the eye because this swan exists only in the eye, it is a creature of the imagination, of poetic vision. The pool upon which the swan's image reflects is 'this pool of opened eye / In us' (this is where 'this object bares its image awakening / ripples of recognition'), and the possible enjambment over the line ending can be read as double syntax, in which the flicker of hesitation foregrounds a reader's uncertainty as to whether this 'pool of opened eye' is something 'out there' in the real world, or an object which exists only in the mind's eye, coming into existence in the reading process itself. When the real bird has disappeared, passed 'out of sight', the mental image passes into 'reflection' and into 'memorial shades' before 'going out of mind'. The stress in such words as 'mind', 'memorial', 'reflection', 'recognition' is on mental processes rather than physical events. The poem does not just record a perception: it is *about* the process of perception. As a visual icon of a swan and its shadow on the water the poem would simply be a visual trick, but as a performance of the temporal process of glimpsing, recognising, remembering and then forgetting the swan, the poem generates an immediacy which no other form could produce.

It may seem odd to talk of 'enjambment' in a poem such as this – a poem with no metre, and where the verse lines seem so obviously organised to create a purely visual pattern. But, as we have tried to show, the line divisions have a complex and productive relationship to the syntactic structure, serving either to invite or to resist a 'pause of suspension', and so forcing us to work out how a word or a phrase connects with what precedes or follows it. This, remember, is exactly what we drew attention to in reading such metrical verse as Milton's. We suggest that you might find it interesting to re-read Hollander's poem now, and see whether you leave a 'pause of suspension' at any more of the line end-ings. Do these coincide with syntactic pauses? Can they be heard only if you read the poem aloud? Try reading the poem out loud to a friend who has never seen it, and see whether she or he can tell from the way you read it that it is poetry. Having done this, you might discuss what the results of this experiment suggest about poetic form.

▦ The Double Pattern and the Romantic Imagination

The 'double pattern' which we are recognising in these poems has to do with the question of whether poems are experienced primarily as spatial or as tem-poral forms. This, in turn, affects the relationship between syntax and the poetic line, which – we are arguing – is a fundamental part of the experience of reading poetry (because it is divided into lines) which is not found in other forms of language. As we have seen, this double pattern of form (or poetic line) and meaning can be found even in lines such as Hollander's which are not metrical. But, although this double pattern would seem to be a feature of poetry *per se*, it could have different functions at different historical periods, and we should perhaps recall the idea we floated at the beginning of this chap-ter – that poetic form might need to be understood in terms of the ideological or historical context in which the poem was written.

We have already hinted, for instance, that Milton's choice of blank verse was politically motivated, since the prefatory note on 'The Verse' in which he at-tempted to justify that choice ends by claiming that, far from being a defect, this 'neglect of rhyme . . . is to be esteem'd an example set, the first in English, of ancient liberty recovered to heroic poem from the troublesome and modern bondage of rhyming'. Phrases like 'ancient liberty' and 'modern bondage' have special significance in the writing of someone like Milton, who spent much of his life working and arguing for a particular concept of liberty in the English Revo-lution. By contrast, the eighteenth-century preference for closed rhyming couplets, in which the sense is contained within the verse unit (the couplet), may reflect not just a different version of the double pattern of line and sense but also a different politics, a politics of containment, of fixed forms and fixed meanings.

That is not to say that there is any inevitable correlation between poetic form and political vision – a fluid syntax is not necessarily a threat to the established order of things (that would be a foolish claim). But it does seem suggestive that the poet in whose work double syntax has been most commonly identified, after Milton, as an integral structural principle should be a poet who, like Milton, aspired to play an active part in revolutionary politics, namely William Wordsworth, who was instrumental in reintroducing blank verse as a medium for English poetry at the very end of the eighteenth century. A fuller history of English versification – or at least of attitudes towards blank verse and the heroic couplet from Milton through Pope to Wordsworth – might reveal that the way the double pattern changes through history has an implicit politics.[14] This would be a more ambitious enterprise than we can embark on here, but the examination of double syntax in Wordsworth which follows will show, we think, that the way syntax relates to verse form in his poetry is closely related to the claims his poetry makes about historically important philosophical and ideological issues.

Double syntax may be found in the following lines from 'Home at Grasmere' (probably written between 1800 and 1806, though not published in Wordsworth's lifetime). Wordsworth is describing how the image of wooded mountains, on which the trees shine with melted hoarfrost, is reflected in a lake:

> all the distant grove
> That rises to the summit of the steep
> Shows like a mountain built of silver light!
> See yonder the same pageant, and again
> Behold the universal imagery
> Inverted, all its sun-bright features touched
> As with the varnish and the gloss of dreams;
> Dreamlike the blending also of the whole
> Harmonious Landscape, all along the shore
> The boundary lost – the line invisible
> That parts the image from reality;
> And the clear hills, as high as they ascend
> Heavenward, so deep piercing the lake below.[15] (567–79)

---

14 Bradford, *Linguistic History of English Poetry*, goes some way in this direction, though its emphasis is not primarily political.

15 This part of the poem is not included in all printed versions, which use different manuscripts as their base. Our text is that of MS.D, as reproduced in Wordsworth, *Home at Grasmere*, in *The Cornell Wordsworth*, ed. Beth Darlington (Ithaca, NY: Cornell University Press, 1977), pp. 87–9.

Ricks's discussion of lines 574–7 ('Dreamlike the blending . . . That parts the image from reality') suggests that there is a parallel between the effect of the line boundaries and the effects of landscape being described:

> The boundary is also that which we cross when we pass from one 'line' to another; the 'line invisible' (following the dash –) is also that which separates one line from another, 'invisible' because it is emblematised on the page by the white space. Invisible, but not non-existent; there is no thing solidly there, no formal punctuation, but there is nevertheless the parting – by means of a significant space, a significant vacancy – of one thing from another.[16]

Ricks's analysis defines the effects of these lines as static or spatial (the 'white space' on the page at the end of line 576), but it seems more accurate to interpret them as a moment of syntactic hesitation. In lines 574–75, for example, the reader may provisionally take the word 'whole' to be a noun until the next line persuades us to reinterpret it as an adjective:

> Dreamlike the blending also of the whole
> Harmonious Landscape . . .

Both the succeeding lines encourage an enjambed reading across a line ending which, in every case, separates (or joins? – but that ambiguity is the point) shore from lake, visible from invisible, 'image' from 'reality':

> all along the shore
> The boundary lost – the line invisible
> That parts the image from reality; . . . (575–77)

Is this a boundary that separates ('parts'), or does the fact that it is lost and invisible mean that image and reality are joined? It should be clear that this is not a purely formal effect, nor is it simply pictorial. Instead, it has potential thematic and philosophical implications for a writer whose poetry develops a philosophical view of nature as a unified, organic and living whole, and explores the ambiguities involved in the perceptual relation between viewer and landscape – these lines are about a 'Dreamlike' effect which problematises the distinction between 'image' and 'reality'. These philosophical assumptions and questions are somehow acted out in the metrical structure of Wordsworth's verse, which is why formal analysis is not something you can forget when you are concentrating on the 'bigger' issues of a writer's beliefs, message or historical importance.

---

[16] 'Wordsworth: "A Pure Organic Pleasure from the Lines"', in Christopher Ricks, *The Force of Poetry* (Oxford: Oxford University Press. 1984), p. 95.

We can perhaps support this claim by looking at an example of double syntax in a poem which has often been seen as one of the best introductions to Wordsworth's philosophy, 'Tintern Abbey' (1798). We can find the same kind of syntactic slide in a central passage of this poem, where Wordsworth is trying to sum up what the love of nature has meant to him as a man and as a poet:

> Therefore am I still
> A lover of the meadows and the woods,
> And mountains; and of all that we behold
> From this green earth; of all the mighty world
> Of eye and ear – both what they half create,
> And what perceive . . . (102–7)

Notice how many of the syntactic units – clauses, phrases, sentences – begin in mid-line. This inevitably means that they run over into the next line more often than not. At the end of line 103 ('A lover of the meadows and the woods, / And mountains') the comma encourages us to take a pause which could be either grammatical or metrical, only to find that Wordsworth has added the mountains to his list of things – 'meadows' and 'woods' – that he loves. This seems to be mere amplification, continued in the repeated 'all' of this and the following line – indeed, this 'mighty' world seems to be getting bigger and bigger as we read on. A second enjambment comes at the end of line 104: 'of all that we behold / From this green earth'. The most interesting enjambment for our current reading, however, is the one at the end of line 105: 'of all the mighty world / Of eye and ear'. What interests us about this line break is the way it manages (very quietly) to transform the outer world of nature – meadows, woods and mountains – into an inner, perceptual world of human experience (you might recall our claim that Hollander's 'Swan and Shadow' does something similar). The parallelism established in the repetition of 'all that . . . all the' (104–5) leads us to take the phrase 'mighty world' as belonging with the preceding syntax as the last of a string of phrases which refer to the external world. But the transformation that takes place over the line ending, as the qualification 'Of eye and ear' forces us to redefine this as the internal universe of the human observer, demands a syntactic revision which leaves us in what we can only call a state of semantic shock. This is no longer the world of meadows, woods and mountains; it has suddenly become the 'mighty world / Of eye and ear'. What Wordsworth says immediately following this – that the eye and ear (of the poet? of all of us?) 'half create' what they 'perceive' – clearly involves ideas about creation and perception which would be highly interesting to any reader who wanted to work out the epistemological assumptions (that is, ideas about how our minds relate to the objective world) of Wordsworth or his fellow Romantic poets. These lines suggest that the 'mighty world / Of eye and ear' is not merely the passive reflection of 'the mighty world' of meadows and woods but is half created by the eye and ear of the observer. Perception thus becomes a creative process rather than a passive reception of images from the external world.

This interests us because the relationship between the human mind and the world of nature is a central issue in Wordsworth's poetry and, indeed, in Romantic poetry generally. Romantic poets were interested in describing the way the mind (particularly the mind of the poet) engages with the outside world in imaginative activity. They claim that this process is neither objective nor subjective, but a complex interaction between subject and object of the kind we saw in Chapter 1 in Keats's response to the nightingale in his 'Ode'. Wordsworth explores this process in many places, but the following passage from *The Prelude* (1805), describing a young child's response to nature, indicates the reciprocal nature of the relationship between perceiving subject and perceived object:

> From nature largely he receives; nor so
> Is satisfied, but largely gives again,
> For feeling has to him imparted strength,
> And powerful in all sentiments of grief,
> Of exultation, fear, and joy, his mind,
> Even as an agent of the one great mind,
> Creates, creator and receiver both,
> Working but in alliance with the works
> Which it beholds. – Such, verily, is the first
> Poetic spirit of our human life . . . (II, 267–76)

The way Wordsworth and his contemporaries saw the imaginative interaction between the mind and the world, and the value they placed on it, produced a revolution in received ideas about poetic description and the imagination which constitutes a large part of what we mean by the 'Romantic revolution' in poetry. Clearly it is exciting to find such a major epistemological shift reflected in or acted out by the dynamic interaction between syntax and metre in Wordsworth's poetry. As we have suggested, the effects of this double pattern may dramatise the intimate interdependence of poetic form and the largest questions which poetry raises and explores.

Exercises

1 Read the following poem by Eleanor Brown (1996) and then try to answer the questions that follow. The point of this exercise is to try to work out relationships between form and content, between the poem's use of formal devices and what it is about.

Waltz

Final embraces that taste even ultimate;
fierce as the night was seized, urgent & intricate;
shot with the consciousness 'we have been intimate' –
skirting the issue, how nonchalant, delicate,
laughingly, reelingly, visit me, *do* visit,
thinking it haltingly, slowly in triplicate,
this is goodbye is it, this is goodbye is it,
this is goodbye, is it?

(a) Work out the poem's metrical form using the methods of analysis presented in Chapter 2.

(b) What relationship, if any, can you discern between the poem's metre and its meaning?

(c) Why is the poem called 'Waltz'?

(d) What happens in the last line?

2 For the following exercise we have written out a poem by William Carlos Williams as though it were prose, adding punctuation where prose would seem to require it; we have also reproduced it as it was printed when published in 1923. Read both versions carefully, and then try to answer the questions.

(a) By the road to the contagious hospital, under the surge of the blue, mottled clouds driven from the northeast – a cold wind. Beyond, the waste of broad, muddy fields, brown with dried weeds, standing and fallen, patches of standing water – the scattering of small trees. All along the road the reddish, purplish, forked, upstanding, twiggy stuff of bushes, and small trees with dead, brown leaves under them, leafless vines. Lifeless in appearance, sluggish, dazed spring approaches.

(b)   **Spring and All**

By the road to the contagious hospital
under the surge of the blue
mottled clouds driven from the
northeast – a cold wind. Beyond, the
waste of broad, muddy fields   5
brown with dried weeds, standing and fallen

patches of standing water
the scattering of trees

All along the road the reddish
purplish, forked, upstanding, twiggy   10
stuff of bushes and small trees

> with dead, brown leaves under them
> leafless vines –
>
> Lifeless in appearance, sluggish,
> dazed spring approaches –   15

(i)   If you did not know that passage (a) was a prose version of a poem, would you still be able to identify it as poetry? If so, what features suggest this? If not, what other kind or kinds of writing might it be? (For instance, an extract from a novel, a diary, a letter, an official report, a newspaper column.)

(ii)   In order to turn Williams's poem into more-or-less conventional prose, we had to modify the punctuation at two or three places. Identify those places, and try to see why we decided to alter the punctuation. Why can the poem itself avoid conventional punctuation? What differences, if any, does our punctuation make to the meaning? Are there any places where you would have punctuated the prose differently? If so, why?

(iii) Identify as many examples of double syntax as you can find in the poem. Then try to sum up the effect of the double syntax, both in the particular places you have identified and, if possible, in the poem as a whole.

(iv)   Try to identify the verse form of Williams's poem. What principle or motive governs the division of the poem into lines?

(v)   Does the poem Williams actually wrote seem more interesting or effective than our prose version? If so, what effects does his form achieve that ours lacks?

(vi)   Think about the significance of the poem's title. Does anything you have said about the form of the poem – its punctuation, syntax, line breaks – in previous questions help you to explain its title?

(vii) In the light of your responses to the previous questions, would you say that the form of this poem has any relationship to its meaning? (You may want to refer back to our summary of the various ways form can relate to meaning in poetry at the beginning of this chapter before answering this question.)

(viii) In 1916 a controversy developed in the United States about the difference between free verse and prose. The critic John Livingstone Lowes declared of Amy Lowell's poetry: 'Miss Lowell's free verse may be written as very beautiful prose; George Meredith's prose may be written as very beautiful free verse. Which is which?' Lowell replied: 'there is no difference. . . . Whether a thing is written in prose or verse is immaterial' (quoted in Peter Jones, ed., *Imagist Poetry* (Harmondsworth: Penguin, 1972), p. 34). From what you have discovered in this exercise on Williams's 'Spring and All', would you agree with Lowes and Lowell?

3 We suggested in the previous chapter that the notion of the prose poem is a contradiction in terms in that the absence of lineation prevents such a text from making use of 'the subtle interplay between poetic language and the poetic line that we claim is characteristic of poetry' (p. 64). In order to allow you to test that claim for yourselves, we would like you to read the following selected passages from a prose poem by Kenneth Koch called 'My Olivetti Speaks' (1998) and then try to answer the questions that follow. The full text consists of fifty-seven prose sections of varying lengths, each one of which is about poetry.

My Olivetti Speaks

Birds don't sing, they explain. Only human beings sing.

. . .

The very existence of poetry should make us laugh. What is that all about? What is it for?

. . .

'I bring fresh showers for thirsting flowers.' Poetry sometimes seems part of an enormous game of Fill in the Blanks. Let every emotion, idea, sensation be covered (filled in) and may none escape. When we have totally completed this board, when all is color, line, and shading, no blank spaces at all, we may, then, see what this great solved jigsaw puzzle means. (I already have one idea: the refreshment of childhood grossly modified by social and historical change.) The Last Judgment is nothing compared to what then we shall see! Otherwise (if there is no puzzle of this sort) why is Shelley disguising himself as a cloud? Wouldn't that be a waste of time?

The awakening of sexual feelings in a hedgehog is a poetic subject possibly not yet covered. This doesn't imply, however, that we should concentrate our efforts on covering it, though someone may, and if he is as good a poet as Ronsard, and has a thriving tradition behind him, he may do it well.

. . .

Once I taught polar bears to write poetry. After class each week (it was once a week) I came home to bed. The work was extremely tiring. The bears tried to maul me and for months refused to write a single word. If refused is the right term to use for creatures who had no idea what I was doing and what I wanted them to do. One day, however, it was in early April, when the snow had begun to melt and the cities were full of bright visions on windowglass, the bears grew quieter and I believed that I had begun to get through to them. One female bear came up to me and placed her left paw on top of my head. Her mouth was open and her very red tongue was hanging out. I realized that she, and the other bears, must be thirsty, so I procured for them several barrels of water. They drank thirstily and looked up at me from time to time gratefully but even then they wrote no poems. They never did write a word. Still I don't think this teaching was a waste of time, and I'm planning on continuing it in the future if I find I have the necessary strength. For hard and exhausting it is to attempt something one knows it is impossible to do – but what if one day these bears actually started to write? I think we would all put down our Stefan George and our Yeats and pay attention! What wonders might be disclosed! what dreams of bears!

. . .

Poetry, which is written while no one is looking, is meant to be looked at for all time.

(a) Read these selections from 'My Olivetti Speaks' a number of times in order to gain a preliminary understanding of each section.

(b) Highlight or underline all the text's poetic features that you can find (drawing on what you already know about poetry, on our discussion of poetry in the first three chapters, and even on our discussion of poetry in the chapters that follow).

(c) Having carried out the activity suggested in (b), would you be prepared to label this text a prose poem?

(d) Divide up or rearrange one or two of the text's longer sections into poetic lines (creating free verse, four-beat verse, or iambic pentameter).

(e) Try to give reasons for the metrical or non-metrical form you have chosen. Have you: (i) imposed line divisions arbitrarily on the text? (ii) created line divisions in response to the shapes and rhythms that are already there in the text? (iii) created line divisions in response to the text's meanings? (iv) introduced line divisions that attempt to add to the text's meaning or effects (for example by creating double syntax)?

(f) Compare and contrast the original prose text with the verse text you have made out of it. Which of the two would you describe as more 'poetic'? Would you describe your verse text as a 'poem'?

(g) Having carried out this exercise, would you change your answer to question (c)? Would you be prepared to call 'My Olivetti Speaks' a poem (even though it is written in prose)? Does the text make any use of what we have called significant form? Is the 'prose' form itself significant (i.e., is there some kind of correlation between form and meaning)?

(h) What is the meaning of the text's title? How does it relate to the text's content and form?

Chapter 4

Creative Form and the Arbitrary Nature of Language

▦ End-rhymes and the Ends of Rhyme

If the only essential difference between poetry and prose is the fact that poetry is cut up into lines, then it should not surprise us to find that line endings are the place where the relationship between a poem's metre and its meaning most often becomes apparent. This is why discussion of metre led us very quickly in our previous chapter away from conventional stress-counting or 'prosody' to look at various ways, such as end-stopping, enjambment and double syntax, in which sense and syntax may be articulated at line endings in poetry. Reformatting the printed layout of poems – writing them out as prose – will often serve to highlight what is lost to the dynamics of the reading process when all the hints and hesitations of a potential pause at line endings are typographically removed. As we saw, those hesitations could be significant even in free verse, where there is no regular stress pattern or syllable count to govern line length. All our examples of double syntax were, in fact, taken from unrhymed free verse and blank verse (except the passage from 'The Lads', which uses free end-rhyme), but a large proportion of English verse is end-rhymed, and if we are serious about line endings as a site of special interest for any understanding of how metre relates to meaning in poetry then it is high time we said something about rhyme.

Most poetry handbooks distinguish between and discuss different types of rhyme (end-rhyme, internal rhyme, half-rhyme, **feminine rhyme**, *rime riche*, eye-rhyme, for instance) and particular rhyme schemes (heroic couplet, *terza-rima*, **quatrain**, **Spenserian stanza**, **rondeau**, **rhyme royal**, sonnet, etc.).[1] But you are unlikely to find many books or journal articles on rhyme as such in

---

[1] For all these terms, and more, see our Glossary entry, 'stanza forms'.

your university library. Fortunately, there are some good introductions to poetry currently in print that explore the dynamic effects of rhyme and its potential relationships with meaning.[2] This is fortunate because students from high school onwards are often encouraged to look at the way poems rhyme: you earn Brownie points in any assessment if you can say something about the way the sound of a poem relates to its sense (rhyme is the most important or prominent device of sound or sound effect, though devices such as assonance, alliteration or onomatopoeia may also add to a poem's overall 'soundscape'). In discussing a poem's 'rhyme' we tend to think we are discussing the most poetic thing about it since, after all, the word 'rhyme' in everyday English is virtually a synonym for poetry. In practice, however, it often turns out to be difficult to say anything sensible or insightful about a poem's use of rhyme, especially if we are concerned to identify some kind of relationship between rhyme and meaning. Because of this, we think that it is high time that teachers were honest and up-front about the theoretical problems of assessment criteria that encourage students to find (or invent) relationships between sound and sense in poetry. This is not to say that there never is a relationship between rhyme and meaning in poetry, but to warn students and teachers against turning the search for it into a free-for-all game in which fantasy overrides common sense. One of our aims in this chapter is to examine some of the reasons, in linguistics and literary theory, why claims about the significance of rhyme sounds in poetry are often problematic or unconvincing whilst at the same time trying to show what real scope there might be for analysing the relation of rhyme to reason in particular poems. That phrase 'rhyme or reason' is itself, of course, proverbial: it's a cliché. You will find it surfacing in titles of the few books and articles that, to date, have discussed the poetics of rhyme.[3] But, like many such alliterative phrases, it has its own rhetorical force which, we want to suggest, will take us directly to the heart of the problem of how sound might relate to sense, or metre to meaning. (As you can see, such alliterative pairings can become addictive.)

The first thing to realise is that there is, normally, no direct link between what a word sounds like and what it means. (We shall look at the theoretical reasons for this later in the present chapter: they are rooted in linguistics and philosophy.) Yet the kind of alliterative phrases we used at the end of the previous

---

[2] See, for example, Jeffrey Wainwright, *Poetry: The Basics* (London and New York: Routledge, 2004), pp. 102–120, and John Strachan and Richard Terry, *Poetry* (Edinburgh: Edinburgh University Press, 2000), pp. 59–74.

[3] See, for instance W.K. Wimsatt, 'One Relation of Rhyme to Reason' in *The Verbal Icon*, pp. 153–68; Wimsatt's essay remains one of the clearest demonstrations of the ways in which, as he puts it, 'the equalities of verse coincide with the parallels of meaning' in poetry (p. 154). John Hollander's *Rhyme's Reason* exploits the parallelism in its title, though it does not restrict itself to discussing rhyme.

paragraph set up a parallelism between the sounds of two words which encourages us to believe that there might be some natural or logical connection between their meanings. The same may be true of rhyme as well. Such rhyming or alliterative patterns, which foreground the materiality of language (its sound), are by no means unique to poetry, however, and to see how they work we could do worse than examine how they function in 'normal' everyday usage, where they can most often be found in some very un-poetic contexts – advertising logos, political slogans or banner headlines as well as proverbial and idiomatic expressions. Here are a few examples (you could make up your own list):

'Hero to Zero' – newspaper headline on a celebrity who got it wrong.

'Let the train take the strain' – advertising hoarding on a motorway to get us to abandon our cars.

'Smart Thinking: City Linking' – advertisement playing on the 'Citylink' logo of a British rail franchise.

'Big Green Parcel Machine' – commercial logo painted on the side of delivery vans belonging to a road transport company that paints its vans bright green.

'Twenty's Plenty' – sign put up in urban streets to signal a lower than usual speed limit for motorists.

'Snack Attack' – header for magazine feature in which 'Six top writers reveal their food cravings'.

'Shop till you drop' – consumerist slogan.

'Waste not, want not' – traditional proverbial saying.

'No pain, no gain' – common expression in all kinds of places, becoming proverbial.

'Pain in Ukraine' – headline signalling Scottish football team losing important overseas match.

Advertising copywriters earn good money making up such slogans, for reasons which are easy to summarise: they catch the attention and they are memorable – there is not much point in an advert no one notices or remembers. Find a good rhyme for 'Coca-Cola' and you'll probably make your fortune. (Try it now.)

Perhaps the most persuasive effect of such **rhetoric**, however, is its quasi-logical function. We have a tendency to assume that there might be some deeper connection between the two words or phrases that are linked together by assonance, alliteration or rhyme. That is why they work proverbially: 'No pain, no gain' must be true, we feel, because the words go together so well, even though we know you can prove almost anything in proverbs. Yet we are calling this a *quasi*-logical effect because there is no logical reason why words that sound the same should have any connection: the effect is at best merely rhetorical. Might this quasi-logical effect be the way rhyme and other sonic echoes work in poetry? The answer, as we shall see, is 'sometimes, but not always'.

There is no doubt that rhyme and other devices of sound assist memory; any folk-singer will tell you that you get to memorise song lyrics by remembering their rhymes (remember what we said in Chapter 2 about the close connections between poetic rhythms and musical forms). Poetic traditions in nearly all languages started out as oral traditions, in which poetry was recited or sung and where the ability to memorise often very long texts seems to have determined the forms which later writers inherited. Rhyme is not used in all poetic traditions (ancient Greek, Latin and Hebrew poetry does not use end-rhyme at all), but poetry's exploitation of the sound-properties of language explains why some of the deepest roots of poetic form go back to poetry's origins as an oral/aural medium of communication that has to be memorable. (As we saw in Chapter 2, p. 59, while ancient Hebrew poetry did not use rhyme, it did use other repeated sound devices, such as parallelism.) Learning poetry by heart and reciting it aloud were once common practices, but they are now seen as quite out of place in the classroom. This is a great loss since such practices put students and other readers more closely in touch with the essential nature and roots of what, as we shall see, is now called 'the poetic function' than modern educators seem to realise.

We have seen that rhyme, like other sound patterning, pairs up words in order to suggest that there is some kind of parallelism of meaning between them (this is the quasi-logic of advertising logos and commonplace phrases). If we find that at least some of the rhyming words in a poem have parallel (or, indeed, opposed) meanings then this would offer some scope for the type of analysis that examines how rhyme relates to meaning. If we are lucky, the rhyming pairs may help us to identify some of the poem's central themes or the 'logic' of its argument. The following example is a modern love sonnet from Eleanor Brown's 1996 collection entitled *Maiden Speech* (we have already looked at two poems from this collection). The title of the collection is relevant to the subject matter and to the speaker's voice in the poem itself (it's also a nice example of ambiguity – think about it):

Probably the most human thing I do,	[a]
apart from dancing; and the only time	[b]
I'm not engaged in finding words for you,	[a]
or for myself, or fishing for a rhyme.	[b]
'The perfect sexual experience'?	[c]
Perhaps you misinterpret my ideal;	[d]
ecstasy, angel choirs, no preference	[c]
of mine: the act, ridiculous and real.	[d]
In retrospect, that first, unfortunate	[e]

5

and technically disastrous time, when we   [f]   10
were stripped of glamour, robbed of dignity –   [f]
my giggling fit, and the importunate   [e]
telephone, and your three-times-lost erection: [g]
that time, perhaps, was closest to perfection.   [g]

The poem has a complex rhyme scheme over its fourteen lines (ababcdcdef-fegg) which we have signalled here so that you can easily see which lines rhyme with which. The pattern conforms to a traditional scheme that we shall explain and analyse more fully in Chapter 12 on 'The Sonnet'. The only rhyming pair that we would call your attention to for the moment is (of course!) the concluding couplet (gg). Could we say that a woman poet who rhymes 'perfection' with 'erection' might be trying to tell her lover (the **addressee** in this sonnet) something about the difference between male and female sexuality? Or at least between his erotic ideals and her own? If we apply to this rhyme-pairing the same quasi-logical assumption that we identified for advertising slogans and marketing logos, we might say that in concluding her sonnet by rhyming these two words Brown is challenging us to think about their meaning and relationship. Do they go together, like 'rhyme' and 'reason'? Or 'perhaps' (14) not . . . It should be clear that in asking such questions we are not just discussing the sound of the words, but the meaning and tone of the whole poem. The relationship between these two words – similarity or difference? – is at the heart (quite literally!) of what the whole poem is about. We might summarise by saying that although her partner assumes that 'erection' is 'perfection', she herself finds that 'the perfect sexual experience' (5) is something else. Her attitude is rather different from his: for him the two words chime, but for her it is only ironically that they rhyme. We shall have more to say about attitude, **irony** and the way poems are voiced by speakers in Chapter 7, 'Hearing Voices', all of which would take us a long way with this superbly voiced sonnet. We shall also learn that one of the received conventions of sonnet form is that, quite often, the final couplet of a sonnet sums up or resolves its central question or theme. Brown's sonnet is a very 'modern' poem in some ways, but it is using a traditional poetic form with a sure-footed sense of how it works. Finally, you might notice the way the run-on line ending (12–13) leads into this closing couplet with a strong enjambment: 'my giggling fit, and the importunate / telephone'. Having recognised in the previous chapter the way Satan's pause on the brink of chaos mimes his hesitation over a line ending in *Paradise Lost*, we might now feel more confident about analysing the way this 'importunate' telephone call intrudes into the climactic final couplet by stepping over a line ending in the closing lines of this sonnet as if it were miming the dynamics of the interruption itself. Earlier, the speaker describes herself as a poet 'fishing for a rhyme' (4), and there might be a sense in which the whole poem is as much about poetry and making rhymes as it is about making love. We can now see how much of the interest of reading such a poem depends not just on understanding *what* it says but on responding to the *way* it says what it says – how its 'meaning' is embodied in the poetics (we could say the 'dynamics') of its language and its form.

It needs to be said, however, that to find quite such a rewarding relationship between the significance of paired rhyme words is rather exceptional, and you may have to search long and hard in English poetry before finding any really significant pairings. Even good poets may struggle to find words that fit both the rhyme sound and the meaning. Thus the idea that all rhymes in poetry set up binary patterns of semantic parallelism or opposition is nonsense: the meaning of rhymed words is normally quite diverse; only rarely do they set up binary pairs.

■ End-rhyme and Poetic Endings

Rhyme also has other effects, however. One of these is what, in our final chapter, we call 'closure'.[4] In Shakespeare's early plays, for instance, although the dialogue is usually in blank verse, the last two lines of any scene often form a rhyming couplet: Elizabethan audiences were apparently primed to listen to the verse, and a rhymed couplet said 'End of scene' if not exactly 'Curtains!' An end-rhyme in poetry may or may not complete the sense of a syntactical unit – phrase, clause or sentence – but in any regularly rhymed verse we come to expect (if we are reading properly for the sound) any unrhymed end-of-line word to – eventually – find its partner; when it does so, there is a sense of closure (as we will see later in this chapter in Browning's 'Meeting at Night'). We can perhaps see how this works in a poem written in 1930 by William Soutar, which attracts our attention for other reasons in this chapter since it is so clearly structured in binary units that display a type of parallelism which, as we shall see, has been claimed by some literary theorists to be fundamental to the poetic function of language. Its rhyme pattern plots these parallels.

He Who Weeps for Beauty Gone

He who weeps for beauty gone
Hangs about his neck a stone.

He who mourns for his lost youth
Daily digs a grave for truth.

---

[4] For more on the theory of closure, see Barbara Herrnstein Smith, *Poetic Closure: A study of how poems end* (Chicago: University of Chicago Press, 1968).

He who prays for happy hours 5
Tramples upon earthly flowers.

He who asks an oath from love
Doth thereby his folly prove.

Mourn not overmuch, nor stress
After love or happiness. 10

He who weeps for beauty gone
Stoops to pluck a flower of stone.

This is a poem that seems to be delivering a moral message; indeed, it seems to be saying the same thing six times. We may not find that message very original or subtle – it seems more proverbial and general – but it is worth noting that it was written by a man who spent the last twenty years of his life on his sickbed with an incurable illness. We might see the four-beat couplet form and the successive rhymes in purely formal terms: they cement the structure if not the (quasi-)logic of the repetitions ('he who does A gets B'), and the rhetoric is not dissimilar to what we found in some of our slogans such as 'No pain, no gain'. The repetitious syntactical and metrical structure of the two-line stanzas is varied by presenting a different example of human aspiration or loss in each stanza and a correspondingly different rhyme sound. The only exception to this is in the first and last stanzas, which use not only the same opening formula ('He who weeps for beauty gone'), but also the same rhyme words: 'gone' and 'stone'. The effect of this is to signal closure: the repetition signals to us that the poem has reached its end and completed its point, just as a rhyming couplet signalled to an Elizabethan audience that a scene in the theatre had ended. There is still some sameness-with-difference, since to 'pluck a flower of stone' (12) varies the opening image in 'hangs about his neck a stone' (2), and as with any binary system it is all a question of 'compare and contrast', identity and difference, parallelism and opposition. Rhyme affords poets just one way of setting up such patterns and effects.

We find something similar in the way George Herbert's 'Mortification' (1633) uses end-rhyme.

Mortification

How soon doth man decay!
When clothes are taken from a chest of sweets
To swaddle infants, whose young breath
Scarce knows the way;
Those clouts* are little winding sheets, *cloths 5
Which do consigne and send them unto death.

When boyes go first to bed,
They step into their voluntarie graves,
   Sleep binds them fast; onely their breath
      Makes them not dead: 10
  Successive nights, like rolling waves,
Convey them quickly, who are bound for death.

    When youth is frank and free,
And calls for musick, while his veins do swell,
   All day exchanging mirth and breath   15
      In companie;
  That musick summons to the knell,
Which shall befriend him at the house of death.

    When man grows staid and wise,
Getting a house and home, where he may move   20
   Within the circle of his breath,
      Schooling his eyes;
  That dumbe inclosure maketh love
Unto the coffin, that attends his death.

    When age grows low and weak,   25
Marking his grave, and thawing ev'ry yeare,
   Till all do melt, and drown his breath
      When he would speak;
  A chair or litter shows the biere,
Which shall convey him to the house of death.   30

    Man, ere he is aware,
Hath put together a solemnitie,
   And dressed his herse, while he has breath
      As yet to spare:
  Yet Lord, instruct us so to die,   35
That all these dyings may be life in death.

This is, clearly, another poem about ending; its argument is an article of faith in the Christian church, at least traditionally, requiring us to believe that in the midst of life we are in death and that the true life is in the hereafter. Herbert's speaker preaches this received doctrine by finding different things in each of the five traditional 'ages of man' (infancy, childhood, youth, maturity, old age) which somehow anticipate death and remind us of our mortality, hence the poem's title 'Mortification'. (If you are not sure what this word means, look it up in a good dictionary – by using a historical dictionary such as the *OED* you might find a number of different meanings that were available to seventeenth-century readers that are highly relevant to Herbert's poem.) But whilst this might be a reasonable way of summing up the poem's message, we suggest that any discussion which did not comment on the way that central message is reflected in the poem's use of rhyme would be missing something interesting and important. Once again it is a matter of repetition and variation: analysis of the rhyme scheme reveals that each stanza rhymes *abcabc*, but the more interesting thing to notice is the way each of the stanzas uses the same two words for the '*c*' rhyme: 'breath' and 'death'. If we apply to this pairing the same test that we learned for our other examples ('No pain, no gain'), all we need ask is: is there any parallelism or opposition between these two terms? And we find that just as 'pain' and 'gain' are opposites, so are 'breath' and 'death' since 'breath' suggests (indeed might be called a synonym for) life. Hence we have a rhymed pairing of opposites running through the poem which insists on the poem's central message that life, at every stage, is a journey towards death, that death is implicit in our every breath. The binary pattern that controls the poem's argument and the structure of each stanza is centred in its obsessive return to this insistent rhyme: this is another poem that says the same thing (more or less) six times. Moreover, at the end of this poem about ending we find the opposition summed up in the phrase 'life in death'. Yet while the whole poem has been about the idea of death-in-life, the final phrase ('all these dyings may be life in death') reverses and overcomes this gloomy message by suggesting that death may lead to life in a new sense. The last two lines are a prayer based on Christian teaching that, if we are mindful of our mortality whilst in this life, we may earn our salvation in the next: 'Yet Lord, instruct us so to die, / That all these dyings may be life in death'.

The examples we have looked at suggest that there are times when poets make significant use of rhyme words to stage the argument of their poems and that if, as readers, we fail to register the way such rhymes are working through their binary patterns of parallelism or opposition between sound and sense then we are missing something of fundamental importance to the poem. However, we do want to stress (again) that not many poems make such strategic use of rhyme. More often you are unlikely to be able to find any such clear-cut binary patterns in the interplay of sound and sense in a poem. Often, all you can do with a rhyme scheme is to work out its algebra ('algebra' since we use the alphabet to assign a different letter to each of the different rhyme sounds) and then find out whether such a rhyme pattern corresponds to any of the conventional verse forms listed and explained in our Glossary. Whilst any student of poetry should learn how to recognise such traditional stanza forms, and any enthusiastic reader will surely want to, the question of whether or not they are worth analysing in a particular poem is not answerable in advance. It may not always be easy, or indeed possible, to say very much about how **verse form** relates to a poem's meaning. In traditional forms the rhyme scheme is part of a fixed metrical pattern, which is why most discussions of 'rhyme' will be found in handbooks on metre. We shall have something to say about such fixed forms in our later chapters on genre since many poetic genres have fixed forms and we offer a guide to most of these in our Glossary (s.v. 'stanza forms').

But for now we want to return to the wider question of poetic form and its relation to meaning: rhyme or reason? Not every kind of poetry or theory about poetry assumes that form embodies content. There are even theories which hold that poetic or textual form resists or disrupts a poem's meaning. In what follows, we want to show that the debate over poetic form needs to be seen in terms of an equally long-standing debate in philosophy and linguistics about the nature of language itself. The claim that the form of language used in poetry is somehow significant has to be tested against the long history of philosophical and theological arguments over the possibility that the relationship between words and ideas or the world is merely arbitrary and conventional. This debate has been going on at least since Plato's *Cratylus*, written more than three hundred years before the birth of Christ.

■ The Arbitrary Nature of Language

Although we tend to assume the opposite, there are strong arguments in favour of the view that language is an arbitrary system which has no intrinsic relation to the world or to our ideas. The sound of the word 'tree', for example, has no inevitable connection either with a real tree or with the idea of a tree in our minds. The sound evokes the idea by association rather than by any necessary connection. This becomes obvious when we remember that each language in the world will use a different sound pattern for the 'same' concept. The fact that English speakers automatically associate the concept of 'tree' with the particular pattern of sounds or letters of /tree/ is due to education and habit rather than to any intrinsic connection. A language works not because it has any natural relation to the world or to meaning, but because its signs and rules are shared and implicitly agreed upon by the members of a language-speaking community.

The Swiss linguist Ferdinand de Saussure made an influential contribution to this argument. In his *Cours de linguistique générale* (1916), Saussure distinguishes the linguistic sign into two aspects: the sound image (our mental image of a word's sound), and the concept (the meaning of the word) and points out the arbitrary or conventional nature of the connection between them. Saussure's names for these two aspects of the sign have been translated as the 'signifier' (the sound of a word or its 'sound image') and the 'signified' (the idea or concept). In an often-quoted formula, Saussure says: 'The bond between the signifier and the signified is arbitrary'; he goes on to say: 'Since I mean by sign the whole that results from the associating of the signifier with the signified, I can simply say: *the linguistic sign is arbitrary.*[5]

It is sometimes thought that this declaration of the arbitrary nature of the linguistic sign is the distinguishing and revolutionary aspect of Saussure's linguistics. Yet, as we have suggested, philosophers had debated this possibility for over two thousand years. At the end of the seventeenth century, for example, John Locke, in his *An Essay Concerning Human Understanding* (1690), produced a particularly important argument in favour of the arbitrary nature of the linguistic sign. The challenging aspect of Saussure's thought is his discussion of the implications of the sign's arbitrary nature. Whereas Locke and others assume that ideas pre-exist language (for Locke they are derived from sensory impressions) and are simply named by language, Saussure argues that ideas are shaped or even produced by the language system itself.

It is clear that the sounds we can make with our mouths are not meaningful in themselves but become meaningful through the conventions of a particular language. Thus, for example, the sound clusters /tree/, /true/, /tray/ and /try/ are signifiers in English, whereas /tra/ is not.[6] In Saussure's terms, the first four sound clusters are meaningful because each change of sound produces a change of meaning: in other words, it is the *differences* between them that produce significance. For Saussure, these very similar sounds become meaningful because English recognises the differences between them as significant. Saussure argues that a similar thing happens on the 'other side' of the sign. The conceptual **field** is not simply a collection of independent, intrinsically different concepts simply waiting there to be assigned an arbitrary name. Instead, each language divides up the conceptual field according to its own arbitrary system. Thus the distinctions English makes between 'tree', 'shrub' and 'bush' and between these and other kinds of plant are not already there in the world, or in our brains, but are generated by the way the language structures our ideas about these living organisms. Other languages might make quite different distinctions among perennial plants having a trunk, bole or woody stem with branches forking out at some distance above the ground.

In other words, in the same way that sounds become signifiers through the way a language makes the differences between them significant, so do concepts or signifieds arise through the way a language divides up the conceptual world on the basis of differences which that language itself has made significant. This is why Saussure says that language is a system of differences without positive terms:

[5] Ferdinand de Saussure, *Course in General Linguistics*, trans. Wade Baskin (New York: McGraw-Hill, 1959), p. 67. For an excellent introduction to *Saussure*, see Jonathan Culler, *Saussure* (Glasgow: Fontana, 1976).

[6] We have avoided using the established system for designating phonetic sounds on the supposition that most of our readers will not be familiar with it. We hope that the point we are trying to make is clear enough.

in language there are only differences without positive terms. Whether we take the signified or the signifier, language has neither ideas nor sounds that existed before the linguistic system, but only conceptual and phonic differences that have issued from the system. (p. 120)

Saussure's linguistic theories have radical consequences for the study of literature, many of which have been explored by the theoretical movement known as 'Structuralism'.[7] For our present purposes, we wish to concentrate on their implications for a study of literary form. In most uses of language we scarcely pay attention to the signifiers in themselves; they automatically summon in our minds the signifieds with which they are associated and in which we are primarily interested. In poetry, however, as we saw in Chapter 3, the organisation of words into lines draws attention to the material nature of the signifier. We have seen that this has apparently paradoxical effects. In the first instance, it seems to make the language opaque and difficult to read – it arrests our habitual desire to 'get at' the meaning as quickly and efficiently as possible. Yet we also saw that if we understand the poetic conventions being employed, and if we are prepared to read with a heightened attention, the materiality of the sign within the poetic line can become aesthetically pleasurable in its own right and can simultaneously produce a heightened sense of the world and the way human beings experience it. Paradoxically, then, the more poetic language becomes opaque, the more 'communicative efficacy' it seems to have.[8] One way of understanding this is to say that poetic language is somehow able to overcome the arbitrary nature of language. As Derek Attridge points out,

> The idea that the distinctiveness (and special pleasurability) of poetic language lies in its capacity to heal, at least momentarily, the breach between signified and signifier, to produce a revitalized language that is not arbitrary and conventional but motivated and natural, echoes through discussions of poetry down the ages.[9]

Poets and critics have repeatedly claimed that poetry, or sometimes literature in general, is a discourse which uniquely motivates or naturalises the relationship between signifier and signified, sound and sense, word and idea, form and meaning. In what follows, we want to sketch a history of such claims in order to show that the arbitrary nature of language has been understood differently at different historical moments and that the attempt to overcome it takes

---

[7] For an account of structuralist literary theory, see Jonathan Culler, *Structuralist Poetics: Structuralism, linguistics and the study of literature* (London: Routledge & Kegan Paul, 1975).

[8] The phrase 'communicative efficacy' is taken from I.A. Richards, 'Communication and the Artist' (1924), reprinted in Lodge, *Twentieth Century Literary Criticism*, p. 108.

[9] Derek Attridge, *Peculiar Language: Literature as difference from the Renaissance to James Joyce* (Ithaca, NY: Cornell University Press, 1988), p. 132.

different forms according to the different philosophical, theological and ideological assumptions which inform poetic theory at any particular time.[10]

We will also be stressing, however, that poetry achieves this effect through employing conventional rhetorical strategies and formal techniques. These conventional strategies and techniques require readers to employ certain reading conventions in order to become effective. This is why poets and readers have to learn the various technical conventions which have been developed in the history of poetry even, or especially, if they seek to resist or subvert those conventions. Our history will reveal that some conventions of reading and writing have celebrated the conventional nature of language, and revelled in the possibilities it opens up for poetry.

◼ Neoclassicism: Language as the Dress of Thought

The philosophy, linguistics, literary theory and literary practice of the eighteenth century were significantly shaped by the philosophical system of Locke's *An Essay Concerning Human Understanding*. Locke's account of the arbitrary nature of linguistic signs led him to distrust language in general and literary language in particular. He denounced rhetorical and figurative language as a 'perfect cheat', and recommended that all discourses should employ a language of clarity and sense.[11] Locke's denunciation of the pleasurable but deceptive nature of literary language clearly left poets with a problem. If language is arbitrary, and acceptable only when used in straightforward, rational ways, what justification could there be for poetry? Alexander Pope's response to this problem was to propose a model of poetry in which truth, clarity and sense predominated, and figurative language and all the other 'embellishments' of poetry were kept duly subservient. This allowed Pope to distinguish 'good' poetry from 'bad' on the basis that it was only the latter that exhibited all the faults which Locke had identified with poetry in general. Pope's model of good poetry is presented in a poem, *An Essay on Criticism* (1709), which sets out to exemplify the precepts he lays down. In an often-quoted couplet (we will return to it more than once in this book), Pope prescribes the proper relation between language and thought in poetry:

---

[10] Although the arbitrary nature of language has been recognised throughout the history of Western culture from Plato to Saussure, there have always been alternative theories which have argued that language has intrinsic and essential relationships with our ideas and with the world 'out there'. See Hans Aarsleff, *From Locke to Saussure: Essays on the study of language and intellectual history* (Minneapolis: University of Minnesota Press, 1982).

[11] Locke, *An Essay Concerning Human Understanding*, ed. Peter H. Nidditch (Oxford: Oxford University Press, 1984), p. 508.

> Expression is the Dress of Thought, and still
> Appears more decent as more suitable. (318–19)

Shortly afterwards he articulates what has become one of the best-known claims about the relation between sound and meaning in English poetry: in poetry, he says, 'The Sound must seem an Eccho to the Sense' (II, 365). Pope attempts to exemplify his theory in lines in which the poetry apparently *does* what it *says*:

> When Ajax strives, some Rock's vast Weight to throw,
> The Line too labours, and the Words move slow;
> Not so, when swift Camilla scours the Plain,
> Flies o'er th'unbending Corn, and skims along the Main. (370–73)

In order fully to appreciate the point here, we need to know that Ajax was the strongest of the Greek warriors in the war against Troy in Homer's *Iliad* and that Camilla was a swift messenger of the goddess Diana in Roman mythology. Pope is attempting to show aspiring poets how the language of poetry can give the impression that it echoes what it refers to. One of the techniques he uses to demonstrate this in these lines is to modify the basic metre of the poem (iambic pentameter). In the line about Ajax's labour, for example, Pope attempts to give the impression that the line itself labours (or is laborious to read). This is achieved through making virtually every word in the line a monosyllable with almost equal semantic importance, and by phrasing the line in a way which makes us want to give it more stresses than usual in iambic pentameter:

>   - / -   /   -   /   /   /   -   /
> When Ajax strives, some Rock's vast Weight to throw
>   b   b   b   b   b

The tension here between meaning and the conventions of the iambic penta-meter is most patent in the word 'vast'. The semantic importance of 'vast' (this is a *vast* weight) makes us want to give it a full stress. But this would produce three stressed monosyllables in a row – which clashes with the natural rhythms of English as well as with the requirements of the iambic pentameter. The demands of the metre thus mean that, although we stress this semantically important word, it is 'demoted' to serve as an offbeat. Thus a tension is set up between the natural rhythm and the metrical beat. This is one of the reasons why the line can seem 'slow' and 'difficult' to read (especially aloud).

If this effect is achieved by, as it were, packing more into the iambic penta-meter line than usual, the line depicting Camilla's unimpeded movement modifies the iambic pentameter in a different way by adding an extra beat and two extra syllables:

```
 /  -    - /  -  /  -   /  - /      - /
Flies o'er th'unbending corn, and skims along the main
   b       b    b        b   b       b
```

As our beat markers indicate, this is a six-beat line (traditionally called a 'hexa-meter'); but although this line is therefore actually longer than the surrounding five-beat lines, it somehow seems shorter to read. At the beginning of the line, several devices work together to give a sense of rapid and easy movement. In our reading, the line begins with a beat and then immediately merges into a rising metre. After the initial beat, the use of elision reduces the double-syllable word 'over' into the one syllable 'o'er', and merges the monosyllable 'the' into the first syllable of 'unbending'. The result is that what would normally be a four-syllable sequence ('over the un-') is compressed into two syllables: 'o'er th'un-'; and these two syllables have to be slightly rushed in a reading because they serve to realise a single offbeat. The momentum which results from these techniques continues unimpeded through the rest of the regularly metrical line. The overall effect is to produce a sense of rapid, unimpeded movement which seems to correspond appropriately with the image of Camilla skimming along the main.

Our analysis shows that Pope sought to make the sound seem an echo to the sense through the skilful manipulation of the poetic form and poetic line. Yet we should take note of Pope's use of the word 'seem': he acknowledges that this effect is an *illusion* produced by the formal devices of poetry. And although Pope sounds as if he is prescribing for poetry in general, we need to remember that his theory of the relationship between form and meaning, sound and sense, emerged in specific historical conditions. Pope is promoting a particular assumption about poetry which might not apply to all kinds of poetry or to all historical periods.

■ Romanticism: Language as the Body of the Spirit

Romantic poets and theorists in the late eighteenth and early nineteenth century rejected Pope's account of the relationship between sound and sense (along with Locke's philosophy and linguistics) as a mechanistic account of poetic language. Instead of seeing thoughts, ideas or meaning as a 'body' which is then 'dressed' by language, Romantic theorists shifted the metaphor by arguing that authentic poetic language 'embodies' the 'spirit' of the mean-ing. In the third of his 'Essays Upon Epitaphs' (written 1809–10), Wordsworth suggests that the writing of poetical epitaphs in the eighteenth century was thoroughly tainted by the artifices which have overrun our writings in metre since the days of Dryden and Pope. . . . [In such writings] those expressions which are not what the garb is to the body but what the body is to the soul, themselves a constituent part and power or function in the thought . . . are abandoned for their opposites.[12]

Wordsworth goes on to argue that 'If words be not . . . an incarnation of the thought but only a clothing for it, then surely will they prove an ill gift.' Similar claims made by other Romantic poets confirm that the Romantics were primarily concerned to make the signifier a 'constituent part' of the signified or an 'incarnation of the thought'. Coleridge recommended the Bible and idealist philosophy as a 'counterpoise' to what he called the 'mechanic philosophy' of the eighteenth century and the growing commercialism of the nineteenth. The contents and language of the Scriptures, he claims, 'are the living *educts* of the imagination', and the imagination is a power which 'gives birth to a system of symbols harmonious in themselves, and cosubstantial with the truths of which they are the conductors'. For Coleridge, the poetic symbol 'always partakes of the reality which it renders intelligible; and while it enunciates the whole, abides itself as a living part in that unity of which it is the representative'.[13] (We will return to the Romantics' account of poetic language in Chapters 5 and 6.)

The Romantic poets' claim that poetic language is the incarnation of thought implies that such language overcomes the arbitrary nature of the sign. At the same time, however, the Romantics tended to see poetic form as merely a way of clothing poetic language – as, in Wordsworth's term, something 'superadded' to poetry. This is why Wordsworth can assert that even the best poetry, 'even of Milton himself', differs in no essential respect from that of prose.[14] Shelley too says that 'it is by no means essential that a poet should accommodate his language' to metrical form.[15] Despite such pronouncements, however, the Romantic poets actually experimented widely with poetic forms.[16] And we have seen that Keats and Wordsworth use metrical form in ways which, far from merely 'dressing' their poetry, play a constitutive part in producing the effect of a spontaneous overflow of powerful feelings or act out,

---

[12] Wordsworth, *Selected Prose*, ed. John O. Hayden (Harmondsworth: Penguin, 1988), pp. 360–61.

[13] From *The Statesman's Manual* (1816), in Coleridge, *The Oxford Authors: Samuel Taylor Coleridge*, ed. H.J. Jackson (Oxford: Oxford University Press, 1985), pp. 660–61.

[14] For Wordsworth's discussion of the relation of metre to poetry, see 'Preface to Lyrical Ballads' (1800), in *The Lyrical Ballads*, pp. 251–4, 261–5.

[15] Shelley, *Shelley's Poetry and Prose*, ed. S. Reiman and J. Powers (New York: Norton, 1977), p. 484.

[16] See Stuant Curran, *Poetic Form and British Romanticism* (Oxford: Oxford University Press, 1986).

through double syntax, the subtleties of their philosophical speculations about the intimate relationship between the human observer and the natural world. A poet's pronouncements about poetic theory are not always a reliable guide to his or her poetic practice.

■ Gerard Manley Hopkins: Parallelism

The poetry of Gerard Manley Hopkins (1844–89) is sometimes said to anti-cipate the technical experimentation of twentieth-century modernism, but more interesting for our current discussion is the fact that he was a pioneering theorist of poetic form. Perhaps more than that of any other poet in English, Hopkins's poetry foregrounds and thickens the language in ways which make it seem sinuously material. The following sonnet, 'God's Grandeur' (1877), exhibits this aspect of Hopkins's style, though not so emphatically as some of his other poems:

> The world is charged with the Grandeur of God.
>   It will flame out, like shining from shook foil;
>   It gathers to a greatness, like the ooze of oil
> Crushed. Why do men then now not reck his rod?
> Generations have trod, have trod, have trod;   5
>   And all is seared with trade; bleared, smeared with toil;
>   And wears man's smudge and shares man's smell: the soil
> Is bare now, nor can foot feel, being shod.
>
> And for all this, nature is never spent;
>   There lives the dearest freshness deep down things;   10
> And though the last lights off the black West went
>   Oh, morning, at the brown brink eastward, springs –
> Because the Holy Ghost over the bent
> World broods with warm breast and with ah! bright wings.

This poem exploits a range of linguistic devices open to the poet, building into each line the sound textures of palpable rhythms, end-stopped and run-on lines, enjambment, end-rhymes and internal rhymes, repetition and insistent alliteration. This draws our attention to the textures of the language and the way they relate dynamically with the metrical form. For Hopkins this linguistic and poetic patterning is done not for its own sake but to create a formal equi-valent to the living textures and tensions of the natural landscape. Hopkins's view of nature is a deeply vitalistic and theological one: 'There lives the dearest freshness deep down things' (10) within nature because 'The world is charged with the Grandeur of God' (1).

In his prose speculations, as W.H. Gardner reports, Hopkins searched for ways of describing the relationship between the outward appearance of objects in the natural world and his sense of the living, spiritual principle which informs them:

> As a name for that 'individually-distinctive' form (made up of various sense-data) which constitutes the rich and revealing 'oneness' of the natural object, he coined the word *inscape*; and for that energy of being by which all things are upheld, for that natural (but ultimately supernatural) stress which determines an *inscape* and keeps it in being – for that he coined the name *instress*.[17]

Hopkins valued the unique 'inscape' and 'instress' of natural objects both for their own sake and for the sense they give that God's shaping power is immanent within them. In his poetry, Hopkins tried not merely to describe this but to create a linguistic equivalent which would produce an analogous effect for his readers, allowing them to experience the instress of the world through the inscape of his poetry:

> No doubt my poetry errs on the side of oddness. . . . But as air, melody, is what strikes me most of all in music and design in painting, so design, pattern or what I am in the habit of calling *inscape* is what I above all aim at in poetry. (quoted by Gardner, p. xxii)

As Gardner puts it: 'The main reason for the initial strangeness of his style is the serious artistic purpose of "inscaping" into a perfect unity (i) the inward fusion of thought and feeling, and (ii) the corresponding outward harmony of rhythm and sound-texture' (p. xxii).

Hopkins, then, extends the spiritual organicism of the Romantics to include every aspect of poetic form. Metre and the cluster of sound effects which are shaped by it are no longer seen as the apparel or dress of poetry. For Hopkins, their combination, unique in each instance, produces an inscape which is 'the very soul of art' (quoted by Gardner, p. xxii). In arguing this, and in foregrounding form so drastically in his poetry, Hopkins paved the way for twentieth-century theories about the relationship between poetic form and meaning.

Hopkins's most influential speculations in this respect include his account of the role of parallelism in the structure of poetry:

> The artificial part of poetry . . . reduces itself to the principle of parallelism. . . . But parallelism is of two kinds necessarily . . . the first kind . . . is concerned with the structure of verse – in rhythm, the recurrence of a certain sequence of syllables, in metre, the recurrence of a certain sequence of rhythm, in alliteration, in assonance and in rhyme. Now the force of this recurrence is to beget a recurrence or parallelism answering to it in the words or thought and, speaking roughly, . . . the more

---

[17] Hopkins, *Poems and Prose*, ed. W.H. Gardner (Harmondsworth: Penguin, 1984), p. xx.

marked parallelism in structure . . . begets more marked parallelism in the words and sense. . . . To the [other] kind of parallelism belong metaphor, simile, parable, and so on, where the effect is sought in likeness of things, and antithesis, contrast, and so on, where it is sought in unlikeness.[18]

Rather than sound echoing sense, Hopkins is positing that parallelism of sound in a poem may 'beget' some parallelism in meaning (which can involve marked similarity or marked dissimilarity). We can perhaps understand this claim as suggesting that when we are struck by an unusual parallel in sound (say, in rhyme) we are prompted to ask whether the meanings of the words are also related in some way – whether, as Hopkins puts it, the words are being compared 'for likeness' sake' or 'for unlikeness' sake'.

We can perhaps illustrate this by looking at a concrete example. The most important thing about Wilfred Owen's poetry would seem to be its message about the horror and futility of war. The fact that Owen's poems use interesting formal devices – even the fact that he chose to use poetic form at all – would seem to be of secondary importance. Owen himself wrote: 'Above all I am not concerned with Poetry. My subject is War, and the pity of War. The Poetry is in the pity.'[19] Yet if we look, for example, at the ending of Owen's 'Strange Meeting' (1919), there are several formal features which seem more than merely decorative. The poem imagines a 'strange meeting' between the speaker and the ghost of an enemy soldier he has killed in action. The ghost's message ends as follows:

> 'I am the enemy you killed, my friend.
> I knew you in this dark; for so you frowned
> Yesterday through me as you jabbed and killed.
> I parried; but my hands were loath and cold.
> Let us sleep now . . .' (40–44)

One of the formal features which is most noticeable here is the use of an unusual kind of end-rhyme. Rhyme between one-syllable words usually consists of a similarity between the vowel sounds and between the final consonant sound (as in beat/heat). In Owen's rhymes, however, the vowel sounds are different, and the echo consists of similarities between consonants (friend/frowned, killed/cold). This device, which is used throughout the poem, is variously called 'consonance' or 'half-rhyme'. Because this is a more unusual

---

[18] Quoted by Roman Jakobson, *Language in Literature*, ed. K. Pomorska and S. Rudy (Cambridge, MA: Harvard University Press, 1987), pp. 82–3.

[19] Draft preface for a collection of war poems, in *The Poems of Wilfred Owen*, ed. Jon Stallworthy (London: Chatto & Windus, 1990), p. 192.

device than proper rhyme, it draws particular attention to itself. The fact that it almost seems as if the same word is being repeated prompts us to think about the similarities and differences in meaning of the words brought together in this way.

In the passage quoted, the near-coincidence of sound between 'friend' and 'frowned' draws attention to the fact that these words seem incompatible with each other (a frown is not a sign of friendliness). This encourages us to think more carefully about the implications of the fact that the dead man calls his killer 'my friend': is this ironic, or a sign of how the dead man is now able to transcend the fact that they are supposed to be enemies? Whereas the coincidence in sound between 'friend' and 'frowned' emphasises their contrast in meaning, that between 'killed' and 'cold' points to the association between them (the dead are cold). Yet these lines tell us that the man's hands were already 'cold' before he was killed – in fact, their being cold was one of the reasons he was unable to parry his opponent's attack. The word cold, then, becomes ambiguous, since although it refers to the harsh conditions of war in the trenches, it also becomes a metaphor for the enemy soldier's reluctance to fight ('my hands were *loath* and cold'). If, as we suggested at the start of this chapter, full rhyme can, at least sometimes, exploit parallels or coincidences of meaning between paired rhymed words, it becomes easier to see how Owen's half-rhymes in 'Strange Meeting' relate to the ambiguities which are at the heart of the poem. Paying close attention to **pararhyme** in this poem brings out the poem's subtleties of meaning and implication in a way that would not be possible in non-poetic language.

Hopkins's theory of poetic form paved the way for the New Critics' account of how all aspects of poetic form cohere into an organic unity (see Chapter 3). The influence of Hopkins on New Criticism can perhaps be seen in W.K. Wimsatt's discussion in *The Verbal Icon* (1954) of the sound–sense relations produced by the sound parallelism of rhyme. In an essay whose title – 'One Relation of Rhyme to Reason' – neatly encapsulates the issues we are exploring, Wimsatt argues that the so-called 'musical' qualities of rhyme in poetry are not worth commenting on, and that the only interest in rhyme is when it forces the reader to consider the interrelationship set up between similarity of form and similarity (or difference) of meaning: 'The words of a rhyme, with their curious harmony of sound and distinction of sense, are an amalgam of the sensory and the logical . . . they are the icon in which the idea is caught' (p. 165). Our discussion of Owen's poem would seem to support the New Critical argument that content and form, in a 'good' poem, are inseparable. If we rewrote Owen's poem with standard rhymes or in blank verse, it would be problematic to claim that it would still be exactly the 'same' poem. We could perhaps reproduce Owen's 'message' in prose, but we would lose the poem's particular impact. Indeed, this means that we can reverse Owen's motto: if the poetry is in the pity, the pity is also in the poetry. (In fact, you might notice that Owen employs half-rhyme in this motto in a way which signals the deep interrelationship between poetry and pity in his poems.)

Wimsatt's assertion that rhyme fuses the sensory (sound) and the logical (meaning) is indicative of the fact that New Criticism represents another phase in the history of attempts to claim that the language and form of poetry have a motivated rather than an arbitrary relationship to meaning. New Criticism differs from our previous case studies by being a way of reading poetry rather than a theory about how it gets written. It seeks to interpret the conventions of poetic form (such as rhyme) as meaningful, and does so through employing a set of reading strategies which are themselves conventional rather than inevitable. But to say that this particular way of reading poetry achieves its ends through employing reading conventions is not to dismiss it. On the contrary, we want to stress in this book that all methods of reading use reading conventions as ways of processing the conventions of poetic language. We are already beginning to see that conventions may change through history, and we hope to show that there may be different conventions of reading and writing within any particular cultural milieu. As we shall see at the end of this chapter, some of these alternative reading conventions reject the idea that poetic language fuses signifier and signified into an organic whole, and celebrate instead the way certain kinds of poetry playfully use the arbitrary nature of the sign to disrupt meaning and produce aesthetic pleasure.

■ Foregrounding and Defamiliarisation

An alternative to the Anglo-American attempt to discover the iconic significance of poetic form originates in discussions of literature in Russia in the second decade of the twentieth century. Asking the same question as the New Critics, the so-called Russian Formalists came up with apparently the same answer: literature is distinguished from non-literary uses of language through its emphasis on form and technique. But instead of seeking to discover an organic relationship between form and content in poetry, the Russian Formalists considered poetry (and literature in general) as a verbal art which foregrounds its devices and techniques in order to 'defamiliarise' our response to the world and to language itself.

In 'ordinary' language we value economy of effort: we desire that the ideas or information will be delivered to us efficiently. We don't want to have to struggle with the signifiers, but to get on to the signifieds as fast as possible. In such language, the signifiers become so familiar and habitual that we no longer take notice of them. Worse still, language becomes a series of clichés which never require us to think about the ideas they convey, or really look at the state of affairs in the world they refer to. As Victor Shklovsky puts it, 'as perception becomes habitual, it becomes automatic'.[20] The role of art in general is to remove this veil of familiarity, to re-alert us to the objects, ideas and events which no longer make an impression: 'art exists that one may recover the sensation of life; it exists to make one feel things, to make the stone *stony*' (p. 20).[21] Art does this by employing the range of techniques and devices at its disposal in ways that impede and disrupt our familiar responses: 'The technique of art is to make objects "unfamiliar", to make forms difficult, to increase the length of perception' (p. 20). Such defamiliarisation can be achieved by using surprising figurative language which draws attention to itself, by using an unusual point of view or poetic speaker, and by the range of poetic devices which foreground the sounds of the language. Thus pronunciation should be made difficult through the 'roughening' effects achieved by the repetition of identical sounds (rhyme, alliteration, and so on), and poetic rhythm should avoid the potentially lulling effect of regular prose rhythms by 'disordering' rhythm. In sum, 'Poetic speech is formed speech' (p. 28).

◼ Roman Jakobson: The Poetic Function

One of the leading thinkers in the Russian Formalist group was Roman Jakobson. Jakobson moved to Prague in 1920 and then in 1941 to the United States, where he became enormously influential in the development of Structuralist poetics. Jakobson's life work was devoted to the linguistic analysis of verbal art. He sought to develop a linguistic rather than an impressionistic account of the nature and effects of poetic language and drew on a range of different theories and poetic traditions. One of Jakobson's most important articles, 'Linguistics and Poetics' (1960), stresses the need for literary critics to adopt the methods of structural linguistics in the description and analysis of how poetry works. He fuses Structuralist assumptions with ideas from New Criticism and Russian Formalism in order to formulate a provocative account of the characteristic interplay between poetic form and meaning.

Perhaps the key concept developed in Jakobson's article is the notion of the 'poetic function' of language. Language is used differently for different purposes, and our response as readers or listeners is shaped by our perception of how and why the language is being used. In Jakobson's terms, language has a range of different 'functions', each of which foregrounds different aspects of language.[22] Among the various functions Jakobson identifies are the following:

[20] See Shklovsky, 'Art as Technique' (1917), reprinted in Lodge, *Modern Criticism and Theory*, pp. 16–30 (19).

[21] For a thorough discussion of the political implications of Russian Formalism, see Tony Bennett, *Formalism and Marxism* (London: Methuen, 1979).

[22] See 'Linguistics and Poetics', in Jakobson, *Language in Literature*, pp. 62–94, especially pp. 66–71. This article is also reprinted in Lodge, *Modern Criticism and Theory*, pp. 32–61.

1 The *referential function*: in referential uses of language, we are primarily interested in the relationship between language and the world (as in science or history); we ask: *is this true?*
2 The *conative function* ('conation' means endeavour – that is, the attempt to achieve something): in conative uses of language we are interested in what it achieves, what its effects are on the reader or listener (as in education, or political persuasion); we ask: *how effective is this – does it educate or persuade?*
3 The *emotive function*: in emotive uses of language, we are primarily interested in the relationship between language and the speaker (as in autobiography, diaries, confession); we ask: *is this sincere?*
4 The *poetic function*: in poetic uses of language, our primary interest is in the artistic nature of the language itself; we ask: *how does this language work as verbal art?*

Jakobson makes it clear that the poetic function occurs in discourses outside poetry, something we tried to suggest early on in this chapter when we listed a few of the many examples of rhyme, assonance and alliteration which we had noted in commercial logos, advertising copy, newspaper headlines, and so on. But although poetic techniques and effects may be found in such discourses, they do not constitute their primary *raison d'être* (advertisements are primarily designed to sell products). We should also bear in mind that poetry involves functions 1, 2 and 3: at different points in the history of speculations about poetry, each of these functions has been stressed more than the others (since the Romantic period, for example, poetry has been strongly associated with the emotive or expressive function). What is startlingly different about Jakobson's argument is that although he admits that poetry may be expressive, referential or persuasive, he argues that these are not the dominant or defining functions of poetic language: 'The poetic function is not the sole function of verbal art but only its dominant, determining function, whereas in all other verbal activities it acts as a subsidiary, accessory constituent' (*Language in Literature*, p. 69).

Jakobson's description of the poetic function makes it central to the questions we are exploring in this chapter. The primary orientation of the poetic function, he says, is 'toward the message as such, focus on the message for its own sake' (p. 69). This is slightly ambiguous, since it is not quite clear what is meant by the 'message as such'. Jakobson seems to clarify this by going on to say: 'This function, by promoting the palpability of signs, deepens the fundamental dichotomy of signs and objects' (pp. 69–70). In other words, the poetic function foregrounds the acoustic or material nature of words rather than seeing them as merely transparent windows onto the world. But although some commentators have interpreted this as implying that poetry foregrounds the signifier at the expense of the signified, Derek Attridge has shown that

Jakobson was primarily interested in describing the way the poetic function makes verbal art meaningful without reducing it to a referential representation of the real world (see *Peculiar Language*, pp. 127–32). As Jakobson says later in the article, there is no justification for 'attempts to confine such poetic conventions as meters, alliteration, or rhyme to the sound level'. He cites Hopkins's account of parallelism with approval, suggesting that a sound effect such as rhyme 'necessarily involves a semantic relation between rhyming units' (p. 81).

Jakobson develops his notion of the poetic function into a general description of how poetry works by specifically attending to the linguistic processes through which poetry is generated. Consider the following basic sentences:

The	child	sleeps
A	baby	naps
The	kid	awakes
(article)	(subject)	(verb)

Each of these sentences takes the same basic combinatory form: article followed by noun (the subject or agent) followed by verb. We could go on producing similar sentences by selecting related nouns and verbs. It thus becomes apparent that language chains (sentences) are put together through processes of *selection* and *combination*. Combination proceeds according to the demands of syntax and purpose – we cannot combine parts of speech in any order we wish: 'the sleeps child' would not be a sentence. The selection of words for each place in a sentence normally occurs according to principles of equivalence (similarity or dissimilarity): 'child', 'baby' and 'kid' are all equivalent to one another, and although there is an obvious dissimilarity between 'awakes' and 'sleeps' they are drawn from the same semantic field (they are related to each other in meaning) and perform equivalent functions in the sentence. But something more interesting takes place in sentences such as the following:

The kid lies and cries in its cradle.

In this example, the combination seems to have been made partly on the basis of equivalence – successive words have been selected because they are *similar* to each other in sound (through alliteration and rhyme). The fact that this makes this sentence seem more 'poetic' than the ones above helps us to understand Jakobson's otherwise difficult statement that 'The poetic function projects the principle of equivalence from the axis of selection into the axis of combination' (p. 71).

Jakobson claims that this process of combining units which are in some way equivalent to each other happens on all levels of poetic texts – not only in terms of sound (rhythm, metre, rhyme, alliteration, and so on) but also in terms of meaning. In other words, all the successive units of a poem (lines, syntactic units, images, and so on) may be combined together according to principles of equivalence (similarity and difference). We can test this claim by analysing the following brief poem:

In a Station of the Metro
The apparition of these faces in the crowd;
Petals on a wet, black bough.
(Ezra Pound, 1916)

One of the challenges of this enigmatic poem is how to make sense of it. Its enigma lies in the way it simply offers two successive images without any signals about how (or whether) we are supposed to connect them (the semicolon is much more neutral here than, say, a colon or a dash would be). The interpretative strategy most readers are likely to employ is to attempt to discover some relation (some kind of equivalence) between the poem's two lines. Indeed, the poem seems to invite us to imagine a visual similarity between 'these faces in the [metro] crowd' and 'petals on a wet, black bough'. Thus the relationship between these images can be interpreted as a *metaphorical* one: the first line can be read as a metaphor (or implicit **simile**) for the second. In fact, the metaphorical equivalences between these lines can be more precisely stated:

faces (A) = petals (A^1)
crowd (B) = wet, black bough (B^1)

The parallels between these lines are even more exact, since the equivalent terms occupy similar places in the clauses and are connected by prepositions:

The apparition of these (A) in the (B);
(A^1) on a (B^1).

This analysis of Pound's poem reveals that semantic equivalence (items in the second line can be read as metaphors for items in the first) coincides with grammatical and spatial equivalence in the two lines. In addition, the parallelism between 'crowd' and 'bough' at the end of each line is reinforced by the fact that there is an aural echo between them – the similarity of vowel sounds (or assonance) makes this a species of half-rhyme. Both Pound's and Owen's poems would thus seem to support Jakobson's claim that 'In poetry, any conspicuous similarity in sound is evaluated in respect to similarity and/or dissimilarity in meaning' (p. 87). The crucial thing to remember, however, is that all these effects and reading strategies are based on the fact that Pound's images are set out in poetic lines. It is this physical fact which makes all the other parallels (aural, grammatical, figurative) salient or interpretable. If these images appeared in a prose description of an experience in the Paris Metro we would be more likely to interpret them simply as successive details rather than as metaphorical equivalents.

■ Parallelism in Robert Browning's 'Meeting at Night'

Jakobson's account of the poetic function can be understood as an elaboration of Hopkins's notion of parallelism. Poetry works by putting words, images, phrases, sentences, lines, stanzas, and so on in parallel with each other in ways which imply that there is some kind of semantic relationship between them. In what follows, we will analyse a poem – Robert Browning's 'Meeting at Night' (1845) – in which a variety of parallelisms occur between its two stanzas. As we shall see, this poem (or our analysis of it) suggests that Jakobson's claim about the structure of poetic texts is an illuminating one. We shall also see, however, that the poem's use of parallelism at all levels of form is related not only to its meaning or effect but also to the historical and cultural context in which it was produced (that is, mid-Victorian Britain).

Meeting at Night

The grey sea and the long black land;
And the yellow half-moon large and low;
And the startled little waves that leap
In fiery ringlets from their sleep,
As I gain the cove with pushing prow,   5
And quench its speed i' the slushy sand.

Then a mile of warm sea-scented beach;
Three fields to cross till a farm appears;
A tap at the pane, the quick sharp scratch
And blue spurt of a lighted match,   10
And a voice less loud, thro' its joys and fears,
Than the two hearts beating each to each!

Our analysis of this poem needs to begin by establishing what is being described. The poem seems to give us access to a male speaker's thoughts and impressions as he journeys across a landscape to meet a woman for what seems like a clandestine love affair. But if this is an accurate statement of the poem's 'content', it is nevertheless only the beginning of an analysis of the poem – which will necessarily involve discussing how its form relates to this 'content'. The poem is, of course, about desire – the speaker's desire to be with his lover – and the fact that he has to cross sea and land works to delay him, and perhaps to increase his sense of expectation. This sense of heightened expectation and anticipation is indicated by the traveller's intensely alert response to the scenery around him, and this contributes to the poem's highly charged atmosphere. One of the ways this atmosphere is produced is by the use throughout the poem of alliteration, internal rhyme and onomatopoeic effects.[23] Alliteration occurs when there is an echo between the initial consonant sounds of nearby words (or stressed syllables). In the first three lines of 'Meeting at Night', there is a cluster of alliterating words beginning with 'l' sounds:

> The grey sea and the long black land;
> And the yellow half-moon large and low;
> And the startled little waves that leap . . . (1–3)

There are also other kinds of echo between words in these lines: there is internal rhyme between 'yellow' and 'low', and a kind of half-rhyme between 'startled' and 'little'. It might be tempting to suggest that this systematic repetition of 'l' sounds is meant to mimic the sound of the lapping waves. In later lines, alliteration combines with onomatopoeic effects which also seem to mimic the sound of what is being described:

> As I gain the cove with **pushing** prow,
> And **quench** its speed i' the **slushy** sand. (5–6)
>
> A **tap** at the pane, the **quick sharp scratch**
> And blue **spurt** of a lighted match. (9–10)

But although there are onomatopoeic effects here, we need to recognise that this is not the way sound-patterning generally works. It would be difficult to make such a claim about the alliteration of 'f' sounds in the second stanza: 'Three fields to cross till a farm appears'. A more interesting reading of these sound effects would be to suggest that instead of reproducing the sound of the actions in the poem, they work to convey a sense of the speaker's heightened

---

[23] One of the ways in which language might seem to escape Saussure's theory of the conventional nature of the sign is through onomatopoeia. Students are often taught to look out for onomatopoeic effects in poetry; consequently they tend to 'discover' it wherever they look. But Saussure points out that onomatopoeia is exceptional rather than intrinsic to language, that it is quite rare, and that onomatopoeic words 'are only approximate and more or less conventional imitations of certain sounds' (*Course in General Linguistics*, p. 69).

perceptions as he moves through this landscape. In other words, such techniques help to make the speaker's experience seem vividly present to the reader.

Our analysis thus far of the formal features of this poem's language is not particularly unusual. Such procedures are commonly taught in the classroom. In what follows, we want to demonstrate that the analysis of poetic form can go further than this, and that it can be much more revealing and interesting. In order to do this we will need to develop a more systematic analysis of the interdependence of form and content in this poem. In particular, we want to explore how the poem exploits the possibilities of parallelism at every level of the text – in its use of stanzas, metre, rhyme scheme, punctuation, enjambment and syntax, as well as in its use of figurative language and imagery. What we want to reveal is the way all these features and devices work together not only to give the poem a sense of 'atmosphere', but also to make reading it a dynamic experience which is intimately related to what is being described.

Perhaps one of the most obvious but not immediately interesting facts about the poem is that it is divided into two stanzas. This becomes more interesting when we discover that almost everything in one stanza has its parallel in the other. At the level of 'content', for example, each stanza deals with different but similar stages in the lover's journey towards the farm where his beloved lives. In the first stanza, he crosses the 'grey' moonlit sea in a boat and arrives on the beach. In the second stanza, he crosses 'Three fields' and arrives at the farm. This parallel between events is enhanced by what we might call the descriptive dynamics of each stanza. Each stanza opens with an impression of the expansiveness of the landscape and the distance to be covered ('The grey sea and the long black land' and the 'mile of warm sea-scented beach') and quickly moves on to images that are immediately to hand and more vividly realised (the waves, the prow of the boat, the 'tap at the pane', the 'lighted match').

More specifically, the dynamic movement of each stanza is concerned with encountering and overcoming restrictions or obstacles. We want to argue that this is not just a matter of content, since certain formal features of the poem can be seen to reproduce this dynamic movement as an effect of reading. In other words, we want to show that we do not just read about this but are induced to experience its equivalent in the reading process. As we shall see, this effect is produced by the combined forces of a number of formal features.

The poem's metre is basically a four-beat rising metre which varies between duple and triple rhythms (this variation can be seen by the fact that the total number of syllables per line varies between 8 and 10). But this basic metre is modified at different strategic points in the stanza in order to produce contrasting effects of restriction and release (using much the same techniques which we have seen in Pope's *An Essay on Criticism*). A mechanical analysis of the metre of the eight monosyllabic words of the poem's opening line would predict the following stress pattern:

     /   /   /   /

The grey sea and the long black land

Yet our experience of reading the rhythm of this line is likely to be significantly different:

     / /   /   /   /

The grey sea and the long black land
     b b   b   b

In other words, the semantic values of these words modify the metre in order to produce clusters of stressed syllables which give a sense that the line is 'difficult' or 'slow' to read. The bunching together of the two beats in 'grey sea' squeezes out an offbeat, and thus inhibits the sense of easy forward motion achieved by rising duple metre. This is compounded by the actual rhythm of 'long black land', with its three stressed syllables in a row. Although an adjective–adjective–noun combination of monosyllabic words is perhaps the most common instance where demotion occurs (the second adjective has to be stressed, but does not carry a beat), it nonetheless works to slow down the movement of the line. The rhythmic effects of the phrase thus seem to emphasise its meaning by producing a sense that the 'long black land' restricts the forward momentum of the reading experience as well as the lover's journey. In the second stanza, the 'mile of warm sea-scented beach' seems to inhibit forward progress even more than the 'long black land' because a double adjective combination which includes a hyphenated adjective is more unusual than a simple double adjective. This sense of restriction at the beginning of each stanza is increased by the way the first two lines in each case are both end-stopped with a semicolon. Just as the lover has a series of physical obstacles to overcome, so too is the reading momentum repeatedly blocked by punctuation.

By contrast, a sense of release and free movement is produced in the third and fourth lines of each stanza. This is achieved through the interaction of a number of formal features: (i) the fact that the third line in each case is a run-on line whose movement is not restricted by any punctuation; (ii) the use (for the only time in the poem) of successive end-rhymes (leap/sleep, scratch/match); and (iii) the fact that 'leap' and 'scratch' are verbs of action:

> And the startled little waves that leap
> In fiery ringlets from their sleep (3–4)

> A tap at the pane, the quick sharp scratch
> And blue spurt of a lighted match. (9–10)

The form, syntax and meaning of both these couplets thus produce a sense of rapid forward momentum which 'leaps' over the line break. Notice that 'quick sharp scratch' has the same structure and rhythm as 'long black land', but seems much quicker because of the overall rhythm of the line it appears in, the run-on line, and the meaning of the phrase itself. The fact that similar constructions work differently in different contexts proves that specific effects are not intrinsic to a particular formal construction, but depend on the interaction between a combination of formal factors and the actual meaning. This sense of tension released is enhanced by the way both stanzas delay the introduction of the first verb – especially in the first stanza, where 'leap' is delayed till the end of the third line (these are examples of what we called suspended syntax in Chapter 3).

It is also productive to examine how the poem's rhyme scheme contributes to this overall effect. In our earlier discussions of rhyme we concentrated on how sound echoes between rhyming words can point to similarities or differences of meaning. But we should stress that this is not invariably the case. In Browning's poem, there do not seem to be any interesting semantic relationships between the rhyming words (except perhaps between 'leap' and 'sleep'). Yet the *pattern* which the rhyme scheme forms is of interest here. As we have seen earlier, in order to describe a rhyme scheme, all you have to do is write 'a' against the last word of the first line and against all the other end-of-line words which rhyme with it. You then write 'b' against the next set of rhymes, and so on. In Browning's poem, this method ends up describing the rhyme scheme as *abccba, deffed*. In other words, we have to wait until the last word in each stanza before the rhyme scheme is completed. In reading a stanza whose rhyme scheme is *abccba*, the reader may well be unconsciously looking forward to the completion of the pattern – which is delayed until the last word. In fact, this point about the rhyme scheme coincides with the way each stanza delays the resolution of tension and expectation until the final word of each stanza. This is because the 'goal' of each stanza is deferred until its final word completes the rhyme scheme and the action at one and the same moment (the prow of the boat comes to rest in the sand, the two lovers finally come together with 'hearts beating each to each').

In other words, the dynamic movement produced by the various formal features of each stanza gives a sense of the overcoming of restrictions in order to reach a goal. And, of course, this corresponds completely with the speaker's movement across the landscape. But the poem is doing more than providing a formal equivalent to the speaker's journey. However vivid the descriptive language, it seems to give us less a sense of the place or journey itself than a sense of the state of mind of the speaker. In fact, the poem's formal features can be seen as producing a formal equivalent of the speaker's sense of expectation and eventual fulfilment. This is because the formal features we have analysed thus far can be thought of as seeking to produce a sympathetic sense of expectation and desire in the reader. Our argument, then, is that a wide range of formal devices combine in this poem to make the reading of it a dynamic emotional experience in which the reader is coaxed into empathising with the desires and expectations of the male protagonist. Thus we could say that the emotional dynamic of this poem is generated by the dynamics of its form.

The fact that there are so many formal parallelisms between the two stanzas (metre, punctuation, rhyme scheme, syntax, and so on) invites us to look for parallelism of imagery and figurative language. The most dense concentration of figurative language in the poem comes in the middle two lines of the first stanza, which concern the speaker's impression of the waves as he crosses the sea:

> And the startled little waves that leap
> In fiery ringlets from their sleep. (3–4)

In these lines the metaphors used for the waves ('startled', 'leap', 'fiery', 'ringlets', 'sleep') are mainly animistic or humanising metaphors – it is as if the boat crossing the water is *awakening* the waves from sleep. More interestingly still, the metaphors figure the waves as a woman (or a woman's hair): the 'fiery ringlets' of the waves are being aroused 'from their sleep'. And if we look at the equivalent lines in the second stanza, we see that what is metaphorical in the first stanza becomes literal in the second:

> A tap at the pane, the quick sharp scratch
> And blue spurt of a lighted match. (9–10)

The metaphor of 'fiery' from the first stanza is made literal by the vivid image of the lighting of the match, and we may be lured into thinking that the woman has been literally aroused from sleep by the 'tap at the pane' (there is no textual evidence for this, however).

And since this is a poem about love and desire, it is perhaps worth remembering that, as we shall see in Chapter 5, fire often carries **connotations** of sexual passion and arousal. Thus this poem appears to be talking about male sexual passion, but in a roundabout and metaphorical way. Our analysis of the stanza structure would support such a reading, since we have discovered that it somehow creates a sense of desire raised by delay which is eventually fulfilled. But if we admit this interpretation, the poem's climax seems particularly sentimental or euphemistic:

> And a voice less loud, thro' its joys and fears,
> Than the two hearts beating each to each! (11–12)

Yet if these lines are anticlimactic, the poem's systematic use of parallelism perhaps encourages us to discover a metaphorical version of the climax in the two equivalent lines in the first stanza:

> As I gain the cove with pushing prow,
> And quench its speed i' the slushy sand. (5–6)

In a revealing way, the man identifies himself here with the boat – it seems as if it is *his* 'pushing prow' which penetrates the 'slushy sand' in a way that seems to offer a displaced but more suggestive 'climax' to the poem.

In order to account for this indirect approach to sexuality and the displacement of the poem's climax, we perhaps need to remember that Victorian Britain had a censorious and prudish attitude towards sexuality and that any writer who wanted to write about 'adult themes' in polite literature had to do so very carefully. This may be why Browning's poem about this clandestine meeting at night contrives to talk about sexuality by displacing it on to the description of the journey itself – giving the landscape and the man's movement through it a powerful erotic charge. In other words, this poem manages to say what it wants to say, but it does so through using figurative and formal devices arranged in the parallel structures we have discovered. Such poetic techniques allow this poem to say things which cannot be said directly, or which the dominant values of its social context do not want to hear. It might be said, then, that the way the poem employs the poetic function is informed by the conflict within Victorian society between the desire to explore sexual love in poetry and the dominant sexual taboos. The subtle techniques of Browning's poem can thus be interpreted as ways of getting round social censorship. In fact there are arguments which imply that the poetic function always operates within specific social contexts which are characterised by ideological and linguistic conflict.[24]

What began as a discussion of formal devices and effects has led to much larger questions about the relationships between language and desire, poetry and society. But if there is a crucial interplay between this poem's use of form, its subject matter, and the historical context in which it was written, it may be that we also need to consider the historical, political and social contexts in

---

[24] This claim can be followed up by examining the Marxist rereading of 'Russian Formalism and Saussurian linguistics' in V.N. Volosinov, *Marxism and the Philosophy of Language*, trans. L. Matejka and I.R. Titunik (New York: Seminar Press, 1973). Yet the creative tension between sexual desire and censorship can also be read in psychoanalytic terms. A first step for such a reading would be Freud's intriguing account of the *ars poetica* in 'Creative Writers and Daydreaming', in Lodge, *Twentieth Century Literary Criticism*, p. 42.

which the poem is read. Our examination of the poem's use of the poetic function underlines the fact that the protagonist is male and that the journey across the landscape is a formal and metaphorical equivalent of male sexual desire and fulfilment. If, as we have suggested, the poem works by inviting the reader to share in the protagonist's experience, we can say that it constructs its reader as male. An interesting empirical, historical and theoretical question would be to ask how Browning's Victorian female readers might have read this poem. We also need to recognise our own historical difference from the Victorian period. How do female readers in the early twenty-first century read the poem? Do they accept its invitation to empathise with its male protagonist in his sexual quest? If a female reader did this, would she then be reading 'as a man'? If she reads 'as a woman', does the poem become a disorientating experience? Is she driven to adopt a reading which resists the effect of the various techniques which we have analysed?

These questions come into sharper focus in considering the poem Browning wrote as a companion piece to 'Meeting at Night'. In 1845, he published 'Meeting at Night' as the first of a pair of poems called 'Night and Morning'. Here is the companion poem, sometimes printed under the title 'Parting at Morning':

II – Morning
Round the cape of a sudden came the sea,
And the sun looked over the mountain's rim:
And straight was a path of gold for him,
And the need of a world of men for me.

In the context created by the second poem, the romantic tone of 'Meeting at Night', with the speaker rowing on to a beach and crossing the moonlit fields in eager anticipation of a meeting with his beloved, is qualified somewhat by his equal eagerness to return to the 'world of men' the next morning. It is important to recognise that the juxtaposition of 'Parting at Morning' with 'Meeting at Night' supplies an element of historical insight in its own right. This juxtaposition does not simply suggest something about the character of the speaker, but also reveals that there was a clear demarcation between the private world of love and the public 'world of men' in the Victorian period. The poem indicates that women inhabited the private world while men could range between private and public worlds. The juxtaposition of these two poems in itself dramatises the sexual division of labour in the Victorian period in a particularly vivid way. In fact, we could use this poem as a way of beginning to map the cultural construction of gender roles in Victorian society. We could begin this simply by listing the different things which the poems associate with the male and female worlds:

world of men	*world of women*
action (rowing boats, etc.)	passivity (waiting)
daytime	night
the sun	the moon
being outdoors	being inside a house
business	love, pleasure
the city	the natural world

In fact, this list can be compared with a similar list produced by the French feminist critic Hélène Cixous as a general description of the gender assumptions of Western patriarchy:

Where is she?
Activity/passivity,
Sun/Moon,
Culture/Nature,
Day/Night,

Father/Mother,
Head/heart,
Intelligible/sensitive
Logos/Pathos.[25]

This list might help us to understand the way Browning's poem subliminally represents the sexual union between the male protagonist and the woman he visits as the coming together of the boat (a product of culture) and the slushy sand (part of nature). And this may alert us to other figurative parallels between woman and nature in the poem – as in the image of 'the startled little waves that leap / In fiery ringlets from their sleep'. Such considerations suggest that the discussion of poetic form is not an artificial academic activity but is deeply implicated with all the other kinds of question which poems raise and which we need to ask. An intelligent analysis of poetic form will inevitably open out to questions of meaning, gender, historical context – and vice versa.

■ Peculiar Language

All the examples of poetic language examined in this chapter and in Chapter 3 exhibit two simultaneous features. On the one hand, poetic form serves to foreground the signifier or the sounds of language. On the other hand, such language produces a heightened sense of meaning and responsiveness to experience. The result is a seeming **paradox**: attention to the materiality of the

---

[25] Cixous, 'Sorties', in Elaine Marks and I. de Courtivron, eds, *New French Feminisms* (Sussex: Harvester, 1981), pp. 90–98 (90).

signifier does not draw attention away from the signified but enhances it. This gives us the sense that the arbitrariness of the sign is overcome in a moment of authentic representation or imitation. Yet if we accept the arbitrary nature of the sign and recognise that the strategies of poetic form which we have examined are conventional, then we cannot understand this peculiar effect of poetic language in terms of realistic imitation. Nor can we say that the sounds of the language are foregrounded for their own sake independently of meaning. In language, the signifier and the signified operate simultaneously and, as Saussure argued, the one cannot exist without the other since they are mutually defining.

The most convincing account of the phenomenon we are discussing is given by Attridge, who suggests that it can be thought of as the effect of two simultaneous and reciprocal processes:

> The mind, in responding to the semantic content of the verbal sequence, is sensitized to certain physical properties of speech; simultaneously, in responding to the foregrounding of the physical properties of speech achieved by the unusual patterning of phonemes, it is sensitized to certain features of the semantic content. (*Peculiar Language*, pp. 152–3)

The result 'is neither direct apprehension of the physical world nor a focus on the sounds of speech as sounds; rather, it might be called a heightened experience of language *as language* . . . language in the act of *producing meaning*' (p. 152). Our peculiar pleasure and sense of heightened attention, then, arises not in response to the way poetic language imitates the world but in response to the creative power of language itself. Poetic language does not simply dress preexisting meanings, or even embody them, but *generates* meaning as we read:

> it is that focus on the materiality of language *as it does its work of bringing meaning into being* that has so often been interpreted as mimetic or iconic representation, because the experience is unquestionably one of increased vividness or intensity of signification. (p. 154)

Yet even if this is a more satisfying account of the phenomenon we have been tracing through the history of poetics, Attridge warns us that it applies only to 'a particular literary tradition and a particular mode of reading. . . . [and hence] cannot be used as a litmus test of what is and is not literature' (p. 155). In the final section of this chapter, we will look briefly at an alternative way of reading which claims that literature exploits and revels in the arbitrary nature of the linguistic sign rather than attempting to overcome it.

■ Christina Rossetti and the Play of the Signifier

Christina Rossetti's 'Winter: My Secret' (1866) contrasts with Browning's 'Meeting at Night' in a number of ways – not least by offering an alternative insight, from a woman's perspective, of sexual politics in the Victorian period. A second contrast is the very different way Rossetti's poem uses language and poetic form.

Winter: My Secret

I tell my secret? No indeed, not I:
Perhaps some day, who knows?
But not to-day; it froze, and blows, and snows
And you're too curious: fie!
You want to hear it? well: 5
Only, my secret's mine, and I won't tell.

Or, after all, perhaps there's none:
Suppose there is no secret after all,
But only just my fun.
To-day's a nipping day, a biting day;   10
In which one wants a shawl,
A veil, a cloak, and other wraps:
I cannot ope to every one who taps,
And let the draughts come whistling through my hall;
Come bounding and surrounding me,   15
Come buffeting, astounding me,
Nipping and clipping through my wraps and all.
I wear my mask for warmth: who ever shows
His nose to Russian snows
To be pecked at by every wind that blows?   20
You would not peck? I thank you for good will,
Believe, but leave that truth untested still.
Spring's an expansive time: yet I don't trust
March with its peck of dust,
Nor April with its rainbow-crowned brief showers,   25
Nor even May, whose flowers
One frost may wither through the sunless hours.
Perhaps some languid summer day,
When drowsy birds sing less and less,
And golden fruit is ripening to excess,   30
If there's not much sun nor too much cloud,
And the warm wind is neither still nor loud,
Perhaps my secret I may say,
Or you may guess.

On one level, this poem may be read as spoken by a female speaker who is resisting the importunities of a male suitor pressing her to tell her secret. There are strong hints that this secret is of a sexual nature, and that to 'know' it would be to 'know' the speaker in a sexual way. For the speaker to allow the man to penetrate her secret would be equivalent to, or even the same as, allowing him to penetrate the secret of her body: 'I cannot ope to every one who taps, / And let the draughts come whistling through my hall' (13–14). The man is figured as winter 'Nipping and clipping through my wraps and all' (17), and the sexual parallel is continued through the wordplay on 'pecked' (to strike with a beak) and 'peck' (to kiss). But as well as the speaker defending her secret (whatever it is), there is also an element of flirtation: the speaker is 'raising the price' of the secret by refusing to tell it and by hinting that she might 'Perhaps' tell it when the weather is just right. Yet the conditions she specifies are so exacting that it doesn't seem very likely that she will ever tell. The last lines seem to hold out some prospect of her secret being revealed, but the language playfully undermines that prospect at the same time. In saying that 'you may guess' when the time is right, she might equally be saying you may go on guessing.[26]

There is also a hint that there might not be a secret: 'Suppose there is no secret after all, / But only just my fun' (8–9). The fun in this poem comes through the delight in word play: 'it froze, and blows, and snows' (3); 'bounding and surrounding me, / . . . buffeting, astounding me' (15–16); 'shows . . . nose . . . snows . . . blows' (18–20). The use of 'peck of dust' in line 24 echoes with the pun on 'peck' in line 21 in a way which works entirely at the level of sound (there is no semantic relationship between 'to peck' and a measure of dry goods). On the one hand, this play with the sounds of words can be read as a way of fending off the man's curiosity and desire; on the other hand, such 'fun' whets curiosity just as concealment arouses desire. Of the many items of clothing mentioned in the poem, a veil and a mask are less useful for keeping out the cold than for simultaneously keeping out and attracting prying eyes – both concealing and revealing at the same time. The language of the poem, then, works both to conceal and to reveal the secret – or perhaps both to defer its revelation and to create the illusion that there is something to tell. In a sense, poetic form here is used playfully in order to defer rather than embody or heighten meaning. In this way, Rossetti's exploitation of poetic form works in a quite opposite way from Browning's. In 'Meeting at Night' poetic form works to produce an effect of sexual consummation; in 'Winter: My Secret' poetic form works to defer sexual and semantic consummation. Thus we might say that these very different uses of the poetic function dramatise two quite different positions in relation to Victorian sexuality.

---

[26] This suggestion comes from Isobel Armstrong's impressive reading of the interrelation between this poem's linguistic playfulness and the sexual politics of Victorian England; see Isobel Armstrong, *Victorian Poetry: Poetry, poetics and politics* (London: Routledge, 1993), pp. 357–9.

It is even possible to suggest that the poem constitutes an **allegory** of itself – that is, it becomes a poem about itself or about our own experience of reading it. The poem potentially produces an ambiguous response in its readers in terms of whether we identify with the speaker or with the inquisitive or amorous suitor. This is not entirely a matter of whether the reader is male or female (though this will be a factor), but an effect of the poem itself. On the one hand, we may be led to identify with its speaker (as we often are with first-person speakers); on the other hand, we are cast in a similar role to the suitor to the extent that we are lured into desiring to know what the speaker's and the poem's 'secret' is. Our habits of reading, combined with the poem's rhetorical strategies, may lure us into desiring to know the poem's secret and may leave us wondering whether there is one after all. The poem implies that it has a secret meaning through its playful language, but that same playfulness defers and resists our attempt to grasp that secret. Perhaps the poem has no hidden meaning, and is just linguistic fun. Thus we can imagine that the speaker speaks for the poem as well ('I tell my secret? No indeed, not I'), and that the 'you' may also refer to us as readers. Such a reading of such a poem would imply that the foregrounding of the signifier here does not give us a sense of enhanced meaning but a sense of being caught up in an intriguing and pleasurable game. These signifiers, rather than striving to embody the signifieds, making them 'more fully present', actually work endlessly to defer meaning, keeping us guessing for ever.

Our reading of this poem in this way is influenced by a set of assumptions about language and literature which come under the umbrella term 'Post-Structuralism'. We will be returning to post-structuralist ideas about literature throughout this book. For now, all we wish to say is that Post-Structuralism accepts Saussure's notion of the arbitrary nature of the sign, but goes on to undermine his claim that the arbitrary bond between signifier and signified is a secure and stable one. Post-Structuralists claim that there is always a certain amount of slippage or 'play' in the language system: the relationship between signifiers and signifieds changes through history and according to the context in which they are used. Normally, this play is kept under control by various methods. In conversation, we can always clear up ambiguities which inevitably arise – unless, that is, we decide to play with them. In expository discourses, such as this book, care is taken to limit the unpredictable meanings which language seems prone to generate. In literary texts the conditions which normally give a degree of stability to language (such as the presence of the speaker) are often absent, and our attempts to fix meaning may not be at all secure. In fact, Post-Structuralists celebrate those texts which seem to exploit the play that is inherent in language and that seem to invite us to play with and within them.

The French writer Roland Barthes was one of the most influential, and accessible, of the post-structuralist thinkers. In an essay called 'From Work to

Text' (1971), Barthes tries to enunciate his conception of text or textuality in opposition to traditional ideas about the literary 'work'. Whereas the work (say, 'Meeting at Night') 'closes on a signified', the 'text' (such as 'Winter: My Secret')

> practises the infinite deferment of the signified . . . its field is that of the signifier and the signifier must not be conceived of as 'the first stage of meaning', its material vestibule, but, in complete opposition to this, as its deferred action.[27]

Barthes stresses that the 'text' plays with and at the level of the signifier, and that reading consists in participating in this play, keeping the game going. This involves an understanding of reading which is quite different from traditional models. 'Our goal', he says elsewhere, 'is not to find *the* meaning, nor even *a* meaning of the text. . . . Our goal is ultimately to conceive, to imagine, to experience the plurality of the text, the open-endedness of its *signifying process*'.[28]

One of the undoubted benefits of such post-structuralist assumptions is that they encourage us to dwell with the playfulness, subtlety and contradictions of the language of texts, and to resist the desire to arrest or overlook these effects in an impatient and aggressive desire to 'penetrate' to the meaning. As Barthes puts it, 'the space of writing is to be ranged over, not pierced'.[29] This seems particularly apt for our reading of 'Winter: My Secret', which has suggested that to 'penetrate' its 'secret' would be a violation of the poem akin to the suitor's desire to violate the speaker.

Exercises

1 Read the following poem several times.

An Irish Airman Foresees His Death
I know that I shall meet my fate
Somewhere among the clouds above;
Those that I fight I do not hate,
Those that I guard I do not love;
My country is Kiltartan Cross,   5
My countrymen Kiltartan's poor,
No likely end could bring them loss
Or leave them happier than before.

---

[27] 'From Work to Text', in Roland Barthes, *Image–Music–Text* (London: Fontana, 1977), p. 158.

[28] 'Textual Analysis of a Tale by Edgar Allan Poe', in Barthes, *The Semiotic Challenge*, trans. R. Howard (Oxford: Blackwell, 1988), p. 262.

[29] 'The Death of the Author', in Barthes, *Image–Music–Text*, trans. Stephen Heath p. 147.

> Nor law, nor duty bade me fight,
> Nor public men, nor cheering crowds,   10
> A lonely impulse of delight
> Drove to this tumult in the clouds;
> I balanced all, brought all to mind,
> The years to come seemed waste of breath,
> A waste of breath the years behind   15
> In balance with this life, this death.
>
> (W.B. Yeats, 1919)

The 'Irish airman' in this poem is usually taken to refer to Major Robert Gregory, the son of Yeats's friend and patron Lady Augusta Gregory, who was killed in action in the First World War in Italy in January 1918. Although Ireland had been promised limited Home Rule in 1914, it was still part of the United Kingdom of Great Britain and Ireland during the First World War, and over 100 000 Irishmen volunteered to fight in the British forces. The excessive repression of the 1916 Easter Rising, however, led to a resurgence of nationalist feeling which resulted in the formation of a provisional Irish Government in 1919. Kiltartan Cross is a village near the Gregory estate in County Galway in western Ireland.

(a) What is the airman's attitude towards what he is doing? Why is he doing what he is doing? What is his state of mind? How does the historical information just given help you to answer these questions?

(b) Go though the poem looking for parallelism of meaning (similarity with difference) between phrases (both within lines and between different lines). It may help to mark them with a pencil or highlighter. For each set of parallel phrases, try to say (i) what is similar between them; and (ii) what is different. When you have done this, try reading through the poem again. Has your understanding of or feeling for the poem changed in any way?

(c) Try to work out the poem's metrical form by using the methods described in Chapter 2. Read through the poem again and try to say how the metrical form relates to the airman's state of mind. Are there any lines in the poem which deviate from the regular metrical pattern? If so, how does each deviation relate to the line's meaning?

(d) Go through the poem marking all the devices of sound which you can find (rhyme, rhyme scheme, alliteration, and so on). Now try to decide whether these formal devices are arranged in parallel patterns. Use a pencil or highlighter in order to make those parallel patterns more explicit or visible.

(e) Is there any interrelation between the parallel patterns of sound you have discovered and the parallels between phrases? If so, what is this interrelation?

(f) From what you have discovered in this process, do you think there is any relationship between the poem's use of parallelism and the airman's state of mind? Do the last four lines help you to answer this question?

(g) What relationship might there be between the formal structure of this poem and the historical information given above?

2 Read the following poem several times.

One Art

The art of losing isn't hard to master;
so many things seem filled with the intent
to be lost that their loss is no disaster.

Lose something every day. Accept the fluster
of lost door keys, the hour badly spent.
The art of losing isn't hard to master.

Then practice losing farther, losing faster:
places, and names, and where it was you meant
to travel. None of these will bring disaster.

I lost my mother's watch. And look! my last, or
next-to-last, of three loved houses went.
The art of losing isn't hard to master.

I lost two cities, lovely ones. And, vaster,
some realms I owned, two rivers, a continent.
I miss them, but it wasn't a disaster.

– Even losing you (the joking voice, a gesture
I love) I shan't have lied. It's evident
the art of losing's not too hard to master
though it may look like (*Write* it!) like disaster.

(Elizabeth Bishop, 1976)

(a) This poem is about losing things and it uses a lot of repetition and parallelism. Go through the poem highlighting, or otherwise noting, as many of the repetitions and parallelisms as you can find. Then make a list of all the things the speaker says she has learned how to lose. How do the repetitions relate to the list of lost things you have noted? Are all the losses equivalent?

(b) What is her attitude towards these losses and what she calls 'The art of losing'? Does it involve a **paradox**? (Look up this word in our Glossary if you don't understand it.) Try to explain the poem's title.

(c) Analyse the metre and rhyme scheme (identify any half-rhymes). Do you think there is any semantic equivalence between the rhyme words of the kind we discussed earlier in this chapter? You might also want to note the effect of any enjambments or end-stopping.

(d) Look up '**Stanza forms**' in the Glossary at the end of this book. Can you identify the stanza form Bishop is using here? Try to summarise what advantages the use of this particular stanza form has for what the poem is trying to say (or do) in the light of your answers to questions (a) and (b).

(e) Finally, check our Glossary entry for the particular stanza form you have now identified and check our index for any other examples of this form that are quoted or discussed elsewhere in *Reading Poetry*. Compare Bishop's use of this stanza form with the way other poets use it (you could do a library- or a web-search for other examples of this poetic form). In the light of your analysis and comparisons, how far does the use of a traditional 'fixed form' restrict what a poet is able to say in a poem? What advantages might the use of such a 'fixed form' have?

3 Return to the exercise on Eleanor Brown's 'The Lads' at the end of Chapter 2. In the light of what you have learned in Chapters 3 and 4, try again to answer the question there about the relationship between the poem's use of form (metre, lineation, rhyme, and so on) and its meanings or the speaker's attitude towards the lads and/or their poetry. Has your answer to this question changed or developed?

4 Try to find any effective and interesting poem which seems to use none of the techniques we have discussed in this and the previous chapter. If your poem manages to meet both criteria – that it be interesting and effective without setting up any significant relationships between form and content – what do you conclude from this? What is it that makes the poem poetic?

Part Two

TEXTUAL STRATEGIES

Chapter 5

Figurative Language

We have argued in the first four chapters of this book that the only substantial difference between poetry and other uses of language is the fact that the rhythms of poetry are organised into lines. We have seen that this is not a trivial difference but one which provides the framework for a range of other devices of sound and syntax that together constitute a 'creative form' which is specific to poetry (and perhaps song). Yet, in the course of our historical examination of poetry's attempts to overcome the arbitrary nature of language, we discovered that some theories of poetry in some historical contexts relegate poetic form as something merely 'superadded' to poetry, and argue instead that poetry can be characterised as a special use of figurative language. For Coleridge, poetry employs a special kind of figure – the poetic symbol. Shelley claims, as we shall see below, that the language of poets 'is vitally metaphorical'.[1] And Hopkins's account of the defining principle of poetry – parallelism – includes the parallelisms of figurative language as well as of sound: 'To the [other] kind of parallelism belong metaphor, simile, parable, and so on'.[2] In a pioneering work of twentieth-century literary theory, René Wellek and Austen Warren echo Max Eastman's claim that 'The two main organizing principles of poetry . . . are metre and metaphor'. They argue that poetry is distinguished from 'scientific' discourse by being a kind of 'thinking by means of metaphors'. The goal or purpose of poetic metaphor, they argue, is deeply related to 'the whole function of imaginative literature'.[3] Yet because figurative language is to

---

[1] 'A Defence of Poetry' (1821), in Shelley, *Poetry and Prose*, p. 482.

[2] Hopkins, *Journals and Papers*, quoted by Jakobson, *Language in Literature*, pp. 82–3.

[3] René Wellek and Austin Warren, *Theory of Literature* (Harmondsworth: Penguin, 1949, repr. 1985), pp. 186, 193, 197.

be found in all kinds of language use, we need to ask whether or not poetry really does use figurative language in distinctive ways. In order to do this, we will explore what figurative language is and how it works in various kinds of discourse.

◼ Figurative Language: the Acid Test

'Figurative language' is a general term for a group of linguistic devices called 'figures of speech'. A figure of speech is a word or phrase which is not meant to be taken literally in the context in which it is being used. If, after the break-up of a relationship, someone announces that 'there are many more fish in the sea', no one is likely to take it as a comment about fish stocks in the Atlantic. As this example indicates, figures of speech occur in all kinds of language uses and situations. We are quite good at knowing when to interpret something figuratively, but it is worthwhile trying to make it clear how we do this. We know that a word, phrase or statement is figurative *when it cannot be taken literally in the context in which it is being used*. Some figurative words or phrases cannot be literally true in any circumstance. When we hear the commonplace phrase 'love is blind', we do not stop and wonder how love could have eyes and how it could have been blinded. The statement cannot be literally true, and we automatically understand it in a figurative sense. Other figurative phrases can be literally true in some contexts, but we realise that they must be understood figuratively in the context in which they are used. It may or may not be true that there are many more fish in the sea, but that is not much consolation to the person suffering from the break-up of a relationship. The phrase 'look before you leap' could be used literally in a specific situation, but in most contexts (where no actual leaping is involved) we automatically interpret it figuratively.

In everyday language uses, we are generally quite good at deciding whether something is to be understood literally or figuratively. But when it comes to reading poetry, many readers seem to put this skill to one side. Students often assume that exercises in interpretation require them to find some hidden meaning in a poem, and the easiest way to do this, often enough, is to read the poem metaphorically ('Although Keats's poem appears to be about a nightingale, it is *really* about the Industrial Revolution'). Such interpretation can seem very clever, but it is ultimately futile: the only effective way to read is to read accurately, and the acid test for metaphor is always: 'Can this word or phrase have its ordinary, literal meaning here?' If so, then the literal interpretation is, at least, accurate. Only when the word or phrase cannot have its literal meaning in the context can we be sure we have a metaphor.

There are many different kinds of figures of speech, some of which we encounter quite frequently in everyday life. These are distinguished from each other on the basis of how they work, and they are given names derived from studies of rhetoric in classical Greece. Many of these terms, such as metaphor or irony, may already be familiar to you. From the large catalogue of different kinds of figures identified and bequeathed to us by classical rhetoric, metaphor has come to dominate the discussion of poetry in the twentieth century. This is why a good deal of our discussion will focus on metaphor, yet we will also be looking at some other important figures (simile, **metonymy**, **synecdoche**, symbol, allegory and apostrophe), only some of which you will have heard of (we will discuss irony in Chapter 8).

◼ Metonymy and Synecdoche

An important and influential distinction between kinds of figures is that between metaphor and metonymy. This distinction is based upon a difference in how these two figurative devices work. Metonymy means 'change of name': it is a figure of speech in which the name of one thing is used to name something which is associated with it – as in 'the pen is mightier than the sword'. This cannot literally be true – imagine trying defend yourself with a pen against an assailant with a sword. To understand the phrase we automatically associate 'pen' with published writing and 'sword' with war or violence in general. Metonymy thus works on the basis that things may be associated with each other in common experience (usually in place or time). Thus we can say 'the White House denied all rumours' without implying that the building itself spoke. This is because of the commonplace association between the US president and the building in which he or she lives. If we hear that someone looks 'down-at-heel' we understand the figure through the association between worn-out shoes and poverty. If we say we are going 'back-packing', our listener will automatically associate this reference to rucksacks with a certain kind of holiday.

A figure which is related to metonymy is 'synecdoche'. Synecdoche works mainly through two associative principles: 'part for the whole', and 'container for contained'. The call for 'all hands on deck' is readily understood as summoning all the sailors to work (and not just their hands!). If our host or a friend in a bar invites us to 'have another glass' we will expect a glass filled with the particular (usually alcoholic) drink which we have been drinking, not another empty glass.

Although – as these examples show – metonymy and synecdoche tend to be confined to familiar phrases and associations, it is possible to use these figures in more interesting ways – as in Antony's rallying call to the Roman citizens in Shakespeare's *Julius Caesar*:

> Friends, Romans, countrymen, lend me your ears. (III. ii)

In this phrase it is clear that Antony is trying to get the attention of his audience rather than seeking to borrow their ears. In the following comment, Thomas Traherne uses a familiar but interesting metonymy:

> You never enjoy the world aright, till the sea itself flows in your veins.

Clearly, this statement could not be literally true (we would die!). To understand it, we have to infer that 'the sea' metonymically stands for 'the experience of going to sea' (while 'flows in your veins' is a metaphor meaning something like 'becomes a part of you'). We can now see that Keats's call in 'Ode to a Nightingale' for a 'beaker full of the warm South' is a metonym, since he is making an imaginative association between wine and the vineyards of southern Europe. Metonymy, then, can be an important and effective device in poetry.

◼ Metaphor

Whereas metonymy works on the basis of association, metaphor works on the assumption that there are similarities between things. In the familiar proverb 'Make hay while the sun shines' we recognise that we are being advised to act while we have the opportunity, and we realise this through the similarity between our own situation and that of the farmer. Many clichéd phrases are examples of what are called 'dead metaphors' (because they have become so familiar that we hardly notice their metaphorical status). For example, we frequently use dead metaphors to describe the way we are feeling: we say that we are 'all cut up', 'head over heels', 'down in the dumps', 'under the weather', 'feeling low', 'getting high', 'over the moon', and so on.[4] None of these phrases (except in unusual circumstances) is likely to be literally true, yet we do not regard the person who utters such statements as a liar. Instead, we automatically understand them as metaphorical ways of indicating how the person is feeling. (This is not to say that metaphor is always a matter of feeling – as we shall see.)

Metaphors are used in all kinds of language. In everyday speech we tend to use metaphorical language frequently, though we are not always aware that we are doing so. Almost all discourses use their own characteristic metaphors – sports commentary, gardening books, weather forecasts, music journalism, literary criticism, and so on. Although science is often assumed to use language

---

[4] Many of these metaphors are based on a more fundamental set of metaphors which assume that height and depth have symbolic connotations. For a discussion of this, see 'Orientational Metaphors' in George Lakoff and M. Johnson, *Metaphors We Live By* (Chicago: University of Chicago Press, 1980), pp. 14–21.

in objective, rational and literal ways, it actually uses a range of (often dead) metaphors: we are told that an electrical 'current' 'flows', that opposite magnetic poles 'attract' each other, that genes can be 'selfish', that a star is 'born', that atomic particles can be 'excited' or have 'charm', that our bodies have a 'biological clock', and so on. This use of metaphor in science is quite revealing about metaphor in general. Such metaphors suggest that we can visualise abstract ideas only in terms of the concrete things we already know. In fact, it has been suggested that metaphor is necessary in scientific thought, not only as a means of explanation but as one of its instruments of enquiry.[5] In other words, metaphor might be a means of thought rather than simply a way of conveying preconceived ideas.

One of the interesting things about metaphors is that they tend to influence the way we understand something even when we do not recognise that a metaphor is being used. This affective power is one of the reasons why poets make precise uses of metaphor, but it is also why politicians, advertisers and journalists use metaphor frequently. In the 1991 Gulf War the military press conferences described the bombing raids on Iraqi installations as 'surgical strikes'. This metaphor suggests that the bombing raids were in some way similar to surgery. Its effect was to claim that the bombing was scientifically precise and professional, and so managed to destroy ('cut out') enemy soldiers and equipment (the 'diseased' parts) while leaving the population (the 'healthy body') unharmed. The metaphor played a part, therefore, in the attempt to reconcile the Western public to the 'Desert Storm' (another interesting metaphor in this respect). The fact that one airman metaphorically described air raids on retreating Iraqi soldiers as a 'turkey shoot' did not quite fit with these official metaphors about the war.

Metaphors, then, are found in all language uses. In fact, once we become alert to the presence of dead metaphors, we are likely to discover that far more of our language is metaphorical than we ever realised. Before we go on to examine the use of metaphor in poetry, we therefore need to explore the nature and effects of metaphor in general. From what we have seen thus far, we can suggest that there are two kinds of metaphor: metaphors which have become 'dead' through overfamiliarity, and metaphors which somehow retain their metaphorical 'vitality' through being relatively new or unusual. What we can call the 'metaphorical effect' occurs when a metaphor produces a new insight or pleasure by making us see an unexpected 'similarity in difference'. But unless the metaphor is particularly interesting, this metaphorical effect will gradually wear off until we fail to recognise that a metaphor is present at all. (In the previous sentence, 'wear off' is just such a dead metaphor.) Yet both

---

[5] See Thomas S. Kuhn, *The Structure of Scientific Revolutions* (Chicago: University of Chicago Press, 1970).

kinds of metaphor play significant roles in the way we think about and understand the world we live in. Every metaphor tells a story, whether we realise it or not.

The Analysis of Metaphor: Tenor, Vehicle, Ground

Metaphor generally works by claiming that there is a similarity between two disparate things or ideas. This makes the technical analysis of metaphor a relatively easy process. Once we have identified that a metaphor is being used, we need to ask what kind of relationship there might be between the metaphor and what is actually being said. Let us take a once familiar metaphorical proverb: 'An Englishman's home is his castle'. This metaphor's 'story' is spelled out by James Boswell in his *Life of Johnson* (1791): 'In London . . . a man's house is truly his *castle*, in which he can be in perfect safety from intrusion.' It is possible to analyse this metaphor into two different terms: *what* is being talked about ('an Englishman's home') and the metaphorical *way* it is talked about ('a castle'). This distinction is the basis of an influential method of analysing metaphor developed by I.A. Richards.[6] As a kind of shorthand, he used the term '**tenor**' for what is being talked about and '**vehicle**' for the metaphorical way it is talked about. There must also be some relationship between tenor and vehicle, otherwise the metaphor would make no sense. Richards called this relationship the '**ground**' of the metaphor. This term can be better understood if we realise that it is itself a metaphor which reminds us that there needs to be some 'common ground' between the tenor and the vehicle. As we have already suggested, the ground of a metaphor will always be some kind of similarity. (In a metonymy, of course, the ground will be some kind of association.)

In the metaphor we are looking at, Richards's analysis would be as follows:

tenor (literal term) = 'an Englishman's home'
vehicle (metaphorical term) = 'his castle'
ground = the similarities between tenor and vehicle (in both, the Englishman is supposed to be in 'perfect safety from intrusion' and to be 'lord and master').

This analysis indicates that the most important thing in analysing any metaphor is to work out the ground. To understand the ground is to understand the figure.

---

[6] See I.A. Richards, *The Philosophy of Rhetoric* (New York: Oxford University Press, 1965; 1st ed 1936), pp. 96–7, 117.

▣ Simile

Since the ground of metaphor is similarity, it is closely related to simile. A famous poetic simile begins Robert Burns's song 'A Red, Red Rose' (1796):

> O my luve's like a red, red rose,
> That's newly sprung in June.

We can analyse this as follows:

tenor (literal term) = my luve
vehicle (metaphorical term) = a red, red rose . . .
ground (similarity) = ?

In this simile there is an interesting ambiguity about the tenor. Does 'my luve' refer to 'my emotional feeling' or 'the woman I love'? Since both meanings of 'luve' are used in the rest of the song, we should perhaps understand the word in both senses in the opening line. In order to work out the ground, we could make a list of all the features of the vehicle (a red, red rose) and decide which are relevant and which are not:

red, nice smell, petals and thorns, tall and thin
with a big head, beautiful, prickly to touch, fresh,
budding, short-lived, precious, delicate . . .

The aspects in this list which may be appropriately transferred to the tenor include nice smell, beautiful, fresh, budding ('newly sprung') and short-lived. (He could also be saying that the woman he loves is tall and thin with a big head, but we doubt it.) Whether all these are relevant in this particular simile would depend on how you understand 'luve' (woman or feeling?) and whether or not you think Burns wants to tell this woman that either she or his love for her is short-lived (such an interpretation is not borne out by the rest of the poem).

This analysis may seem somewhat artificial in that you probably feel you understood Burns's simile without it (one of the reasons for this instant understanding is that the comparison of love or a woman with a rose is a highly conventional device which has a long history). We certainly do not envisage you analysing each metaphor or simile in such a painstaking way, but what the analysis does offer is a slow-motion action replay of the cognitive process which happens in your mind when you read the simile. This is helpful because it reveals that we work out the ground of a simile or metaphor by rapidly sorting out which aspects of the vehicle are relevant and which are not. Only some aspects will be relevant, because there are always differences as well as similarities between the vehicle and tenor of a metaphor or simile.

■ Explicit and Implicit Metaphors

Although all metaphors are based on similarity, there are different kinds of metaphor and it will be a great help if we spend some time examining these different kinds. An important structural difference is between *explicit* and *implicit* metaphors. We have seen that metaphor is a two-part structure in which one thing is likened to another. Yet if we compare two of our examples, we will see a fundamental difference in the way they work:

> An Englishman's home is his castle.

> We made two surgical strikes this afternoon.

In the first of these we are given both sides of the equation: we are told that 'an Englishman's home' (the tenor) is in some way equivalent to 'a castle' (the vehicle). We call this an *explicit* metaphor because both halves of the metaphor are present in the text, and it is clear what is being compared with what: one thing is said to *be* another thing. Such metaphors are not entirely explicit, of course, since they still require us to infer the ground (the similarity between tenor and vehicle).

In the second example, however, we are given only one side of the equation – 'surgical strikes' – and we are expected to infer the other ('accurate bombing raids'). The figurative half of the equation is left to work on its own, there is no connecting form of the verb 'to be', and what is actually being referred to is left implicit (our interpretation of the phrase is thus largely dependent on the context in which it is being used). In such a metaphor it seems as though the vehicle (the figurative term) has substituted for the tenor (what is actually being referred to) in the same way as an on-field player in a team game can be swapped with a substitute player from the bench. Because what is actually being referred to or said is left implicit, this second kind of metaphor is called an *implicit* metaphor. All the following phrases use implicit metaphors:

> 'We made two *surgical* strikes.'
> 'Time *flies*.'
> 'Her luck *ran out* in the end.'
> 'There are many more *fish* in the *sea*.'

These are all implicit metaphors, because we have to imagine what literal word or phrase has been substituted by each of them. Implicit metaphors, then, ask us to do more interpretative work than explicit metaphors because we have to complete the metaphorical equation for ourselves:

'luck is *running out*' = 'luck is . . . ?'

The usefulness of the distinction between explicit and implicit metaphors lies in the frequency with which poetry uses the latter kind of metaphor as a way of leaving its meanings implicit. An example would be the following line from W.H. Auden's sonnet 'Our Bias' (1940):

> The hour-glass whispers to the lion's roar.

The verb 'whispers' must be a metaphor because an 'hour-glass' cannot literally 'whisper'. To infer the tenor we have to read the phrase as a whole and ask what interaction there could be between an hour-glass and a lion's roar. The lion is 'king of the jungle' and announces this by its roar. An hour-glass measures an allotted amount of time by allowing sand to run from one glass bulb to another. The fact that the latter 'whispers' to the former suggests that it has a message for the lion – presumably that, however fiercely and loudly it roars, its life (and its 'reign') won't last for ever. The use of the metaphor 'whispers' also stresses how quietly the sand runs through the glass in comparison with the lion's roar, and this makes it all the more ironic that the lion cannot resist its message.

A revealing experiment would be to try to substitute a literal word or phrase in place of 'whispers' which would convey the same meanings. We believe that it would be impossible to do this. Try it! We predict that every word or phrase you come up with will be another metaphor! (And you might ask whether this new metaphor is as effective as 'whispers'.) In other words, it seems impossible to supply a single tenor (literal meaning) for this metaphorical vehicle. Similar problems arise with many implicit metaphors: try the same exercise with 'time flies' or 'luck is running out'. (By contrast, it seems relatively easy to translate 'fish' as potential lovers and 'the sea' as the social world.) If it is true that we cannot make an accurate non-figurative paraphrase for many implicit metaphors, then this may have radical consequences for our understanding of metaphor and of language in general. It might suggest that we do not construct metaphors by first thinking literally and then finding a suitable metaphor, but that we *think with metaphors*.

Metaphors, we have suggested, always need to be understood in terms of the context in which they appear. In the line we have quoted from Auden, the lion and its roar might be literal (the poem may be about lions), but it is doubtful that the poem is staging a literal encounter between a lion and an hour-glass. It is much more likely that we have to understand 'hour-glass' as a metonym for 'time' (on the basis of association). In the context of the poem as a whole, however, there are hints (but they are only hints) that the lion and its roar might be figurative too:

Our Bias

The hour-glass whispers to the lion's roar,
The clock-towers tell the gardens day and night,
How many errors Time has patience for,
How wrong they are in always being right.

Yet Time, however loud its chimes or deep,   5
However fast its falling torrent flows,
Has never put one lion off its leap
Nor shaken the assurance of a rose.

For they it seems care only for success:
While we choose words according to their sound   10
And judge a problem by its awkwardness;

And time with us was always popular.
When have we not preferred some going round
To going straight to where we are?

In the context of the whole poem, which seems to be some sort of meditative reflection on the different relationship 'they' and 'we' have to time and its messages, there are hints that the lion and the rose are implicitly figurative. The lion and the rose may stand for those living things (and those people?) which are not troubled by a sense of time, whose power and beauty have an unshakeable assurance and who 'care only for success'. In contrast, 'we' (who?) seem inhibited by time, language and problems, and are unable to emulate the lion or the rose. (Although we feel that the lion and rose here are figurative, we are not wholly convinced that they are metaphorical: later in the chapter we will suggest that they are more like symbols.)

■ Metaphors as Different Parts of Speech

The difficulty of analysing and understanding implicit metaphors can be eased somewhat by the fact that in any metaphor, tenor and vehicle will be the same part of speech. This is clear in explicit metaphors, where both vehicle and tenor are present:

An Englishman's *home* [noun] is his *castle* [noun];

Life [noun] is *an incurable disease* [adjective + noun = noun phrase].

In fact, *all* explicit metaphors are made up of nouns, pronouns or noun phrases. Their general formula is:

(pro)noun/noun phrase [tenor] = noun/noun phrase [vehicle].

But although all explicit metaphors are made up of nouns, not all noun metaphors are explicit. Sometimes nouns are used as implicit metaphors, and we have to infer the noun or noun phrase which is being referred to – as in 'there are many more fish [potential lovers] in the sea [social world]'. Nouns, then, can form both explicit and implicit metaphors.

All other parts of speech form implicit metaphors: if the metaphorical term or phrase you are trying to interpret is a verb, adjective or adverb, then the metaphor will be implicit and you will have to infer the tenor (which will be the same part of speech as the vehicle). In the verb metaphor 'luck is running out', the tenor is not 'luck' (don't let the verb 'is' fool you here), but a verb or verb phrase which could appropriately replace 'running out'. In the adverbial metaphor 'he thinks deeply', the tenor will be an adverb or adverbial phrase which could appropriately replace 'deeply'. And so on. The following metaphors are all implicit:

Pronouns/nouns: 'I am the *vine*, ye are the *branches*'

Verbs: 'time *flies*'; 'the hour-glass *whispers*'

Adjectives: 'a *golden* opportunity'; '*water-tight* logic'

Adverbs: 'he may talk *smoothly*, but he thinks *deeply*'

■ The Transfer of Connotations

Our analysis of Burns's simile indicates that figurative language works by exploiting the connotations of particular words and the things they refer to. A word's 'denotation' is its primary significance, reference or meaning, while its 'connotations' are the 'secondary or associated significances and feelings which it commonly suggests or implies' (see 'Connotations' in *Abrams*). The term metaphor derives from the Greek *metaphora*, which means 'to transfer': a metaphor works by transferring the connotations of one thing or idea to another. In a metaphor such as 'the onward *march* of liberty', some of the connotations of marching are transferred to the idea of liberty, making it seem like an irresistible army moving forward. If we were to talk of the '*blossoming* of liberty', however, we would be giving 'liberty' a significantly different set of connotations. The power metaphor has to persuade us to see a thing in a particular way derives from this transference of connotations. To call bombing raids 'surgical strikes' is to transfer the positive connotations of surgery (scientific accuracy, medical treatment, benevolence) to bombing. When Keats calls wine 'the warm South', the positive connotations of southern Europe (poetry, dance, 'sunburnt mirth', and so on) are transferred to the wine.

As a kind of case study, we would like to consider the range of connotations which 'fire' has in our culture and the host of metaphors it has led to. One of the primary definitions of 'fire' is 'a state of combustion', but while this denotation is rather uninspiring, the connotations of 'fire' are rich and varied, and have led to a number of different metaphorical usages:

excitement (to catch fire, set the world on fire)

danger (play with fire, go through fire and water, out of the frying pan into the fire)

religious punishment (fire and brimstone)

strong emotion (a fiery temper)

sexuality (to kindle desire, the flames of passion, a smouldering look)

the cosiness of home (keep the home fires burning)

life itself (fire of life)

The connotative richness of 'fire' is one of the reasons it is used so frequently in poetry and other 'poetic' discourses. Yet not all its connotations will always be appropriate to every usage: in analysing any metaphor you need to assess what connotations are being transferred in each particular case (as we saw in looking at Burns's simile). Try to decide what fire or burning connotes in each of the following passages:

It is better to marry than to burn.
        (I Corinthians)

Thou art a soul in bliss; but I am bound
Upon a wheel of fire, that mine own tears
Do scald like molten lead.
    (Lear to Cordelia, *King Lear* IV.vii. 7, 46–48)

Tyger! Tyger! burning bright
In the forests of the night,
What immortal hand or eye,
Could frame thy mortal symmetry?
        (Blake, 'The Tyger')

    Years steal
Fire from the mind as vigour from the limb.
        (Byron, *Childe Harold*, III)

Not till the fire is dying in the grate, Look we for any kinship with the stars.
        (George Meredith, *Modern Love*)

I confess to pride in this coming generation. You are working out your own salvation; you are more in love with life; you play with fire openly, where we did in secret, and few of you are burned!

(Franklin D. Roosevelt, 1926)

Some of these uses overlap with each other, but their meaning in context may be quite different. You might, for example, compare the passage from I Corinthians with that from Roosevelt.

■ The Cognitive Power of Metaphor

One of the most important powers of metaphor is that it enables us to talk about intangible or abstract things in concrete ways. This is presumably why we tend to use concrete metaphors when we are trying to describe intangible feelings, experiences or ideas. As you might expect, philosophical and religious discourses make frequent use of concrete metaphors in order to talk about intangible concepts:

> The mind is a kind of theatre, where several perceptions successively make their appearance; pass, re-pass, glide away, and mingle in an infinite variety of postures and situations . . . [but]. . . . The comparison of the theatre must not mislead us. They are the successive perceptions only, that constitute the mind; nor have we the most distant notion of the place, where these scenes are represented, or of the materials, of which it is compos'd.[7]

> Yea, though I walk through the valley of the shadow of death, I will fear no evil: for thou art with me; thy rod and thy staff they comfort me.
>
> (Psalm 23)

Although both these examples use concrete metaphors to talk about abstract things, the metaphors work quite differently. In the Psalm, the metaphors work emotively, offering what have become commonplace concrete metaphors for spiritual states or experiences. Hume is using a concrete metaphor for cognitive purposes – he is trying to give us a mental picture of something (our own mind) which we find it hard to think about. But he warns us not to be misled by his metaphor, since it is *only* a metaphor for something which we cannot otherwise imagine.

Concrete metaphors also play an important role in poetry, for the same reasons. This can be seen in Hopkins's 'Heaven-Haven' (1865–66), the title and subtitle of which provide the clue for interpreting its metaphors:

---

[7] David Hume, *A Treatise of Human Nature* (1739), ed. Ernst C. Mossner (London: Penguin, 1969), p. 301.

Heaven-Haven

A nun takes the veil

I have desired to go
   Where springs not fail,
To fields where flies no sharp and sided hail
   And a few lilies blow.

And I have asked to be   5
   Where no storms come,
Where the green swell is in the havens dumb,
   And out of the swing of the sea.

Hopkins's title combines both kinds of parallelism which he identified as characteristic of poetic art: the similarity of sound emphasises the fact that in this poem (as in much Christian thought) heaven is figured as a haven from the storms of life. In the second stanza in particular, the primary meaning of haven as a harbour giving shelter for ships is used to develop what is called an *extended metaphor*. Most of the metaphors we have looked at thus far have involved a single pairing of vehicle and tenor. In Hopkins's second stanza, however, the metaphor of heaven as a haven is extended through a series of related metaphors: the nun imagines herself as a ship (or passenger in a ship) which has been searching for a haven 'Where no *storms* come', where the '*green swell*' of the storm-tossed waves cannot be heard, and where the '*swing of the sea*' cannot be felt. Each of the metaphors develops or extends the notion that heaven is a place of refuge from the storms of the world which threaten the spiritual destruction of the individual soul.

■ Dead Metaphor and Poetic Metaphor

We have seen that metaphor is an extremely powerful and flexible device which features in all kinds of language use. The host of dead metaphors which make up a far larger proportion of our language than we generally realise tend to influence and shape the way we perceive the world and the everyday stories we tell about it. In fact, the extent to which language in general is metaphorical raises problems for the straightforward distinction between literal and figurative with which we began this chapter. The late-nineteenth-century German philosopher Friedrich Nietzsche suggested that virtually all language is metaphorical, and that the truths which we take to be self-evident are actually dead metaphors:

> What, then, is truth? A mobile army of metaphors, metonyms, and anthropomorphisms – in short, a sum of human relations, which have been enhanced, transposed, and embellished poetically and rhetorically, and which after long use seem firm,

canonical, and obligatory to a people: truths are illusions about which one has for-gotten that this is what they are; metaphors which are worn out and without sensu-ous power; coins which have lost their pictures and now matter only as metal, no longer as coins.[8]

Here Nietzsche is pointing out the ideological power which dead metaphors have over society and over our thoughts – they seem 'obligatory' truths to a people precisely because they are no longer recognised as metaphors. If this is the case, if the dead metaphors of our language do a great deal of our thinking for us without our knowing it, then it would seem urgent to become as alert as possible to the metaphorical undercurrents of our language, and to 'coin' new metaphors which tell alternative stories and resist the process of 'defacement' which Nietzsche's own metaphors describe. If the distinction between literal and figurative is problematic, that between dead and living metaphor is crucial.

Metaphor, then, may be radical or conservative – it may either reaffirm con-ventional ways of thinking (through dead metaphors, idiomatic phrases) or challenge such conventions by inviting us to look at something in a new way. The role poetry is assumed to play in this struggle is influentially described by Shelley in the passage we have already quoted from his *A Defence of Poetry* (1821). Shelley stresses the importance of original metaphor in poetry, anti-cipating the Russian Formalists' concept of defamiliarisation by claiming that 'Poetry lifts the veil from the hidden beauty of the world, and makes familiar objects be as if they were not familiar' (*Shelley's Poetry and Prose*, p. 487). One of the ways poetry does this is through a special use of metaphor. The lan-guage of poets, he claims,

> is vitally metaphorical; that is, it marks the before unapprehended relations of things and perpetuates their apprehension, until words, which represent them, become, through time signs for portions or classes of thought, instead of pictures of integral thoughts; and then, if no new poets should arise to create afresh the associations which have been thus disorganised, language will be dead to all the nobler purposes of human intercourse. (p. 482)

Shelley is claiming here that the 'vital' metaphors of poets alert us to relations between things which no one had ever recognised before, and he assumes that new metaphors produce new thoughts (or new connections between thoughts). In time, however, our sense of these relations gets lost (perhaps by degenerat-ing into dead metaphors) and new poets are needed to 'revitalise' the language through creating new poetic metaphors. For Shelley, then, poetic metaphor keeps the language 'alive'. He even suggests that the ability of poetic metaphor continually to generate new ways of thinking is crucial to social and political

---

[8] Friedrich Nietzsche, 'On Truth and Lies in an Extra-Moral Sense', in *The Portable Nietzsche*, ed. Walter Kaufmann (New York: Viking Penguin, 1954), pp. 42–47.

renovation, and even revolution. This allows him to claim that 'All the authors of revolutions in opinion are . . . necessarily poets' (p. 485) and hence that 'Poets are the unacknowledged legislators of the World' (p. 508). Shelley's account of the role of poets and the nature of poetic metaphor involves characteristically Romantic assumptions, and we shall see in Chapter 6 that these assumptions have not been shared throughout history. Since the Romantic period, however, most poets and critics have assumed that poetry should be original and innovative (though Shelley's sense of the political potential of poetic metaphor has usually been overlooked).

■ Metaphor in Poetry

Many twentieth-century critics and theorists recognise that metaphor permeates all language; but they try nonetheless to distinguish the poetic from the 'everyday' metaphor in ways which more or less reiterate Shelley. While non-literary metaphors are held to be dead and ineffective, 'the literary metaphor *par excellence*' is regarded as 'an image freshly created in the imagination of the poet'.[9] Our own discussion has sought to show that it is problematic to differentiate between the language of poetry and that of other discourses on the basis that the former is metaphorical while the latter is not, or by saying that the one uses 'fresh' metaphors while the other uses dead metaphors. Dead metaphors often appear in poetry, and fresh metaphors may be coined by military press officers as well as by poets.

Yet poetic metaphor does seem qualitatively different from metaphor outside poetry. Winifred Nowottny distinguishes between metaphors which are boring or ham-fisted and those which, in Ezra Pound's words, give a 'sense of sudden liberation'.[10] Some metaphors are more powerful or suggestive or provocative than others; although such metaphors are not necessarily confined to poetry, they play an important role in poetry. The difference between metaphors inside and outside poetry lies in the way they are used and the way readers respond to them according to different sets of expectations. Outside literature, metaphors are usually regarded merely as vehicles for meaning. In reading literature, however, and especially poetry, readers tend to pay more attention to the metaphors on the assumption that they are of interest in their own right. Literary texts often use difficult or complex metaphors which force us to attend to them in this way. Such metaphors differ from 'dead' metaphors in several ways: their unexpectedness 'announces' the fact that they are

---

[9] Leech, *Linguistic Guide to English Poetry*, p. 196.

[10] Winifred Nowottny, *The Language Poets Use* (London: The Athlone Press, 1962), p. 57. Nowottny's two chapters on metaphor in poetry (pp. 49–71 and 72–98) are extremely useful.

metaphors; they require an effort of analysis and imagination to be understood; they stimulate new ideas or ways of thinking about something; they produce an emotive effect – whether it be provocative, disturbing, thrilling, or whatever.

Yet even if individual poetic metaphors are qualitatively different from non-poetic metaphors, they nevertheless gain their power by drawing on the store of figures and connotations in 'everyday' language. Often, a poetic metaphor does not merely involve a one-to-one link between vehicle and tenor but makes available to the poet a range of interlocking terms which can, for example, be used in an extended metaphor (as in Hopkins's 'Heaven-Haven'). As Nowottny puts it,

> The merit of a particular metaphor from the poet's point of view may not simply be that there are 'links' between [for example] love and a journey in a boat, but also that there is a much larger range of specialized terminology connected with boats and the sea than there is with love. (p. 67)

(Nowottny's point here sheds further light on the way the metaphors work in Browning's 'Meeting at Night'.) An individual metaphor in a poem, then, may work as part of a network of figures drawn from a particular area of experience and forming a web of interconnections within the poem. One way this might happen is when a poem reanimates a dead metaphor by combining it with an unusual metaphor drawn from the same source. Nowottny's example is from Shakespeare's Sonnet 30:

> When to the sessions of sweet silent thought
> I summon up remembrance of things past.

There is a kind of interanimation between these metaphors: the commonplace metaphor of 'summoning up' memories is reactivated by having this take place in the 'sessions' of thought – which suggests that meditation can be thought of as a court of law able to summon up memories as witnesses of things past. This is just one small example of a general trend in the way poetic metaphor is organised in poetry. Nowottny argues that poetic metaphors need to be understood in terms of the way they participate within poetic structure as a whole:

> in my own opinion the chief difference between language in poems and language outside poems is that the one is more highly structured than the other, and the more complex organisation set up in poems makes it possible for the poet both to redress and to exploit various characteristics of language at large. (p. 72)

The figures of a poem form a kind of 'network' or 'tissue' which allows multiple interactions between the figures as their connotations play off against one another, bringing 'into play an aura of their suggestions' (p. 84). Furthermore, poetry often foregrounds the process by which it makes and explores metaphors – as is clearly signalled in the first line of Shakespeare's Sonnet 18: 'Shall I compare thee to a summer's day?' In doing this, poetic metaphor resists attempts to treat it merely as a 'peephole' onto the real world, and allows us to experience language in the process of creating meaning (p. 87).[11]

▪ The Political Possibilities of Poetic Metaphor

Nowottny's claim that poetic metaphors draw on the store of figures in the language in general, but work differently in poetry by the way they interact with each other within a poem's overall structure, can be tested through an analysis of the role and effect of metaphors within a particular poem. The poem we have chosen to look at, Adrienne Rich's 'Song' (1973), has a fairly straightforward structure in which each stanza tries out an apparently straight-forward figure for the same basic thing – the nature of the poetic speaker's loneliness. Metaphors in poems often do several different things at the same time. They may simultaneously represent something in the world and reveal the state of mind of the speaker viewing the world. In addition, as we have suggested, they may work to confirm, revise or challenge the conventional ways in which we think, and hence resist or promote cultural, social or polit-ical change. Rich's 'Song' presents itself as a response to someone who has wondered if the speaker is lonely; rather than denying it, the speaker uses a series of figures which seek to define exactly what kind of loneliness she experi-ences. In doing this, the poem can be seen as resisting conventional (usually negative) images of what it means for a woman to live or act alone and as telling a new and enabling story about and for such women.

> **Song**
> You're wondering if I'm lonely:
> OK then, yes, I'm lonely
> as a plane rides lonely and level
> on its radio beam, aiming
> across the Rockies   5
> for the blue-strung aisles
> of an airfield on the ocean
>
> You want to ask, am I lonely?
> Well, of course, lonely
> as a woman driving across country   10

---

[11] For a more recent and theoretically sophisticated suggestion that poetic metaphor stages and performs the process by which language creates meaning, see Derek Attridge, 'Performing Metaphors: The Singularity of Literary Figuration', in *Paragraph*, 28, ii (July 2005), 18–34.

day after day, leaving behind
mile after mile
little towns she might have stopped
and lived and died in, lonely

If I'm lonely   15
it must be the loneliness
of waking first, of breathing
dawn's first cold breath on the city
of being the one awake
in a house wrapped in sleep   20

If I'm lonely
it's with the rowboat ice-fast on the shore
in the last red light of the year
that knows what it is, that knows it's neither
ice nor mud nor winter light   25
but wood, with a gift for burning

The poem is organised into four stanzas, each of which answers the interrogator's question by introducing and extending a different basic figure. Each figure offers a concrete vehicle (a plane, a woman driving, waking up, a rowboat) for the abstract tenor (loneliness). In the first section, the speaker says that she is

> lonely
> as a plane rides lonely and level
> on its radio beam, aiming
> across the Rockies

In order to understand this simile, we need to ask what connotations are transferred from this image of the flying plane to the woman's loneliness. Our list would include being on course, being purposeful, level, having a positive goal, crossing a huge barrier, heading for a slightly mystical destination, and a sense of release. Clearly, these connotations ask us to see this loneliness in very positive ways.

In the second section, the speaker responds by saying that she is

> lonely
> as a woman driving across country
> day after day, leaving behind
> mile after mile
> little towns she might have stopped
> and lived and died in, lonely

Again, we need to ask what the connotations are of this simile. The speaker says that she is lonely as a woman who is *driving*, crossing enormous distances, leaving behind all possibilities of a settled life in which she would experience a different kind of loneliness (the loneliness of a woman living and dying alone in a small town). The simile thus draws on the range of connotations from American books and films of being 'on the road'. This is a conventional image of freedom, but it is one used more often for men rather than women. The poem therefore anticipates the way the film *Thelma and Louise* (MGM, 1991) appropriates this conventionally masculine image of freedom in order to transform it into an available image for women.

The third stanza switches from these pioneering images to a seemingly cosy domestic interior. If she is lonely, then it is

> the loneliness
> of waking first, of breathing
> dawn's first cold breath on the city
> of being the one awake
> in a house wrapped in sleep

These lines could be read literally, but it is more interesting for our own argument if we read 'waking first' and 'being awake' as metaphors – that is, as suggesting that this woman is alone because she is more aware than the people she is closest to (she is *awake* in a metaphorical sense).

But the most interesting of the figures comes in the last stanza:

> If I'm lonely
> it's with the rowboat ice-fast on the shore

We can perhaps read 'with' here as suggesting that there is a certain similarity between the speaker's loneliness (abstract condition) and a particular rowboat in a particular situation. This is a complex figure which needs to be read very carefully. The rowboat is interesting in that it is a vehicle (in two senses) which would normally allow the speaker to leave her situation (like the plane, like the car). Yet we are told that the boat is 'ice-fast on the shore'. In other words, it is stuck, frozen, bound by ice. What are the connotations of this image of being frozen in place?

The rowboat is said to be 'in the last red light of the year', so we also have to add connotations of winter and the idea of one year coming to an end and another about to begin. We also need to think about the connotations of 'red' in this phrase, and to add them to the equation. In the lines that follow, the rowboat is itself personified – it has a very clear sense of its own identity as separate from everything which surrounds and restrains it. The rowboat

> knows it's neither
> ice nor mud nor winter light
> but wood

Thus we are invited to see a further similarity between the woman and the rowboat – she too, the poem implies, is very self-aware and sure of her identity (she knows what she is), even though she is apparently trapped.

But it is the last image – the final extension of the metaphor – which is the most intriguing, suggestive and ambiguous. To say that the rowboat knows that it is made of wood 'with a gift for burning' seems to imply a number of possibilities which derive from the multiple connotations of fire and burning:

1 It/she has a gift for giving out warmth;
2 It/she has a gift for sexual passion;
3 It/she has a gift for self-destruction;
4 It/she has a gift for freeing itself/herself from the ice (even though it would destroy itself in the process);
5 It/she has a destructive potential, which perhaps implies that such women have a revolutionary power.

The image also alludes to the idiomatic phrase 'to burn one's boats', which is a metaphor for leaving something behind and destroying any possibility of returning. Thus the last extended metaphor is much more complex and ambiguous than the relatively straightforward and confident similes and metaphors in the first three stanzas. Because of this, the last stanza becomes a powerful and open-ended conclusion to the poem.

■ Poetic Symbol

Metaphor is not the only kind of figure that has been said to be unique to, or definitive of, poetry. We have seen that Coleridge tried to argue that the characteristic figure of poetry is the symbol, and many poets and critics have followed suit. The Coleridgean symbol 'always partakes of the reality which it renders intelligible; and while it enunciates the whole, abides itself as a living part in that unity of which it is the representative'.[12] Such a symbol seems to escape from the arbitrary nature of language because it is supposed to be part of ('cosubstantial with') its spiritual or abstract meaning. Thus we could imagine that a flower – say a rose – could be used to symbolise the whole of nature: it would then both 'stand for' nature yet also be a 'part of' nature. Wellek and Warren, in general agreement with Coleridge, offer the example of religious

---

[12] From *The Statesman's Manual* (1816), in *The Oxford Authors: Samuel Taylor Coleridge*, pp. 660–61.

symbols which, they claim, 'are based on some intrinsic relation between "sign" and thing "signified", metonymic or metaphoric: the Cross, the Lamb, the Good Shepherd'.[13]

The term symbol derives from the Greek verb *symballein*, 'to put together'; a *symbolon* was a 'half-coin carried away as a pledge by each of the two parties to an agreement' (see 'symbol' in *Princeton*). The *symbolon*, then, was a concrete object which symbolised an abstract situation (an agreement). As a general definition of symbol, *Princeton* says that it is 'a kind of figurative language in which what is shown (normally referring to something material) means, by virtue of some sort of resemblance, suggestion or association, something more or something else (normally immaterial)' (*Symbol*). Wellek and Warren suggest that in literary theory the term symbol should be used to define 'an object which refers to another object but which demands attention also in its own right' (pp. 188–89).

Symbols derive their meaning from the conventions of the culture in which they appear. In Western countries, and elsewhere, certain kinds of cars are regarded as 'status symbols', and the car in general has come to symbolise individual freedom (regardless of whether it actually delivers it). If a car is used in this way in a film, advertisement or poem, it is (to combine the above definitions) an object which 'demands attention in its own right' but it also refers to 'something more or something else'. The connection between the object and the 'something else' can be of various kinds: Wellek and Warren say that it might be 'metonymic or metaphoric', while *Princeton* posits 'some sort of resemblance, suggestion, or association'. But although this indicates the close relationship between symbol and metaphor or metonymy, there is a crucial difference. The car in the film, advertisement or poem has to be regarded as a literal object in its own right as well as having additional associations and connotations.

Symbols, then, draw on what we could call the contemporary mythology of a culture, but they may also draw on historical and even prehistorical associations.[14] Thus, for example, a journey (especially one crossing water) can symbolise a transition in life. A white wedding veil in some cultures symbolises purity. The lily has a similar symbolic meaning for similar reasons (the 'few lilies' in Hopkins's 'Heaven-Haven' can be regarded as symbols of spiritual purity). Fruit in general (especially the apple) can symbolise temptation in

---

[13] Wellek and Warren, *Theory of Literature*, p. 188. For a further discussion of poetic symbolism, see Nowottny, *The Language Poets Use*, pp. 174–222.

[14] For an analysis of a range of modern myths or symbols, see Roland Barthes, *Mythologies*, trans. Annette Lavers (London: Granada, 1973). For a discussion of literary symbols and their mythical dimension, see Northrop Frye, *Anatomy of Criticism* (Princeton, NJ: Princeton University Press, 1957), pp. 71–128.

Christian and Jewish cultures. For Christians, the cross symbolises the complex set of ideas and meanings involved with Jesus's crucifixion. A set of scales can symbolise justice; the Statue of Liberty has an obvious symbolic value.

Poetry makes use of such public and conventional symbols, but it also uses symbols which are less easily translated into specific symbolic meaning. The rose has a long and varied history of figurative meanings in Western culture, and it has often been used as a symbol.[15] Yet consider Blake's use of it in 'The Sick Rose' (1794):

> O Rose, thou art sick.
> The invisible worm
> Which flies in the night
> In the howling storm:
>
> Has found out thy bed   5
> Of crimson joy,
> And his dark secret love
> Does thy life destroy.

Although the general cultural meanings associated with the rose will inevitably influence a reader's response to this poem, it is mainly the way the rose is used in the poem itself which makes it seem symbolic. It would seem wrong to treat the rose as an implicit metaphor, merely a vehicle for an unspecified tenor, because, on one level, this rose *is* a rose. Yet readers also tend to feel that Blake's rose is additionally referring to some undefined – perhaps undefinable – aspect of sexuality, morality or spirituality. We cannot turn to a dictionary of symbols to find the 'key' to such a poem. Although the poem makes the rose seem meaningful, any attempt to specify what the rose 'means' or 'stands for' is quickly frustrated by the poem itself. This indicates that such symbols 'suggest a direction or a broad area of significance' rather than any specific reference (see 'symbol' in *Abrams*).

Such symbols appear quite frequently in Romantic poetry because of their suggestive power. Blake in particular developed an extensive and complicated symbolic system. In France in the second half of the nineteenth century the poetry of the **Symbolist Movement** – which included Charles Baudelaire, Arthur Rimbaud, Paul Verlaine, Stéphane Mallarmé and Paul Valéry – systematically made things such as birds and flowers central to their poetry because of their suggestive symbolic resonance (or what Baudelaire called their 'evocative bewitchment'). English-language poets such as Yeats and Eliot were influenced by this movement, and included Symbolist elements in their own poetry.

---

[15] See Barbara Seward, *The Symbolic Rose* (New York: Columbia University Press, 1960).

Yeats, for example, redeployed the Symbolists' use of the swan in several of his own poems. There is, perhaps, an element of Symbolism in Auden's 'Our Bias'. The 'hour-glass' is, of course, a conventional metonymic symbol for time or for time's passing. It is thus the same kind of conventional, public symbol as the scales of justice, and we found it relatively easy to provide its symbolic meaning. But it is less easy to provide a meaning for the lion and the rose:

> Yet Time, however loud its chimes or deep,
> However fast its falling torrent flows,
> Has never put one lion off its leap
> Nor shaken the assurance of a rose. (5–8)

The lion and the rose may be working as implicit metaphors in the poem, but it is far from easy to supply tenors for them. Lions as well as roses are often used as conventional symbols (the Wars of the Roses, the British Lion), and it may be that they carry elements of these uses into the poem (or into our reading of the poem). But we would claim that the lion and rose in 'Our Bias' are more like Symbolist symbols, working suggestively to evoke symbolic meanings which draw on their symbolic connotations outside the poem but need to be understood primarily in terms of the way they work in the poem itself.

■ Poetic Allegory

An allegory is a fictional narrative, dialogue or scene which works on two parallel levels of meaning at one and the same time. The characters, speech, action and setting make coherent sense on a literal level, but there are usually strong signals in the text that we need to translate each detail of the surface story into another equally coherent story. Usually, those signals also provide a kind of implicit code which prescribes the way we translate each detail into the parallel story. Abrams, *allegory* distinguishes two main types of allegory: (i) historical and political allegory, in which the surface story needs to be read as a transposed version of political and historical events and characters; (ii) the allegory of ideas, 'in which the literal characters represent abstract concepts and the plot exemplifies a doctrine or thesis'. The central device of the second type is **personification**, in which abstract ideas or entities are personified as characters. Sometimes this is quite explicit, as in Bunyan's *The Pilgrim's Progress* (1678–84), in which the central character, who is called Christian, flees the City of Destruction and goes on a journey in quest of the Celestial City. *En route*, he meets with allegorical characters (including Mr Worldly-Wiseman, Hypocrisy, Help and Faithful) and passes through an allegorical landscape (which includes places such as the Slough of Despond and the Valley of the Shadow of Death).

Spenser's *The Faerie Queene* (1590–96) is a long allegorical poem in which the surface story of chivalric adventure is both engaging in itself and yet also requires to be read as a fusion of moral, religious, historical and political allegory. In the thirteenth-century *Romance of the Rose*, a long medieval dream vision, the rose is neither a metaphor nor a symbol but an explicitly allegorical **emblem** of a woman and her love which features in a sustained allegorical narrative about courtship. In one sense, then, allegory is closely related to symbol in that something physical (an object, character or action) stands for some other meaning (political, historical, religious, moral, and so on). Allegory sometimes makes use of conventional symbolism such as the quest journey. Yet allegory differs from the kind of poetic symbolism we have examined in that it tends to offer a code of interpretation which guides our translation of the surface details into a set of meanings which are limited and precise rather than suggestively imprecise.

Coleridge rejected allegory as a mechanistic process of composition which makes arbitrary connections between textual details and their allegorical meaning, and developed his notion of the symbol as a positive alternative.[16] Romanticism's rejection of allegory and elevation of the symbol in this way had a decisive effect on post-Romantic poetics (for example, in Symbolism). As a consequence, allegory was relegated as an inferior mode of composition (it is revealing that there is no reference to allegory in the index of Wellek and Warren's *Theory of Literature*).[17] Yet this 'official' account of the development of poetics ignores the fact that allegory was by no means consigned to the 'graveyard' of medieval, Renaissance and neoclassical poetry. In fact, Romantic poets and their successors continued to use allegory, in new ways, for their own ends. Shelley's *Prometheus Unbound* (1820) can be read as a sustained political allegory, and Keats uses allegory and allegorical personifications in his odes (such as 'To Autumn' and 'Ode on a Grecian Urn'). Christina Rossetti's 'Up-Hill' (1858) is a subtle example of spiritual allegory in the form of a dialogue between the speaker and an unspecified interlocutor:

> Does the road wind up-hill all the way?
>> Yes, to the very end.
> Will the day's journey take the whole long day?
>> From morn to night my friend.

[16] See Coleridge, 'Lay Sermons', in *The Oxford Authors: Samuel Taylor Coleridge*, pp. 660–62.

[17] Paul de Man sought to deconstruct the Romantic elevation of symbol over allegory by demonstrating that its organicist rhetoric makes misleading and mystificatory claims about poetic language. De Man also sought to reinstate allegory as a way of describing the self-reflexivity of the most 'self-knowing' literary texts. See Paul de Man, *Blindness and Insight: Essays in the rhetoric of contemporary criticism*, 2nd edn (London: Routledge, 1983), pp. 187–228 and Paul de Man, *Allegories of Reading: Figural language in Rousseau, Nietzsche, Rilke, and Proust* (New Haven, CT: Yale University Press, 1979), pp. 188–245.

But is there for the night a resting place?   5
   A roof for when the slow dark hours begin.
May not the darkness hide it from my face?
   You cannot miss that inn.

Shall I meet other wayfarers at night?
   Those who have gone before.   10
Then must I knock, or call when just in sight?
   They will not keep you standing at that door.

Shall I find comfort, travel-sore and weak?
   Of labour you shall find the sum.
Will there be beds for me and all who seek?   15
   Yea, beds for all who come.

On the surface this dialogue consists of the poetic speaker enquiring about a journey she is contemplating or on the point of making. As such, every detail makes realistic sense, and the whole coheres into what sounds like a quite ordinary exchange between a prospective traveller and someone who knows the way. Yet there are clues throughout the poem which guide us to read it as a religious allegory about the journey through life to death. These clues are perhaps partly reliant on the reader being familiar with similar allegories, such as *Pilgrim's Progress*, or with the general tendency of understanding life as a journey. Yet it is the text itself which guides us into understanding this particular journey as allegorical. Such clues include the following: the journey is up-hill all the way and takes the whole day (invoking notions of Christian fortitude); the journey begins in the morning and ends at night (thus invoking general cultural associations between times of day and periods of life); the end of the journey will bring an end to labour at 'a resting place' which cannot be missed and in which there are 'beds' (graves?) 'for all who come'.

Rossetti's poem can be said to be allegorical because the two meanings run neatly in parallel with each other, each detail of the surface meaning can be translated into its corresponding meaning, and the second meaning is not simply suggestive or open-ended, but extremely precise. Although journeys can be used metaphorically or symbolically, the fact that this poem limits the possible meanings of the journey to a one-to-one correspondence between real journey and implied journey allows us to describe it as allegorical. Yet it is the case that allegory has largely disappeared from modern poetry. As Billy Collins puts it in his poem 'The Death of Allegory' (1991), all those allegorical figures who used to 'parade about on the pages of the Renaissance' – such as Truth, Chastity and Villainy – 'are all retired now, consigned to a Florida for tropes' (3, 11).

▪ Poetic Apostrophe

An apostrophe is a rhetorical figure in which the poetic speaker addresses something non-human or abstract, or someone who is either absent or dead. We have already seen examples of this. In Chapter 1 we noted in passing that the whole of 'Ode to a Nightingale' is based on this figure: the poem's speaker addresses the nightingale not necessarily in expectation of a reply (that is not part of the convention!) but as if the nightingale could understand the speaker's words. Blake's 'Sick Rose' is an apostrophe to the rose – as the first line ('O Rose, thou art sick') announces.

Apostrophe is not entirely confined to poetry: we sometimes address pet animals or dead relatives; prayer can be thought of as a kind of apostrophe; we sometimes write diaries as if to absent or imaginary friends (Anne Frank's diary is a moving example) or even address the diary directly ('Dear Diary . . .'). One of the interesting things about these examples is the sense of privacy which surrounds them: we might well feel embarrassed if someone overhears us talking to the dog, praying to a god or cursing a bus which seems never to arrive.[18]

Apostrophe seems to hark back to magic ritual and to primitive ideas that the absent, the dead, the inanimate or the non-human can be contacted and their aid invoked. Yet the thing which is humanised retains a sense of mysterious otherness, as if it might have power over us (as the dead do in some religions). This is perhaps why, in prayer and in poetry, the apostrophised addressee is referred to in the respectful second person 'thou' rather than 'you': 'O Rose, *thou* art sick'; 'Away! Away! for I will fly to *thee*'. The effect is formal but impassioned – as the frequent use of the vocative 'O' or the exclamatory 'Oh' suggests. The combination of ritualistic formality and passionate exclamation is exemplified in Shelley's 'Ode to the West Wind' (1820): 'O wild West Wind, thou breath of Autumn's being'.

Apostrophe can appear in all kinds of poetry, and can be addressed to all kinds of physical things or abstract entities: Chaucer addresses a 'Complaint to His Purse'; in 'The Author to Her Book' Bradstreet addresses a book she had written; in 'Coda', Pound addresses his own poetry: 'O my songs'; in 'The Sun Rising', Donne addresses the sun; Whitman's 'Crossing Brooklyn Ferry' addresses the flood-tide, the clouds, the sun and the crowds, in quick succession. Interestingly, there is some correlation between kinds of apostrophe and genre. In some genres the poet calls on the help of the muse in what is called an **invocation** – Milton calls on the 'Heavenly Muse' at the beginning of *Paradise Lost*: 'I thence / Invoke thy aid to my adventurous song' (I, 12–13). Such an invocation was the conventional way of beginning epics. Odes, as we have seen, are frequently constituted as apostrophes to non-human or inanimate

---

[18] For a discussion of this last apostrophic situation, see Jonathan Culler, *The Pursuit of Signs: Semiotics, literature, deconstruction* (London: Routledge, 1981), pp. 141–2.

things: there are odes which apostrophise cats, birds, urns, winds, abstract concepts, and so on. Love poetry often apostrophises the absent beloved, and elegies may address the dead person as if he or she were still alive.

The apostrophic address to the dead person in elegies is particularly interesting, since it harks back to primitive feelings about the continuing existence of the dead, and even serves to maintain the illusion that they are still alive. The first forty lines of Ben Jonson's **elegy** 'To the Memory of my Beloved, the Author Mr William Shakespeare' (1623) apostrophise the recently dead playwright as if he were still living:

> Soul of the age!
> The applause! delight! the wonder of our stage!
> My Shakespeare, rise; I will not lodge thee by
> Chaucer or Spenser, or bid Beaumont lie
> A little further to make thee room:
> Thou art a monument without a tomb,
> And art alive still while thy book doth live,
> And we have wits to read and praise to give. (17–24)

The convention of apostrophising the dead can still be found in elegies, even though our culture is perhaps not so fortified by religious faith, or faith in the power of art to immortalise the artist, as was the Renaissance. The bulk of Theodore Roethke's 'Elegy for Jane: My Student Thrown by a Horse' (1953) recognises her death by referring to her in the past tense. In the last two sections, however, the sense of her absence is paradoxically recorded in an address which implicitly imagines her as present:

> My sparrow, you are not here,
> . . .
> If only I could nudge you from this sleep,
> My maimed darling, my skittery pigeon.
> Over this damp grave I speak the words of my love:
> I, with no rights in this matter,
> Neither father nor lover. (14–22)

There is a surprising dearth of critical discussion of apostrophe prior to the recent attention of deconstructive critics. This is surprising because, as Jonathan Culler points out, apostrophe is such a common feature of lyric poetry that it is almost possible 'to identify apostrophe with lyric itself' (*Pursuit of Signs*, p. 137). Culler suggests that traditional critics have found the device embarrassing, a hangover from the past which serves no function in modern poetry. For Culler, however, the figure is central to poetry because it foregrounds the fact that the poem is an event of language rather than a description or narrative of experience, and because it dramatises the speaker's aspiration to poethood. To hail the west wind or to call on the heavenly Muse is to announce oneself as a poet and to lay claims to the power of poetry to animate the inanimate, to humanise the inhuman. It exposes the pretensions of the speaker to be a 'visionary poet who can engage in dialogue with the universe' (p. 143). Culler maintains that apostrophe embarrasses critics because it makes it all too obvious that the visionary power of poetry depends on a figurative or rhetorical device which is so explicitly conventional.

Exercises

1 Read the following poem several times and then try to answer the questions which follow.

Crossing the Bar

Sunset and evening star,
   And one clear call for me!
And may there be no moaning of the bar,
   When I put out to sea,

But such a tide as moving seems asleep,   5
   Too full for sound and foam,
When that which drew from out the boundless deep
   Turns again home.

Twilight and evening bell,
   And after that the dark!   10
And may there be no sadness of farewell,
   When I embark;

For though from out our bourne of Time and Place
   The flood may bear me far,
I hope to see my Pilot face to face   15
   When I have crossed the bar.

                (Tennyson, 1889)

(a) What does it literally mean to cross a bar?

(b) Underline, highlight or circle all the words and phrases which seem obviously metaphorical to you.

(c) Having done this, try to say what the poem is about and how the metaphors contribute to the poem.

(d) Is there anything in the poem which suggests that the journey it describes might be an extended metaphor? What features seem to suggest this?

(e) If it is an extended metaphor, what is it a metaphor for? What evidence is there to support your reading?

(f) Go through the poem once again marking the words and phrases that you now consider to be metaphorical. What differences are there between your results now and the results you got for (b)?

(g) How would you respond to someone who said that the poem is (i) literally about a sea journey? or (ii) allegorical? or (iii) symbolic?

2 Read the following poem several times and then answer the questions that follow.

Spring

To what purpose, April, do you return again?
Beauty is not enough.
You can no longer quiet me with the redness
Of little leaves opening stickily.
I know what I know.   5
The sun is hot on my neck as I observe
The spikes of the crocus.
The smell of the earth is good.
It is apparent that there is no death.
But what does that signify?   10
Not only under ground are the brains of men
Eaten by maggots.
Life in itself
Is nothing,
An empty cup, a flight of uncarpeted stairs.   15
It is not enough that yearly, down this hill,
April
Comes like an idiot, babbling and strewing flowers.
(Edna St Vincent Millay, 1920)

(a) Try to identify as many examples as you can of (i) apostrophe, (ii) metaphor, (iii) simile, (iv) symbol. Give reasons why each instance you discover is figurative and why you decided to classify it in the way you did.

(b) Try to say whether each figure that you have found supports or undermines conventional ways of representing what is being figured.

(c) To what extent can the poem be understood as an attempt to replace a conventional set of figures with an unconventional and challenging set?

Chapter 6

Poetic Metaphor

In Chapter 5 we examined the nature of figurative language in general, exploring the relationship between figurative language inside and outside poetry and looking at how a number of different figures operate in poetry. In this chapter we want to trace the way shifting historical concepts of the nature of poetry and metaphor have influenced metaphor's role in poetry. Through detailed readings of the use of metaphor in particular poems from different historical periods, we hope to offer a preliminary map of the history of poetic metaphor. It should be said at the outset that we are not attempting to write a comprehensive history of poetic metaphor, nor to cover all the important contributions which recent theories have made to an understanding of metaphor in poetry. Such aims are, unfortunately, beyond the scope of a book of this kind.

■ Metaphor in the Renaissance

To a large extent, the Renaissance which transformed European culture in the period from the mid-fourteenth century to the end of the sixteenth century was triggered by the rediscovery of classical writers and texts of Greece and Rome. One of the most important disciplines of the Classical period was rhetoric, which was concerned with the production and analysis of figures of speech in the art of persuasion. Classical rhetoric provided the basis for understanding figurative language in European literature from that of the Classical Greeks down to modern times. The pioneering rhetorical theorist was Aristotle (384–322 BCE), whose *Rhetoric* analysed the techniques which orators used to persuade audiences, and whose *Art of Poetry* described the internal mechanisms of tragic drama and epic poetry (the *Art of Poetry* was rediscovered in 1500). Although Roman rhetoricians were influenced by Aristotle, they also significantly modified his rhetorical system.[1] Rhetorical treatises such as Cicero's *De Oratore* (55 BCE) and Quintilian's *On the Training of an Orator* (ACE 96) had a major impact on Renaissance literature, oratory and education. Rhetoric, along with grammar and logic, formed a central part of the classical education which boys of privileged backgrounds received at the humanist schools in Europe in the fifteenth and sixteenth centuries. Pupils were taught to think, write and speak in persuasive and imaginative ways through exercises in rhetorical technique. Rhetoric was distinguished into invention, disposition (style) and eloquence (delivery). Invention was concerned with the content of a speech, style with presenting that content in effective language, and delivery with the performance of the speech. Rhetoric and poetry used the same techniques of composition, often for the same ends – that is, to persuade.

Writers on rhetoric and poetics in the Classical and Renaissance periods treated figurative language as a crucial element of style or disposition. Figurative language was held to have a number of different functions and effects: it served as ornamentation; it lent vividness to the material; it had the power to dignify and lend brilliance to style and to make it more varied and novel; it helped to clarify one's argument or subject matter and lend it force; and (occasionally) it was used or held to express feeling. Since metaphor was thought to be a deviation from proper meaning – 'the artistic alteration of a word or phrase from its proper meaning to another' (Quintilian) – and to intrude into one's discourse like an unannounced guest (Cicero), the rhetoricians stressed that care needs to be taken to make metaphor appropriate to what is being said (as appropriate clothes may enhance the beauty and dignity of the body), and warned writers to avoid metaphors that are far-fetched, obscure, incongruous or disproportionate to the thing to which they are applied.

An important aspect of the rhetorical training of the humanist schools in the Renaissance was the absorption of large numbers of received conventions or commonplaces of description (such as traditional similes) called *topoi*. All Renaissance students were taught, as part of their basic training, to amplify, vary and enrich these *topoi* or received ideas in novel and copious ways. Shakespeare's Sonnet 73 (1609) can be seen as a virtuoso example of this Renaissance rhetorical training exercise in which the poem's speaker attempts to persuade the addressee to regard him in a certain way.[2]

---

[1] See H.C. Lawson Tancred's introduction to Aristotle, *The Art of Rhetoric* (Harmondsworth: Penguin, 1991), pp. 53–8.

[2] This sonnet, for obvious reasons, has been frequently discussed by critics. See for example Nowottny, *The Language Poets Use*, pp. 76–86, and Buchbinder, *Contemporary Literary Theory and the Reading of Poetry*, pp. 26–32.

That time of year thou mayst in me behold
When yellow leaves, or none, or few, do hang
Upon those boughs which shake against the cold,
Bare ruined choirs, where late the sweet birds sang.
In me thou see'st the twilight of such day   5
As after sunset fadeth in the west;
Which by and by black night doth take away,
Death's second self, that seals up all in rest.
In me thou see'st the glowing of such fire,
That on the ashes of his youth doth lie,   10
As the deathbed whereon it must expire,
Consumed with that which it was nourished by.
    This thou perceiv'st, which makes thy love more strong,
    To love that well which thou must leave ere long.

This sonnet is typical of the genre at this period in so far as it is an address to a beloved (see Chapter 12). Less typical is the fact that the beloved in the majority of Shakespeare's sonnets is a young man. The purpose of the sonnet seems to be an attempt to influence the way the young man (the addressee) perceives the speaker, and to say something like 'your love for me is all the more "strong" because you continue to love me even though you see that I am old and will soon die'. The poem's main means of doing this is through its use of metaphor.

Shakespeare developed his own version of the sonnet by dividing its fourteen lines into three groups of four lines (called quatrains) followed by a concluding couplet. Each of these quatrains contains a different, extended metaphor for the speaker's age or condition: (i) as *late autumn*, (ii) as *twilight*, (iii) as a *dying fire*. All three metaphors are commonplace ways, or received *topoi*, of representing old age, yet the interesting thing about the poem is that it revitalises these 'old' or 'tired' metaphors by extending them, and making them precise and specific rather than vaguely general. One of the paradoxes of the poem, then, is that it employs these dead metaphors for approaching death in ways which make them seem new and refreshingly alive. It is also worth noting that these are all implicit metaphors: the tenor which is common to all the poem's metaphors – which we take to be 'old age' – is never actually given in the poem. Instead we are presented with a series of concrete metaphors which not only attempt clearly to define the speaker's age but also seem calculated to have an effect on the listener or addressee.

Let us begin with the first quatrain:

That *time of year* thou mayst in me behold
When yellow leaves, or none, or few, do hang

> Upon those boughs which *shake against the cold*,
> *Bare ruined choirs*, where late the sweet birds sang. (1–4)

Any direct statement of the *topos* 'autumn of life' is avoided here through the way the lines develop an extended, concrete metaphor for autumn. The vague metaphor of 'time of year' is made precise and vivid by the image of the trees in the process of shedding their last remaining leaves. This is made still more vivid by introducing two subsidiary metaphors within the primary metaphor: first, the boughs of the trees are said to 'shake against the cold' (only animals or humans shake *against* the cold); secondly, the boughs are then said to be 'bare ruined choirs, where late the sweet birds sang'. It is probably clear that the boughs of trees cannot be similar in any way to a 'company of singers, birds, angels, etc.' (one of the dictionary's definitions of choir). The fact that 'sweet birds' have recently (lately) sung here indicates that the boughs are being compared with a choir in the sense of a 'chancel of cathedral, minster, or large church' (a chancel is an enclosed part of a church where the choir sits). The fact that these boughs are *'bare ruined* choirs' which have been abandoned by the birds adds to the dark and desolate image of autumn which these lines conjure up.

In the second quatrain, the speaker explores a different metaphor for his age, one which shifts from the larger scale of the seasons to the more immediate image of fading day. As Nowottny points out, this second stanza 'increases the degree of figuration superimposed upon the basic metaphor' (p. 79):

> In me thou see'st the *twilight* of such day
> As after sunset fadeth in the west;
> Which by and by black night doth *take away*,
> *Death's second self*, that *seals up* all in *rest*. (5–8)

Again, the basic metaphor of 'I am in the twilight of my life' (another *topos*) is reanimated by the vivid particularity of the image. It is not any old twilight but the twilight of *'such* day', and we are told exactly what kind of day. We are reminded of the precise meaning of twilight – that brief moment between the end of sunset and the onset of night – and the addressee is invited to reflect on its implications for the speaker. Furthermore, this is the kind of twilight in which the coming of 'black night' seems like the coming of death. Again, this particularisation is achieved through employing secondary metaphors within the primary metaphor: 'black night' is said to be *'Death's second self'*, its alter ego, and so both night and death are personified through a humanising metaphor – black night is said to 'take away' the twilight and to 'seal up all in rest'. This last image is disturbingly ambiguous. Although it could simply mean that night brings on sleep (which is also like a 'second self' to death) and that everyone and everything is cosily and safely sealed up in rest, it also alludes to the fact that dead people are 'sealed up' in their coffins and that 'rest' is a common euphemistic metaphor for death.

The third stanza repeats the pattern of the first two, but shifts attention to an even more immediate image and adds still more supplementary figuration to produce what Nowottny calls an 'almost unanalysable intricacy' (*The Language Poets Use*, p. 79):

> In me thou see'st the *glowing* of such *fire*,
> That on the *ashes of his youth* doth lie,
> As the *deathbed* whereon it must *expire*,
> *Consumed* with that which it was *nourished* by. (9–12)

Once more, this stanza invokes a commonplace concretive metaphor or *topos* for old age – 'my fire is burning low'. Yet this is not the glowing of any old fire – this is 'the glowing of *such* fire'. We have already looked at the metaphorical possibilities of 'fire' in Chapter 5, and you might want to think about its connotations in this instance. Although this particular fire is 'glowing', secondary, humanising metaphors tell us that it is on its 'deathbed' and that this deathbed is made up of the 'ashes of his youth'. In its 'youth' the fire was 'nourished' with fresh fuel and burned bright, but the brightness of its burning 'consumed' the fuel and turned it into 'ashes'. These ashes now form a 'deathbed' which chokes or 'consumes' the fire itself, and will eventually cause it to 'expire'. In an interesting turnaround, then, the human (the speaker's age) is first made inanimate (as fire, ashes), then the inanimate image is humanised (youth, deathbed, expire, nourished). The speaker seems to be saying that the very brilliance of his youthful burning is now the cause of his fading (in a colloquial metaphor, he has 'burnt himself out').

In each of these metaphors, then, secondary or internal metaphors develop, extend, or qualify the primary metaphors. The purpose of these metaphors seems to be to make the poem's addressee perceive the speaker in a certain way. This is stressed in each quatrain ('thou mayst in me behold', 'In me thou see'st', 'In me thou see'st') and in the concluding couplet:

> This thou perceiv'st, which makes thy love more strong,
> To love that well which thou must leave ere long. (13–14)

The final couplet in a **Shakespearian sonnet** typically works as a 'punch line' which either clarifies or gives a new twist to the preceding twelve lines. If this is so, what exactly is the beloved supposed to understand by this couplet (and hence the whole poem)? Is it an attempt to praise the beloved for being faithful to an old man? Is it a bid to persuade or encourage the young man to continue loving well? Is it an elaborate plea for sympathy? Or, paradoxically, is the whole poem a virtuoso display of the speaker's capacity for producing vivid, vital metaphors out of dead metaphors for his own old age?

■ The Metaphysical Conceit: John Donne

Some of John Donne's poetry, published in 1633, must have been written almost contemporaneously with Shakespeare's, yet it is sufficiently different from Renaissance poetry for critics to claim that it inaugurates a new kind of poetry or period. In 1692, Dryden mocked Donne's love poetry for introducing 'metaphysics' (or philosophical speculations) in a way which 'perplexes the minds of the fair sex' for which they were supposedly written. What began as mockery became an accepted critical label for a small group of so-called 'metaphysical' poets writing in the seventeenth century (they include Donne, George Herbert and Andrew Marvell). **Metaphysical poetry** is characterised by a dramatic use of intellectual ingenuity, irony and paradox, and uses figurative language in explicitly argumentative and pseudo-logical ways. Such techniques can be found both in love poetry and in religious poetry, and are exhibited most clearly in what are known as 'metaphysical **conceits**'. The conceit is

> A complex and arresting metaphor . . . which stimulates understanding by combining objects and concepts in unconventional ways . . . the term denotes a rhetorical operation which is specifically intellectual rather than sensual in origin. Its marked artificiality appeals to the power of reason to perceive likenesses in naturally dissimilar and unrelated phenomena. ('Metaphysical Poetry' in *Princeton*).

The conceit in Metaphysical poetry yokes together, in Samuel Johnson's eighteenth-century condemnation, 'the most heterogeneous ideas'. In talking of love, the speaker of a Metaphysical poem might draw on the most incongruous of disciplines for comparisons – 'scholastic philosophy, Renaissance logic and rhetoric, the "new science" of the seventeenth century, and Reformation and Counter-reformation theology' ('Metaphysical Poetry' in *Princeton*). Even though the poet displays wit and ingenuity in demonstrating the 'logic' of such conceits, the fact that they involve such far-fetched metaphors indicates the way Metaphysical poetry breaks with some of the assumptions of Renaissance rhetoric. For Jeffrey Wainwright, the literary conceit is connected with the idea of being conceited: 'the working through of the metaphor is likely to display an ingenuity which some readers will find affected and self-admiring, as though the poet is keener to show off than to say something significant' (*Poetry: The Basics*, p. 158).

Some of the most famous examples of 'metaphysical' metaphors or conceits can be found in Donne's 'A Valediction: Forbidding Mourning' (1633). It will help you to know that 'valediction' means bidding farewell:

As virtuous men pass mildly away,
    And whisper to their souls to go,
Whilst some of their sad friends do say
    The breath goes now, and some say, No;

So let us melt, and make no noise,   5
    No tear-floods, nor sigh-tempests move,
'Twere profanation of our joys
    To tell the laity our love.

Moving of th'earth brings harms and fears,
    Men reckon what it did and meant;   10
But trepidation of the spheres,
    Though greater far, is innocent.

Dull sublunary lovers' love
    (Whose soul is sense) cannot admit
Absence, because it doth remove   15
    Those things which elemented it.

But we by'a love so much refined
    That our selves know not what it is,
Inter-assured of the mind,
    Care less, eyes, lips, and hands to miss.   20

Our two souls therefore, which are one,
    Though I must go, endure not yet
A breach, but an expansion,
    Like gold to airy thinness beat.

If they be two, they are two so   25
    As stiff twin compasses are two;
Thy soul, the fixed foot, makes no show
    To move, but doth, if th'other do.

And though it in the centre sit,
    Yet when the other far doth roam,   30
It leans and hearkens after it,
    And grows erect, as that comes home.

Such wilt thou be to me, who must
    Like th'other foot, obliquely run;
Thy firmness makes my circle just,   35
    And makes me end where I begun.

As in Shakespeare's Sonnet 73, the speaker is using metaphor here to persuade his beloved into accepting a certain point of view. It seems that the speaker is about to go on a journey, while the woman must wait at home for his return. The poem is set at the point of farewell (the valediction), and we 'overhear' the speaker 'forbidding' his beloved's 'mourning'. He does this by using figurative language in a persuasive argument. The poem starts with a simile (signalled by 'As' and 'So') which indicates what their parting ought to be like:

> *As* virtuous men pass mildly away,
>   And whisper to their souls to go,
> Whilst some of their sad friends do say
>   The breath goes now, and some say, No;
>
> *So* let us *melt*, and make no noise,
>   No *tear-floods*, nor *sigh-tempests* move,
> 'Twere *profanation* of our joys
>   To tell the *laity* our love. (1–8)

The simile suggests that their parting should be as quiet as the parting of soul from body at the death of 'virtuous men', whose virtue means that they welcome death and 'whisper to their souls to go'. This parting is so subtle that the 'sad friends' who watch at the deathbed are unable to say whether it has happened or not. The second half of the simile (signalled by 'So' at the beginning of the second stanza) introduces several metaphors in support of the simile. The speaker says 'let us *melt*' away, like the parting of body and soul described in the first stanza. Mocking the conventional hyperbolic metaphors used in such situations, he says: let us not have 'floods' of tears or sighs like 'tempests'. The second half of the stanza introduces a new metaphor in the service of the same argument. In saying that it would be '*profanation* of our joys / To tell the *laity* our love', Donne is implicitly saying that their love is sacred, and that it would be polluted if the 'laity' were to hear about it. (Donne quite frequently uses metaphorical equations between sacred and profane love – see, for example, 'The Canonisation' (1633).)

The speaker compliments the addressee by saying that their parting cannot threaten a love 'so much refined / That our selves know not what it is' (17–18). This is reiterated by the simile in stanza six, where the listener is challenged to imagine their unity-in-separation as 'Like gold to airy thinness beat' (24). The vehicle of this simile is drawn from the art of gilding – the decoration of ornaments or furniture with gold leaf made though hammering gold to a thin foil. The phrase 'airy thinness' asks us to imagine this foil as beaten out so thinly as to be virtually immaterial, and it is this strange idea which justifies the argumentative logic of the simile, since such a subtle immateriality would correspond to the spirituality he is claiming for their love. Like the earlier deathbed simile, this simile seems to be trying to articulate a kind of transitional moment or state which is so subtle that we can hardly imagine it or decide if it is physical or metaphysical, material or spiritual, sacred or profane. Donne's repeated exploration of such paradoxical states was one of the characteristics which provoked readers to call his poetry, and poetry like it, 'metaphysical'.

Something similar happens in the most famous and often-discussed conceit in the poem – the final extended simile in which the parted (yet still joined) lovers are compared to a pair of compasses:

> If [our souls] be two, they are two so
> As *stiff twin compasses* are two;
> Thy soul, the *fixed foot*, makes no show
> To move, but doth, if th'other do.
>
> And though it *in the centre sit,*
> Yet when the other *far doth roam,*
> It leans and *hearkens* after it,
> And grows erect, as that comes *home.*
>
> *Such* wilt thou be to me, who must
> Like th'other foot, *obliquely run;*
> Thy *firmness* makes my *circle just,*
> And makes me end where I begun. (25–36)

Perhaps the most striking feature of this simile is the way it challenges the reader to visualise exactly how a compass turns and inclines when it is being used by a cartographer or navigator (which reinforces the parallel between the movement of the compass and that of the traveller). Indeed, it is only through the imaginary realisation of such movement that the reader can recognise the grounds of the simile. This comparison is used and extended in such a way that what may initially seem a bizarre comparison turns out to have an impressive emotional logic. The woman staying at home becomes the 'fixed foot' which sits 'in the centre' while 'th'other foot' (the travelling man) 'far doth roam'. Just as the 'firmness' of the compass's fixed point is crucial to the other foot, making the circle it describes 'just', so is the woman's 'firmness' (her fixed place and her emotional strength and reliability) crucial to the speaker, making his own circle just and eventually bringing him home (where he began).

Our discussion of this extended simile or conceit would seem to support commonplace claims that Donne's poetry works through a kind of 'intellectual probing' or logic which marks a decisive break with Renaissance rhetoric. Yet although Donne's figures are undoubtedly conceptual and intellectually challenging, it is by no means clear that they are being used logically rather than rhetorically. After all, the speaker's ostensible purpose in the poem is to persuade a woman that their love will endure this temporary separation: this is a rhetorical, not a logical argument. Although the compass simile might seem strange to us, it actually draws on a symbolism which was quite conventional in the Renaissance: the circle was a standard symbol of perfection, and had already been associated with the compass image in numerous emblems of constancy. Yet a closer scrutiny of this conceit reveals that its persuasive power relies on the way it handles and embellishes this received idea, this *topos*, rather than on its logical consistency. The more we try to visualise what the compass is doing in these lines, the more problems we are likely to have with the logic of the argument. For you cannot draw a perfect circle when one foot of a pair of compasses 'comes home' to the other – that will produce only a squiggle or an ellipse. And if you draw a perfect circle, the roving foot will never come home to join the fixed foot. Donne is trying to get his image to illustrate two incompatible arguments, both of which depend on what are, essentially, only figures of speech. On the one hand, if the fixed foot stays in position, the roving foot will describe a perfect circle (which will demonstrate the perfection of their love). On the other hand, while the fixed foot stays in position, the speaker claims, the roving foot will eventually come back to it (this shows the lover's fidelity). But these two arguments and images are clearly incompatible with each other: they can't both happen at the same time.

A close scrutiny of Donne's figures, then, reveals that they are more pseudo-logical than logical. Donne's conceits exhibit an inventive exuberance designed to generate as much argumentative power as possible, even if it becomes self-contradictory. Such rhetorical resourcefulness is a large part of what seventeenth-century poets, and especially the 'Metaphysical' poets, meant by 'wit', a term they used to refer to the invention of apparently far-fetched conceits for essentially rhetorical ends.

■ Eighteenth-century Metaphor: Neoclassicism

There are several reasons why the period from 1660 to the late eighteenth century is called the 'Neoclassical period' – one of them being that eighteenth-century writers rigorously followed the Classical rhetoricians' attitude towards metaphor. Samuel Johnson, the dominant critic of the period, attacked Shakespeare's and Donne's use of figurative language, claiming that their metaphors tended to be violently or comically inappropriate for their subject matter. In his *Dictionary* (1755), Johnson defines 'metaphor' almost as an abuse of language: 'The application of a word to an use to which, in its original import, it cannot be put'. In 1690, John Locke, the most influential philosopher of the period, held that figurative language inevitably distorts the truths of empirical experience. He argued that figurative language could be avoided because it was confined to an inferior and superficial faculty of the mind which he called 'Wit'. Wit, he suggests, constructs and relates ideas according to processes of metaphor and metonymy:

> *Wit* [can be discerned] most in the assemblage of *Ideas*, and putting those together with quickness and variety, wherein can be found any resemblance or congruity, thereby to make up pleasant Pictures, and agreeable Visions in the Fancy.

The faculty of rational judgement, by contrast, separates ideas according to the differences between them, and hence helps us avoid the deceptions of figurative language:

> *Judgment*, on the contrary, lies quite on the other side, in separating carefully, one from another, *Ideas*, wherein can be found the least difference, thereby to avoid being misled by Similitude, and by affinity to take one thing for another. (*Essay Concerning Human Understanding*, pp. 508, 156)

Locke's argument, together with the negative example of the extravagances of Metaphysical wit, provoked early-eighteenth-century writers to try to distinguish 'true wit' from 'false wit'. Perhaps the most influential early example of this is a series of periodical essays by Joseph Addison, published in 1711. Addison quietly resists Locke by saying that true wit has 'its foundation in the nature of things', and that 'the basis of all [true] wit is truth'.[3] This is because true wit consists in an actual resemblance between ideas – although the ideas brought together in true wit 'should not lie too near one another in the nature of things; for where the likeness is obvious, it gives no surprise' (Addison, 1970, p. 16). False wit, by contrast, consists in a resemblance of words (as in puns) rather than ideas, and therefore compares with each other things which have no resemblance in reality. Even Shakespeare, Addison says, was given to this kind of false wit – which reveals that even the 'greatest genius' needs to be 'subdued by reason, reflection and good sense' and be 'cultivated by the rules of art' (p. 12). This stress on the curbing of genius by good sense and the rules of art provides a key to understanding Neoclassical poetics and poetry. In any comparison, both the idea and the figure used to convey it have to be decorous and rational, and the relationship between vehicle and tenor has to be appropriate and founded in truth.

Published in the same year as Addison's papers on true and false wit (but written two years previously), Pope's *An Essay on Criticism* sought to define true wit as a poetic practice whose figurative language works to illustrate pre-established truths in precisely the way Addison prescribes:

---

[3] *The Spectator*, Friday 11 May 1711, in Joseph Addison, *Critical Essays from the Spectator*, ed. Donald F. Bond (Oxford: Oxford University Press 1970), p. 19.

> True Wit is Nature to Advantage drest,
> What oft was Thought but ne'er so well Exprest (297–8).
>
> Expression is the Dress of Thought, and still
> Appears more decent as more suitable. (318–19)

The following passage, in which Pope is describing the changing perspective of poets as they mature, contains a memorable simile which apparently exemplifies this limited use of figurative language ('tempt' here means 'attempt'):

> Fir'd at first Sight with what the Muse imparts,
> In fearless Youth we tempt the Heights of Arts,
> While from the bounded Level of our Mind,
> Short Views we take, nor see the Lengths behind;
> But more advanc'd, behold with strange Surprize
> New, distant Scenes of endless Science rise!
> So pleas'd at first, the towring Alps we try,
> Mount o'er the Vales, and seem to tread the Sky;
> Th' Eternal Snows appear already past,
> And the first Clouds and Mountains seem the last:
> But those attain'd, we tremble to survey
> The growing Labours of the lengthen'd Way,
> Th' increasing Prospect tires our wandring Eyes,
> Hills peep o'er Hills, and Alps on Alps arise! (219–32)

In these lines, Pope's point (the more you know the more there is to know) is established in the first six lines and merely explained and exemplified in the eight-line simile which follows. Rather than being used to persuade or argue a point (as it would be in Shakespeare or Donne), the simile serves simply to illustrate and expand upon it in a memorable way. And although the comparison between advancing in the art of poetry and climbing mountains may initially appear surprising, it is made to seem entirely appropriate and congruous (it is not far-fetched in the way that Donne's compasses are).

Yet a closer analysis of the lines reveals that figurative language may be playing a more active and constitutive role than Neoclassical theory would seem to allow. The sense of congruity between the two halves of the simile is an illusion created by the fact that the comparison between advancing in the poetic craft and climbing a mountain is already built into the first six lines through metaphors such as 'the heights of arts' and 'the bounded level of our mind'. These metaphors appear to *constitute* the idea rather than merely 'dressing' a pre-existing idea. It is not clear that Pope could make his point without these metaphors, and this suggests that metaphor cannot be restricted to the secondary role to which strict Neoclassical theory would confine it. As we suggested in Chapter 5, and despite Locke's warnings, it would seem to be impossible to think without metaphor.

Romantic Metaphor

Whereas eighteenth-century thinkers attempted to see metaphor as an embellishment of language, a dressing of thought, the Romantic poets regarded metaphor as fundamental to language and to thought itself. In his *Defence of Poetry* (1821) Shelley echoes Locke by stressing that the mind operates according to two different principles: reason and the imagination. The imagination, working on 'the principle of synthesis', establishes new links between ideas according to relations of similarity. Reason, by contrast, analyses 'the relations borne by one thought to another'. But Shelley reverses Locke's scheme by making imagination the primary mode of thought and relegating reason to a secondary role. While the imagination actually composes new thoughts through metaphor, reason simply analyses existing thoughts: 'Reason is to Imagination as the instrument to the agent, as the body to the spirit, as the shadow to the substance' (*Shelley's Poetry and Prose*, p. 480). Shelley thus overturns Locke's attempt to make imagination and metaphor mere aberrations of the rational mind. Poetic metaphor becomes the primary means through which we apprehend the world and discover or produce new truths. Reason is left to play a secondary role, becoming a kind of analytic commentator on the metaphorical productions of the imagination. Romantic linguistic theory, then, reverses the conventional idea that metaphor is a secondary deviation from literal language: for the Romantics, metaphor comes first, and rational distinctions and literal meanings are developed subsequently.

Influenced by Rousseau's suggestion that civilisation had corrupted humanity's original nobility, Romantic writers searched for ways of reconnecting with humanity's authentic nature. This is why they were interested in 'uncivilised' people, in the 'natural innocence' of childhood, and in the 'wilds' of nature. Along with the assumption that the language of 'primitive' peoples must be poetic, the Romantics held that the poetic imagination arose out of the individual's inner self in so far as it had escaped the corrupting forces of society. These ideas can be seen in one of the pioneering documents of English Romanticism, the 'Preface to *Lyrical Ballads*' (1800), where Wordsworth explains that he had tried in the *Lyrical Ballads* to reject the artificial 'figures of speech which . . . have long been regarded as the common inheritance of Poets' in order to employ 'a selection of the real language of men in a state of vivid sensation'. He explains that he has written about 'Low and rustic life' because 'in that condition, the essential passions of the heart . . . are under less restraint, and speak a plainer and more emphatic language'. For such reasons, Wordsworth believed that his poetry would be 'alive' with natural metaphors:

if the Poet's subject be judiciously chosen, it will naturally, and upon fit occasion, lead him to passions the language of which, if selected truly and judiciously, must necessarily be dignified and variegated, and alive with metaphors and figures. (*Lyrical Ballads*, pp. 254–5)

The result of Wordsworth's 'experiment' was a pared-down poetic language which, at its best, uses figurative language in simple but moving ways:

Song

<blockquote>

She dwelt among th' untrodden ways
   Beside the springs of Dove,
A Maid whom there were none to praise
   And very few to love.

A Violet by a mossy stone   5
   Half-hidden from the Eye!
– Fair, as a star when only one
   Is shining in the sky!

She liv'd unknown, and few could know
   When Lucy ceas'd to be;   10
But she is in her Grave, and Oh!
   The difference to me.

</blockquote>

In this 'song' the figurative language seems to arise out of the situation rather than being imported into the poem from the 'stock' of available poetic figures. The figures are limited to the middle stanza, and make disarmingly simple comparisons between Lucy and natural objects. These seemingly 'natural' figures reveal not only the solitude of Lucy's situation and the harmony between her and the natural environment, but also the 'authentic' way the speaker perceives her.

In his *Biographia Literaria* (1817), Coleridge develops a philosophical account of the Romantic imagination which rigorously differentiates it from the fancy or wit of eighteenth-century poetry. The fancy, he suggests, is a passive and merely mechanical mental faculty which arranges the ideas stored in the memory according to associations of space and time (as such, it might remind us of metonymy). Such a process cannot produce new ideas, but simply points out pre-existing connections between received ideas. The imagination, by contrast, is an active living power which shapes and transforms ideas in a creative way, and reveals the natural or organic coherence between ideas and between things (as such, metaphor is its characteristic means). Metaphors produced by the imagination also reveal the sympathetic interaction between the natural world and the human mind.

Coleridge's theory of the imagination and of the nature of metaphor which it entails can be seen in action in Wordsworth's *The Prelude* (1805). Perhaps the major poetic achievement of English Romanticism, *The Prelude* is a poem of eight-and-a-half thousand lines, divided into thirteen 'books', which Wordsworth presents as an autobiographical account of the growth of his own mind. In Book IV Wordsworth develops an intriguing simile for the poem's relation to the past events it ostensibly records:

> As one who hangs down-bending from the side
> Of a slow-moving Boat, upon the breast
> Of a still water, solacing himself
> With such discoveries as his eye can make,
> Beneath him, in the bottom of the deeps,
> Sees many beauteous sights, weeds, fishes, flowers,
> Grots, pebbles, roots of trees, and fancies more,
> Yet often is perplexed, and cannot part
> The shadow from the substance, rocks and sky,
> Mountains and clouds, from that which is indeed
> The region, and the things which there abide
> In their true dwelling; now is crossed by gleam
> Of his own image, by a sunbeam now,
> And motions that are sent he knows not whence,
> Impediments that make his task more sweet;
> – Such pleasant office have we long pursued
> Incumbent o'er the surface of past time
> With like success . . . (IV, 247–64).[4]

There are two things which we want initially to point out about these lines: the structure of this simile puts the figurative side before the literal, the vehicle before the tenor; the figurative vehicle is extended over fifteen lines. The combined effect of these two features is that unlike Pope's simile, which supposedly serves merely to illustrate a point already made, Wordsworth's simile does a great deal of conceptual work *prior to* the literal point, and goes on at such length that we tend to forget that we are reading a simile and respond to the first fifteen lines as being of interest in their own right. And when the tenor of the simile does arrive – telling us that the attempt to discern the past is as complicated as the attempt to distinguish underwater objects from a boat – that tenor turns out to employ a metaphor which is derived from the simile: the poem's speaker and reader have been 'Incumbent o'er [leaning over] the

---

[4] For a brilliant discussion of these lines, to which we are partly indebted, see Isobel Armstrong, *Language as Living Form in Nineteenth-Century Poetry* (Sussex: Harvester, 1982), pp. 29–32.

surface of past time' (263). Both sides of the simile, then, employ the same figure, and it becomes impossible to maintain any straightforward distinction between literal and figurative, or between what the poem itself calls shadow and substance. Instead, an exchange or interchange occurs between literal and figurative in a way which suggests an 'organic' or inevitable connection between the two. This is wholly characteristic of Romantic metaphor. If Classical and Neoclassical accounts of metaphor urge us to recognise the difference between tenor and vehicle (as in the difference between dress and body) so that we may not be misled by metaphor's potentially deceptive power, Romanticism tends to collapse the difference between tenor and vehicle, stressing the interchange between them and seeing metaphor as intrinsic to creative thought rather than a kind of lie.

The priority (both in sequence and length) given to the vehicle of this simile means, as we have said, that it does a large amount of conceptual work and becomes of interest in its own right. This is entirely appropriate, since the fifteen lines of the first part of this simile stage an exploration in miniature of Romantic theories of perception and epistemology (or theory of knowledge). We are not simply being presented with a 'nice' image of someone drifting on a 'slow-moving Boat' and idly gazing beneath the water. Instead, this situation is used in order to explore in a concrete way the Romantics' assumption that human beings are not detached, objective observers of objects in the world but, rather, that our very presence as observers changes what we observe so that perception is itself a creative rather than a passive process. The person in this boat looks under the water and makes 'discoveries' with 'his eye' and 'Sees many beauteous sights'. Wordsworth lists a number of these objects which the viewer is likely to see, but interestingly he ends the list with 'and fancies more'. Yet this apparently straightforward distinction between real and 'fancied' objects, or between seeing and imagining (Wordsworth did not follow Coleridge's strict distinction between fancy and imagination), is complicated in the subsequent lines. We are told that the man

> often is perplexed, and cannot part
> The shadow from the substance, rocks and sky,
> Mountains and clouds, from that which is indeed
> The region, and the things which there abide
> In their true dwelling . . . (IV, 254–58)

In these lines, the man has difficulty in distinguishing between the objects which are really there under the water and the reflections of 'rocks and sky, / Mountains and clouds' on the water's surface. In terms of the larger simile, this suggests that it is difficult to distinguish in memory between the things which really happened in the past and the things which we project upon the past in attempting to remember it. In terms of the exploration of perception, it suggests that it is difficult to discern absolutely between what we actually see and what our minds add to what we see (you might think back here to our discussion of Wordsworth's poetry in Chapter 3).

That word 'perplexed' is quite suggestive in this context. Its primary meaning is the familiar one of being puzzled or bewildered. But a second meaning indicated by the *OED* – of being entangled or intertwined – allows us to think of this observer as being entangled or intertwined within that which he sees (in philosophical terms, the perceiving subject is not detached from but intertwined with the objects which he views). This possibility is supported by the following lines, where we are told that the man's attempt to discriminate the 'shadow from the substance' is complicated by his own physical presence within the scene he is trying to observe:

> now [he] is crossed by gleam
> Of his own image, by a sunbeam now,
> And motions that are sent he knows not whence. (IV, 358–60)

His own image (reflection) appears within the scene he is trying to observe, and hence further perplexes him (in both the senses just mentioned). In addition, 'motions' also complicate his task – motions, presumably, of the water itself produced by the 'slow-moving Boat' and perhaps originating in his own slight movements as he tries to see into the water. In other words, the observer's very presence *within* the scene being observed affects that scene: the viewing subject is part of that which he views. This problem is not regretted by the Romantic thinker – these 'Impediments . . . make his task more sweet' (261). This, in the nutshell of these few lines, is the Romantic revolution in epistemology.

This figure in *The Prelude* carries out, and requires the reader to carry out, an enormous amount of conceptual work. Yet there are potential problems with the Romantic account of metaphor. Metaphor, as we have seen, is a twofold structure made up of a relationship between figurative and literal, vehicle and tenor. Part of the intellectual and emotional effect of metaphor arises through this doubleness – through the difference as well as the similarity between vehicle and tenor. Neoclassical writers attempted to keep vehicle and tenor clearly distinguished in order not to be deceived. Romantic writers tended to downplay or overlook the literal in a way which potentially undermines the difference between metaphorical and literal. In the most extreme case – in the poetry of Shelley – metaphor seems completely unfettered by considerations of literal meaning and can result in thrilling but opaque poetry. One of Shelley's best-known poems is his 'Ode to the West Wind' (1820), of which we will quote only the first two of five sections:

1

O wild West Wind, thou breath of Autumn's being,
Thou, from whose unseen presence the leaves dead
Are driven, like ghosts from an enchanter fleeing,

Yellow, and black, and pale, and hectic red,
Pestilence-stricken multitudes: O Thou,   5
Who chariotest to their dark wintry bed

The winged seeds, where they lie cold and low,
Each like a corpse within its grave, until
Thine azure sister of the Spring shall blow

Her clarion o'er the dreaming earth, and fill   10
(Driving sweet buds like flocks to feed in air)
With living hues and odours plain and hill:

Wild Spirit, which art moving everywhere;
Destroyer and Preserver; hear, O hear!

2

Thou on whose stream, 'mid the steep sky's commotion,   15
Loose clouds like Earth's decaying leaves are shed,
Shook from the tangled boughs of Heaven and Ocean,

Angels of rain and lightning: there are spread
On the blue surface of thine aery surge,
Like the bright hair uplifted from the head   20

Of some fierce Maenad, even from the dim verge
Of the horizon to the zenith's height,
The locks of the approaching storm. Thou Dirge

Of the dying year, to which this closing night
Will be the dome of a vast sepulchre,   25
Vaulted with all thy congregated might

Of vapours, from whose solid atmosphere
Black rain and fire and hail will burst: O hear!

There are a number of things about this poem which an extended reading ought to attend to, including the dynamic use of ***terza rima*** to create a sonnet-like structure in each of the sections, and the question of the relation between the poem and its political context.[5] But for our present purposes, we will limit the discussion to the question of how Shelley uses metaphor. The ode is constructed as a continuous apostrophe to the west wind in a way which metaphorically humanises an inanimate phenomenon. Having begun with this address, the speaker immediately offers a metaphor for that metaphor: in the first line, the humanised wind is said to be the '*breath* of Autumn's being' (which also figures Autumn as an animate creature). This wind blows the vari-coloured autumn leaves as an 'enchanter' drives 'ghosts' (3), but it also drives (or chariots) seeds to their 'wintry bed' (6). Each seed remains 'like a corpse within its grave' (8) until the warm Spring wind will cause it to sprout – or, as the poem puts it, until it calls them from their graves with a 'clarion' (trumpet call):

> until
> Thine azure sister of the Spring shall blow
> Her clarion o'er the dreaming earth, and fill
> . . .
> With living hues and odours plain and hill. (8–12)

Thus far it has been relatively easy to 'make sense' of Shelley's poem by offering paraphrases of the metaphors. Yet if we attend to the bracketed line which Shelley embeds between the last two of the lines just quoted, we are faced with something of a puzzle. The metaphor we have been tracing suggests that the spring wind will act like a trumpet blast which will call the seeds from their beds/graves and that their blossoming will result in 'plain and hill' being filled with 'living hues and odours'. But the parenthesis in brackets simultaneously suggests that the spring wind will act like a shepherd, 'Driving sweet buds like flocks to feed in air' (11). We can visualise the 'azure sister' doing both things, but being asked to imagine that the 'sweet buds' will somehow be like flocks of sheep feeding 'in air' is, as we say, stretching it a bit – especially since we are being asked simultaneously to imagine them as people leaving their beds and as corpses rising from their graves.

In the second section things get still more complicated because of the rapid slippage from one opaque metaphor to another. Here we are asked to see the wind as having (or perhaps being) a 'stream' upon which 'Loose clouds' are 'shed' as if they were 'decaying leaves' (15–16). Although it is possible to supply grounds for the clouds–leaves simile, the metaphor is extended into obscurity

---

[5] See our Glossary for *terza rima* and sonnet. As for the poem's politics, 'Ode to the West Wind' needs to be read in relation to Shelley's other poems written shortly after the so-called Peterloo Massacre of August 1819, in which troops in Manchester charged into a peaceful demonstration in support of parliamentary reform (see 'The Mask of Anarchy' and 'England in 1819'). The poem's last line in particular – 'If Winter comes, can Spring be far behind?' – allows the poem to be read as an extended metaphor for imminent revolution.

by suggesting that these loose clouds have been 'Shook from the tangled boughs of Heaven and Ocean' (17). In what way can the interaction between the air and the ocean be like the tangling of the boughs of a tree? Immediately after this, we are forced to readjust our image of these clouds as leaves on a stream to seeing them as 'Angels' – heavenly messengers whose message consists of 'rain and lightning' (18). This metaphor, too, is immediately discarded, since lines 18–21 ask us to see these clouds as being 'spread' on the sky 'Like the bright hair uplifted from the head / Of some fierce Maenad' (a frenzied dancing priestess of Dionysus, god of wine and fertility). These hair-like clouds then become 'The locks of the approaching storm' (23).

There has been a long line of negative criticism of Shelley's poetry which runs through the Victorian period (Lamb, Carlyle, Arnold) and into the twentieth century (Eliot and the New Critics). In 1936, F.R. Leavis contributed to that negative criticism with a dismissive reading of the figurative language of the second stanza of 'Ode to the West Wind'. Leavis argued that Shelley's poetry is 'unreadable' in the sense that if we put aside the emotional power of the poetry and ask 'obvious questions', we will discover his metaphors have hardly any basis in the real world:

> What . . . are those 'tangled boughs of Heaven and Ocean'? They stand for nothing that Shelley could have pointed to in the scene before him: the 'boughs', it is plain, have grown out of the 'leaves' in the previous line, and we are not to ask what the tree is.

Leavis suggests that the obscurity of this figure is characteristic of Shelley's use of figurative language in the rest of the poem and elsewhere:

> In the growth of those 'tangled boughs' out of the leaves, exemplifying as it does a general tendency of the images to forget the status of the metaphor or simile that introduced them and to assume an autonomy and a right to propagate, so that we lose in confused generations and perspectives the perception or thought that was the ostensible *raison d'être* of imagery, we have a recognised essential trait of Shelley's: his weak grasp of the actual.[6]

Leavis's critique here presents an insightful account of the way Shelley's figurative language operates. Using an apt figure of his own, Leavis suggests that the 'tangled boughs' appear in the poem not because of any likeness they might have with what Shelley is referring to, but because they 'have grown out of' (follow on from) the 'leaves' in the previous line. Leavis thus signals his objection to the way Shelley's figures 'assume an autonomy and a right to propagate' themselves by a joke at Shelley's expense: these boughs 'have grown out of' these leaves in a reversal of the natural order of things. Just as leaves grow out of boughs, Leavis suggests, so should metaphors 'grow out of' the literal nature of the 'actual' world and not be allowed to 'propagate' themselves. In the

---

[6] Leavis, *Revaluation*, pp. 192–4.

'confused' self-generation of Shelley's figures, he argues, 'the status of the meta-phor or simile that introduced them' is lost, along with 'the perception or thought that was the ostensible *raison d'être*' or justification of the figures in the first place.

Yet although this is an accurate analysis of the way Shelley's figurative lan-guage tends to work, we might ask whether Leavis is being too literal-minded in his demand that Shelley's metaphors ought to 'stand for' something that he 'could have pointed to in the scene before him'. This implies that figurative language should always be in the service of realistic descriptions of the world – that this is its only *raison d'être*. Leavis notes the tumultuous energy of Shelley's poem, but suggests that it simply distracts us from asking the right questions. Poetry, Leavis implies, should make sense by being subject to rational thought, mimesis and moral concerns. His objection to Shelley's poetry is that it revels in the generative power of metaphor unfettered by the demands of lit-eral sense and sensory perception – that its figurative language does not remain subservient to pre-existing 'perception or thought'. Leavis is thus rejecting Romanticism's tendency to reverse the subordination of figurative to literal. What Leavis fails to register is that the tumultuous virtuosity of Shelley's metaphors reproduces in the reading experience the tumult of the storm and its effects on the poem's speaker. He is also implicitly rejecting Shelley's claim in the *Defence of Poetry* that the *raison d'être* of poetic metaphor is not to serve established sense but to revitalise the language and expand the individual imagination by creating fresh thoughts and new correspondences between thoughts. This was where the revolutionary potential of poetry lay for Shelley, not in its slavish relation to reality or common sense.

Metaphor in Victorian Poetry

To a certain extent, Victorian poetry can be understood as both a continuation of Romanticism and a reaction against the extremes of Romantic metaphor. Although the Romantic poets are often thought to be concerned with 'nature', their poetry typically uses nature as a trigger for inner speculations, and natu-ral objects quickly become metaphors for the speaker's mental landscape. (We have seen this in Keats's 'Ode to a Nightingale'; it can also be seen in Shelley's 'Ode to the West Wind' and in Wordsworth's 'Tintern Abbey'.) By contrast, one strand of Victorian poetry tends to establish the speaker's place and pur-pose in the 'real world', and only then to use that as the ground for metaphor.[7] A characteristic example of this is Matthew Arnold's 'Dover Beach' (1867).

> The sea is calm tonight.
> The tide is full, the moon lies fair

[7] This argument is influenced by a slightly different argument in Bradford, *Linguistic History of English Poetry*, pp. 133–53.

Upon the straits; on the French coast the light
Gleams and is gone; the cliffs of England stand,
Glimmering and vast, out in the tranquil bay.   5
Come to the window, sweet is the night air!
Only, from the long line of spray
Where the sea meets the moon-blanched land,
Listen! you hear the grating roar
Of pebbles which the waves draw back and fling,   10
At their return, up the high strand,
Begin, and cease, and then again begin,
With tremulous cadence slow, and bring
The eternal note of sadness in.

Sophocles long ago   15
Heard it on the Aegean, and it brought
Into his mind the turbid ebb and flow
Of human misery; we
Find also in the sound a thought,
Hearing it by this distant northern sea.   20

The Sea of Faith
Was once, too, at the full, and round earth's shore
Lay like the folds of a bright girdle furled.
But now I only hear
Its melancholy, long, withdrawing roar,   25
Retreating, to the breath
Of the night wind, down the vast edges drear
And naked shingles of the world.

Ah, love, let us be true
To one another! for the world, which seems   30
To lie before us like a land of dreams,
So various, so beautiful, so new,
Hath really neither joy, nor love, nor light,
Nor certitude, nor peace, nor help for pain;
And we are here as on a darkling plain   35
Swept with confused alarms of struggle and flight,
Where ignorant armies clash by night.

The poem's first section firmly establishes the speaker's location in a specific natural landscape which is imbued with cultural and ideological resonances: the poetic speaker and his 'love' (29) are standing at the window of a house overlooking the cliffs and beach at Dover, and looking out across the Channel towards the French coast. Although metaphor is used in this section, it simply enhances the description or, through controlled uses of personification, prepares for the metaphorical reflections which will follow later: although the 'sea is *calm*' (1), there is a 'grating *roar*' (9) of pebbles which 'bring / The eternal *note of sadness* in' (13–14). The shift from itemised description to metaphorical reflection is mediated by the comparison with Sophocles in the second section: we are able to find such a thought in the sound of this 'distant northern sea' because, for Sophocles, the same sound in the Aegean 'brought / Into his mind the *turbid ebb and flow* / Of human misery' (16–18). Thus the conditions are carefully prepared for the third section, which extends the metaphor of the 'Sea of Faith' (21) through eight lines. For the speaker of this poem there is no 'ebb and flow' of human misery but simply the 'melancholy, long, withdrawing roar' of the 'Sea of Faith' as it retreats, in an awesome metaphor,

> to the breath
> Of the night wind, down the vast edges drear
> And naked shingles of the world. (25–28)

This horrifying image allows the speaker to realise in the final section that the apparently 'calm' landscape is a fragile illusion, only barely disguising the insecurities and deceptions of the real world. The only refuge is in love, but even then the couple are said to be beset with danger in the final chilling simile:

> we are here as on a darkling plain
> Swept with confused alarms of struggle and flight,
> Where ignorant armies clash by night. (35–37)

■ Modernism and Metaphor

In the second decade of the twentieth century a group of poets calling themselves the 'Imagists' reacted against what they saw as 'the verbose and abstract language into which much of the poetry of the nineteenth century had declined' ('imagists' in *Princeton*). Ezra Pound, in 'A Few Don'ts By An Imagiste' (1913), produced a kind of manifesto of the short-lived, but highly influential, Imagist movement. Stressing that poetry should consist of vividly 'concrete' images, and that all abstractions should be purged, Pound advises would-be poets how to avoid the third-rate Romanticism of contemporary poetry:

Use no superfluous word, no adjective, which does not reveal something.

Don't use such an expression as 'dim land of peace.' It dulls the image. It mixes an abstraction with the concrete. It comes from the writer's not realizing that the natural object is always the *adequate* symbol.

Go in fear of abstractions.[8]

---

[8] Quoted by Jones, *Imagist Poetry*, p. 131.

In a letter written in 1915, Pound recommends 'Objectivity and again objectivity. . . . Language is made out of concrete things. General expressions in non-concrete terms are a laziness' (quoted by Jones, p. 20). In a 1914 article on another pre-modernist movement – 'Vorticism' – Pound asserts: 'The "Image" is the furthest possible remove from rhetoric. Rhetoric is the art of dressing up some unimportant matter so as to fool the audience for the time being' (quoted by Jones, p. 21). These comments suggest that **Imagism** can be seen both as a modern version of the distrust of figurative language which periodically surfaces throughout the history of Western culture and as an attempt to overcome the arbitrary nature of the sign.

The most famous Imagist poem is Pound's 'In a Station of the Metro', and you may find it interesting to go back to our discussion of it in Chapter 4 in order to consider it alongside Pound's statements about Imagism. In a letter written to Harriet Monroe in 1912, Pound enthused over the poetry of Hilda Doolittle (H.D.), saying that it was 'Objective – no slither; direct – no excessive use of adjectives, no metaphors that won't permit examination' (Jones, p. 17). H.D.'s poem 'Sea Rose' (1916) gives an idea of what he was getting at:

> Rose, harsh rose,
> marred and with stint of petals,
> meagre flower, thin,
> sparse of leaf,
>
> more precious   5
> than a wet rose
> single on a stem –
> you are caught in the drift.
>
> Stunted, with small leaf,
> you are flung on the sand,   10
> you are lifted
> in the crisp sand
> that drives the wind.
>
> Can the spice-rose
> drip such acrid fragrance   15
> hardened in a leaf?

Apart from its use of apostrophe (which you might want to compare with Blake's apostrophe to a rose), this poem seems to purge its language of all trace of 'poetic' metaphors: metaphors such as 'you are flung on the sand' are a long way from the abstractions of 'dim land of peace' and from Shelley's extraordinary use of metaphor in 'Ode to the West Wind'. 'Sea Rose' resists using the natural image as a vehicle for metaphysical speculations (in the way Arnold does with the 'Sea of Faith'). Instead of using the rose as a metaphor, and instead of producing metaphors about the rose, this poem seeks, as far as is possible in language, to present a 'concrete' image of the rose itself. The natural image is presented as if it were poetic in its own right. Only the word 'precious' hints at traditional ways of poeticising roses, and then it is used precisely to claim that this rose is more precious – because of its meagreness – than the kind of roses usually eulogised in poetry.

Imagism's rejection of 'poetic' metaphor in favour of 'concrete' images set a benchmark for the Modernist poetry of Eliot, Pound, Stevens, Williams and others. The difficulties of Modernist poetry arise, for the most part, from factors other than its use of metaphor. Yet it is possible to find extraordinarily difficult metaphors in Modernist poetry which resemble the conceits of the Metaphysical poets. A second factor in the early phase of the development of Modernism was the arrival in England from the United States of the young T.S. Eliot in 1914, along with some poems which Pound hailed as 'modern' and contrived to get published. 'The Love Song of J. Alfred Prufrock' (1917) updates the Victorian **dramatic monologue** (see Chapter 7) in order to treat contemporary urban life in an experimental poetry which seems to abandon both metrical form and the imperative of making sense. Eliot argued that modern poetry must be difficult if it is to be responsive to the complexities of the twentieth century, and 'Prufrock' is a pioneering example of such difficult poetry. The poem offers a different alternative to the abstract tendencies of 'poetic' metaphor from that offered by Imagism by presenting a series of memorable metaphors and similes whose tendency, however, is to be so strange that it becomes difficult to say what they 'mean' (in Leavis's sense).[9]

We will begin by looking at the first twenty-two lines:

> Let us go then, you and I,
> When the evening is spread out against the sky
> Like a patient etherized upon a table;
> Let us go, through certain half-deserted streets,
> The muttering retreats   5
> Of restless nights in one-night cheap hotels
> And sawdust restaurants with oyster shells:
> Streets that follow like a tedious argument
> Of insidious intent
> To lead you to an overwhelming question . . .   10
> Oh do not ask, 'What is it?'
> Let us go and make our visit.

[9] That Leavis celebrated Eliot's poetry while condemning Shelley's may reveal a political side to his poetic judgments. See F.R. Leavis, *New Bearings in English Poetry* (1st ed, 1932), pp. 60–100.

> In the room the women come and go
> Talking of Michelangelo.
>
> The yellow fog that rubs its back upon the window-panes   15
> The yellow smoke that rubs its muzzle on the window-panes
> Licked its tongue into the corners of the evening,
> Lingered upon the pools that stand in drains,
> Let fall upon its back the soot that falls from chimneys,
> Slipped by the terrace, made a sudden leap,   20
> And seeing that it was a soft October night,
> Curled once about the house, and fell asleep.

In the famous opening simile, the sheer difference between vehicle ('a patient etherized upon a table') and tenor ('the evening . . . spread out against the sky') seems to allow for no grounds upon which any similarity could be imagined. The extended metaphor of the yellow fog/smoke as a cat rubbing its back or muzzle on the window-panes, and so on, makes poetic sense without making any other kind of sense. In what way could the fog lick its 'tongue into the corners of the evening'? And what are 'the corners of the evening'? Such figures seem to break with the very nature of metaphor – that is, the positing of a degree of significant resemblance between different ideas or things.

One way of understanding these figures would be to see them as an extreme response to the post-Romantic emphasis on originality, the pressure to produce new metaphors summarised in Pound's call to 'make it new' or in Russian Formalism's account of defamiliarisation. Yet these figures produce not so much defamiliarisation as disorientation, less new insight than a resistance to insight. A more interesting way of understanding such metaphors is to abandon trying to work out whether they offer surprising but revealing ways of looking at the evening or the fog and to think of them as combining to connote a 'psychological atmosphere' which allows an insight into the character of the invented poetic speaker. The claim that the evening sky is like a patient etherised upon a table might tell us more about Prufrock than it does about the evening sky. As we read more of the poem we gain the impression of Prufrock as a pathetic, ineffectual character who is incapable of fully engaging with other people or making sense of his place in the world. Prufrock seems unable to make decisions or take decisive action: although the first section ends with him urging 'Let us go and make our visit', there is nothing in the rest of the poem to suggest that Prufrock ever does 'go'. But not only is Prufrock himself like an etherised patient, so too is his language: the opening simile simply does not work; its two sides remain isolated from one another as if the simile itself were etherised.

Eliot himself might have approved of this method of reading the figures in 'Prufrock', since we have effectively treated the opening simile as an example of what he later called an 'objective correlative':

The only way of expressing emotion in the form of art is by finding an 'objective cor-
relative'; in other words, a set of objects, a situation, a chain of events which shall be the
formula of that particular emotion; such that when the external facts, which must
terminate in sensory experience, are given, the emotion is immediately evoked.[10]

To a certain extent, Modernist writing tried to reproduce the quirky processes
of the human mind – as in, say, the 'stream-of-consciousness' techniques of
Woolf and Joyce. Yet Modernist writers pushed their experiments beyond this
to produce texts – such as Eliot's *The Waste Land* (1922) or Joyce's *Ulysses*
(1922) – which cannot be made to cohere in terms of the experience of a single
consciousness. Pound's extraordinary poetry in *The Cantos* (1925–69) takes
Modernist techniques of collage to a point where no ingenuity of the reader
could unify the disparate kinds of language or imagine that they originate in
the mind of an invented speaker. Although 'Prufrock' is, by comparison with
these 'high Modernist' texts, a relatively modest experiment, the poem's ending
opens it out to irresolution and incoherence:

> I have heard the mermaids singing, each to each.
>
> I do not think that they will sing to me.
>
> I have seen them riding seaward on the waves
> Combing the white hair of the waves blown back
> When the wind blows the water white and black.
>
> We have lingered in the chambers of the sea
> By sea-girls wreathed with seaweed red and brown
> Till human voices wake us, and we drown.

The perplexing and intriguing thing about these lines is that they seem reson-
antly meaningful without our being able to say what they mean, metaphori-
cally suggestive without allowing us to see what is literally being suggested.
Rather than coming to a conclusion – a final moment of insight which would
resolve its difficulties – the poem opens out to an incoherence and inconclu-
siveness which cannot be wholly accounted for by reference to Prufrock's
'character'.

The critical theory and practice of New Criticism was partly developed as a
response to the difficulties of Modernist poetry. Cleanth Brooks, for example,
argued that neither Neoclassical nor Romantic assumptions about poetic
metaphor are appropriate for understanding the 'obscure' metaphors of
Modernist poetry. Instead, he suggests, Modernist metaphor needs to be

[10] 'Hamlet' (1919) in Eliot, *Selected Prose of T.S. Eliot*, pp. 45–9 (48).

thought of as analogous to the conceits of the Metaphysical poets which, as we have seen, use apparently incongruous and 'unpoetic' comparisons in ways which become justified through their contribution to the meaning and effects of the poem as a whole. Donne's compasses, he argues, 'are poetic in the only sense in which objects can ever be legitimately poetic – they function integrally in a poem'.[11] He claims that the startlingly 'obscure' metaphors of Modernist poetry – such as Eliot's comparison of the evening sky with a patient etherised upon a table – work in the same way as Metaphysical conceits: they set up an interplay between intellect and emotion, and are justified by the fact that they can be shown to 'contribute to the total effect' of the poems they appear within (p. 15). It is this similarity in technique and outlook, Brooks suggests, which is the real reason why Donne became important for the Modernist poets.

Yet there are important differences between Metaphysical and Modernist uses of metaphor. Whereas Donne's poem works to justify its startling metaphors, the metaphors and similes of 'Prufrock' are presented without any such justification. The reader is simply confronted with obscure and apparently incongruous similes and metaphors and left to work them out for him- or herself. This is why the New Critical technique of 'close reading' was developed: starting out with the assumption that every detail of a 'good' poem will be integral to its overall meaning and effect, the New Critics set about interpreting such metaphors in ways which would demonstrate their implicit relationship to the 'total context' of the poem as a whole. The opening simile of 'Prufrock', then, might be 'justified' by claiming that, rather than revealing anything about the evening sky, it reveals something about the psychological nature and condition of Prufrock himself.

New Criticism, then, developed powerful techniques for processing the obscurities of Modernist poetry, turning apparent incoherence into complex unity. Yet the New Critical attempt to interpret Modernist metaphors in this way (and so integrate Modernism into the poetic tradition) serves to smooth over what is most challenging about Modernist poetry. Poems such as Eliot's 'Prufrock' or *The Waste Land* (along with the poetry of other Modernists such as Pound and Wallace Stevens) potentially undermine our habitual assumptions that poems can be understood as the speech of poets or invented poetic speakers and unsettle the belief of critics such as Leavis that poetic metaphor can be justified only if it reveals something about the world and/or the person viewing the world.

Post-structuralist literary theory can be seen as a different kind of response to Modernism which seeks to celebrate and sustain its tendency towards

---

[11] 'Metaphor and the Tradition', in Cleanth Brooks, *Modern Poetry and the Tradition* (Chapel Hill: University of North Carolina Press, 1967), pp. 1–17 (12).

productive incoherence. Although Saussure argued that the relationship between signifier (the aural or written aspect of a word) and signified (the conceptual meaning of a word) is merely conventional, this conventionality binds signifier to signified like two sides of a piece of paper. Each signifier is thus unproblematically linked to its signified, and competent users of the language, by definition, will all agree about which signifier is linked with which signified. But this description of language overlooks the complexities, ambiguities and multiple meanings which feature in the way language is actually used. Metaphor, for example, complicates Saussure's model by claiming that two quite different signifiers are somehow equivalent to one another, or that one signifier can substitute for another, or that a signifier can have a different, unpredictable meaning according to the context in which it is used.[12]

Yet although metaphor potentially interferes with the stable relationship between signifier and signified, in many instances it seems to work in the same way that Saussure claims language works in general. In other words, the vehicle–tenor relationship can be thought of as a version of the signifier–signified relationship. Interpreting a metaphor, then, simply involves treating the vehicle as a signifier for which the implied meaning or tenor would be the signified. Yet we have seen that this apparently straightforward passage from vehicle to tenor, or from signifier to signified, becomes impeded in certain kinds of poetic metaphors (such as Shelley's or Eliot's). In Chapter 5 we found that Auden's 'The hour-glass whispers to the lion's roar' presents several problems for any attempt to translate vehicle into tenor: it is difficult to supply a wholly satisfactory signified for the signifier 'whispers' and, in any case, whatever signified we might come up with will probably turn out to be another metaphor or signifier; we also suggested that the lion and its roar might be a poetic symbol for which we are unable to specify any precise signification.

For Roland Barthes, in his post-structuralist phase, these features of Shelley's or Eliot's or Auden's metaphors – the resistance they offer to any attempt to state their 'meaning' – would constitute precisely their interest. As we saw in Chapter 4, Barthes celebrates the way a certain kind of 'text'

> practises the infinite deferment of the signified, is dilatory; its field is that of the signifier and the signifier must not be conceived of as 'the first stage of meaning', its material vestibule, but, in complete opposition to this, as its *deferred action* . . . the *infinity* of the signifier refers not to some idea of the ineffable (the unnameable signified) but to that of a *playing*; the generation of the perpetual signifier . . .[13]

---

[12] For a philosophical discussion of the contextual nature of metaphor and the way the multiple meanings it introduces disrupt Saussure's linguistic theories, see Paul Ricoeur, *The Rule of Metaphor: Multi-disciplinary studies of the creation of meaning in language*, trans. Robert Czerny (London: Routledge, 1986), especially pp. 120–25.

[13] 'From Work to Text', in Barthes, *Image–Music–Text*, p. 158.

While Leavis deplores the way Shelley's metaphors seem to generate themselves with no reference to 'sense', Barthes would no doubt have celebrated this as 'the generation of the perpetual signifier'. And Barthes's remarks also seem appropriate to the metaphors in 'Prufrock', which do not operate simply as the first stage of meaning – a figurative way of referring to something which we simply translate back into its 'proper' meaning – but as elements in the text which resist being translated into 'literal meanings', signifiers which refuse to yield up their signifieds. The effect of this is both aesthetic and cognitive. Readers may experience a unique kind of pleasure in reading such poetry which is derived not from reducing each element of the figurative language to single, stable meanings but from the way the figures intrigue us *because* they resist final closure and disclosure.

Exercises

1 Read the following poem several times, then carry out the instructions which follow.

> I wandered lonely as a cloud
> That floats on high o'er vales and hills,
> When all at once I saw a crowd,
> A host, of golden daffodils;
> Beside the lake, beneath the trees,   5
> Fluttering and dancing in the breeze.
>
> Continuous as the stars that shine
> And twinkle on the milky way,
> They stretched in never-ending line
> Along the margin of a bay: 10
> Ten thousand saw I at a glance,
> Tossing their heads in sprightly dance.
>
> The waves beside them danced; but they
> Outdid the sparkling waves in glee;
> A poet could not but be gay,   15
> In such a jocund company;
> I gazed – and gazed – but little thought
> What wealth to me the show had brought:
>
> For oft, when on my couch I lie
> In vacant or in pensive mood,   20
> They flash upon that inward eye

> Which is the bliss of solitude;
> And then my heart with pleasure fills,
> And dances with the daffodils.
>
> (Wordsworth, 1807)

(a) Go through the poem marking or highlighting all the metaphors which the speaker uses for the daffodils. Is there any consistent pattern or trend in the way the flowers are figured? What connotations are transferred to the daffodils?

(b) Analyse the simile in the poem's first two lines: what connotations are transferred onto the speaker and his wandering?

(c) Compare the way the speaker figures himself with the way he figures the daffodils. What does this reveal about the speaker's relation to the daffodils?

(d) Look at the metaphor in the poem's last line. In what way does this metaphor resolve the 'problem' which the poem explores?

(e) Would you say that the poem's metaphors and similes are far-fetched and incongruous or do they seem appropriate and natural?

(f) If you did not know that the poem was by Wordsworth, is there anything about its use of metaphor which would lead you to suspect that it is a Romantic poem (or even a Wordsworth poem) rather than a Renaissance, Metaphysical, Neoclassical or Modernist poem?

2 Read the following poem several times and then carry out the instructions which follow.

Pet Panther

My attention is a wild
animal: it will if idle
make trouble where there
was no harm: it will

sniff and scratch at the   5
breath's sills:
it will wind itself tight
around the pulse

or, undistracted by
verbal toys, pommel the   10
heart frantic: it will
pounce on a stalled riddle

and wrestle the mind numb:
attention, fierce animal
I cry, as it coughs in my   15
face, dislodges boulders

in my belly, lie down, be
still, have mercy, here
is song, coils of song, play
it out, run with it.   20
(A.R. Ammons, 1983)

(a) Begin by concentrating on the poem's initial metaphor. Would you say that it is far-fetched or appropriate? What is the ground of the metaphor – that is, what similarity is there between vehicle and tenor? What connotations are transferred from vehicle to tenor?

(b) Now go through the poem highlighting or marking all the other metaphors. To what extent can the poem be seen as an extended metaphor which elaborates the initial metaphor?

(c) For each metaphor, try to decide if it is far-fetched or appropriate by asking what similarity there is between vehicle and tenor. Are there any metaphors which seem particularly incongruous?

(d) Would it be accurate to describe the poem as playfully extending an initially congruous metaphor in ways which lead to incongruity?

(e) To what extent do the metaphors in the poem's last lines resolve the 'problem' which the poem deals with? Is it possible that these lines offer a metaphor for the use of metaphors in the poem as a whole?

(f) In what way do the poem's metaphors characterise it as a twentieth-century poem?

3 Read the following poem several times and then carry out the instructions which follow.

Fetching Cows

The black one, last as usual, swings her head
And coils a black tongue round a grass-tuft. I
Watch her soft weight come down, her split feet spread.

In front, the others swing and slouch; they roll
Their great Greek eyes and breathe out milky gusts   5
From muzzles black and shiny as wet coal.

The collie trots, bored, at my heels, then plops
Into the ditch. The sea makes a tired sound
That's always stopping though it never stops.

A haycart squats prickeared against the sky.   10
Hay breath and milk breath. Far out in the West
The wrecked sun founders though its colours fly.

The collie's bored. There's nothing to control . . .
The black cow is two native carriers
Bringing its belly home, slung from a pole.   15

(Norman MacCaig, 1965)

(a) This poem is full of figures and images, but before looking at these we want
to anticipate some of the things we shall be attending to in our next chapter
by asking you to identify the speaker. Who is 'fetching cows' in the poem?
Who is the 'I' who addresses us at the end of line 2? Can you situate the
speaker in relation to the things he is observing or talking about? Where is
the action occurring? (It may or may not help you to know that MacCaig
was a Scottish poet.)

(b) Try to identify any images in the poem which have to be seen as metaphors
(or similes) and not as literal descriptions. Look up in a dictionary any words
you are not sure you understand, e.g. 'founders', or any words that might
have secondary meanings that you are not aware of, e.g., 'colours' (12).
Remember our 'acid test' for identifying metaphors which we offered early
on in Chapter 5 and also what we say there about 'Metaphors as Different
Parts of Speech'.

(c) Select three or four of the most striking or interesting of the metaphors or
similes you have identified and analyse them into tenor, vehicle and ground.
Then try to describe the meaning or effect of each metaphor in the context
of the poem as a whole.

(d) Identify any images in the poem that can be read literally and not figura-
tively. What do they contribute to our overall impression of the cows or the
scene as a whole?

(e) Are all the poem's images or metaphors visual? Can we speak of 'auditory
images'?

(f) What, in the light of your answers to these questions, is the speaker's atti-
tude towards 'fetching cows'? How do the ways he describes them or his
surroundings – whether literal or metaphorical – express this attitude?

(g) Might there be some ambiguity in the title? Try looking up 'fetch' and 'fetching' in your dictionary, even though you think you know what they mean. Which of the various meanings are appropriate to the poem? How do these meanings affect your sense of the poem's tone (i.e., the speaker's attitude towards his job or towards the cows)? (Thinking about this poem's use of figurative language and images has necessarily led to questions of tone, attitude and ambiguity – the topics of the next three chapters.)

Chapter 7

Hearing Voices in Poetic Texts

In his *Glossary* entry on 'Persona, Tone, and Voice', M.H. Abrams points out, 'we tend to think of all works of literature . . . as a mode of speech' (p. 155), or , as Patricia Parker puts it, 'in the absence of contrary indications, we infer a voice even though we know that we are reading words on a page'.[1] In reading poetry, this tendency can perhaps be related to the origins of poetry in oral performance, though we will argue that there are other factors at work as well. But if reading does consist in the automatic translation of writing into imaginary speech, then it seems possible to ask two questions: 'Who speaks the words on the page?' and 'How did we come to "overhear" these words?'

■ Voices from Beyond the Grave[2]

We can usefully ask these questions of a poem by Chidiock Tichborne, who was executed in 1586, shortly after the poem was written.

Tichborne's Elegy
WRITTEN WITH HIS OWN HAND
IN THE TOWER BEFORE HIS EXECUTION

My prime of youth is but a frost of cares,
My feast of joy is but a dish of pain,

---

[1] Patricia Parker, introduction to Chaviva Hošek and P. Parker, eds, *Lyric Poetry: Beyond the New Criticism* (Ithaca, NY: Cornell University Press, 1985), p. 16.

[2] For a lively discussion of the notion that all texts 'can be thought of as involving a voice from beyond the grave', see Andrew Bennett and N. Royle, *An Introduction to Literature, Criticism and Theory: Key critical concepts* (Hemel Hempstead: Harvester Wheatsheaf, 1995), pp. 57–64.

My crop of corn is but a field of tares,
And all my good is but vain hope of gain;
The day is past, and yet I saw no sun,   5
And now I live, and now my life is done.

My tale was heard and yet it was not told,
My fruit is fallen and yet my leaves are green,
My youth is spent and yet I am not old,
I saw the world and yet I was not seen;   10
My thread is cut and yet it is not spun,
And now I live, and now my life is done.

I sought my death and found in it my womb,
I looked for life and saw it was a shade,
I trod the earth and knew it was my tomb,   15
And now I die, and now I was but made;
My glass is full, and now my glass is run,
And now I live, and now my life is done.

In reading this poem, do you infer or imagine that it is being spoken? If so, who speaks the words of this poem which has been printed on the page you are reading? And is the speaker speaking to you, to someone else, or to no one at all? Pause for a moment and try to answer these questions.

If Abrams is correct in his supposition that we tend to think of written literary texts as being spoken, it is likely that you will have experienced 'Tichborne's Elegy' as speech. And because we tend to think of texts as being spoken by their author you may have decided that it is Tichborne himself who is speaking the text. But you may have more difficulty in deciding who he is speaking to. We might imagine that there was someone in the Tower of London with him at the time (perhaps a confessor), but the poem seems more like the kind of solitary self-reflection which might be stimulated by the imminent prospect of being executed. Yet if it is that, how is it that we come to 'hear' (or 'overhear') this speech more than four hundred years after the author's death? Speech is an ephemeral medium – it perishes in the moment it is uttered. If the poet *spoke* the words in 1586, then he cannot be *speaking* them in 2006 (as we re-write this book), or in whatever year you come to read it. Unless, that is, we think of the poet as continually speaking to us from beyond the grave.

The poem's title and epigraph were supplied by its early publisher (they are clearly not by Tichborne, since they refer to him in the third person). 'Elegy' is a generic term which usually refers to a 'lament in verse for a particular person' (Abrams, *Glossary*). We thus have the unusual situation here of the poet writing his own elegy in anticipation of his coming death. The epigraph indicates the mode of his death and stresses the context in which the poem came to be written. We do not know why Tichborne wrote the poem, though it may have been for private circulation among his family or friends. But the poem also has similarities with the kind of consoling or commemorative inscriptions scratched on the walls and windows of the Tower of London and other places of confinement (examples survive). All these circumstances might lead us to suppose that this was a highly personal poem in which the author sums up his feelings at a moment of overwhelming personal crisis in his life. Yet these circumstances also remind us that this poem was *written*, not spoken, and we are forced to recognise that the words of the poem were probably never spoken by its author. And if the author did not speak the words in 1586, he is clearly not speaking them as you read the poem in the twenty-first century. Thus we are forced to recognise the gulf between the long-dead person who once *wrote* this poem and the imaginary voice we hear when we *read* it. In fact, this writing does not record a speech event which once took place in the Tower of London, but *creates* the effect of a speech event whenever it is read. This is why, throughout this book, we distinguish between a poem's author and its speaker. Our experience of hearing (or overhearing) a voice in this text, then, is an illusion created by ourselves because of the way we have been trained to read all writing as if it were speech. Rather than hearing voices from beyond the grave, we create those voices ourselves through an interpretative interaction with written words on a page.

In what follows, we want to stress that 'Tichborne's Elegy' is not an exceptional case. The points we have made can be generalised – not simply because most of the poems we read and study are by poets who are dead but, rather, because the academic study of poetry is mostly devoted to written poetry, poetry on the page. And writing, as Roland Barthes has pointed out in his essay 'The Death of the Author', entails the absence and metaphorical 'death' of the author, whether or not he or she is still alive.[3] The same could be said of an audio-recording of a poet reading his or her poems – the sound of the voice in such a situation does not entail the presence of the author.

■ Voice and Genre

We tend to assume that it is obvious who is speaking in a text. Yet we have seen that asking this question and thinking about our answer can be quite productive. One of the things which this question can lead to is a way of thinking about genre. Narrative fiction, drama and poetry can be distinguished in terms of how they present themselves as speech. Narrative fiction typically consists of the voices of characters framed by a narrator's voice. Drama consists of the

---

[3] Barthes, 'The Death of the Author', in *Image–Music–Text*, pp. 142–8.

voices of characters without a narrator (although the stage directions in play texts have a narrative function, as does the 'chorus' used in some plays). Although we may be tempted to think of poetry as consisting of the direct, unmediated voice of a single poetic speaker, poetry can actually be distinguished into three main genres or kinds: narrative, dramatic and lyric. The distinctions between these genres can be thought of in terms of who speaks the words on the page. Each genre employs its own characteristic way of presenting itself as 'speech', though we need always to remember that none of them presents actual speech but only representations of speech. As Barbara Herrnstein Smith puts it:

> The various genres of literary art can to some extent be distinguished according to what types of discourse – for example, dialogues, anecdotes of past events, public speeches, and private declarations – they characteristically represent. Thus lyric poems typically represent personal utterances.[4]

The fact that 'Tichborne's Elegy' presents itself as an 'utterance by a single speaker, who expresses a state of mind or a process of perception, thought, and feeling', and that the speaker is 'musing in solitude' (see 'elegy' in *Abrams*), marks it out as a lyric poem ('elegy' is one of the sub-genres of lyric). Lyric poetry, then, has its own characteristic way of presenting itself as speech. Keats's 'Ode to a Nightingale' is an example of the Romantic lyric in that it seems to give us access to the speaker's inmost experience in such a way that it appears obvious to assume that the speaker is its author, John Keats. Because the kind of poetry familiar to most modern readers is lyric poetry – and thus resembles 'Tichborne's Elegy' and 'Ode to a Nightingale' – there is a tendency to think that all poetry is like this. We want to show, however, that there are other kinds of poetry which are, in their own way, just as important and interesting as lyric poetry, and that part of their interest is in the different ways they present themselves as speech.

■ Voices in Narrative Poetry

Narrative and dramatic poetry, in contrast with lyric poetry, are organised not as expressions of a single speaker's inner state but as stories involving events and characters. In dramatic poetry, the story is presented through the actions and speech of characters; in **narrative poetry**, the actions and speech of characters are presented through a narrator (the storyteller). When we read a play it is easy to accept the fiction that the words are spoken by the characters, the *dramatis personae*, and that their dialogue is 'overheard' as though the reader were part of the audience. (More problematic, however, are the stage directions

---

[4] Smith, *On the Margins of Discourse* (Chicago: University of Chicago Press, 1978), p. 8.

which are frequently included in play texts, since they do not seem to be spoken at all.) In novels, it is usually possible to interpret the words on the page as either the speech of characters or the words of the narrator. In everyday life we sometimes tell stories about things that have happened to or involved ourselves ('I knocked on the door', or 'we were completely lost', and so on): literary critics call this 'first-person' narration (because it involves the grammatical first person – I, we). But we can also tell stories about things we had no involvement in ('then she started the car . . .' or 'they washed up on an island', and so on): literary critics call this 'third-person' narration (because it involves the grammatical third person – she, he, they). Narrators are thus distinguished into first-person and third-person narrators. First-person narrators are often presented as if they were characters telling the story – Conrad's narrator in *Heart of Darkness* (1899) tells a story about things which happened to him in the Congo, but the novel also includes the circumstances in which he tells the story (he is on a boat on the Thames with some friends). Third-person narrators are more problematic in this respect, since such narrators never refer to themselves in the first person. To a certain extent the third-person narrator is a fiction created as much by the reader as by the author. Indeed, this is a good example of our tendency to process writing as if it were speech. This same habit explains why some readers tend to imagine that the voice of the third-person narrator is that of the author. But academic teachers encourage students to distinguish a novel's fictional narrator from its author because the narrator is always part of a novel's fictional world and effect.

Dramatic and narrative poems resemble plays and novels in terms of how they organise and present themselves as the speech of characters and narrators. The epic narrative poetry and the verse drama of ancient Greece and Rome have been hugely influential on literature in English. Indeed, the Western literary tradition is often said to be founded on the epic narrative poems attributed to Homer, a Greek poet who lived at least 700 years before Christ. Homer's poems – despite the fact that they would probably have been sung 'live' – resemble historical novels narrated in the third person. We can see this from the following passage, taken from a modern translation of the final book of *The Iliad* (*c.* 750 BCE), in which the dead body of the hero Hector is taken back into the city of Troy, which he has been defending:

> The girl wailed and cried
> to all the city: 'Oh, look down, look down,
> go to your windows, men of Troy and women,
> see Lord Hector now! Remember joy
> at seeing him return alive from battle,
> exalting all our city and our land!'
> Now, at the sight of Hector, all gave way

> to loss and longing, and all crowded down
> to meet the escort and body near the gates,
> till no one in the town was left at home.[5]

Narrative poetry appears throughout the English poetic tradition. Popular ballads are typically narrative poems which were once sung or recited by 'bards' who made no claim to be the poem's author. Ballads tend to employ either first-person or third-person narration in fairly strict ways. A good example can be seen in the first two stanzas of the Scottish ballad 'Bonny Barbara Allan':

> It was in and about the Martinmas time,
>   When the green leaves were a falling,
> That Sir John Graeme, in the West Country,
>   Fell in love with Barbara Allan.

> He sent his man down through the town,
>   To the place where she was dwelling:
> 'O haste and come to my master dear,
>   Gin* ye be Barbara Allan'   *if

In the literary tradition, pure third-person narration is comparatively rare in poetry, although Shakespeare's narrative poems, *Venus and Adonis* (1593) and *The Rape of Lucrece* (1594), are early examples. In most of the major narrative poems in English prior to the Romantic period – such as Chaucer's *The Canterbury Tales* (c. 1387–94) and *Troilus and Criseyde* (c. 1385), Spenser's *The Faerie Queene* (1596), Marlowe's *Hero and Leander* (1598), Milton's *Paradise Lost* (1667) and Pope's *The Rape of the Lock* (1712) – the presence of a first-person narrator intrudes in one way or another into what would otherwise be third-person narrative. The use of the 'I' narrator in these poems, however, is typically restricted to a prologue or a preparatory invocation of the Muse, though it occasionally recurs at the end in order to enclose the third-person narrative within a first-person 'frame'.

Under the dual influence of Classical art and the Enlightenment emphasis on reason, much of the poetry produced in the late seventeenth century and much of the eighteenth century tends to be impersonal and hence to be presented in the third person. At the same time, however, the narrative element begins to disappear (perhaps under the influence of the rise of the novel). In this period, long poems presented in the third person tend to be discourses or descriptive

---

[5] Homer, *The Iliad*, trans. Robert Fitzgerald (Oxford, Oxford University Press, 1984), pp. 440–41.

poems rather than narratives. John Dryden pioneered this development in such poems as *Religio Laici* (1682), and it was continued by Alexander Pope in his poetic 'essays' and his various 'epistles'. The trend is well represented by Samuel Johnson in moralising poems such as *The Vanity of Human Wishes* (1749), which begins as follows:

> Let Observation, with extensive view,
> Survey mankind, from China to Peru;
> Remark each anxious toil, each eager strife,
> And watch the busy scenes of crowded life;
> Then say how hope and fear, desire and hate
> O'erspread with snares the clouded maze of fate.

Typical of such poetry at this period is the way the poem claims to rise above the limited view of a single observer in order to 'watch' and 'survey' the whole of 'mankind'. The general moral truth derived from this is presented as the discovery of some impersonal abstraction called 'Observation' rather than the insights of the poet or a first-person narrator.

This stress on impersonal observation can also be found in James Thomson's *The Seasons* (1726), which elevated third-person description of the landscape into a major genre. The following lines from 'Winter' give an idea of this:

> The cherished fields
> Put on their winter robe of purest white.
> 'Tis brightness all; save where the new snow melts
> Along the mazy current. Low the woods
> Bow their hoar head; and, ere the languid sun
> Faint from the west emits his evening ray,
> Earth's universal face, deep hid and chill,
> Is one wild dazzling waste that buries wide
> The works of man. (232–40)

The Seasons was an influential work in what would come to be recognised as a new sub-genre – the loco-descriptive or topographic poem, in which the observation of landscape is coupled with moral observation (John Denham's *Cooper's Hill* (1642) was the English-language pioneer in this genre). Later poems such as Thomas Gray's 'Elegy Written in a Country Churchyard' (1751), Oliver Goldsmith's 'The Deserted Village' (1784) and William Cowper's *The Task* (1785) adapt this genre to their own ends, but more or less retain its 'third-person' technique.

Narrative poetry made an interesting comeback at the end of the eighteenth century, partly because the Romantic poets took a renewed interest in popular ballads and began to write their own ballad-like poems. Wordsworth and Coleridge included ballad-like poems, such as Coleridge's 'The Rime of the Ancient Mariner', in their *Lyrical Ballads* (1798/80). Burns's 'Tam O'Shanter' (1790) imitates the third-person narrative technique of the ballad form. As well as writing intensely first-person lyric poems like 'Ode to a Nightingale', Keats also wrote third-person narrative poems such as *Endymion* (1818) and literary ballads such as 'La Belle Dame sans merci' (1819). In fact, the Romantic poets' renewed interest in narrative poetry suggests that the common view of the Romantic period as concerned solely with lyrical expression is a misreading of Romanticism (partly encouraged by the Romantics themselves). In the Romantic period itself, the Romantic lyrics which we now value were thought to be less original than the narrative poems of Sir Walter Scott such as *Marmion* and 'The Lady of the Lake', or the verse tales of George Crabbe – which are now largely neglected.[6] And by far the most popular poems in the Romantic period were Byron's long narrative poems such as *Don Juan, Childe Harold's Pilgrimage* and *The Corsair*.[7]

One of the purposes of this historical survey of narrative poetry up to the Romantic period is to emphasise that there are other kinds of poem than the Romantic lyric, and many kinds of poetry in which the central interest is not the poetic sensibility of the poet. This needs to be said, because – for reasons which we will touch on – dramatic and narrative poetry have come to be regarded as lesser genres in comparison with the lyric.

▓ The Speech Situation: Voices in Lyric Poems

A glance at recent accounts of the lyric suggests that it is impossible to give an all-encompassing definition of the genre which would fit all sub-genres or individual examples (see 'Lyric' in *Princeton*). A lyric poem is not a song lyric, yet this use of the term lyric for the words of songs points to the history of the lyric as a poetic genre. In ancient Greece, a lyric was sung to the accompaniment of a musical instrument – usually a lyre. The lyric entered English in the form of the songs of wandering minstrels and balladeers. In the Early-Modern

---

[6] In 1812, Francis Jeffrey, one of the leading reviewers of the period, wrote that Crabbe was 'the most original writer who has ever come before us'. There are signs that the critical neglect of Crabbe is coming to an end; his *Selected Poems*, edited by Gavin Edwards, appeared in a Penguin edition in 1991.

[7] The story of narrative poetry does not end with Byron but continues through the Victorian period, when Tennyson's *Idylls of the King* were immensely popular, to the present day. We suggest that you look at poems such as Arthur Hugh Clough's *Amours de Voyage* (1849), Elizabeth Barrett Browning's *Aurora Leigh* (1856), Christina Rossetti's 'Goblin Market' (1862), T.S. Eliot's 'Journey of the Magi' (1927), and many others.

or 'Renaissance' period, however, with the development of printing, the lyric underwent a crucial historical transformation which involved an increasing dissociation between song and lyric. The Renaissance also witnessed a new focus on the individual as a unique human being or subject ('subject' here is a philosophical term meaning something like 'self'– hence 'subjective'). This important development is most clearly manifested in Renaissance portraiture, where the individual personality of the sitter is captured by the artist in a way that was quite unprecedented in the painting of earlier periods. We find a similar development in the lyric's potential for expressing individual selfhood in the poetry of this period, which was also largely unprecedented. Thus a huge range of internal thoughts and feelings – including philosophical questions, religious experience, love, lust, mourning, political comment, and more – became characteristic themes and occasions of lyric expression. But although the lyric thus evolved into a flexible vehicle for a wide variety of thoughts and emotions, and although the Renaissance period has been described as 'the most lyrical of England's poetic eras' (*Princeton*), the lyric was not considered as 'elevated' a genre as drama or epic. This is why the major works of the Renaissance through to the eighteenth century were in verse drama (such as Shakespeare's plays), or in forms which had some affinity with epic narrative.

It is only in the Romantic period – the second great lyrical era – that the lyric (especially the lyric of feeling and meditation) became the pre-eminent poetic genre. Indeed, the major poem of the period – Wordsworth's *The Prelude* (1805) – is a remarkable generic achievement in that it consists of an autobiographical narrative with epic elements mixed in with some of the most wonderful lyric passages in the English language. The potential of the Renaissance lyric for representing individual subjectivity was taken up in the Romantic period in order to explore the central concern of Romanticism: the relationship between individual subjectivity and the processes of imaginative creation (as we saw in 'Ode to a Nightingale'). The lyric speaker thus became associated more than ever with the poet. This association has continued up until the present day in the minds of poets, critics, teachers, students and general readers. We want to stress that this association is not inevitable, and that it came about through historical processes and the promotion of a theory of poetic creativity and reading which has been increasingly challenged from the middle of the twentieth century onwards.

The following poem is an example of a Romantic lyric (which is, in fact, another elegy):

> A slumber did my spirit seal;
> I had no human fears:
> She seemed a thing that could not feel
> The touch of earthly years.

No motion has she now, no force;   5
  She neither hears nor sees;
Rolled round in earth's diurnal course,
  With rocks, and stones, and trees.
          (William Wordsworth, 1800)

Who speaks the words of this poem which has been printed on the page you
are reading? And is the speaker speaking to you, to someone else, or to no one
at all? Pause for a moment and try to answer these questions.

For many students and critics of poetry, the answer to the first of these ques-
tions seems so obvious that the question itself would not seem worth asking.
This question is nevertheless interesting because the 'obvious' answer to it can
differ quite radically according to the reader's underlying assumptions about
poetry. In fact, there are two influential 'interpretive communities'[8] whose very
different answers to this kind of question constitute the opposing sides of a
critical debate which shaped the study of poetry in Anglo-American educa-
tional institutions in the twentieth century. For one set of readers, a (lyric)
poem's speaker is the poet expressing his or her unique and intimate feelings
and experience. For such readers, this seems so obvious that it has become the
very definition of poetry itself, and is often the motivation for reading poetry
in the first place.[9] Such an approach would therefore assume that the first-
person pronouns in 'A slumber did my spirit seal' refer to Wordsworth himself,
and would value the poem because it appears to put us in touch with the pro-
found experience of a profound genius.

A less frequently asked question is how we have come to be privy to these
innermost thoughts of the poet. Do we imagine that Wordsworth is speaking
directly to us in a way which miraculously erases the two-hundred-year gap
between the moment of writing and the moment of reading? Even if we imag-
ine this, is there any sign in the poem that Wordsworth is concerned with
addressing a reader or an audience? Does he not seem, in fact, to be too caught
up in his own sense of love and loss to worry about who 'hears' him? In fact,
our sense of the 'sincerity' of the poet's emotions probably inclines us towards
the latter position, since we tend to believe that sincere feeling is compromised
if the speaker is concerned to 'display' that feeling.

These assumptions about poetic sincerity, solitary emotion and lack of con-
cern about impressing a reader or an audience can be called 'Romantic'

---

[8] This expression was developed by Fish, *Surprised by Sin: The reader in Paradise Lost*,
pp. 325–9.

[9] In 'The Two Kinds of Poetry' (1833), John Stuart Mill claimed that 'Lyric poetry, as it was the
earliest kind, is also . . . more eminently and peculiarly poetry than any other' (in Mill, *Essays
on Poetry*, ed. F. Parvin Sharpless (Columbia: University of South Carolina Press), pp. 28–43
(36)). See also 'genre' in Abrams, *Glossary*.

because they were influentially articulated by the Romantic poets themselves. Perhaps the most famous statement of such beliefs is Wordsworth's assertion (in a preface to the volume of poems in which 'A slumber' first appeared) that 'poetry is the spontaneous overflow of powerful feelings'. The idea that the reader of poetry accidentally 'overhears' a poet's spontaneous overflow was memorably articulated by Shelley in 1818:

> A poet is a nightingale, who sits in darkness and sings to cheer its own solitude with sweet sounds; his auditors are as men entranced by the melody of an unseen musician, who feel that they are moved and softened, yet know not whence or why. (*Shelley's Poetry and Prose*, p. 486)

Thus the poet 'sings' in solitude with no concern for an audience. Readers or 'auditors' simply 'overhear' the poet's self-communion. In 1833, John Stuart Mill developed these ideas into a general definition of poetry:

> Eloquence is *heard*, poetry is *overheard*. Eloquence supposes an audience; the peculiarity of poetry appears to us to lie in the poet's utter unconsciousness of a listener. Poetry is feeling confessing itself to itself, in moments of solitude.[10]

In contrast to eloquence or rhetoric, then, which is designed to impress or move an audience, poetry is supposed to be the private meditation of the poet, produced spontaneously and with no consciousness of, or designs upon, a listener or reader. In fact, it is probably our assurance that we are 'overhearing' spontaneous feeling uttered without any design upon us that allows us to be so moved by it.

The extent to which we share these Romantic assumptions indicates how successfully Romanticism broke the Renaissance connection between poetry and rhetoric. The reason why most contemporary readers are likely to agree with the assumptions of Wordsworth, Shelley, Mill, and others is that these assumptions came to dominate the way poetry was taught in student textbooks, and in British and American schools and universities, until about 1940. Even today, such assumptions continue to be promoted in schools, colleges, universities and popular films, and in most 'handbooks' and 'guides' to poetry.[11]

Yet there is another interpretative community of university-trained readers and teachers who would not agree with such 'Romantic' answers to our questions. Between about 1940 and 1970 the set of reading assumptions and practices which called itself 'New Criticism' encouraged university students of

---

[10] Mill, 'Poetry and its Varieties' (1859), reprinted in Edmund Jones, ed., *English Critical Essays: Nineteenth century* (London: Oxford University Press, 1950), pp. 341–67 (347).

[11] In 1985, Herbert Tucker noted that such assumptions still shaped the expectations of students entering undergraduate classes in the United States; see Tucker, 'Dramatic Monologue and the Overhearing of Lyric', in Hošek and Parker, *Lyric Poetry*, pp. 226–43 (229).

poetry – particularly in the United States – to put aside their Romantic, subjectivist assumptions. One of the basic tenets of New Criticism is 'to assume always that the speaker [of a poem] is someone other than the poet himself'.[12] With this in mind, Robert Scholes offers the following advice to the apprentice reader: 'In beginning our approach to a poem we must make some sort of tentative decision about who the speaker is, what his situation is, and who he seems to be addressing'.[13] Thus New Criticism makes a clear distinction between the poet who wrote a poem and the 'speaker' who is assumed to speak it. The New Critic can be said to be interested in the **'speech situation'** of the poem, and to argue that this can be worked out from details contained in the poem itself. In other words, even a first-person lyric poem is thought of as a kind of dramatic soliloquy spoken by a speaker who is analogous to a character in a play. According to W.K. Wimsatt and Cleanth Brooks, 'Once we have dissociated the speaker of the lyric from the personality of the poet, even the tiniest lyric reveals itself as drama.'[14]

If we think of the 'I' in 'A slumber did my spirit seal' as referring to Wordsworth himself, we can easily be led into asking whether Wordsworth ever had such an experience, and our admiration of the poem might well be affected by the answer. New Critics would argue that such a question may be of interest to a biographer, but not to a literary critic. Attempting to understand the speech situation in Wordsworth's poem allows us to shift away from simply 'appreciating' the poem. If we think of the speaker and the speech situation as aspects of the poem which Wordsworth has created rather than experienced, Scholes's questions can become the starting point of interpretation.

The nature and situation of the speaker of 'A slumber' can be inferred from the poem itself. Unless there is evidence to the contrary, we usually assume that the speaker is the same sex as the author. The location of the speaker's brief but enigmatic meditation on the death of this unidentified female is not, perhaps, the most important question, though we could infer that he is standing by her graveside, since he seems painfully aware that she is now as inanimate as things like 'rocks, and stones, and trees'. A number of critics have sought to identify the 'she' of the poem. Critics problematically associate her with the 'Lucy' of various other poems which Wordsworth wrote about someone called 'Lucy'. Critics make the inference because Wordsworth wrote the 'Lucy poems' at the same time, because he published them more or less as a group, and because the other poems are about the death of Lucy and its effects on the

[12] Laurence Perrine, *Sound and Sense*, 2nd edn (New York: Harcourt Brace Jovanovich, 1963), p. 21.

[13] Robert Scholes, *Elements of Poetry* (New York: Oxford University Press, 1969), pp. 11–12.

[14] W.K. Wimsatt and C. Brooks, *Literary Criticism: A short history* (London: Routledge, 1965), p. 675.

speaker. Biographical research, however, has failed to identify Lucy with a single girl or woman in Wordsworth's life, while other kinds of research have suggested that the name Lucy is partly drawn from several earlier poems by different writers. Coleridge, to whom Wordsworth sent a copy of the poem shortly after it was written, speculated in a letter that 'Most probably in some gloomier moment [Wordsworth] had fancied the moment in which his Sister might die' (Coleridge to Thomas Poole, 6 April, 1799). Although this comment has prompted some rather far-fetched speculations about the poem by recent critics, Coleridge seems to have had no inside information to support his notion. Critics and biographers alike have to remain content with the fact that we shall never know to whom 'she' refers – or even whether 'she' refers to anyone at all.[15]

More interesting than these biographical questions about the 'external' speech situation is the speaker's 'internal situation' – the emotional dilemma of trying to come to terms with the fact that the girl or woman he once thought immortal has died, and is now equivalent to all the other inanimate objects which the earth carries round in its endless turning. Yet such a paraphrase hardly begins to touch upon the ambiguities of the text and the speaker's ambivalences which we infer from them. Thus, for example, we need to ask whether the speaker is blaming himself for 'slumbering' – for the fact that when she was alive he was somehow unaware of her mortality, and hence of how precious she was:

> A slumber did my spirit seal;
>   I had no human fears:
> She seemed a thing that could not feel
>   The touch of earthly years. (1–4)

What, we might ask, does 'human fears' imply in the context of this poem? Is it that the speaker blames himself for being in some way 'inhuman' because his 'spirit' slumbered when she was alive and with him? Or is it that he never fully recognised her humanity – both as someone uniquely valuable and as someone mortal? This ambiguity and ambivalence resonate through the third and fourth lines, which can be read both as a statement of how she seemed eternally young and full of life and as a terrible indictment of the speaker for thinking of her as a 'thing that could not feel' (this is another example of double syntax). And the poignant irony of the second stanza is that she has now become just such an 'immortal' thing:

---

[15] See Brian G. Caraher, *Wordsworth's 'Slumber' and the Problematics of Reading* (Pennsylvania: Pennsylvania State University Press, 1991), pp. 41–2.

> No motion has she now, no force;
>   She neither hears nor sees;
> Rolled round in earth's diurnal course,
>   With rocks, and stones, and trees. (5–8)

These lines memorialise her as being at one with the elemental, unchanging things of nature, but they are also an ironic reflection on the speaker's sense of his inability, when she was alive, fully to realise her mortality and humanity.

Thinking of the voice in 'A slumber did my spirit seal' as that of an invented speaker who is *part of* the poem (rather than its creator) has enabled us to focus on that speaker's emotional drama as the central interpretative interest of the poem. In this way, we have tried to show the kinds of reading which can result from adopting the New Critical assumption of the 'poetic speaker' – even in reading poems (such as Romantic lyrics) in which the voice seems closely identifiable with the poet. Although Romantic lyrics – but not all Romantic poems – seem to present themselves as the intimate speech of the poet, there may be an interpretative payoff for suspending our belief and treating the poetic voice as an invented speaker. On a more general level, there are various theoretical and practical problems involved with the assumption that the speaker is the poet:

1 The assumption that all poems simply recount the author's own feelings or experience excludes the possibility that poets can imagine and write about experiences they have not had and might invent speakers different from themselves for the particular purpose of the poem;
2 We often have no way of telling whether the speaker's experience, feelings and opinions are those of the poet, and it often does not matter: whether or not Wordsworth himself experienced the emotional dilemmas of 'A slumber did my spirit seal' does not affect the poem's power or the way we might interpret it;
3 It is important to maintain the distinction between the voice *in* the poem and the human being who wrote it, because the sense of a human voice speaking a poem is an effect created by the poem: written poems, for the most part, are not recordings of actual speech acts but fictional utterances in which the utterance itself is part of the fiction, part of the poem's effect and meaning.

This last point attempts to stress that poems are not the written records of actual speech acts, but written texts which present themselves *as if* they were speech acts. Lyric poems are not real utterances but fictional representations of utterances.

Some of these points can be supported through looking at some poems in which it would clearly be an interpretative error to believe that the speaker is the author. Emily Dickinson's 'I heard a Fly buzz – when I died' (*c.* 1862) is a case in point:

I heard a Fly buzz – when I died –
The Stillness in the Room
Was like the Stillness in the Air –
Between the Heaves of Storm –

The Eyes around – had wrung them dry –   5
And Breaths were gathering firm
For that last Onset – when the King
Be witnessed – in the Room –

I willed my Keepsakes – Signed away
What portion of me be   10
Assignable – and then it was
There interposed a Fly –

With Blue – uncertain Buzz –
between the light – and me –
And then the Windows failed – and then   15
I could not see to see –

In fact, such a poem reveals some of the problems of the division of poems into the generic categories of dramatic, narrative and lyric. Although this poem would be classed as a lyric, it clearly has narrative and dramatic elements since the speaker can be thought of only as a dramatic character or a fictional narrator who recounts what amounts to a story about her own death. As Dickinson herself suggested, the speaker of a poem is 'a supposed person'.[16]

Dickinson's poem is not an isolated or extreme case, but typical of a large body of lyrical poems spoken by obviously fictional speakers. Indeed, the invention of poetic speakers can be seen as one of the richest and most fundamental aspects of poetic creativity. In many cases – as in 'I heard a Fly buzz' – the whole poem seems to be generated out of the invention of the speaker. Langston Hughes's 'The Negro Speaks of Rivers' (1926) is another example:

The Negro Speaks of Rivers
(TO W.E.B. DUBOIS)

I've known rivers:
I've known rivers ancient as the world and older than the
    flow of human blood in human veins.

My soul has grown deep like the rivers.

---

[16] Letter to T.W. Higginson, July 1862, in *The Letters of Emily Dickinson*, ed. Mabel L. Todd (London: Victor Gollancz, 1951), p. 257.

I bathed in the Euphrates when dawns were young.
I built my hut near the Congo and it lulled me to sleep.   5
I looked upon the Nile and raised the pyramids above it.
I heard the singing of the Mississippi when Abe Lincoln

went down to New Orleans, and I've seen its muddy
bosom turn all golden in the sunset.
I've known rivers:
Ancient, dusky rivers.

My soul has grown deep like the rivers.   10

Although this poem is spoken in the first person, the speaker's claims about his experience clearly go beyond what is possible for an individual human being. The longer central section of the poem suggests that this consciousness has lived through all of black history, from the origins of life in Africa through to the construction of the pyramids. It also takes in the American experience of slavery and the struggle against it. Thus this speaker identifies himself with and speaks for all African-Americans, and the poem works to raise and expand political consciousness and to celebrate the African and American history of black people. Yet the speaker goes beyond even this by claiming that his experience of rivers has allowed him to become 'deep like the rivers' and to know and identify with rivers which are 'ancient as the world and older than the flow of human blood in human veins'.

▧ Voices in Dramatic Poetry

In this book we do not pay much attention to poetic drama (such as Shakespeare's plays) on the basis that they are plays in verse designed primarily for the stage. Yet there is a significant body of dramatic poetry, as opposed to poetic drama, which also complicates the question of 'who speaks?' So-called 'closet drama' is written in the form of drama, but designed to be read rather than performed. There are important examples of closet drama written in verse, such as Milton's *Samson Agonistes* (1671) and Shelley's *Prometheus Unbound* (1820). Yet this is not the only kind of dramatic poetry.

Some dramatic poetry resembles drama by placing two or more speakers in dialogue with one another. Sometimes the dialogue is made explicit – as in Samuel Daniel's 'Ulysses and the Siren' (1605), a restaging of Ulysses' temptation by the Siren which first occurs in Homer's *Odyssey*. This is the first exchange in a dialogue that extends to seventy-two lines:

SIREN. Come, worthy Greek, Ulysses, come,
Possess these shores with me;

The winds and seas are troublesome,
And here we may be free.
Here may we sit and view their toil   5
That travail in the deep,
And joy the day in mirth the while,
And spend the night in sleep.

ULYSSES. Fair nymph, if fame or honour were
To be attained with ease,   10
Then would I come and rest me there,
And leave such toils as these.
But here it dwells, and here must I
With danger seek it forth;
To spend the time luxuriously   15
Becomes not men of worth.

Other multi-voiced poems leave the reader to identify the situation and charac-
terise the different voices – as in Josephine Miles's 'Reason' (1956):

Said, Pull her up a bit will you, Mac, I want to unload
    there.
Said, Pull her up my rear end, first come first serve.
Said, Give her the gun, Bud, he needs a taste of his own
    bumper.
Then the usher came out and got into the act:

Said, Pull her up, pull her up a bit, we need this space,
    sir.   5
Said, For God's sake, is this still a free country, or
    what?
You go back and take care of Gary Cooper's horse
And leave me handle my own car.

Saw them unloading the lame old lady,
Ducked out under the wheel and gave her an elbow,   10
Said, All you needed to do was just explain;
Reason, Reason is my middle name.

▢ The Dramatic Lyric, the Addressee and the Reader

If such poems seem to stretch conventional definitions of the lyric to the limit,
the genre is also creatively modified in the so-called 'dramatic lyric'. In one
kind of dramatic lyric, the speaker addresses another person in a specific situ-
ation; although the 'addressee' is implicitly present, he or she makes no reply.

There are numerous examples of this kind of dramatic lyric, but it can be exemplified by the first two lines of Marvell's 'To His Coy Mistress' (1681), which quickly establish the dramatic situation:

> Had we but world enough, and time,
> This coyness, lady, were no crime.

Dramatic lyrics in which male speakers attempt to woo or seduce female characters who are implicitly present were quite common in the sixteenth and seventeenth centuries. Such poems can usefully alert us to the importance of distinguishing between the addressee and the implied reader. The way in which the situation of the speaker is dramatised in such seduction scenarios means that it is not just the speaker who is presented as a character placed in what is evidently a fictional or dramatic situation, but also the woman he is addressing. In such cases the addressee – the woman – is as much an imaginary construct as the speaker. This fictional, dramatised addressee needs to be distinguished from the audience or readership for which the poem was written. In this example, while the addressee is the (fictional) woman whom the speaker is trying to seduce, the poem's intended readership might well be a group of (mostly male) readers who would be expected to admire the speaker's seductive strategies. Scholars sometimes search out evidence for the actual readership – in contemporary documents such as catalogues of people's libraries, correspondence, and the like. And they may also try to discover the 'real' identity of a poem's addressee – as in the search to identify the young man or the 'dark lady' of Shakespeare's sonnets. But such evidence is external to the poem, and doesn't affect our reading of it as a poem (as opposed to a historical document). The characteristics of a poem's intended reader can often be derived from implicit clues in the poem itself. Similar effects in novels led Wolfgang Iser to develop the notion of the 'implied reader'.[17] The implied reader of a poem is an imaginary reader whose world view and reading experience are appropriate for responding to the poem in the appropriate way. Thus if a poem makes use of, say, double syntax or a rhyme pair that sets up a significant semantic relationship between the paired words, the poem anticipates a reader (an implied reader) who is capable of spotting and understanding such devices. It is thus to be hoped that readers of the present book are equipping themselves to become more and more like the implied readers for whom poets design their poems. Having said this, there might be some cases where the reader might wish to distance him or herself from the implied reader.

The identification of the implied reader becomes most interesting where his or her sex, social class or cultural and political status are different from those

---

[17] Wolfgang Iser, *The Implied Reader: Patterns of communication in prose fiction from Bunyan to Beckett* (Baltimore, MD: Johns Hopkins University Press, 1974).

of the addressee. This can, perhaps, be seen in Donne's 'The Flea' (1633), in which the speaker uses the actions of a flea as the occasion for a series of conceits designed to seduce the female addressee:

> Mark but this flea, and mark in this,
> How little that which thou deny'st me is;
> Me it sucked first, and now sucks thee,
> And in this flea, our two bloods mingled be;
> Confess it, this cannot be said   5
> A sin, or shame, or loss of maidenhead,
>   Yet this enjoys before it woo,
>   And pampered swells with one blood made of two,
>   And this, alas, is more than we would do.
>
> Oh stay, three lives in one flea spare,   10
> Where we almost, nay more than married are.
> This flea is you and I, and this
> Our marriage bed, and marriage temple is;
> Though parents grudge, and you, we're met,
> And cloistered in these living walls of jet.   15
>   Though use make you apt to kill me,
>   Let not to this, self-murder added be,
>   And sacrilege, three sins in killing three.
>
> Cruel and sudden, hast thou since
> Purpled thy nail, in blood of innocence?   20
> In what could this flea guilty be,
> Except in that drop which it sucked from thee?
> Yet thou triumph'st, and say'st that thou
> Find'st not thyself, nor me the weaker now;
>   'Tis true, then learn how false, fears be;   25
>   Just so much honour, when thou yield'st to me,
>   Will waste, as this flea's death took life from thee.

The dramatic situation in this poem is more fully developed than it is in most examples of this tradition of seduction lyrics, such as Marvell's 'To His Coy Mistress', in so far as each stanza develops the speaker's argument one stage further in response to an implied action on the part of the woman. Line 10, 'Oh stay, three lives in one flea spare', for instance, requires the reader to imagine that she has just attempted to squash the flea, whereas the last stanza implies that she has disregarded his plea and has killed it: 'Cruel and sudden, hast thou since / Purpled thy nail, in blood of innocence?' (19–20). Much of the wit of the poem relies on the speaker's rhetorical skill in capitalising on these imaginary actions by turning them to his own argumentative advantage.

227

The way he offers reassurance to the woman by trying to convince her that submission to him will not compromise her moral and religious scruples also offers us – by implication, at least – some impression of her character. Thus in the first stanza he argues that it would be no 'sin, or shame, or loss of maidenhead', and in the second the metaphors of 'marriage temple' and 'cloistered' walls imply that their union would somehow not violate her religious scruples (though there is a paradox here, since 'cloistered' implies a monastic chastity which is incompatible with marriage). But if such gestures of assurance are clearly addressed to the woman, it is less easy to say with any confidence for whose benefit the wit is being manifested. The speaker could, of course, be trying to laugh her into bed, but it is equally possible to argue that the wit in such a poem is being displayed for the entertainment of an implied reader who is not the woman, and that it is possibly being displayed at her expense. It makes some difference to the sexual politics of such a poem if we assume that the implied reader is probably male. We are not arguing that this is the only way of reading the poem, or that all Donne's love lyrics imply a male reader, but we do want to stress that it could be important to make a distinction between the addressee and the implied reader, particularly when the speaking voice in the poem is as strongly dramatised as it is in 'The Flea'.

Not all love lyrics of this period deny the female addressee a voice. In Sir Walter Ralegh's 'The Nymph's Reply to the Shepherd' (1600), the nymph responds to Christopher Marlowe's 'The Passionate Shepherd to His Love' (1599). Marlowe's shepherd attempts to woo 'his love' by promising her all the pleasures of a pastoral existence:

> Come live with me and be my love,
> And we will all the pleasures prove. (1–2)

Ralegh's 'nymph' replies in a sceptical vein:

> If all the world and love were young,
> And truth in every shepherd's tongue,
> These pretty pleasures might me move
> To live with thee and be thy love. (1–4)

All such dialogues are the voices of invented, fictionalised or dramatic speakers: Marlowe's shepherd is as much a **persona** as Ralegh's nymph.

■ The Dramatic Monologue

In the nineteenth century a number of poets developed the dramatic lyric into what we now call the dramatic monologue. This kind of poem, which is similar to a speech in a play, usually has the following features:

1 The poem is uttered by a single speaker who is clearly not the poet, and the utterance takes place in a specific situation at a critical moment;
2 The speaker addresses and interacts with one or more auditors, although this is revealed only by what the single speaker says (the auditor's 'replies' are not given as such in the text);
3 The speaker's utterance reveals his or her character to the reader.

Points (1) and (3) are supposed to distinguish the dramatic monologue from the dramatic lyric, but there is clearly a varying amount of overlap between specific examples of the two sub-genres.

Isobel Armstrong has suggested that the dramatic monologue was invented by women poets in the early nineteenth century.[18] A major pioneer was Felicia Hemans, whose collection of fifty-seven poems, *Records of Woman: With Other Poems* (1828), includes a number of poems in which real historical women are given imagined speeches in imagined situations.[19] Poems such as 'Properzia Rossi' can be seen as establishing the generic conventions of the dramatic monologue. Working out the speech situation of 'A Spirit's Return' is one of its major challenges, but the realisation that it is a dramatic monologue is a hugely important step in understanding how this poem significantly reworks the conventions of Romantic poetry. Later users of dramatic monologue include Charlotte Brontë and Tennyson, but Robert Browning is the poet who has become most closely identified with the genre. His 'My Last Duchess' (1842) has become the genre's model poem:

My Last Duchess
FERRARA

> That's my last Duchess painted on the wall,
> Looking as if she were alive. I call
> That piece a wonder, now: Frà Pandolf's hands
> Worked busily a day, and there she stands.
> Will't please you sit and look at her? I said   5
> 'Frà Pandolf' by design, for never read
> Strangers like you that pictured countenance,
> The depth and passion of its earnest glance,

---

[18] Armstrong, *Victorian Poetry*, pp. 325–6. The standard discussion of the genre is Robert Langbaum, *The Poetry of Experience: The dramatic monologue in modern literary tradition* (Chicago: University of Chicago Press, 1957). There is a case, we suggest, for arguing that the prologues of Chaucer's *Canterbury Tales* (c. 1387) can be regarded as dramatic monologues (see the exercise at the end of Chapter 16 of the present book).

[19] See Felicia Hemans, *Records of Woman: With Other Poems*, ed. Paula R. Feldman (Kentucky: University of Kentucky Press, 1999).

But to myself they turned (since none puts by
The curtain I have drawn for you, but I)   10
And seemed as they would ask me, if they durst,
How such a glance came there; so, not the first
Are you to turn and ask thus. Sir, 'twas not
Her husband's presence only, called that spot
Of joy into the Duchess' cheek: perhaps   15
Frà Pandolf chanced to say 'Her mantle laps
'Over my lady's wrist too much,' or 'Paint
'Must never hope to reproduce the faint
'Half-flush that dies along her throat': such stuff
Was courtesy, she thought, and cause enough   20
For calling up that spot of joy. She had
A heart – how shall I say? – too soon made glad,
Too easily impressed; she liked whate'er
She looked on, and her looks went everywhere.
Sir, 'twas all one! My favour at her breast,   25
The dropping of the daylight in the West,
The bough of cherries some officious fool
Broke in the orchard for her, the white mule
She rode with round the terrace – all and each
Would draw from her alike the approving speech,   30
Or blush, at least. She thanked men, – good! but thanked
Somehow – I know not how – as if she ranked
My gift of a nine-hundred-years-old name
With anybody's gift. Who'd stoop to blame
This sort of trifling? Even had you skill   35
In speech – (which I have not) – to make your will
Quite clear to such an one, and say, 'Just this
'Or that in you disgusts me; here you miss,
'Or there exceed the mark' – and if she let
Herself be lessoned so, nor plainly set   40
Her wits to yours, forsooth, and made excuse,
– E'en then would be some stooping; and I choose
Never to stoop. Oh sir, she smiled, no doubt,
Whene'er I passed her; but who passed without
Much the same smile? This grew; I gave commands;   45
Then all smiles stopped together. There she stands
As if alive. Will't please you rise? We'll meet
The company below, then. I repeat,
The Count your master's known munificence
Is ample warrant that no just pretence   50

> Of mine for dowry will be disallowed;
> Though his fair daughter's self, as I avowed
> At starting, is my object. Nay, we'll go
> Together down, sir. Notice Neptune, though,
> Taming a sea-horse, thought a rarity,   55
> Which Claus of Innsbruck cast in bronze for me!

One of the reasons why this poem might seem initially inaccessible is that it only gradually releases the clues which allow us to work out who the speaker is, what his situation is, and whom he seems to be addressing. Piecing together the clues, we can infer that the speaker is showing a stranger around his house, and has drawn back a curtain before a picture of his 'last duchess' painted by a certain Frà Pandolf. The stranger seems to have been struck by the look on the woman's face (the 'glance' or 'spot of joy'), which must be quite striking since everyone who sees it apparently wishes to know how it 'came there' (6–12). The Duke answers at some length that such a look was always on her face because she was always flirting with all the men she encountered – including the artist on the day he painted her. Not willing to lower himself ('to stoop') in order to correct her in this, the Duke tells his auditor: 'I gave commands; / Then all smiles stopped together' (45–46). This is a chilling moment in the poem because the Duke seems to have revealed – whether inadvertently or not – that he had his wife killed because of her behaviour. This moment of horror is compounded by the way he reverts to polite affability with the stranger, and returns to a topic of conversation which they have evidently been pursuing:

> Will't please you rise? We'll meet
> The company below, then. I repeat,
> The Count your master's known munificence
> Is ample warrant that no just pretence
> Of mine for dowry will be disallowed;
> Though his fair daughter's self, as I avowed
> At starting, is my object. Nay, we'll go
> Together down, sir. (47–54)

We infer from this that the stranger is the representative of a Count, that the two of them are negotiating a marriage settlement between the Duke and the Count's daughter, and that the Count and his daughter are waiting 'below'. This gives a horrifying twist to the monologue since it offers a whole new perspective on what has gone before.

In the course of this conversation about the painting of his previous wife, then, the Duke does indeed reveal his character. An inevitable question is whether he does it deliberately or whether it is accidental. On the one hand, it would seem a terrible blunder to reveal, in the midst of marriage negotiations, that he had his last wife murdered because she enjoyed the attentions of other men. On the other hand, however, such a hint might well serve as a warning to his wife-to-be about what she can expect if she behaves in a similar way. Whichever way we answer this question, the Duke emerges as a terrifyingly powerful and callous man, sexually jealous and possessive, able to use his power and wealth to commit murder with impunity, and feeling a certain 'disgust' for women and sexuality. Although he seems to be a lover of art, the objects he collects seem designed merely to demonstrate his power and wealth. Having had his wife murdered because he was unable to control her and keep her from responding to the looks of other men, he now controls the display of her portrait by unveiling it to selected guests. And in a revealing ambiguity, he tells the Count's representative that his 'object' (the material thing which is his aim) is the Count's 'fair daughter's self' (52–53).

This rather disturbing poem, then, seems a long way from the Romantic lyric. It is hard to imagine that the speaker is representative of any aspect of the poet's own self. And even the way the poem's knotty syntax is locked within the rhymed iambic pentameter seems to prevent any feeling of spontaneous flowing verse. Even though the Victorian period as a whole was heavily influenced by the Romantic poets, we can thus trace a significant strand of ambivalent revolt in Browning's exploration of the possibilities of the dramatic monologue.[20] It was this attempt to develop a poetic form which broke with Victorian Romanticism which attracted the Modernist poets of the early twentieth century to the dramatic monologue. We have already looked at the best-known and most influential Modernist dramatic monologue – Eliot's 'The Love Song of J. Alfred Prufrock' (1917). The poem's opening lines signal both their genre and their Modernist anti-lyricism:

> Let us go then, you and I,
> When the evening is spread out against the sky
> Like a patient etherized upon a table.

If Browning's Duke of Ferrara alludes scathingly to a nexus of Renaissance and Romantic lyrics in dismissing his wife's response to 'The dropping of the daylight in the West' (26), Prufrock's description of the evening seems utterly devoid of any nostalgia for Romanticism.

---

[20] For an interesting discussion of the way Browning's dramatic monologues constitute an ambivalent resistance to Romantic lyricism, see Tucker in Hošek and Parker, *Lyric Poetry*, pp. 226–39.

◼ Challenges to Reading Poetry as Speech: Modernism and Intertextuality

Modernist poetry constitutes a crucial episode in the story we are telling in this chapter. We have seen that each of the three main poetic genres – narrative, dramatic and lyric – is fundamentally bound up with the understanding of poetry as speech. Poems such as Eliot's *The Waste Land* (1922) and Ezra Pound's *The Cantos* (1921–69) refuse to conform to any of these genres, breaking up and toying with each genre in ways which result in a poetry that refuses to comply with our habitual desire to translate writing into speech. *The Waste Land* is a poem made up of a multiplicity of anonymous 'voices' woven in with quotations and allusions from all kinds of texts. The overall effect is that the reader finds it impossible to construct a coherent narrative or lyric experience, or to imagine that the poem could somehow represent the speech of a single narrator, lyric speaker or poetic voice.

In the later *Cantos* this process is taken to extremes, especially in Pound's frequent use of Chinese writing. Chinese writing consists of ideograms which are not based, as most Western writing is, on a phonetic alphabet. This means that the Chinese ideogram cannot be seen as merely the written representation of speech, but is irreducibly graphic and even pictorial. For English-speaking readers, such ideograms are literally unreadable writing. Yet even the first **cantos** of Pound's huge 'poem' can be seen to play with and foreground the fact that they are made up of writings which cannot be reduced to speech or be seen as originating in a single human consciousness. The first sixty-seven lines of *Canto* I (1921) consist of what could almost be understood as a dramatic monologue spoken by Odysseus (except that other characters speak to him towards the end). But rather than being an 'original' poem which imagines Homer's hero in a new situation, like Tennyson's 'Ulysses',[21] Pound's text consists of his own translation of a sixteenth-century Latin translation of part of Book XI of Homer's Greek text in which Odysseus descends to the underworld. In this way Pound breaks with our idea that a poem should be an author's original creation. He also hints at the written, textual nature of 'his' poem by referring to the translator in the poem itself. At the end of the translation of the translation, a new 'speaker' makes the following enigmatic comment:

> Lie quiet Divus. I mean, that is Andreas Divus,
> In officina Wecheli, 1538 out of Homer. (68–69)

---

[21] Odysseus is an alternative name for Ulysses, the speaker of Tennyson's dramatic monologue 'Ulysses'. Odysseus/Ulysses is the central character in Homer's epic poem *The Odyssey*.

In these lines, Pound addresses and reveals his 'source' – Andreas Divus being the translator of the text he has 'borrowed' from, and Wechel being a famous sixteenth-century French printing-house ('officina'). The canto then ends as follows:

> And he sailed, by Sirens and thence outward and away
> And unto Circe.
>   Venerandam,
> In the Cretan's phrase, with the golden crown, Aphrodite,
> Cypri munimenta sortita est, mirthful, orichalchi, with golden
> Girdles and breast bands, thou with dark eyelids
> Bearing the golden bough of Argicida. So that: (70–76)

Ending on a colon like this, the poem seems to be torn from a larger written text. Its intertextual nature is exemplified in that word 'Venerandam', which the poem itself tells us is a 'Cretan's phrase'. The editors of the *Norton Anthology of Poetry* (4th edition) present the following information in a footnote:

> 'Worthy of worship,' applied to Aphrodite. This, like the Latin words and phrases in the next lines, derives from a Latin translation of two Hymns to Aphrodite (among the so-called Homeric Hymns, dating from the eighth to sixth century B.C.). This translation by Georgius Dartona Cretensis was contained in the volume in which Pound had found Divus's translation of the *Odyssey*. (p. 1201)

Pound and Eliot, then, developed a collage technique of assembling poems which effectively breaks the association between literature and speech that had held since Homer. Appropriately enough, this is done through recycling bits and pieces of text taken from the whole written tradition, from Homer to the early twentieth century. In doing this, they worked against the grain of a tradition of Western thought exhibited not only in literature but throughout the history of Western culture.

Pound's and Eliot's avant-garde experiment with poetry has been continued in some recent 'postmodern' poetry but, for reasons we have already suggested, the majority of poets, critics, teachers, students and readers in the early twenty-first century continue to hold what are effectively late-Romantic views about poetry as the precious speech of special beings. In doing so, such readers not only ignore the Modernist experiment and the huge body of non-lyrical poetry in the tradition since Homer, but have also avoided the kinds of questions with which we began this chapter. Although there are poems in the tradition which announce themselves as written – such as Anne Bradstreet's 'A Letter Written to Her Husband, Absent Upon Public Employment' (1678) or Shelley's 'Lines Written in Dejection, Near Naples' (1818) – most poems silently ignore their own written status, and we usually conspire with them.

In announcing the 'death' of the 'Author' in 1968, Barthes was partly summarising the consequences of the Modernist trends we have traced in writers such as Pound and Eliot. Drawing together ideas from Saussurian linguistics and the notion of 'intertextuality' developed by Julia Kristeva (which we will examine further in Chapter 13), Barthes and others produced a 'post-structuralist' literary theory appropriate for the literary practices of European Modernism. Barthes argues that to ask who is speaking the words of a literary text is an undecidable question, since any statement in a text is inextricably shaped by the innumerable 'voices' which inhabit our culture. Nothing that we say or write can be wholly original, he suggests, because the whole of language is ceaselessly recycled throughout our text-saturated culture. This means that 'a text is a multi-dimensional space in which a variety of writings, none of them original, blend and clash'. The writer does not originate writing out of the depths of his or her soul, but simply mixes pre-existing writings, as we have seen in Pound's *Cantos*. Furthermore, writing entails the absence or loss of the speaking voice: when writing begins, Barthes posits, 'the voice loses its origin' (*Image–Music–Text*, pp. 146, 142). As we saw in our discussion of 'Tichborne's Elegy', writing entails and presupposes the 'death' of the author.

The advent of such post-structuralist theory in France in the late 1960s and early 1970s, and its absorption thereafter by many literary critics and theorists in Britain and the USA, has meant that a theoretical gap has opened up between what many academic teachers assume about literature in their own published research and the assumptions of students entering university and college. In a nutshell, while many teachers assume that literature is an *intertextual* field of writing, many students assume that literature is a mode of intimate speech in which authors communicate their inner selves to the inner self of the reader in what is effectively an *intersubjective* process.

By making its intertextual patchworking unmistakable, Modernist poetry such as Pound's and Eliot's foregrounds its written nature and undermines our attempt to translate it into the speech of a poet or poetic speaker. Post-structuralist accounts of writing and intertextuality claim that these techniques are not confined to Modernism but actually foreground the nature of all writing. In this way, Pound's and Eliot's poetry exposes the problems with attempting to read any poetry as speech. But this is not to say that their poetry is 'better' than poetry which seeks to maintain and exploit the illusion that it is unmediated speech. Nor are we suggesting that you must abandon reading first-person lyric poetry as the unmediated voice of the poet. We do think, however, that you ought to be aware of the problems involved with this assumption, and realise that it is simply one reading strategy among others. And we are also not suggesting that the textual experiments of Pound and Eliot, reinforced by post-structuralist literary theory, mean that we should abandon altogether the New Critical notion of the 'speaker' as a naive attempt to rescue poetry from the impersonality and loss of control entailed by writing. The notion of the 'speaker' is one of the strategies and effects available to poetry, and it helps to account for our sense that poetry can be an intersubjective experience or process. Indeed, as we have suggested, working out a poem's 'speech situation' is usually a crucial step to understanding it – even if the poem works to challenge the idea that poetry equals speech.

Nonetheless, the assumption that poetry is intersubjective does not sit easily alongside the idea that it is an intertextual discourse which apparently problematises the very idea of 'voice' in texts. This leaves theoretically inclined university teachers (and writers of books about poetry such as the present one) with a problem. When we teach students, do we have to abandon the theoretical ideas which we find productive and exciting? Herbert Tucker believes that it only *seems* incumbent on critics and university teachers that they

> choose between intersubjective and intertextual modes of reading, between vindicating the self and saving the text . . . [or become] by turns intertextual readers in the study and intersubjective readers in the classroom.
>
> (Tucker, in Hošek and Parker, pp. 242–3).

Tucker believes that we do not have to choose between these options because recognition of the textuality (written nature) of poems entails recognising that the notion of the speaker is one of the *effects* of that textuality:

> while texts do not absolutely lack speakers, they do not simply have them either; they invent them instead as they go. Texts do not come from speakers, speakers come from texts. . . . To assume in advance that a poetic text proceeds from a speaker is to risk missing the play of verbal implication whereby character is engendered in the first place. . . . At the same time, . . . the ghost conjured by the textual machine . . . remains the articulate phenomenon we call character: a literary effect we ignore at our peril.
>
> (*Lyric Poetry*, p. 243)

We hear voices in written poems, then, not only because we have been trained to do so, but because such ghostly voices are one of the most powerful effects which poems create.[22] In reading poetry, we need to be attentive to the way it dramatises the process by which language creates voices (rather than the other way round). As Tucker puts it, 'Texts do not come from speakers, speakers

---

[22] The claim that voices in poems are textual effects rather than the voices of their authors remains valid even for confessional poetry such as that of Sylvia Plath. While we should not ignore the anguish Plath experienced, nor try to claim that her poetry is not informed by that anguish, we do need to retain the sense that disturbing poems such as 'Elm' (1962/65) or 'Daddy' (1962/65) construct voices rather than giving us an unmediated access to the dead poet's own voice. This point also touches on the way some recent feminist criticism has sought to direct attention to neglected or undervalued poetry by women by arguing that such poetry represents a storehouse of recorded women's voices and experience.

come from texts'. Our task, and our pleasure, as readers is to trace 'the play of verbal implication' that engenders character in poems. And although literary Modernism sought to empty poems of character, more recent poetry has found new ways of exploiting the literary effect we call character. The poetry of Carol Ann Duffy, for example, is particularly inventive in terms of its generation of voice and character. This is most obvious in collections such as *The World's Wife* (1999), which consists of poems that invent scripts for the wives of famous male figures (historical and fictional) – such as 'Mrs Midas' and 'Mrs Darwin'. Yet her poetry in general brings into being a kind of rogues' gallery of strange invented speakers. The following poem, 'Boy', from her 1990 collection *The Other Country*, is simply one example of many:

> I liked being small. When I'm on my own
> I'm small. I put my pyjamas on
> and hum to myself. I like doing that.
>
> What I don't like is being large, you know,
> grown-up. Just like that. Whoosh. Hairy.
> I think of myself as a boy. Safe slippers.
>
> The world is terror. Small you can go *As I*
> *lay down my head to sleep, I pray* . . . I remember
> my three wishes sucked up a chimney of flame.
>
> I can do it though. There was an older woman
> who gave me a bath. She was joking, of course,
> but I wasn't. I said *Mummy* to her. Off-guard.
>
> Now it's a question of getting the wording right
> for the Lonely Hearts verse. There must be someone
> out there who's kind to boys. Even if they grew.

The most striking thing about this poem is the way the language generates a sense of the speaking character (who is obviously not the poet). We will be using this poem for one of the exercises on tone at the end of the following chapter. For now, read it carefully in order to discern the nature and character of the speaker that emerges from it.

Exercises

1 Read the following poem several times, then answer the questions that follow:

Not Waving But Drowning
Nobody heard him, the dead man,
But still he lay moaning:

> I was much further out than you thought
> And not waving but drowning.
>
> Poor chap, he always loved larking
> And now he's dead
> It must have been too cold for him his heart gave way,
> They said,
>
> Oh, no no no, it was too cold always
> (Still the dead one lay moaning)
> I was much too far out all my life
> And not waving but drowning.
>
> (Stevie Smith, 1957)

(a) How many different voices or speakers can you discover in the poem? Label each voice 1, 2, 3, and so on, and mark where each voice begins and ends.

(b) Try to say *why* you think there are different speakers in the poem. (What is it about the language which makes you think there are different speakers?)

(c) Try to define each speaker more exactly. For example, is the speaker first or third person? Try to say who you think each speaker is. Does the poem have a narrator? If so, what kind? Give textual evidence for each decision.

(d) What is the attitude of each speaker to the drowning man (serious, ironic, sympathetic, and so on)? Give textual evidence to support your decision.

(e) What does 'drowning' mean in this poem?

(f) Try to sum up what you think this poem is saying. What contribution does the use of different voices make to this?

2 Read the following poem several times, then answer the questions that follow by quoting or referring to evidence from the text:

What Song the Sirens Sang

> I genuinely wanted them to come.
> It's most important that you understand
> there was no malice in it. Only loss,
> each time, and every time the loss was mine.
> How could it have succeeded, otherwise?   5
> Who embraces death on the strength of some
> lukewarm invitation? No bald command,
> no whore's cold patter gets a man to toss
> his life away. Accident, not design,
> flooded and burst their lungs; I sang no lies.   10

I never lied. I told them what I'd done,
each time. But who was listening to me?
I pointed out my island's grisly necklace
of wave-washed bones; sometimes I even cried,
sincerely, urgently, please, do not come!   15
On the knife horizon, the evening sun
slit his own throat and bled into the sea,
while they, the foolish, fascinated reckless,
jumped in to drown. I watched them as they died,
praying to all the gods to strike me dumb.   20

You understand, I had a job to do.
I did it very well – which doesn't mean
that I was ever satisfied. It was
no joy to me to see what I desired
struggle, fail, die, drift too late to my shore.   25
Why should I bother saying this to you?
Because in all my life I've never been
heard, when I warned 'I'm trouble.' Or because
I want you not to come to me. I'm tired.
I do not want to do this anymore.   30

(Eleanor Brown, 1996)

(a) Who is the speaker of this poem?

(b) Who or what were the Sirens? To answer this, you may need to use a dictio-
nary of classical mythology or the Internet. Also see Samuel Daniel's 'Ulysses
and the Siren' discussed earlier in the present chapter.

(c) How does identifying the speaker help you understand or interpret this
poem?

(d) What is the Sirens' song (both in the myth and in this poem)?

(e) Who is the poem's addressee?

(f) Is the speaker reliable?

(g) What is the poem's genre? How does identifying the poem's genre help you
understand or interpret it?

(h) Does this poem: (i) have a feminist project? (ii) have something to say about
sexual relations in the twenty-first century? How does your answer to these
questions relate to the poem's speech situation?

Chapter 8

Speakers with Attitude: Tone and Irony

In Chapter 7 we examined the arguments for, and the advantages of, regarding poems as fictional representations of different kinds of speech situation. Although we also looked at some poetry and some literary theory which challenge the very basis of this assumption, it nevertheless remains true that most poetry presents itself as some form of speech. Assuming this to be the case, the New Critics went on to suggest that interpreting a poem consists primarily in 'working out, from the textual evidence and from our knowledge of speakers, the nature of the speaker's attitude'.[1] To ask about a speaker's attitude is, as we will show, to ask about his or her tone. This is why, for the New Critics, the question of tone became virtually the central question in the interpretation of lyric poetry. In this chapter, we will examine the way attention to tone – especially irony – can lead to productive readings of poetry which can lead beyond New Criticism's understanding of tone.

▇ Tone in Speech

The word 'tone' primarily refers to qualities of sound. Amplifiers on most sound systems have a tone control which allows you to modify the sound of the music by giving more emphasis either to the low frequency (the bass) or to the high frequency (the treble). Tone is also used to refer to qualities of the human voice. Tone – or intonation – is used specifically to refer to those modulations of voice which we use to convey certain emotions or meanings above and beyond those denoted by the actual words used. Thus we can use the sound of our voice to indicate how we are feeling about ourselves, about the

---

[1] This is Jonathan Culler's succinct summary of the New Critical approach; see Culler, 'Changes in the Study of the Lyric', in Hošek and Parker, *Lyric Poetry*, pp. 38–54 (39).

topic being discussed, or about the person we are addressing: we can speak impatiently, imploringly, despondently, suspiciously, sexily, formally, intimately, solemnly, playfully, angrily, lovingly, seriously, ironically, and so on.

Being alert to tone in everyday conversation is crucial, because tone can convey meanings which may modify or even contradict the literal meaning of what is said. Depending on the context and the relationship between speakers, the same phrase can be said in a range of different tones, and the addressee (the person spoken to) is expected to interpret not merely the statement itself but the way it is modified through tone. Sometimes the tone in which we say something can be completely at odds with the surface meaning of the words we are using. Thus, for example, it is possible to imagine situations in which the way 'I *hate* you!' is said might convey a quite opposite meaning to its face value. Sarcasm is a familiar attitude which exhibits itself by forcing us to reverse the literal meaning of what is said. Depending on tone and context, phrases like 'that's a nice shirt' or 'that was intelligent of you' can be quite the opposite of compliments.

Attention to tone, therefore, reveals that speech is usually produced by what we might call 'speakers with attitude'. A speaker's tone is a clue to her or his attitude: 'The tone of a speaker's voice . . . reveals information about her attitudes, beliefs, feelings, or intent' ('tone' in *Princeton*). An attitude is always directed towards someone or something, and there are four basic directions in which attitude can be focused. Tone of voice may convey an attitude towards the person being addressed, towards the subject matter being talked about, towards the words being used, or towards the speaker him- or herself.

■ Tone in Writing?

Students are often asked in tutorials, and in essay and exam questions, to discuss the tone of a piece of literature. Yet if tone is basically a feature of sound, and is conveyed in speech by modulations of the voice, how can we talk about or detect tone in writing? It seems that the word 'tone' in discussions of literature can be used only figuratively, since we cannot literally hear any voice in a literary text – let alone its tone. When students are asked about tone in literary texts, they are being asked to *imagine* the speaker's tone of voice. This is possible because – as we have seen – tone is primarily a matter of attitude. Thus the question of tone in literature involves working out the general attitude of a text, poetic speaker, narrator or character by making inferences based on the text's language and genre, and the context in which the words are uttered or the text was produced. As in real speech, this attitude may be directed towards the person being addressed (this may be a character, an addressee or the reader), the subject matter being talked about, the words being used or the speaker him- or herself.

▨ Verbal Irony

The New Critics claimed that irony is the most 'mature' literary tone. The term irony comes from the Greek *eironeia*, meaning 'dissimulation in speech'. The verbal dissimulation we call irony typically takes the form of an understatement (or sometimes an overstatement) in which the actual or intended meaning is often the opposite of the apparent meaning. If the price of something you are interested in buying turns out to be far higher than you had imagined, and you say to the shopkeeper something like 'I hope you are making enough profit out of this', then you are ironically implying the opposite – that you think he or she is making far too much profit.

Thus irony can be defined as a figure of speech in which the ironic meaning (what is meant) is the opposite of the literal meaning (what is said). Irony is not lying, however, because the ironist wishes his or her true meaning to be inferred by the addressee, and indicates that meaning through tone of voice, emphasis and gesture. Another important factor in the production and understanding of irony is the context in which the statement is made (as in our example about price). The very disparity between what you say and what you mean has to be recognised, otherwise the irony will be missed. And the point of using irony is to make your real opinion understood in a way which is more effective than straightforward statement. Irony seems to conceal what is really meant, only more effectively to reveal it. It is a mask which is not meant to deceive (Leech, *Linguistic Guide to English Poetry*, p. 171).

The kind of irony we have looked at so far is usually called 'verbal irony' because it relies on a perceived disparity between what someone says and what they mean. Verbal irony can be thought of as a figurative device because the words it uses are not to be taken literally or at face value. Such irony depends on the listener's or reader's skill in detecting the implied meaning behind the actual words used. Irony is thus a kind of linguistic game which requires the participation of the listener or reader in what Abrams calls 'an ultimate test of skill in reading between the lines' (see 'irony' in *Abrams*).[2] As we will see, poetic speakers in lyric poems often make use of verbal irony.

▨ Situational or Structural Irony

In verbal irony, the speaker knowingly produces the irony and recognises the difference between what they say and what they mean. But irony can also be

---

[2] Verbal irony is not the only kind of irony, and we will be looking at some of the others in this chapter. For more inclusive general introductions to irony in literature, see D.C. Muecke's two books *The Compass of Irony* (London: Methuen, 1969) and *Irony* (London: Methuen, 1970). A more advanced discussion is Wayne C. Booth, *A Rhetoric of Irony* (Chicago: University of Chicago Press, 1974). A whimsical, ironic and often insightful discussion may be found in D.J. Enright, *The Alluring Problem: An essay on irony* (Oxford: Oxford University Press, 1968).

produced when a speaker or character says something with sincerity (says it straight) but which is made ironic by the situation – usually because he or she lacks a vital piece of knowledge (which is available to the reader or audience) which would allow them to realise that what they have said cannot be taken seriously as a true view of the situation. In such a situation, the reader or audience sees the irony, while the character or speaker is entirely serious and sincere. It is the reader or audience who sees that matters are actually the opposite of what the character or speaker believes. Such irony is produced by the situation that the text has set up and is therefore called situational or structural irony.

Situational or structural irony, then, is produced when a character or speaker says or does something which we recognise as having an ironic significance of which he or she is unaware. As such, situational irony is often generated in narrative texts where the presence of a narrator gives the reader access to knowledge that may not be available to the characters. One of the great exponents of structural irony in narrative fiction is Jane Austen. In *Emma* (1816), for example, although the eponymous character seems to believe in the self-satisfied self-image she has created for herself, the text allows us to see her in a different, ironic light. Thus we share the ironic attitude of the novel's narrator towards Emma and her actions. In fact, the whole novel can be thought of as an ironic game designed to 'correct' Emma's faults by having her actions ironically rebound on herself in order eventually to make her a fit partner for Mr Knightley. The use of structural irony in *Emma*, then, sets up a distance between the reader and its ironised central character because we are prevented from sharing her opinion of herself. At the same time, however, the novel as a whole balances its ironic criticism of Emma by also encouraging us to empathise with her, and to care about her fate. The overall tone of the novel can therefore be described as a blend of ironic criticism of, and sympathy with, its heroine.

Structural irony can also be created in novels through using a fallible or naive narrator 'whose invincible simplicity or obtuseness leads him to persist in putting an interpretation on affairs which the knowing reader . . . just as persistently is called on to alter and correct' (Abrams, *Glossary*). In such cases we cannot share or sympathise with the narrator's views and so take up an ironic stance towards them. In Mark Twain's *Huckleberry Finn* (1885), however, although we are likely to feel ironically distant from Huck's absurd moral dilemmas over the fact that he has helped a black slave to escape, we cannot help also feeling sympathy towards Huck precisely because of his engaging naivety.

A very different kind of structural irony is at work in Swift's 'A Modest Proposal' (1729), an essay which Swift presents as being written by a 'reasonable' person who has come up with an eminently reasonable and economical solution to the problem of poverty in Ireland – namely, that the children should be converted into butcher's meat. The savagery of Swift's **satire** counts on the reader's ability to measure the distance between the narrator's point of view and the author's. Although Swift's ingenuous Proposer is a very different character from Huck, both are naive narrators and we are not meant to take their views seriously.

■ Dramatic Irony

Dramatic irony is similar to structural irony in narrative fiction. It occurs when the audience or the reader of a play knows more than a character does about the character's situation. There are two main conditions in which dramatic irony arises: when the spectators recognise that what a character is saying or doing is completely at odds with the real circumstances; and when there is an ironic discrepancy between what a character believes about his or her actions and what the play demonstrates about them. Our attitude towards the character in such situations depends upon whether we pity him or her (tragic irony) or enjoy a joke at his or her expense (comic irony).[3] We experience dramatic irony in watching or reading *Othello* because we are made fully aware of Iago's deception of Othello, and so realise that Othello's jealous interpretation of events and eventual murder of Desdemona is a mistake of tragic proportions.

■ Tone in Narrative Poetry

The various kinds of situational irony that are generated in narrative prose fiction are also exploited in narrative poetry. Situational irony can arise when the reader or audience knows the outcome of the story beforehand and thus knows more than the characters in the thick of the action. This situation is quite typical of the narrative poetry and drama of ancient Greece, which normally took the form of retelling a familiar historical or mythological story. Homer's *Iliad* (*c.* C8 BCE), for example, is a long narrative poem in twenty-four books of six-beat verse that recounts an episode in the Trojan War in which the Greeks defeated the Trojans and destroyed the walled city of Troy. Homer's intended audience (the Greeks of his own time) would have known the end of the story before they gathered to hear it recited. The interest, then, was not in what happens but in *how* the familiar story is told – not in the content but in the form, or rather in the poetry. One of the poetic effects made possible by this situation is situational irony. One revealing example comes in book X, when Hector, the Trojan hero and commander, proposes that

---

[3] For further discussions of dramatic irony, see Muecke, *Compass of Irony*, pp. 104–7; and B.O. States, *Irony and Drama: A poetics* (Ithaca, NY: Cornell University Press, 1971).

someone ought to go out on a night patrol to see if the Greek ships are well guarded. The Trojans seem reluctant to volunteer for this dangerous mission until a man called Dolon steps forward, attracted by the excitement but also anticipating success and asking Hector for a reward (the chariot and horses of the Greek hero Achilles) when the Greeks are finally defeated. The irony of the passage is well brought out in the following modern translation:[4]

> The listening Trojans all grew mute and still.
> Among them there was one by the name of Dolon;
> rich in gold, and rich in bronze, this man
> was heir to the great herald called Eumedes,
> and a good runner, puny though he seemed,
> an only son, with five sisters.
>   He spoke
> before the Trojans in response to Hector:
> 'Hector, pride and excitement urge me on
> to make this night-patrol close to the ships
> for information. Only, lift up your staff
> and swear that my reward will be that team
> and brazen car that bear the son of Peleus.
> For my part, I take the oath not to be blind
> on this patrol, or let you down. I'll make it
> straight through all the camp until I reach the ship
> of Agamemnon. There the Achaean captains
> must be debating battle or retreat.'
>   Hector complied, held up his staff, and swore:
> 'May Zeus in thunder, consort of Hera, witness
> this: no other Trojan rides that car
> behind that team. I say that you will do so.
> It is to be your glory.'
>   So he swore
> an oath to incite the man – and swore in vain. (X, 313–35)

Homer's audience would have seen the situational irony here in the way Dolon anticipates his reward for a successful mission and hence anticipates the defeat of the Greeks and the distribution of their treasures. Although Homer's audience might not know the result of Dolon's mission, they would know that Achilles and the Greeks would win the war and that the Trojans were doomed. If you like, Dolon is counting his chickens before they have hatched and the

[4] Homer, *The Iliad*, trans. Robert Fitzgerald (Oxford and New York: Oxford University Press, 1984), p. 172.

audience knows that they will never hatch. For the same reasons, Hector's vow and promise, meant sincerely, is also made ironic for the audience (who knows that Hector too will fall in battle). But if the audience is not attentive enough to these ironies, the narrator highlights them with that brief and chilling comment: 'So he swore / an oath to incite the man – and swore in vain'. (In fact, in the following hundred lines or so, we see that Dolon's patrol fails and he his captured and killed.)

A particularly interesting narrative poem in terms of ironic technique is Byron's *Don Juan* (1819–24), a long poem which traces the life and amorous adventures of its hero. Byron's persona or narrator is a master of irony, and nothing is safe from his all-pervasive ironic vision. He can be ironic about his characters, about the social values and habits of 'good society', about other poets, and even about himself. The first Canto concerns Don Juan's upbringing and first amorous affair. When he reaches the age of sixteen, he attracts the attentions of a woman who is 'married, charming, chaste, and twenty-three' (I, 472). Byron ironically mocks the woman's self-deceptive attempts to quell her interest in this young boy by praying to the Virgin Mary. As so often in structural irony, the irony arises through the disparity between what characters want to believe about themselves and what their actions reveal:

> She vowed she never would see Juan more,
>   And next day paid a visit to his mother,
> And looked extremely at the opening door,
>   Which, by the Virgin's grace, let in another;
> Grateful she was, and yet a little sore –
>   Again it opens, it can be no other,
> 'Tis surely Juan now – No! I'm afraid
> That night the Virgin was no further prayed. (I, 601–18)

Meanwhile, Byron has the young Juan wandering in the woods, unable to understand his own longings and acting out all the clichés of conventional lovers. In describing Juan's confused thoughts, Byron ironically mocks not only the emotions of first love but the philosophical reflections of contemporary poets such as Wordsworth and Coleridge:

> Young Juan wandered by the glassy brooks,
>   Thinking unutterable things; he threw
> Himself at length within the leafy nooks
>   Where the wild branch of the cork forest grew;
>   . . .
>
> He thought about himself, and the whole earth,
>   Of man the wonderful, and of the stars,

> And how the deuce they ever could have birth;
> And then he thought of earthquakes, and of wars,
> How many miles the moon might have in girth,
> Of air-balloons, and of the many bars
> To perfect knowledge of the boundless skies; –
> And then he thought of Donna Julia's eyes.
>
> In thoughts like these true Wisdom may discern
> Longings sublime, and aspirations high,
> Which some are born with, but the most part learn
> To plague themselves withal, they know not why:
> 'Twas strange that one so young should thus concern
> His brain about the action of the sky;
> If you think 'twas Philosophy that this did,
> I can't help thinking puberty assisted. (I, 713–44)

In these stanzas Byron ironically undercuts the seriousness of young love and philosophical poetry by 'sending it up' and setting it up for a fall. This fall typically occurs in the last line of the stanza, although Byron allows a mocking tone to seep through into the most 'serious' of moments – as when the phrase 'how the deuce' undermines the 'dignity' of young Juan's cosmological speculations (a sudden switch between registers can be a good indicator of irony, since register often implies attitude).

Yet this ironic Byronic narrator can also invite ironic reflections on himself by adopting an urbane, reasonable, innocent voice whose statements about himself we are clearly not meant to take seriously:

> Such love is innocent, and may exist
> Between young persons without any danger.
> A hand may first, and then a lip be kissed;
> For my part, to such doings I'm a stranger,
> But *hear* these freedoms form the utmost list
> Of all o'er which such love may be a ranger:
> If people go beyond, 'tis quite a crime,
> But not my fault – I tell them all the time. (I, 633–40)

The Canto ends with a few self-reflections which we cannot help but take ironically after what we have read:

> For my part, I'm a moderate-minded bard,
> Fond of a little love (which I call leisure);
> I care not for new pleasures, as the old
> Are quite enough for me, so but they hold.

Oh Pleasure! you're indeed a pleasant thing,
　　Although one must be damned for you, no doubt:
I make a resolution every spring
　　Of reformation, ere the year run out,
But somehow, this my vestal vow takes wing,
　　Yet still, I trust, it may be kept throughout:
I'm very sorry, very much ashamed,
And mean, next winter, to be quite reclaimed. (I, 941–52)

■ Political Irony in Lyrics

Like other forms of figurative language (such as metaphor), irony is often a more effective way of conveying a point than direct statement. Irony is often used for social or political criticism, and there is a substantial body of lyric poetry which uses political irony. Shelley's sonnet 'Ozymandias' (1818) is a good example:

> I met a traveller from an antique land
> Who said: Two vast and trunkless legs of stone
> Stand in the desert . . . Near them, on the sand,
> Half sunk, a shattered visage lies, whose frown,
> And wrinkled lip, and sneer of cold command,　　　　　5
> Tell that its sculptor well those passions read
> Which yet survive, stamped on those lifeless things,
> The hand that mocked them, and the heart that fed:
> And on the pedestal these words appear:
> 'My name is Ozymandias, king of kings:　　　　　　10
> Look on my works, ye Mighty, and despair!'
> Nothing beside remains. Round the decay
> Of that colossal wreck, boundless and bare
> The lone and level sands stretch far away.

Rather than making a direct statement or commenting on the traveller's story, Shelley simply juxtaposes the image of the broken statue and its inscription with the image of the empty desert, and leaves it to the reader to work out the point. The irony here could be called 'historical irony', because it is produced through the discrepancy between the boastful inscription on the pedestal and the way the passage of time has left no evidence of the king's 'works' except the 'colossal wreck' of the statue. Instead of impressive works, the statue is surrounded by 'lone and level sands' which are 'boundless and bare'. Because of this, the once proud boast on the pedestal has become ironic. Time has played an ironic joke on the king, giving the inscription a new meaning for all kings: rather than despairing because the works of Ozymandias overshadow anything they can do, kings now need to despair because even the works of such a mighty king are subject to the ruins of time. The poem makes this point not through stating it but through ironically juxtaposing the inscription with a description of its setting. By asking readers to get the point for themselves, such ironic juxtaposition is far more effective than a direct statement of the point.

A similar use of historical irony for political effect can be seen in Elvis Costello's song 'Peace In Our Time' (from *Goodbye Cruel World* (F-Beat Records, 1984), one of the most powerful responses in pop music to the threat of nuclear war in the period prior to the collapse of the Soviet Union:

Peace In Our Time

Out of the aeroplane stepped Chamberlain with a condemned
    man's stare
But we all cheered wildly, a photograph was taken, as he
    waved a piece of paper in the air
Now the Disco Machine lives in Munich and we are all
    friends
And I slip on my Italian dancing shoes as the evening
    descends

And the bells take their toll once again in a victory
    chime   5
And we can thank God that we've finally got peace in our
    time.

There's a man going round taking names no matter who you
    claim to be
As innocent as babies, a mad dog with rabies, you're
    still part of some conspiracy
Meanwhile there's a light over the ocean burning brighter
    than the sun
And a man sits alone in a bar and says 'Oh God, what have
    we done?'   10

[Chorus]

They're lighting a bonfire upon every hilltop in the land
Just another tiny island invaded when he's got the whole
    world in his hands
And the Heavyweight Champion fights in the International
    Propaganda Star Wars
There's already one spaceman in the White House, what do
    you want another one for?

[Chorus]

In the first verse, Costello employs historical irony by referring to a famous incident which occurred just before the outbreak of the Second World War. Nazi Germany had threatened to invade and annex part of Czechoslovakia, and Neville Chamberlain, then British Prime Minister, had met Hitler in Munich in order to avoid war by assuring him that Britain would not intervene. The incident to which Costello refers was filmed and is often shown on television; it involves Chamberlain stepping out of an aircraft on 30 September 1938, having just returned from the meeting with Hitler. Chamberlain waves a piece of paper in the air and claims that it contains a signed agreement with Hitler which guarantees 'peace for our time'. (These are Chamberlain's actual words, though the phrase is generally misquoted.) Although Chamberlain presumably believed Hitler, and used these words sincerely, the words and the gesture were soon made ironic by the turn of events – the German invasion of Poland and the outbreak of war a year later.[5] In fact, when we see the film of the incident we experience something like dramatic irony. Because we know that his triumphant gesture will soon be undermined by events, we view Chamberlain like an actor in a play and respond to his claim about 'peace for our time' ironically. Because of this, we share the singer's ironic attitude towards these solemn words (Chamberlain was making an allusion to the Book of Common Prayer). When Costello sings 'we can thank God that we've finally got peace in our time', we know we are not meant to take the words literally or seriously – partly because of the historical context, and partly because of the way the song treats that context and those words.

One of the ironies on which Costello is drawing is the fact that we have all become 'friends' after such a terrible war – that Munich, the site of the fatal meeting between Hitler and Chamberlain, is now the home of the 'Disco Machine'. In fact, we can understand the song as an ironic comment on the previous fifty years in the history of the West, and the way this history was used to justify the arms race and restrictions of freedom in Britain and the USA. To thank God that we've finally got peace in our time is ironically to mimic the claim that the nuclear deterrent kept peace in Europe for forty years. The song points out that at the same time that this was being said, the United States invaded 'tiny' islands (such as Grenada) which did not fall into line with its world-view, produced ever more powerful nuclear weapons, and even began to develop the Star Wars project. The song thus points out the ironic mismatch between the official language of peace and the reality which that language tried to camouflage.

The fact that irony can be far more effective than straightforward statement is vividly illustrated in the following sonnet by Hugh MacDiarmid (1935). This

[5] For contemporary news reports of these incidents, see Derrick Mercer, ed., *Chronicle* of *the Twentieth Century* (London: Dorling Kindersley, 1995), pp. 500–2, 513–17.

251

sonnet is a good example of a poem in which the question of tone involves asking about the speaker's attitude towards the subject matter and towards the words being used.

In the Children's Hospital

Does it matter? Losing your legs? – SIEGFRIED SASSOON

Now let the legless boy show the great lady
How well he can manage his crutches.
It doesn't matter though the Sister objects,
'He's not used to them yet,' when such is
The will of the Princess. Come, Tommy,   5
Try a few desperate steps through the ward.
Then the hand of Royalty will pat your head
And life suddenly cease to be hard.
For a couple of legs are surely no miss
When the loss leads to such an honour as this!   10
One knows, when one sees how jealous the rest
Of the children are, it's been all for the best! –
But would the sound of your sticks on the floor
Thundered in her skull for evermore!

Like most sonnets (see Chapter 12), this is organised into two sections in which the second section is a kind of answer to the first. In this case, the sonnet 'turns' in the last two lines (as Shakespeare's Sonnet 73 does). The voice of the first twelve lines seems to be that of a reasonable person who tries to persuade the 'legless boy' that it really was worth losing his legs, since it has led to this meeting with a Princess. Yet the absurdity of such an attitude encourages us to believe that we are not meant to take it seriously – especially in the following lines:

> For a couple of legs are surely no miss
> When the loss leads to such an honour as this!
> One knows, when one sees how jealous the rest
> Of the children are, it's been all for the best! (9–12)

In seeming to be enthusiastic about the benefits of royal visits, the speaker exaggerates these benefits (this is irony as overstatement) in a way which forces us to see how incongruous this attitude is with the boy's actual situation. In this way, statements which seem enthusiastic about royal visits turn out to be powerful criticisms of this kind of attitude and language. Yet this poem also demonstrates the power of irony in a seemingly unintentional way by reverting to straight criticism in the last two lines. Although we seem to be expected to take these lines as the poem's punch line, they are actually less effective as criticism than the irony used in the bulk of the poem.

◼ New Critical and Deconstructive Ironies

In Chapter 7 we pointed out some of the reasons why lyric poetry has come to be almost synonymous with poetry itself. This was reinforced by New Criticism, which placed lyric poetry at the centre of the canon and the curriculum, and made the poetic speaker the primary interest of the lyric. Because of this, the first concern of the New Critic became the interpretation of the tone of the lyric speaker's utterance. As in real speech situations, tone in lyric poetry relies on our being alert to the way the context or speech situation the poem sets up is likely to affect what a speaker says. It is also important to ask whether the speech situation involves an addressee. Such an addressee is usually part of the fiction of the poem – for instance, a lover who is being wooed – although poems sometimes directly address the reader. We can also ask whether the speaker is trying to influence the addressee in some way. Each of these questions may help in assessing a lyric poem's tone. In trying to analyse tone in a lyric poem, we may need to think about the poetic speaker's attitude: (1) towards the addressee; (2) towards the subject of the poem; (3) towards the words he or she is using; (4) towards the speaker him/herself.

A New Critical perspective would attempt to assess whether the tone of a poem is 'complex' and 'mature' or 'idealistic' and 'naive'. This is because the kind of tone exhibited by a poetic speaker became the criterion for judging whether or not a poem was 'mature' or 'immature'. In an influential discussion of 'The Imagination', I.A. Richards suggests that there are two types of poetry: sentimental or naive poetry, which attempts to ignore and exclude anything that might compromise its stance, and mature poetry, which imaginatively includes potentially damaging viewpoints and resolves them into a complex unity. Richards suggests that the naive poem is vulnerable to external irony – that is, to the ironic responses of readers who are not willing to accept its sentimental idealism. The mature poem, by contrast, is said to have an ironic tone because it precludes attacks from the outside by already including, and holding in balance, potentially ironic reflections on itself. In a sense, then, the ironic poem is more on its guard than the naive poem, less committed to any single position, idea or emotion. For Richards, poetic irony becomes a means of internal reconciliation and balance rather than a way of presenting a critical comment on the world outside the poem:

> Irony in this sense consists in the bringing in of the opposite, the complementary impulses; that is why poetry which is exposed to it is not of the highest order, and why irony itself is so constantly a characteristic of poetry which is.
>
> (*Principles of Literary Criticism*, p. 197)

This notion of irony as a means of internally reconciling opposing viewpoints in a state of tension or balance was taken up by New Critics such as Cleanth Brooks in order to valorise the ironic wit of poets such as John Donne over the naivety of 'sentimental' poetry:

> [Immature, sentimental poetry] is incapable of enduring an ironical contemplation because in such poetry the complementary impulses have been excluded from the poem. The accidental introduction of the poem into a context where they occur means the destruction of the poem. . . . The sentimental experience . . . always has to be viewed in the 'right' perspective – else it crumbles. Richards' poetry of synthesis, on the other hand, is impervious to irony for the very reason that it carries within its own structure the destructive elements – the poet has reconciled it to them. We may go further and say that the poet has included enough of the context in his experience so that the poem can never be thrown, raw and naked, into a new context in which it may appear foolish and ridiculous.[6]

The New Critics, therefore, valued irony as the most mature poetic tone because it allows the speaker to take up a knowing, balanced, perhaps non-committal attitude not only towards the addressee or theme but also towards the speaker's own position. Such self-ironic poetry will never commit itself wholeheartedly to love or to any political cause without some qualifying irony lest, in some contexts, it might appear sentimental and naive.

Richards's and Brooks's conception of irony, then, is significantly different from the kind of irony we have looked at in Shelley's and MacDiarmid's sonnets. In these poems, it is possible to discern a single, committed stance 'behind' the irony. In the poetry that the New Critics valued most, by contrast, the tone was supposed to be complex and varied. Although there are significant differences in the political points being made in 'Ozymandias' and 'In the Children's Hospital', there are similarities in their use of irony. This is because it is possible, by reading 'between the lines', to discern the serious point which each text is making, which is stable and not itself subjected to irony. Such irony is therefore called 'stable irony'.[7] While the New Critics valued poems in which the irony was stable it also had to be ambiguous, complex, and varied. As we have seen, Richards and Brooks regarded irony precisely as the sign and means of achieving unity through the reconciliation of opposites into an 'organic unity'. A good poem's ambiguous, complex and varied irony could be regarded as stable because it was held to be the complex expression of a single, mature poetic speaker in which varied impulses were reconciled.

---

[6] Brooks, *Modern Poetry and the Tradition*, p. 44. Also see Brooks, 'Irony as a Principle of Structure', in M.D. Zabel, ed., *Literary Opinion in America*, 3rd edn (New York: Harper, 1962), pp. 729–41.

[7] For a discussion of 'stable irony', see Booth, *Rhetoric of Irony*, pp. 1–86.

Yet there have been significant changes in the study of lyric poetry since the heyday of New Criticism (see Culler in Hošek and Parker, pp. 38–54). Post-structuralist literary criticism, under the influence of Paul de Man, argued that the kind of 'close reading' advocated by New Criticism, if it is pushed far enough, will tend to reveal a poem's internal disunity rather than an 'organic unity'. Rather than being signs of the mature balance of a poetic speaker, a careful reading of irony, complexity and ambiguity in poems will reveal that these features tend to lead to discontinuity. As de Man puts it,

> As it refines its interpretations more and more, American criticism does not discover a single meaning, but a plurality of significations that can be radically opposed to each other. Instead of revealing a continuity affiliated with the coherence of the natural world, it takes us into a discontinuous world of reflective irony and ambiguity.[8]

Taking his cue from the notion of Romantic irony (examined below), de Man argues that irony – far from being a means of structural coherence and stability – is a rhetorical process which disrupts the illusion of a text's seamless unity and announces the difference between textual artifice and 'natural' experience.[9] Irony, in this sense, is sometimes called 'new' or 'unstable' irony.[10]

■ Undecidable Ironies and Sexual Politics

The complexities and ambiguities of irony can be especially intriguing when they are not resolved or held in 'balance' by a poem (or by a critic). An interesting example of this would be Adrienne Rich's 'Orion' (1965), especially since it raises questions about sexuality and sexual politics in intriguing and provocative ways. What is interesting for us is that its tone becomes ambiguous or even undecidable in terms of its treatment of the addressee, the subject matter and the speaker herself. 'Orion' is the most prominent constellation which appears in the winter sky in the northern hemisphere; it is named after a giant hunter of Greek mythology, and it is supposed to depict the hunter with his belt and sword hanging down. It quickly becomes clear, however, that the interest of this poem is not in stargazing but in the way the speaker's shifting attitudes towards the constellation invoke different images of and attitudes towards men.

---

[8] de Man, 'Form and Intent in the American New Criticism', in *Blindness and Insight*, pp. 20–35 (28).

[9] See de Man, 'The Rhetoric of Temporality', in *Blindness and Insight*, pp. 187–228 (209).

[10] Although Booth's discussion of 'unstable irony' in *A Rhetoric of Irony*, pp. 223–77, is not at all influenced by post-structuralist thought, his response to the disorientating unstable ironies of modern texts such as Beckett's plays and novels illuminates a 'postmodern' development in literary art which is close to what de Man is getting at.

Orion

Far back when I went zig-zagging
through tamarack pastures
you were my genius, you
my cast-iron Viking, my helmed
lion-heart king in prison.   5
Years later now you're young

my fierce half-brother, staring
down from that simplified west
your breast open, your belt dragged down
by an oldfashioned thing, a sword   10
the last bravado you won't give over
though it weighs you down as you stride

and the stars in it are dim
and maybe have stopped burning.
But you burn, and I know it;   15
as I throw back my head to take you in
an old transfusion happens again:
divine astronomy is nothing to it.

Indoors I bruise and blunder,
break faith, leave ill enough   20
alone, a dead child born in the dark.
Night cracks up over the chimney,
pieces of time, frozen geodes
come showering down in the grate.

A man reaches behind my eyes   25
and finds them empty
a woman's head turns away
from my head in the mirror
children are dying my death
and eating crumbs of my life.   30

Pity is not your forte.
Calmly you ache up there
pinned aloft in your crow's nest,
my speechless pirate!
You take it all for granted   35
and when I look you back

it's with a starlike eye
shooting its cold and egotistical spear

> where it can do least damage.
> Breathe deep! No hurt, no pardon   40
> out here in the cold with you
> you with your back to the wall.

This is a difficult and challenging poem, and we will therefore look at a few lines at a time in order to work out the speech situation and ask about tone. Adapting Scholes's questions, we can begin by asking: 'who is the speaker, what is her situation, and whom is she addressing?' The speaker seems to be a woman (not just because the poet is female but also because of internal indications in the poem), and she is addressing or apostrophising the constellation Orion (she is therefore outside on a winter's night).

In the first stanza, the speaker looks back at her childhood fantasies about the constellation:

> Far back when I went zig-zagging
> through tamarack pastures
> you were my genius, you
> my cast-iron Viking, my helmed
> lion-heart king in prison. (1–5)

For the child (far back), the constellation represented a series of romantic male fantasy figures: it was her own 'cast-iron Viking', her own Richard the Lion-Heart (the 'helmed / lion-heart king in prison'). The child presumably took these fantasies seriously, but what is the speaker's present attitude towards her childhood dreams about romantic heroes? Is it a fond memory, or does she now have an ironic distance towards those fantasies and the child that she once was? The next lines might affect our answers to these questions:

> Years later now you're young
>
> my fierce half-brother, staring
> down from that simplified west
> your breast open, your belt dragged down
> by an oldfashioned thing, a sword
> the last bravado you won't give over
> though it weighs you down as you stride
>
> and the stars in it are dim
> and maybe have stopped burning. (6–14)

Has the tone changed now that the poem has switched to the mature woman's conception of the constellation? What is her present attitude towards this archetypal male figure?

257

The first clue to a possible shift in attitude is that whereas she has got older, it now seems to be 'young'. And though this seems to allow for a different kind of intimacy between them ('he' is now her 'fierce half-brother'), the constellation is no longer the romantic hero figure it was for her as a child. Instead, it is young, is set in the 'simplified west', and is open-shirted and macho, with an 'oldfashioned thing' dangling from its belt – a weapon which he/it takes pride in and won't relinquish. This 'oldfashioned thing' which weighs the young man down as he strides is ostensibly the sword which, in the constellation, hangs down between the hunter's legs and which young men no longer carry in the modern world. At the same time, the speaker also seems to be implying that the young hunter gives far too much emphasis to his sexual prowess (it is 'the last bravado you won't give over'). Both sexual prowess and sword, however, seem more show than substance since 'the stars in it are dim / and maybe have stopped burning'. This can be read in two ways at the same time. On a literal level, the stars which form Orion's 'sword' are indeed faint; furthermore, because of the huge distances between the Earth and the stars in the constellation, the light we see from them was emitted a long time ago, and it could be that the stars themselves might have stopped giving out light. On a figurative level, the suggestion that the stars in the sword are no longer burning reinforces the sexual connotations of these lines since, as we have seen, 'burning' often connotes sexual desire. Thus the tone here may be an ironic one towards male pretensions – whether they be sexual or combative.

But then the tone unexpectedly changes again:

> But you burn, and I know it;
> as I throw back my head to take you in
> an old transfusion happens again:
> divine astronomy is nothing to it. (15–18)

Here, the speaker recognises that he does 'burn' (with desire?) and her possibly sympathetic response compounds the ambiguities of meaning and the tonal ambivalences. To throw back her head to take him in could literally mean that she looks up to see the constellation. Yet it can also be read as developing the ongoing sexual metaphor: figuratively, she positions herself for oral sex or sexual intercourse. (A third possibility is that she 'takes him in' in the sense of deceiving him.) The first and second possible readings are maintained in the lines which describe the result of this action: 'an old transfusion happens again'. What is that 'old transfusion'? Transfusion literally means to transfer fluid from one receptacle or body to another (as in a blood transfusion); figuratively, it is to 'imbue' or 'inspire'. In the double reading we have been suggesting, then, 'taking in' the light from the constellation transfuses inspiration into her in a way analogous to the transfusion of fluids which occurs in sex. This is clearly a wonderful experience, because 'divine astronomy is nothing to it'. Thus the tone of the second and third stanzas, which began in a mocking way, seems to have shifted to a new kind of celebration of this fantasy relation to the constellation.

At this high point of transfusion, the speaker confides to the constellation that her life indoors is somewhat disastrous:

> Indoors I bruise and blunder,
> break faith, leave ill enough
> alone, a dead child born in the dark.
> Night cracks up over the chimney,
> pieces of time, frozen geodes
> come showering down in the grate.
>
> A man reaches behind my eyes
> and finds them empty
> a woman's head turns away
> from my head in the mirror
> children are dying my death
> and eating crumbs of my life. (19–30)

The focal points of home and family which – in 1965, at least – were supposed to ground a woman's identity seem here to dramatise her disintegration and dissolution – as in the disturbing image in which 'children are dying my death / and eating crumbs of my life'. The next stanza begins by recognising that she will get no pity from the constellation, and continues by momentarily reverting (ironically?) to ways of figuring it which recall her childhood fantasies. Emphasising his unresponsiveness, she apostrophises him as 'my speechless pirate' (34) who is 'pinned aloft in your crow's nest' (33). Is she now using such childhood fantasies ironically to dismiss the unresponsive 'pirate', or is she ironically reflecting on herself for looking towards a constellation for comfort?

The fantasy male figure remains utterly aloof from the reality of home and family, and somehow allows her to distance herself from her crisis:

> You take it all for granted
> and when I look you back
>
> it's with a starlike eye
> shooting its cold and egotistical spear
> where it can do least damage.
> Breathe deep! No hurt, no pardon
> out here in the cold with you
> you with your back to the wall. (35–42)

Her 'relationship' with this aloof constellation seems to enable her to become aloof from her own problems. She becomes like the constellation, looking back at it 'with a starlike eye' which shoots 'its cold and egotistical spear' towards 'where it can do least damage'. It thus becomes a kind of therapeutic target at which she can direct her most 'cold and egotistical' shafts – perhaps instead of aiming them at her family. Out 'in the cold' with this cluster of stars, she seems to feel relief from the complexities of human relationships: there is 'No hurt, no pardon'. It is as if she is outside with a secret lover who represents a 'simplified' alternative to her entrapment inside. Yet Orion has his 'back to the wall' – a concluding image whose ambiguity keeps open the questions which the poem raises rather than bringing them to a conclusion: is it a figurative way of describing the way the constellation is spread out against the night sky? Does it carry on the conceit that this is her lover with his back to a wall as they caress? Does it suggest that he is somehow on the defensive?

Since this poem opens up so many questions about sexual politics and sexual relationships it would seem imperative that we try to decide what its overall tone – and hence its 'message' – is. Does the poetic speaker, or the poem itself, develop an ironic attitude towards men? Or does the speaker develop an ironic attitude towards herself for her continued dependence on imaginary male figures? Does the poem itself constitute an ironic comment on this trait in the speaker? What we have tried to show is that it is very difficult to give easy answers to these questions because part of the challenge of this ambiguous and ambivalent poem is that it refuses to yield straightforward answers to the complex questions it opens up. Suggesting that such questions might be 'undecidable', however, is not to evade them but to recognise their complexity in 'real life'.

Irony, then, can be related to a recognition of complexity and ambiguity, but need not necessarily be a 'principle of structure' which holds that complexity in a 'mature' balance or resolves it into an organic unity. And although the irony in 'Orion' is an 'unstable irony' in the sense that it is not clear what 'stance' is being adopted behind the irony, this does not mean that such a poem is not engaged with social and political questions. The 'undecidability' of such a poem seems to make it more rather than less engaged with some of the central, perhaps 'undecidable', questions of our time. In this way, the ironic undoing of easy answers becomes almost synonymous with the critical process called '**deconstruction**'.[11]

---

[11] This point is made in *Princeton*, p. 280. For a suggestion that the undecidability which deconstructive criticism seems to search out and analyse is synonymous with the poetic and the political, see Barbara Johnson, *A World of Difference*, 2nd edn (Baltimore, MD: Johns Hopkins University Press, 1989), pp. 30–31, 193–4. These questions are explored at length in our concluding chapter.

■ 'Romantic' and 'Postmodern' Irony

Unstable irony is not just a modern (or postmodern) phenomenon. Lilian Furst compares it to 'a disease that may long be present in isolated cases and that may then under special circumstances become epidemic'.[12] Isolated 'cases' include Laurence Sterne's novel *Tristram Shandy* (1759–67), but the best-known 'epidemics' have occurred in the Romantic period and throughout the twentieth century. The 'disease' was diagnosed and named in the Romantic period by the German writer Friedrich Schlegel as 'Romantic irony'. Abrams summarises Romantic irony as 'a mode of dramatic or narrative writing in which the author builds up the illusion of representing reality, only to shatter it by revealing that the author, as artist, is the arbitrary creator and manipulator of the characters and their actions' (see 'irony' in *Abrams*).[13] To illustrate Romantic irony, we can return to Byron's *Don Juan*. In addition to all the other ironies which we glanced at earlier, *Don Juan's* self-conscious, self-ironic narrator frequently reveals himself as the arbitrary manipulator of his characters and narration. As with most of the ironic effects in *Don Juan*, it is often in the last line of a stanza that the narrative illusion is ironically dispelled:

> Thus would [Juan] while his lonely hours away
>   Dissatisfied, not knowing what he wanted;
> Nor glowing reverie, nor poet's lay,
>   Could yield his spirit that for which it panted,
> A bosom whereon he his head might lay,
>   And hear the heart beat with the love it granted,
> With – several other things, which I forget,
> Or which, at least, I need not mention yet. (I, 761–68)

The narrator also presents himself as opportunistically manipulating the conventions of poetry:

> And if in the mean time her husband died,
>   But Heaven forbid that such a thought should cross
> Her brain, though in a dream! (and then she sighed)
>   Never could she survive that common loss;

---

[12] Furst, 'Romantic Irony and Narrative Stance', in Frederick Garber, ed., *Romantic Irony* (Budapest: Akademiai Kiado, 1988), pp. 293–309 (307).

[13] For illuminating discussions of Romantic irony, see Muecke, *Compass of Irony*, pp. 159–215; Garber, *Romantic Irony*; Anne K. Mellor, *English Romantic Irony* (Cambridge, MA: Harvard University Press, 1980); Lilian Furst, *Fictions of Romantic Irony in European Narrative, 1760–1857* (London: Macmillan, 1984).

> But just suppose that moment should betide,
>   I only say suppose it – *inter nos*:
> (This should be *entre nous*, for Julia thought
> In French, but then the rhyme would go for nought.) (I, 665–72)

As well as occasionally destroying the illusion in this kind of way, the poem opens with a self-conscious **parody** of epic conventions which ironically foregrounds and plays with them. It begins abruptly with the startling admission 'I want a hero', then sorts through and dismisses various possible heroes before settling on Don Juan:

> I condemn none,
> But can't find any in the present age
> Fit for my poem (that is, for my new one);
> So, as I said, I'll take my friend Don Juan. (I, 37–40)

In other words, rather than presenting us with an already-thought-out story, *Don Juan* seems to present us with the hesitant activity of putting that story together. It therefore foregrounds the problems and processes of poetic creation and implies that the finished product is haphazard and provisional:

> Most epic poets plunge '*in medias res*'
>   (Horace makes this the heroic turnpike road),
> And then your hero tells, when'er you please,
>   What went before – by way of episode,
> While seated after dinner at his ease,
>   Beside his mistress in some soft abode,
> Palace, or garden, paradise, or cavern,
> Which serves the happy couple for a tavern.
>
> That is the usual method, but not mine –
>   My way is to begin with the beginning;
> The regularity of my design
>   Forbids all wandering as the worst of sinning,
> And therefore I shall open with a line
>   (Although it cost me half an hour in spinning),
> Narrating somewhat of Don Juan's father,
> And also of his mother, if you'd rather. (I, 41–56)

All these features are characteristic of Romantic irony. As Lilian Furst explains,

> The Romantic ironist . . . assumes a prominence in his narrative that is the antithesis of the half hidden, reticent position associated with the more traditional ironist. . . .

The narrator holds the centre of the stage, disposing his characters and arranging his materials before our very eyes so that we see not the finished product but the creative process. . . . In the context of the Romantic vision of the artist, irony is the sign of his total freedom, his right to manipulate, to destroy as well as create.

(Furst in Garber, *Romantic Irony*, p. 300)

In contrast with stable irony, Romantic irony leaves no secure place, free from irony, on which narrator and reader may stand:

The signals that [the reader] catches from the mercurial narrator may be loud and manifold, but they are inevitably conflicting and confusing as the narrator himself has no clear and firm position. He stands beside his work, making it, chopping and changing it, improvising or seeming to improvise, launching out into various directions only to retreat again. . . . The problems of interpretation, or reconstructing the intended meaning, become acute at this juncture as we move from the stability of traditional irony operating from its fixed and secure vantage point to the instability of Romantic irony that is riddled with ambiguities. (p. 302)

Although Byron did write some wonderful Romantic lyrics (such as 'She Walks in Beauty'), the radical irony of *Don Juan* clearly does not fit with the image of Romantic lyric sincerity created by Victorian writers such as John Stuart Mill and perpetuated to the present day. It is perhaps revealing that, although Byron was the most popular of the Romantic poets during the Romantic period itself, his popularity subsequently waned, and critical attention shifted to more 'sincere' poets such as Wordsworth and Keats.[14] Yet it has again become possible to revalue Byron's Romantic irony in a cultural and critical climate in which Post-structuralism and Postmodernism have problematised (or shied away from) lyric sincerity in favour of texts and critical approaches which foreground and celebrate self-conscious artifice. Novels such as Alasdair Gray's *Lanark* (1981), films such as Quentin Tarantino's *Pulp Fiction* (Miramax, 1994), or TV series such as *The Singing Detective* or *Moonlighting*, are just a few examples which indicate the way Romantic irony has come into its own again as 'Postmodernism' or 'new irony'. Such a revolution in artistic production and critical taste also allows us to reassess texts from the past which did not fit the twin Victorian criteria of realism and Romantic lyricism, such as Sterne's novel *Tristram Shandy*. Bob Hope and Bing Crosby's 'Road' movies of the 1940s and 1950s can suddenly seem precociously experimental in the way they ironically play with the conventions of

---

[14] It is revealing that one of the best modern critics of Romanticism, David Simpson, could have written a book called *Irony and Authority in Romantic Poetry* (London: Macmillan, 1979) that mentions Byron only twice in passing. The book nonetheless presents an important reading of the other major Romantic poets as Romantic ironists. A similar attempt is made by Anthony Thorlby, 'Imagination and Irony in English Romantic Poetry', in Garber, *Romantic Irony*, pp. 131–55.

Hollywood realism. It is no coincidence that poems such as *Don Juan* seem uncannily similar to some of the self-consciously textual and ironic texts which are said to exemplify our postmodern condition. The ironic consciousness which enjoys films that foreground their own filmic status rather than continuing the escapist fantasy of 'realist' films is analogous to the Byronic persona which leaves no illusions – not even about the self or about art – intact. Yet, in Byron as in *Tristram Shandy*, this ironic consciousness leads not to despair and indifference but to engagement and celebratory comedy.

Exercises

1 Read the following untitled sonnet by Edna St Vincent Millay (1930) several times, then answer the questions.

> I dreamed I moved among the Elysian fields,
> In converse with sweet women long since dead;
> And out of blossoms which that meadow yields
> I wove a garland for your living head.
> Danaë, that was the vessel for a day   5
> Of golden Jove, I saw, and at her side,
> Whom Jove the Bull desired and bore away,
> Europa stood, and the Swan's featherless bride.
> All these were mortal women, yet all these
> Above the ground had had a god for guest;   10
> Freely I walked beside them and at ease,
> Addressing them, by them again addressed,
> And marveled nothing, for remembering you,
> Wherefore I was among them well I knew.

(a) Try to identify or characterise the speaker and the addressee, and then describe what the relationship is between them. Then describe the tone of the poem, bearing in mind that tone involves the speaker's attitude towards (i) the addressee, (ii) the subject matter, (iii) the speaker him- or herself.

(b) The classical allusions can be identified as follows:

'Elysian fields' (1): the otherworld, home of the happy dead.
'Danaë' (5): woman seduced by Jove, who descended upon her in a golden shower.
'Europa' (8): a girl abducted by Jove in the shape of a bull.
'Swan's featherless bride' (8): Leda, who was raped or seduced by Jove in the shape of a swan.

What characteristic or characteristics do all these myths have in common? Now re-read the poem, in order to register how these allusions might apply to the speaker's own situation. Does this information about the allusions change your sense of the poem's tone in any way? If so, how and why?

(c) If you now believe the poem to be ironic, try to locate the irony by identifying any words, phrases or lines which seem particularly ironic. Then attempt to classify the irony as closely as possible, bearing in mind the categories introduced in this chapter: verbal, structural, political, stable or unstable, Romantic, New Critical, Deconstructive. This may not be easy, but it could be a fruitful area for class discussion.

2 Re-read Brown's 'The Lads' from exercise 2 at the end of Chapter 2, then try to answer the following questions.

(a) Try to identify the speech situation by deciding who is speaking to whom and in what setting.

(b) What is the speaker's attitude towards (i) the lads and (ii) their poetry? Is this attitude consistent throughout? Is there any ambivalence?

(c) Go through the poem identifying its various registers. How far does the use of register support your claims about the speaker's attitude/tone?

(d) At the end of Chapter 2 we asked you to work out the poem's use of different kinds of metrical form. Do the shifts between metrical forms relate to the question of tone?

(e) When the speaker says 'that yours will never be to reason why' she is making an allusion to a famous poem. Try to track down the source of that allusion, perhaps by using the Internet. How does your discovery of the source text for this allusion affect your sense of the speaker's attitude/tone towards the lads? (For allusion, see Chapter 13, and our Glossary.)

3 Re-read Duffy's 'Boy' printed at the end of Chapter 7.

(a) Is it possible to distinguish between the speaker's tone and the poem's tone? In other words, is the speaker's attitude towards himself the same as the poem's attitude towards him?

(b) What attitude or attitudes does the poem invite us to take towards the speaker?

(c) What is your attitude towards the speaker?

(d) Is there a difference between your answer to questions (b) and (c)? If so, why?

Chapter 9

Ambiguity

In several chapters of this book we have suggested that features such as double syntax, metaphor and tone can lead to ambiguity. In what follows, we will explore the way twentieth-century literary criticism came to regard certain kinds of ambiguity as effective poetic devices which enrich a poem or help it to articulate things that are outside the scope of more 'straight-talking' language. Yet we shall also see that there is some confusion and controversy among literary critics about what ambiguity is. Thus one of the aims of the following discussion will be to distinguish between a number of different terms and concepts which tend to get confused with each other.

■ The Dream of Single Meaning and Perfect Communication

It is a natural enough assumption, if we do not think about it too much, that individual words and the sentences they make up will normally have single or obvious meanings, and that the overall meaning when such sentences are joined together into a discourse will be clear and unambiguous. This is what teachers look for in students' essays, and this is our goal in writing the chapters of this book. Yet it may be that unambiguous clarity is an ideal which should be aimed at but can never be achieved. Language is inherently prone to ambiguity for at least two reasons: (1) language is not like mathematics or geometry, whose signs and concepts have single and exact definitions agreed on by all users; (2) discourse is often interpreted in contexts which unpredictably affect how it is understood.

Because of these factors, a great deal of effort goes into trying to reduce the potential ambiguity of discourse. In most speech situations it is possible to clear up confusions by asking the speaker what she or he means. Almost any kind of conversation or interview may have an ongoing process of mutual clarification taking place within it, since speech can generate misunderstanding as well as understanding. A great deal of political discussion, argument and antagonism is generated out of the ambiguities to which speech can give rise. Politicians are vigorously interviewed on TV by journalists intent on either eliminating or discovering ambiguities in what they say. Their spoken comments are turned into 'sound bites' which are broadcast in different programmes and become open to different interpretations by different commentators and factions. An apparently clear statement in one context or to one kind of audience seems to become ambiguous or to mean something quite different in another context or to another kind of audience. Thus ambiguity becomes the very stuff of politics. Whether or not the ambiguity is really there in the original statement appears to be less important than the way that statement can seem, or be made to seem, ambiguous by contending political groups.

Most of the time, fortunately, we do not need to scrutinise each other's language with quite the same care as in delicate political situations. In ordinary language usage we tend to accept a certain amount of slippage or ambiguity – we do not, for the most part, demand that the other person continually defines his or her terms. This is partly because factors such as shared context, inference, tone of voice, mutual trust and interpretive generosity allow us to understand and communicate with each other. Most of the time we automatically filter out alternative meanings by selecting those meanings that are appropriate to the context. If this was not the case, however, even everyday discourse might break down in the way political discussions often do.

Writing has different kinds of advantages and constraints from speech. In a book like the one you are now reading, it is obviously desirable to be as clear and unambiguous as possible. In order to achieve this, the text has gone through several stages of revision in which the elimination of potential ambiguities was always high on the agenda. One of the reasons why such care is needed is that writing, once it leaves the author, has to stand on its own feet. As a reader, you are not able to ask us what we mean by a particular word, sentence or chapter. So we have attempted to become critical readers of our own writing and to put ourselves in your shoes in order to anticipate and eliminate the ambiguities you may experience as a reader.

In most situations the context of a piece of writing appreciably reduces the scope for any ambiguity or misunderstanding. Newspaper headlines, traffic notices, advertisements, and so on come to us in ready-made contexts which help to determine and delimit our interpretation. In poems, however, we often have to infer the context from the text itself – as we did in looking at Wordsworth's 'A slumber did my spirit seal' in Chapter 7. Perhaps more than with any other kind of text, the primary contextual evidence for understanding poems is implied within the text itself. And because poems leave a lot to the imagination and rely on rhetorical devices such as metaphor and irony, they become especially open to ambiguity. Indeed, it has been argued that poets consciously build ambiguity into poems as one of the most effective poetic devices.

■ Ambiguity as Characteristic of the Language of Poetry

Although we regard ambiguity as a fault of style in those discourses in which clarity is important, literary criticism in the twentieth century came to regard ambiguity in poetry as one of its most characteristic and valuable features. In 1936, I.A. Richards pointed out that the 'new' literary criticism being developed in the early twentieth century had reversed prevailing assumptions about ambiguity established in Classical rhetoric:

> where the old Rhetoric treated ambiguity as a fault in language, and hoped to confine or eliminate it, the new Rhetoric sees it as an inevitable consequence of the powers of language and as an indispensable means of our most important utterances – especially in Poetry and Religion.[1]

This revolution in critical assumptions was initiated by William Empson's *Seven Types of Ambiguity* (1930), which posited that 'the machinations of ambiguity are among the very roots of poetry'.[2] Although the details of Empson's argument have been criticised, his general claims about ambiguity in poetry have been largely accepted. Ambiguity has come to be regarded as a central feature of art in general and of poetry in particular. In 1957, Northrop Frye claimed that 'The conclusion that a work of art contains a variety or sequence of meanings seems inescapable.'[3] In 1975, H.G. Widdowson announced that 'It is in the nature of poetry to be ambiguous and no one interpretation can capture the meaning of a poem in its entirety.'[4]

There are probably several reasons for this development in literary criticism. Freud's claims that double meanings and linguistic 'slips' of all kinds are not a meaningless nuisance but profoundly revealing about the individual psyche had a seminal influence on twentieth-century thought. Literary practice, too, underwent something of a revolution after the First World War. The experimentation of Modernist writing included a new zest for wordplay which culminated in James Joyce's *Finnegans Wake* (1939) – an inexhaustible treasure house of jokes, puns and ambiguities. Forerunners of New Criticism such as I.A. Richards sought to differentiate the language of literature from the language of the sciences, arguing that whereas the goal of scientific discourse is

[1] I.A. Richards, *The Philosophy of Rhetoric*, p. 40.
[2] Williams Empson, *Seven Types of Ambiguity* (London: Penguin, 1961), p. 3.
[3] Frye, *Anatomy of Criticism*, p. 72.
[4] H.G. Widdowson, *Stylistics and the Teaching of Literature* (London: Longman, 1975), p. 114.

clarity, that of poetry is the exploration of areas of human experience inaccessible to science. This is the assumption supporting Richards's belief that ambiguity is 'an indispensable means of our most important utterances – especially in Poetry and Religion'. Such an assumption is compounded by Eliot's claim in 1921 that life in the twentieth century had become especially complex and that twentieth-century poetry had to reflect that complexity.[5] Winifred Nowottny concludes that 'the richness or manysidedness of language . . . enables the poet to declare our own inchoate and complex experience in a verbal form' (*The Language Poets Use*, p. 149).

Yet although the celebration of ambiguity in literature is largely a twentieth-century development, creative writers throughout history have exploited ambiguity for various literary effects. Although Classical and Neoclassical rhetoric sought to eliminate ambiguity as a fault, not all writers followed the rules of propriety. Shakespeare played with the ambiguities of language almost as much as Joyce. And although Samuel Johnson rebuked Shakespeare for indulging in punning, such pillars of **Augustan** poetry as Alexander Pope made brilliant use of puns and double meanings. In this sense, twentieth-century literary criticism can be said to have 'caught on' at last to an important aspect of literary practice which earlier critics had either disapproved of or been blind to. As Mahood observes,

> Where the Augustans disapproved of Shakespeare's wordplay and the Victorians ignored it, we now acclaim it. A generation that relishes *Finnegans Wake* is more in danger of reading non-existent quibbles into Shakespeare's work than of missing his subtlest play of meaning.[6]

◾ Ambiguity and Obscurity

In everyday usage, if we describe something as 'ambiguous' we probably mean one of two things: either that it is obscure in meaning or that it seems to have two or more meanings. This ambiguity in the term 'ambiguous' is supported by most dictionary definitions. *Collins English Dictionary* defines ambiguous as 'doubtful or uncertain; of doubtful significance; equivocal; obscure in meaning; susceptible of two or more meanings'. Unfortunately, but perhaps inevitably, literary critics have perpetuated rather than clarified the obscurity of the term 'ambiguity'. M.H. Abrams's definition, however, can help us to clear up this confusion. Ambiguity, he says, is a poetic device which uses 'a single word or expression to signify two or more distinct references, or to express two or more diverse attitudes or feelings' (see 'ambiguity' in *Abrams*). Ambiguity as a poetic device, then, has nothing to do with obscurity or doubtful

[5] 'The Metaphysical Poets', in Eliot, *Selected Prose* (Harmondsworth: Penguin, 1953), p. 118.
[6] M. Mahood, *Shakespeare's Wordplay* (London: Methuen, 1957), p. 94.

meaning. In fact, we will argue that there is a great deal of precision in poetic ambiguity. As Abrams puts it, ambiguity is a word or expression which signifies 'two or more *distinct* references'. For the references to be distinct from one another, we need to be able to distinguish what they are. In Rich's 'Orion', for example, we claimed that the phrase 'I throw back my head to take you in' is ambiguous because, in the context of the poem, it can be read in at least two distinct ways which can be precisely described.

■ Ambiguity and Ambivalence

Ambivalence is not the same as ambiguity. Whereas ambiguity is a feature of language, ambivalence is a quality of *feeling*. Ambivalence is the coexistence in one person of opposite feelings towards an object, person or situation. An ambivalent feeling might result in, or be revealed by, an ambiguous statement, but not necessarily. And by the same token, we cannot assume that an ambiguous phrase or text indicates ambivalent feelings in the speaker or writer.[7] The ambiguous phrase 'I throw back my head to take you in' does not seem to indicate ambivalent feelings in the speaker. By contrast, the meaning of the first section of Rich's 'Orion' is straightforward enough even though the speaker may well be feeling ambivalent towards the constellation and/or her childhood fantasies:

> Far back when I went zig-zagging
> through tamarack pastures
> you were my genius, you
> my cast-iron Viking, my helmed
> lion-heart king in prison.

■ Ambiguity and Multiple Meaning

Having distinguished ambiguity from obscurity, doubtful meaning and ambivalence, we still need to differentiate between ambiguity and multiple meaning. Although Abrams regards multiple meaning as an alternative term for ambiguity, there is a wide range of ways in which a piece of text can have multiple meaning without being ambiguous. Irony, for example, can be thought of as a kind of multiple meaning, since a reader has to distinguish between an apparent meaning and an implied meaning.

Although Empson's *Seven Types of Ambiguity* transformed the critical attitude towards ambiguity, it is a very confused book which tends to equate

---

[7] Nowottny makes a similar point in her chapter on 'Ambiguity', *The Language Poets Use*, pp. 146–73.

ambiguity with all kinds of multiple meaning. This can be seen in his account of the 'first type' of ambiguity:

> First-type ambiguities arise when a detail is effective in several ways at once, e.g. by comparisons with several points of likeness, antitheses with several points of difference . . . 'comparative' adjectives, subdued metaphors, and extra meanings suggested by rhythm. (p. v)

Empson goes on to say that 'The fundamental situation, whether it deserves to be called ambiguous or not, is that a word or a grammatical structure is effective in several ways at once' (p. 2). His first example of this 'simplest type of ambiguity' is the fourth line from a Shakespeare sonnet with which we are already familiar (see Chapter 6):

> That time of year thou mayst in me behold
> When yellow leaves, or none, or few, do hang
> Upon those boughs which shake against the cold,
> Bare ruined choirs, where late the sweet birds sang. (1–4)

Empson claims that the last of these lines is ambiguous:

> the comparison holds for many reasons; because ruined monastery choirs are places in which to sing, because they involve sitting in a row, because they are made of wood, are carved into knots and so forth, because they used to be surrounded by a sheltering building crystallised out of the likeness of a forest, and coloured with stained glass and painting like flowers and leaves, . . . and for various sociological and historical reasons (the protestant destruction of monasteries; fear of puritanism); . . . these reasons, and many more relating the simile [metaphor!] to its place in the Sonnet, must all combine to give the line its beauty, and there is a sort of ambiguity in not knowing which of them to hold most clearly in mind. (pp. 2–3)

It is difficult not to admire Empson's ingenuity here in teasing out all these implications from the line, even though we may find some of them odd or far-fetched. But instead of exposing ambiguities, he is simply thinking of as many grounds as he can for the metaphorical comparison of wintery 'boughs' with 'Bare ruined choirs' and assembling the multiple connotations which the vehicle imports into the poem. As he himself concludes, 'Clearly this is involved in all such richness and heightening of effect, and . . . covers almost everything of literary importance' (p. 3). He also admits that he is not wholly confident that such a range of multiple connotations and implications 'deserves to be called ambiguous'. In fact, we would suggest that Empson's analysis of the line reveals no ambiguity in the sense in which we wish to define it.

Multiple connotations do not necessarily constitute ambiguity. If they did, we would have to admit, with Empson, that every literary effect could be called ambiguous, and this would make the term so general as to render it use-less and leave us unable to discuss real ambiguity. This is the problem with many accounts of ambiguity which repeat Empson's confusion. Nowottny accepts the fact that ' "ambiguity" is now associated with such concepts as ambivalence, tension, paradox and irony, and with interest in metaphor and symbol as means by which the poet can evade or transcend univocal assertion' (p. 147). Her concern is with the negative associations of the term ambiguity rather than with the fact that it has become a general term for a whole range of multiple meanings. In our own definition of ambiguity, we will distinguish it from most kinds of multiple meaning by saying that ambiguity consists of *two or more distinctly different meanings sustained by the same piece of text which cannot be resolved into a single meaning*. This definition is influenced by Soon Peng Su's redefinition of ambiguity:

> An item is ambiguous when the two conditions below are fulfilled: (a) semantically, it is capable of having two or more distinctly different meanings (senses or references), and (b) pragmatically, the different meanings of (a) can be interpreted as tenable in a given context.[8]

Ambiguity as a Form of Multiple Meaning

We have argued that multiple meanings in poems are not always ambiguous, and have therefore proposed a general definition of ambiguity which will dis-tinguish it from other types of multiple meaning (such as irony or allegory). Yet ambiguity is, of course, a *type* of multiple meaning.[9] And although the other kinds of multiple meaning are not necessarily ambiguous, they can become 'rich sources of potential ambiguity':

> the confusion that ambiguity is equivalent to multiple meaning . . . can be resolved by considering ambiguity as a form of multiple meaning, different from, but capable of being evoked by, other forms of multiple meaning such as irony, paradox, alle-gory and so on.
>
> (Su, *Lexical Ambiguity in Poetry*, pp. 11–12)

Recognising ambiguity as a form of multiple meaning entails that we establish its difference from other forms. Let us look again at our definition of ambigu-ity: 'two or more distinctly different meanings sustained by the same piece of text which cannot be resolved into a single meaning'. This description does not hold good for other kinds of multiple meaning, because in each of them we are

---

[8] Soon Peng Su, *Lexical Ambiguity in Poetry* (London: Longman, 1994), p. 59. This study of poetic ambiguity is extremely useful in sorting out the confusions in literary criticism over the notion of ambiguity, and has greatly helped us in writing this chapter.

[9] For a useful discussion of multiple meaning and ambiguity in twentieth-century poetry, see Lesley Jeffries, *The Language of Twentieth-Century Poetry* (London: Macmillan, 1993), pp. 79–91.

required to discriminate the 'real' from the apparent meaning. In the irony of MacDiarmid's sonnet (discussed in Chapter 8), it would be a mistake to think that the speaker really is saying that it was a good thing for the boy to lose his legs since it has led to an encounter with a Princess. Hence, the poem's 'double' meaning resolves itself into a single meaning. In reading a metaphor, we should not lose sight of the fact that the metaphor is a way of talking about something literal rather than a means of saying two different things at once. (Having said this, it sometimes happens that a passage can be read as metaphorical and literal at one and the same time and hence is ambiguous.) And the multiple connotations which Empson teases out of Shakespeare's line add extra shades of significance and implication, but these do not become *alternatives* to one another.

In allegory, too, the surface narrative consists of a series of figurative vehicles whose tenors we are expected to keep in mind throughout (or retrospectively to recognise at some moment of revelation). George Herbert's 'Redemption' (1633), for example, weaves an allegory out of the fact that the word 'redeem' has a range of literal and metaphorical meanings: (1) buy back, recover by expenditure, convert tokens into cash; (2) fulfil promise; (3) purchase the freedom of another by ransom; (4) save, rescue, reclaim, deliver from sin; (5) make amends for.

> Having been tenant long to a rich lord,
>   Not thriving, I resolved to be bold,
>   And make a suit unto him, to afford
> A new small-rented lease, and cancel the old.
> In heaven at his manor I him sought;   5
>   They told me there that he was lately gone
>   About some land, which he had dearly bought
> Long since on earth, to take possession.
> I straight returned, and knowing his great birth,
>   Sought him accordingly in great resorts;   10
>   In cities, theatres, gardens, parks, and courts;
> At length I heard a ragged noise and mirth
>   Of thieves and murderers; there I him espied,
>   Who straight, *Your suit is granted*, said, and died.

This poem initially looks as if it is about the socioeconomic relationship between tenants and 'rich lords' in the period in which the poem was written, especially in the way the tenant has to pluck up courage to 'make a suit unto' the lord to grant him 'A new small-rented lease, and cancel the old' (3–4). It is important to realise that to make a suit *unto* someone is not the same as to make a suit *for* someone. The potentially ambiguous nature of this phrase is eliminated by the preposition and by the context: 'suit' here means a request or petition rather than a set of clothes. The speaker of this poem is petitioning or requesting his lord to cancel their old economic contract, under which he was 'Not thriving' (2), and to replace it with a better deal. (This shows that our search for ambiguities in poems cannot ride roughshod over the conventions of grammar and context.)

The first clue which indicates that this tenant–lord relationship is an allegory or extended metaphor for something else is the speaker's surprising statement that he sought his lord's 'manor' 'In heaven' (5). The fact that the lord himself is not currently 'in heaven' because he has gone on a business trip to 'take possession' of 'some land which he had dearly bought / Long since on earth' (6–8) is another clue about the real situation being dramatised in the poem. This is clearly no ordinary lord, and his business trip is no ordinary one. The identity and true business of this lord are finally confirmed when the tenant finds him among 'thieves and murderers', and by the manner in which the speaker's suit is granted: 'there I him espied, / Who straight, *Your suit is granted*, said, and died' (13–14).

To make sense of this ending, the reader has to supply the implied context – which is indicated by the presence of this lord among 'thieves and murderers' and by the fact of his death. Both these points are allusions to Christ's crucifixion as recounted in the Gospels. Once we recognise this, we realise that everything that has gone before is an allegory which uses the economic sense of 'redemption' in order to dramatise an individual instance of spiritual redemption. Thus the economic and spiritual readings of the poem are not alternative interpretations which have equal weight or validity. The potential ambiguities are resolved into allegory, and the socioeconomic story becomes a vehicle for restaging a story of Christian belief. In terms of what the poem is really about, then, there is no ambiguity. In fact, Barbara Herrnstein Smith claims that the poem's ending is 'an extraordinarily moving conclusion' which we experience 'with a double shock of surprise and recognition'.[10]

Our discussion of Herbert's poem indicates that effects of ambiguity or clarity are bound up with questions of context. Herbert was writing in a period and for a readership where he could take it for granted that his analogy between Christian belief and the tenant–landlord relationship in seventeenth-century England would be immediately understood. Christ is thought to have secured the redemption of humankind (and of individual believers) by paying with his life on the cross. This economic metaphor and the spiritual economy of this act of redemption by the 'redeemer' is the central principle of Christianity. This is how God, in the words of the poem, 'dearly' buys and 'takes possession' of the earth. Given this, the conclusion of Herbert's 'Redemption' is truly conclusive, since it re-enacts the Christian economy in an

---

[10] Smith, *Poetic Closure*, pp. 125–26.

individual instance. Christ grants the tenant's suit through and in the act of dying; the act of redemption *is* the act of dying, and so the poem closes its account, as it were, with the word 'died'.

Thus Herbert uses the double meaning of 'redemption' to make his meaning conclusive and clear – in much the same way as a *double entendre* can serve as the punch line of a joke and achieve instant recognition. Yet poems, like jokes, often depend on readers having specific knowledge if they are to have the desired effect. Both jokes and poems are largely context-dependent. Problems of interpretation may therefore arise when readers read the poem in quite different contexts, and with quite different assumptions or knowledge, from the ones Herbert anticipated and built into his poem. (Indeed, this demonstrates the importance of the distinction between the intended or implied reader and the actual reader.) But could the poem then be said to be ambiguous in a negative sense for actual readers who do not share Herbert's assumptions? We would say not. Although the poem might be confusing or obscure to a reader who does not 'get it', that is the reader's confusion, not the poem's ambiguity.

▧ Ambiguity as 'Either/Or' or 'Both/And'?

We have discovered that the thing which distinguishes ambiguity from other forms of multiple meaning is the relationship between the two or more meanings involved. The multiple meanings of ambiguity need to be distinctly different from one another, and they need to resist being resolved into a single meaning. Being more precise, we can say that in ambiguity the various meanings have to be equally possible in the context (*both* x *and* y are possible meanings), and that these possible meanings exist in an either–or relationship with each other (the meaning could be *either* x *or* y).[11] In such cases, we have no warrant for choosing between the different meanings. This is ambiguity.

We can try this out with our example from Rich's 'Orion': 'I throw back my head to take you in'. We argued in Chapter 8 that there are at least two ways of interpreting this, since 'take you in' can mean both 'absorb you intellectually' and 'admit you sexually' (with a further possible meaning of 'deceive you'). Since there is a clear difference between the two acts, and since one excludes the other, the meaning of the phrase has to be *either* one *or* the other. Yet we suggested that *both* are possible in the context of the poem. In other words, this fulfils both our criteria for ambiguity.

The degree of difference or mutual exclusion between the meanings in ambiguity can vary. The most extreme difference is when the meanings exist as logical opposites which contradict one another – as in the following example of 'disjunctive ambiguity'. In Shakespeare's *Henry VI Part Two*, which is about

---

[11] This approach to ambiguity is influenced by that in Su, *Lexical Ambiguity* pp. 43–60.

the struggle for power between Henry VI and the Duke of York, a spirit is asked to reveal the fate of the King and responds as follows:

> The Duke yet lives that Henry shall depose,
> But him outlive, and die a violent death. (I. iv. 31–32)

Line 31 can be read in two quite opposite and mutually exclusive ways: (1) 'The Duke who will depose Henry is still living'; (2) 'The Duke whom Henry will depose is still living'. Such cryptic ambiguity is quite typical of the prophecies made by spirits and witches in Shakespeare's plays (as in *Macbeth*). In this instance, both the King's and the Duke's supporters are able to interpret it as foretelling the victory of their leader. This is possible because the spirit's prophecy exhibits grammatical ambiguity – its grammatical structure can be interpreted in two quite opposite ways in terms of who does what to whom (we have slightly simplified the sentence):

> There is a Duke (object) that Henry (subject or agent)
>   shall depose (verb).
> There is a Duke (subject or agent) that Henry (object)
>   shall depose (verb).

This ambiguity is more possible in sixteenth-century English, when word order was more flexible; the phrase 'that Henry shall depose' would have been more easily understood as saying 'that shall depose Henry' than it can be in modern English. The important thing, however, is that these two possible meanings are clearly in logical opposition to each other.

Another kind of either–or relationship is when the ambiguous meanings are mutually exclusive without being logical opposites. An example discussed by Su is the following:

> The soldiers took the port at night.

The word 'port' is ambiguous because, in the context we are given, it can mean either 'harbour' or 'a kind of alcoholic beverage' (Su, *Lexical Ambiguity in Poetry*, p. 26). In this case the ambiguity is not grammatical (a matter of word order and sentence structure) but lexical – it depends on the various meanings of the word 'port' which can be found in a dictionary. In most kinds of discourse the potential ambiguity or confusion aroused by the word 'port' in this sentence would be eliminated by the larger context – the nature of the general incident being described and the relationship of the sentence to those which surround it. Yet it is also possible to create a context which would hold open both these possible meanings of 'port'. Such a strategy is a characteristic of puns. Pope uses this pun in *The Dunciad* (1743) in a satirical description of Cambridge University as a place of refuge for one of its scholars:

> Where Bentley late tempestuous wont to sport
> In troubled waters, but now sleeps in port. (IV, 201–2)

Derek Attridge provides a succinct analysis of this pun:

> In most of our encounters with the word *port*, the context in which it occurs . . . suppresses large areas of its potential signification; Pope's achievement in this couplet is to leave unsuppressed two apparently incompatible fields of meaning . . . by inventing a context in which both are simultaneously acceptable. The noble conception of the tempest-tossed bark at last lying peacefully in harbour is radically undercut by the unseemly image of the great scholar reduced to drunken slumber by nightly overindulgence, and the movement between the two is as inescapable as it is perpetual.[12]

Discussion of this kind of ambiguity often makes reference to those visual puns which oscillate uncontrollably from one image to another as we look at them. The best discussion of this effect is E.H. Gombrich's account of the visual pun of the rabbit–duck image:

> We can see the picture as either a rabbit or a duck . . . the shape transforms itself in some subtle way when the duck's beak becomes the rabbit's ears and brings an otherwise neglected spot into prominence as the rabbit's mouth. . . . We can switch from one reading to another with increasing rapidity; we will also 'remember' the rabbit while we see the duck, but the more closely we watch ourselves, the more certainly will we discover that we cannot experience alternative readings at the same time.[13]

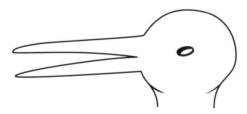

To say that this picture is 'really' a duck or 'really' a rabbit would be to miss the whole point. Nor can we say that the two pictures or readings are somehow blended together. Instead, they coexist as contradictions of each other. This is ambiguity.

---

[12] Attridge, 'Unpacking the Portmanteau, or Who's Afraid of *Finnegans Wake*?', in Jonathan Culler, ed., *On Puns: The foundation of letters* (Oxford: Blackwell, 1988), pp. 140–55 (141).

[13] E.H. Gombrich, *Art and Illusion: A study in the psychology of pictorial representation*, 5th edn (London: Phaidon, 1977), pp. 4–5.

◼ Lexical and Syntactical Ambiguity

There are two basic reasons why ambiguity is possible in language: first because syntax and grammatical structure can be open to different readings, and secondly because individual words can have more than one meaning. It can sometimes be useful to make a distinction between syntactical and lexical ambiguity. The example from *Henry VI Part Two* discussed above was syntactically (that is to say, grammatically) ambiguous. The following statements are further examples:

> The shooting of the hunters was terrible.
> Visiting relatives can be tedious.[14]

The first of these can be read as saying either that 'it was terrible that the hunters were shot' or that 'the shooting which the hunters did was terrible'. This is because the syntax does not allow us to decide whether the hunters are the agents or the objects of shooting. In the second example, the ambiguity pivots over the word 'visiting', which can be read either as an action or as an adjective.

Lexical ambiguity draws on the fact that the English language is replete with words which have more than one meaning and with different words which have the same sound (and often the same spelling). Open a dictionary at random, choose any word, and it is quite likely that your choice will have more than one – perhaps several – distinctive meanings listed under that entry. An example discovered at random is 'submit' (which means both to put forward for consideration and to surrender). You may also find two different words with exactly the same spelling and pronunciation listed one after the other as separate entries. An example of the latter, discovered at random, is 'hop' (to spring on one foot) and 'hop' (a climbing plant with bitter cones used to flavour beer). Words with more than one meaning are called 'polysemous'; different words with the same sound are called 'homonyms'.

◼ Homonyms and Polysemous Words

In homonyms, then, two different words have the same sound (and perhaps spelling). Examples include 'port', 'hop', 'ball' (spherical object, dance), 'mail' (post, armour), 'cape' (garment, promontory), 'till' (cash register, until, to cultivate, boulder clay), 'vice' (failing or bad habit, device for clamping things), 'graft' (to toil, to transplant living tissue). Because the meanings of homonyms are usually completely unrelated to one another, they are a fruitful source of

---

[14] These examples, which were originally discussed by the linguist Noam Chomsky, are taken from Attridge, in Culler, *On Puns*, p. 141.

ambiguity. In some rare but interesting cases, the two meanings of a homonym are opposites – as in 'cleave' (to split asunder) and 'cleave' (to adhere closely).

Polysemous words, by contrast, are single words with different meanings. Examples include 'vision' (the act or faculty of seeing, a thing seen, an imaginary sight, insight or foresight), 'sentence' (a combination of words expressing a thought, a judgment passed on a criminal by a court, to pass sentence), 'suit' (the act of suing, a petition, an action in a court of law, a series of things of the same kind or material, to fit, to be adapted to, to please), 'score' (a cut on the surface of something, a tally mark, the number twenty, number of points, goals, etc., written music, plus all the verbs associated with these things). Because the meanings of polysemous words are usually related to each other in some way (if they were not, they would be different words), and because that degree of relation can vary from quite distinct to quite close, it may become unclear in some instances whether the meanings are far enough apart to allow for ambiguity.

Neither homonyms nor polysemous words are ambiguous in themselves. Usually, the context in which they are used excludes those meanings which are not relevant. They become ambiguous only when, whether by accident or by design, the context allows two or more of the meanings to be equally relevant and possible. With homonyms, as we have seen, there is usually no overlap between meanings, and this means that homonyms can provide the raw material for clear-cut ambiguity when the context allows it – as in the cases of 'port' (sorry!) examined above. With polysemous words, however, the ambiguities can be less obvious, more subtle, and occasionally debatable. An example arises in Burns's 'A Red, Red Rose' (1796):

> O my luve's like a red, red rose,
>   That's newly sprung in June;
> O my luve's like the melodie
>   That's sweetly sung in tune.
>
> As fair art thou, my bonnie lass,   5
>   So deep in luve am I;
> And I will luve thee still, my dear,
>   Till a' the seas gang dry.
>
> Till a' the seas gang dry, my dear,
>   And the rocks melt wi' the sun: 10
> O I will luve thee still, my dear
>   While the sands o' life shall run.
>
> And fare thee weel, my only luve,
>   And fare thee weel awhile!
> And I will come again, my luve,   15
>   Though it were ten thousand mile.

In everyday usage, love (or 'luve') is used as a verb ('I love you') and as a noun which can refer either to the emotion of love ('I am in love') or to the person loved. In 'Red, Red Rose', Burns uses 'luve' in all these senses. In the second stanza, it appears both as emotional state ('So deep in luve am I') and as verb ('I will luve thee'). In the final stanza, however, the speaker refers to his beloved as 'luve': 'fare thee weel, my only luve'. These different uses are all clearly distinguished from each other. But in the first stanza it is not clear whether 'luve' refers to the speaker's emotional state or to his beloved: 'O my luve's like a red, red rose'. That Burns uses 'luve' in both senses in subsequent stanzas does not help us to resolve this. Nor is the ambiguity resolved by the fact that stanzas two to four are addressed to his beloved, since it does not follow that the first stanza is also addressed to her. Thus the double meaning of 'luve' in the first stanza remains unresolved, and perhaps unresolvable. Yet the two distinct meanings of 'luve' are not in conflict with one another and they add up to a coherent poetic statement. In fact, the second stanza seems to suggest that there is a direct ratio between the extent of her beauty and the depth of his love: 'As fair art thou, my bonnie lass, / So deep in luve am I'. In examining a similar double usage of 'love' in Blake, Su concludes that these possible senses are incompatible on one level (one reference is to an emotional state, the other to a human being) and so ambiguous. But she also recognises that 'The two senses for love . . . can be compatible, as one can tell one's love (person) about one's love (state of emotion)'. Since she accepts that Blake's usage of 'love' is ambiguous (we would say the same for Burns's), she concludes that the meanings in question do not have to be contradictory or even incompatible to create ambiguity: *'difference between senses which are distinct and disparate* is a sufficient condition for ambiguity to occur' (*Lexical Ambiguity in Poetry,* p. 47).

■ Ambiguity of Connotations as Well as Denotations?

Su argues that ambiguity should be reserved as a description of divergent relations between denotations (as in the homonym 'port' or the polysemous 'love' examined above). This is because ambiguity, she claims, is established not by connotation but by denotation. The phrase 'a human elephant' is ambiguous because it denotes either an elephant which is in some way like a human being or a human being who is in some way like an elephant. Although the connotations associated with 'elephant' and 'human' will come into play in either case, they are not involved in producing the ambiguity (see Su, pp. 23–4). She also argues that, in any case, 'connotative meaning is subjective: it is apt to vary from individual to individual, from period to period, or from community to community. This makes it too unstable and open-ended to constitute a major factor in ambiguity' (p. 23).

Su seeks here to distinguish between the clear-cut nature of denotative ambiguity and the 'open-ended' nature of connotative implications. Yet we would argue that 'ambiguous connotation' generates some of the most subtle ambiguities in poems. For an example of this, we can turn back to our discussion of the last stanza of Rich's 'Song' in Chapter 5:

> If I'm lonely
> it's with the rowboat ice-fast on the shore
> in the last red light of the year
> that knows what it is, that knows it's neither
> ice nor mud nor winter light
> but wood, with a gift for burning

We claimed in Chapter 5 that this final image is ambiguous because it 'seems to imply a number of possibilities which derive from the multiple connotations of fire and burning':

1 It/she has a gift for giving out warmth;
2 It/she has a gift for sexual passion;
3 It/she has a gift for freeing itself/herself from the ice;
4 It/she has a gift for self-destruction;
5 It/she has a gift for leaving everything behind and destroying any possibility of returning (through an allusion to the idiomatic phrase 'to burn one's boats');
6 It/she has a gift for destroying things that surround it/her.

All these possible connotations are relevant to the context and, although there is some overlap, there are enough differences between them to make it impossible to reduce the ending to a single meaning which would include all these potential meanings. And because we have no reason to justify choosing one at the expense of the others, we can say that the ending is ambiguous at the level of the connotations.

▮ A Word of Caution

It is easy to become overenthusiastic in the search for ambiguity in poems, so it needs to be stressed that the words and phrases used in poetry are not always ambiguous. And although poetry often exploits the ambiguous possibilities inherent in language itself, this does not mean that each word or phrase in a poem has as many meanings as we can find for it. As always, we need to interpret the individual word or phrase within the context of the whole poem, and sometimes we might need to consider the historical context in which the poem was written. Words continually change their meaning or develop new meanings, so words which were unambiguous at the time of writing may seem potentially ambiguous at the time of reading.

Sometimes, the effect of a word in a poem arises because of the way its various possible meanings are *excluded* in order to leave a single, incisive meaning. Poets cut away extraneous meanings as often as they exploit multiple meanings. A good example can be found in Donne's 'A Valediction: Forbidding Mourning' (which we discussed in Chapter 6):

> Our two souls therefore, which are one,
>   Though I must go, endure not yet
> A breach, but an expansion,
>   Like gold to airy thinness beat. (21–24)

In general usage, the word 'beat' may have one of several meanings according to the context in which it is used (punishment, competition, music, and so on). In Donne's poem, however, the word does not ask us to think about all the possible meanings of 'beat'. And although it is used as a past tense of 'to beat' in the sense of to strike or hit repeatedly, the way it is used in the poem excludes any association with pain or violence. Only *one* of the possible meanings of 'beat' is appropriate in this context – to shape and thin (gold) by blows with a hammer. This is a delicate action, since it transforms gold 'to airy thinness'. Thus, although we are encouraging you to be alert to potential ambiguities in poems, and to use a dictionary in this quest, we also urge you to test out possible ambiguities against the actual context formed by the poem's language.

Our experience of teaching Herbert's 'Redemption' alerts us to another way in which inexperienced readers can 'discover' ambiguity which is not there. Although we have claimed that the poem is not ambiguous, and that it achieves 'closure' at the end, we have seen some readers find it confusing or 'ambiguous'. It is therefore worth examining how the poem could be thought ambiguous. There are two factors involved. The first factor is that some readers do not see the theological significance of the ending because, for one reason or another, they are either not aware of the Christian story of the death of Jesus on the cross or not familiar with what we can call the 'spiritual economy' which is supposed to be enacted by that death. Such readers have reported a shock of surprise that the poem should end in death but have enjoyed no shock of recognition. The second factor is that without the safeguard of this recognition, readers seem to find the syntax of the conclusion a source of confusion. This can leave readers unsure about who it is that has died (is it the lord or the tenant?). These factors may lead such readers to claim that the poem is ambiguous.

But although syntax can be a significant source of ambiguity in poems, we want to show that the syntax here is not at all ambiguous. Let us examine it carefully:

> there I him espied,
> Who straight, *Your suit is granted*, said, and died.

There are four verbal phrases here ('espied', 'is granted', 'said' and 'died'), and we need to ask who is the agent of these verbs – that is, who does these things? Who says the italicised phrase? Who dies? We can begin to answer these questions by dividing the lines into phrases in order to display their syntax:

> there I him espied,
> Who straight, Your suit is granted, said,
> and died.

Now try answering the question yourself: who is the agent in each phrase – that is, who does the action in each case?

Our answers to these questions are as follows. The first phrase seems clear enough if we rearrange the syntax into a more conventional pattern:

the speaker ('I') caught sight of ('espied') the lord ('him') 'there' (amongst 'thieves and murderers')

The analysis of the second phrase can be taken in two stages. First, we can clarify the syntax by rearranging it:

who immediately ('straight') said 'Your suit is granted'

Secondly, we need to decide to whom 'Who' refers. There are two clues to this. The first depends on the grammatical relationship between the first and second phrases:

I espied him, who said . . .

'Who' must therefore be 'him' (the lord). This is supported by the second clue – the actual content of the direct speech which is marked off from the rest of the text by the use of italics: 'Your suit is granted'. We know from the rest of the poem that the speaker is making a suit 'unto the lord', and that he hopes that the lord will grant that suit. The lord does so in the direct speech indicated in the last line. The interlocking grammar of the poem's concluding lines now makes the analysis of the last phrase clear:

> I caught sight of the lord; he said 'Your suit is
> granted' and [then] died.

Unravelling the syntax of this line-and-a-half has involved quite a lengthy ana-lysis, and many readers will have realised the syntactic structure without it. But the process has shown that, although the syntax here may be unconventional, it is not at all ambiguous. If readers feel that these lines are 'ambiguous' they are really saying that they find them difficult or obscure. Ambiguity, as we said above, is something which exists in a text. A reader's confusion is not a text's ambiguity.

For the most part, syntax in poetry follows the basic conventions of syntax in general. Although it often takes poetic liberties, and although it is sometimes archaic or elaborate, poetic syntax can usually be followed in the same way as syntax in any other discourse. This needs to be stressed, because the division of poetry into lines can lead readers to confine their attention to individual lines and thus overlook the way an elaborate sentence may stretch across many lines and still need to be read *as a sentence*. This is not to say that the use of lines does not interfere with and creatively modify the way we read poetic syntax (as we saw in Chapter 3), but it is to insist that we should always try to work out the syntax of sentences in poems.[15] Passages in poems which seem ambigu-ous or confusing – or are potentially misleading – may suddenly resolve them-selves through careful analysis of syntax.

■ New Criticism: Interpreting Ambiguity as Organic Unity

The New Critics made ambiguity (along with the related effects of irony and paradox) the defining characteristic of poetic language. Yet although the New Critics were exceptionally sensitive to ambiguity in poems, they were equally committed to producing interpretations which resolved those ambiguities into a complex organic unity. Cleanth Brooks, our archetypal New Critic, reveals the New Critical line on ambiguity in a discussion of Wordsworth's 'Ode: Intimations of Immortality' (1807):

> The poem . . . displays a rather consistent symbolism. . . . more surprising is the fact that the symbols reveal so many ambiguities. In a few cases, this ambiguity, of which Wordsworth . . . was apparently only partially aware, breaks down into outright confusion. Yet much of the ambiguity is rich and meaningful . . . and it is in terms of this ambiguity that many of the finest effects of the poem are achieved.[16]

---

[15] For a difficult but brilliant discussion of the production of ambiguity through syntax in nine-teenth-century poetry, see Armstrong, *Language as Living Form in Nineteenth-Century Poetry*.

[16] 'Wordsworth and the Paradox of the Imagination', in Brooks, *Well Wrought Urn*, pp. 114–38 (115).

For the New Critics, then, ambiguity can be of two kinds. The ambiguity of 'outright confusion' is problematic, and arises out of a poet's failure to resolve all the contradictions opened up by the poem. The ambiguity which is 'rich and meaningful', by contrast, produces poetry's 'finest effects'. Brooks anticipates that his readers might be surprised by his claims that there are enriching ambiguities in Wordsworth's poem because those readers had been trained to think of Wordsworth as a sincere and straightforward poet. Yet Brooks seeks to argue that good ambiguity is the sign of good poetry and of the poetic imagination at work. He values the 'good' ambiguities in Wordsworth's 'Ode' because, he claims, they display the poem's central theme – which he takes to be the processes of the poetic imagination itself. Brooks assumes that these processes are in themselves ambiguous and paradoxical. In another essay, 'The Language of Paradox', he claims that the poetic imagination unifies through welding together 'the discordant and the contradictory' in a 'fusion which is not logical'. He supports this through quoting Coleridge's account of the unifying power of the imagination, which 'reveals itself in the balance or reconcilement of opposite or discordant qualities' (*Well Wrought Urn*, p. 17).

The 'Intimations Ode' is too long and complex to present and discuss at length here, but it is possible to quote enough to be able to examine the assumptions about ambiguity which inform Brooks's insightful reading of it. The poem opens with Wordsworth's sense that he has lost forever the visionary powers he claims to have had as a child (in much Romantic poetry, there is a tendency to elide the difference between poet and speaker):

> There was a time when meadow, grove, and stream,
> The earth, and every common sight,
>   To me did seem
>   Apparelled in celestial light,
> The glory and the freshness of a dream.
> It is not now as it hath been of yore –
>   Turn whereso'er I may,
>   By night or day,
> The things which I have seen I now can see no more. (1–9)

For Brooks, the central question which this stanza opens up is who or what once 'apparelled' the earth in 'celestial light'. Being 'celestial', the light apparently comes from heaven (*either* from a divine source *or* from the sun and moon). Wordsworth's later reference to his loss of the 'visionary gleam' (57) echoes with 'seem' and 'dream', and raises the question of the substantiality and value of this vision. Is it that the earth only *seemed* to be clothed in glory, and that this was in fact merely a dream, or does this indicate the fleeting fragility of genuine revelation? In the fifth stanza, Wordsworth claims that we are born into the world 'trailing clouds of glory . . . / From God' (65–66). Brooks links this image with the poem's many images of the sun and moon – 'The sunshine is a glorious birth' (16) – in order to suggest that the child may be a source of light, like the rising sun 'which brings its radiance with it' (p. 119). In other words, the source of the visionary gleam which appareds the earth in childhood becomes ambiguous: is it from a celestial source (God or the sun and moon), or does it come from within the child himself?

The poem develops the parallel between the child and the sun to imply that just as the glorious light of dawn 'fades' into the common light of day, so too does the child's world lose the visionary gleam as he matures into adulthood. With the loss of visionary insight, the adult grows accustomed to the everyday sights of the earth, but always feels a sense of loss. (This, incidentally, demonstrates that Wordsworth was far from being a 'nature poet' – in his poetry, nature bereft of imaginative vision is radically impoverished.) Stanzas 3 and 4 indicate this loss of vision by shifting their emphasis from sight to the sounds of the world. In the sixth stanza, the earth attempts to accustom the growing child to itself and make him forget his visionary heritage, and the seventh stanza traces the growth from childhood to old age as if it were a series of theatrical roles which have to be learnt but are alien to the soul's true nature. Stanzas nine to eleven are the so-called 'recovery' stanzas in which Wordsworth attempts to revivify at least the 'embers' (131) of childhood vision:

> . . . those first affections,
> Those shadowy recollections,
> Which, be they what they may,
> Are yet the fountain light of all our day,
> Are yet a master light of all our seeing. (150–54)

The final stanza apparently brings full recovery and resolution:

> I love the Brooks which down their channels fret,
> Even more than when I tripped lightly as they;
> The innocent brightness of a newborn Day
>   Is lovely yet;
> The clouds that gather round the setting sun
> Do take a sober colouring from an eye
> That hath kept watch o'er man's mortality;
> Another race hath been, and other palms are won.
> Thanks to the human heart by which we live,
> Thanks to its tenderness, its joys, and fears,
> To me the meanest flower that blows can give
> Thoughts that do often lie too deep for tears. (195–206)

Brooks argues that this stanza dramatises the imagination at work in its process of reconciling opposites. The poem has, in effect, raised the question of how the imagination works by asking whether the visionary gleam is projected on to nature by the child or whether it results from an innocent way of looking which yields insights into nature's divinity to which others are blind. Brooks cites I.A. Richards's claim that Wordsworth's and Coleridge's theory of the imagination involved both doctrines at various moments, and then argues that Wordsworth's 'Ode' reconciles them through its system of ambiguous symbols:

> If the poem is about the synthesizing imagination . . . the reason for the major ambiguities is revealed. These basic ambiguities . . . assert themselves as the poem ends. Just before he renders thanks to the human heart . . . the poet says that the clouds do not give *to*, but take *from*, the eye their sober coloring. But in the last two lines of the stanza, the flower does not take *from*, but gives *to*, the heart. We can have it either way. Indeed, the poem implies that we must have it *both* ways.
>
> (*Well Wrought Urn*, p. 136)

Brooks is therefore saying that the poet's recovery from his crisis is achieved through regaining the simultaneous 'give-and-take' of imaginative vision, which both confers colour on the world (in the way that the setting sun confers colour on the clouds) and receives impressions from the world (from even the 'meanest flower') which are far more profound than those of ordinary sight.

Thus Wordsworth's 'Ode' opens up huge questions, only to attempt to stage recovery and achieve resolution through reconciling its central ambiguities in a dramatisation of imaginative vision. To the extent that it achieves such closure, Brooks admires the poem. Yet although he celebrates the ending, he feels that the 'solution is asserted rather than dramatized' and is not therefore poetically justified. He claims that 'some of the difficulties we meet in the last stanzas appear not enriching ambiguities but distracting confusions' (p. 137). One of these unresolved 'confusions' arises from the fact that whereas Wordsworth had earlier hailed the child as 'Thou best Philosopher' (112) because he has not yet lost the visionary power, in the penultimate stanza he celebrates the 'years that bring the philosophic mind' (188). Another 'confusion' which Brooks does not mention, but one which would affect his reading, is the fact that when he presents his 'fallen' state in stanza four, Wordsworth attempts to rejoice in the way 'Earth herself is adorning' (44). If the earth can adorn itself, this contradicts the suggestion in the first stanza – on which Brooks's reading depends – that the earth is 'appareled' by some outside agency (such as the child).

Thus, as Brooks puts it, even though the 'Ode' consists of great poetry 'sustained almost throughout the poem', nevertheless 'there is some vagueness . . . and there are some loose ends' (p. 138). These present 'difficulties' for Brooks because his programme of interpretation and his underlying assumptions about poetry lead him to expect that a 'good poem' will yield to interpretation a wholly unified meaning where all the loose ends are woven into a consistent pattern which is sustained throughout. Ambiguities, then, are of value only when they are resolved by the poem – or, more precisely, resolvable by interpretation. The 'good' ambiguities in the poem are held together in a coherent unity because they are supposedly produced by the imagination and display its characteristic nature. The 'bad' ambiguities in the poem are, by contrast, logical inconsistencies and distracting confusions which leave loose ends unresolved (pp. 133–8).

For Brooks, then, ambiguity ought to enrich a poem's central theme, idea or meaning, and ambiguities which cannot be incorporated in this way are held to produce confusion or incoherence and hence a degree of poetic failure. Good poetry is richly ambiguous; bad poetry is incoherently ambiguous. New Criticism's understanding of ambiguity is therefore reminiscent of its treatment of irony in that both are valued in so far as they contribute to a poem's internal consistency. In fact, it seems as if the New Critics sought to resolve the either/or of ambiguity into the both/and logic of a weak version of paradox. As Brooks says of the conclusion to the 'Ode', 'We can have it either way. Indeed, the poem implies that we must have it *both* ways.' For Brooks, this is precisely the 'paradox' of the imagination. A paradox, for Brooks, is 'the assertion of the union of opposites'. This is why paradox and ambiguity supposedly indicate a *unified* rather than a contradictory experience: 'If the poet, then, must perforce dramatize the oneness of the experience, even though paying tribute to its diversity, then his use of paradox and ambiguity is seen as necessary' (pp. 194, 195). As Timothy Bahti has argued, 'Brooks's paradox does not preserve or otherwise unfold ambiguity, but rather enfolds and smothers or cancels it. There is, in fact, nothing uncertain or self-contradictory about Brooks's "paradox".'[17] There may be ambiguities in poems, but they are 'solved' by the critical interpretation (Bahti, pp. 212–13). Impressive though Brooks's interpretations of poems are, then, it should be recognised that their attention to ambiguity is concerned primarily with interpreting away the self-contradictory status of ambiguity into the resolution of poetic 'closure'.

▮ The 'Duck–Rabbit Effect' of Strong Ambiguity

New Criticism, then, drew attention to ambiguity in poetry in order to resolve it through interpretation. We would suggest that an alternative, more exciting, response to ambiguity in poems is to attempt to hold it open and remain alert to the way the poem itself keeps it open. In fact, it is only by resisting the

---

[17] Timothy Bahti, 'Ambiguity and Indeterminacy: The Juncture', *Comparative Literature* (1986) 38, p. 211.

desire to resolve ambiguity through interpretation that we can remain 'faithful' to the text's challenge.

A poem which sustains a 'duck–rabbit' effect at the level of connotation throughout its three stanzas is Leonard Cohen's 'As the Mist Leaves No Scar' (1961). On the face of it, this seems to be a straightforwardly simple poem, yet a close reading indicates that the same words can be read as having two quite opposing but equally possible connotations.

> As the mist leaves no scar
> On the dark green hill,
> So my body leaves no scar
> On you, nor ever will.
>
> When wind and hawk encounter,   5
> What remains to keep?
> So you and I encounter,
> Then turn, then fall to sleep.
>
> As many nights endure
> Without a moon or star,   10
> So will we endure
> When one is gone and far.

In this seemingly tender love lyric, a speaker is addressing his beloved about the quality of their love. As in many such poems, the speaker employs a series of similes which liken their love to natural phenomena. Yet this quite conventional device is brought to life again by a certain haunting ambiguity in the poem. Let us read it image by image.

The claim 'my body leaves no scar / On you, nor ever will' (3–4) can be read in two ways in the context of the rest of the poem: (1) my physical love for you has no violence in it – it will not wound you or your body, and it never will; (2) my physical love for you will not leave a lasting impression on you; it will leave no trace and when I am gone it will be as if I had never been. Both these opposite readings can be supported by the other half of the simile: 'As the mist leaves no scar / On the dark green hill'. Their coming together in love is likened to the impact the mist has on the hill. Is this impact beautiful, or merely ephemeral?

The second stanza introduces a new natural simile for their lovemaking: 'When wind and hawk encounter, / What remains to keep?' (5–6). This simile for the sexual encounter between the lovers likens their lovemaking to the powerful image of a hawk balanced and suspended in the wind. Again, this can be read in two opposite ways: (1) as a pure and exhilarating encounter which leaves both wind and hawk proudly free; (2) as a coming together with no significance or consequence beyond the immediate moment. And does the fact that they turn from each other and fall asleep suggest how satisfying their lovemaking is, or how indifferent they are to each other after lovemaking?

The third stanza suggests that the lovers endure each other's absence as the night has sometimes to endure the absence of moon or stars. As with any simile, we need to decide what features are transferred from vehicle to tenor. A crucial question concerns whether the lovers' coming separation will be temporary or permanent. Are we meant to assume that they will be reunited after a separation in the same way the stars can only ever be temporarily absent from the night? This question is kept open by the ambiguity which arises from the different possible ways of interpreting the line 'So will we endure'. As a dictionary reveals, 'endure' (which comes from the Latin *durare*, harden) has two main groups of meanings: (1) undergo pain, tolerate, submit to; (2) remain in existence, last a long time. The speaker could be invoking both meanings simultaneously in an effort of reassurance: although our separation will cause us pain, we will survive it. Yet it is not clear whether they are to endure a temporary or a permanent separation. Both possibilities are kept open by the last line: 'When one is gone and far'. 'When' here does not specify the nature of the separation (contrast it with '*while* one is gone and far'). This ambiguity is also kept open by the use of 'we' in 'So will *we* endure'. Will they endure (survive) as a couple, or endure as individuals going their separate ways? And if it is the latter, is the tone reassuring or cynical – saying something like 'Don't worry, we'll get over it, it's not such a big thing'?

Given these two alternative, apparently equally supportable, interpretations of the poem, we can ask about its tone. Is it loving and celebratory, or indifferent and cynical? To choose one reading over the other would be to ignore the other possible reading – which might tell us something about ourselves, but only at the cost of failing to recognise something interesting and challenging about the poem itself. The poem's tone, we suggest, is irresolvably ambiguous in the sense that the words make it impossible for us to decide how the speaker feels towards the addressee. (This is not to decide that the lover is ambivalent towards his beloved, but that the poem's tone is ambiguous.)

Our reading of Cohen's 'As the Mist Leaves No Scar' has claimed that the poem makes possible two readings which are completely at odds with one another. Rather than choosing between these readings, or attempting to resolve them into a coherent interpretation, we have chosen instead to attempt to describe how both readings are made possible by the poem. In other words, rather than interpreting the poem, we have sought to analyse the way it generates reading possibilities. This shift from interpretation to analytic description entails thinking of poetry not simply as a means of conveying a message or expressing a meaning, but as a discourse which uses language to produce intellectual and aesthetic effects. In Cohen's poem, whatever its message might be to the beloved, the fascination for us is the way it draws on the storehouse of ambiguities inherent in language in order to produce ambiguities which resist being reduced to singular meaning.

In poetry, then, ambiguity can serve to enrich and complicate meaning in ways which may allow us to re-read poems many times without feeling that they have become obvious or stale. It is often the ambiguity of a poem which gives it its subtle charge, or makes it challenging and continually interesting and stimulating. An ambiguous moment in a poem can continue to intrigue us even after reading (and teaching) it many times. In fact, we would conclude by arguing that the ability to remain open to potential ambiguity, rather than attempting to find the 'proper' meaning, is one of the skills or attitudes which is most crucial to develop in reading poetry. In this way, we would be developing a response towards poems reminiscent of Keats's description of what he called '**Negative Capability**':

> at once it struck me, what quality went to form a Man of Achievement especially in Literature & which Shakespeare possessed so enormously – I mean *Negative Capability*, that is when a man is capable of being in uncertainties, Mysteries, doubts, without any irritable reaching after fact & reason.[18]

Exercises

1 Read the following poem (by Edwin Muir, 1925) and then try to answer the questions that follow.

Childhood

Long time he lay upon the sunny hill,
    To his father's house below securely bound.
Far off the silent, changing sound was still,
    With the black islands lying thick around.

He saw each separate height, each vaguer hue,   5
    Where the massed islands rolled in mist away,
And though all ran together in his view
    He knew that unseen straits between them lay.

Often he wondered what new shores were there.
    In thought he saw the still light on the sand,   10
The shallow water clear in tranquil air,
    And walked through it in joy from strand to strand.

[18] Letter of 21 December 1817 to George and Thomas Keats, in Keats, *Letters*, p. 43.

> Over the sound a ship so slow would pass
> > That in the black hill's gloom it seemed to lie.
> The evening sound was smooth like sunken glass,   15
> > And time seemed finished ere the ship passed by.
>
> Grey tiny rocks slept round him where he lay,
> > Moveless as they, more still as evening came,
> The grasses threw straight shadows far away,
> > And from the house his mother called his name.   20

(a) Spend some time reading and re-reading this poem, trying to understand it. Make sure you consider (i) what is happening, (ii) where it is set, (iii) the symbolic connotations of the poem's metaphors and images, and (iv) what it is saying and/or suggesting about the boy's situation in life and/or his inner life.

(b) Are there any words or phrases that are ambiguous? If so, (i) try to spell out or paraphrase the various meanings and (ii) try to decide whether these various meanings are equally possible and relevant in the context of the poem.

(c) Is the ambiguity at the level of denotation or connotation?

(d) Are the various meanings or connotations of each ambiguous phrase (i) logically contradictory, (ii) mutually exclusive, or (iii) simply distinct senses?

(e) Does the ambiguity work as 'both/and' or 'either/or'?

(f) For each ambiguity, try to say how it relates to what the poem is saying about the boy's situation in life and/or his inner life.

(g) Is there a relationship in the poem between ambiguity and ambivalence?

(h) Are there any words or phrases in the poem that could be ambiguous in a different context but which should not be read as ambiguous in this poem? Identify one such word or phrase, explain how it could be ambiguous in another context, and say why it is not ambiguous in the poem.

2 Read the following poem – Shakespeare's sonnet 138, first published in 1599 when Shakespeare was thirty-five – and then try to answer the questions that follow.

> When my love swears that she is made of truth,
> I do believe her, though I know she lies,
> That she might think me some untutored youth,
> Unlearnèd in the world's false subtleties.
> Thus vainly thinking that she thinks me young,   5
> Although she knows my days are past the best,

Simply I credit her false-speaking tongue:
On both sides thus is simple truth suppressed.
But wherefore says she not she is unjust?
And wherefore say I not that I am old?   10
Oh, love's best habit is in seeming trust,
And age in love loves not to have years told.
  Therefore I lie with her and she with me,
  And in our faults by lies we flattered be.

(a) After reading the poem carefully, try to sum up what the speaker is saying about (i) his love, (ii) himself, (iii) his relationship with his love.

(b) Make sure that you understand the meaning of all the words and phrases in the poem; if necessary, look them up in a good dictionary (e.g., the *Oxford English Dictionary*).

(c) Are there any words or phrases that are ambiguous or have multiple meanings in the poem? Try to paraphrase the different meanings and say how they might be equally relevant to the overall poem.

(d) Are the multiple meanings you have found achieved though lexical or syntactic ambiguity? Do they make use of homonyms and/or polysemous words? Are they puns?

(e) How do the ambiguities you have discovered relate to (i) the speaker's self-image, (ii) the speaker's image of his love, (iii) the speaker's feelings about his relationship with her, or (iv) the speaker's general attitude towards the relationship between men and women?

3 Choose two homonyms and two polysemous words (perhaps by using a dictionary) and, for each one, try to invent a pun or a line of poetry that makes effective use of these multiple meanings. Using one or more of your examples, try to write a short poem in which ambiguity or multiple meaning plays a significant role.

Part Three

TEXTS IN CONTEXTS/CONTEXTS IN TEXTS

Chapter 10

Introducing Contexts

In this chapter we want to draw attention to the impact upon poetry of the different contexts in which it is written and read. 'Context' is a term traditionally used by literary critics to identify a range of external factors which formed a 'background' at the time when a text was written and can be shown to have had some kind of impact on its writing or meaning. In this section of the book we examine in some depth a range of different kinds of context which may shape the writing of poetry and which readers may need to consider. It would seem, then, that we are embarking on a major shift of emphasis in our discussion. In the previous chapters we have stressed the central importance of close and detailed attention to elements which are internal to poems themselves (metre, metaphor, ambiguity, tone, and so on). From now on, we will be introducing factors which are ostensibly outside individual poems (social context, political and historical events, other literary texts, and so on). This will help us to argue that the close *textual* reading of poetry needs to be supplemented with appropriate *contextual* knowledge of various kinds.

The distinction between factors which are internal and those which are external to a text is one of the basic moves of literary criticism. In their *Theory of Literature* (1949) René Wellek and Austin Warren divide the study of literature into 'The Extrinsic' and 'The Intrinsic' approaches. The extrinsic approach includes examining the various relationships between literature and non-literary contexts in chapters such as 'Literature and Biography', 'Literature and Society', 'Literature and Ideas' and 'Literature and the Other Arts'. Wellek and Warren point out that the extrinsic approach had hitherto dominated the study of literature and claim that, although it had undoubtedly thrown light on the conditions under which literature has been produced, it had not contributed much to the actual study of literary texts. Such scholarship, they suggest, does not in any way prepare scholars for the reading of literary texts themselves: they mention 'the astonishing helplessness of most scholars when confronted with the task of actually analysing and evaluating a work of art'.[1] This is why Wellek and Warren devote the bulk of their book to discussing the intrinsic approach to literature, which involves looking at features which are internal to individual literary texts or to literature in general (chapters are devoted to issues such as 'Rhythm and Metre', 'Image, Metaphor, Symbol, Myth', 'Literary Genres' and 'Literary History').

Wellek and Warren's book encouraged New Criticism's attempt to downplay interest in external factors by making the close reading of 'the words on the page' the central and characteristic activity of literary study. For New Criticism, external approaches were, at best, only an aid to criticism and, at worse, bad substitutes for it. The New Critics temporarily won the argument about the proper focus of literary studies because they presented a coherent and teachable practice – the close reading of poems – and because the contextual study of literature at the time was little more than a mishmash of different approaches with little theoretical coherence or identifiable methodology.[2] Yet we shall see in subsequent chapters that New Criticism's overemphasis on text at the expense of context has itself been found wanting by more recent approaches which have developed new and compelling accounts of the importance of reading literature within its various contexts of production and reception.

A poem's date of composition is a necessary first clue to establishing the historical context in which it was produced. That context may include historical, political, social and cultural factors, as well as various literary and discursive elements. A poem's literary context may include the other literature produced in the same period (including other texts by the poem's author), along with various kinds of intertextual connections between the poem and other literary texts in the 'tradition'. We also want to show that literature is not a hermetically sealed discourse but porous to, even shaped by, the larger cultural and discursive activity going on in the society in which it is produced. The term 'discursive' is the adjective from 'discourse', a word which in recent literary theory has had its original sense extended to become an umbrella term for the whole range of written and cultural texts produced within a society at any particular historical moment. A poem's 'discursive context', then, can include all the kinds of writing being produced at the time when it was written.

In the chapters that follow we shall begin by looking at how the production and reception of poetry are affected by literary and more general discursive

---

[1] Wellek and Warren, *Theory of Literature*, p. 139.

[2] See John Crowe Ransom, 'Criticism Inc.', reprinted in Lodge, *Twentieth Century Literary Criticism*, pp. 228–39.

networks, examining the contexts created by genre, allusion and intertextuality. We shall then extend our investigation by looking at larger questions of history and politics. As the discussion develops, the provisional – but heuristically useful – distinctions we have just outlined will turn out to be complex and even problematic. We shall have to recognise, for example, that the distinction between historical and discursive contexts does not hold in any sustained examination of context. This is because history and politics impact upon our consciousness though various kinds of representation. We shall also be led to reconsider the very basis of the distinction between text and context. As we have seen throughout this book, attention to 'intrinsic' factors such as metaphor or metre has inevitably led us to consider the relationship between poetry and 'extrinsic' things such as society.

■ 'Ode to a Nightingale' and the Intertextual Context of Romanticism

In order to open up these questions, we want to return to and expand upon the discussion of Keats's 'Ode to a Nightingale' initiated at the beginning of this book. In Chapter 1 we suggested that Keats's Romantic poem conforms to many of our received ideas about poetry in general because those received ideas are themselves derived from Romantic theories about poetry. We also argued that the poem is not only an example of Romantic poetry but a poem which explores the assumptions and limits of Romantic theories about poetry.

One way of substantiating and developing this account of the poem would be to concentrate more on the significance of the nightingale both within and beyond the poem. We have seen that Keats's speaker imagines that this bird is immortal and that its song has consoled people of all classes (from emperors to simple country people) through all time:

> The voice I hear this passing night was heard
>   In ancient days by emperor and clown:
> Perhaps the self-same song that found a path
>   Through the sad heart of Ruth, when, sick for home,
>   She stood in tears amid the alien corn. (63–67)

The emphasis here is on the affective power and longevity of the bird's song and voice. This, together with the way the speaker imagines that the bird's song will become his own 'high requiem' (60) at his death, suggests that this bird is being imagined as some kind of creative being. To develop this line of interpretation we need to go outside the poem to examine what we can call its 'intertextual literary context' (that is, the way it interrelates with other literary texts). If this image of the singing nightingale is placed alongside one of the most characteristic statements of Romantic poetic theory – from Wordsworth's influential 'Preface to the *Lyrical Ballads*' of 1800 – we arrive at an intriguing interpretation. Since Wordsworth claims that poetry is 'the spontaneous overflow of powerful feelings', we might speculate that Keats's nightingale – which is 'pouring forth' its soul 'In such an ecstasy' – is being figured as an ideal image of the Romantic poet.

We can get further support for this interpretation by looking at how birds (especially the nightingale) are represented in other Romantic poems. The nightingale has had a particular significance in the history of poetry. Brewer's *Dictionary of Phrase and Fable* tells us that the Greeks called the nightingale 'Philomel' (which means 'lover of song') after a woman in one of the myths of ancient Greece who was raped, had her tongue cut out so she could not inform on her violator, and was then turned into a nightingale by the gods. Because of this, the nightingale became associated with melancholy song in English Renaissance poetry – as in Milton's 'Il Penseroso' (1645), where the nightingale is described as 'Most musical, most melancholy!' As Andrew Ashfield notes, 'There was no shortage of poems to nightingales in the eighteenth century although their significance is a neglected area in Keats scholarship given the canonical status of his "Ode to a Nightingale".'[3] Ashfield names fifteen eighteenth-century poets who wrote poems to the nightingale, including Charlotte Smith. Keats was probably familiar with Smith's 'On the Departure of the Nightingale', published in her *Elegiac Sonnets* (3rd edn, 1786), in which the speaker bids 'a long adieu' to the nightingale as 'The gentle bird, who sings of pity best'. Of more interest to our present discussion is that she calls the nightingale the 'Sweet poet of the woods'.[4] Keats was almost certainly familiar with at least the second of Coleridge's two poems about the nightingale. In the first, 'To the Nightingale' (1796), Coleridge hails the nightingale as 'Sister of love-lorn Poets, Philomel', and echoes the poetic tradition in calling it 'melancholy'. In the second, 'The Nightingale' (1798), however, he rejects this tradition by saying that the nightingale is called melancholy only by poets who have never actually listened to the bird's song (this is an example of the way poems can revise the literary tradition rather than merely repeat it). Coleridge's poem forms an important precedent to Keats's suggestion in the 'Ode' that the bird is singing out of sheer happiness:

[3] Andrew Ashfield, ed., *Romantic Women Poets, 1770–1838: An anthology* (Manchester: Manchester University Press, 1995), p. 307, n.77. For an alternative anthology see Jennifer Breen, ed., *Women Romantic Poets, 1785–1832: An anthology* (London: J.M. Dent, 1992).

[4] Charlotte Smith, 'Sonnet: On the Departure of the Nightingale', reprinted in Ashfield, *Romantic Women Poets*, p. 35.

'Tis the merry Nightingale
That crowds, and hurries, and precipitates
With fast thick warble his delicious notes,
As he were fearful that an April night
Would be too short for him to utter forth
His love-chant, and disburden his full soul
Of all its music! (43–49)

Coleridge recommends that poets ought to imitate the nightingale's example and write poetry out of their full souls rather than repeating the inaccurate images of past poets.

Another important 'bird poem' of the Romantic period – Shelley's 'Ode to a Skylark' – cannot be thought of as having had an influence on Keats's poem since it was written in June 1820, about a year after Keats's 'Ode' was first published.[5] Yet we can suggest that Shelley's poem has an *intertextual* relationship with Keats's. A couple of stanzas from Shelley's poem will make this clear:

Hail to thee, blithe Spirit!
  Bird thou never wert,
That from Heaven, or near it,
  Pourest thy full heart
In profuse strains of unpremeditated art.
. . .
Like a Poet hidden
  In the light of thought,
Singing hymns unbidden,
  Till the world is wrought
To sympathy with hopes and fears it heeded not: (1–5, 36–40)

In his *Defence of Poetry*, as we saw in Chapter 7, Shelley suggests that 'A poet is a nightingale, who sits in darkness and sings to cheer its own solitude with sweet sounds' (*Shelley's Poetry and Prose*, p. 486) – a passage that may well have been influenced by Keats's 'Ode to a Nightingale'.

A number of Romantic poets, then, represented birds as idealised poet figures and thus established a figurative parallel between birds and bards: Smith calls the nightingale a 'poet of the woods'; Coleridge recommends the

---

[5] 'Ode to a Nightingale' was first published in *Annals of the Fine Arts* (July 1819), and was republished in Keats's *Lamia, Isabella, The Eve of St Agnes, and Other Poems* (1820). See *The Poems of John Keats*, ed. Miriam Allott (London: Longman 1970; New York: Norton, 1972), pp. 523–4.

nightingale as a model for would-be poets; and Shelley calls the poet a night-ingale and hails the skylark as an ecstatic poet whose 'hymns' are so powerful that all the world is coaxed into listening. By examining these poetic birds, we can get some idea of how the Romantic poets wished to represent themselves and their poetry. Coleridge's nightingale seems driven to express its urgent feelings – 'to utter forth / His love-chant, and disburden his full soul / Of all its music!' Shelley's skylark is apparently inspired by the same need: he hails it as pouring out its 'full heart / In profuse strains of unpremeditated art'. And Keats's nightingale is said to be 'pouring forth [its] soul abroad / In such an ecstasy' (57–58). Romantic poetry, then, represents itself as striving towards the natural, spontaneous, 'unpremeditated art' of birdsong – towards the music of uncontainable feeling rather than the language of thought.

But if this is the literary context which informs Keats's treatment of the nightingale, the 'Ode' gains its special interest from the way it investigates and finds problematic some of the assumptions which it shares with that context. This is partly because Keats's poem, as we have seen, demonstrates the limitations of certain Romantic conceptions of poetry and the Romantic quest to transcend the individual self. As the speaker ruefully puts it towards the end of the poem, 'The fancy cannot cheat so well / As she is fam'd to do, deceiving elf' (73–74). The speaker cannot literally become one with the nightingale, and cannot permanently escape the cares of life through the poetic imagination. In other words, we can think of 'Ode to a Nightingale' not just as a Romantic poem which displays certain features which are common to the Romantic period, but as a Romantic poem which investigates and finds wanting some basic assumptions of Romanticism. In this way, we can say that 'Ode to a Nightingale' is a 'self-reflexive' poem which 'critiques' its own assumptions about poetry. The poem both accepts and undermines the Romantic conventions of treating birds as ideal poet figures. The nightingale in the poem does not allow itself to be appropriated in this way: it flies away in the last stanza, leaving the poetic speaker alone and forlorn. What this indicates is that the speaker's fascination with the nightingale arises not because it is an available role model but because it is elusive and unattainable. It is the bird's 'otherness' which is so compelling, and this suggests that the imagination's impulse arises from a realisation that the natural world is radically different from, or *other* than, the human, and cannot be so easily appropriated for human ends.

By moving to and fro between a close analysis of the individual poem and an examination of one aspect of the literary context in which it participates, we have been able to refine our reading of the poem. We have shown that the poem shares a number of assumptions which were common to Romanticism, but we have also shown that it reworks or questions some of those assumptions in interesting ways. In other words, poems need to be seen not as unique objects produced wholly from within the experience and consciousness of individual poets but as part of a more general network of literary themes and conventions. At the same time, knowledge of such themes and conventions, gained through reading other poems, reveals how the individual poem is not only deeply informed by the larger literary context but can subtly revise or criticise the conventions it works with. In the case we have examined it is clearly helpful, even crucial, to have some general notions of Romanticism. Nevertheless, it would be fatal to allow this knowledge to inhibit close attention to the text of the poem itself. You should never assume that a poem will simply or straightforwardly conform to any general description of the literary period or movement in which it participates, yet you will not be able fully to respond to a poem's impact if you cannot see how it works within and reworks the conventions of its literary context.

■ Resisting the Literary Tradition: The Neoclassical Context

A poem's literary context is formed not only by the literature which is contemporary with it, but also by the literature of the past. One of the informing contexts for British Romanticism was the set of cultural assumptions which dominated the eighteenth century and which Romanticism rejected and defined itself against. These cultural assumptions were powerfully articulated in the poetry of the eighteenth century, as we can see by looking at a few definitive examples. Alexander Pope's *An Essay on Criticism* (1709, 1711) was one of the most influential poems of the early eighteenth century, setting the critical standards and criteria for other poets to follow. The poem is divided into three parts, and contains nearly seven hundred and fifty lines. We will examine thirty or so lines from the second part, using a modern edition of Pope's poetry which attempts to give you some idea of how the poem appeared on the page in his time.[6] Modern print, spelling and punctuation conventions had not yet been established, so there are words which begin with capital letters which would not do so now, words which are italicised for no apparent reason, words which we would consider misspelt, and some punctuation which seems odd by today's conventions. Some recent editions smooth out these features and make the text appear modern and more readable, but we feel that it is important for you to realise that the changes in typographical and punctuation conventions through history also constitute a kind of context which ought to inform our reading of texts from the past.

> *True Wit* is *Nature* to Advantage drest,
> What oft was *Thought*, but ne'er so well *Exprest*,
> *Something*, whose Truth convinc'd at Sight we find,

[6] *The Poems of Alexander Pope*, ed. John Butt (London: Methuen, 1963), pp. 153–4.

That gives us back the Image of our Mind:
As Shades more sweetly recommend the Light,
So modest Plainness sets off sprightly Wit:
For *Works* may have more *Wit* than does 'em good,
As *Bodies* perish through Excess of *Blood*.
    Others for *Language* all their Care express,
And value *Books*, as Women *Men*, for *Dress*:
Their Praise is still – *The Stile is excellent*:
The *Sense*, they humbly take upon Content.
Words are like *Leaves*; and where they most abound,
Much *Fruit* of *Sense* beneath is rarely found.
False Eloquence, like the *Prismatic Glass*,
Its gaudy Colours spreads on *ev'ry place*;
The Face of Nature we no more Survey,
All glares *alike*, without *Distinction* gay:
But true *Expression*, like th' unchanging *Sun*,
Clears, and *improves* whate'er it shines upon,
It *gilds* all Objects, but it *alters* none.
Expression is the *Dress* of *Thought*, and still
Appears more *decent* as more *suitable*;
A vile Conceit in pompous Words exprest,
Is like a Clown in regal Purple drest;
For diff'rent *Styles* with diff'rent *Subjects* sort,
As several Garbs with Country, Town, and Court.
. . .
In *Words*, as *Fashions*, the same Rule will hold;
Alike Fantastick, if *too New*, or *Old*;
Be not the *first* by whom the *New* are try'd,
Nor yet the *last* to lay the *Old* aside. (297–336)

We have already glanced at some of these lines at several points in this book. In Chapter 6 we examined the poetic and philosophical context which informs Pope's definition of 'wit' in these lines and saw that, for Pope and his contemporaries, 'wit' did not mean what it means for us (though there is some overlap) but referred to the inventive faculty of the mind which creates poetry. Here, we wish to examine the whole passage in order to trace the connections between the theory of poetry it promotes and the political and cultural context in which it was produced. Underlying the obvious differences of diction between Pope and Keats is a very different 'poetic ideology'. Pope's lines contain some of the most concise expressions of a theory of poetry which dominated writing in England before the Romantic 'revolution'. His *Essay* is both an essay about the proper way to criticise poetry and a kind of manifesto about, and model of, what good poetry should be like. For Pope, true poetry consists of impressive expressions not of new thoughts but of 'What oft was thought'. Expression is likened (and the rhyme supports this) to the *dressing* of nature 'to advantage'. Thus we can already see how this conception of poetry is radically different from the Romantic claim that poetry involves 'Pouring forth thy soul abroad / In such an ecstasy'. In effect, the differences between Pope and Keats, and between Neoclassicism and Romanticism, can be thought of as being grounded in the differences between wit and imagination: whereas Neoclassical wit is characterised by an elegant and inventive decoration of socially established truths, the Romantic imagination is thought of as the unique expression of new insights and feelings which either well up from within the poet or are produced by a capacity for extraordinary empathy.

The metaphor of 'dress' is extended throughout this passage. Poetry is nature well-dressed, and to be well-dressed is not to be gaudy or over-done, since 'modest Plainness sets off sprightly wit' (302). In this metaphor, dress refers to language while the meaning or 'sense' is the body (this is an eighteenth-century version of a commonplace but problematic distinction between form and content, language and meaning). Attention to dress, we are warned, should not be at the expense of the body of sense:

> Others for *Language* all their Care express,
> And value *Books*, as Women *Men*, for *Dress*:
> Their Praise is still – *The stile is excellent*;
> The sense, they humbly take upon content. (305–8)

Pope condemns those readers who too easily agree with the meaning (or sense) of a poem merely because they are impressed by its style, and he likens such readers to the conventional idea that women (at least in the eighteenth century) are attracted to men not for their substance (their sense) but for the way they dress. Poetry should be stylish, but it ought not to be *merely* stylish – we still make that connection between 'style' and fashion-sense which Pope is exploiting here, even if we are unlikely to apply it to poetry. As well as eighteenth-century sexism, Pope also promotes eighteenth-century conservatism. Just as dress (Pope suggests) should always be decent and suited to the occasion and the person, so too should language be appropriate to the thought it expresses:

> Expression is the *Dress* of *Thought*, and still
> Appears more *decent* as more *suitable*;
> A vile Conceit in pompous Words exprest,
> Is like a Clown in regal Purple drest;
> For diff'rent *Styles* with diff'rent *Subjects* sort,
> As several Garbs with Country, Town, and Court. (318–23)

It should be noted that 'clown' here – as in 'Ode to a Nightingale' – means a countryman (and perhaps an uncouth man) as well as a jester.[7] Whereas Keats's 'Ode' suggests that the nightingale's egalitarian song has consoled both emperors and clowns throughout history, Pope suggests that there is a proper way for a 'clown' to dress, which is quite different from the dress of monarchs. Pope's eighteenth-century readers might have recognised that he is also reinforcing the strict genre codes of eighteenth-century poetic theory, which carefully distinguished between the language thought suitable for 'low' and for 'high' poetic genres (see Chapter 11 on 'Genre'). This political and poetic conservatism can also be seen in the final use of the dress metaphor in this passage:

> In *Words* as *Fashions* the same Rule will hold;
> Alike Fantastick if *too New* or *Old*;
> Be not the *first* by whom the *New* are try'd,
> Nor yet the *last* to lay the *Old* aside. (333–36)

(We should note that Pope's use of 'fantastic' here does not have the positive connotations of its modern usage; among the meanings available to Pope listed in the *Oxford English Dictionary* are 'capricious', 'foppish', 'eccentric', 'quaint' and 'grotesque'.)

Our analysis thus far indicates an important point: while the close reading of poems can be enhanced by paying attention to their informing context, such close reading can also reveal things about that informing context. Pope's tone and assumptions about poetry can be regarded as evidence, provisionally at least, about the cultural presuppositions of his society. In Britain in 1711, a poet could claim to represent the dominant cultural consensus. Most writers were part of the 'establishment' and generally supported the status quo, although they sometimes criticised society in their writings. And while satiric criticisms of society increased after political power passed from the Tory party into the hands of the more progressive (or, for some, corrupt) administration of Sir Robert Walpole and the Whigs in 1721, writers on all sides of the argument still seem to have felt that they were playing a central role in the social formation. By 1819, however, the writer's relationship to society had shifted significantly. As Britain continued to transform itself into a capitalist, industrialised, but still deeply conservative society, literature became more marginal and many writers found themselves in the role of critical outsider. This is not to say that they were not socially committed (writers were perhaps more committed to social intervention in the Romantic period than at any other time),

---

[7] Evidence for earlier meanings and usages of words in poems may be given by the editor of the edition you are reading; if not, the best resource is the *Oxford English Dictionary*.

nor to say that there was no readership for literature (there was in fact an unprecedented expansion of literacy). And it is certainly not to suggest that writing was considered aloof from society, or politically ineffectual (the range of government institutions – from censorship to critical journals – set up to curb radical writing refutes any such idea).[8] Shelley's assertion in 1821 that 'Poets are the unacknowledged legislators of the World'[9] indicates not only the marginalisation of poets but also Shelley's own belief (wishful, perhaps) that poetry continued to play a central role in the formation of the public sphere.

We can trace signs of this difference in the writer's social position in the poems we are looking at. Whereas Keats's poet figure experiences his poetic moment in a natural environment isolated from society, Pope claims that poetry is fundamentally part of the society in which it is produced:

> *True Wit* is *Nature* to Advantage drest,
> What oft was *Thought*, but ne'er so well *Exprest*. (297–98)

Pope's use of 'Nature' here is quite different from Keats's, and should not be confused with our own idea of nature. The meaning of nature changes through history in ways which accord with ideological, cultural and scientific changes.[10] For Pope's contemporaries, nature was valued mainly when it was cultivated – for example, in the eighteenth-century cult of formally stylised landscape gardens – and civilisation itself was seen as a 'natural improvement' on nature ('improvement' was also an economic term in the period). The scientific discoveries of contemporaries such as Isaac Newton (1642–1727) simply confirmed for Pope that the 'laws' of 'Nature' were equivalent to God's laws:

> Nature, and Nature's Laws lay hid in Night;
> God said, Let Newton be! and All was Light!
> ('Epitaph for Sir Isaac Newton', 1730)

For Pope, nature connotes an abstract system of fixed laws which manifest God's laws and shape the 'constitution' of the natural and human world. In the first 'Epistle' of his *An Essay on Man* (1733), subtitled 'Of the Nature and State of Man, With Respect to the Universe', Pope stresses that the laws of God and Nature have allotted mankind a particular place in the order of things, and any attempt to aspire beyond our place would break those laws:

---

[8] See the various essays collected in David B. Pirie, ed., *The Romantic Period* (Harmondsworth: Penguin, 1994); Pirie's introduction, pp. vii–xix, is excellent.

[9] 'A Defence of Poetry' (1821) in *Shelley's Poetry and Prose*, p. 508.

[10] For a fascinating account of the way 'keywords' like 'nature' change through history, see Raymond Williams, *Keywords: A vocabulary of culture and society* (London: Fontana, 1983).

And who but wishes to invert the laws
Of order, sins against the Eternal Cause. (129–30)

The general order, since the whole began,
Is kept in Nature, and is kept in man. (171–72)

From Nature's chain whatever link you strike,
Tenth or ten thousandth, breaks the chain alike. (245–46)

This stress on the necessary order of the universe and humankind's fixed place within it is used to justify the fixed laws and order of human society, and leads to the quaint assertion that if any individual strives to rise above (or sinks below) his or her allotted place, then the whole cosmic order will collapse into chaos. For Pope, then, it is clear that nature and society are not opposed, but the same thing. That which 'oft was thought' – by society (or a certain part of society) rather than by individuals – is equated in the lines quoted above with nature itself.

Pope's understanding of nature is quite different from that of the Romantics about a hundred years later, and this difference indicates a fundamental change in cultural assumptions between the two periods. One of the sources of the Romantics' understanding of nature was Jean-Jacques Rousseau who, in 1755, influentially argued that civilisation had corrupted humanity and that human beings had once lived in a 'state of nature' and been naturally good.[11] Rousseau was thus a thinker who began the process of overturning eighteenth-century conceptions about the relationship between nature and society. He argued this so persuasively that he initiated a vogue for 'untamed' nature – the wild areas of the world which have not been spoiled by human 'improvement'. For the Romantics (and this is something else we have inherited from them), 'nature' connotes the opposite of the society in which they lived (and all things related to it, such as industry). For Wordsworth, nature was a benevolent force which allowed the individual to get in touch with his or her own profound inner nature (see the discussion of 'Tintern Abbey' in Chapter 3).[12]

■ Periodisation: Constructing Contexts

We are beginning to see that poems absorb and rework the language and assumptions of the general discursive context which surrounds them – even 'nature' becomes a changing discursive construct rather than something

---

[11] See Rousseau, *A Discourse on the Origins and Foundations of Inequality Among Men*, trans. Maurice Cranston (Harmondsworth: Penguin, 1984).

[12] Although we have inherited the Romantic idea of nature, it has since been complicated by the theory of evolution developed in the nineteenth century by writers such as Charles Darwin, in which nature is seen as a harsh environment in which only the fittest survive.

outside discourse altogether. This means that we need to find out about the distinguishing features of a cultural context within which a particular poem was produced. In order to be able to identify and characterise a cultural context, you need either to know some cultural history or know where you can read up on the cultural features of the historical period you are interested in. Such historical knowledge has conventionally been divided up into literary history and social, economic and political history. The history of English literature is traditionally distinguished into different 'periods', each of which is thought to display some typical features which differentiate it from the periods which precede and follow it. Thus you will often find scholars referring to the Renaissance (1500–1660), which in England normally includes the Elizabethan, Jacobean, Caroline and Commonwealth periods. The Neoclassical period (1660–1785) takes in the Restoration and Augustan periods and the Age of Sensibility. The Romantic and Victorian periods cover the nineteenth century, while the twentieth century can be divided into the Edwardian, Georgian, Modern and Postmodern periods (critics remain divided on whether the latter term is the best way of labelling the period in which we are living). The two poems we are looking at were therefore produced in two different 'periods': Pope's in the Neoclassical period (or, to be more precise, the Augustan period); Keats's in the Romantic period.

The periodisation of literary history is usually achieved by identifying certain common assumptions and features which seem to have been shared by a majority of the writers of the time. An attempt is sometimes made to relate these shared literary 'paradigms' to the larger historical context. Even short entries about literary periods or movements in glossaries such as Abrams or *Princeton* can therefore be useful in helping us begin to orientate ourselves in the unfamiliar terrains of the past. To some extent, however, the division of cultural history into watertight periods is a retrospective fiction imposed upon the past by critics. Yet it is the case that, although culture is continually being transformed through history, there are some periods in which changes simply modify existing cultural theory and practice, and other periods in which the basic cultural paradigms are radically transformed. The Neoclassical and the Romantic periods were two such periods of relative stability, whereas the transformation between them was radical enough to mean that while we still share many cultural assumptions with the Romantic period, the culture of the Neoclassical period is likely to seem quite alien to readers coming to it for the first time. This is why it will be particularly helpful for you to look up the descriptions in Abrams, *Glossary* or in *Princeton* of any pre-Romantic period in which you happen to be interested.

Yet two words of warning need to be issued. The first concerns the problems involved in describing the characteristic features of any culture or period in history. Just as there is a huge diversity of different, even radically incompatible, cultural assumptions competing with each other in our present historical moment (whatever country we happen to live in), so too were the cultures of the past diffuse and diverse. In fact it might be more accurate to define cultures in terms of their conflicts rather than their agreements (such conflicts are often signs of a culture's vitality). Generalisations about a period's 'mind-set' threaten to reduce cultural complexity and diversity to a set of crude, self-fulfilling observations. (In this respect, it is encouraging that the *Princeton* entry on Neoclassical Poetics continually qualifies its discussion by attending to cultural trends in Neoclassicism which complicated and contradicted its 'official' assumptions.) This does not mean that it is pointless trying to define a cultural context (we have shown that it can be crucial for the reading of individual poems), but it does mean that we should be wary of relying on a simplified description of that context. Because of this, you should treat such thumbnail sketches as simply the first provisional step in finding your way into the history of a period. There is no substitute for your own wide and thorough reading of texts – poetic and otherwise – drawn from the various cultural contexts in which you become interested. More detailed 'maps' of literary history can be found in general histories of literature.[13] And specialised critical studies of the cultural context you are interested in will be even more helpful.[14] As well as reading literary history, it is equally important to read books on political, social, and intellectual history because historical contexts are usually more complex and interesting than studies devoted primarily to literature often acknowledge.[15] The deepening historical knowledge gained from such research

[13] Brief sketches of the histories of various poetic traditions (including English Poetry, American Poetry, and Scottish Poetry) may be found in *Princeton*. Useful histories of literature in English include David Daiches, *A Critical History of English Literature* (London: Secker & Warburg, 1969); Alastair Fowler, *A History of English Literature: Forms and kinds from the Middle Ages to the present* (Oxford: Blackwell, 1987); and *The Penguin History of Literature* in 10 volumes (various editors and dates of publication). For the American tradition see D. Stauffer, *A Short History of American Poetry* (New York: Dutton, 1974), and E. Elliott *et al.*, eds, *Columbia Literary History of the United States* (New York: Columbia University Press, 1988). The standard history of Scottish Literature is Cairns Craig, ed., *The History of Scottish Literature* (Aberdeen: Aberdeen University Press, 1987–89).

[14] A useful introduction to the cultural context of eighteenth-century poetry is Paul Fussell, *The Rhetorical World of Augustan Humanism*. For the intellectual context of Romanticism, see M.H. Abrams, *The Mirror and the Lamp: Romantic theory and the critical tradition* (Oxford: Oxford University Press, 1953); for the political and social context, see Marilyn Butler, *Romantics, Rebels, and Reactionaries* (Oxford: Oxford University Press, 1981), and David B. Pirie, ed., *The Romantic Period*. Stephen Prickett, ed., *The Romantics* (London: Methuen, 1981), contains chapters on art, religion, philosophy, literature and the historical context.

[15] For a revealing historical study of eighteenth-century social and political thought, see J.G.A. Pocock, *Virtue, Commerce and History: Essays on political thought and history, chiefly in the eighteenth century* (Cambridge: Cambridge University Press, 1985).

will have profound effects on your response to literary texts, and help put you in touch with current historical and historicist trends in literary studies.

Our first word of warning leads on to the second: you should not allow summaries of the cultural 'background' or contextual information to serve as a rigid template into which you force the poem you are trying to read. Just as any culture is made up of diverse elements, so any individual text is not likely to comply neatly with our predetermined notions about the culture within which it was produced (as we have seen with 'Ode to a Nightingale'). The most interesting poems, indeed, are those which resist or undercut their period's dominant preconceptions and which force us to revise what Wordsworth called 'our own pre-established codes of decision'.[16]

To try to explore why particular cultures such as eighteenth-century England generally share a set of relatively stable assumptions, and why such a culture should eventually be displaced, is beyond the scope of this book. What is clear is that cultural forms such as poetry participate in much larger cultural and political movements, regardless of whether individual poems deal explicitly with such issues. Abrams has influentially argued that the quite distinct theories of poetry which Pope and Keats held need to be seen as part of a larger philosophical shift in the way human beings conceived and represented the relationship between the human mind and the outside world. Abrams shows that the dominant conception of the human mind in the eighteenth century was Locke's suggestion that it is a passive receiver of images from the outside world; when the mind expresses its ideas it is therefore acting as a kind of *mirror*, reflecting back (perhaps modified) images it has received from the outside world. Romanticism reacted against this conception of the human mind by arguing that the mind is a living source of original ideas which it projects out into the world like a lamp (see Abrams, *The Mirror and the Lamp*). For Michel Foucault, however, the difference in poetic theory between Pope and Keats would be just one symptom of a total transformation in the fundamental paradigms of human knowledge and discourse which can be traced across a range of discourses about language, economics, the natural world, and so on.[17] A Marxist historian would argue that such huge cultural changes need to be examined in terms of the growth of capitalism and manufacturing in England in the eighteenth century, together with the impact of such developments as the American and French revolutions and the expansion of print media and literacy.[18]

[16] 'Advertisement' to first edition of *Lyrical Ballads*, in Wordsworth, *The Lyrical Ballads*, p. 7.
[17] See Foucault, *The Order of Things: An archaeology of the human sciences* (London: Tavistock, 1970).
[18] See Eric Hobsbawm, *The Age of Revolution, 1789–1848* (New York: New American Library, 1962); Raymond Williams, *Culture and Society: Coleridge to Orwell* (London: Hogarth, 1987); and Pirie, ed., *The Romantic Period*.

■ Genre

At this point we would like to introduce another kind of literary context – that formed by genre. Genre simply means 'kind', and any particular example of a genre will have some sort of relationship (of similarity or difference) to others of its 'kind'. It is easy to see that the two poems we have been looking at differ in their genre because it is announced in their titles: one is an 'ode'; the other is an 'essay'. These two genre names may be familiar to you already, because you may well have been required to write an essay at some point in your formal education and because the term 'ode' is often used as a 'poetic' term in the title of popular poems. But these genre names have, in fact, more specialised uses in the academic discussion of poetry. An ode may be defined as a fairly long lyric poem on a serious theme written in elevated language and with a complex stanza form. Abrams remarks that 'Romantic poets perfected the personal ode of description and passionate meditation, which is stimulated by . . . an aspect of the outer scene and turns on the attempt to solve either a personal emotional problem or a generally human one' (see 'ode' in *Abrams*). An essay is quite a different genre: it's a short discursive composition that attempts to develop a convincing argument. Abrams notes that 'The formal essay . . . is relatively impersonal: the author writes as an authority, or at least as highly knowledgeable, and expounds the subject in an orderly way. . . . Pope adopted the term for his expository compositions in verse . . . but the verse essay has had few important exponents after the eighteenth century' (see 'essay' in *Abrams*).

The poet's choice of genre involves relating his or her poem in some way to the conventions of that genre and to the history of poems in that genre. Poets like Pope and Keats were, in their different ways, highly conscious of the cultural baggage that went with each particular genre. Pope's and Keats's poems conform in several ways to these descriptions of the genres they belong to. While Keats's isolated, highly personal lyric speaker muses in the solitude of nature, Pope's relatively impersonal speaker adopts a position of cultural authority about poetry and claims to represent the general views of his society. But genre is not simply a context knowingly invoked by a writer. Genre conventions are also shared by readers, and set up particular reading expectations (our reading experience will have taught us – or will teach us – to expect that an ode will differ from an essay). In other words, genre is a context which affects a poem's reception as well as its production. (For more on genre, see Chapter 11.)

■ Other Kinds of Context

We could add other kinds of contexts to the ones we have looked at. Sometimes a poem's purpose, place, occasion or setting can be considered as informing contexts. A poem's author can also become or be treated as a context in various ways. Although there have been important criticisms of author-centred approaches to literature, the social identity of a poet (in terms of nationality, class, sex or race) can sometimes be thought of as an influential contextual factor.[19] The poet's biography is also considered by many readers as an important context for understanding poems (witness the attempt to 'explain' parts of 'Ode to a Nightingale' by the fact that Keats had recently watched his brother die of tuberculosis). The author's other poems and writings can be considered as an available context (for instance, in the way we looked at Keats's letters in Chapter 1, or some of Pope's other poems in the present chapter). In addition, it is possible to discern the way an author's 'cultural aura' affects our response to his or her writings. Keats's very name invokes cultural associations which are very different from those of Alexander Pope, and inevitably influence the way we read his poetry. All such contexts, of course, need to be treated with the same caution as the other contexts we have examined.

■ 'September Song': A Contextual Reading

To conclude this chapter, we would like to develop a case study of a relatively recent poem in order to show that contextual information can be as important for the reading of poems produced in our own period as it is for poems from the past. 'September Song' by Geoffrey Hill was published in 1968.

September Song
Born 19.6.32 – Deported 24.9.42

Undesirable you may have been, untouchable
you were not. Not forgotten
or passed over at the proper time.

As estimated, you died. Things marched,
sufficient, to that end.   5
Just so much Zyklon and leather, patented
terror, so many routine cries.

(I have made
an elegy for myself it
is true)   10

---

[19] T.S. Eliot stressed that 'Honest criticism and sensitive appreciation is directed not upon the poet but upon the poetry' ('Tradition and the Individual Talent', in Eliot, *Selected Prose of T.S. Eliot*, p. 40). More radical critiques of author-centred approaches to literature are Roland Barthes, 'The Death of the Author', and Michel Foucault, 'What is an Author?', in Lodge, *Modern Criticism and Theory*, pp. 167–72 and 197–210.

> September fattens on vines. Roses
> flake from the wall. The smoke
> of harmless fires drifts to my eyes.
>
> This is plenty. This is more than enough.

Before we look at how our interpretation of this poem can be aided by relating it to various contexts, we suggest that you spend a few moments reading it.

Historical Moment? The period in which this poem was written – the late 1960s – was an exciting and turbulent one in Europe and the United States. Many young people, especially students, took to the streets in the USA and Britain in protest against the Vietnam War and in Paris against the conservative political and educational system, and youth culture – pop music, pop art, fashion – seemed the most exciting and innovative area of culture. Yet this context does not appear to be particularly relevant to an understanding of Hill's poem. Much more relevant, in fact, are the dates at the beginning of the poem which apparently refer to dates in the life of the poem's addressee. The way these dates are presented may remind us of an inscription on a tombstone – except that this person is said to have been 'deported' on the second date rather than having 'departed'. Whether deported or departed, however, it is indicated that this occurred during the Second World War.

Although the language seems simple enough, there are several reasons why it may be quite puzzling to readers encountering the poem for the first time. As we shall see, the poem's ambiguous obscurity does not wholly clear up with contextual information and careful interpretation. The only obviously strange word is 'Zyklon', and it would seem important to find out what it means. In fact, this word turns out to be the major clue about the context to which the poem refers, and hence to an understanding of it. If you have a good knowledge of German you will know that *der Zyklon* means 'cyclone', although the ominous implications of this will not yet be clear. The *Oxford English Dictionary* tells us that Zyklon is a name for hydrogen cyanide, which is 'used as a fumigant and formerly as a poison gas'. The list of uses after the definition makes it clear that Zyklon was the poisonous gas used by the Nazis in the extermination camps in the Second World War. This piece of information about the historical context to which the poem refers, together with the date of 'deportation' and the fact that the speaker says 'As estimated, you died' (4), allows us to realise that the addressee of the poem died in a gas chamber in a German concentration camp. The term 'deported', then, could refer to the date the victim was removed to the camp, but the way the dates are presented at the head of the poem suggests that 'deported' means 'died': yet the implication is that the child (aged ten) did not simply 'depart' this life (as the usual euphemism has it) but was actively 'deported' by the Nazis.

Genre? The poem claims that its genre is a song, but it is difficult to imagine how or why anyone could sing it. In fact, the poem violates almost every convention associated with songs: its rhythmic structure is irregular, occasionally awkward, and not at all song-like, and there are no rhymes or refrain. Perhaps, then, the poem's title is bitterly ironic: how could we ever sing a song about such an event? The poem also announces that it is an 'elegy', and at first sight this would seem appropriate, since an elegy is a poetic lament for someone who has died. Yet even here the poem unsettles our generic expectations – we will have to return to the puzzling statement by the author/speaker to the effect that 'I have made / an elegy for myself' (8–9).

Author? Quite often, detailed information about authors can be distracting if such contextual information deflects attention from the poem itself. Having said that, we must add that experienced readers of poetry do tend to pick up knowledge about canonical authors (partly through reading a range of their poems), and this can help or inform the reading process. With more contemporary poets, such knowledge, if desired, often needs to be actively sought out. This can be done through the various reference books available about contemporary poets, through reading criticism (if available), through reading other poems by the same author, or by searching on the Internet (many contemporary poets have homepages).[20] Even a glancing familiarity with Hill's other poems reveals that the Holocaust is one of his ongoing preoccupations. His first collection of poems, *For the Unfallen* (1959), contains a poem called 'Two Formal Elegies (For the Jews in Europe)', and there are several poems in *King Log* (1968), from which 'September Song' comes, which deal with the Holocaust. Even given this, however, we may still be curious about how and why Hill came to write about a child murdered twenty-six years prior to the act of writing. In this case, the most trivial-seeming biographical detail may be the most revealing – the fact that Hill was born on 18 June 1932 (one day before the birth date given in the subtitle).

Poem's purpose? The purpose of an elegy, as we have seen, is usually to lament the death of a particular person and to derive some kind of consolation at the end. The near coincidence in Hill's and this child's birth dates may suggest that some kind of imaginative relationship is being posited between author and child, even though we have no reason to suspect that there was any real-life connection. You might ask whether any consolation is found at the end of the poem – indeed, whether any consolation could be possible in such a case.

---

20 Reference books include James Vinson, *Contemporary Poets* (London: Macmillan, 1980) and Michael Schmidt, ed., *A Reader's Guide to Fifty Modern British Poets* (London: Heinemann, 1979). Both have useful entries about Hill. There is a short but interesting discussion of Hill's poetry in Neil Corcoran, *English Poetry Since 1940* (London: Longman, 1993), pp. 112–27. For an excellent discussion of 'September Song', see Ricks, *The Force of Poetry*, pp. 296–304.

But although the different kinds of contextual information we have looked at are crucial, they *enable* an interpretation of the poem to develop rather than adding up to an interpretation in themselves. We always need to introduce such contextual information into a textual engagement with the poem itself. As a conclusion to this chapter, we want to develop a more extended reading of Hill's 'September Song' in order to explore how contextual information can work hand in hand with textual analysis. The opening sentence – 'Undesirable you may have been, untouchable / you were not' – fuels speculation about the child's identity. Knowledge of the racist ideology which led to the Holocaust suggests that the child was Jewish, and these lines imply that she was female. Anyone who has seen *Schindler's List* (Universal Pictures, 1993) (and this experience can provide a useful context for our attempt to read this poem) will recall the Nazis' ambivalent response to Jewish women. While they found some of them desirable, the Nazis' ideology told them that the Jews were less than human. This is illustrated in Spielberg's film when Schindler is jailed for kissing a Jewish woman, and when the German commandant wrestles with contradictory feelings of desire and revulsion towards his Jewish servant woman. Officially, then, Jewish women were 'undesirable'. The fact that the child in Hill's poem is ten years old raises the horrifying prospect that even a ten-year-old could have been subject to the Nazis' sexual abuse. Yet 'undesirable' can also mean not wanted in a different sense: the Nazis attempted to exterminate the Jews as an 'undesirable' race. The term 'untouchable', too, has contextual resonances which reverberate within the poem. 'Untouchable' is a term for the lowest caste in the Hindu caste system in India. Yet although the Jews held that place for the Nazis, they were not untouchable in several senses: they were not safe from the Nazis' reach, nor were they immune from sexual abuse, violence and murder. This is stressed in the next two lines, which underline the cold efficiency of the extermination process: 'Not forgotten / or passed over at the proper time' (2–3). Reading these lines in the context of Jewish traditions adds a grim irony to these lines: Passover is 'a feast of the Jews to commemorate the time when God, smiting the first-born of the Egyptians, passed over the houses of the Israelites' (*Collins English Dictionary*).

The second section compounds the horror of the child's death by stressing how efficient and routine the extermination of millions of people became:

> As estimated, you died. Things marched,
> sufficient, to that end.
> Just so much Zyklon and leather, patented
> terror, so many routine cries. (4–7)

The representation of the mass extermination of human beings as 'Just so much Zyklon and leather' foregrounds its nature as a kind of industrial process: the phrase might be interpreted as saying that an exact amount of Zyklon produced an exact amount of leather (the skin of Jews was said to have been used by the Nazis to manufacture articles like lightshades). The continuation of the line also produces a bizarre and chilling echo of 'patent leather' – which might recall the Nazi uniforms – and the fact that Zyklon was a patented product. The phrase 'so many routine cries' could apply both to the routine commands of the German soldiers as they sent millions to their death and to the many ('so many') cries of their victims which became, horrifyingly, routine to their murderers.

'September Song', then, is a chilling reminder of German atrocities in the Second World War, and although it is disturbing to read (and to write about) that very effect testifies to the poem's importance. Yet Hill's poem builds unexpected complexities into itself. The fact that the speaker addresses the dead child directly (as 'you') is not an unusual device in poetry (we have seen that such apostrophes are fairly common in elegies), yet in this instance there is something disturbing about the idea of conversing with a victim of the Holocaust. We have suggested that the near coincidence of birth dates between the poet and this victim of the gas chambers may well have been a motivation for the writing of the poem. There is evidence in the poem itself that the author/speaker is exploring the differences between his own fate and the child's, and this introduces all kinds of disturbing ambiguities into the poem. The penultimate section seems to stress the contrast between the poet's current situation and the child's fate:

> September fattens on vines. Roses
> flake from the wall. The smoke
> of harmless fires drifts to my eyes. (11–13)

These lines conjure up images of a peaceful, routine day in a rural setting in late September. The 'harmless fires' connote seasonal work in gardens or fields, and emphasise the contrast between the poet's lot and the horrors of the child's death. Yet this Keatsian autumn day (see Keats's 'Ode to Autumn') is also an anniversary of the child's death: while this September is fattening, the dates at the head of the poem tell us that the child died (was 'deported') on 24 September 1942.

The poem's last line is as ambiguous as any other, yet our whole understanding of the author/speaker's attitude towards the child, towards his own position, and towards the poem itself rests upon it. The presentation of these two abrupt sentences – 'This is plenty. This is more than enough' – as a single line finally destroys any remaining possibility that this 'song' could ever actually be sung. One way of interpreting the line is that the author/speaker is saying that these brief images of the child's death speak for themselves and further commentary is unnecessary. Yet we could imagine a quite different tone, and hence a quite different meaning: 'This will do! – I won't bother going on with this "song".' A different but equally unsettling way of reading the same words would be to imagine them as a statement of the poet's satisfaction with the 'plenty' that he has (the bountifulness of his comfortable rural existence) and/or with the quality of what he has written.

The last of these possibilities may be supported through one way of interpreting that curious middle section:

> (I have made
> an elegy for myself it
> is true) (8–10)

We have already noted that the poem can be seen as an elegy, but there is a certain ambiguity in the phrase 'I have made / an elegy for myself'. This could be read as meaning that the elegy is not for the child but for the poet. This meaning bifurcates into either (a) this elegy (like all elegies) is really written to console the speaker/poet, since the person elegised is beyond consolation; or (b) this elegy is for me because, in slightly different circumstances, I could have been the one who died. A wholly different way of reading the phrase, however, which relies on a different reading of 'it / is true', would be to suggest that the poet/speaker feels a certain satisfaction at having produced a successful elegy – at having demonstrated his skill at his craft.

In some ways, then, the second half of the poem is even more disturbing than the first, since it raises all kinds of unsettling questions about the way we attempt to represent events of the Holocaust (this debate was restimulated by *Schindler's List*), and about our relationship to it. The poem seems to suggest that even if we were not born at the time or were too young to know about the Holocaust, we cannot escape our sense of guilt about what happened, or about the fact that we were not victims. In one sense, this is the inescapable experience of what has been called 'the postmodern condition'. As Abrams *Glossary* puts it,

> The term postmodernism is sometimes applied to the literature and art after World War II (1939–45), when the effects on Western morale of the first war [1914–18] were greatly exacerbated by the experience of Nazi totalitarianism and mass extermination.

He goes on to list other threats which have undermined still further our sense of certainty and security – 'the threat of total destruction by the atomic bomb, the progressive devastation of the natural environment, and the ominous fact of overpopulation' (p. 120).

There are two ways of responding to the relentless use of ambiguity in Hill's poem. We could see it as a self-indulgent playfulness which has no place in a poem about such a subject. Alternatively, we could see this unsettling and disturbing feature as precisely foregrounding and acting out the inescapable ambiguities of our relationship to the Holocaust, especially when we attempt to represent or write about it. Theodor Adorno famously asserted (in a book translated into English the year before Hill published 'September Song') that 'To write poetry after Auschwitz is barbaric'.[21] This can be understood as saying that it would be barbaric to carry on producing culture as if nothing had happened, and perhaps that poetry is the most irresponsible of luxuries. It seems that no representation of the Holocaust could do justice to it (witness the criticism that *Schindler's List* concentrated on an unrepresentative event, or that it was 'too beautiful'), but it is also clear that we have a moral responsibility to go on trying to represent it. Hill is writing poetry which confronts this impossible but necessary task while seeming to be deeply aware of Adorno's point. The self-reflexivity of Hill's poem seems to recognise that, in the aftermath of the Holocaust, we are all implicated in the guilt – that simple distinctions between innocence and guilt are no longer viable.[22] 'September Song' seems to be saying that we cannot write about or represent this event without reflecting upon these issues or reflecting on the problems and responsibilities involved. This means that such poetry will inevitably need to be both responsive to the event itself and self-critical about the act of writing about it. In a sense, any poem about the Holocaust has also to be about poetry itself – scrupulously self-analytical about the reasons for and consequences of writing poetry about such an event.

Hill's poems, then, are not just poems 'about' the Holocaust but poems whose poetics are shaped by the political and cultural impact of the Holocaust. As Neil Corcoran puts it:

> the difficulties of interpretation . . . [and] undecidability of tone [in Hill's poetry] . . . are perhaps the inevitable result of as sophisticated a verbal and poetic intelligence as Hill's coping with the conviction that any more univocal English would be pretence and delusion after what history has inflicted on the language. His work seems to embody at its source the conviction that, from where we are now, there is no center of value to be finally located, no model of utterance which can create an innocent space, no articulation free of guilt or impure motive.
>
> (Corcoran, *English Poetry Since 1940*, p. 126)

---

[21] Adorno, *Prisms: Cultural criticism and society*, trans. S. Weber (London: N. Spearman, 1967), p. 34.

[22] See Barbara Johnson's reflections about Paul de Man's collaboration with the Nazis in his native Belgium during the war in the preface to the paperback edition of her *A World of Difference*.

This refusal of clear-cut certainties and the possibility of objectivity, together with an exploration of indeterminate ambiguities and a foregrounding of textual self-awareness, are all features of postmodernist art. According to Jean-François Lyotard, these features arise because our contemporary, postmodern world has lost faith in what he calls 'the Grand Narratives' – that is, the certainties which once allowed us to believe in various stories about humanity's confident progress towards perfection (whether these narratives were Christian, scientific, Marxist, nationalist, or whatever).[23] Postmodernism is often said to involve irresponsible playfulness, but for many commentators its undoing of certainties arises out of a historical context in which the facts of the Holocaust finally put an end to any illusions about humankind or its destiny – especially since those atrocities were carried out in the name of perfecting the race.

Exercises

1 Read the following poem by Seamus Heaney several times, then try to answer the questions which follow. In conformity with general practice, this poem appears in Heaney's *North* (1975) without any contextual information.

Punishment

I can feel the tug
of the halter at the nape
of her neck, the wind
on her naked front.

It blows her nipples   5
to amber beads,
it shakes the frail rigging
of her ribs.

I can see her drowned
body in the bog,   10
the weighing stone,
the floating rods and boughs.

Under which at first
she was a barked sapling
that is dug up   15
oak bone, brain-firkin:

---

[23] See Lyotard, *The Postmodern Condition: A report on knowledge*, trans. Geoff Bennington and Brian Massumi (Manchester: Manchester University Press, 1984).

her shaved head
like a stubble of black corn,
her blindfold a soiled bandage,
her noose a ring   20

to store
the memories of love.
Little adulteress,
before they punished you

you were flaxen-haired,   25
undernourished, and your
tar-black face was beautiful.
My poor scapegoat,

I almost love you
but would have cast, I know,   30
the stones of silence.
I am the artful voyeur

of your brain's exposed
and darkened combs,
and your muscles' webbing   35
and all your numbered bones:

I who have stood dumb
when your betraying sisters,
cauled in tar,
wept by the railings,   40

who would connive
in civilized outrage
yet understand the exact
and tribal, intimate revenge.

(a) Try to develop an interpretation of the poem by using the techniques and principles of textual analysis presented in this book. What would you say the poem is about, and what are the textual features which reveal this for you?

(b) Do you think that this poem has anything in common with Geoffrey Hill's 'September Song' (even though Heaney's poem is clearly not about the Holocaust)? Do you think our description of the general context of Hill's poem (published just seven years before) can be regarded in any way as an informing context for Heaney's poem?

(c) Are there any aspects of 'Punishment' which you find puzzling and which you feel might be cleared up by some contextual information? Where do you think you might find such information?

(d) Our own suggestions about further research would include:
  (i) reading the episode recording Jesus's forgiveness of the woman taken in adultery in the Gospel According to St John 8: 1–11.
  (ii) reading the short entry on Heaney in James Vinson, ed. (1980) *Contemporary Poets*;
  (iii) reading other poems by Heaney, especially those collected in *North*;
  (iv) reading the chapters on *North* in Neil Corcoran, *Seamus Heaney* (London: Faber, 1986) and in Michael Parker, *Seamus Heaney: The making of the poet* (Basingstoke: Macmillan, 1993).

(e) Having done your contextual and critical research, return to the poem and try to gauge how the information you have discovered and the interpretations you have read have helped in your reading of it. Has your reading of the poem changed in any way? Which kind of contextual research has been most productive? Would you now change your responses to questions (a) and (b)? What would you say is the most crucial context for understanding the poem?

2 Read the following poem by Thomas Hardy then answer the questions. The date that follows the poem as printed here was included when the poem first appeared in a collection entitled *Poems of the Past and the Present* (1901) and should therefore be seen as contextual information supplied by the poet himself.

The Darkling Thrush
I leant upon a coppice gate
    When Frost was spectre-grey,
And Winter's dregs made desolate
    The weakening eye of day.
The tangled bine-stems scored the sky   5
    Like strings of broken lyres,
And all mankind that haunted nigh
    Had sought their household fires.

The land's sharp features seemed to be
    The Century's corpse outleant,   10
His crypt the cloudy canopy,
    The wind his death-lament.
The ancient pulse of germ and birth
    Was shrunken hard and dry,
And every spirit upon earth   15
    Seemed fervourless as I.

At once a voice arose among
   The bleak twigs overhead
In a full-hearted evensong
   Of joy illimited;   20
An aged thrush, frail, gaunt, and small,
   In blast-beruffled plume,
Had chosen thus to fling his soul
   Upon the growing gloom.

So little cause for carolings   25
   Of such ecstatic sound
Was written on terrestrial things
   Afar or nigh around,
That I could think there trembled through
   His happy good-night air   30
Some blessed Hope, whereof he knew
   And I was unaware.
31 December 1900

(a) Go through the poem in order to establish what we might call its 'internal context': (i) where is the speaker? (ii) what is the time of year? (iii) what is the time of day? (iv) what is the speaker's response to his context?

(b) The beginnings of an answer to the last question in (a) might be derived from asking more questions: how does the speaker represent (i) the landscape and (ii) the thrush? To answer these questions, you should look at the figurative language. Is there any common theme that links a number of the metaphors? Do the metaphors link together into an extended metaphor? If so, highlight all the figures and images that are included in, or associated with, that extended metaphor.

(c) Compare and contrast Hardy's representation of the thrush in this poem with the Romantics' representation of birds (as examined in Chapter 1 and earlier in the present chapter). Is Hardy's thrush similar to Keats's nightingale or significantly different? What are the consequences (in the poem) of that similarity or difference? In answering these questions, think about the title: what does it mean? Could Hardy's 'darkling thrush' be described as a 'symbol'? If so, what does it stand for?

(d) What is the speaker's tone or mood? That is, what is his attitude towards (i) the world and (ii) the thrush?

(e) What is the significance of the date appended to the poem? Does it help us to understand the speaker's situation and mood in the poem itself?

(f) Is it reasonable to assume that there was any particular event or development – public or personal – that would account for Hardy's (or the speaker's) outlook at the dawn of the new century? Do some research in your library, or on the Internet, to see if you can find any contextual information that might explain or justify this outlook. Biographies and critical works on Hardy, and also more general accounts of late-nineteenth-century political, social or intellectual history, are likely to be useful in this research. Using the sources you have found, try writing two or three paragraphs on 'The world view of Thomas Hardy'.

(g) Try to summarise the conclusions you have arrived at in response to the above questions so as finally to produce an interpretation of the poem which is not only based on close reading of the text itself, but also on relevant information about its historical and its literary (or intertextual) contexts.

Chapter 11

Genre

■ Genres in General

In making choices about which television programmes to watch, what films to go to see, what records to buy, and what books to read, our selection is typically guided by preferences for certain types over others. There is a wide range of different kinds of television programme – soaps, documentaries, news, light entertainment, drama, reality TV – and our ideas of what type a new programme is are guided by television listings, by the programme's title, and by experience of seeing other programmes of the same kind. The fact that viewers know what to expect from these different kinds of programme helps to guide viewing choices, and we generally know if we are 'in the mood' to watch, say, a game show or a documentary. Similarly, we know what to expect of a film by the kind of film it is – Western, spy thriller, road movie, comedy. Record shops and charts are often organised into different kinds of music – pop, rock, punk, hip-hop, house, rap, indie, folk, blues, jazz, classical, and so on. Books are also organised into different kinds, and marketed accordingly – bookshops are usually arranged into sections such as science, travel, sport, art, prose fiction. In the prose fiction section you might find subdivisions such as horror, romance, adventure, science fiction. The literature section will usually be divided up into novels, drama and poetry. These in turn may be further subdivided according to various principles.

This way of organising cultural products into different kinds is done partly in order to sell more products by making our choices easier. At the same time, such distinctions indicate real distinctions between different kinds (of, say, music) and reveal real similarities between products of the same kind (all examples of, say, rap music have something in common). Our knowledge of this, and the way we use this knowledge in making our choices, indicates that we have internalised a range of different expectations about different kinds of cultural product. These expectations govern what kinds of product we choose to see or listen to at any particular time, and also shape the way we understand and respond to what we have chosen.

The different kinds of music mentioned above could be called musical genres, and you could subdivide several of these into smaller categories. Jazz, for instance, includes bebop, traditional, west coast, swing, and possibly rhythm and blues and jazz-rock. There are more genres of classical music than we could possibly list here – symphonies, fugues, concertos, programme music, chamber music, oratorios, operas, even 'tone poems'. The different kinds of prose fiction just mentioned could also be called genres. 'Genre' is a French word which simply means 'kind', from the Latin *genus*, meaning 'type' or 'species'. Poetry, we have suggested, is one of the major genres of literature, distinct from other genres of prose fiction and drama. In Chapter 7 ('Hearing Voices') we suggested that poetry itself could be divided into three major genres according to the way they present themselves as speech: lyric, narrative and dramatic poetry. But these poetic genres can also be further subdivided into a number of different kinds, and when people talk about poetic genres it is generally these subdivisions that they are referring to.

Students of literature are often expected to recognise the genre of a work and to use its conventional name. There are quite a lot of poetic genres and genre names, and many of these names are taken from foreign languages. But is it really necessary to learn a lot of obscure technical terms for different poetic genres? Do we really need to know what an ode is, or an elegy, an epigram, a **villanelle**, an **eclogue**, a sonnet, an epithalamium, a dramatic monologue (to name but a few)? Couldn't we try to demystify the business of genre by using simpler terms? Or, better still, couldn't we forget about 'genre' altogether and read every poem on its own terms? This chapter will explore these questions.

▦ Genres with Fixed Forms: The Limerick

Some poetic genres identify themselves through their use of a fixed form – they are (almost) invariably written in a particular stanza form, with a specific number of lines and a predetermined metre and rhyme scheme. The sonnet might be the best example of such a fixed form – which is why we shall be devoting the whole of the next chapter to it as a representative poetic genre – but other examples might include the villanelle, the sestina, the limerick, the clerihew, the **haiku** (if you don't recognise some of these terms, look them up in our Glossary). It might be objected that these are not really genre terms so much as the names of stanza or verse forms which might better belong in our chapter on metre. However, there may be good reasons for insisting that these particular names also involve assumptions about characteristic subject matter and the way the poem handles it. The type of subject a poem deals with and the way it handles it are themselves a large part of what is normally meant by 'genre'.

The limerick, for instance, always (or nearly always) consists of a single five-line stanza with the stress pattern 3 + 3 + 2 + 2 + 3 and rhymed *aabba*, but it also tends to treat a particular type of subject in a very specific way:

> There was a young lady of Norway,
> Who hung from her toes in a doorway;
> She said to her beau:
> 'Come over here, Joe,
> I think I've discovered one more way!'
> (A.C. Swinburne, 1837–1909, attrib.)

Limericks are 'light verse' or 'comic verse' (these are also generic names), and you will sometimes find them in places you wouldn't expect to find most other genres of poetry. The earliest limericks we know of were printed in the 1820s, and the form was later popularised by Edward Lear (*Book of Nonsense*, 1846) as a sub-type of what has become known as 'nonsense verse' – which can itself be thought of as a distinctive genre (see 'Nonsense Verse' in *Princeton*). Even though the limerick might not be 'serious poetry', it can tell us much about the way genres operate more generally in literature. We might be persuaded that we should regard such fixed forms as something more than metrical patterns, something closer to genres, if it could be demonstrated that they often show other conventional features which may be normalised and varied. For instance, most limericks begin with a fixed syntactic formula with the pattern: 'There was a young/old man/woman of [place-name] [line break] Who . . .'. That is a fairly rigid, artificial formula. They also use triple rhythm:

>   -   / - -   / - - /   -
> There was a young lady of Norway . . .

Early examples tend to repeat the first line at the end – an example of formal closure – but later writers of the limerick, as in the example we have quoted above, found it more effective to conclude the poem with a surprising reversal or revelation of the witty point. The fact that the last line returns to the rhythm of the first helps to persuade us that the culminating point is somehow appropriate, and the closing rhyme, through its echo of the chosen proper name, finally cements the 'logic' of what is normally an outrageous conclusion. Clearly this is a purely poetic 'logic' that depends on readers' willingness to assume those links between sound and sense which, we suggested in earlier chapters, play a large part in the formal organisation of poetry – this might be described as one more 'Relation of Rhyme to Reason' (see Chapter 4). This interplay of metrical and conceptual patterns, of established convention and variation, of reader expectation and response, is exactly the experience of genre. For well-tuned readers the interplay between these things is a large part of the experience of literature itself since, as we have tried to show throughout this book, the reading of poetry is largely a matter of registering the relations between form and function, system and event, or (in Reader Response criticism, especially) expectation and surprise.

In thinking about fixed or artificial forms, it is sometimes assumed that it is only the more sophisticated genres that are governed by complex rules and conventions. Some genres appear to be more artificial than others, their conventions more strange to us and hence more difficult to come to terms with. But one of the reasons why we have chosen to discuss popular genres such as the limerick in this chapter, rather than 'high' forms such as epic, or ode, or sonnet, is precisely because they challenge this prejudice. There are good reasons for thinking that some of the genres of popular culture are highly conventional, and that 'artificial' forms are not exclusive to high art. The formula for starting a limerick, for instance, is quite rigid, but it is quite easy to make up new limericks once you have learned it. The first step is to think of a proper name that fits the metre; you then have to find a word that rhymes with it and see what kind of story or joke the rhyme word suggests. If the subject or denouement is scandalous, or bizarre or surprising, so much the better since limericks are expected to be slightly *risqué* or shocking, and the success of your poem will depend to a large extent on how successfully it meets, or manipulates or (if you're good enough) challenges those expectations. Here is a particularly witty example of a limerick which plays upon and subverts our generic expectations (we quote the whole poem):

> There was a young lady of Crewe
> Whose limericks stopped at line two.[1]

If we are correct in defining the limerick as a 'fixed form' with a specific number of lines and a predetermined metre and rhyme scheme, how could we claim that this two-line poem is still a limerick? How far can a poem depart from the conventions which define a genre before it ceases to belong to that genre at all? One of the best anthologies of limericks – *The Penguin Book of Limericks* – has whole sections of 'extended' limericks, *haiku*-shaped limericks and upside-down limericks.[2] Here is an 'extended' limerick:

[1] Quoted in Alastair Fowler, *Kinds of Literature: An introduction to the theory of genres and modes* (Oxford: Clarendon Press, 1982), p. 173, from Martin Gardner, *Scientific American* (April 1977), p. 134.
[2] E.O. Parrott, ed., *The Penguin Book of Limericks* (Harmondsworth: Penguin, 1983), pp. 248, 249–50, 251–2.

There was a strange student from Yale,
Who put himself outside the pale.
  Said the judge: 'Please refrain
  When passing through Maine,
  From exposing yourself again in the train,
Or you'll just have to do it in jail.'
(Anon., *Penguin Book of Limericks*, p. 248)

It is probably worth noticing how this example varies the form not only by adding an extra line which prolongs the 'b' rhyme and delays the final denouement, but also by extending the extra line to four beats rather than two. This line contains an internal rhyme ('again' and 'train') which further accentuates the 'b' rhyme, before the poem finally satisfies our expectation of closure with the return of the 'a' rhyme in the last line. It might not be easy to say precisely what the rhetorical effect of these variations is, or how they relate to the 'message' of the poem, but you might want to think about the 'message' of the last line itself. (Is it a satirical point about sexuality in prisons? Does it hint at the hypocrisy and double-standards of the judge? Or are all such 'serious' questions out of place when reading 'light verse' such as limericks?)

A different kind of variant form is the haiku-shaped limerick, invented by a certain Ted Pauker, who called this hybrid-genre the 'Limeraiku'. Here is an example:

In Arabia,
Baby, a girl *must* get dust
In her labia.
(Gertrude Gerard, no date, *Penguin Book of Limericks*, p. 249)

The haiku is a traditional Japanese poetic genre that normally consists of a three-line poem that records a Zen-like response to the natural world and in which the number of Japanese phonetic characters is tightly controlled. English poets and translators generally try to emulate the traditional haiku form by making the English haiku consist of a seventeen-syllable poem in three lines of five, seven and five syllables.[3] As we can see, the above 'Limeraiku' substitutes the stanza form associated with the limerick with three lines that adhere to the

---

[3] In *The Haiku Handbook: How to Write, Share, and Teach Haiku* (Tokyo, New York and London: Kodansha, 1985), William J. Higginson and Penny Harter point out that Western authors and critics are mistaken to assume 'that the haiku is a seventeen-syllable poem in lines of five, seven, and five syllables' because Japanese poets do not count syllables but *onji*, that is 'the phonetic characters used in writing Japanese phonetic script' (p. 100). Against this, it might be said that the conventions of the *English* haiku are that it consists of a seventeen-syllable poem in lines of five, seven, and five syllables.

formal conventions of the English haiku (try counting the syllables in each line). But instead of offering a Zen-like insight, this poem echoes some of the limerick's conventions: there's the place name at the end of the first line and a rhyme for it in the last line; there's the close proximity of rhymes in the middle of the poem (must/dust); and there's the *risqué* subject matter. Thus we could say that the 'Limeraiku' is a hybrid genre which, however unlikely, tells us something about how genres can cross-fertilise with one another in order to create new genres. As we will see, such processes have taken place throughout literary history. The real question is whether the 'Limeraiku' will survive by being taken up by poets in the future, or whether it is simply an interesting cross-breed that will die out.

The inclusion of such variant forms in a collection of limericks might be thought to undermine everything we have said about the limerick as a fixed form, but it should be apparent that the capacity of fixed forms to subvert their own conventions is one of the advantages they have over less strictly regulated genres. The point about such violations is that they work only for readers who recognise the conventions they are subverting. To break a rule in such a way does not invalidate it; on the contrary, such subversions are themselves rule-dependent. The question to be asked is whether such poems, however aberrant, would work as effectively if the reader did not recognise them as limericks. We suggest that they would not. We shall have more to say about this when we come to examine variations of sonnet form in the next chapter.

One of the conventions of the limerick, which has evidently suggested witty possibilities that have themselves congealed into a minor variant, is that the opening line should end with a proper noun – a personal or place name. Quite a lot of limericks display their wit by choosing a place name that is quite difficult to find a rhyme for – the concluding rhyme then becomes all the more surprising, and its reversal all the more effective. 'Uttoxeter' (a town in England) offers a recurrent challenge, and the *Penguin Book of Limericks* assembles no fewer than twelve examples that rise to this challenge, finding such outrageous rhymes as 'cock-sitter', 'baroque sweater', 'pox hit her' and 'John Knox at her'. If the limerick poet can introduce a proper noun that is not pronounced as it is spelled (for instance, a foreign name), so much the better: there are limericks in which Nantes rhymes with 'aunt', and Antigua with 'what a pig you are'; 'Dun Laoghaire' is an obvious challenge, but anyone from Ireland could tell you that Multerry rhymes with adultery. The number of limericks that set themselves the task of meeting this rhyming challenge suggests that it might have evolved into one of the 'optional' conventions of the genre. It is much easier to make up a limerick if the 'young lady' or 'young man' comes from Bude, because then she or he will inevitably be nude or lewd and your poem will be rude. The objection to limericks as 'serious' poetry might be, precisely, that their argument (or their humorous point) is so evidently rhyme-led

– that is, their form drives their content. But, we suggest, it is precisely this fact that makes them formally and theoretically interesting, since it foregrounds that uncertain yet productive relationship between sound and sense which, we have repeatedly suggested, is fundamental to many kinds of poetry.

▨ Neoclassical Genre Theory

The criteria for judging the success of a limerick are surprisingly close to those which Neoclassical critics brought to the evaluation of literature as a whole. Although the term Neoclassicism is usually reserved for the late-seventeenth- and eighteenth-century revival of Classical styles in the arts generally, a similar Classical revival was also fundamental to the earlier Renaissance of the sixteenth and seventeenth centuries; indeed, the term 'Renaissance' refers to the *rebirth* of Classical culture. This 'rebirth' can be seen, for instance, in the way Renaissance poets adapted Classical genres for their modern vernacular poetry. Critics of the Renaissance and Neoclassical periods influenced the way writers used genres, so it is helpful to know something about their genre theory when we read poetry written from the sixteenth and to the eighteenth century. Such critics also raised issues about genre which are still in theoretical debate. Neoclassical poets and critics advocated the imitation of Classical models, and their concept of influence laid great importance on defining the different kinds of writing which were practised by the ancient poets. The task of defining the different genres was taken up by Renaissance Italian critics such as Julius Caesar Scaliger, who described more than a hundred genres in the sixteenth century, although he totally ignored modern kinds of vernacular writing, including the sonnet (Fowler, *Kinds of Literature*, p. 26). The fact that most of the national traditions in modern Europe established their literary canon under the influence of Renaissance and Neoclassical assumptions helps to explain why so many of our own genre terms remain closely linked to Classical models.

Neoclassical writers tended to see literature as a finite repertoire of fixed forms. They may not always have been able to agree on the number or the names of those forms, but they assumed that genres are historically unchanging, and modern writers were valued according to the fidelity with which they imitated those ancient forms, the conventions of which were abstracted and laid down as 'rules' for the modern writer. French literature of the seventeenth century was more Neoclassical than English literature, largely because French culture as a whole became more authoritarian in the reign of Louis XIV, when the *Académie française* was instituted, among other things, to regulate precisely such matters. In English culture there was never universal agreement as to how strictly modern writers should be bound by the rules and conventions which were thought to govern Classical genres, though many of the 'new' kinds of English poetry, even before the strictly 'Neoclassical' period

331

(1660–1800), are self-conscious imitations of Classical models – Donne's *Elegies* and *Satires*, Jonson's *Epigrams*, Cowley's *Odes*.

Many Neoclassical writers assumed that the whole of literature was a hierarchical system in which some genres were more serious than others; they put epic and tragedy up at the top of the scale, and 'low' genres such as burlesque (though not necessarily satire) at the bottom. Each genre had its appropriate level of linguistic style (modern linguistics would call it 'register'), and this match between genre and style is what the word '**decorum**' referred to. Modern readers generally feel unsympathetic towards this Neoclassical class system, which had its ideological and political motivations, but it is worth pausing to ask whether we have similar prejudices about some genres being superior to others. Are all genres equally valued? One could explore these questions by thinking about television genres. Which of these types of programme is more likely to count as 'serious' television: opera, soap opera, documentary, classic serial, sitcom, chat show, panel game, news and current affairs? And, as far as literature is concerned, was our choice of the limerick to illustrate the notion of literary genre at all surprising?

Modern readers are not likely to share the Neoclassical view that literature is a rigid system of fixed forms. Genre rules seem too prescriptive or restrictive, and they ignore our sense that the most interesting – and arguably the most successful – literary works often do not seem to conform to any of the established kinds. We tend to assume that creativity is a matter of breaking stereotypes and that fixed kinds are a sign of fixed minds. Fixed genre rules also ignore the manifest evidence that genres evolve – not only as new forms are invented and interact with the old, but also as innovative writers break the rules and so establish new benchmarks for subsequent writers. In assigning particular poems to a recognised genre which had its place within a rigid hierarchy of fixed forms, Neoclassical theory was resisting the possibility that the genre system might be dynamic and continually evolving. As we tried to show in the case of the limerick, even such a recognisably fixed form has evolved variants and hybrid types within a relatively short period after its invention.

But the question of whether poems can be assigned to a particular genre is not rendered invalid by the inadequacy of the Neoclassical system. There *are* distinct poetic genres, even if they change through history and through interacting with each other, and poets have continued to write with genre models in mind up to the present day.[4] Indeed, our recognition that the genre system is not fixed but continually evolving can be seen in the fact that we are constantly

---

[4] For an excellent collection of poetry that is organised into different poetic forms and genres and demonstrates how poets up to the present day have used and developed highly conventional poetic forms, see Mark Strand and Eavan Boland, *The Making of a Poem: A Norton Anthology of Poetic Forms* (New York and London: Norton, 2000).

inventing names for new genres as they emerge – war poetry, concrete poetry, the limerick, free verse, confessional poetry, nonsense verse, Beat poetry, Imagist poetry, Black-Mountain verse, Symbolist poetry, performance poetry, **dub poetry**, and so on. Some of these categories might be thought to identify a school or movement rather than a genre, but one of the things that distinguishes a movement is, after all, its use of distinctive kinds of writing.

■ Recognising a Poem's Genre: The Ballad as an Example

To see why it might be useful to recognise a poem's genre, we shall look at a particular example of the ballad genre. Here is the whole text of the poem whose opening stanza we printed as prose in Chapter 2, when we wanted to find out how easy it is for readers to recognize the 4×4 metrical form.

Lord Randal

'O where ha' you been, Lord Randal, my son?
And where ha' you been, my handsome young man?'
'I ha' been at the greenwood; mother, mak my bed soon,
For I'm wearied wi' huntin', and fain wad lie down.'

'And wha met ye there, Lord Randal, my son?   5
And wha met you there, my handsome young man?'
'O I met wi' my true-love; mother, mak my bed soon,
For I'm wearied wi' huntin', and fain wad lie down.'

'And what did she give you, Lord Randal, my son?
And what did she give you, my handsome young man?'   10
'Eels fried in a pan; mother, mak my bed soon,
For I'm wearied wi' huntin', and fain wad lie down.'

'And wha gat your leavin's, Lord Randal, my son?
And wha gat your leavin's, my handsome young man?'
'My hawks and my hounds; mother, mak my bed soon,   15
For I'm wearied wi' huntin', and fain wad lie down.'

'And what becam of them, Lord Randal, my son?
And what becam of them, my handsome young man?'
'They stretched their legs out and died; mother, mak my bed soon,
For I'm wearied wi' huntin', and fain wad lie down.'   20

'O I fear you are poisoned, Lord Randal, my son!
I fear you are poisoned, my handsome young man!'
'O yes, I am poisoned; mother, mak my bed soon,
For I'm sick at the heart, and I fain wad lie down.'

'What d'ye leave to your mother, Lord Randal, my son?   25
What d'ye leave to your mother, my handsome young man?'
'Four and twenty milk kye; mother, mak my bed soon,
For I'm sick at the heart, and I fain wad lie down.'

'What d'ye leave to your sister, Lord Randal, my son?
What d'ye leave to your sister, my handsome young man?'   30
'My gold and my silver; mother, mak my bed soon,
For I'm sick at the heart, and I fain wad lie down.'

'What d'ye leave to your brother, Lord Randal, my son?
What d'ye leave to your brother, my handsome young man?'
'My houses and my lands; mother, mak my bed soon,   35
For I'm sick at the heart, and I fain wad lie down.'

'What d'ye leave to your true-love, Lord Randal, my son?
What d'ye leave to your true-love, my handsome young man?'
'I leave her hell and fire; mother, mak my bed soon,
For I'm sick at the heart, and I fain wad lie down.'   40

In the case of the limerick we stressed that it was the metrical form, stanza
structure and rhyme pattern which play a large part in the definition of the
genre. We might therefore ask how far these features would help us to cate-
gorise 'Lord Randal' as a ballad. Simply reading the poem aloud will probably
allow you to recognise that this is a four-beat metre. When we analysed this
poem in Chapter 2, we found a strongly accented stress pattern, with an irre-
gular number of unstressed syllables between the beats. There are lines in the
poem that stretch this metrical pattern to the limit – it is difficult to imagine
that we would scan line 19 as a four-beat line if it did not appear within a
poem that has already established the insistent 4 × 4 pattern:

$$\text{- } / \quad \text{- } (/) \text{ - - } / \quad (/) \text{ - } / \quad \text{- - } /$$
They stretched their legs out and died; mother, mak my bed soon

Our analysis in Chapter 2 identified this as a strong-stress (sometimes called
'accentual-syllabic') metre, in which it is the stresses that count, while the
number of unstressed syllables can vary. Even so, it is rare to find four
unstressed syllables in a row: our analysis shows that the underlying metrical
pattern can only be sustained by demoting two stressed syllables, which is why
this line is particularly awkward. Ballads often use this strong-stress metre in
4 × 4 stanza patterns, though the term **'ballad metre'** is conventionally used for
stanzas with the 4,/3,/4,/3 metrical pattern (which, as we saw in Chapter 2, is a
variant of the 4 × 4 stanza). Thus, although 'Lord Randal' is not in 'ballad

metre', this does not disqualify it from being a ballad. (By the same token, the fact that many popular poems use the ballad metre does not automatically mean that they are ballads.)

Identifying the metrical form of 'Lord Randal', then, does not get us very far towards understanding its genre. Nor has it got us very far towards understanding how the poem presents its subject matter or how it uses the wider (and, arguably, more interesting) conventions of its genre. How might a reader gain some familiarity with those conventions? For some readers this might not be a problem, since the ballad is a genre which is still alive in our culture. Popular music – both in the folk traditions of Britain and the United States, and in more commercial derivatives – still produces 'ballads'. The term 'ballad' in rock music usually connotes a slow, romantic number, but this usage is misleading since such ballads have little in common with the ballad tradition. Songs such as 'The Ballad of Bonnie and Clyde', Bob Dylan's 'Ballad of Hollis Brown' (1964) or 'Ballad of a Thin Man' (1965), or John Lennon's 'Ballad of John and Yoko' (1969) are closer to the ballad tradition in the way they tell their stories. Some readers will be familiar with ballads such as 'Casey Jones', 'Frankie and Johnny' or 'John Henry', and you may well have read further poems from the 'literary' canon which describe themselves, or have been described as, ballads. By using such examples we could try to work out what features they had in common and so attempt to build up a description, if not a definition, of the ballad genre. Certainly, genre recognition depends on wide reading and/or listening and a willingness to make comparisons between works that seem to resemble each other so that we can begin to generalise the characteristics they share. That willingness can often be productive, even if it gets only as far as saying, 'This poem reminds me of . . .'. But the number of literary genres is probably too great, and the process of deciding which features are specific to a particular genre too laborious, for most of us to undertake such a painstaking empirical process. Most of us take a short cut by consulting a dictionary of literary terms or a glossary (such as the one at the end of this book). By doing this, and testing out those definitions on actual examples, you will sharpen your sense of the characteristics of recognised genres.

The *Princeton* entry for 'Ballad' offers a useful summary of its generic features. The ballad is a short narrative poem or song that has its roots in the orally transmitted folk ballads that circulated in the illiterate and semi-literate people of late medieval Europe. *Princeton* identifies three characteristics 'which seem to hold for all genuine specimens':

(1) [Ballads] focus on a single crucial episode. The [ballad] begins usually at a point where the action is decisively directed towards its catastrophe. Events leading up to this conclusive episode are told in a hurried, summary fashion. Little attention is given to describing settings; indeed, circumstantial detail of every sort is conspicuously absent. (2) [Ballads] are dramatic. We are not told about things happening; we

are shown them happening. Every artistic resource is pointed toward giving an intensity and immediacy to the action and toward heightening the emotional impact of the climax. Protagonists are allowed to speak for themselves, which means that dialogue . . . bulks large. At strategic moments, dialogue erupts into the narrative. Such speeches are sparingly tagged; frequently we must deduce the speaker from what is being said. (3) [Ballads] are impersonal. The narrator seldom allows his or her own attitude toward the events to intrude. Comments on motives are broad, general, detached. There may be an 'I' in a ballad, but the singer does not forget his or her position as the representative of the public voice. Bias there is in [ballads], of course, but it is the bias of a party, community, or nation, not an individual's subjective point of view.

Princeton goes on to identify a number of other features which have some relevance to 'Lord Randal': there is a sparsity of figures of speech in ballads, and little time for 'careful delineation of character or exploration of psychological motivation'. Perhaps most relevant to 'Lord Randal' is *Princeton*'s comment on 'the heavy amount of repetition and parallelism characteristic of the ballads'. This repetition is not ornamental but frequently emphatic – reiterating something which can be seen as a focal point of the action or of the emotions which it arouses. The traditional ballad is an orally transmitted popular song which has been handed down from singer to singer, and one of the functions of such repetition was to assist the reciter's memory. Specific to the ballad is the device modern ballad-collectors and scholars call 'incremental repetition', in which a phrase within a line, or the line itself, is repeated with additions that take the story forward by introducing a significant variation of detail. The fact that each stanza will also repeat the accompanying tune makes it easy for certain verbal phrases to get attached to the musical phrase at particular points in the song (indeed, that is how refrains tend to get remembered in modern community singing, where the audience joins in the chorus – 'chorus' in this sense is another term for what in poetry is called the 'refrain'). The fact that many of the traditional popular ballads in English were first recorded in the Scottish borders, and are sometimes called 'Border ballads' (though the ballad is practised much more widely), may also help us to account for the language of 'Lord Randal': only Scots pronunciation would be likely to rhyme 'soon' and 'down'.

Let us see how many of the characteristics *Princeton* identifies can be found in 'Lord Randal'. The poem is about a sensational event in which a handsome youth has been poisoned by his lover, and his mother's anxious questioning reveals that he is dying. This is what *Princeton* calls the 'single crucial episode' on which this ballad focuses. The poem pretends to be recited at the very moment when this revelation occurs (indeed, it is itself that revelation which we overhear), and the fact that the whole poem is a dialogue, with no narrator's voice whatever, gives it that dramatic immediacy which *Princeton*

identifies as typical of ballads. The poem shows us a story as though its climac-
tic events were taking place in front of us. The fact that Lord Randal has been
poisoned by his lover and is confessing this to his mother suggests that the
poem is appealing to sensationalist and sentimental tastes in potential listeners.
It would not be difficult to imagine the kind of tabloid headline a modern
newspaper might use for such a story. (Why not try inventing such a headline?)

The poem makes extensive use of repetition (with a refrain) in regularly
rhymed stanzas, all of which repeat the same four rhyming words with a kind
of relentless insistence. Incremental repetition shows itself in the way the whole
poem is constructed out of the repeated question-and-answer formula. It is,
then, full of repetition and parallelism, none of which is 'ornamental rhetoric'
(*Princeton*) but is wholly geared towards heightening the emotional atmo-
sphere and revealing the plot ('Plot', says *Princeton*, 'is the central element' in
ballads). The variation of these insistent repetitions signals important stages in
the development; for instance, the major shift in the refrain takes place after
line 24, where the repeated formula 'For I'm wearied wi' huntin'' changes to
'For I'm sick at the heart'. The shift is triggered by the mother's expression of
her realisation in the previous stanza that her son has been poisoned, and that
realisation is itself prompted by Lord Randal's response to her final question of
this series, in line 17 ('And what becam of them, Lord Randal, my son?'), as he
reveals that his hawks and his hounds have died after being fed the remains of
his meal ('They stretched their legs out and died; mother, mak my bed soon').
The ballad's questions thus far have been carefully staged to lead up to the
gradual realisation, on the part of the reader and of Lord Randal's mother, of
the enormity of the crime committed. From this point on, the conclusion of the
refrain, 'I fain wad lie down', takes on a sinister implication which goes
beyond the mere weariness of the hunter. The mother's questions shift, imme-
diately following this revelation that he is dying, to his testamentary bequests
(he's making his will), but the sequence of 'mother', 'sister' and 'brother' in the
formulaic variations of the remaining stanzas – so that 'what d'ye leave to your
true-love' is reserved for the final variation in the last stanza – effectively
brings the whole poem to its climax in the way he curses the agent of his
destruction. The whole poem has led up to that final revelation of an unanti-
cipated bitterness which switches the tone and is quite different from the
weariness he expresses in the preceding stanzas.

There is a spareness or terseness to the dialogue of 'Lord Randall' which is
characteristic of ballads. We learn of the hero's relationship to his mother and
to his lover, and the mother's simultaneous awareness of these two things
might be thought to inform her two alternate forms of address: 'Lord Randal,
my son' and 'my handsome young man'. This is a poem about sons and lovers,
and its focus, for all its simplicity, is elemental not elementary. This narrative is
wholly uninterested in character and motive; we learn nothing more of the

relationship than this, and we are not told why the Lord has been poisoned by his lover. The amount of information that is withheld contributes to the air of mystery and unaccountable aura of emotion which surround the poem. That, too, is typical of ballads.

It is worth asking, at this point, what a reader gains by recognising that 'Lord Randal' is a ballad. We want to suggest that attuning ourselves to the characteristics which are typical of the genre has not only taught us something about genre, but has improved our responsiveness to the poem itself. One way of putting this would be to say that the poem's genre is a context which has allowed us to read the text with greater confidence and insight. We do not claim that our commentary has uncovered everything of interest in 'Lord Randal', or even that it has identified all the features that are specific to ballads. You might want to re-read the poem now in order to find anything we have missed. You could do this by going through it checking off the 'ballad characteristics' which we have identified from the *Princeton* description. Or, alternatively, you could try to find ways of reading the poem which make no reference to its genre – for example, by writing a commentary which makes no mention of the word 'ballad' or the characteristic features of ballads but still seems to cover what you take to be the most interesting and important things in the poem. We anticipate that you may find this quite difficult (and not only because we have now alerted you to regard the poem as a ballad).

◾ Genres in History: The History of a Genre

Genres have histories. We may need to study such histories because it is important to recognise that the naming and identification of genre types is itself a historically relative process, and the application of genre names often shows a revealing instability over the centuries. Our usage of the word 'ballad', for instance, to describe a form of popular narrative verse for which the normative models would be such poems as 'Lord Randal' or 'Sir Patrick Spens' would have seemed curious to any reader before the eighteenth century. English is unique in its usage of 'ballad' as the word for what in French, German and Scandinavian languages are merely called 'songs'. As G.H. Gerould says, 'only the Anglo-Saxons have chosen to adopt a foreign term for a sophisticated product and apply it without discrimination to at least five or six different sorts of verse'.[5] The word 'ballad' is derived from a word meaning a song to be danced to, an association we still preserve in 'ballet' and in 'ball' (for the kind of event at which people engage in 'ballroom dancing'). In the Middle Ages, French and English poets composed 'ballades', a strict form in regular metre with a concluding *envoi* – a short postscript or coda consisting of a stanza

[5] G.H. Gerould, *The Ballad of Tradition* (Oxford: Oxford University Press, 1957), p. 235.

which sends the poem about its business by addressing it to its patron or summing up its message. Only in the late sixteenth century did the word 'ballad' come to refer to a (particular kind of) story told in song, although 'ballad' could still refer at this time to a whole variety of lyric and narrative forms.

With the invention of printing it became profitable to circulate single sheets or chapbooks containing popular songs, jests, romantic tales and sensational or topical stories. These are known as 'broadside ballads', because they were printed on broadsheets – that is to say, on one side of a single sheet of paper not designed to be folded or bound. But the word 'ballad' came to be used to describe any such ephemeral production sold by chapmen or itinerant print-sellers. The Stationers' Register records that between 1557 and 1709 more than three thousand such 'ballads' were licensed for printing. Broadside ballads have important connections with the form we now designate 'traditional ballads', often using its metre, sometimes set to the same traditional tunes, and appealing to many of the same tastes. But broadside ballads also included other types of subject matter – romances, riddles and jests, even preaching. They often included journalistic reportage, and they have an important place in the development of the newspaper – the fact that we could imagine Lord Randal's story as a potential newspaper item may suggest why. Broadside ballads are written rather than oral compositions, specifically composed for the print medium and appealing to a predominantly urban rather than a rural readership, and this introduced some fundamental differences from the traditional oral ballad. Modern students of literature are unlikely to read any broadside ballads, but that is entirely a result of the fact that the 'traditional' ballad was the form which, in the late eighteenth and nineteenth centuries, became assimilated to high culture and absorbed into the canon of 'English literature'. That process is worth studying, because it can tell us quite a lot about the continuing commerce between popular and high culture, and about the historical revaluation of genres that is part of the ongoing process of defining and redefining literature itself though history.

Ballad scholars have noted that Shakespeare's references to ballads always use it as a term of reproach (Gerould, p. 237). Falstaff, for instance, speaks of ballads 'sung to filthy tunes'. The history of the ballad is largely the story of its rehabilitation and acceptance into the literary canon. That process is already foreshadowed in Sir Philip Sidney's confession in *The Apology for Poetry* (1595) that 'I never heard the old song of Percy and Douglas that I found not my heart moved'. But this confession is accompanied by condescension towards the 'barbarousness' and 'rude style' of 'that uncivil age' (what we call the Middle Ages – many traditional ballads were composed in the late fifteenth or early sixteenth century). Sidney does not call it a ballad, but the 'old song' he is referring to is the ballad we know as 'Chevy Chase', and his praise gave the lead to such later apologists as Ben Jonson. Joseph Addison singles out the same ballad of 'Chevy Chase' as suited to the refined tastes of his readers in a couple of *Spectator* essays of 1711.

Educated interest first showed itself in the collecting of written records of ballads, which began before the end of the seventeenth century and continued through the eighteenth, among antiquarians such as Samuel Pepys and Thomas Percy. Such collections were based on whatever printed and manuscript sources their compilers could lay hands on, and for this reason contained a preponderance of broadside ballads, together with a variety of heterogeneous popular forms. Modern ballad scholars tend to reproach these collections for the impurity of their sense of the ballad as a genre, but a large part of the interest of such collections as Percy's *Reliques of Ancient English Poetry* (1765) lies precisely in the evidence its heterogeneous content affords us of the ballad's changing historical affiliations with other popular forms in a more extended genre system. Percy gave his collection the running title 'Ancient Songs and Ballads', but some of his contemporaries were already beginning to distinguish between popular songs and ballads, even though ballads were traditionally set to music and sung. In 1761 the poet William Shenstone wrote to Bishop Percy as follows: 'It has become habitual to me, to call that *Ballad*, which describes or implies some action; on the other hand, I term a *Song*, that which contains only an expression of sentiment.' In 1783 another anthologist, J. Ritson, stressed that 'With us, songs of sentiment, expression, or even description, are properly termed *Songs*, in contradistinction to mere narrative compositions, which we now denominate *Ballads*' (cited in Gerould, p. 252). These comments are evidence of the slow emergence of genre distinctions. Today we would probably agree with Ritson's distinction by noting that expressive songs – love songs, expressions of grief, loss, or personal betrayal – are likely to be voiced in the first person, whereas the ballad singer or narrator usually adopts an impersonal narrative voice. Though we might still describe both as types of lyric poetry, we need to recognise how far our own definition of 'lyric' has been influenced by the way nineteenth-century writers redefined lyric as, above all, the medium for personal expression. As John Ruskin put it, 'lyric poetry is the expression by the poet of his own feelings' (cited in Fowler, *Kinds of Literature*, p. 137). That definition of 'lyric' would have surprised an eighteenth- or, indeed, a seventeenth-century reader. The point is that not only genres themselves, but also our conceptions of them change through history.

To recognise how the late eighteenth century understood the distinctions and associations between different kinds of poetry in this genre system is probably crucial if we are to understand the way the ballad came to be used when, very shortly thereafter, it finally made its way into the canon of approved poetic genres in the work of the Romantic poets and their successors. The important thing to recognise is that no 'serious' poet before the closing years of the eighteenth century would have dreamed of writing a ballad. From

Wordsworth onwards, however, the ballad becomes a recognised member of the genre system of English poetry. Use of its conventions becomes so natural to poets that the name 'literary ballad' has been invented for this sub-genre in order to distinguish it from the authentic folk songs which devotees of the emerging discipline of folklore were increasingly beginning to record from the lips of surviving ballad singers. The assumptions about the ballad which made it an appropriate genre for the Romantic poets might be summarised as follows. First, it was a popular form – Wordsworth and Coleridge's title, *Lyrical Ballads*, for their collection of poems in 1798 was intended to send a clear signal that the forms of expression used by ordinary people were more appropriate to poetry in an age of revolution than the eighteenth-century genres they had inherited from the Neoclassical canon. Secondly, the ballad's similarities with the medieval romances, some of which were included in the eighteenth-century 'ballad' collections, appealed to nineteenth-century poets' taste for 'Gothic' and medieval subjects. Ballads and **romances** are both narrative genres recording the exploits of heroic or chivalric characters in settings which seemed mysteriously remote from the modern world, and hence appealed to the imagination of nineteenth-century poets and their readers. And the fact that, as we have seen with 'Lord Randal', ballads often call up intense emotions in response to the actions they are recording had a strong appeal at a time when poetry's capacity to evoke powerful feelings was highly valued. Since the time of Coleridge and Wordsworth the ballad form has had a continuing influence on the mainstream of poetry in English, and poets such as Keats, Rossetti, Meredith, Swinburne, Yeats, Housman and Auden have produced examples of the 'literary ballad' or poems which use its conventions. At the same time, the popular ballad has survived both in oral and 'folk' traditions in particular areas of Scotland, Ireland and the United States, as well as in popular music, including jazz and rock.

■ A Family of Related Genres: Towards a Literary System

What matters about this brief history of a poetic genre in the present context is not so much what it tells us about the history of the ballad as what it might suggest for our understanding and use of genre concepts. We seem to have discovered that the ballad – despite our suggestion when reading 'Lord Randal' that it was a fixed, readily identifiable genre – turns out not to be so stable as we implied. Not only has the word's meaning shifted throughout its history, but at any one time it seems to have been associated with a shifting matrix or family of different genres. In modern critical usage there are various kinds of ballad which we might distinguish by different qualifying adjectives: there is the traditional ballad, which for us (but not for Shakespeare, or for readers long after him) now supplies the normative model; there is the broadside ballad (not an oral form, but written for the print medium); there are Robin Hood ballads, which use different narrative conventions from the traditional ballad; and there is the literary ballad, which is the name we give to the belated appropriation of the conventions of the traditional ballad by high culture. We are thus able to identify various species of the genus – various subordinate kinds of ballad. Such distinctive variants of a literary genre are called 'sub-genres'.

At various periods in its history (or in the history of its reception) the ballad has also been associated with various forms which we would now be inclined to exclude from the genre altogether – expressive songs, popular romances, riddles, jests and comic tales, campfire songs, Negro Spirituals, Blues. But other variants can be seen as authentic members of the genre system, even though their subject matter and target audience may be somewhat different from those of the traditional ballad. Bob Dylan's 'A Hard Rain's A-gonna Fall' is a protest song about nuclear or ecological disaster written during the Cuban missile crisis of October 1962. Its repeated question-and-answer formula is a clear echo of 'Lord Randal': 'Oh, where have you been, my blue-eyed son? / Oh, where have you been, my darling young one?' Such an echo might, perhaps, be regarded as an 'allusion' since, as we shall explain in Chapter 13, 'allusion' refers to moments when one text deliberately echoes another without actually quoting it. The question-and-answer formula could certainly be seen as functioning as what we might call a genre marker, signalling the relationship of Dylan's lyric to its traditional ballad models.[6]

■ The Literary System

Genres, then, can be thought of as existing within family networks. Individual genres can be divided into sub-genres, but they are also related, through similarities and differences, to all the other genres in the literary system. There have been a number of attempts to describe such family relationships in a systematic way. The hierarchical ranking of the Neoclassical critics was one such system, and various theorists in the twentieth century sought to map the literary system as an orderly structure of interrelated genres. The most ambitious of these was Northrop Frye's *Anatomy of Criticism* (1957), which reduces all literary genres to four mythical archetypes identified with the four seasons and to five narrative modes depending on the status of the hero.[7] But none of these systems has won wide support, largely because the assumption that the

---

[6] The language of Bob Dylan's songs is usefully discussed by Christopher Ricks in 'American English and the Inherently Transitory', in Ricks, *The Force of Poetry*, pp. 417–41. In his more recent book-length study of Dylan's lyrics, *Dylan's Visions of Sin* (London: Penguin, 2003), Ricks discusses 'A Hard Rain's A-gonna Fall' as a reworking of 'Lord Randal' (pp. 329–44).

[7] Northrop Frye, *Anatomy of Criticism* (Princeton, NJ: Princeton University Press, 1957).

received repertoire of generic categories is fixed and universal, rather than historically changing, matches neither our actual experience of literary kinds nor the kind of historical transformations we have traced in the ballad.

It is certainly interesting to speculate on the fundamental principles of genre, but a lot depends on what axis is chosen as the basis for any comparisons. We could range the genres on a sliding scale between fictionality and documentary, or between narrative and non-narrative kinds, or between popular and élite, instructive and entertaining, Classical and Romantic, naive and sentimental.[8] But most of these criteria seem equally arbitrary, and it would no doubt be all too easy to find individual literary texts that would disrupt such systems. Alternatively, we might decide that the medium of presentation was fundamental to genre, so we could separate written from oral, pictorial from verbal media, manuscript genres from print genres, electronic from print media. But again, while there are times when it is possible to show quite interesting and important changes to genres as they cross media boundaries, the fact that they do frequently cross such boundaries suggests that medium is not fundamental to their definition. For instance, both narrative and drama can cross to and fro from one medium to another – as with the film of the book and the book of the film. A Western film may use some different conventions from those found in a Western novel, but the fact that we think of both as Westerns suggests that the medium is not definitive as a principle of genre difference. It is that capacity of the work to transgress boundaries that makes genres such protean and paradoxical conventions. The system is dynamic, multidimensional, constantly changing.

■ Structuralist Theories of Genre

In some theories of literature a description of the underlying generic codes and conventions which shape the way particular texts represent human experience has been seen as a primary task of analysis, a task which extends at least as urgently to contemporary works in popular media as to works in the literary tradition. Structuralism, in particular, insists that we have no unmediated knowledge of social meaning or truth; what we assume to be true is wholly constructed for us by our culture's repertoire of symbolic conventions, which are largely dependent on the network of generic codes. The job of identifying and analysing those codes was a primary goal of Structuralist criticism of the 1950s and 1960s.

---

[8] Schiller's essay 'Über naive und sentimentalische Dichtung' (1795–96) divides all poets into two classes: 'naive' writers who have an immediate and intuitive closeness to nature, and 'sentimental' ones who strive to recapture such a sense through cultivated and artificial forms.

For Structuralism, genre can be seen precisely as a set of conventions which enable readers to 'naturalise' texts, since those conventions shape readers' expectations of what is plausible or 'natural' to human experience in discourse of various kinds. The Structuralist term 'verisimilitude' refers to this capacity of a text to conceal its own conventional strategies, and thus make what it presents seem natural and inevitable. Definitions of the term include 'whatever tradition makes suitable or expected in a particular genre'.[9] The concept of verisimilitude extends beyond genre to cover virtually the whole literary system, and it has often been more productively applied to mimetic and narrative modes such as the novel, film and advertising, whose conventionality is less obvious than is the case with most poetic genres. But Jonathan Culler's summary of the aims of the Structuralist project may indicate why concepts of genre should have taken on so much importance in Structuralist thinking:

> there is a kind of attention which one might call structuralist: a desire to isolate codes, to name the various languages with and among which the text plays, to go beyond manifest content to a series of forms and then to make these forms, or oppositions or modes of signification, the burden of the text.
>
> (*Structuralist Poetics*, p. 259)

The recognition that what we can say, in any medium, is determined largely by the discourses available to us led to the characteristic Structuralist insistence that the point of origin of all meanings lies not in the speaking individual but, rather, in linguistic, literary and cultural systems; indeed, the very identity of the individual speaker or author is said to be constructed by that system.

Gérard Genette offers the following account of the Structuralist concept of the literary system in an essay entitled 'Structuralism and Literary Criticism' (1964):

> literature is not only a collection of autonomous works, which may 'influence' one another by a series of fortuitous and isolated encounters; it is a coherent whole, a homogeneous space, within which works touch and penetrate one another; it is also, in turn, a part linked to other parts in the wider space of 'culture,' in which its own value is a function of the whole. Thus it doubly belongs to a study of structure, internal and external.[10]

As Genette notes, classical rhetoric formalised this system in its theory of genres, but it failed to recognise that, as we have seen with the ballad, both genres and the system which connects them evolve and change through history: 'What was lacking in this theory [Classical rhetoric] was the temporal dimension, the idea that the system could evolve' (Genette, in Lodge, *Modern*

---

[9] Culler, *Structuralist Poetics*, p. 139.
[10] Genette, 'Structuralism and Literary Criticism', reprinted in Lodge, *Modern Criticism and Theory*, pp. 62–78 (73).

Criticism and Theory, p. 74). The system of relationships between genres as it exists at any one time, along with the codes and conventions of each genre, is what Structural linguistics calls a 'synchronic' structure. The way a particular genre develops or evolves through history is, by contrast, 'diachronic'. More traditional scholars had already charted the diachronic or historical evolution of particular genres, but some Structuralists aimed to go beyond this to map both the synchronic structure at any one point in time and the diachronic development of the whole system through history. This is what we might think of as a three-dimensional model of literary history:

> The structuralist idea, in this matter, is to follow literature in its overall evolution, while making synchronic cuts at various stages and comparing the tables one with another. Literary evolution then appears in all its richness, which derives from the fact that the system survives while constantly altering.
>
> (Genette, in Lodge, *Modern Criticism and Theory*, p. 74)

As Genette says, such an approach transforms literary history into 'the history of a system' (p. 75).

It hardly needs to be said that this is a highly ambitious project, and forty or so years after its inception it remains largely unfulfilled. As Genette's statement above suggests, historical study involves not just tracing the distinctions (and connections) between those genres which are 'internal' to 'the literary field', but also 'the much wider division between literature and everything that is not literature; this would be, not literary history, but the history of the relations between literature and social life as a whole: the history of the *literary function*' (p. 76). These relations were, in fact, what we were attending to when we traced the changing history of attitudes towards the ballad which, as we saw, was 'not literature' prior to the late eighteenth century, but became part of the accepted repertoire of 'literary' genres (at least in some of its developments and sub-genres) thereafter. This raises the question whether some literary genres might (like the ballad) have 'poor relations', while others (odes? epics?) are wholly 'literary'. Structuralism's recognition, in attempting to describe literature as a discrete system of genres, that many of these genres have sometimes crossed the frontiers between literature and non-literature through their history has opened up the possibility that all such frontiers are arbitrary and movable. This argument has been most consistently developed, as we shall see, by Tzvetan Todorov.

■ Literary Competence

Genette's (and French Structuralism's) redefinition of the goals of literary history has to be seen in the context of literary studies as practised in France, where 'literary history' remains more firmly instituted as the basis of the academic discipline than it has become in the United States or Britain. Students in British and North American universities are likely to spend less time thinking about the history of literature than about problems of close reading, interpretation and analysis of individual texts. The part of Structuralist genre theory that is more directly relevant to these activities is its theory of literary competence. The idea of 'competence' derives from linguistics and refers to the fact that in order to understand even a simple sentence the speaker of a language must have internalised a whole range of phonological, syntactic and semantic codes and structures. As Culler notes, 'Without this implicit knowledge, this internalized grammar, the sequence of sounds does not speak to [a user of a language]' (*Structuralist Poetics*, p. 113). This 'internalized grammar' is what linguistics calls 'linguistic competence'. Structuralist literary theory argues that although literature uses language, linguistic competence will only 'take one a certain distance in one's encounter with literary texts' (p. 114). In order to understand literary texts, a reader also needs 'literary competence'. This is because 'literature is a second-order semiotic system':

> To read a text as literature is not to make one's mind a *tabula rasa* and approach it without preconception; one must bring to it an implicit understanding of the operations of literary discourse which tells one what to look for. (pp. 113–14)

This 'implicit understanding' or 'literary competence' depends on a reader's familiarity with the codes and conventions of the literary system which, as we have seen, is a system of genres. Genre study, then, is something more than a system of classification (a descriptive or scientific taxonomy); rather, it involves the identification of those codes and conventions which competent readers need to have internalised. This is why, in our discussion of 'Lord Randal', we wanted to know whether the identification of its ballad features leads to a more competent reading of the poem than we could have gained simply by reading it as a unique utterance. We implied that a reading of the poem which did not recognise its use of ballad conventions would not be a fully competent one. As Culler puts it, 'The semiological approach suggests . . . that the poem be thought of as an utterance that has meaning only with respect to a system of conventions which the reader has assimilated' (p. 116). That system of conventions is largely made up of the conventions of particular genres. Indeed, one of the aims of the present book is to help its readers develop and become conscious of their literary competence in order to become better readers of poetry.

■ Genres as Discourse: Tzvetan Todorov

The recognition that some (if not all) literary genres have non-literary 'relatives' or variants has led Tzvetan Todorov into a radical critique of Structuralism's systematising project – i.e., its attempt to see literature as a self-contained structure of related, if shifting, genres.[11] Todorov's position is best summed up in his statement that 'If one opts for a structural viewpoint, each type of discourse usually labelled literary has nonliterary "relatives" that are closer to it than are any other types of "literary" discourse' (*Genres in Discourse*, p. 11). He offers the example of lyric poetry which has, he suggests, more conventions in common with prayer (a non-literary discourse) than it has with the historical novel (a literary genre). We have seen in this chapter that a form such as the ballad has particularly close affinities with a number of genres – popular song, reportage, sensational journalism – which would not normally be included in the literary canon, and our history of this genre reveals that it was not until some centuries after its emergence that the ballad itself came to be regarded as a serious literary form. Todorov therefore suggests that genres are, fundamentally, not discrete literary forms but products of discourse – that is, of the various discursive choices which a given culture makes available to the members of a linguistic community. Those possibilities are much wider than the literary system, since 'The literary genres, indeed, are nothing but such choices among discursive possibilities, choices that a given society has made conventional' (p. 10). As a consequence, 'there is no reason to limit this notion of genre to literature alone; outside of literature the situation is no different.' Such a theory redefines genre as a socio-cultural phenomenon and suggests that departments of literature need to make way for a broader-based discipline which will explore 'the theory of discourse and . . . the analysis of its genres' (p. 12). Some of the consequences of this theory may be recognised in the way university syllabuses have extended their remit in recent years to embrace previously marginalised genres, and the way some academic departments of literature have expanded into Cultural or Media Studies.

Todorov argues that genres can be defined not only in terms of their structure but also in terms of their function. The concept of function is largely indebted to modern speech-act theory, which investigates the different things we use language for: praising, thanking, narrating, describing, cursing, offering, seducing, bewitching, and so on. All discourse, and all genres, are specialised or conventionalised forms of these functions, appropriate to particular occasions. Many genres, both literary and non-literary, originate in discourses which have a specific social function and occasion. We have not yet identified the occasion of poems as a feature of genre, though, clearly, what a poem is used for affects its genre; it is only because we think of poetry as 'literature' that we forget that many poems have (or originally had) specific functions and occasions. Indeed, many genre names identify those functions: people recited

---

[11] Todorov's concern with genre criticism is developed in a number of essays, particularly 'The Notion of Literature' and 'The Origin of Genres', in Todorov, *Genres in Discourse*, trans. Catherine Porter (Cambridge: Cambridge University Press, 1990).

epithalamiums at weddings, elegies or obsequies at funerals, odes when power-ful people had to be praised for anything, carols at Christmas. A poem's form may reflect that function, and its conventionalised structure may be preserved as a convention of the genre long after its successors have lost their original function.

Although Todorov argues that there are no structural differences which dis-tinguish literature from other discourses, he does not, in fact, deny the exis-tence of literature outright. Literature becomes the shifting body of discursive practices ('genres of discourse') to which any culture, at a particular moment, assigns a 'literary' function. What applies to literature as a whole also applies, not surprisingly, to poetry in particular. Todorov argues that 'Poetry in general does not exist, but variable conceptions of poetry exist and will continue to exist, not only from one period or country to another but also from one text to another' (p. 71). What this means is that the study of literature, or of poetry and its particular genres, has to involve the history of changing conceptions of the literary, the poetic and the generic. As he says, 'There has never been a literature without genres; it is a system in constant transformation, and his-torically speaking the question of origins [where genres come from] cannot be separated from the terrain of the genres themselves [what they include]' (p. 15). That is why 'history' can no longer be separated from 'conventions' or from 'theory'. We have repeatedly tried to indicate this in the present book, and this is why we have included some account of the history of the ballad in this chap-ter alongside theoretical reflections on the notion of genre. As Todorov puts it, 'Poetry is its own genres, poetics is the theory of genres' (p. 15). Far from dismissing genre to the margins of the discipline, then, this theory places it at the centre of the agenda for literary studies.

Exercises

1 Read the following poem by John Keats (written in 1819) carefully several times. Then re-read 'Lord Randal' before answering the questions.

La Belle Dame sans Merci: A Ballad

O what can ail thee, knight at arms,
　　Alone and palely loitering?
The sedge has wither'd from the lake,
　　And no birds sing.

O what can ail thee, knight at arms,　　　　　　　　　　5
　　So haggard and so woe-begone?
The squirrel's granary is full,
　　And the harvest's done.

I see a lily on thy brow
    With anguish moist and fever dew,   10
And on thy cheeks a fading rose
    Fast withereth too.

I met a lady in the meads,
    Full beautiful, a fairy's child;
Her hair was long, her foot was light,   15
    And her eyes were wild.

I made a garland for her head,
    And bracelets too, and fragrant zone;
She look'd at me as she did love,
    And made sweet moan.   20

I set her on my pacing steed,
    And nothing else saw all day long,
For sidelong would she bend, and sing
    A fairy's song.

She found me roots of relish sweet,   25
    And honey wild, and manna dew,
And sure in language strange she said –
    I love thee true.

She took me to her elfin grot,
    And there she wept, and sigh'd full sore,   30
And there I shut her wild wild eyes
    With kisses four.

And there she lulled me asleep,
    And there I dream'd – Ah! woe betide!
The latest dream I ever dream'd   35
    On the cold hill's side.

I saw pale kings, and princes too,
    Pale warriors, death pale were they all;
They cried – 'La belle dame sans merci
    Hath thee in thrall!'   40

I saw their starv'd lips in the gloam
    With horrid warning gaped wide,
And I awoke and found me here
    On the cold hill's side.

> And this is why I sojourn here,   45
>   Alone and palely loitering,
> Though the sedge is wither'd from the lake,
>   And no birds sing.

(a) Keats's poem is sometimes sub-titled 'A ballad'. Which of the genre-specific characteristics of the ballad can you identify in the poem? We have listed them below, as a reminder. Go through the poem and tick off each feature which you find.
    (i)   focus on a single crucial episode;
    (ii) dramatic immediacy, sometimes assisted by dialogue;
    (iii) impersonal narration;
    (iv) plot as central;
    (v) few arresting figures of speech;
    (vi) much repetition and parallelism, which is not ornamental but advances the plot and heightens atmosphere;
    (vii) appealing to a popular audience, but describing the adventures of aristocratic or heroic participants.

(b) From what you have discovered in (a), would you describe Keats's poem as a ballad? Does it have any features which make such a description problematic?

(c) Now compare Keats's poem with 'Lord Randal'. Make a list of the similarities and differences between the poems. If you find similarities between them, do you think that this can be explained by saying that they both use the general conventions of the ballad form, or would you say that Keats's poem is actually modelled on 'Lord Randal'?

(d) Assuming that Keats's poem is a 'rewrite' of 'Lord Randal', try to identify how Keats modifies the action and characterisation of the earlier poem. Then compare the way both poems are narrated.

(e) Now read the ballad 'Thomas the Rhymer' (below). Compare this poem with Keats's by applying the instructions in (c) and (d).

(f) Apart from the fact that it is not anonymous, are there any features of Keats's poem that would lead you to suspect that it is not really a traditional ballad? What other kinds of writing, if any, do such features recall? These may be something less specific than a genre and might be influenced by your knowledge of the poem's author or the period at which it was written. (Think back to 'Ode to a Nightingale'.)

(h) Try to develop an overall interpretation of 'La Belle Dame sans Merci'. You should spend some time on this.

(i) What, if anything, does Keats's use of the conventions of the ballad genre (including any modifications of those conventions) contribute to your interpretation of the poem in the previous question?

(j) Traditional ballads habitually describe the adventures of aristocratic or heroic participants. Bearing this in mind, try to describe the attitudes towards class, gender, religious belief and moral or social action implied in 'Lord Randal' and/or 'Thomas the Rhymer'. How far might one or both of these poems be seen as confirming or reinforcing such attitudes, even if they are not an overt theme? Now do the same for Keats's 'La Belle Dame sans Merci'.

(k) Try to sum up, in the light of all your answers to the above questions, what a reader gains by recognising the genre of Keats's poem?

Thomas the Rhymer

True Thomas lay on Huntlie bank,
   A ferlie* he spied wi' his e'e   *wonder
And there he saw a ladye bright
   Come riding down by the Eildon Tree.*   *hills near
                                 Melrose, Scotland

Her shirt was o' the grass-green silk,   5
   Her mantle o' the velvet fyne;
At ilka tett* of her horse's mane   *every tuft
   Hung fifty siller* bells and nine.   *silver

True Thomas, he pull'd aff his cap
   And louted* low down to his knee   *bent   10
All hail, thou mighty Queen of Heaven!
   For thy peer on earth I never did see.

O no, O no, Thomas she said,
   That name does not belang to me;
I am but the Queen of fair Elfland   15
   That am hither come to visit thee.

Harp and carp*, Thomas, she said   *sing
   Harp and carp along wi' me,
And if ye dare to kiss my lips,
   Sure of your bodie I will be.   20

Betide me weal, betide me woe,
   That wierd* will never daunton* me.   *fate; daunt
Syne* he has kissed her rosy lips   *since
   All under the Eildon Tree.

Now ye maun* go wi' me, she said,   *must 25
    True Thomas, ye maun go wi' me;
And ye maun serve me seven years
    Thro' weal or woe, as may chance to be.

She mounted on her milk-white steed,
    She's ta'en True Thomas up behind;   30
And aye whene'er her bridle rung
    The steed flew swifter than the wind.

O they rade on, and farther on –
    The steed gaed* swifter than the wind –   *went
Until they reach'd a desart wide   35
    And living land was left behind.

Light down, light down now, True Thomas
    And lean your head upon my knee;
Abide and rest a little space
    And I will show you ferlies three.   40

O see ye not yon narrow road
    So thick beset with thorns and briers?
That is the path of righteousness,
    Though after it but few enquires.

And see not ye that bonny road   45
    That winds about the fernie brae?
That is the road to fair Elfland,
    Where thou and I this night maun gae.

But Thomas, ye maun hold your tongue
    Whatever ye may hear or see,   50
For if you speak word in Elflyn land
    Ye'll ne'er get back to your ain countrie.

O they rade on, and farther on,
    And they waded through rivers aboon* the knee   *above
And they saw neither sun nor moon   55
    But they heard the roaring of the sea.

It was mirk, mirk night and there was nae stern* light   *star
    And they waded through red blude to the knee;
For a' the blude that's shed on earth
    Rins through the springs o' that countrie.   60

Syne* they came on to a garden green   *since
    And she pu'd an apple frae a tree:
Take this for thy wages, True Thomas,
    It will give thee tongue that can never lie.

My tongue is mine ain*, True Thomas said,   *own 65
    A gudely gift ye wad gie* to me   *give
I neither dought* to buy nor sell   *dare
    At fair* or tryst where I may be;   *market

I dought neither speak to prince or peer
    Nor ask of grace from fair ladye.   70
Now hold thy peace, the lady said,
    For as I say, so must it be.

He has gotten a coat of the even* cloth   *smooth
    And a pair of shoes of velvet green;
And till seven years were gane and past   75
    True Thomas on earth was never seen.

2 In order to get some sense of how easy – or how difficult – it is to write in a fixed form, we would like you to try to write an original limerick.

   (a) Using our description of the limerick above, try to write an original limerick which would display as many of the conventions of the genre as possible. Make a checklist of the limerick conventions you have used in your poem.

   (b) In our description of the limerick, we stated that certain kinds of subject matter are appropriate to the genre. Does your limerick conform with such conventional subject matter? In order to test the assumption that only non-serious subjects are suitable for limericks, we would now like you to try to write a serious poem using the limerick form. Try to write a limerick dealing with terrorism, global warming, AIDS, love or any other serious topic of your own choice.

   (c) Did you experience any difficulties in writing your serious limerick? Do you think your limerick is wholly successful, or is there a mismatch between form and content? If there are problems with your poem, try to say why these occur. Is it because the limerick genre comes to us already invested with a weight of tradition, leading us to expect certain kinds of conventional subject matter and response? Or is there something intrinsic to its metrical form and stanza pattern which does not lend itself to the serious treatment of serious subjects? If you think your poem is wholly successful, try to explain how it overcomes the potential mismatch between form and content.

3 Although we have discussed only the limerick and the ballad in this chapter, elsewhere in this book we attend to the genre-specific features of a number of different poetic genres. You can therefore use this book as a resource for discovering things about other genres by using the index and the Glossary. We suggest that you look up the following genre terms in the index and Glossary, and so piece together our scattered discussions of various genres: dramatic lyric, dramatic monologue, elegy, essay, haiku, lyric, narrative poetry, ode, sestina, sonnet, and so on. For any *one* of these, (a) summarise the genre's conventions, (b) find a poem that is written in that genre, and (c) examine whether or not the poem conforms with or breaks from the genre's conventions.

Chapter 12

The Sonnet

▣ The Sonnet as a Fixed Form

In continuing our discussion of genre, we could spend time on any number of recognised poetic kinds. We have chosen the sonnet as a case study, however, because it is in many ways a representative form as well as a distinctive genre. The sonnet, like the limerick, is another example of a fixed or 'closed' form because its defining characteristics are largely formal. That is why an examination of its genre-specific characteristics in this chapter will, necessarily, pick up on quite a lot of the issues raised in earlier chapters on poetic form. Arguably, it is possible to make sense of many poems without consciously identifying their genres, but to read a sonnet without recognising that it is a sonnet is likely to frustrate any competent understanding.

The close relationship between form and meaning which is characteristic of sonnets may be seen in Shakespeare's Sonnet 18, first printed in 1609. This poem shows most of the conventions characteristic of the form and might serve as a normative model.

> Shall I compare thee to a summer's day?
> Thou art more lovely and more temperate:
> Rough winds do shake the darling buds of May,
> And summer's lease hath all too short a date:
> Sometimes too hot the eye of heaven shines, 5
> And often is his gold complexion dimmed;
> And every fair from fair sometimes declines,
> By chance or nature's changing course untrimmed;
> But thy eternal summer shall not fade,
> Nor lose possession of that fair thou ow'st*; *ownest 10

> Nor shall death brag thou wander'st in his shade,
> When in eternal lines to time thou grow'st:
> So long as men can breathe, or eyes can see,
> So long lives this, and this gives life to thee.

Sonnet 18 is part of a sequence of one hundred and fifty-four sonnets, more than half of which are addressed to Shakespeare's patron, the same young man ('Mr. W.H.') to whom the whole sequence is dedicated (the rest are addressed to a mysterious 'dark lady'). Read in the immediate context of the sequence, it is clear that this sonnet is addressed to the young man. (As we will see, the fact that Shakespeare addresses love sonnets to both a young man and a dark lady does not necessarily mean that he or his speaker was bisexual.) The poem's fourteen lines can be conveniently divided into sections which the rhyme scheme identifies for us. If you analyse the rhyme scheme in the way we recommended in Chapter 4, you will find that it conforms to the following pattern: *abab cdcd efef gg*. It is not difficult to show how this structure of three quatrains and a final couplet corresponds to particular developments in the argument of the sonnet. In the first quatrain the speaker ponders on whether to use a particular simile in a compliment to his addressee, but immediately has reservations about it because the addressee is 'more lovely and more temperate' and more long-lasting, than a summer's day or even the whole summer. The second quatrain develops these reservations, finding more and more reasons for rejecting the comparison initially proposed. In the third quatrain, however, the speaker turns from listing the disadvantages of 'a summer's day' to identify the one advantage which the addressee has over the passing season – that the addressee's 'eternal summer shall not fade / . . . When in eternal lines to time thou grow'st' (9–12). In the context of other poems in the sequence, 'eternal lines' may be interpreted in two senses. The speaker is trying to preserve the young man's beauty and sometimes recommends him to marry and have children and so preserve his likeness in the 'eternal lines' of subsequent generations. But the speaker also suggests that his own poetry will perpetuate the man's beauty in its own 'eternal lines'. The final couplet confirms the second of these meanings by confidently claiming the enduring life of the poem we are reading.[1]

---

[1] The idea that poetry has a permanence not shared with the passing seasons is a conventional argument or **topos** (see Glossary), which we are not invited to question. The assumption that poetry can outlast more substantial memorials goes back to a claim made by Horace, who boldly asserted that he had created in his verses a monument 'more lasting than bronze' ('Aere perennius', *Odes*, 3.30.1). The expression became proverbial; Shakespeare uses it in Sonnet 55: 'Not marble, nor the gilded monuments / Of princes, shall outlive this powerful rhyme'.

As this brief analysis shows, the overall argument of the poem has a logical structure which corresponds to the divisions of the verse form into three four-line sections and a final couplet. Each quatrain contains a stage of the argument, or a unit of sense that is syntactically complete by the end of the quatrain. Shakespeare's argument depends on a contrast between the tenor and vehicle of his proposed metaphor, a contrast which turns on the word 'But' at the beginning of line 9. That **turn** in the argument occurs at the place which had become the most important of the structural divisions in the sonnet form as it had evolved in Italy and elsewhere in the two hundred years or more before 1609.

With Shakespeare's sonnet in front of us, we can usefully offer a general description of the sonnet genre, which will serve as a point of reference for the further examples we shall be analysing in this chapter. A sonnet is a fourteen-line poem in iambic pentameter, which can often be divided into two parts known as the '**octave**' (the first eight lines) and the '**sestet**' (the last six). There are two principal kinds of sonnet form in English: the 'English' or 'Shakespearian' sonnet – consisting of three quatrains and a couplet and usually rhymed *abab cdcd efef gg*, as in the above example – and the 'Italian' or 'Petrarchan' sonnet – comprising two quatrains and a sestet (rhymed *abba abba cde cde*). The rhyme scheme of the Italian form appears to insist more strongly than the Shakespearian on a division between octave and sestet, which is why Italian readers coined the term '**volta**' ('turn') to refer to this shift which the introduction of new rhyme sounds appears to signal after line eight. In the Shakespearian sonnet each quatrain introduces new rhyme sounds and the major formal break appears to be the shift from the three alternately rhymed quatrains to the final rhymed couplet, which is why some textbooks define the 'turn' in an English sonnet as occurring after line twelve.

▇ Finding the Volta: Form and Meaning

If things were this simple, we could end this chapter here. Needless to say, they are not. For a start, the division between octave and sestet in the sonnet is not just a matter of a shift in the rhyme pattern. In most **Petrarchan sonnets** that shift corresponds to a turn in the syntax or grammar, a change in the argument or subject matter. And we have seen that, although Shakespeare's Sonnet 18 does not use the Italian rhyme pattern, it nevertheless exhibits such a turn in its argument at precisely the point required by the octave–sestet structure of the **Italian sonnet** form. This turn in the argument and grammar of Shakespeare's sonnet is clearly signalled by the word 'But' at the beginning of line 9. Such a turn is very common in sonnets of all types and there is thus a good case for using the 'Italian' terminology – octave, volta, sestet – to refer to many English as well as Petrarchan sonnets. The terminology is useful because it can refer not just to sonnets' rhyme scheme, but also to the conventionalised structure of their arguments. Whether or not a sonnet's rhyme scheme corresponds with, or runs counter to, that semantic shift is always likely to be of interest, for the point about sonnets is that their conventional verse pattern traditionally relates to the organisation of meaning in ways which are more direct than is the case with almost any other poetic genre. It is quite a good idea when reading any sonnet to get into the habit of looking first at line nine to see whether there is any turn in the grammar and thus how its argument is structured. As the poet Eleanor Brown once said to us, sonnets tend to have a critical 'G-spot'.

In Shakespeare's Sonnet 130 (1609), which is one of those addressed to a 'dark lady', the volta is delayed to line 12, where the change from quatrains to final couplet coincides with the most decisive turn in the argument:

> My mistress' eyes are nothing like the sun;
> Coral is far more red than her lips' red;
> If snow be white, why then her breasts are dun;
> If hairs be wires, black wires grow on her head.
> I have seen roses damasked, red and white,   5
> But no such roses see I in her cheeks;
> And in some perfumes is there more delight
> Than in the breath that from my mistress reeks*.   *exhales
> I love to hear her speak, yet well I know
> That music hath a far more pleasing sound;   10
> I grant I never saw a goddess go*;   *walk
> My mistress, when she walks, treads on the ground.
>   And yet, by heaven, I think my love as rare
>   As any she* belied with false compare.   *woman

Our statement that the volta is 'delayed' in this sonnet certainly begs the question of how one chooses to apply this Italian term to the English sonnet. The volta is 'delayed' only if the reader expects it to come at the end of line eight. If the expected place for a volta in such English sonnets is the end of line twelve, then clearly this sonnet meets those expectations. It is probably important at this point to recall what we said in Chapter 11 about genre conventions being a matter of readers' expectations. One advantage of thinking that the volta is delayed in this Shakespearian sonnet, however, results from the fact that the poem's rhetorical strategy depends so heavily on keeping the reader guessing. This is a sonnet which plays games with conventional expectations about the subject matter for sonnets. Love sonnets normally praise the mistress, but this one does so through what we might call negative comparison. Like Sonnet 18, the poem is trying out conventional comparisons for the addressee, but in this poem the addressee is found to fall short of them: the colour of her breasts does not match up with the conventional claim that they be white as snow; her cheeks are not like roses; her breath is not as sweet as perfume (but note that 'reeks' does not have its modern connotations at this date). The longer Shakespeare can keep up this game before turning the whole poem round into a conventional – if paradoxical – compliment the better.[2] For that reason it probably makes it more effective if the reader expects some kind of about-turn after line eight, only to find it delayed to line thirteen (which begins with the turning phrase 'and yet').

The Shakespearian sonnet, with its summative final couplet, certainly helped to make a turn in line 13 an available convention and Shakespeare's sonnets vary the placement of the volta, sometimes turning the grammar in line 9, sometimes in line 13, and sometimes both. Whether or not Sonnet 130 can be described as varying the conventions of sonnet form, it certainly varies the conventions governing its choice of subject matter. It does so precisely by inverting them. The description of the woman violates the established conventions of love sonnets at this period, which often praised the mistress by comparing the brightness of her eyes to the sun, the fairness of her skin to snow, her blonde hair to gold thread and so on. But though this speaker denies that his mistress has any of these conventional marks of beauty, his wit depends on his readers' familiarity with the very conventions, the clichés of description, which he is subverting. This way of praising a woman by singling out different parts of her body in a list and finding appropriate metaphors to compare them with has a long history and is known as a '**blason**'. It had been turned to satirical purposes long before Shakespeare wrote (not that we think Shakespeare is necessarily being satirical here). Shakespeare is using a highly conventional genre to make claims for the truthfulness, sincerity and unconventionality of his own feelings (and his expression of those feelings) by defining them against the comparisons that had become conventional to the genre. We shall look at several other sonnets which do something similar in the course of this chapter; the sonnet tends to be a somewhat introverted, self-regarding form of writing and often works by playing with the conventions established in previous sonnets.

Another example of how the syntactic structure and argument of a sonnet correspond to its verse form is Shakespeare's Sonnet 29 (1609):

> When in disgrace with fortune and men's eyes,
> I all alone beweep my outcast state,
> And trouble deaf heav'n with my bootless* cries,   *futile

---

[2] The praise is paradoxical, yet still conventional, in a sense that was familiar to sixteenth-century readers. Traditional rhetoric defined 'paradox' as any argument which reversed the conventional grounds for an argument, and Renaissance writers produced many examples of the 'paradoxical encomium', as in Erasmus's *In Praise of Folly* (1510), which praises something – folly – that is conventionally the opposite of praiseworthy.

And look upon myself and curse my fate,
Wishing me like to one more rich in hope,   5
Featured like him, like him with friends possessed,
Desiring this man's art, and that man's scope,
With what I most enjoy contented least,
Yet in these thoughts myself almost despising,
Haply I think on thee, and then my state,   10
Like to the lark at break of day arising
From sullen earth sings hymns at heaven's gate,
   For thy sweet love rememb'red such wealth brings,
   That then I scorn to change my state with kings.

This sonnet expresses the contrasting feelings of disappointment and delight of a speaker whose actual circumstances are not fully revealed to us (we are not told what occasioned his misfortune). At first sight it might look like another conventional lover's complaint. In the octave the speaker laments his lack of success compared with other men and this could be read as a figure for the lover's exile from his beloved's favour. The sestet overturns this reading by affirming that despite his ill-fortune the mere thought of his beloved is enough to transform his mood, so that he 'sings hymns at heaven's gate'. The major shift in the argument thus takes place between the octave and the sestet: the octave concentrates wholly on the speaker's unhappiness, his lack of fortune and worldly success and only in the sestet do we learn that the poem is not just an expression of personal anguish or worldly disappointment but an elaborate compliment to an unidentified addressee. The strong contrast between the unhappiness of the first eight lines and the joy of the last six turns on the qualifying conjunction 'Yet' at the beginning of line nine – the argument of the sonnet and its syntax, turn on that word. Certainly, the final couplet also stands apart in some ways by presenting a final resolution of the argument, identifying – for the first time – the 'love' which explains and motivates the turn, justifies the compliment and finally reveals that this sonnet is some kind of love poem.

However, other ways of reading this sonnet are possible. Again, the immediate context of the sonnet sequence makes it clear that this sonnet is addressed to Shakespeare's patron rather than the dark lady. In the literary system of Shakespeare's day, writers dedicated their work to wealthy patrons in the hope of preferment or monetary reward. Read in this context, such phrases as 'in disgrace with fortune', 'rich in hope' and 'such wealth brings' take on a literal rather than a metaphorical sense. If they are taken literally, it is the patron's generosity, and not just his 'sweet love', that causes the speaker to sing 'hymns at heaven's gate'. Poems in praise of the patron at this period use many of the conventional topics of **panegyric** (or praise) which were also available to the love poet praising his mistress – encomiastic or complimentary rhetoric was common to both modes of address, which may be why the discourse of patronage in this sonnet seems so close to the language of love.[3] Whichever way we interpret this sonnet, however, our point is that it displays in a particularly clear way the relationship between the formal and argumentative structures which the sonnet form makes possible. The shifts of mood, argument and syntax in this case are signalled by the conjunctions 'When . . . Yet . . . For' at the beginning of lines 1, 9 and 13 (the beginning of the octave, sestet and final couplet respectively). The kind of formal resolution we find in the final couplet is entirely characteristic of the way the closing couplet functions in a conventional 'English' sonnet. The couplet is syntactically complete and summative; you could easily detach it from the preceding lines and might well feel that in doing so you had abstracted the poem's essential point.

This particular sonnet is by no means exceptional, for that accommodation of meaning to form – or form to meaning – is crucial to the sonnet as a genre. Learning how to recognise and analyse this interplay of form and meaning is the fundamental skill required of any competent reader of sonnets. As with any genre convention, it is a matter of programming your expectations as a reader, and this is best done (as we saw with the ballad) by reading as many 'normative' examples as you can. A useful exercise right now might be to look at a few more sonnets by Shakespeare. See how many examples you can find where the sestet or the final couplet begins with a strong qualifier – words like 'then', 'yet', 'but' and 'so'. Notice how often line 8, or line 12, ends with a full stop or semicolon. You might then try to describe or paraphrase the relationship between the argument of the octave and that of the sestet in one or two of the examples you have identified.

■ Identifying the Speaker

There are some further normative characteristics of Shakespeare's Sonnet 29, besides its use of the sonnet structure, that are worth calling attention to before we move on. Perhaps the most important of these is the character of the poetic speaker. Most sonnets are presented as the speech of a first-person speaker and seem to give us access to personal thoughts and feelings which are addressed directly to the reader, to a third party, or to himself or herself. As Michael Spiller puts it, 'The sonnet, because of its brevity, always gives an impression of immediacy, as if it proceeded directly and confessionally or conversationally from the speaker and therefore from the creator of that

---

[3] For a close reading of this sonnet which clarifies its use of the discourse of patronage see John Barrell, *Poetry, Language and Politics* (Manchester: Manchester University Press, 1988), pp. 18–43.

speaker'.[4] But Spiller's 'as if' is important, since the voices that can be used in any genre are constructed largely by the conventions of the genre itself. Shakespeare's Sonnet 29 does not merely express its speaker's thoughts and feelings, but examines and rationalises them in order to come to some kind of conclusion in the final couplet. Speakers in sonnets are likely to be arguing with and attempting to persuade the addressee, often the 'mistress' in a love sonnet. Alternatively the speaker will appear to be thinking about his own personal feelings in order to reach some kind of conclusion about them. Our suggestion that the speaker in Shakespeare's sonnets was likely to be a male lover addressing a 'mistress' was influenced by the fact that the normative type of the sonnet in Shakespeare's day was the love sonnet. As we have seen, even though some of Shakespeare's sonnets are not conventional love sonnets addressed to a 'mistress', they use the same discourse of complaint, compliment and reflective self-communing.

■ Donne's 'Holy Sonnets': A Hybrid Form?

The love sonnet is the most common type in the Renaissance, when it became a fashionable courtly form in all the major European languages; it is what we might call the 'default' type of sonnet. But occasionally we find poets using this courtly and secular form to handle different types of subject matter, as with John Donne's 'Holy Sonnets' (1633) which reflect not on the love of a mistress but on the love of God. However, we find in these religious poems the same accommodation of thought and feeling to the structure of the sonnet that we demonstrated in Shakespeare's love sonnets. It is striking how often the sestet of Donne's sonnets begins with such words as 'only', 'yet', 'then', 'but'. In the following example the speaker apostrophises the angels and the dead in the octave, urging them to prepare for the general resurrection at the end of time, only to pray to God in the sestet to defer the apocalypse for a while so that he can atone for his own sins.

> At the round earth's imagin'd corners, blow
> Your trumpets, Angels, and arise, arise
> From death, you numberless infinities
> Of soules, and to your scattered bodies go;
> All whom the flood did, and fire shall, o'erthrow,   5
> All whom war, dearth, age, agues, tyrannies,
> Despair, law, chance hath slain, and you whose eyes
> Shall behold God, and never taste death's woe.
> But let them sleep, Lord, and me mourn a space;

---

[4] Michael Spiller, *The Development of the Sonnet* (London: Routledge, 1992), p. 6.

> For, if above all these, my sins abound,   10
> 'Tis late to ask abundance of Thy grace
> When we are there. Here on this lowly ground,
> Teach me how to repent; for that's as good
> As if Thou' hadst sealed my pardon with Thy blood.

This sonnet turns very decisively on the 'But' of line 9. The octave confidently anticipates the general resurrection which the Book of Revelation in the Bible forecasts as the triumphant end of history for the church. This moment of general salvation of the elect is an article of Christian doctrine, and Donne appears so confident of its imminence in the octave that his enthusiasm runs away with his logic, since his list of those he calls on to arise from death includes some who have not yet died. This inventive exuberance contrasts strongly with the quiet penitence and self-doubt of the sestet, where Donne remembers his own unworthiness and asks God for more time to work out his own salvation. Thus the volta at the octave–sestet division stages a dramatic swing in the mood and tone of the poem. The final couplet then achieves some kind of middle ground between these two extremes, as Donne remembers that Christ's atonement alone secures our salvation. But this resolution is nothing like the resolution we saw in the summative final couplet of Shakespeare's sonnets. This couplet is not, like Shakespeare's, a complete, detachable semantic unit – indeed, the last sentence begins in the middle of line 12.

This sonnet's structure combines elements of the 'English' and the 'Italian' sonnet. Although the three quatrains and couplet structure might suggest the Shakespearian pattern, which would be confirmed by the *cdcd ee* of the sestet, the *abba abba* of the octave conforms to the Italian pattern.[5] The structure thus appears to consist of an Italian octave followed by an English sestet and the turn in the syntax or argument at the beginning of line 9 coincides with the way the third quatrain breaks away from the tight, infolded rhymes of the octave. All Donne's 'Holy Sonnets' use this structure, the only variation being that sometimes the third quatrain has the same infolded rhyme pattern (*cddc*) as the two previous 'quatrains' (it nevertheless introduces new rhyme sounds).

This hybrid form of sonnet suggests that the rules of this genre were never as rigid as some modern textbooks, with their clear distinction between the 'Petrarchan' and 'Shakespearian' forms, would have us believe. Indeed, sixteenth- and seventeenth-century writers did not distinguish between the two types of sonnet, or use our names for them. Different English sonnets vary

---

[5] In seventeenth-century pronunciation, which had broader vowel sounds than modern English, the 'b' rhymes are all good rhymes, not half-rhymes, and there is no 'poetic licence' involved – 'infinities' (3) and 'tyrannies' (6) rhyme with 'arise' (2) and 'eyes' (7), and 'good' (13) rhymes with 'blood' (14).

from their Italian progenitor in different ways. English sonneteers did not invent a wholly different set of genre conventions from their foreign originals, but adapted those conventions to new circumstances. Whether they staged a turn in the syntax or argument of the sonnet at the beginning of line 9 was an option that always remained open to them, whatever the rhyme pattern used. Although, as we have stressed, this is among the most fixed of poetic forms, it thus appears to have more flexibility than one might have supposed.

■ Expectation and Variation

So far we have suggested the extent to which reading sonnets involves analysing the fit between syntactic, semantic and formal units. But the great advantage of genre conventions for poets is that they can be varied; and the stricter the rules are, as with the sonnet, the more salient and significant it becomes when they are broken. For the reader, the advantage of a normalised pattern is that it can function as a kind of control model against which deviations can be measured. If the reader of a sonnet expects a turn in the argument after line 8, it can be highly effective, as we saw with Sonnet 130, if those expectations are frustrated. Yet we have also seen that the sonnet form has not always been as fixed as the normative models we have defined would suggest. The sonnet is a more protean form (always changing its shape) than our normative description allows. The two types we have identified – Italian and English – are by no means the only forms which the sonnet has assumed. Edmund Spenser, for instance, invented a rhyme scheme which linked the quatrains together (*abab bcbc cdcd ee*). This is often identified in student guidebooks as the third normative type, the 'Spenserian sonnet'. Sir Philip Sidney wrote one sonnet (in *Arcadia* [1580]) which has only one rhyme throughout (*aaaa aaaa aaaa aa*) and Blake wrote a fourteen-line poem, 'To the Evening Star' (1783), which has some claim to be read as a sonnet but uses no rhymes at all. The earliest sequence of love sonnets in English, Thomas Watson's *Hekatompathia* (1582), consists of poems that are eighteen lines long. Watson had no hesitation in calling them sonnets, although at this time the word 'sonnet' was often used to refer to poems in a variety of forms – a habit that lasted at least until 1633, when the posthumous collection of Donne's love lyrics, none of which is in sonnet form, were published with the title 'Songs and Sonets'.

Some of these variations might be regarded as aberrations, exceptions that prove the rule, since the existence of deviations does not necessarily invalidate the idea of a normative model; indeed, the very idea of deviation relies on the fact that there must be known conventions to deviate from. Although it can often be instructive to see how individual poems conform to or deviate from the received conventions of the genre, it is also important to recognise how the normative models of the sonnet themselves have been subject to historical redefinition. For that reason, as we saw with the ballad, it could be important to identify the continuities and changes that have influenced the conventions of the sonnet throughout its long history.

▨ A History of the Genre: Petrarchan Conventions

The sonnet form was already three hundred years old when it reached England in the early sixteenth century. When Sir Thomas Wyatt and the Earl of Surrey wrote the first English sonnets in the 1530s, the genre already carried a heavy freightage of established subject matter and treatment from its use in continental Europe. The earliest sonnets were written in the first half of the thirteenth century by a group of poets in the Sicilian court of the Emperor Frederick II. This school of courtly Italian poetry was itself influenced by the troubadour poets of the South of France, who spoke and wrote in the Provençal language, composing songs which typically dealt with the unrequited love of an eloquent and courtly speaker for an unattainable lady of a higher social status than himself. This social and erotic paradigm had a wide-ranging and long-lasting influence on European literature, to which it has become customary to refer under the catch-all title 'courtly love'. The impulse to link the detached moments which individual sonnets record in the love life of the poet, or his constructed persona, to a spiritual autobiography centred on the love of a named and idealised woman was developed by Italian *stilnovisti* ('new style') poets in the late thirteenth and early fourteenth century, such as Guido Cavalcanti and Dante Alighieri. These poets used the sonnet as the favoured medium for love poetry in which the lady is idealised and spiritualised, becoming a radiant image or revelation of heavenly and religious truth. Dante's *La Vita Nuova* ('The New Life') (*c.* 1292–1300) was a collection of narrative prose pieces, *canzone* (lyric poems) and sonnets in which the speaker (a version of Dante aged seventeen) writes of his love for Beatrice (also seventeen), who remains an unattainable and, in the end, a spiritual love. One of the interesting aspects of *La Vita Nuova* is the way Dante analyses his own sonnets, as in the following modern translation of the sonnet in section XXI:

> The power of love borne in my lady's eyes
>   imparts its grace to all she looks upon;
>   men turn to gaze at her when she walks by;
>   the heart of him she greets is made to quake,
>   his face to whiten, forcing down his gaze;
>   he sighs as all his defects flash in mind;
>   all pride and indignation flee from her.
> Help me to honour her, most gracious ladies.

365

> All sweet conception, every humblest thought
> blooms in the heart of one who hears her speak,
> and man is blessed at his first sight of her.
> The image of her when she starts to smile
> breaks out of words, the mind cannot contain it,
> a miracle too rich and strange to hold.[6]

The most striking thing about this sonnet is the way the speaker exalts the woman he worships from afar. And while this modern translation has obscured the rhyme scheme of the original, the poem's layout still emphasises the octave–sestet division. In addition, Dante goes on (as with all the other sonnets in the sequence) to analyse the poem into its constituent parts:

> This sonnet has three parts. In the first part I tell how this lady animates this power by the use of her most munificent eyes; in the third I tell how she does the same thing, only this time by the use of her most gracious mouth; and between these two is a very small part, which is like a beggar asking aid from the preceding and following parts, and it begins here: 'Help me to honour her'. The third part begins here: 'All sweet conception'.

> (*Vita Nuova*, p. 41)

It would thus appear that the sonnet was conceived from very early on as a poetic form in which the interplay between formal divisions and the stages in the 'argument' were considered by one of its main practitioners as worthy of notice. Dante was in fact teaching his readers how to read his sonnets in a way that anticipates the way we are encouraging our readers to read sonnets.

The next major practitioner of the sonnet was Francesco Petrarch (1304–1374), whose *Canzoniere* consists of a sequence of three hundred and sixty-six poems, three hundred and seventeen of which are sonnets addressed to a real but idealised and unattainable woman called 'Laura' (one hundred and three were written after she died); the following sonnet is a modern translation of poem 140:

> Lord Love, who holds the chief place in my mind
> and lives and reigns inside my very heart,
> comes sometimes to my face, armed head to foot,
> and camps there where his standard is displayed.
>
> She who teaches that love must be endured,
> and thinks desire and smouldering hopes should be
> restrained by reverence, sense, and modesty,
> is angered by our boldness, deep inside.

[6] Dante, *Vita Nuova*, trans. Mark Musa (Oxford and New York: Oxford University Press, 1992), p. 40.

366

> So Love retreats into the heart in fear,
> his purpose lost, and stays there to lament;
> there hides himself, and does not reappear.
>
> What can I do, now my lord's full of fear,
> but be with him until the bitter end?
> For he dies well whose love is strong and pure.[7]

There are a number of things we might notice about this sonnet, including the personification of 'Lord Love' and the extended metaphor that suggests that a man's attempt to woo his beloved is a kind of warfare that is defeated by her modesty. In face of this defeat, love retreats into the male speaker's heart and he asserts his constancy by insisting that his love will remain pure and strong until he dies. This content is shaped into the octave–sestet structure by the rhyme scheme (this translation approximates the original Petrarchan rhyme scheme) and the turn in the argument signalled by 'So' at the beginning of line nine.

Petrarch was crowned laureate on the Capitoline Hill in Rome in 1340 and for the next 200 years he was regarded as the poet who had most successfully established the reputation of Italian as a literary language. It is no coincidence that in one language or national tradition after another, from the fourteenth century to the seventeenth, the moment poets dreamed of initiating a poetic renaissance in their own tongue, one of the first genres they chose to write in was the sonnet. If you wanted to put a date to the beginnings of a national tradition in modern English poetry – or French, or Spanish, or German, or Dutch – you could do a lot worse than discover who wrote the first sonnets in those languages. When poets wanted to create a national literature they could and did imitate the classics, but they also imitated Petrarch's sonnets.

By the end of the sixteenth century Petrarch's *Canzoniere* or *Rime* were thought to have established the pattern for love sonnets in all the major European languages. The normative conventions of the love sonnet, which we refer to as 'Petrarchan conventions', include the adoration of an idealised and largely unresponsive mistress; the use of conventional conceits drawn from Petrarch, most of which express the conflicting hopes and despondencies of the necessarily unsatisfied lover; the assumption of a direct autobiographical and confessional narrative voice; the grouping of sonnets in an extended sequence into which a number of other poetic forms – *canzoni*, madrigals, songs, or 'ballads' – may be strategically interspersed.

In its early history the sonnet normally assumes a strongly gendered voice, a male speaker who typically pleads with a remote or inaccessible woman whose

---

[7] Petrarch, *Canzoniere*, trans. J.G. Nichols (Manchester: Carcanet, 2000), p. 134. Both Wyatt and Surrey translated this sonnet in the sixteenth century.

very inaccessibility is imposed on her largely by the pedestal upon which the speaker places her. Given this sexual paradigm, only a limited number of possible reactions are open to the speaker – when he is not simply exalting or pleading, he can reproach her for her cruelty, blame himself for the futility of his love or delight in its inevitability and reflect on her controlling influence on his writing, or on the likely effect or lack of effect of his poetry on her. Almost any one of these reactions can be played off against another, typically between the octave and sestet of the sonnet, and the moment of resolution or persuasion which any particular sonnet reaches is always likely to be undone or reversed in subsequent sonnets of a sequence. All potential solutions to the problems of the Petrarchan erotic paradigm are unstable or provisional. In all this frantic emotional and intellectual business, the woman's role is essentially passive: she is its object, compelled or required by the paradigm to remain remote and largely unresponsive.

The Petrarchan mode was introduced to English readers through the imitations and translations of Wyatt and Surrey, which first became available in the pioneering anthology known as *Tottel's Miscellany* of 1557 (Tottel included thirteen of Surrey's and twenty-seven of Wyatt's sonnets). It was Tottel's actual title, *Songs and Sonettes*, that supplied the title formula for the earliest edition of Donne's love poems in the following century and neither title intends to restrict the word 'sonnet' to the fourteen-line imitations of Petrarch. At this period 'sonnet' can still mean any short lyric poem. This has led some historians, mistakenly, to claim that the English Renaissance had no proper name for this kind of poem, which it produced in such large numbers. However – as Spiller shows – from the last quarter of the sixteenth century onwards, though it could still be used more loosely, 'sonnet' normally meant what we still understand it to mean (*Development of the Sonnet*, p. 96). Seventeen of Wyatt's thirty-two sonnets are modelled on particular sonnets of Petrarch. It was the Earl of Surrey who first relaxed the tight, infolded rhyme scheme of the Italian sonnet to what was to become the characteristic 'English' pattern of four unlinked quatrains plus a final couplet (*abab cdcd efef gg*). The reason for this loosening was probably that it is easier in Italian to sustain rhyme sounds over many lines than it is in English, Italian having a greater percentage of similarly sounding word endings.

The great Elizabethan sonnet vogue owes something to Wyatt and Surrey, but was truly initiated by Sir Philip Sidney's *Astrophel and Stella* (1591), a sequence of one hundred and eight sonnets and eleven 'songs'. The fashion lasted for only a few years, the majority of its products being written in the four to five years between 1593 and 1597; by 1650, when Milton produced his sonnets, the great Elizabethan outpouring of sonnets had largely subsided and the form was not revived until the closing years of the eighteenth century.

▩ Constructing Voices: An Example from Sir Philip Sidney

The way an Elizabethan sonneteer defines a poetic voice is well illustrated by the opening sonnet of Sidney's *Astrophel and Stella*, the sonnet sequence which supplied the model for most of its Elizabethan successors:

> Loving in truth, and fain in verse my love to show,
> That she, dear she, might take some pleasure of my pain,
> Pleasure might cause her read, reading might make her know,
> Knowledge might pity win, and pity grace obtain,
>   I sought fit words to paint the blackest face of woe: 5
> Studying inventions fine, her wits to entertain,
> Oft turning others' leaves, to see if thence would flow
> Some fresh and fruitful showers upon my sunburn'd brain.
>   But words came halting forth, wanting invention's stay;
> Invention, Nature's child, fled stepdame study's blows;   10
> And others' feet still seem'd but strangers in my way.
> Thus great with child to speak, and helpless in my throes,
> Biting my truant pen, beating myself for spite:
> 'Fool,' said my Muse to me, 'look in thy heart and write!'

Sidney's sequence, like Petrarch's, professes to be the record of an actual love affair with a particular woman – in Sidney's case Penelope Devereux, Lady Rich, eldest daughter of the first Earl of Essex, whom he met at court in 1581, the same year she married Lord Rich. But if we ask how the experience which this opening sonnet presents might relate to Sidney's own personal experience, the first thing we have to do is recognise that all such apparently autobiographical confessions in sonnet sequences of this period are undoubtedly fictionalised. The only evidence that Sidney ever had an actual love affair with Penelope Rich is in these sonnets themselves. We should remember that Petrarch's sonnets also purport to record his love affair with a woman who was already married and with whom he had nothing that we would call a 'relationship'. The advantage of writing Petrarchan sonnets to a woman who was already married was precisely that she was likely to be inaccessible – a situation which is fundamental to what we called the sonnet's 'erotic paradigm'. So to ask what it was in Sidney's relationship with Lady Rich which made him assume, as he does in this opening poem, that she would be likely to scorn his verse, taking 'pleasure' in his 'pain', is to ask an irrelevant question. The Petrarchan lover suffers and his mistress is cruel and unresponsive to his pleas for favour, because that is the name of the game. In so far as there is any autobiographical basis to the relationship which these sonnets record, it has already been conventionalised, is already 'literary'.

The definition of an appropriate speaker for this conventionalised address might be seen as the essential purpose of this opening sonnet. Sidney presents himself as labouring to write his love sonnet (both labouring in the study and metaphorically being 'great with child to speak') and the lines read laboriously. That mannered laboriousness is captured in the very movement of the verse, the way each phrase in lines 3–4, for instance, is cantilevered out on the one before as if to lead the lover inexorably, if precariously, to the object of his desire – though 'object' may be too physical a word to use for what the poem tactfully calls 'grace':

> Pleasure might cause her read,
>   reading might make her know,
>   Knowledge might pity win,
>   and pity grace obtain.

Such labour contrasts with the simplicity and directness of the poem's last line, every one of whose words is a monosyllable: '"Fool," said my Muse to me, "Look in thy heart and write!"' The whole art of this sonnet could be seen as preparing the way for this rhetorical volte-face. Thus if we wanted to locate the turning point in the argument of this 'English' sonnet, we might say that it is delayed – not to the final couplet, but to the very last line. But as soon as we start looking for the volta, which is perhaps the first thing a sonnet-reader should do, we might notice that, as in so many sonnets, the sestet begins with a strong qualifier, 'But' and that the sestet announces the futility of the poetic labour of the octave. Yet the sestet seems as laborious as the octave and the speaker's frustration appears to be sustained and prolonged by the suspended present participles 'Loving', 'Studying', 'Biting', all of which are finally resolved in the peremptory imperative 'write!' with which the sonnet ends. That movement from conflict to resolution is something which, as we have seen, the octave–sestet division of the sonnet form is well adapted to handle. Although Sidney adapts the sonnet structure to his own purposes, then, we might conclude that what he was adapting was nevertheless already a received convention.

In fact this sonnet about writing a sonnet is also about originality and convention. When Sidney's speaker says that he has been studying 'inventions fine' (6), he means poetic ideas and expressions already created by other writers. Renaissance theories of writing, including Sidney's own, often insisted that the best way of learning how to write was to copy what other people had written, a process known as 'imitation'. The sestet is preoccupied with such theories of composition: the 'others' feet' that stand in Sidney's way are the poems of other writers which he is attempting to imitate – as the pun on metrical 'feet' indicates. The sonnet is perhaps the ideal genre in which to dramatise this debate about imitation and originality, precisely because so many of its conceits were recognised, even at this early stage of its development in England, as intertextual. The voice that was available to the poet was known to be largely, if not wholly, constructed by the genre's past practitioners. To compose sonnets at this period was, almost inevitably, to speak not with one's own voice but with Petrarch's. Sidney distances himself in a later sonnet (no. 15) from poets 'that poor Petrarch's long deceased woes / With new-born sighes and denizen'd wit do sing'. But for all its pretence of an escape from rhetorical *imitatio*, Sidney's erotic paradigm is strictly Petrarchan, strictly literary. We can see that the opening sonnet's skilful use of rhetorical figures is very far from the simplicity that the Muse herself is advocating in the last line. That technique of cantilevered phrasing in lines 3–4, for example, conforms to a rhetorical figure known in this period as *gradatio* (a Latin word that literally means 'ladder', though it is amusing in this context to learn that one of its alternative names was 'climax'). Sidney's poem turns out to be an argument for artlessness of expression which wants readers to admire its own artfulness.

Sidney's argument in this sonnet seems to recognise one of the abiding problems in sonnet theory, which has wider implications for the whole issue of writing in fixed forms: namely, the question of how a poet can find his or her own voice in a medium whose conventionality is so apparent. As we have seen, the sonnet had always appeared to favour the expression of emotion, defining the confessional 'I' of its persona in ways that encouraged readers to take it as the expression of a reflective, emotive consciousness. We could say that Sidney flirts with generic conventions, distancing himself from them even as he uses them, deviating from their strict application without wanting to escape completely. That may be why this opening sonnet to a sequence in which most of its successors are in the conventional sonnet metre (iambic pentameter) is written in hexameters (six-beat, twelve-syllable lines). Hexameters often seem laboured and less 'natural' to the speaking voice in English poetry than pentameters and it would be much more difficult to stage the measured parallelism of the *gradatio* in lines 3–4 in pentameters. The choice of an aberrant metre was certainly not accidental: Sidney's techniques and effects are all what this sonnet would call 'studied'.

▦ Modifying the English Sonnet: John Milton

The last major English poet to make use of the sonnet form before it became unfashionable and went into cold storage for a hundred years or more was Milton, who wrote twenty-four occasional sonnets on various subjects. Milton favoured the Italian rather than the English sonnet form; but though this might lead us to expect the Petrarchan voice and conventions, his sonnets are among the least Petrarchan of English sonnets in their choice of subject matter and their way of handling it. Milton's most striking innovation is that he makes the sonnet political and it was this innovation, as we shall see, that led Wordsworth to take Milton as his model when attempting to revive the sonnet as a vehicle for political comment in the early nineteenth century. Milton also departs from the received conventions in the radical way his syntax overrides the formal structures of the sonnet form. We can see this in the following example (*c.* 1652):

> When I consider how my light is spent,
>   Ere half my days, in this dark world and wide,
>   And that one Talent which is death to hide
>   Lodg'd with me useless, though my Soul more bent
> To serve therewith my Maker, and present   5
>   My true account, lest he returning chide,
>   Doth God exact day-labour, light deny'd,
>   I fondly ask; But Patience to prevent
> That murmur, soon replies, God doth not need
>   Either man's work or his own gifts, who best   10
>   Bear his mild yoke, they serve him best, his state
> Is kingly. Thousands at his bidding speed,
>   And post o'er Land and Ocean without rest:
>   They also serve who only stand and wait.

If we analyse the way the syntax of this poem relates to its verse form, as we did in discussing the relationship between metre and syntax in Chapter 3, we notice that the units of sense override the conventional divisions of the sonnet's structure more consistently than is the case with any of the examples we have examined so far. The strong enjambment at the end of line 8 ('But Patience to prevent / That murmur') completely overrides the conventional division between octave and sestet, though this is only the strongest of several power-fully run-on line endings (at the end of lines 3, 4, 5, 9, 10 and 11). In addition, new clauses and sentences often begin in mid-line, creating strong caesuras at various points.

A useful kind of exercise with this and sonnets like it might be to break down the sense units in order to see how they correspond with or override the conventional divisions of the verse structure. The verse units are the individual line boundaries, together with the conventional divisions of the octave, sestet and final couplet. The sense units are groups of words which belong together – individual phrases and clauses which it would be difficult to separate without a feeling of grammatical fragmentation and incompleteness. Sense units are not wholly discrete, since clearly all parts of a sentence are linked together to some degree and the divisions that follow are not the only way one might break up

Milton's sentences. One test of whether a sense unit is (at least provisionally) complete would be to ask whether it would be natural to take a pause after it when reading aloud. Our way of dividing up the sense units of Milton's sonnet is as follows (line divisions are marked '/', while the conventional divisions of the sonnet are marked '//'):

> When I consider how my life is spent,/
> Ere half my days,
>   in this dark world and wide,/
> And that one Talent
>   which is death to hide/
> Lodg'd with me useless,
>   though My Soul more bent/ To serve therewith my Maker,
>   and present/ My true account,
>   lest he returning chide,/
> Doth God exact day-labour, light deny'd,/
>   I fondly ask;
>   But Patience to prevent// That murmur,
>   soon replies,
>   God doth not need/ Either man's work or his own gifts,
>   who best/ Bear his mild yoke,
>   they serve him best,
>   his state/ Is kingly.
>   Thousands at his bidding speed,/
> And post o'er Land and Ocean without rest:/
> They also serve who only stand and wait.

By laying out the sonnet in this way, we are foregrounding the poem's syntactic structure at the expense of its metrical form. In Chapter 3 we argued that some of the most interesting and fundamental effects of poetic form result from the interplay between metre and syntax. In the present case our analysis exhibits the interplay between the syntactic or sense units (the sentences and phrases) and the verse units (the lines). In the octave, four out of the eight line endings correspond with syntax divisions, but from line 8 to line 10 there is no such correspondence and the octave–sestet division is completely overridden. The comma after 'speed' (12) is a very weak syntax division and hardly prevents our reading line 13 as a run-on line. Thus it is only the last line that re-establishes structural stability. In the context of this urgent movement the monumental assurance of the self-contained aphorism of the last line seems all the more impressive.

It is important to ask, as always, how this use of sonnet form affects the subject matter and argument of the poem. The first line refers to Milton's blindness and the sonnet is asking how Milton can serve God now that he is disabled (Milton went blind in 1650–51 at the age of forty-two). 'Talent' in line 3 alludes to the biblical parable of the talents (Matthew 25: 14–30), which advises Christians that they will be required to render an account to God of how they have used their gifts in serving Him in this world. We might say that the poem is about patience, about coming to terms with a disability and finding out how to serve God. In exploring this question the poem exhibits that expression of emotion, of conflict and division, that rational reflection leading towards some resolution or conclusion, which we have seen as characteristic of the sonnet form. The aphoristic last line, which has almost become proverbial in English since Milton coined it in this poem, sends a strong signal of completion, resignation and closure. It could be interesting to ask how this closure resolves the swings of mood, the open syntax and the tensions between sonnet form and subject matter which the rest of the sonnet dramatises.

One way of answering this question would be to return to the sonnet's volta, since this often represents the moment where a sonnet's argument turns towards its resolution. If we look for a qualifying conjunction signalling the turn of the syntax and argument, we can certainly find one – but not at the beginning of line 9, where all we find is a strong enjambment. The turning word 'But' is not even at the beginning of a line but occurs at a strong caesura in the middle of line 8. One reason for this premature appearance of the volta, we might suggest, is that this is a sonnet about patience and frustration. The volta is perhaps anticipated because it is acting out the very manner in which 'Patience' (8) intervenes to 'prevent / That murmur'. 'Patience' is the sestet's answer to the octave's question and patience here is impatient. ('Prevent' in Milton's usage means 'anticipate', from the Latin *praevenio*, to 'come before' and 'murmur' is a word which, for Milton, tends to imply sacrilegious dissatisfaction with or rebellion against God's will.)

Related to enjambment is the suspended syntax. Several of Shakespeare's sonnets, including Sonnet 29, open with a 'When' clause – a subordinating conjunction whose completion the reader has to await, or comes to expect, in the resolution of the sestet. Milton's syntax is more puzzling, however, and it may be difficult for us to work out exactly how its opening 'When' clause gets resolved. It is followed by a series of qualifications and elaborations – 'Ere half my days . . .' (2); 'And that one Talent . . . (3); 'though my Soul . . .' (4); 'lest he returning' (6). It is only in line 8 that we finally get the main clause – 'I fondly ask' ('fondly' means 'foolishly') – and the reader has to work out that the overall syntax of this sentence is: 'When I consider how my light is spent, I fondly ask: "Doth God exact day-labour, light deny'd"?' In other words: 'When I think about how blind I am, I foolishly ask whether God requires the disabled to do their duty'. This question is clearly Milton's and the reply that follows can be assigned to 'Patience'. Modern punctuation would probably place quotation marks round Patience's reply, although there have been critical disputes about whether or not Patience speaks the whole of the last six-and-a-half lines.[8]

The Second Coming of the English Sonnet

After Milton, English poets had little time for the sonnet until the latter half of the eighteenth century. It had what we might think of as an unfavourable brand image. In 1742 Thomas Gray wrote a sonnet on the death of his friend, Richard West, but it was some years before there was any sustained revival. The earliest sonnets in this revival were produced in 1777 by Thomas Warton, followed by further examples from a number of poets, including Charlotte Smith (*Elegiac Sonnets and Other Essays*, 1784), Anna Seward (*Original Sonnets on Various Subjects*, 1799), Helen Maria Williams and William Lisle Bowles. These writers adapted the sonnet to a new kind of subject-matter. Recognising that the form was closely attuned to the expression of personal feelings, they used it for elegies to deceased friends or to record the speaker's response to natural scenery. As Stuart Curran says,

> Sonnets of sensibility flooded forth like tears. Starting in the 1780s and continuing for some four decades of rediscovery, this most exacting small form of the British tradition was bent, stretched, reshaped, rethought. Its rebirth coincides with the rise of a definable women's literary movement and with the beginnings of Romanticism.[9]

The sonnets of Charlotte Smith and of the poets who followed her influenced Coleridge, who wrote a number of sonnets himself at this period; in 1793 he collected fifty or so 'Sonnets by Various Authors' into a pamphlet which has been described as 'a virtual manifesto of early Romanticism' (Curran, p. 35). In the preface Coleridge describes the sonnet as 'a small poem, in which some lonely feeling is developed' and which works best when 'moral Sentiments, Affections, or Feelings, are deduced from, and associated with, the scenery of Nature' (quoted in Curran, p. 36). This definition clearly marks a significant change in the sonnet's subject matter compared with its use in the Renaissance. Such a change can be recognised in Charlotte Smith's 'Sonnet: Composed during a Walk on the Downs, in November 1787':

> The dark and pillowy cloud; the sallow trees,
> Seem o'er the ruins of the year to mourn;
> And cold and hollow, the inconstant breeze
> Sobs through the falling leaves and withered fern.

---

[8] Interpretations which assign the whole of the last six-and-a-half lines to Patience are questioned by Stanley Fish, 'Interpreting the Variorum', reprinted in Lodge, *Modern Criticism and Theory*, pp. 310–29. Though this essay is an important contribution to Reader–Response Theory, we are not wholly convinced by Fish's reading of this sonnet.

[9] Curran, *Poetic Form and British Romanticism*, p. 31.

> O'er the tall brow of yonder chalky bourn,   5
> The evening shades their gathering darkness fling,
> While, by the lingering light, I scarce discern
> The shrieking night-jar, sail on heavy wing.
> Ah! yet a little – and propitious Spring
> Crowned with fresh flowers, shall wake the woodland strain;   10
> But no gay change revolving seasons bring,
> To call forth pleasure from the soul of pain,
> Bid siren Hope resume her long lost part,
> And chase the vulture Care – that feeds upon the heart.

The poem's 'argument' depends on an identification of the speaker's mood with the mournful winter landscape: thus the trees seem to 'mourn' (2) and the breeze sobs (4). (The idea that the natural world sympathises in this way with the perceiving subject became part of the stock in trade of Romantic and Victorian poets – John Ruskin later dismissed this convention as 'The Pathetic Fallacy'.[10]) Although the season responds to the speaker's mood in the octave, the sestet reflects bitterly that it will not do so when spring returns. While the spring will bring the landscape back to life, it will not change the speaker's mood – it will not renew 'Hope' or chase away 'vulture Care' (13–14). These personified abstractions apparently refer to the speaker's strong feelings, though they offer no clue as to the circumstances that occasioned those feelings – indeed, their status as generalised abstractions serves to deter or deflect such particular enquiry. If we were intent on discovering what motivated this despair, we would have to look for some context outside the poem. One of Smith's modern editors offers a biographical note which suggests that her sonnets, 'with their pervading themes of melancholy and isolation', were 'possibly intensified by her own confinement within an unhappy marriage and in the debtor's gaol'.[11] A different, more literary context would be the growing fashion towards the end of the eighteenth century of 'sensibility', which encouraged melancholy reflection in solitary surroundings in just such sonnets as this.

How far readers are entitled to supply such contexts or allow them to inform their reading of such a poem is an open question and one which we raised in Chapter 10. But as far as sonnet conventions are concerned, it should be clear that sonnets, traditionally, had never felt obliged to identify the personal or biographical circumstances that motivated their speakers' reflections.

[10] Ruskin introduced this phrase in vol. 3, ch. 12 of *Modern Painters* (1856) to describe the tendency of poets to attribute their own emotions to nature; 'pathetic' is etymologically linked with words such as 'sympathy' and 'empathy' – in the pathetic fallacy nature supposedly empathises with human feelings, but it also usually implies *pathos* in the sense that such feelings are generally sad. Ruskin saw it as a 'fallacy' because he believed it was not true to nature.

[11] Ashfield, *Romantic Women Poets*, p. 33.

Sonnets are too short for such narrative detail. All the sonnet requires is the articulation of conflicting thoughts or feelings and a move towards some kind of resolution of that conflict. Smith's sonnet clearly meets that formal requirement and responds to the type of analysis we have been recommending throughout this chapter. The octave establishes the identification of its speaker's mood with the winter landscape in two sentences which fill each of the first two quatrains. The turn towards 'propitious Spring' takes place in the opening line of the sestet, though the qualifying 'But' – the type of word that often introduces a sonnet's volta – is delayed to line 11. That delay has its own logic since, although line 9 is where the speaker's thoughts turn from winter to spring, the argument requires a more decisive turn in which the speaker anticipates the coming disengagement of her feelings from the season and the landscape which the octave has so successfully connected.

■ Finding a Voice: Wordsworth and Milton

Wordsworth's *Poems in Two Volumes* (1807) contains forty-seven sonnets, divided into 'Miscellaneous Sonnets' and 'Sonnets on Liberty'. Although he had written a number of 'juvenile' sonnets at an earlier period he subsequently disowned them and his decisive turn to the sonnet dates from the year 1802, when he began to use it to work out his troubled sense of the poet's engagement with the issues of nationalism and revolution during the war against Napoleonic France. Perhaps the most important thing to realise in order to understand why Wordsworth should have begun using this genre for working out his problems in 1802 is the fact that all his sonnets are modelled on those of Milton. At this period Milton still had a reputation as a champion of English liberty in the revolutionary and religious struggles of the seventeenth century which, many of Wordsworth's contemporaries felt, prefigured the turbulent politics of their own time. Many of Milton's sonnets, such as 'On the late Massacre in Piedmont' (1655) or 'On the new Forces of Conscience under the Long Parliament' (1646?), address political issues directly. The subject matter of most of Wordsworth's sonnets of the early years of the nineteenth century was also political – the problem of defining a British response to recent events in France, particularly the Peace of Amiens, which secured Napoleon's hold on power.[12]

---

[12] In 1843 Wordsworth added a note to one of his sonnets in which he recalls that 'one afternoon' in 1801 (actually May 1802) his sister read him the sonnets of Milton: 'I was particularly struck on that occasion by the dignified simplicity and majestic harmony that runs through most of them'. He immediately composed three sonnets in imitation. Yet he also possessed a copy of Charlotte Smith's sonnets, which he had annotated in 1789 and was re-reading in 1802; he admired the sonnets of Helen Maria Williams and was critical of the subsequent neglect of these female pioneers of the sonnet's revival (see Ashfield, *Romantic Women Poets*, pp. 34, 67).

Milton not only supplied the model for Wordsworth's sonnets in their use of the 'Italian' verse form and in their approach to questions of national destiny, but he is also named or addressed directly in the sonnets, most memorably in 'London, 1802', which begins: 'Milton! thou shouldst be living at this hour: / England hath need of thee.' One of the persistent themes of Wordsworth's political sonnets of this period is the necessity for poets or imaginative writers to find a voice that could address the urgent problems of contemporary politics, defining British interests and the nation's distinctive ideals and radical traditions at a time when it was becoming increasingly clear to former revolutionaries (like Wordsworth) that the French Revolution was going badly wrong and that Britain, the last bastion of liberty, was itself now under threat from France and from reactionary forces within. It is this anxiety about Britain which is explored in the following sonnet (1802):

> It is not to be thought of that the Flood
> Of British freedom, which, to the open Sea
> Of the world's praise, from dark antiquity
> Hath flowed, 'with pomp of waters unwithstood',
> Road by which all might come and go that would,   5
> And bear out freights of worth to foreign lands;
> That this most famous Stream in Bogs and Sands
> Should perish; and to evil and to good
> Be lost for ever. In our halls is hung
> Armoury of the invincible Knights of old: 10
> We must be free or die, who speak the tongue
> That Shakespeare spake; the faith and morals hold
> Which Milton held. – In every thing we are sprung
> Of Earth's first blood, have titles manifold.

The sestet begins in mid-line, a favourite trick of Milton's. And we might notice the same kind of suspended syntax that we saw in Milton's sonnet on his blindness, making us wait for the delayed verb. The resolution certainly comes in this case, but only after an enjambment that trickles the syntax over the volta into the sestet: 'It is not to be thought of that . . . British freedom . . . Be lost forever'. Having broached this unthinkable possibility in the octave, the sestet offers a succession of confident reminders of the enduring symbols of British fortitude and independence and the talismanic contribution that the great national poets had made to this. The quotation marks in line 4 acknowledge that Wordsworth is quoting from Samuel Daniel's poem on the *Civil Wars between Lancaster and York* (1595 and 1609), thus associating his own poetic voice with that of his predecessors. The stream of national liberty is identified in the sestet with 'Knights of old' and with Shakespeare, Milton and the

English language itself. The stream of liberty becomes one of hereditary breeding, a tradition of great writers and a national literature in which practitioners of the sonnet form have assumed a prominent place. Wordsworth's Miltonic sonnets can thus be read as staking his own claim to succeed Shakespeare and Milton and become a new champion of British liberty in face of this new threat.

The poem's syntax and sonnet form register the speaker's vacillations of confidence and doubt as he attempts to weigh up Britain's and his own responsibilities. It might help us overcome potential distaste for the overt jingoism of Wordsworth's sonnets if we attend to the ways in which sonnet form can register such vacillation. This will alert us to the political instabilities and personal insecurities which the movement of the verse in these sonnets so often reveals behind the apparent assurance of their patriotism. 'England! the time is come' is the rallying opening apostrophe in a sonnet of 1803 whose argument revolves around an anxiety that England should be so clearly unfit for its role as the last bastion of liberty and it ends with the despairing exclamation: 'Oh grief that Earth's best hopes rest all with Thee!' One of the fascinating things about this sonnet 'sequence' is how successive poems, with their appended dates of composition, register the way the political outlook was changing from one month to the next and dramatise Wordsworth's own shifting responses to those changes.

■ Romantic Sonnets: John Keats

Keats's sonnets confirm that the sonnet had become an important genre in the Romantic period. Keats discusses the possibilities of sonnet form in his sonnet 'On the Sonnet' (written 1819, printed 1848), another of those self-reflexive meta-statements to which sonnets are prone:

> If by dull rhymes our English must be chain'd,
> And, like Andromeda, the Sonnet sweet
> Fetter'd, in spite of pained loveliness,
> Let us find out, if we must be constrain'd,
> Sandals more interwoven and complete   5
> To fit the naked foot of Poesy:
> Let us inspect the Lyre, and weigh the stress
> Of every chord, and see what may be gain'd
> By ear industrious, and attention meet;
> Misers of sound and syllable, no less   10
> Than Midas of his coinage, let us be
> Jealous of dead leaves in the bay wreath crown;
> So, if we may not let the Muse be free,
> She will be bound with garlands of her own.

Here Keats debates the merits of using a fixed form, as Sidney does in 'Loving in truth . . .' and as Wordsworth does in 'Nuns fret not at their Convent's narrow room (in which the confinement of the sonnet form is compared to monastic confinement). In Keats's sonnet, 'Fetter'd' (3) goes with 'Sandals' (5) and 'naked foot' (6) to create an extended metaphor for the metrical and rhyme patterns of the poem itself. This sonnet has a closely interwoven rhyme scheme, but one which is quite different from any conventional sonnet rhyming pattern: *abcabdcabcdede*. Clearly there is no pattern to these rhymes to indicate any of the quatrain divisions or the octave/sestet structure of the conventional sonnet; the rhymes are themselves 'more interwoven and complete' (5), each threading its own way though the traditional divisions of sonnet form so as to break down any mechanically imposed structure. The sonnet is thus bound by 'Sandals' or 'garlands' (14) of its own devising, not fettered by others' chains. The way this sonnet uses its rhyme scheme, run-on lines and suspended syntax to explore the paradox of poetic freedom within formal constraints could be analysed using the same techniques that we have used for the sonnets of all periods examined in this chapter. The very fact that Keats's sonnet seems to call for such analysis, however, suggests that it is making significant use of the formal conventions of the genre even as it distances itself from them. As in 'Ode to a Nightingale', the characteristic sense of Romantic liberty and spontaneous artlessness is produced through staging a dynamic interplay between syntax, metre and poetic form.

The Modern Sonnet

Since the Romantic period the sonnet has never gone out of fashion and has remained one of the established genres available to poets writing in English. In the nineteenth century Elizabeth Barrett Browning wrote a large number of sonnets, including an important sequence of forty-four 'Sonnets from the Portuguese' (1847–50) celebrating her love for Robert Browning. George Meredith's *Modern Love* (1862) is a sequence of fifty sixteen-line 'sonnets' about the break-up of his own marriage. Twentieth-century poets have continually adapted sonnet conventions to new types of subject matter in ways which suggest the continuing vitality of this most traditional of poetic forms. Edna St Vincent Millay (1892–1950), for instance, produced many sonnets written from a woman's point of view which challenge most of the masculine assumptions about sexuality and romantic love which sonnets traditionally tended to uphold (as you may have recognised in the Millay sonnet we set for the exercise at the end of Chapter 8). In the 1930s and 1940s W.H. Auden wrote sonnets which address some of the moral and political issues of the time and make interesting use of metre and sonnet structure (we have quoted one of these, 'Our Bias' (1940), in Chapter 5). In 1964 John Berryman published a sequence of fourteen-line 'Dream Songs' which he describes in a prefatory note as 'essentially about an imaginary character (not the poet, not me) named Henry, a white American in early middle age, sometimes in black face, who has suffered an irreversible loss and talks about himself . . .'. Seamus Heaney's 'Glanmore Sonnets' (1979) record his deep attachment to his native Irish landscape. Geoffrey Hill (born 1932) has made notable use of sonnets to examine the long history of human cruelty and violence and, specifically, the Holocaust. Edwin Morgan published his ten 'Glasgow Sonnets' in 1973 and fifty 'Sonnets from Scotland' in 1984. Eleanor Brown's sequence of 'Fifty Sonnets' (*Maiden Speech*, 1996, pp. 18–43), from which we drew our example of significant rhyme in Chapter 3, consists of a set of modern love sonnets in which a very modern female speaker addresses her lover and charts her shifting experience of a love affair – thus imitating and reversing the speech situation of the Elizabethan sonnet sequences that Brown's sonnets so knowingly allude to. All these examples indicate the extent to which modern writers continue to feel that the sonnet, for all its apparent artificiality and conventionality, is well adapted to address real and relevant issues, whether personal or of wider public importance.[13]

The continuing relevance of the sonnet form to the experience of writers whose cultural identity is very different from those of its courtly originators in the European Renaissance may be seen in the sonnets of the black American poet Gwendolyn Brooks (born 1917). Brooks has made frequent use of the sonnet form and sometimes of the sonnet sequence. The following poem is part of a sequence of sonnets, ballads and other poems called 'The Womanhood':

The Rites for Cousin Vit

Carried her unprotesting out the door.
Kicked back the casket-stand. But it can't hold her,
That stuff and satin aiming to enfold her,
The lid's contrition nor the bolts before.
Oh oh. Too much. Too much. Even now, surmise,   5
She rises in the sunshine. There she goes,
Back to the bars she knew and the repose
In love-rooms and the things in people's eyes.
Too vital and too squeaking. Must emerge.
Even now she does the snake-hips with a hiss,   10
Slops the bad wine across her shantung, talks
Of pregnancy, guitars and bridgework, walks
In parks or alleys, comes haply on the verge
Of happiness, haply hysterics. Is.

---

[13] This impression is sustained by the six hundred or so sonnets collected in *The Penguin Book of the Sonnet: 500 years of a classic tradition in English*, ed. Phillis Levin (London: Penguin, 2001).

This elegiac sonnet is highly successful in bringing Cousin Vit back to life and in celebrating the vitality of that life. The isolation of the last word 'Is' succinctly sums up the speaker's attitude (tone) and the point of the poem: it affirms that Cousin Vit simply 'is' in all the energetic but perhaps self-destructive ways she used to be. Moreover, the rhetorically effective isolation of that conclusive word might alert us to the syntactic movement of the whole poem and its relation to the verse form, which would repay the same kind of analysis we have carried out on most of the other sonnets in this chapter. We do not think we now need to pursue such an analysis at any length, though we recommend that you do so. We will restrict ourselves to making a few suggestions which you might wish to take further. The sonnet uses the Italian rhyme pattern, but though the octave ends with a full stop it may not correspond with the major turn in the argument, which one might prefer to locate in line 5, where the speaker imagines the corpse's liberation from confinement in the coffin. That change from death back to life seems to be the significant and central volta of the poem (signalled by 'Even now . . .'). If there is any shift in argument or attitude after the octave–sestet turn, it might be in the way the lines which follow present a potentially ambivalent attitude towards Cousin Vit. Would it be true to say that there is more approval and celebration of her vitality in the octave, but more criticism and disapproval implied in the sestet? The poem also makes interesting use of enjambment to generate a sense of Cousin Vit's energy – particularly at the end of lines 11–13. And at the end it makes effective use of parallelism and alliteration: Cousin Vit 'comes haply on the verge / Of happiness, haply hysterics'. It would be worth asking whether this parallelism, which suggests that Cousin Vit's exuberance is as likely to take her to the verge of hysterics as to the verge of happiness, relates to any ambivalence in the speaker's attitude and how the last word ('Is') might resolve this ambivalence. Such formal analysis would not be a distraction from the poem's engagement with human experience. On the contrary, the fact that this poem is a sonnet plays a large part in its shaping of the urban experience of black American women in the twentieth century.

Exercises

1 Read the following sonnet by John Berryman (1967) several times. The first four of our questions will prompt you to think about the poem's overall meaning; the later questions ask you to think more specifically about its use of the sonnet form.

Sonnet 23

They may suppose, because I would not cloy your ear –
If ever these songs by other ears are heard –
With 'love' and 'love', I loved you not, but blurred
Lust with strange images, warm, not quite sincere,
To switch the bedroom black. O mutineer   5
With me against these empty captains! gird
Your scorn again above all at *this* word
Pompous and vague on the stump of his career.
Also I fox 'heart', striking a modern breast
Hollow as a drum, and 'beauty' I taboo;   10
I want a verse fresh as a bubble breaks,
As little false . . . Blood of my sweet unrest
Runs all the same – I am in love with you –
Trapped in my rib-cage something throes and aches!

(a) What are lines 1–5 saying about the speaker's motives for not using the word 'love'? Why should the absence of this word in his poetry cause some readers to suppose that it was written 'To switch the bedroom black'? What are the implications of this image?

(b) What is the purpose of the extended metaphor ('mutineer', 'captains', 'gird' and 'stump') in lines 5–8? Who is the 'mutineer' and who are the 'captains'?

(c) Try to summarise the meaning of the first three-and-a-half lines of the sestet.

(d) Why does the speaker use the word 'something' in the last line? What are the effects of this when combined with the use of 'love' in the previous line?

(e) Does this sonnet conform to any of the established forms – Italian, Shakespearian or Spenserian?

(f) Is there a turn in the argument of the poem at any point? If so, how does that turn relate to the poem's overall theme or argument?

(g) Why might it be appropriate that the title of this poem should call attention to its genre? How does your knowledge of sonnet conventions shape your response to the poem?

(h) Re-read Sidney's 'Loving in truth . . .'. Does it have any similarities of either form or content with Berryman's sonnet?

(i) Are there any characteristics that suggest that, for all its relationship with Renaissance sonnet conventions, Berryman's sonnet is a distinctively modern poem?

2 Look up any of the sonnets we have quoted in other chapters of this book and answer the following questions in order to produce an analysis of the way they use sonnet conventions. You can choose from any of the following: Brown, 'Probably the most human thing I do' (Chapter 3); Hopkins, 'God's Grandeur' (Chapter 4); Auden, 'Our Bias' (Chapter 5); Shakespeare, 'Sonnet 73' (Chapter 6); MacDiarmid, 'In the Children's Hospital' (Chapter 8); Shelley, 'Ozymandias' (Chapter 8); Millay, 'I dreamed I moved among the Elysian fields' (Chapter 8); Herbert, 'Redemption' (Chapter 9); Shakespeare, 'Sonnet 138' (Chapter 9).

(a) What type of sonnet is it – Shakespearian, Petrarchan, Spenserian, or some variant of these?

(b) How far does the rhyme pattern indicate the formal divisions of the sonnet's structure? How far is the argument accommodated to this structure? How do the units of sense or syntax relate to the line divisions and to the formal divisions – octave, sestet, final couplet – of the sonnet's structure? To answer this, you might try rewriting the text in the same way that we reformatted Milton's sonnet 'On his Blindness', by laying out each syntactic unit on a separate line.

(c) Does the subject correspond to any of the types of subject matter which became conventional for sonnets at different periods of its history? Pay attention to the date of the poem in answering this question.

(d) What kind of speaker does the poem have? Who is the addressee? Describe the tone of the poem.

3 John Donne once claimed that 'he is a fool which cannot make one sonnet, and he is mad which makes two'. In this exercise we would like you to try to write a sonnet. You may not find it easy, despite Donne's assertion, but we think it might help you to understand something about how ideas and language are fitted into a fixed poetic form. It does not matter what the subject of your sonnet is – if you like, you could write a sonnet about writing a sonnet. You will probably find it best if you start by thinking of an idea or an issue that can be turned round, contradicted, or reversed in a surprising way. That will give you a structure that you can turn across the volta. Try to think about the overall syntax of the sonnet (maybe try a 'When . . . then' sentence structure) and about syntactic suspension, caesura and enjambment. Do not worry too much if your metre is a bit irregular, but do try to follow a predetermined rhyme scheme and see where it takes your argument. If you find yourself having to break the rules, see if you can do it to some purpose. It might be fun (and quite revealing!) to pass the results of this exercise round in class or in a tutorial and to comment on each other's efforts.

Chapter 13

Allusion, Influence and Intertextuality

■ Allusion

We have already mentioned allusion in several earlier chapters. In our discussion of why 'Ode to a Nightingale' seems 'poetic', we noted the contribution made by Keats's use of allusions to classical mythology (as in 'the true, the blushful Hippocrene'). In discussing Elvis Costello's 'Peace in Our Time', we claimed that the title and chorus make an ironic allusion to a political speech which was itself alluding to the Book of Common Prayer. We suggested that the conclusion of Rich's 'Song' is made ambiguous through an allusion to the idiom 'to burn one's boats'. We noted that the climax of Herbert's 'Redemption' clarifies the real situation being re-enacted in the poem through alluding to the Gospel story of Christ's crucifixion. And we argued that the plethora of allusions in *The Waste Land* undercuts our attempt to understand the poem as representing the speech of a single poetic voice.

These examples suggest that allusion can play a number of different roles in poems: it can be a sign of the poetic (Keats); it can work ironically (Costello); it can serve to complicate meaning (Rich) or to clarify meaning (Herbert); and, taken to an extreme, it can challenge conventional conceptions about what poetry is (Eliot). Allusion, then, can be seen as a poetic device alongside metaphor, ambiguity, rhyme, and so on. But the particular nature of allusion means that it is a device which works *between* texts rather than wholly within individual texts. It therefore opens up questions about originality, about the relationship between poems, and about the kinds of knowledge readers are expected to bring to a poem. In this chapter we want to develop these provisional remarks about allusion by examining how it works within and between poems and how critics have traditionally understood it. This will lead us into an examination of other ways in which poems interrelate with other texts (influence) and with discourse in general (intertextuality).

Non-textual allusions involve references to people, events or topics, or to publicly known facts about the poet's life. Costello's allusion refers to a historical event (Chamberlain's return from the Munich conference with Hitler), but also to a textual event – Chamberlain's statement (itself an allusion to the Book of Common Prayer). But although the term 'allusion' is used to include such non-textual references, it is best reserved for those moments when texts refer to other texts or to a particular passage from another text. The passage from the earlier work may be quoted or adapted, but it is not normally identified explicitly. Because they are left implicit, textual allusions can work only if the reader recognises them; they draw on our knowledge of previous literature by demanding recognition of unidentified references, echoes, quotations.

The question of how obscure an allusion can afford to be is always likely to be an issue, and poets may easily misjudge their readers' familiarity with such references, as Edwin Morgan does in one of his 'Glasgow Sonnets' (1972) when he compares a block of high-rise flats to the Dover cliffs described by Edgar to his recently blinded and suicidal father, Gloucester, in *King Lear*. Here is Morgan's sonnet:

> From thirtieth floor windows at Red Road
> he can see choughs and samphires, dreadful trade –
> the schoolboy reading *Lear* has that scene made.
> A multi is a sonnet stretched to ode
> and some say that's no joke. The gentle load   5
> of souls in clouds, vertiginously stayed
> above the windy courts, is probed and weighed.
> Each monolith stands patient, ah'd and oh'd.
> And stalled lifts generating high-rise blues
> can be set loose. But stalled lives never budge.   10
> They linger in the single-ends* that use   *Glasgow tenement flat
> their spirit to the bone, and when they trudge
> from closemouth* to laundrette their steady shoes
>   *common entrance to tenement
> carry a world that weighs us like a judge.

And here is the passage from *King Lear* to which this alludes:

>   How fearful
> And dizzy 'tis to cast one's eyes so low!
> The crows and choughs that wing the midway air
> Show scarce so gross as beetles. Half way down
> Hangs one that gathers samphire – dreadful trade!
> Methinks he seems no bigger than his head. (IV.vi.11–16)

Shakespeare's description is strongly ekphrastic and creates a feeling of vertigo, which is certainly one of the effects that Morgan's allusion is echoing. 'Choughs' are rare birds in Scotland, and 'samphire' is a plant that grows in coastal habitats and was traditionally used in the kitchen. Morgan's sonnet would repay closer reading, not only to explore the effect of his Shakespearian allusion, but also perhaps its wider 'literary' references: the way, for instance, he compares buildings to poems. The point, for now, is simply that allusions only work for those readers who spot them. Despite Morgan's reference to 'the schoolboy reading *Lear*' (3), correspondence in the *Glasgow Herald* newspaper ran for some days from ornithological readers citing Morgan's poem and reflecting on whether or not it proved that 'from the thirtieth floor of the Red Road flats it was still possible in the 1970s to see choughs'. But maybe we shouldn't expect bird-watchers to spot a rare allusion – this perhaps requires more literary twitchers.

To explore more fully how allusions work we would like to look at Wordsworth's allusion in the opening lines of *The Prelude* (1805) to the closing lines of Milton's *Paradise Lost* (1667). Milton's ending describes Adam and Eve leaving Eden after their 'fall':

> The World was all before them, where to choose
> Their place of rest, and Providence their guide;
> They hand in hand with wand'ring steps and slow,
> Through Eden took their solitary way. (XII, 646–49)

At the beginning of *The Prelude* Wordsworth describes his return to the countryside after a period of being a 'captive' in the city:

> The earth is all before me: with a heart
> Joyous, nor scared at its own liberty,
> I look about, and should the guide I choose
> Be nothing better than a wandering cloud,
> I cannot miss my way. (I, 15–19)

We can use this example to make a number of defining points about allusion:

1 Allusion is not, or is only rarely, exact quotation but creatively modifies the wording of the past text to suit the new poetic purpose;
2 Allusion is not an accidental similarity between different texts but a deliberate poetic strategy;
3 Allusion is not plagiarism – the poet expects readers to notice that an allusion is being made and to be able to identify its source.

Allusion, then, differs from other kinds of textual 'borrowings' (such as quotation or plagiarism). And because part of the effect of allusion comes through our recognising its original source, it differs from those kinds of textual sharing in which it is not possible to discover an original – as in the use of *topoi* (typical poetic phrases or images), shared generic features, proverbs or commonplaces. And since we have stressed that an allusion is intentional, we need to distinguish it from unintentional similarities between texts (which may have occurred unconsciously or accidentally). Unfortunately, however, as we shall see, in practice it becomes difficult to distinguish between intentional and unintentional similarities between texts. Allusion, then, foregrounds the problems inherent in interpretations which rely on making claims about authorial intention.

Another theoretical question raised by allusion (and, even more radically, by the notion of intertextuality) is the question of originality. Since originality is a valued feature of art in general, and of post-Romantic poetry in particular, we need to ask why Romantic poets like Wordsworth and Keats rely on past texts in these ways. Doesn't their use of allusion question their claim that poetry is the outpouring of spontaneous feelings? Doesn't the use of so many allusions make 'Ode to a Nightingale' look less like the recording of a unique event and more like a carefully crafted poem which borrows from earlier texts? And doesn't this also mean that a reader needs to supplement any spontaneous response to the poem with an ability to spot allusions that entails bringing knowledge of other texts to the poem?

Allusion implies that poems are not unique objects but gain part of their meaning through their relation to other texts. An allusion to one of Donne's *Devotions* can help to illustrate this: we can say that 'No poem is an island, entire of itself; every poem is a piece of the poetic tradition, a part of the general discourse'.[1] An important question, however, concerns the *attitude* the poem takes towards the earlier text which is being alluded to. In many cases allusions are, as it were, reverential. The texts of the past are seen as impressive and valued achievements, and an allusion can be seen as acknowledging that. This might be one of the effects of Wordsworth's allusion to Milton. In fact, the many reverential references to Milton throughout Wordsworth's poetry indicate the degree to which Wordsworth admired the earlier poet. On one level, then, Wordsworth's allusions can be seen as a process of canon formation, of selecting and celebrating certain works of the past which are to be valued. By looking at the way in which the Romantic poets in general allude to past poets, it would be quite easy to draw up a short list of their favourites. It would certainly include Homer, the Greek dramatists, Virgil, Dante, Chaucer, Spenser, Shakespeare and Milton. (There are also conspicuous absences from this list – the eighteenth-century poets against whom the Romantics rebelled.)

---

[1] This statement is an allusion to John Donne's claim (1623) that 'No man is an Island, entire of itself, every man is a piece of the Continent, a part of the main' (*Devotions*, XVII).

The work of allusion, then, can contribute to the formation and maintenance of a valued literary canon or tradition.

By making allusions to a valued tradition, however, a poet not only attempts to reshape or reaffirm that tradition but implicitly stakes his or her own claim to join it. Wordsworth's *Prelude* is asking us not just to value Milton's poetry but also to recognise its own affiliation with Milton's poetry. Making allusions is like networking: a poem inserts itself within an exclusive textual network by making allusions. In doing so, it is asking us to see it as a new element within a valued and developing poetic tradition. Reading any single poem in this discursive network involves seeing its relationship to the rest of the network. The poet is assuming an 'ideal reader' who will be fully familiar with the poetic tradition or canon.

Yet allusion does not merely look back in reverence to the past, but recycles poetic material in order to refashion it for new poetic purposes. Thus it is often important to look at the relationship between the way the material works in the source text and the way it works in the new text. The ending of *Paradise Lost* imagines the beginning of human history in Christian terms (it alludes to and retells the story of the expulsion from Eden in the Book of Genesis). In being banished from Eden, Adam and Eve have been excluded from a life of easeful joy and are entering a life of hardship and death which will set the pattern for humankind until the coming of Christ. Although the 'World was all before them' and they seem free to choose their own destiny ('guided' by 'Providence'), they are leaving Paradise, entering into a fallen world and initiating a history of 'sin'. Thus they enter this bereft world and history with little enthusiasm: 'with wand'ring steps and slow'. Although the opening of Wordsworth's *Prelude* alludes strongly to Milton's ending, it transforms it into a claim that the present world is a paradise. Wordsworth represents the 'earth' – the natural world – as a place of 'liberty' rather than of banishment from Eden. Wordsworth cannot go astray (as Adam and Eve are supposed to have done) because wherever he wanders in this world he is at home. Thus *The Prelude* transforms Milton's ending into a new beginning by resisting the orthodox Christian thought which shapes Milton's conception of the relationship between human beings and the world. For Wordsworth, the natural world is itself a paradise: we have not been banished from Eden because it is all around us; we are not fallen creatures in need of the guidance of Providence, but can choose to follow even a 'wandering cloud' because we cannot miss our way.

Thus although Wordsworth's allusion to *Paradise Lost* indicates a reverence for Milton and a wish to join him as a canonical poet, there is also a sense in which Wordsworth's allusion stresses his departure from Milton's traditional Christian outlook. Allusion can therefore signal differences as well as allegiances between poets. In fact, Wordsworth's allusion to Milton's greatest epic poem at the opening of his own autobiographical epic suggests that he is seeking to emulate Milton. Wordsworth is striving to equal or surpass the greatest achievement of the poet he most admires.[2] Allusion can, then, signal rivalry between poets as well as affiliation.

■ Influences and Echoes

Just as many contemporary artists – film makers, pop and rock musicians – often talk of the influences which have gone into the development of their individual style, many critics of poetry are keen to trace a poet's 'influences'. Although almost anything could be said to influence an author or a particular text, 'critics now most often use the term to designate the affiliative relations between past and present literary texts and/or their authors'.[3] This notion of influence involves the idea that poets consciously allude to the poets they admire and wish – to a limited extent, at least – to imitate. But influence may also entail unwilling, unconscious or accidental reference by one poet to another – influxes from other texts which the poet does not notice or cannot avoid.

Keats was perhaps the most self-conscious poet of all in terms of his relationships to previous poets. In his letters and poems he repeatedly outlined his ambition to be 'among the English poets', and he set himself programmes of reading and writing which would constitute his poetic apprenticeship. Several of his poems' titles announce their relationship to previous poets and poems, and several use quotations from other poets' texts as epigraphs. The very texture of Keats's language is rich with reworkings of the language of other poets. This is made apparent by the annotations of scholars such as Miriam Allott in her edition of *The Poems of John Keats* (1970). One of the most interesting poems in this respect is 'Ode to Psyche' (1820), the first of Keats's five great odes written in 1819:

> O Goddess! hear these tuneless numbers, wrung
>   By sweet enforcement and remembrance dear,
> And pardon that thy secrets should be sung
>   Even into thine own soft-conched ear;
> Surely I dreamt to-day, or did I see   5
>   The winged Psyche with awaken'd eyes?

---

[2] For a sustained enquiry into the poetic interrelations between *The Prelude* and *Paradise Lost*, see Robin Jarvis, *Wordsworth, Milton and the Theory of Poetic Relations* (London: Macmillan, 1991). The first half of Jarvis's book provides a useful critical survey of most of the theories we will be discussing in this chapter, and develops a theory of its own based on a re-reading of Freud.

[3] Louis A. Renza, 'Influence', in Frank Lentricchia and Thomas McLaughlin, eds, *Critical Terms for Literary Study* (Chicago: University of Chicago Press, 1990), 186–202 (186).

I wander'd in a forest thoughtlessly,
   And, on the sudden, fainting with surprise,
Saw two fair creatures, couched side by side
    In deepest grass, beneath the whisp'ring roof   10
    Of leaves and trembled blossoms, where there ran
      A brooklet, scarce espied:
'Mid hush'd, cool-rooted flowers, fragant-eyed,
   Blue, silver-white, and budded Tyrian,
They lay calm-breathing on the bedded grass;   15
    Their arms embraced, and their pinions too;
    Their lips touch'd not, but had not bade adieu,
As if disjoined by soft-handed slumber,
And ready still past kisses to outnumber
    At tender eye-dawn of aurorean love: 20
      The winged boy I knew;
But who wast thou, O happy, happy dove?
    His Psyche true!

O latest born and loveliest vision far
    Of all Olympus' fading hierarchy!   25
Fairer than Phoebe's sapphire-region'd star,
    Or Vesper, amorous glow-worm of the sky;
Fairer than these, though temple thou hast none,
    Nor altar heap'd with flowers;
Nor virgin-choir to make delicious moan   30
    Upon the midnight hours;
No voice, no lute, no pipe, no incense sweet
    From chain-swung censer teeming;
No shrine, no grove, no oracle, no heat
    Of pale-mouth'd prophet dreaming.   35

O brightest! though too late for antique vows,
    Too, too late for the fond believing lyre,
When holy were the haunted forest boughs,
    Holy the air, the water, and the fire;
Yet even in these days so far retir'd   40
    From happy pieties, thy lucent fans,
    Fluttering among the faint Olympians,
I see, and sing, by my own eyes inspired.
    So let me be thy choir, and make a moan
      Upon the midnight hours;   45
Thy voice, thy lute, thy pipe, thy incense sweet
    From swinged censer teeming;

Thy shrine, thy grove, thy oracle, thy heat
    Of pale-mouth'd prophet dreaming.

Yes, I will be thy priest, and build a fane   50
    In some untrodden region of my mind,
Where branched thoughts, new grown with pleasant pain,
    Instead of pines shall murmur in the wind:
Far, far around shall those dark-cluster'd trees
    Fledge the wild-ridged mountains steep by steep;   55
And there by zephyrs, streams, and birds, and bees,
    The moss-lain Dryads shall be lull'd to sleep;
And in the midst of this wide quietness
    A rosy sanctuary will I dress
With the wreath'd trellis of a working brain,   60
    With buds, and bells, and stars without a name,
With all the gardener Fancy e'er could feign,
    Who breeding flowers, will never breed the same:
And there shall be for thee all soft delight
    That shadowy thought can win,   65
A bright torch, and a casement ope at night,
    To let the warm Love in!

An understanding of some of the central allusions in this poem would appear necessary if we are to be able to understand it at all. As a bare minimum, we probably need to know something about Psyche and the 'winged boy'. Less central, perhaps, are the other allusive names: Tyrian, Olympus, Phoebe, Vesper, zephyrs and Dryads. Keats clearly expected his reader to understand what these names and figures represent, and most of his readers would have gone through the classical education which was standard for men of a certain class in the early nineteenth century. Keats himself did not have such a classical education and learned about these things through second-hand sources – through translations and classical dictionaries.

Very few readers today have a classical education. We can no longer be assumed automatically to recognise these names and recall their significance. Most editions of Keats will present some information about these figures, but if you were using an edition which did not, your best recourse would be to a Classical Dictionary, to *Brewer's Dictionary of Phrase and Fable*, or to the Internet. The editors of the *Norton Anthology of Poetry* give the following information about Psyche: 'In Greek legend, Psyche (meaning "soul") was loved in secret and in darkness by Cupid, the "wingéd" son of the goddess Venus. After many trials Psyche was united with Cupid in immortality' (p. 845). They paraphrase lines 24–25 as referring to Psyche as the 'last of the deities to be added to the company of the Greek Olympian gods' (p. 846). As for the other names, we are given the following information: Tyrian = 'Purple or red, as in the "royal" dye made in ancient Tyre'; Phoebe = the moon; Vesper = the evening star; zephyrs = breezes; Dryads = tree nymphs. Having had these allusions decoded in this way, try reading the poem again in order to see how this information affects your reading. What, for example, has become clearer to you?

With this poem, then, tracking down the story of the central figure (Psyche) in another text (Greek legend) allows some insight into the significance of the subject matter. It allows us to understand the speaker's encounter with the two lovers recorded in the first stanza and to see why Psyche, being the most recent of Olympian gods, has inspired no tradition of ritual worship. It is precisely the fact that she was deified 'too late for antique vows' (36) that allows the poet/speaker to promise that he will set up a new cult in worship of her in which he will be the sole devotee. Furthermore, the fact that Psyche means soul (hence the terms psychology and psychoanalysis) helps us to make sense of the last stanza, in which Keats vows to 'build a fane' (that is, a temple) to his goddess 'In some untrodden region of my mind' (50–51).

Yet above and beyond these explicit allusions whose decoding helps our understanding, the poem contains many references to other texts which, even if we do spot them, do not seem to yield any insight into its meaning but indicate, instead, the various influences which have affected its language. A scholarly editor such as Allott presents an editorial 'apparatus' for each poem which sometimes becomes as bulky as the poem itself. A good deal of her 'apparatus' for 'Ode to Psyche' is given over to spotting 'sources' and 'influences', including Lemprière's *Classical Dictionary* (1788), Apuleius's *The Golden Ass*, various Elizabethan writers, and Milton and Wordsworth. Although she identifies only one Wordsworthian influence, Allott makes good her claim about the Elizabethan and Miltonic influences by tracing five allusions to Milton, three to Spenser and one to Shakespeare and/or George Puttenham. She also suggests that there are allusions in the poem to Collins's 'Ode to Pity' – not to mention self-borrowings, several echoes of the translation of *The Golden Ass*, and the possibility that the imagery of the last stanza may derive 'from lectures on the structure of the brain given at St Thomas's Hospital' (*Poems of John Keats*, p. 519n). Keats's 'Ode to Psyche' thus emerges as a poem which is like the 'wreath'd trellis' of its last stanza – a trellis woven through and through with strands drawn from other texts.

Allott's annotative work is clearly driven by an enthusiasm for seeking out verbal similarities between texts. But although she is an avid literary detective, it is not clear what her assumptions are about the causes and consequences of such textual echoes. Thus at one point she claims that Keats's 'phrasing *suggests a recollection, possibly unconscious*, of Milton's "Nativity Ode" '. She says that Keats's 'mental region . . . *is reminiscent of* Psyche's resting-place in

Adlington's *Apuleius*'. Keats's language is said to be '*echoing* Spenser's "An Hymne in Honour of Love"'. And Keats's reference to Olympus's faded hierarchy '*probably recalled to him* Milton's description, with its repeated negatives, of the disappearance of the ancient Greek deities at the birth of Christ in the "Nativity Ode" 173–80' (pp. 516–21; emphases added). As our emphases indicate, there is some confusion in Allott's assumptions about the causes of these textual echoes. The use of terms like 'probably' indicates the speculative nature of this detection process. This is further complicated by the suggestion that some of Keats's 'recollections' might be 'unconscious' and that some of these connections might be produced (rather than discovered) by the reader (the *reader* may find a line in one poem 'reminiscent' of a line in another).

It is noteworthy that Allott never uses the term 'allusion' to describe the textual relations she discovers. This is perhaps because, as we have seen, allusion implies conscious intention on the part of the author. Whereas allusion is a poetic device, the notion of influence may include unwilling, unconscious and accidental influxes into a poem from other texts. The question of influence thus involves its own particular questions about intention and originality: not only do many elements in a text come from other texts, but we can never be sure whether its author consciously chose to include those elements. More radically still, our examination of Allott's scholarly work on Keats's poem allows us to ask whether the tracing of influential relations between texts may be produced by the reader rather than being an objective fact about the texts themselves.

John Hollander attempts to distinguish clearly between allusion and what he calls 'echoes between texts'. Allusion, for Hollander, is intentional and is meant to be explicit to the well-read reader: 'one cannot . . . allude unintentionally – an inadvertent allusion is a kind of solecism'. Echo, however, 'may be unconscious or inadvertent', and the reader is not expected to spot an echo or work out its significance.[4] Echoes of earlier texts are thus more elusive than allusions, and often have a more remote resemblance to their source. Many titles of twentieth-century novels are allusive: William Faulkner's *The Sound and the Fury* (1929), for instance, relies on the reader recognising that it is an allusion to a well-known speech by Macbeth describing life as 'a tale / Told by an idiot, full of sound and fury, / Signifying nothing' (*Macbeth* V.v. 25–29). One of the narrators of Faulkner's novel is mentally retarded, and his limited understanding of the events he observes controls the reader's response to and understanding of those events. As Hollander points out, it is the unquoted first half of the line that 'points to Faulkner's making the visionary idiot Benjy a significant narrator' (p. 106). In contrast with such explicit allusions, echoes

---

[4] John Hollander, *The Figure of Echo: A mode of allusion in Milton and after* (Berkeley: University of California Press, 1981), pp. 62, 64.

'can be maddeningly elusive'. Hollander examines I.A. Richards's 'overhearing of Tennyson's "Tithonus" sighing behind the first refrain line of William Empson's villanelle "Missing Dates" ' (p. 95):

> 'The waste remains, the waste remains and kills' (Empson)
> 'The woods decay, the woods decay and fall' (Tennyson).

As Hollander says, 'this rebound gives back neither word nor phrase, but instead a kind of cadence, involving phonemic and semantic elements, locked in a syntactic and metrical pattern' (p. 96). There is no suggestion here that the reader is intended to pick up this echo, or that it has any bearing on Empson's meaning.

Such textual echoes are quite different from the deliberate allusion Alexander Pope expects us to recognise in the line we quoted in Chapter 10 from his 'Epitaph for Sir Isaac Newton': 'God said, Let Newton be! and all was Light!' If you turn to the opening verses of the book of Genesis at the beginning of the Bible you will easily be able to identify this allusion: 'God said, Let there be light: and there was light' (1. 3). This is no casual echo but a highly meaningful (and potentially controversial) allusion which you could profitably spend some time analysing. What similarities does the allusion propose between God's creation of light and the scientific study of nature? And what an enormous compliment it is to compare God's creation of Newton with his original creation of the world, as if both were equally momentous events! In our discussion in Chapter 10 we cited this line to illustrate historical changes in the idea of nature and, having identified the allusion, you might now feel inspired to clarify its specific context by finding out what you can about Newton's particular discoveries about the prismatic composition of light. We might now want to say that Pope's line 'alludes' to this particular discovery, except that we are quite keen to reserve the term 'allusion' for inter-textual echoes. We would therefore prefer to say: 'Pope's allusion *refers* specifically to Newton's discoveries concerning the prismatic composition of light'. Texts *refer* to things in the real world; they only *allude* to other texts: we hope this example might explain why it could be important to maintain this distinction. In Chapter 10 we quoted this line in our discussion of the extra-literary contexts in which texts may be situated; questions of allusion and influence, which are our topic now, are concerned with their textual or inter-textual contexts.

The notions of allusion and echo imply that a literary text is at least partly made out of other literary texts, and that a significant part of the 'experience' which a poem is supposed to express is its author's experience of reading. In addition, they also entail a notion of a literary tradition and canon. Literature is seen as a self-enclosed, self-referring system into which individual writers insert themselves by referring to and revising the perceived great writers of the tradition. The status of the new writer is determined according to the way he or she relates to what has gone before: minor writers hand on the baton, while great writers radically reinterpret (Hollander, p. 73). Yet there are interesting problems and contradictions in these assumptions. First, as we have suggested above and will argue again more forcibly, the assumption that literature is a discrete, self-sustaining system existing and perpetuating itself independently from other kinds of discursive activity in society is untenable. Secondly, making authorial intention the directing agent of inter-literary relations serves to deflect attention away from two suggestive problems with the accounts of allusion and echo which we have traced: (1) the difficulty of being certain whether or not the author intended to refer to the previous text; (2) the possibility that inter-literary connections are created in the act of reading as much as in the act of writing. Although traditional accounts of inter-poetic relations seek to repress such possibilities, we will conclude this chapter by examining a more radical theory of 'intertextuality' which celebrates them. Before that, however, we wish to explore further the idea of the 'literary tradition'.

■ The Burden of the Past

Poet-critics such as Sir Philip Sidney (*Apology for Poetry*, 1595), Alexander Pope (*Essay on Criticism*, 1711) and T.S. Eliot ('Tradition and the Individual Talent', 1919) all claim that poets need to establish a relationship to the poetry of the past and that this will have wholly beneficial effects on their own poetry.[5] Thus past poetry becomes a benign 'influence' which will 'inspire' the modern poet. Most critical studies of influence used to assume the same. Walter Jackson Bate's *The Burden of the Past and the English Poet* (1971) challenged this assumption by arguing that poets might experience the poetry of the past as a 'burden' rather than an inspiration. Bate argues that this is a particularly (but not exclusively) modern anxiety, and discovers the first signs of its modern form in the late seventeenth century. The problem became acute for poets in the eighteenth century, since it was 'the first period in modern history to face the problem of what it means to come *immediately* after a great creative achievement'.[6] The great achievement with which eighteenth-century poets had to come to terms was the English Renaissance – a period in which Shakespeare's plays and Milton's *Paradise Lost* represent only the tip of the iceberg. The Renaissance writers themselves had not experienced the past as a

[5] See Sidney, *Prose Works*, p. 42; Pope, *An Essay on Criticism*, I, 189–200; Eliot, *Selected Prose*, pp. 21–30.
[6] Walter Jackson Bate, *The Burden of the Past and the English Poet* (London: Chatto & Windus, 1971), p. 12.

burden: Sidney felt that the English language was virtually an untapped poetic resource, and the precedents he looked to were geographically and historically remote enough to be digested as 'food' for a wholly new poetic 'body'. By contrast, the task of the Restoration and early-eighteenth-century poets was to try to create their own 'space' after the colossal achievement of the Renaissance. As Dryden put it, Shakespeare and his contemporaries seemed to have exhausted the major possibilities of dramatic poetry, leaving nothing to their 'children':

> We 'acknowledge them our fathers', but they have already spent their estates before these 'came to their children's hand'. As a result our present choice is 'either not to write at all, or to attempt some other way'.
>
> (Bate, p. 26, quoting Dryden)

The creative solution of poets such as Dryden and Pope was to return to the Classical poets in order to become more 'Classical' than the Renaissance (which made a rather freewheeling use of the classics). Influenced by French Neoclassicism, the English Neoclassical poets and critics stressed the 'Classical' virtues of order, propriety and decorum. Thus by 'leapfrogging' over their immediate predecessors, the Neoclassical poets were able to draw on their 'ancestors' in order to distance themselves from their 'fathers' (see Bate, pp. 18–22). This does not mean that Dryden and Pope ignored the Renaissance, but that they creatively responded to and 're-read' it. Pope's poetry alludes to Shakespeare and Milton, but adapts them to his early-eighteenth-century needs;[7] Dryden had already anticipated him by rewriting selected bits of his English predecessors – Chaucer, Shakespeare, Donne – in the 'improved' Neoclassical style.

Although the Romantic period is often thought of as breaking with the Neoclassical reverence for tradition in favour of originality, the Romantics were in fact equally concerned to insert themselves into a poetic tradition. The difference is that they assumed that some English poets (Shakespeare and Milton) had written poetry which had equalled or even surpassed the poetry of Classical Greece and Rome. This led to a rejection of Neoclassical poets like Pope in favour of poets such as Shakespeare and Milton, who were assumed to have emulated rather than merely imitated the poets of the past. But in doing this, the Romantic poets had to face up to the achievements of the Renaissance rather than sidestep them as the Neoclassical poets had done. What is more, the Romantic poets were, by definition, even more belated than the Neoclassical poets. And the Romantic poets became especially conscious of the burden of the past because Romanticism, for the first time in history, made originality the necessary ideal for poetry (Bate, pp. 106–7). Rather than imitating the

---

[7] See Reuben A. Brower, *Alexander Pope: The poetry of allusion* (Oxford: Oxford University Press, 1959).

poets of the past, the Romantic poets set themselves the task of emulating them (in the same way as they felt that Renaissance poets had emulated the Classical poets). This burden and self-imposed ideal forced the Romantic poets into developing extraordinary creative solutions. Bate argues that the Romantic poets, by finding these new creative spaces for themselves, allowed themselves to believe that they imaginatively joined with the poets of the past whom they admired.

Just as the Neoclassical poets had sought to carve out their own space, so too did the Romantics open up a kind of double territory which seemed to contain wholly new poetic possibilities: the natural world and the 'inner nature' of the human mind. The sense of release which Wordsworth celebrates at the beginning of *The Prelude* exemplifies the Romantic exploration of these two territories as mirror-images of one another. Wordsworth naturalises the old idea of poetic inspiration by saying that the 'breeze / That blows from the green fields' (1–2) upon his body awakens a 'corresponding mild creative breeze' (43) within himself. In the 'Prospectus' to *The Excursion* (1814), Wordsworth articulates his poetic ambitions and assumptions, telling us that he seeks to dwell on and in 'the individual Mind that keeps her own / Inviolate retirement' and explaining that 'the Mind of Man' is 'the main region' of his song (19–20, 40–41). Bate cites 'Ode to Psyche' as Keats's analogous attempt to appropriate for himself this new Poetic territory:

> Yes, I will be thy priest, and build a fane
> In some untrodden region of my mind (50–51).

■ The Anxiety of Influence

Bate accepts at face value the Romantics' imaginative solution to their problem and thus emerges as something of a Romantic thinker himself. This is perhaps why he has virtually nothing to say about how post-Romantic poetry coped with the added burden of Romantic poetry itself. Harold Bloom, who became the foremost critic of poetic influence with a series of important books in the 1970s, makes crucial transformations of Bate's position which allow him to account for the way poets continue to create imaginative space for themselves within and after Romanticism.[8] Rather than imagining the poet as gazing on past poets with loving admiration and emulation, Bloom takes up Bate's use of paternal metaphors in order to argue that the relationship between poetic 'sons' and 'fathers' is analogous to the Oedipal struggle which Freud claims

---

[8] See Harold Bloom, *The Anxiety of Influence* (Oxford: Oxford University Press, 1973), *A Map of Misreading*, (Oxford: Oxford University Press, 1975), and *Poetry and Repression: Revisionism from Blake to Stevens* (New Haven, CT: Yale University Press, 1976).

shapes father–son relationships in real life. In other words, for the 'son' to overcome the debilitating and inhibiting presence of the 'father' (the precursor poet) he has symbolically to 'murder' him and take his place. It must be remembered that, as in Freud's own thought, such struggles and desires are largely unconscious, and that an excessive love of the precursors may work to mask unconscious hostility. And since this struggle for identity and originality is a psychologically violent one, only 'strong' poets emerge from it with the illusion of originality, while 'weak' poets remain thoroughly traditional and conventional.

Like Bate, Bloom believes (or initially believed) that this scenario became most acute in the Romantic period.[9] Yet he also posits that Milton's *Paradise Lost* gains its supreme power through its successful struggle with such mighty precursors as Moses and Spenser.[10] In fact, *Paradise Lost* becomes a poem which explicitly dramatises the dilemma and strategies of the belated poet in the figure of Satan who, in his struggle with God (the original creator), attempts to resist the fact of his own inevitable belatedness through the construction of a powerful myth of the self and its origins:

> . . . who saw
> When this creation was? Remember'st thou
> Thy making, while the maker gave thee being?
> We know no time when we were not as now;
> Know none before us, self-begot, self-raised
> By our own quickening power . . . (V, 856–61)

For Bloom, Satan becomes the archetype of the strong poet (see *A Map of Misreading*, p. 37). Just as Satan creatively misreads his belated relationship to God, so do belated poets misread their precursors in order to claim originality for themselves.

Although it might initially seem unattractive and improbable, Bloom's theory leads to persuasive readings of poems and of the history of poetry which transform our sense of what poetry is and how it works. For Bloom, poems – or at least what he calls 'strong poems' – are not about poetic themes (such as love or daffodils), nor even about themselves, but 'are necessarily about *other poems*; a poem is a response to a poem' (*Map of Misreading*, p. 18). This response is not signalled by verbal resemblances: instead, a strong poem achieves its power through rewriting the past poem in its own terms. This is how the poet achieves his or her own 'individual voice'. Thus the New Critical

---

[9] Bloom's extension of his theory backwards to include pre-Enlightenment canonical texts can be seen in his *Ruin the Sacred Truths: Poetry and belief from the Bible to the present* (Cambridge MA: Harvard University Press, 1989).

[10] See 'Milton and His Precursors' in Bloom, *A Map of Misreading*, pp. 125–43.

attempt to understand a poem as a thing in itself, an 'autotelic' object whose 'telos' (purpose and meaning) is internal to itself, is quite misleading.

Keats's letters and poetry reveal that he had a strong sense of his own belatedness in respect to the poets of the past. An unashamedly ambitious poet who sought to be included among the English poets after his death, Keats was acutely aware of the problems involved with that ambition. These problems were less to do with doubts about his own capacity than with his recognition of the achievements of past poetry. As he matured as a poet, Keats developed a peculiar 'love-hate' relationship with Milton in particular. This can be seen in the rapid transformation of his response to Milton in letters written during the period of composition of his epic fragment *The Fall of Hyperion*:

> Shakespeare and the paradise Lost every day become greater wonders to me – I look upon fine Phrases like a lover. (14 August 1819)

> the Paradise Lost becomes a greater wonder. The more I know what my diligence may in time probably effect; the more does my heart distend with Pride and Obstinacy. (24 August 1819)

Here Keats exhibits both love for his precursors and a sense of growing pride in his belief that he may come to emulate them. On 21 September 1819, however, he says that he has abandoned *The Fall of Hyperion* because 'there were too many Miltonic **inversions** in it'. In a journal-letter in the same month, he writes:

> I have but lately stood on my guard against Milton. Life to him would be death to me. Miltonic verse cannot be written but in the vein of art – I wish to devote myself to another sensation.[11]

This startling turn against Milton seems to act out Bloom's claim that 'Poetic influence, in its first phase, is not to be distinguished from love, though it will shade soon enough into revisionary strife' (*Map of Misreading*, p. 12).

Keats was an even more belated poet than Wordsworth precisely because he faced not only the colossal tradition which Wordsworth encountered, but also Wordsworth's own achievement. Keats's extraordinary move, in the face of this, was to return to Greek mythology in order to create a mental landscape which was different from the Christianising Milton and the naturalising Wordsworth. Keats uses mythological figures not because they are 'poetic', but in order to re-explore the dynamics of poetic creativity. At the height of his ambition, for example, Keats twice attempted to write an epic – *Hyperion* and *The Fall of Hyperion* – based on the Greek myth about the overthrow of the original gods (the Titans) by a new race of gods (the Olympians). He focused his poems on the displacement of the old sun-god Hyperion by the new sun-god Apollo. Since Apollo is also the god of music and poetry in Greek

[11] Keats, *Letters of John Keats*, pp. 277, 281, 292, 325–6.

myth, Apollo's struggle with Hyperion can be seen as a figure for Keats's own struggle as an aspiring poet with his precursors. Thus the poem resembles *Paradise Lost* in the sense that it is about the struggle between two opposing groups of supernatural beings which focuses on the encounter between an original creator and an ambitious, revolutionary poet.

Keats employs the Greek myth of Psyche for similar ends in 'Ode to Psyche', in which – Bloom posits – he successfully cleared an imaginative space for himself and attained poetic maturity. In an essay called 'In the Shadow of Milton', Bloom argues that 'The first of [Keats's] great odes, the "Ode to Psyche," takes belatedness as its overt subject and struggles with the shadows of Milton and Wordsworth' (*Map of Misreading*, p. 152). Bloom suggests that Keats's voyeurism in the first stanza is a kind of internalised identification with Satan, who spies on Adam and Eve in Book IV of *Paradise Lost*. It is important that Keats sees and recognises Psyche with his own eyes because she is to be his Muse figure. The poem is addressed to and inspired by her and, as the ending promises, this is simply the preparation for more poetry to come. Psyche is an appropriate and enabling Muse for Keats because, just as he is a belated poet, so Psyche is a belated goddess – she is the 'latest born' who now outshines 'all Olympus' faded hierarchy' (25). Keats's recognition of his 'true muse' is thus 'a moment of poetic self-recognition' (*Map of Misreading*, pp. 153–4). By emphasising, through its series of negatives, that no one has ever sung for Psyche, that no 'pale-mouth'd prophet' has ever 'dreamed' of her, the second stanza clears the decks, as it were, for Keats to step forward not as belated but as a first-comer to offer to be her pale-mouthed poet-prophet. This is achieved in the third stanza which, emphasising her lateness ('Too, too late for the fond believing lyre'), cancels all the negatives of the previous stanza in order for Keats to claim that he is inspired by his 'own eyes' (or by the fact that they allow him to see his 'own' Muse):

> I see, and sing, by my own eyes inspired.
>   So let me be thy choir, and make a moan
>   Upon the midnight hours;
> Thy voice, thy lute, thy pipe, thy incense sweet
>   From swinged censer teeming;
> Thy shrine, thy grove, thy oracle, thy heat
>   Of pale-mouth'd prophet dreaming. (43–49)

In the last stanza, as we have already mentioned, the poem employs the Romantic metaphor of an internalised nature in order to discover an 'untrodden region' within and out of which to create poetry. For Bloom, this is a particularly extraordinary example of internalisation because it almost makes us forget that 'this landscape, and this oxymoronic intensity, are wholly inside his psyche' (*Map of Misreading*, pp. 154–5):

> Yes, I will be thy priest, and build a fane
>   In some untrodden region of my mind,
> Where branched thoughts, new-grown with pleasant pain,
>   Instead of pines shall murmur in the wind:
> Far, far around shall those dark-cluster'd trees
>   Fledge the wild-ridged mountains steep by steep;
> And there by zephyrs, streams, and birds, and bees,
>   The moss-lain Dryads shall be lull'd to sleep . . . (50–57)

Bloom suggests that Keats here is internalising a Wordsworthian landscape in a way which seems wholly successful and that Keats has therefore coped with Wordsworth's inhibiting influence. Nonetheless, it remains a figurative strategy, a necessary fiction, and Keats's strength is that he is not deluded by his own imaginative illusion. The poem's last lines end not by claiming that there really is such a place in his mind but by implying that it is a fantasy place in which poetry 'will' and 'shall' be produced in some unspecified future:

> And in the midst of this wide quietness
>   A rosy sanctuary *will I* dress
> With the wreath'd trellis of a working brain,
>   With buds, and bells, and stars without a name,
> With all the gardener Fancy *e'er could* feign,
>   Who breeding flowers, will never breed the same:
> And *there shall be* for thee all soft delight
>   That shadowy thought can win,
> A bright torch, and a casement ope at night,
>   To let the warm Love in! (58–67; emphases added)

These lines can seem at once wholly persuasive in their apparent triumph over belatedness and, as the tenses reveal, quite self-conscious of their own rhetorical feigning. As Bloom puts it,

> There is past time here, in the anterior feignings of the gardener Fancy, and there is a promised future, . . . but clearly there is no present time whatsoever. . . . but even as there is no present moment so there is no place of presence, nor perhaps will there ever be.
>
> (*Map of Misreading*, p. 155)

Yet this necessary fiction is effective. In anticipating the poetic activity to come, the poem itself becomes an example of that poetry. This poem's 'tuneless numbers' are already addressed to Psyche, already an example of this poet's service to his Muse.

In his turn, Keats (along with Shelley) represented yet another strong poet for subsequent poets to cope with. Each new poet who comes along has to find his or her own strategy for coming to terms with this ever-increasing belatedness. But because finding a poetic voice is achieved though 'misreading' precursors, it would seem that there is always scope for the really strong poet to succeed. Yet Bloom believes that only a few poets survive the recognition of their own belatedness and achieve the status of strong poets. This is partly because the tradition continues to accumulate and the institutions of education and criticism continue to proliferate, making it harder and harder to develop successful strategies for becoming original. Thirty years ago, Bloom found contemporary American poetry to be in only a precariously healthy state: 'Even the poets I most admire, John Ashbery and A.R. Ammons, are rendered somewhat problematic by a cultural situation of such belatedness that literary survival itself seems fairly questionable' (*Map of Misreading*, p. 38). Fortunately, like most predictions of impending doom, Bloom's anxiety about the future of poetry seems to have been unfounded. In the last thirty years, American poetry – along with poetry throughout the English-speaking world and beyond – has continued to flourish and poets, strong and not so strong, continue to fashion their individual voices out of their engagement with the poetry of the past.

■ A Poetry of Their Own?[12]

Bloom is wholly committed to the notion of poetic tradition and the canon of great poets. His thought knowingly resists and challenges the various ways in which the very notions of tradition and canon have come increasingly under attack in recent decades. For Bloom, the ongoing production of literature itself depends on the existence of a canon:

> What happens if one tries to write, or to teach, or to think, or even to read without the sense of a tradition?
>
> Why, nothing at all happens, just nothing. You cannot write or teach or think or even read without imitation, and what you imitate is what another person has done, that person's writing or teaching or thinking or reading.
>
> (*Map of Misreading*, p. 32)

The fact that this process has taken place for twenty-five hundred years since the Greeks first took Homer as an educational resource suggests to Bloom the silliness of 'passionate declarations that poetry should be liberated from the academy' (p. 34). To believe that poetry, and culture in general, is a matter of the internal life of individuals is to be a naive reader of the Romantic poets.

---

[12] The title of this section is an allusion to Elaine Showalter, *A Literature of Their Own* (Princeton, NJ: Princeton University Press, 1977), a pioneering critical work in the feminist attempt to argue for a distinct female literary tradition. For a feminist account of women's poetry and its history, see Jan Montefiore, *Feminism and Poetry: Language, experience, identity in women's writing* (London: Pandora, 1987).

In arguing that 'everyone who now reads and writes in the West, of whatever racial background, sex or ideological camp, is still a son or daughter of Homer' (p. 33), Bloom is responding to the various politically orientated critiques of the canon which have emerged from black, feminist and Marxist criticism over the last few decades. But although it is reductive and inaccurate to describe the canon as made up solely of the writing of 'dead, white, middle-class men' (as is sometimes said), it is nonetheless true that writing by white males is predominant in literary histories and academic syllabuses. Some feminist critics argue that Bloom's theory of the making of strong poets through competitive struggle works to perpetuate critical neglect of women writers through a kind of 'patriarchal blindness'.[13] Louis A. Renza summarises the argument as follows: 'surely his oedipal or father–son reformulation of textual relations presupposes a "sexist" or fixed Freudian paradigm of Western literary history that minimises and misreads the situation of women writers in this same tradition?' (in Lentricchia and McLaughlin, *Critical Terms for Literary Study*, p. 197).

Sandra Gilbert and Susan Gubar's *The Madwoman in the Attic* (1979) is often assumed to be just such a feminist critique of Bloom. In fact, Gilbert and Gubar claim that 'Bloom's model of literary history . . . is not a recommendation for but an analysis of the patriarchal poetics (and attendant anxieties) which underlie our culture's chief literary movements.' Bloom analyses and explains a fact which other theorists ignore: that 'Western literary history is overwhelmingly male – or, more accurately, patriarchal'.[14] Although this is a useful insight, we would suggest that its focus is slightly askew. While Bloom is not recommending a patriarchal poetics, he *is* recommending a 'strong' poetics. Bloom is primarily interested in 'strong' poetry because he finds it powerfully moving – because it produces sublime effects. He says that he believes that 'Milton's Satan . . . remains the greatest really Modern or post-Enlightenment poet in the language', because 'I respond to Satan's speeches more strongly than to any other poetry I know' (*Map of Misreading*, p. 37).

Bloom is not particularly interested in the sex of the poet but, rather, in his or her capacity to assume and produce 'Satanic power'. He uses Freud's account of Oedipal relations between fathers and sons as an *analogy* for the relationship between poets. Bloom seems to have no qualms about claiming that certain women poets have achieved the status of strong poets within the tradition – his repeated example is Emily Dickinson. In his account of the way strong American poets knowingly write 'In the Shadow of Emerson', Bloom chooses to examine Dickinson's 'Because I Could Not Stop For Death'

---

[13] See Annette Kolodny, 'A Map for Rereading: Or, gender and the interpretation of literary texts' in *New Literary History: A journal of theory and interpretation* (1990) 11, pp. 451–67, 587–92.

[14] Sandra Gilbert and Susan Gubar, *The Madwoman in the Attic* (New Haven: Yale University Press, 1979), pp. 45–6.

alongside poems by Walt Whitman and Wallace Stevens 'because they are as strong as any written by the strongest of our poets' (*Map of Misreading*, p. 177). In fact, Bloom makes claims for Dickinson which surpass anything he says about such male poets:

> Her stance is rarely belated, because of her exquisite good fortune in having only precursors who were merely male. . . . What can our map of misreading do to or for her, or does her originality extend so far that she passes beyond our revisionary model? Often she does . . . (p. 184).

Gilbert and Gubar's *The Madwoman in the Attic* can be read as a hugely extended account of how Dickinson – given her personal circumstances and the general circumstance of women poets in the nineteenth century – came to achieve such poetic power. Although they are concerned primarily with nineteenth-century women writers, Gilbert and Gubar's sense that literary writing is enabled (or sometimes disabled) by tradition leads them to examine the work and fate of women writers prior to the nineteenth century. They argue that the discovery of a female literary tradition was important for women poets because the image of women presented in male-authored texts was disabling for the aspiring woman writer. Rather than suffering an anxiety of influence, they suggest, women writers suffered an anxiety of authorship which the discovery of predecessors could help to alleviate. Virginia Woolf believed that the greatest difficulty facing women novelists in the early nineteenth century was not the discouragement and criticism of men, but the fact that

> they had no tradition behind them, or one so short and partial that it was of little help. For we think back through our mothers if we are women. It is useless to go to the great men writers for help, however much one may go to them for pleasure.[15]

But although women writers played a significant part in the establishment of the novel as a serious literary genre in the eighteenth century, women poets had a much harder time of it. The fact that so few women poets succeeded in making an impact within the patriarchal literary establishment which actively resisted them meant that women poets in the nineteenth century could look to no sustained tradition of women's poetry.[16] As Elizabeth Barrett Browning wrote, 'England has had many learned women, not merely readers but writers of the learned languages, and yet where are the poetesses? . . . I look everywhere for grandmothers and see none' (quoted in Gilbert and Gubar,

---

[15] Virginia Woolf, *A Room of One's Own* (London: Grafton, 1977), p. 34. The whole of this short text is of immense interest to students of the history of women's fiction and poetry.

[16] Recent feminist-inspired scholarship has begun to reconstruct a female poetic tradition. This has resulted in anthologies such as Germaine Greer, *et al.* eds, *Kissing the Rod: An anthology of seventeenth-century women's verse* (London: Virago, 1988), and Ashfield, *Romantic Women Poets.*

Madwoman in the Attic, pp. 539–40). Gilbert and Gubar argue that the poetry of even the most prominent women poets of the nineteenth century tended to comply with an 'aesthetics of renunciation' as a way of coping with their exclusion from the patriarchal tradition. Barrett Browning's verse-novel *Aurora Leigh* (1856), however, can be more confidently seen as 'an epic of feminist self-affirmation' whose 'compromise aesthetic of service conceals (but does not obliterate) Aurora Leigh's revolutionary impulses' (*Madwoman in the Attic*, pp. 575–9). *Aurora Leigh* is a first-person autobiographical account of the development of a female poet in relation to the historical and ideological contexts of nineteenth-century Europe. As such, it is both a fictionalised autobiography of Barrett Browning herself and a self-conscious reworking of the literary tradition. While Barrett Browning admired several female poets from the immediate past, none of them could provide a precedent for her large-scale narrative poem of more than 10 000 lines. Unable to find pioneering 'grandmothers', she drew on and transformed the tradition which was available to her. Most obviously, *Aurora Leigh* is a female version of or alternative to Wordsworth's account of his own development as a poet in *The Prelude* – which was first published in 1850.[17] It was also influenced by narrative poems by Byron, Tennyson and Arthur Hugh Clough, and by contemporary novels written by both men and women. Indeed, *Aurora Leigh* has been likened to a patchwork quilt of 'Romantic and Victorian texts reworked from a woman's perspective'.[18]

In writing *Aurora Leigh*, Barrett Browning confirmed her status as a major Victorian poet and became herself an enabling pioneer for subsequent women poets. As Gilbert and Gubar put it, 'Barrett Browning, while looking everywhere for "grandmothers," became herself the grand mother of all modern women poets in England and America. Certainly, she was the spiritual mother of Emily Dickinson' (p. 580). It is generally thought that the 'Foreign Lady' in Dickinson's 'I think I was Enchanted' (*c.* 1862) refers to Barrett Browning:

> I think I was enchanted
> When first a sombre Girl –
> I read that Foreign Lady –
> The Dark – felt beautiful –
>
> And whether it was noon at night –   5
> Or only Heaven – at Noon –
> For very Lunacy of Light
> I had not power to tell –

---

[17] For the parallels and differences between *Aurora Leigh* and *The Prelude*, see Kerry McSweeney's introduction to Barrett Browning, *Aurora Leigh* (Oxford: Oxford University Press, 1993), pp. xvi–xvii, xxvi–xxvii.

[18] See Cora Kaplan's introduction to Barrett Browning, *Aurora Leigh and Other Poems* (London: The Women's Press, 1978), pp. 5–36.

The Bees – became as Butterflies –
The Butterflies – as Swans –   10
Approached – and spurned the narrow Grass –
And just the meanest Tunes

That Nature murmured to herself
To keep herself in Cheer –
I took for Giants – practising   15
Titanic Opera –

The days – to Mighty Metres slept –
The Homeliest – adorned
As if unto a Jubilee
'Twere suddenly confirmed –   20

I could not have defined the change –
Conversion of the Mind
Like Sanctifying in the Soul –
Is witnessed – not explained –

'Twas a Divine Insanity –   25
The Danger to be Sane
Should I again experience
'Tis Antidote to turn –

To Tomes of solid Witchcraft –
Magicians be asleep –   30
But Magic – hath an Element
Like Deity to keep –

This poem presents the effect of reading Barrett Browning on Dickinson as if it
were a poet's version of St Paul's conversion on the road to Damascus. The
world is changed utterly into poetic sublimity and the sounds of nature are
transformed into Titanic opera and poetry. Yet Dickinson's poem is quite dis-
similar to the poetry of Barrett Browning. Dickinson is inspired by her precur-
sor not to imitate in a weak way but more powerfully to experience and
articulate her own unique poetic vision.[19]

[19] For a discussion which questions or complicates the idea that Dickinson straightforwardly
responded to Barrett Browning as a benign influence, see Betsy Erkkila, *The Wicked Sisters*:
Women poets, literary history and discord (Oxford: Oxford University Press, 1992), pp. 68–
79. Erkkila challenges the general feminist model of women poets as a supportive sisterhood or
as a line of mother–daughter relations: 'this study seeks to reclaim women's literature and women's
literary history as a site of dissension, contingency, and ongoing struggle rather than a separate
space of some untroubled and essentially cooperative accord among women' (pp. 3–4).

Ellen Moers's *Literary Women* (1976) argues that Dickinson was relatively poorly read in the male American tradition available to her and that 'Instead she read and reread every Anglo-American woman writer of her time'.[20] Yet this emphasis on Dickinson's reading of women's writing, though important, is not the whole story.[21] Gilbert and Gubar stress that Dickinson was inspired by the novels of authors such as the Brontës and George Eliot, but they also point out her reading of the line of male poets from Shakespeare to Emerson. It is clear, then, that Dickinson did not write entirely within a female tradition. She drew on the dominant male tradition as well as on the fragmented tradition of women writers which was available to her. In forging her own unique and powerful poetic voice in this way, she helped to make possible the tradition of women's poetry in North America and Britain which flourished in the twentieth century. Clearly, as Bloom argues, nothing happens without a tradition. But what Bloom fails to recognise is that there are *traditions* rather than a single tradition. Black and women poets in the English-speaking world do write in relation to the tradition which began with Homer – as the poetry of the Caribbean poet Derek Walcott exemplifies – but they also write within and out of other traditions which the mainstream Anglo-American tradition has largely ignored. Yet we need to recognise that these different traditions overlap and interact with each other in productive ways. Just as no poem is an island, no tradition is an island either.

■ The Poetics and Politics of Intertextuality

The term 'intertextuality' was introduced into critical discourse by Julia Kristeva and became widely known in Anglophone countries through translations of Roland Barthes. Intertextuality is sometimes used as an umbrella term for all the different ways in which texts interrelate with each other (allusion, imitation, influence, parody, and so on). In this wider sense, intertextuality has been known and thought about in different ways from Plato onwards.[22] Yet in Kristeva's and Barthes's essays, intertextuality represents a radical break with such notions. The post-structuralist thought which Barthes represents understands 'text' in a much wider sense than literature or even writing in general,

---

[20] Ellen Moers, *Literary Women* (London: The Women's Press, 1978), p. 61.

[21] For a thorough account of Dickinson's reading, see Jack L. Capps, *Emily Dickinson's Reading* (Cambridge, MA: Harvard University Press, 1966).

[22] For a succinct history of intertextuality in this wider sense, see Judith Still and M. Worton, eds, *Intertextuality: Theories and practices* (Manchester: Manchester University Press, 1990), pp. 1–44. For theoretical reflections on influence and intertextuality, see Clayton and Rothstein, 'Figures in the Corpus: Theories of Influence and Intertextuality', in Jay Clayton and E. Rothstein, eds, *Influence and Intertextuality in Literary History* (Madison: University of Wisconsin Press, 1991), pp. 3–36.

expanding it to include all kinds of language use – written documents, everyday speech, songs, advertisements, and so on. In this sense, we live in a text-saturated environment. And because language gets endlessly recycled through this environment, our words have always already been used elsewhere. To take an obvious instance: whenever we say 'I love you' we are using a phrase which has been iterated countless times and gains its modern resonance through its use in films, songs, soap operas, and so on. It is this fact which allows us to use the phrase meaningfully, to know when and how it should be used, and to interpret its significance. But this also means that we cannot use the phrase innocently – it always comes loaded with associations from the ways it is used in our culture.

For Barthes, literary texts can be understood as a weaving together of such culturally and socially saturated words and phrases into unique combinations:

> the Text [is] . . . woven entirely with citations, references, echoes, cultural languages (what language is not?), antecedent or contemporary, which cut across it through and through in a vast stereophony. The intertextual . . . is not to be confused with some origin of the text: to try to find the 'sources', the 'influences' of a work, is to fall in with the myth of filiation; the citations which go to make up a text are anonymous, untraceable, and yet already read: they are quotations without inverted commas.[23]

This description of the intertextual nature of texts is clearly not to be confused with the kinds of literary relations we have traced above: in this theory 'the citations which go to make up a text are anonymous, untraceable'. Any text – a poem, say – can be seen as 'a tissue of quotations drawn from the innumerable centres of culture' (p. 146), shot through with other kinds of discourse (everyday speech, philosophy, science, social rituals, religious doctrine, and so on). One of the effects of this is radically to dissolve the boundaries between literary and non-literary texts. Literature is no longer seen as a self-contained, self-referring discourse. Another effect is, as Barthes intimates, to do away with the notion of origins and originality: no text can be wholly original, an author cannot claim to be the originator of the text's language, and it is impossible to trace its original sources. This theory thus abandons the author-centred, psychologising models of textual relations we have examined above: the author is radically decentred from what is primarily a textual, linguistic and cultural phenomenon.

One way of clarifying these claims is to think about a particular kind of text. Love poetry, for example, has a huge intertextual resonance in our culture. We somehow know (from our culture) that one of the things we can do when we are in love is write poetry or a love song. Such poems and songs seem

---

[23] Barthes, 'From Work to Text', in *Image–Music–Text*, pp. 155–64.

to come from the heart: they articulate our love to ourselves and express our love to the beloved. We can also buy ready-made poems in Valentine cards, or lovers may choose a popular hit as 'their' song. Such cultural activity has a long history, and has a parallel or interconnected history in literary tradition(s). In a sense, the way we behave when we are in love is shaped by the history of love poetry in our culture and by the way it is interwoven with other cultural representations of love (such as films). We understand the gestures and rituals of love by absorbing them from our culture. We know, for example, that courting and wooing may involve the sending of certain symbolic gifts (such as red roses) and the giving and accepting of compliments. Thus we can say that we know the codes and conventions of love, and those codes are shaped by and help to shape our understanding of gender relations. Gender itself can be seen as a discursive product: although our sex is determined by biology (we are either male or female), gender identities (masculine and feminine) and sexual relations are largely shaped by various kinds of discourse – those of religion, medicine, sport, fashion, magazines, psychology, art, and so on. And when we read literary love poetry, our understanding is partly shaped by the way it employs the various codes of love, sex and gender which circulate in our society.

The post-structuralist notion of intertextuality is therefore crucially different from the other ways in which texts interact with each other. Processes of allusion, imitation and influence imply that poetry is a relatively closed system in which individual poems relate mostly to other poems. In the extreme case of Bloom's theory, poems are not about anything but other poems. In contrast, as our example of love poetry indicates, the idea of intertextuality allows us to realise that poetry is a social practice which may engage with all the discourses of our society – both literary and non-literary, high culture and popular culture. Intertextuality in this sense transforms our understanding of the world as well as poetry. For Julia Kristeva, intertextuality 'situates the text within history and society, which are then seen as texts read by the writer, and into which he inserts himself by rewriting them'.[24] Thus our assumptions about love and gender, for example, can be seen as textual constructs rather than as givens which are simply there in the world. And love poems necessarily draw on our society's preconceptions about love and gender in order to reinforce, question or even transform them.

Intertextuality can be a poetically and politically enabling concept for writers from marginalised groups. It invites us to see poetry not as an aloof discourse available only to those who are thoroughly immersed in the dominant tradition

---

[24] Julia Kristeva, *Desire in Language: A semiotic approach to literature and art* (New York: Columbia University Press, 1980), p. 65.

but as a discourse which is more generally available because it relates to all the discourses which surround us. Thus intertextuality may be a democratising concept. Whereas the reader looking for influence needs to be thoroughly educated in the dominant poetic tradition, the intertextual reader is qualified through being alert to the range of discourses which animate our contemporary culture. To read a contemporary love poem, it is at least as important to be aware of how it draws on and reworks the ideologically charged and unstable notions of love and gender which infuse our culture as it is to be aware of the history of love poetry.

The fact that Barthes calls the anonymous citations which make up a text 'already read' indicates the importance of the reader in the theory of intertextuality. This does not mean that the reader should already have read the various texts, literary and otherwise, to which the text in hand might refer. Instead, it means that the reader will bring to a text the reading expectations which have been absorbed from a lifetime of reading (in the most general sense). In order to be intelligible, texts need to employ conventions which readers will automatically process because they *are* conventions. When a child hears the phrase 'Once upon a time,' that child instantly realises that a story has begun. It would be futile to try to track down the origins of that phrase in past texts, or even to try to trace the story in which the child first heard that phrase and began to absorb it as a narrative convention. Such a convention is 'already read', and literature can be said to be constituted by a vast and untraceable 'stereophony' of such already read conventions. Their impact is to suspend the referential possibilities of the language being used in order to promote the literary. When a child hears 'Once upon a time', she or he does not wonder about the date of the events which are about to be narrated.

For Barthes, a literary text is a tissue of such conventions drawn not only from the literary system itself but from a culture's general discursive activity. But because the codes and conventions peculiar to literature suspend the question of reference, literature is freed up to play with the cultural material it absorbs. Thus literature does not simply reproduce the conventions of its society or confirm the expectations of its readers. Although there is a pleasure to be derived from literature which simply conforms with social and readerly conventions (such as the romance novels published by Mills & Boon), the textual pleasures of literature are generated by the way our expectations are played with and upon, and by the way texts engage us in active interpretation. Far from being a conservative process, the intertextuality of texts is for Barthes the means through which a society's codes and conventions are actively unsettled and transgressed.

We can conclude this discussion by looking at a poem by E.E. Cummings (1931) which draws heavily on our culture's codes and conventions of sexual love and love poetry.

somewhere i have never travelled, gladly beyond
any experience, your eyes have their silence:
in your most frail gesture are things which enclose me,
or which i cannot touch because they are too near

your slightest look easily will unclose me   5
though i have closed myself as fingers,
you open always petal by petal myself as Spring opens
(touching skilfully, mysteriously) her first rose

or if your wish be to close me, i and
my life will shut very beautifully, suddenly,   10
as when the heart of this flower imagines
the snow carefully everywhere descending;

nothing which we are to perceive in this world equals
the power of your intense fragility: whose texture
compels me with the colour of its countries,   15
rendering death and forever with each breathing

(i do not know what it is about you that closes
and opens; only something in me understands
the voice of your eyes is deeper than all roses)
nobody, not even the rain, has such small hands   20

It is possible to list some of the 'already read' conventions which this poem cites from our culture's stock of literary and non-literary codes of love poetry, and which we need to be familiar with if we are to understand the poem at all:

1 that the speaker of a love poem addresses the beloved in order to praise and compliment;
2 that a male speaker praises the female addressee's physical and emotional characteristics;
3 that the female addressee is described in terms of natural images (particularly flowers and especially roses);
4 that the effect of love may be described as an opening up of the self and/or the other;
5 that this opening up may be figured as a journey.

Some or all of these conventions circulate endlessly through the cultural practices of the western world in the modern period, so much so that they have become thoroughly naturalised. Interestingly, however, many of them may well derive from the conventions of Petrarchan love that shaped the love sonnets of late Medieval Europe.

Exercises

1 (a) Can you detect any other codes and conventions of love in cummings's poem?

(b) In what ways does cummings's poem resist, play with, or transgress our reading expectations as derived from the codes of love poetry which we have outlined?

(c) If the poem does any of these things, what are the effects?

(d) If you feel that the poem simply repeats the codes and conventions of love poetry, how does that influence your response to the poem?

(e) If you feel that it does creatively rework the conventions it uses, how does that influence your response to the poem?

2 Read the following poem by Edmund Blunden (1928) and then try to answer the questions that follow:

Vlamertinghe: Passing the Chateau, July 1917

'And all her silken flanks with garlands drest' –
But we are coming to the sacrifice.
Must those have flowers who are not yet gone West?
May those have flowers who live with death and lice?
This must be the floweriest place   5
That earth allows; the queenly face
Of the proud mansion borrows grace for grace
Spite of those brute guns lowing at the skies.

Bold great daisies, golden lights,
Bubbling roses' pinks and whites –   10
Such a gay carpet! poppies by the million;
Such damask! such vermilion!
But if you ask me, mate, the choice of colour
Is scarcely right; this red should have been much duller.

(a) What is the poem's setting and historical context?

(b) What is the poem's genre?

(c) What is the poem's speech situation? (who is the speaker? who is the speaker addressing? where are the speaker and the addressee? what is the speaker talking about?)

(d) Sometimes an allusion is signalled by a marked difference in **register** (see Glossary). How would you describe the poem's dominant register? Are there any changes in register? How would you describe these registers? Which register is normal for the speaker? Which register might indicate an allusion or allusions?

(e) Can you spot any potential allusions?

(f) For each possible allusion, try to identify the text that is being alluded to by using hunches, reference books or the Internet (by searching for key words or phrases).

(g) When you have discovered the source text for the allusions in this poem, identify as many allusions to that source text as you can.

(h) How might the lines in the source poem influence the way we interpret Blunden's poem?

(i) How does the conclusion of the source poem influence our understanding of Blunden's poem? Does Blunden's poem accept or reject the 'message' of the closing lines of the source text?

(j) Compare and contrast the way the two poems end.

(k) Try to summarise how spotting the allusions in Blunden's poem helps you understand it.

3 This exercise looks at a type of relationship between poems which we have not considered in this chapter – the fact that poems are sometimes written as responses to other poems. Read the following poems, and then try to answer the questions which follow.

This Is Just to Say

I have eaten
the plums
that were in
the icebox
and which   5
you were probably
saving
for breakfast
Forgive me
they were delicious   10
so sweet
and so cold
(William Carlos Williams, 1934)

Variations on a Theme by William Carlos Williams

[1]

I chopped down the house that you had been saving to live
in next summer.
I am sorry, but it was morning, and I had nothing to do
and its wooden beams were so inviting.

[2]

We laughed at the hollyhocks together
and then I sprayed them with lye.   5
Forgive me. I simply do not know what I am doing.

[3]

I gave away the money that you had been saving to live on
for the next ten years.
The man who asked for it was shabby
and the firm March wind on the porch was so juicy and cold.   10

[4]

Last evening we went dancing and I broke your leg.
Forgive me. I was clumsy, and
I wanted you here in the wards, where I am the doctor!

(Kenneth Koch, 1962)

(a) What kinds of 'already read' codes does Williams's poem employ? (For example, where would you normally expect to find such a text?)

(b) In what ways does Williams employ the codes and conventions of poetry? (For example, what makes us read it as a poem?)

(c) What is the effect of Williams's code mixing here?

(d) What kinds of cultural codes are invoked by Koch's title? (For example, in what kind of cultural practice would such a title normally appear?)

(e) What kind of relation does Koch's poem take up towards Williams? (For example, is it complementary, reverential, ironic, parodic?)

(f) To what extent does Koch's poem depend upon its reader having read Williams's poem? What difference would it make if you had not read Williams's poem?

(g) Are we meant to believe that the things recounted in Koch's poem really occurred?

4 Read the following poem, by Billy Collins (1998), and then try to answer the questions that follow.

Taking Off Emily Dickinson's Clothes

First, her tippet made of tulle,
easily lifted off her shoulders and laid
on the back of a wooden chair.

And her bonnet,
the bow undone with a light forward pull.   5

Then the long white dress, a more
complicated matter with mother-of-pearl
buttons down the back,
so tiny and numerous that it takes forever
before my hands can part the fabric,   10
like a swimmer's dividing water,
and slip inside.

You will want to know
that she was standing
by an open window in an upstairs bedroom,   15
motionless, a little wide-eyed,
looking out at the orchard below,
the white dress puddled at her feet
on the wide-board, hardwood floor.

The complexity of women's undergarments   20
in nineteenth-century America
is not to be waved off,
and I proceeded like a polar explorer
through clips, clasps, and moorings,
catches, straps, and whalebone stays,   25
sailing toward the iceberg of her nakedness.

Later, I wrote in a notebook
it was like riding a swan into the night,
but, of course, I cannot tell you everything –
the way she closed her eyes to the orchard,   30
how her hair tumbled free of its pins,
how there were sudden dashes
whenever we spoke.

What I can tell you is
it was terribly quiet in Amherst   35
that Sabbath afternoon,
nothing but a carriage passing the house,
a fly buzzing in a windowpane.

So I could plainly hear her inhale
when I undid the very top   40
hook-and-eye fastener of her corset

and I could hear her sigh when finally it was unloosed,
the way some readers sigh when they realize
that Hope has feathers,
that reason is a plank,   45
that life is a loaded gun
that looks right at you with a yellow eye.

(a) This poem makes a number of allusions to Emily Dickinson's poetry (includ-
ing a reference to her prolific use of dashes); go through the poem trying to
spot as many passages as you can that you think might be allusions to her
poetry, then try to find some of the original poems that are being alluded to
(beginning with the two Dickinson poems in this book – one in the present
chapter and one in Chapter 7). When you have found the source poems for
some of the allusions, try to work out the point of each allusion by com-
paring and contrasting the two poems brought together by the allusion.
(In doing this, you might look back at our discussion of allusion in the first
section of the present chapter.)

(b) Do you think the use of allusion in this poem serves (i) as a clue to meaning;
(ii) as a kind of in-joke; (iii) to define the implied reader; (iv) to stake a claim
in the American poetic tradition?

(c) Billy Collins is currently the most popular and best-selling poet in America.
What are the implications of the fact that he has written a poem in which
the poet-speaker takes off Emily Dickinson's clothes and, presumably, has
sex with her? (In answering this question, you might re-read parts of the
present chapter, including the sections called 'The Burden of the Past', 'The
Anxiety of Influence' and 'A Poetry of Their Own?'; you might also read up
on Emily Dickinson, perhaps in a good biography or on the Internet.)

Chapter 14

Poetry, Discourse, History

■ Text and Context

In what follows, we shall try to demonstrate some of the benefits of attempting to situate poetry within the historical context in which it was written. This will involve asking what kind of relationship there is between a poetic text and its historical context. Is the historical context merely a 'background' to the more or less independent poem (as many literary critics would claim)? Or is the poetic text simply a historical document which illustrates its context (which is the way many historians might use a poem)? Recent literary critics and theorists have begun to question the very basis of such apparently clear-cut distinctions between literature and history, text and context, intrinsic and extrinsic, foreground and background, poetry and politics, imagination and ideology. Critics inspired by Marxist theories of culture have long argued that cultural practices and products (such as poetry) need to be understood in relation to the material and ideological conditions in which they are produced.[1] Sociological studies of literature examine the way the social institutions of literature have an impact upon the kinds of text produced in a society. Blends of Marxism, sociological approaches, and the theories of 'discourse' developed by thinkers such as Michel Foucault have led to literary theories which have been labelled 'New Historicism' or 'Cultural Materialism'.[2] Such approaches argue that literature is a 'discourse' which always has specific functions within any particular society. As a discourse, literature is shaped by a range of historically specific and changing factors, and needs to be read alongside other discourses

---

[1] For a succinct introduction to Marxist literary theories, see Terry Eagleton, *Marxism and Literary Criticism* (London: Methuen, 1976).

[2] For a useful introductory discussion of the impact on literary criticism of Foucault's notion of 'discourse', see 'Historicism' in *Princeton*.

within the society in which it was produced. These might include religious discourses, medical discourses, discourses about race, class, sexuality, nationalism, and so on. The effect of this is to suggest that literature is not a product of unique individuals which transcends historical differences but part of the varied discursive activity of particular societies. We can illustrate this with a contemporary analogy: it seems clear that pop music is an inextricable part of the world in which it participates – its lyrics reproduce or revise current ideologies of sexual love; it is produced, distributed and consumed according to the principles and technologies of capitalism; and it is one of the most powerful ways in which young people experience and articulate their lives. In similar ways, a poetic text is part of its context and its context is part of the text. Poems are not simply historical documents whose interest lies in the insight they allow on the historical moment but are themselves interpretations, from particular viewpoints, of their historical moment which allow us to see a problem, event or issue in a new way.

But if literary texts are always written from within particular historical contexts, we read and attempt to make sense of them in contexts which are often very different from those original contexts. Yet the assumption that writing and reading are – or ought to be – only marginally affected by the contexts in which they occur survives in the afterlife of New Criticism. It remains a basic premise of the way students of literature are taught and examined in schools in Britain, and it shaped the way deconstructive criticism was understood and practised in American universities. Jacques Derrida's famous statement that 'there is nothing outside of the text' was mistakenly taken to mean business as usual by some teachers and critics in that it seemed to reiterate the basic premises of New Criticism. Critics concerned with political and historical contexts (such as Marxists and feminists) understood Derrida's statement in the same way and this led them to reject deconstruction as ahistorical and apolitical. In its context, however, Derrida's statement is far more suggestive than both sides of this argument have recognised. In saying that 'there is nothing outside of the text [there is no outside-text; *il n'y a pas de hors-texte*]', Derrida is not suggesting that there is nothing outside the book which we hold in our hand (this would be an absurd proposition). Instead, he is saying that we cannot support of our interpretation by referring to any concrete reality which is not in itself already textual. In Derrida's extended sense of textuality, all cultural meanings, all thoughts, are products of language rather than concrete realities which exist outside language.[3] Derrida's thought thus questions our apparently commonsensical distinction between text and context by suggesting that context is itself textual, and that reading is always contextual: 'there is

---

[3] See Jacques Derrida, *Of Grammatology* trans. Gayatri Chakravorty Spivak (Baltimore, MD: Johns Hopkins University Press, 1976), pp. 158–9.

nothing but context, and therefore: there is no outside-the-text'.[4] Contexts are always textual for two reasons: first, because events and ideas are mediated to us through texts (newspapers, books, TV, conversation, the Internet, and so on); secondly, because contexts insinuate themselves within texts. And texts are always contextual, because writing and reading necessarily take place in some context or another; the very possibility of reading depends upon the fact that texts survive their original contexts and can be transported into others. And the fact that a text can be read in different contexts indicates that no single context is wholly determinate of a text's meaning. Thus arguments between, say, New Critics and Marxists as to whether the 'proper' way of reading consists in close reading of 'the text itself' or attention to 'the material context' are based on limited assumptions about texts and contexts. Furthermore, as we have seen in this book, reading poetry is itself a historically conditioned activity: the way poetry is read in different periods and contexts changes according to changing assumptions about what poetry is and what it is for.

■ Poetry and History: Marvell's 'Horatian Ode'

A poem which 'has played a central part in twentieth-century discussions of the relationship between poetry and politics'[5] is Andrew Marvell's 'An Horatian Ode upon Cromwell's Return from Ireland' (written 1650). Readings of the poem have ranged from close New Critical attention to 'the words on the page' to claims that the poem can be understood only through an equally close attention to the minutiae of the events and debates of the English Civil War. In what follows, we want to examine some of the different approaches to the poem in order further to explore the possible ways in which a poetic text may interrelate with its historical context.

But since even New Critical readings depend upon a basic knowledge of the historical figures and issues involved, we will briefly sketch these before presenting the poem itself. The poem concerns Oliver Cromwell (1599–1658), the outstanding Puritan general of the Parliamentary Army which successfully defeated King Charles I and his Royalist forces in the English Civil Wars (1642–46). The King was beheaded in 1649, England was declared a 'Commonwealth', and Cromwell became chairman of a newly created Council of State. In 1653, he became Lord Protector – virtually a military dictator – until his death in 1658. Two years after Cromwell's death the Commonwealth

---

[4] Jacques Derrida 'Biodegradables: Seven diary fragments', *Critical Inquiry* 15 (1989), 812–73 (873).

[5] David Norbrook, 'Marvell's "Horatian Ode" and the Politics of Genre', in Thomas Healy and J. Sawday (eds), *Literature and the English Civil War* (Cambridge: Cambridge University Press, 1990), pp. 147–69 (147).

dissolved and Charles's son was restored to the throne as Charles II. The poem's occasion is Cromwell's return from a successful campaign in Ireland, and reference is made at the end of the poem to his plans to fight the Scots who had supported Charles in the Civil Wars. The poem begins by describing how Cromwell rose from being a farmer to political and military prominence, first by defeating his enemies in his own party and then by defeating the Royalist forces.

An Horatian Ode upon Cromwell's Return from Ireland
The forward youth that would appear
Must now forsake his muses dear,
    Nor in the shadows sing
    His numbers languishing.
'Tis time to leave the books in dust,   5
And oil the unused armour's rust:
    Removing from the wall
    The corslet of the hall.
So restless Cromwell could not cease
In the inglorious arts of peace,   10
    But through adventurous war
    Urged his active star.
And, like the three-forked lightning, first
Breaking the clouds where it was nursed,
    Did thorough his own side   15
    His fiery way divide.[6]
(For 'tis all one to courage high,
The emulous or enemy:
    And with such to enclose
    Is more than to oppose.)[7]   20
Then burning through the air he went,
And palaces and temples rent:
    And Caesar's head at last
    Did through his laurels blast.[8]
'Tis madness to resist or blame   25
The force of angry heaven's flame:
    And, if we would speak true,
    Much to the man is due,

---

[6] After 1644, Cromwell made himself pre-eminent among the parliamentary leaders on 'his own side'.
[7] It is even harder to pen him up than to fight against him.
[8] Refers to Cromwell's defeat and beheading of Charles I; the ancient Romans believed that the laurel tree was immune to lightning (a laurel wreath was worn by the Roman emperors).

Who, from his private gardens, where
He lived reserved and austere,   30
   As if his highest plot
   To plant the bergamot,[9]
Could by industrious valour climb
To ruin the great work of time,
   And cast the kingdom old   35
   Into another mould.
Though justice against fate complain,
And plead the ancient rights in vain:
   But those do hold or break
   As men are strong or weak.   40
Nature, that hateth emptiness,
Allows of penetration less:
   And therefore must make room
   Where greater spirits come.[10]
What field of all the Civil Wars,   45
Where his were not the deepest scars?
   And Hampton shows what part
   He had of wiser art,
Where, twining subtle fears with hope,
He wove a net of such a scope,   50
   That Charles himself might chase
   To Carisbrooke's narrow case:[11]
That thence the royal actor borne
The tragic scaffold might adorn:
   While round the armed bands   55
   Did clap their bloody hands.
He nothing common did or mean
Upon that memorable scene:
   But with his keener eye
   The axe's edge did try: 60
Nor called the gods with vulgar spite

---

[9] The bergamot = species of pear known as the 'prince's pear' or 'pear of kings' – this points to the pun in 'highest plot'.

[10] These lines draw a metaphor from the then current debate in science and philosophy about whether a vacuum was possible in nature, and about the impossibility of two physical bodies occupying the same space.

[11] In 1647 the King fled to Carisbrooke Castle on the Isle of Wight, where he was betrayed by the governor; it has been suggested that Cromwell allowed Charles to escape from Hampton Court in order to demonstrate the King's irresponsibility.

To vindicate his helpless right,
   But bowed his comely head
   Down as upon a bed.
This was that memorable hour   65
Which first assured the forced power.
   So when they did design
   The Capitol's first line,
A bleeding head where they begun,
Did fright the architects to run;   70
   And yet in that the State
   Foresaw its happy fate.[12]
And now the Irish are ashamed
To see themselves in one year tamed:
   So much one man can do,   75
   That doth both act and know.
They can affirm his praises best,
And have, though overcome, confessed
   How good he is, how just,
   And fit for highest trust: 80
Nor yet grown stiffer with command,
But still in the Republic's hand:
   How fit he is to sway
   That can so well obey.
He to the Commons' feet[13] presents   85
A kingdom, for his first year's rents:
   And, what he may, forbears
   His fame, to make it theirs:
And has his sword and spoils ungirt,
To lay them at the public's skirt.   90
   So when the falcon high
   Falls heavy from the sky,

---

[12] These lines refer to an event narrated by various Roman historians. During the preparation of the foundations for the Temple of Jupiter in ancient Rome, workmen dug up a human head, and this was interpreted as an omen foretelling that Rome would become the 'capital place of the whole world' (Livy). This interpretation was based on a pun (the Latin word for head is *caput*) and the temple and the hill on which it stood were consequently named the 'Capitol' or the 'Capitoline'. Marvell adds the details that the head was 'bloody' and that the architects were frightened: these details obviously tie in with the fact of Charles's beheading, but they may also imply some criticism of Cromwell.

[13] Refers to the House of Commons – that part of the English Parliament which supposedly represented the common people, and in whose name Cromwell had fought the Royalists.

She, having killed, no more does search
But on the next green bough to perch,
    Where, when he first does lure,   95
    The falconer has her sure.
What may not then our isle presume
While Victory his crest does plume?
    What may not others fear
    If thus he crown each year?   100
A Caesar, he, ere long to Gaul,
To Italy an Hannibal,[14]
    And to all states not free
    Shall climacteric be.
The Pict no shelter now shall find   105
Within his parti-coloured mind,
    But from this valour sad
    Shrink underneath the plaid:[15]
Happy, if in the tufted brake
The English hunter him mistake,   110
    Nor lay his hounds in near
    The Caledonian deer.[16]
But thou, the Wars' and Fortune's son,
March indefatigably on,
    And for the last effect   115
    Still keep thy sword erect:
Besides the force it has to fright
The spirits of the shady night,[17]
    The same arts that did gain
    A power, must it maintain.   120

---

[14] Cromwell is being likened to Caesar and Hannibal – invaders of Gaul and Italy respectively. We might ask how complimentary this comparison is (and note that Cromwell is likened to Caesar as invader, whereas above Charles was likened to Caesar as civic leader).

[15] Marvell is referring to the fact that Cromwell is about to march on Scotland. Marvell is punning on the Roman name for the Scots ('Picti' – painted men – because they painted their bodies before going into battle) in order to suggest that they were factious – that is, party/ particoloured (like the Plad or plaid – a long woollen garment, usually with a tartan pattern, worn by the Scottish Highlanders). The word 'sad' here is glossed as 'steadfast'. E.N. Williams tells us that in the campaign which Marvell anticipates, 'Cromwell was victorious at Dunbar (3 Sept 1650) and then, luring the Scots S[outh] into England, he defeated them at Worcester on the same day a year later' (Williams, *Penguin Dictionary of English and European History, 1485–1789* (Harmonsworth: Penguin, 1980), p. 111).

[16] Caledonian = Scottish (from Caledonia, the Roman name for Scotland).

[17] The sword held erect forms a cross to ward off evil spirits.

One of the reasons why this poem has been so central to discussions of the relationship between poetry and politics is that it is not at all easy to say where its speaker stands in relation to the most fundamental and controversial political upheaval ever to have occurred in England. On the one hand, the description of the King's dignified behaviour at his execution which forms the centre of the poem (53–64) seems to suggest that the speaker's and Marvell's sympathies lie with Charles. On the other hand, Cromwell is described as a brave, resourceful, active, intelligent, successful and selfless servant of the English state. Does Marvell, then, present a balanced perspective which sees the virtues of both sides? Or is he a Royalist who condemns Cromwell's cause even if he admires the man? Or, conversely, is he a supporter of Cromwell able to be generous to the defeated King? Can he pay respect to the 'ancient rights' (38) which have been displaced while also looking forward to the achievements of the Commonwealth? Is Marvell, or the speaker, a political realist or an opportunist prepared to fall in with whoever is currently in power?

In order to try to solve the political enigma of the 'Horatian Ode', literary critics have tried two different approaches in differing degrees of combination: the close reading of the nuances of the ode itself; and the examination of Marvell's political career and other writings in order to ascertain his politics. The latter method sheds interesting light on the problem, but seems unable to solve it. We know that Marvell became a tutor to a ward of Cromwell in 1653, and took a position (along with Milton) as Latin Secretary to the revolutionary government in 1657. He became an MP for Hull before the restoration of Charles II and, although he continued in the house of Commons until his death in 1678, he became one of the most cutting satirists of the restored monarchy. It is also significant, perhaps, that although the 'Horatian Ode' was written in June or July 1650, and was probably circulated in manuscript, it was never published in Marvell's lifetime. When the first folio edition of Marvell's poetry was published, in 1681, the 'Horatian Ode' – along with two later poems on Cromwell – was cancelled at the last minute from almost all the copies. We do not know why this happened, but it may have been because the publishers thought the poems too controversial.

But if these details point to Marvell as a supporter of Cromwell, some of his poetry before the 'Horatian Ode' appears to support the Royalist cause in the Civil Wars. Although there is some controversy about whether he was the author of 'An Elegy Upon the Death of my Lord Francis Villiers' (1648), most scholars and editors now attribute it to him. The subject of the poem was killed in a Royalist uprising against the Puritan army in July 1648. The poem derives consolation from the idea that this noble lord revenged his own death in advance by killing large numbers of the 'vulgar' Puritan troops, and it closes by suggesting that those who mourn him ought to commemorate him by destroying the whole revolutionary army:

> Such are the obsequies to Francis own:
> He best the pomp of his own death hath shown.
> And we hereafter to his honour will
> Not write so many, but so many kill.
> Till the whole army by just vengeance come
> To be at once his trophy and his tomb. (123–28)

But while Marvell appears to have had violent Royalist sympathies two years before writing the 'Horatian Ode', he went on to publish an anonymous poem five years after it marking 'The First Anniversary of the Government under His Highness the Lord Protector, 1655'. This poem celebrates Cromwell and the Commonwealth he has created as highlighting the inadequacy and tyranny of kings. And in 1659 Marvell published an elegiac 'Poem Upon the Death of His Late Highness the Lord Protector' which unambiguously eulogises Cromwell as 'heaven's favorite' (157) and finds consolation in the fact that Cromwell's son Richard had succeeded his father as head of state (Charles II was to be restored to the throne in 1660). On the evidence of Marvell's political poetry, then, it would seem that between the elegy for Lord Francis Villiers (1648) and the elegy for Cromwell (1659) his political sympathies and allegiances underwent a complete about-turn. Thus we might be tempted to suggest that the ambiguities and ambivalences of tone in the 'Horatian Ode' emerge out of Marvell's own ambivalences at a moment of transition in his feelings. More cynically, we might wonder whether Marvell merely changed his mind according to the way the wind was blowing.

In 1946, Cleanth Brooks used the 'Horatian Ode' as a test case in an attempt to articulate his New Critical understanding of the relationship between criticism and historical studies. For Brooks, although the critic is in debt to the historian for historical information about a poem's context, only the critic, through close reading of the text itself, can say what a poem means, and how the various things it says are unified (remember that unity is one of the defining qualities of a 'good' poem for the New Critics). In a distinction with which we would agree, Brooks stresses that he has 'tried to read the poem, the *Horatian Ode*, not Andrew Marvell's mind'.[18] For Brooks, the 'final appeal' in any question of interpretation 'is not to what Andrew Marvell the Englishman must have thought, or even to what Marvell the author must have intended, but rather to the full context of the poem itself' (in Carey, *Andrew Marvell*, p. 193). The 'full context of the poem', then, is simply 'the poem itself' rather than the context in which it was produced. On this assumption, Brooks proceeds with his task as critic – the close scrutiny of the poem's

---

[18] Cleanth Brooks, 'Literary Criticism' (1946), reprinted in John Carey, ed., *Andrew Marvell: A critical anthology* (Harmondsworth: Penguin, 1969), pp. 179–98 (197).

language. This scrutiny reveals for Brooks a complex ambiguity in the speaker's attitude towards Cromwell. He claims that there is an implicit parallel between Cromwell and the 'forward youth' of the first line, and that 'there lurks' in the word 'forward' the 'sense of "presumptuous", "pushing"'. The description of Cromwell as 'restless' (9) is said to be 'as ambiguous in its meaning as "forward" and in its darker connotations even more damning'. The description of Cromwell climbing through 'industrious valour' (33) – which Brooks finds a 'strange collocation' – seems to indicate Cromwell's aggressive 'thirst for glory' (pp. 184–5).

Brooks's pursuit of complex ambiguity leads him to suggest that the speaker admires as well as criticises Cromwell. If 'industrious valour' is damning, Cromwell also displays an admirable valour which modifies his ambition:

> Cromwell's is no vulgar ambition. If his valor is an 'industrious valour', it contains plain valor too of a kind perfectly capable of being recognised by any Cavalier [i.e. Royalist]:
>
> > What field of all the Civil Wars,
> > Where his were not the deepest scars? (45–6)
>
> If the driving force has been a desire for glory, it is a glory of that kind which allows a man to become dedicated and, in a sense, even selfless in his pursuit of it. (pp. 187–8)

Yet the upshot of Brooks's argument is that whatever the poem finds to admire in Cromwell it ultimately condemns him because his cause is unjust – he offends against 'justice' (37) and the King's 'helpless right' (62). However the speaker might praise Cromwell's industrious, valiant and selfless powers, 'For the end served by those powers, the speaker has no praise at all' (p. 189). For Brooks, then, the poem's Royalist sympathies are not in doubt. Since Cromwell was indisputably in the wrong, the poem's real interest is in a comparative character study:

> the more closely we look at the 'Ode', the more clearly apparent it becomes that the speaker has chosen to emphasize Cromwell's virtues as a man, and likewise those of Charles as a man. The poem does not debate which of the two was right, for the issue is not even in question. In his treatment of Charles, then, the speaker no more than Charles attempts to vindicate his 'helpless right'. Instead, he emphasizes his dignity, his fortitude, and what has finally to be called his consummate good taste. (p. 189)

Although he recognises that right was on the side of Charles, however, the poem's speaker is said to be a political realist who tries to come to terms with the fact that Cromwell is now head of state. The speaker admires many of Cromwell's qualities – such as his apparent willingness to be the state's servant (its falcon) rather than its master (see lines 91–96). But ultimately, Cromwell is guilty in the same way as Macbeth is guilty and, however much we might admire such usurpers, the fact that they rose by the sword means that they will eventually die by the sword (according to Brooks's dubious reading of the poem's closing lines). The complexities of the speaker's response make up the poem's aesthetic effect: 'These implications enrich and qualify an insight into Cromwell which is as heavily freighted with admiration as it is with a great condemnation' (p. 196). Brooks, then, reads the poem as if the speaker were watching a compelling dramatic spectacle rather than being caught up in the midst of pressing events and issues.

Brooks seems correct in suggesting that the most urgent question to ask of the ode is what attitude is adopted towards the two principal figures. We can begin to approach this question through thinking about the poem's genre, since the title tells us that it is a 'Horatian Ode'. This indicates that the poem needs to be read in relation to the way the Roman poet Horace used the poetic genre of the 'Ode'. The modern reader, who is likely to have had a different education from Marvell's classically educated contemporaries, may need to do a bit of homework to find out what kind of poem the Horatian Ode was. Classical odes were used for public utterance on state occasions. The Horatian ode, after the example of the Roman poet Horace, was used to praise public figures such as generals, and was typically contemplative in tone and sentiment. In the first half of the sixteenth century, Horatian odes became strongly associated with Royalism, and this means that the poem's very title would have raised specific expectations in its initial readers. At the same time, since the ode was normally the 'vehicle of praise for victorious generals', the poem's title may indicate that Marvell is praising Cromwell in the way that Horace praised Augustus.[19]

Understanding the history of a poem's genre allows us to see how that poem fits in with, or breaks away from, that genre's conventions. In the case of Marvell's 'Horatian Ode' we have a poem which arguably does not fit neatly and innocently into the genre to which it declares itself to belong. But we still need to decide whether the poem itself is secretly Royalist, ironically subverting Royalist expectations, or implying that Cromwell now needs to be viewed as having taken over the mantle of leadership from the monarchic line. If the poem is supposed to be a Horatian celebration of the returning general, how are we to read the apparently sympathetic lines about the King's execution which form its centre? In fact, it may be that the politics of the ode are 'undecidable' (in a sense which we will develop in the final chapter of this book). Such undecidability does not foreclose politics but keeps political questions open: it is perhaps the ode's undecidability that made it one of the test cases in twentieth-century discussions of the interrelationship between poetry and politics.

---

[19] John M. Wallace, *Destiny His Choice: The loyalism of Andrew Marvell* (Cambridge: Cambridge University Press, 1968), p. 73.

Yet even if its political position is undecidable, we believe that it is important to be more precise about the historical implications of that undecidability. In what follows, we want to try out two different historical approaches to the poem which will situate our analysis within larger historical and political questions. The first, inspired by the Marxist theory of Pierre Macherey, examines the poem in terms of its ideological project – revealed as much by what it *does not say* about its historical moment as by what it does say. The second is informed by more recent discussion about the interrelation between politics and literature which argues that poetry is a discourse that needs to be understood in historical terms, especially in the way it interacts with the other discourses which surround it and make up its historical context.

This next stage in our reading of the poem involved some research in the library looking for studies of Marvell and/or the English Civil Wars and Revolution which might help us to place Marvell's poem within its historical and political context. A series of Advanced Boolean Searches on our university library's computer catalogue produced a number of promising titles, including *Literature and the English Civil War*, *Dragon's Teeth: Literature in the English Revolution*, *Destiny His Choice: The loyalism of Andrew Marvell* and *The Seventeenth Century: The intellectual and cultural context of English literature, 1603–1700*.[20] The next thing was to find the books on the shelves and to scan lists of contents and indexes looking for anything that looked promising. This process led us to several useful and insightful chapters on the politics of the 'Horatian Ode'.

◼ Poetry and Ideology: Significant Omissions

Michael Wilding's reading of the 'Horatian Ode' in his book *Dragon's Teeth: Literature in the English Revolution* is based on a quite different assumption from Brooks's. Wilding concentrates as much upon what the poem *does not say* as upon what it says. This is because what a text leaves out of the historical stories it tells may be as significant as what it includes. As Wilding acknowledges, this approach is influenced by Pierre Macherey's *A Theory of Literary Production* (1966, repr. 1978). In stark contrast with Brooks's New Critical approach, which concentrates on a text as a finished product, Macherey attends to a text's conditions of production. For Macherey, a text's production is not explicable in terms of the imagination of the individual who wrote it. Instead, we need to realise the extent to which the ideological conflicts and repressions which shape and animate a culture at any particular moment also

---

[20] For these books, see Healy and Sawday, *Literature and the English Civil War*; Michael Wilding, *Dragon's Teeth* (Oxford: Clarendon Press, 1987); Wallace, *Destiny His Choice*; and Graham Parry, *The Seventeenth Century* (London: Longman, 1989) in our Bibliography.

shape and animate the literary texts which are produced within that culture. Freud's theory of the unconscious and Marx's description of the workings of ideology suggest that we are not wholly conscious of the desires and thoughts which drive us, nor do they originate wholly from within our individual minds. Both the individual psyche and the ideological life of a society are in conflict with themselves because they are maintained through repression. That which is repressed within the mind or within society continues to have effects precisely because effort is required to keep it repressed. A society employs ideologies which tell reassuring stories about itself by occluding that which cannot be faced. It is possible to think of many examples of this: the ideology of romantic love in the nineteenth century disguised the fact that marriage involved the virtual enslavement of women; the endlessly repeated story that the United States is the land of the free draws attention away from the history of slavery and the genocide of Native American peoples. According to Macherey, literary texts give form to such ideological repressions in ways which allow us to become conscious of them, and of the gaps and internal conflicts which are their *raison d'être*. For Macherey, the critic's job is not (as with Brooks) to demonstrate how a text achieves unity but, precisely, to trace the significance of how a text *fails* to achieve unity. The conflicts and omissions within a text reveal the ideological work which it is trying to carry out:

> We should question the work as to what it does not and cannot say, in those silences for which it has been made. . . . The order which it professes is merely an imagined order, projected onto disorder, the fictive resolution of ideological conflicts, a resolution so precarious that it is obvious in the very letter of the text where incoherence and incompleteness burst forth.[21]

Influenced by Macherey's arguments, Wilding's reading of the text of the 'Horatian Ode' relates its complexities to those aspects of its historical moment which are significantly absent from the poem. This allows him to argue that Marvell's poem, by focusing on the merits of Charles I and Cromwell as individuals, reduces what was actually a much more complex political situation to a simple choice between two men. He begins by examining in greater detail the contemporary resonances of Cromwell's Irish campaign. Cromwell is still thought of in Ireland with bitterness for the way he put down the Irish rebellion. The details are given by E.N. Williams:

> In Ireland (Aug 1649) he broke the back of Irish resistance which had been active since 1641, and achieved lasting notoriety at Drogheda on 11 Sept 1649 when it refused to surrender. He slaughtered the garrison and all the priests he could catch in order to encourage other towns to surrender – and thus save lives by shortening

---

[21] Pierre Macherey, *A Theory of Literary Production* (London: Routledge & Kegan Paul, 1978), p. 155.

the war. On 11 Oct, Wexford received similar treatment. After Cromwell's departure the mopping up was completed, and English Prot[estant]s were settled on land confiscated from Irish Cath[olic]s, while Ireland was united with England (1653–60), sending MPs to the English Parl[iament].

(*Penguin Dictionary of English and European History, 1485–1789*, p. 111)

Wilding seeks to recover the political and symbolic meaning of Cromwell's venture into Ireland. The rebellion there in November 1641, in which thousands of English were killed, was in fact one of the crucial events which sparked off the first Civil War. Puritans in England believed that the King – a Catholic and a Stuart – welcomed the rebellion and was reluctant to respond to it. An opposition group in Parliament 'refused to trust a royal nominee with command of an army to conquer Ireland' (Wilding, *Dragon's Teeth*, p. 118). This raised the question of whether ultimate power in the state lay with the King or with Parliament, and this in turn helped precipitate Civil War and Revolution. Cromwell's victorious return from Ireland after the English Revolution could thus be seen as a symbolic moment in which he demonstrated his ability to cope with problems which the King was thought to have secretly fomented. By concentrating on this symbolic moment, then, Marvell's poem seems to endorse Cromwell's claims to be the man most fitted to become the new ruler of England.

Marvell's poem presents Cromwell as England's only option by ignoring English resistance to the Irish and Scottish campaigns. In particular, the poem occludes the radical arguments of a political movement called the Levellers, who called for a genuinely egalitarian state and criticised the Irish campaign for its tyrannous oppression of the people.[22] The Levellers initially backed Cromwell and Parliament against the King, believing that Cromwell would carry out their radically egalitarian political programme. Cromwell, however, having benefited from their support, turned against them when their radicalism threatened his own programme. Williams usefully summarises:

> Consisting mainly of shopkeepers, artisans, apprentices and yeomen, they represented the grievances and aspirations of social groups who had supported Parl[iament] against the K[ing], but who . . . resented the fact that neither the Long Parl[iament] . . . nor Cromwell and the generals would pay attention to their [democratic] programme as it threatened the rights of property-owners. [The rise of Cromwell to power] merely substituted one tyrant for another in Leveller eyes. . . . In Mar[ch] 1649 Lilburne, Walwyn and other leaders were arrested and the City branch of the movement put down; while in May 1649 the Army Levellers were crushed by Cromwell himself. (pp. 261–2)

---

[22] The name and lyrics of the modern political folk band The Levellers are inspired by this political movement in the English Civil War.

By omitting any hint of the Levellers' alternative voice, and keeping silent about Cromwell's 'savage suppression of Leveller mutiny' within England, Marvell gives the impression that Cromwell is the representative figurehead of all the anti-Royalist positions (Wilding, *Dragon's Teeth*, p. 22).[23] The effect of this is to make it seem inevitable that, with the King dead, Cromwell is the sole option left for England.

Our discussion of what Marvell's ode excludes from the historical story it tells indicates that poems are always interpretations of history at particular moments and from specific positions within history. This means that we need to compare the stories of such poems with other interpretations (found in history books, other poems or other specimens of contemporary discourse). Marvell's poem was written at a crucial moment just after the execution of the King, when the whole political system in England was in the midst of an unprecedented transformation and no one could be sure how things would work out. By shutting out other options (he makes no mention of Charles's son as well as ignoring the Levellers) Marvell seems to imply that there is only one way to respond to the political reality. Thus the poem ends by urging Cromwell to 'March indefatigably on' (114).

■ Poetry as a Discourse in Relation to Discursive Contexts

John Barrell has argued that we ought to ask questions of poems which have been neglected under New Criticism's influence: 'when it was written, . . . whom it addressed, . . . what was the function of any particular literary activity – writing epic poems, reading novels – at any particular period or for any particular kind of reader'.[24] In other words, he is proposing that poems need to be regarded as discursive acts produced within specific institutions and discursive networks. But such an attention to the relationship of poems to historically specific discourses does not mean that we can thereby recover the historical reality to which those poems supposedly refer:

> all we can hope to recover of the past is other representations of it: other texts, other discourses, or other examples of the discourse embodied in the text we are examining. But if we can compare a poem, as a discursive account of reality, with other such contemporary accounts, we can begin to understand it, precisely, as discourse, as the embodiment of a partial view of the world in competition with other partial views; as political, and not as universal.
>
> (*Poetry, Language and Politics*, p. 12)

[23] For a more sustained discussion of Cromwell's Irish campaign and response to the Levellers, see Christopher Hill, *God's Englishman: Oliver Cromwell and the English Revolution* (London: Weidenfeld & Nicolson, 1970), pp. 107–45.

[24] John Barrell, *Poetry, Language and Politics* (Manchester: Manchester University Press, 1988), p. 3.

The major implication of this theory of discourse for our present discussion is the idea that Marvell's poem needs to be understood not in terms of the uniquely individual thought of its author but in terms of the general belief systems of the period as they adapted to historical circumstances. The question which this raises is not whether Marvell was a Royalist or a Cromwellian or a turncoat, but the extent to which his poem draws on the available terms and ways of understanding these circumstances which were circulating at the time.

The original clue which led us towards examining the interplay between Marvell's 'Horatian Ode' and the discourses of its historical moment was found by chance when we were glancing through a literary history of the period which one of us had bought second-hand as a student. In Chapter 9 of *English Poetry and Prose, 1540–1674*, edited by Christopher Ricks, Maren-Sofie Røstvig proposes a solution to the puzzle of Marvell's politics by glancing at what Barrell would call the Royalist and Puritan 'discourses' of the Civil Wars as used in the many pamphlets written on all sides of the question in that period. This discourse suggests that both sides in the Civil Wars interpreted events and figures through a similar Christian perspective:

> If it is conceded that the larger part of the English nation was committed to a religious view of history, the curious passivity of many Royalists at the time of the execution of King Charles I is more easily understood. A religiously-motivated loyalism to the man in power as the leader appointed by God, would explain the ambiguity in Marvell's attitude towards Charles and Cromwell in 'An Horatian Ode . . .'. As soon as their side was favoured by the events of the war, the Parliamentarians were quick to argue that a divine judgment had been passed through trial by battle, and many men of moderation must have shared the sentiments of Thomas, Lord Fairfax, when he wrote the following lines on the issue of the execution:

> > But if the Power devine permitted this
> > His Will's the Law & ours must acquiesse.

> This is the tenor of many Civil War pamphlets, and this is what Marvell, too, states in his Horatian ode:

> > 'Tis Madness to resist or blame
> > The force of angry Heavens flame.[25]

What Røstvig reveals here is that both sides in the English Civil Wars assumed that God was the ultimate arbiter of political fortunes. For the Royalists, kings were chosen by God, but if a king was overthrown God must have allowed it to happen and must have chosen the human being who overthrew and replaced the king. Royalists ought therefore to be loyal to the new regime even while hoping that the usurper would be overthrown and monarchy restored.

---

[25] Maren-Sofi Røstvig, 'Andrew Marvell and the Caroline Poets', in Ricks, ed., *Sphere History of Literature in the English Language*, vol. 2, pp. 206–48 (231).

For the Parliamentarians, the fact that they had prevailed and that Cromwell had gained control of England was a sign of God's approval. Both sides, then, assumed that they ought to be loyal to the new regime. Both could adopt the loyalist assumption that whoever is the head of state deserves loyalty on the basis that he or she must have been elected and appointed by God. (As we will see, however, the concept of loyalism raised its own problems that impact on our attempt to interpret Marvell's poem.)

Our search for books which might shed further light on the religious notion of loyalism in this period led us to two promising titles: *Destiny His Choice: The loyalism of Andrew Marvell* and *God's Englishman: Oliver Cromwell and the English Revolution*. The latter is a biography of Cromwell by Christopher Hill, one of the foremost modern historians of seventeenth-century Britain. The title of Chapter ix, 'Providence and Oliver Cromwell', indicated that it might deal with the kind of issues we were looking for. The chapter begins by explaining that 'Predestination is at the heart of protestantism', and quotes Martin Luther as saying: 'God foreknows and wills all things, not contingently but necessarily and immutably' (*God's Englishman*, p. 219). Those who believe they have been given an insight into God's providence and have been chosen to carry out God's will are the 'elect'; they are the agents through which God achieves what he has ordained. The elect do not wallow in the sense of being saved, but are called to work in order to carry out God's will on earth: 'It is by means of works performed through grace, in Calvin's view, that the elect "make their calling sure"' (p. 220). Puritanism, then, involved ordinary people industriously working in the world with the conviction that they were doing God's will. (This may explain the reference in the poem to Cromwell's 'industrious valour'.) The eventual aim of the strenuous efforts of the elect was to bring about God's historical plan on earth – the building of the New Jerusalem prophesied in Revelation 21. Thus Calvinism entails a teleological theory of history: the elect are working to bring to pass things which God has preordained. Members of God's elect are therefore integrated into the historical process; by co-operating with God's historical plans, they made 'their destiny their choice'.[26]

Cromwell assumed that he was one of God's elect and that God was on his side (or, rather, that he was on God's side) in the war against the Royalist forces. Hill quotes from Cromwell's account of his feelings before Naseby (where, with his New Model Army, he defeated the King on 14 June 1645): 'I could not (riding alone about my business) but smile out to God in praises in assurance of victory . . . and God did it' (pp. 228–9). Cromwell's supporters also believed that they were fighting God's good fight and that Cromwell was

---

[26] 'While her glad parents most rejoice, / And make their destiny their choice' (Marvell, 'Upon Appleton House', 743–44).

God's chosen Englishman. It was in the name of providence and necessity that Cromwell and his supporters in Parliament 'steeled themselves', as Hill puts it, 'to one of the boldest and most epoch-making gestures in history – the public execution of a king by his subjects, for the first time in modern Europe' (p. 233). The Puritans believed that they could carry out such actions without guilt because they were merely the means through which God achieved his ends.

The Puritan doctrine of the individual being chosen or 'elected' by God is not dissimilar to the biblical idea that kings are chosen by God as his representatives on earth. Yet the Bible could also be used as evidence to indicate that God sometimes chooses individuals to chasten kings who step out of line: 'God normally worked through kings, his lieutenants on earth, Thomas Scott wrote in 1623; but he might on exceptional occasions raise up a David to quicken Saul's zeal' (pp. 244–5). What was radical about the Puritan ideology was the Puritans' claim that they were a community of the elect and hence part of a kind of divine aristocracy above, and quite apart from, the worldly aristocracies and monarchies which ruled the world. An important feature of their doctrine was the claim that the outcome of any action would reveal whether or not it was in conformity with God's designs: 'the success of a virtuous human being is at once his victory and the victory of divine grace working in him' (p. 244). To prove that they were of the elect and that they were carrying out God's plans, then, the Puritans tended to use success as 'evidence' of divine approval. As Cromwell claimed, if the cause 'be of God, he will bear it up. If it be of man, it will tumble' (quoted by Hill, p. 237). Cromwell's very success in war and politics was held to demonstrate that he was of the elect.

Yet the argument from success was not the sole prerogative of the Puritans. Monarchists also used this doctrine – through the notion of divine right – in order to justify the arbitrary rule and actions of kings. At the outset of the Civil War, when the King's forces were winning battles, the Royalists taunted the Puritans by claiming that their victories demonstrated that God was on the King's side:

> The outbreak of actual fighting in the civil war naturally gave a great fillip to the argument from success. 'Where is your Roundheads' God now?' asked a triumphant royalist in 1644. 'Hath he forsaken you Roundheads of Bolton now? Sure he is turned Cavalier.' But soon the God of Battles revealed himself consistently on the side of [Cromwell's] New Model Army. . . . The fact of military victories 'continued seven or eight years together' allowed a pamphleteer of 1648 to argue that: 'In such cases successes are to be looked upon as clear evidence of the truth, righteousness and equity of our cause.'[27]

---

[27] Hill, *God's Englishman*, p. 246, quoting G. Ormerod, ed. (1849), *Tracts Relating to Military Proceedings in Lancashire During the Great Civil War*, p. 193 and Anon., *Salus Populi Solus Rex* (17 October 1648).

The belief that Cromwell's success revealed God's support also 'proved convincing, or convenient, for many Royalists and Presbyterians when it came to accepting the Commonwealth' (quoted by Hill in *God's Englishman*, p. 248). Yet the doctrine was to have an unexpected sting in its tail when, after the death of Cromwell, the Commonwealth was overthrown and the son of Charles I was restored to the throne in 1660. Such a reversal demonstrated that 'God's end was not what the radicals had taken it to be', and left radical figures such as Milton desperately trying to justify the ways of God to men.

John M. Wallace begins his book *Destiny His Choice: The loyalism of Andrew Marvell* with a detailed examination of the Civil War pamphlets. The evidence he presents reveals that all sides of the debate shared very similar religious convictions about the origins of secular power. The key text was Paul's Epistle to the Romans 13: 1–2:

> Let every soul be subject unto the higher powers. For there is no power but of God: the powers that be are ordained of God. Whosoever therefore resisteth the power, resisteth the ordinance of God.

This was the 'heart of the matter' for the Royalists, but it was also the basic assumption of even the most radical groups. Wallace maintains that 'Charles and Lilburne [one of the Levellers' leaders] could have shaken hands on the fact that all power was of God: the quarrel was about its distribution, not its origin' (*Destiny His Choice*, p. 12). The quarrel was possible because, although Paul says 'there is no power but of God', he does not specify the nature of the holder of political power. His statement could apply to kings, but equally it could apply to any other form of political power, including parliamentary government.

Another doctrinal (and ideological) problem arose over a set of interrelated questions: whether it was possible, given that kings are elected by God, to depose a corrupt or tyrannous king; whether a benevolent usurper was better than a tyrannous king; and under what conditions a usurper could become a legitimate ruler approved by God. The Royalists were driven to argue that even if a king were a tyrant, and had thereby abused his election, he was still chosen by God and could not be removed. A usurper, by the same argument, could never be God's representative. Even if a usurper flourished, this did not indicate that he was elected by God but that he had been 'permitted' in the same way that God permits evil in the world (p. 18). Critics of the Royalists were quick to point out some major flaws in these arguments. One problem was that it was difficult to distinguish between what God supported and what he merely permitted. A second problem was that even if God established kings on thrones, the Bible showed that he also dethroned them by using chosen agents. A third problem was that the line of English monarchs revealed several usurpations and derived ultimately from the violent usurpation of William the

Conqueror. Pushed on these issues, the Royalists found it impossible securely to distinguish between authentic and unauthentic power, and ended up 'attributing a lawful title to every forced power which had ever succeeded in maintaining itself' (p. 21). One Royalist pamphlet admitted that there was scarcely a kingdom in the whole of Christendom which had not begun through armed usurpation, but asserted that their survival demonstrates God's approbation: 'for though it may be unjust at first in him that invades and Conquers, yet in the succession, which is from him, that providence which translates Kingdomes, manifests it selfe and the will of God'.[28] In other words, the argument of the Royalists became almost identical with that of the Puritan parliamentarians – who went on to argue that Cromwell's success in overthrowing the monarch and setting up a new political power demonstrated that he had God's approbation. In other words, 'The royalists were hoist with their own petard, as they well knew' (p. 27).

When the Royalist forces were defeated and the King was imprisoned, writers on both sides began to look for ways in which the people could come to accept the new political reality, and hence re-establish the state's peace and security. Antony Ascham, a supporter of the Revolution, played a major role in formulating the doctrine of loyalism, arguing that it was better to transfer allegiance to the new power in possession than to leave the country open to the dangers posed by the Levellers. Ascham paved the way for the Royalist pamphleteers such as Sir Robert Filmer, who advised that 'the subjects' obedience to the fatherly power must go along and wait upon God's providence, who only hath right to give and take away kingdoms'.[29] The Royalist clergy followed suit in a series of sermons preached in the autumn of 1649 which recommended loyalism to the power in possession on the basis that immediate peace was crucial, and that the future ought to be left to God's providence. In the last sermon the King was to hear before his execution, the Royalist Henry Ferne 'preached what could well be called a manifesto of loyalist thought' (p. 40).

Immediately following the execution of the King, the House of Commons sought to require anyone entrusted with public office to take an oath of allegiance or 'Engagement'. In October 1649, the House passed a further 'Engagement' resolution which proclaimed that virtually the entire literate population should take a vow to be 'true and faithful to the Commonwealth of England, as it is now Established, without a King or House of Lords' (quoted by Wallace, p. 48). The Engagement was further extended in January to the whole male population aged eighteen or over. Anyone who did not take the

---

[28] Wallace, *Destiny His Choice*, p. 24, quoting Henry Ferne, *Conscience Satisfied* (Oxford, 1643).
[29] Wallace, p. 39, quoting Sir Robert Filmer, *The Anarchy of a Limited or Mixed Monarchy* (Oxford, 1648).

oath was virtually excluded from civil rights: 'anyone who wished or needed to hold a public position of any kind, or who had any cause to seek for redress of grievances at law, was obliged to take the oath' (p. 49).

The Engagement oath stimulated a new flurry of pamphlets both for and against it. Loyalist arguments for accepting the oath more or less reiterated the arguments we have already looked at for accepting the new government after the King's defeat. The peace and security of the state was the prime consideration, the oath could be taken as only provisionally binding, and it was not for human beings to decide whether God sanctioned the new regime or merely permitted it. Thus the loyalist position was one of 'wait and see'. The Royalist opposition to the Engagement came mainly from the Presbyterians, who continued to maintain that Charles's son – who had gone into exile and would eventually become Charles II – was King of England and that the people owed their loyalty to him. Yet their Royalist arguments contained the same internal contradictions as before, and they were not prepared to call for armed rebellion. Thus they more or less suggested that the people should comply with the illegitimate regime without recognising its authority. Cromwell's success in Ireland had a significant impact at this point because it was used by the Puritans and the loyalists as evidence for God's approbation: 'The success of the Irish, and later the Scottish, campaign bolstered the confidence of the government's apologists in God's immediate approval of the new regime' (p. 63).

◼ Reading Marvell's Ode in the Discursive Context of the Civil War Debates

Our examination of the discourse of the Civil War debates allows us to rethink Marvell's 'Horatian Ode' not in terms of its author's personal allegiances and ambivalences with regard to Charles I or Cromwell but in terms of the way the poem draws upon and contributes to the discursive debate about the constitutional crisis. We suggest that this is the context in which Marvell's contemporary readers (if they had seen a copy of the unpublished manuscript) would have understood the poem (unfortunately, there are no known contemporary responses to the 'Horatian Ode'). The questions we need to ask of the poem are the questions which the Civil War pamphlets urgently debated: (1) can Cromwell be interpreted as a necessary evil which God has permitted for his inscrutable reasons? or (2) is Cromwell God's scourge, visited upon England for its sins? or (3) is Cromwell a predestined head of state chosen by God to help England fulfil its part in God's larger plan? or (4) is he even the 'Christian prince' foretold in the Book of Revelation who will help to bring about the New Jerusalem? (That such questions could even be asked reveals the heady presupposition that the English were God's chosen people!) Wallace argues that the ambiguities that so many critics have found in the poem arise not out of Marvell's unique and 'poetic' impartiality but out of 'the nature of circumstances which were popularly understood to be contradictory' (*Destiny His Choice*, p. 71). Arguing that there are 'two Cromwells in the poem, the scourge of God and the leader of his troubled people' (p. 70), Wallace claims that the poem hesitates between options (2) and (3) before opting for the latter.

Yet given the fact that the Civil War pamphlets interpreted the historical moment in Christian terms, it is notable that, as Brooks says, 'Marvell has taken care to make no specifically Christian references in the poem' (in Carey, ed., *Andrew Marvell*, p. 184). Douglas Bush responds by saying that this is 'In keeping with the pagan tone of a Horatian ode', but that 'the reader makes an obvious transfer from pagan Rome to Christian England'.[30] If we translate the pagan images of the poem into Christian ones, it is possible to see how immersed the poem is in the constitutional debate we have traced. Although it does not specifically state that Cromwell is God's Englishman (as Marvell's later poems on Cromwell do), its representation of him as energetic, purposeful, brave, selfless and, above all, irresistibly successful suggests character traits which, in the discursive network we have traced, would have indicated his status either as God's elected scourge or as his predestined head of state.

The first half of the poem deals with Cromwell's rise to power and his success in the Civil War. On the evidence of this alone, people at the time who were not supporters of Cromwell would have thought that he was God's scourge sent to chastise the King and the English people. Cromwell's rise is represented as an uncontainable natural force: he made his 'fiery way' through his own side 'like the three-forked lightning' breaking through clouds (13–16); he then went

> burning through the air . . .
> And palaces and temples rent:
> And Caesar's head at last
> Did through his laurels blast. (21–24)

The representation of Cromwell as 'The force of angry heaven's flame' (26) hints that this awesome force might be an agent of heaven rather than merely a phenomenon of the upper air. Just as lightning was once seen as a sign of the pagan gods' anger, Marvell's metaphor suggests that Cromwell is an agent of the Christian God. The very fact that this lightning was able to blast through Caesar's laurels indicates at the very least that God did not protect the King from Cromwell's onslaught.

The poem then switches from representing Cromwell as a natural force sent from heaven to examining how his qualities as a man have contributed to his

---

[30] Bush, 'Marvell's *Horatian Ode*', in Carey, *Andrew Marvell: A Critical anthology*, pp. 199–210.

rise: 'And, if we would speak true, / Much to the man is due' (27–28). This is a man who

> Could by industrious valour climb
> To ruin the great work of time,
>   And cast the kingdom old
>   Into another mould.
> Though justice against fate complain,
> And plead the ancient rights in vain. (33–38)

The huge scale of Cromwell's achievements indicates an unprecedented degree of 'industrious valour'. This term, which Brooks finds so puzzling, would have had a clear and specific meaning for anyone familiar with the Puritan doctrine of the time. Such qualities and such achievements mark Cromwell as one of God's elect; the 'ancient rights' of kings is a vain plea against such a 'fate' (a concept which Puritanism reinterpreted as 'predestination'). Cromwell is the blacksmith of nations, able through sheer energy to 'cast the kingdom old / Into another mould'. He is also both brave and skilful in war:

> What field of all the Civil Wars,
> Where his were not the deepest scars?
>   And Hampton shows what part
>   He had of wiser art. (45–48)

In contrast with such active qualities of war and statecraft, the King's passive behaviour on the scaffold represents a dignified acquiescence to the irrepressible tide of history.

The rest of the poem sets out to interpret Cromwell's character and achievements as demonstrating his fitness to become head of state rather than simply being God's scourge. Whether or not any Irish people at the time would have 'confessed / How good he is, how just' (78–79), it is clear that Marvell represents the Irish victory as demonstrating Cromwell's qualifications to rule: his achievements are based on wisdom as well as an irrepressible capacity for action (he 'doth both act and know' [76]), and he is 'fit for highest trust' (80) because he is both 'good' and 'just'. Cromwell has also demonstrated his fitness as head of state, the poem claims, because he has shown that he wishes to serve the republic rather than rule over it:

> How fit he is to sway
> That can so well obey.
>   He to the Commons' feet presents
>   A kingdom, for his first year's rents:

> And, what he may, forbears
> His fame, to make it theirs:
> And has his sword and spoils ungirt,
> To lay them at the public's skirt. (83–90)

The change in Cromwell from scourge to fit head of state is measured by the change in the figure which the poem uses to represent him: if in his rise to power he resembled 'angry heaven's flame', he has now become a falcon who, though he still strikes from the skies, is controlled by the falconer and returns to 'the Republic's hand' (82). With such a leader, the poem suggests, England seems destined for great things: 'What may not then our isle presume / While Victory his crest does plume?' (97–98).

By reading the poem in this way, and by linking it to the particular stage of the Civil War debates out of which it emerged, it has been possible to interpret the poem in terms of the ideological work it performs. Without the benefit of hindsight, the poem intervenes at a historical moment in which English citizens were required to respond to Cromwell within the interpretative frameworks which were available to them. In the midst of the critical moment, Marvell's poem suggests that Cromwell was the most powerful man in England who promised to transform England into the most powerful country in the world. The poem therefore recommends its readers to be loyal to him as the predestined head of state.

Yet we have to remember that this is an ideological reading of the moment from within the moment itself. What the poem does is to represent and interpret events so that they tell a certain story. But because this story is in conflict with other stories (those of the Royalists, the Levellers, the Irish, and so on) there are gaps and fissures in the poem which reveal the manufactured nature of the ideological story. Thus it is often possible to reinterpret certain key moments in the poem as potentially telling a quite different story. The claim, for example, that the King's beheading foretells the founding of a prosperous state makes a flattering comparison between England and Rome, but this interpretation of the execution is clearly achieved through a forced rhetorical ruse. And there are moments in the second half of the poem which may be interpreted as suggesting that Cromwell may not always be content with being a servant of the state: for the present, he simply 'forbears' to do what he is capable of doing. There are also indications that Cromwell's success, and England's fortunes under him, may be only temporary: 'What may not then our isle presume / *While* Victory his crest does plume' (emphasis added). And though the final lines urge Cromwell to 'March indefatigably on', there is a suggestion that England will never enjoy peace under him: 'The same arts that did gain / A power, must it maintain' (119–20).

The contradictions of the 'Horatian Ode' can be read, then, not as emerging out of the inner doubts or even-handedness of its author but as dramatising the conflicts within and between contemporary attempts to represent unprecedented political upheavals and to understand Cromwell's long-term significance in a very unstable situation. It seems impossible to decide whether the poem accepts the Puritan version of events or whether it is simply endorsing the loyalist line. But that both interpretations were somewhat forced is registered in the fabric of the poem itself. In this, the poem is very much a text of its moment. It does not stand outside history and politics, but participates within the historical and political struggles and debates of the specific moment in which it was produced.

We have been stressing, however, that a historical reading of poetry needs not only to be responsive to the discursive context in which a poem was produced but also to be aware of the historicity of the act of reading itself. None of today's readers can hope to experience the sense of the immediate press of events under which Marvell wrote. The many revolutions and theories of revolution in the almost three-and-a-half centuries since the English Revolution have transformed our sense of the significance of such political events. Religious interpretations of the world have waned in the West, although millenarianism and religious fundamentalism have re-emerged (yet again!) in the last decade. Many of today's readers of Marvell's poem (and of this book) will not be Christians. Many will not be English. What differences might these factors make? What do English readers feel as they read a poem which so clearly takes it for granted that England has a special destiny which would involve a struggle for world domination? What about Scottish or Irish readers? Or readers in any of the countries in the world (including the United States) which currently speak English as a consequence of England's sense of destiny revealed in the poem? We cannot answer these questions for you, yet we would again urge the point that a historically responsible reading takes account of such factors in order to make sure that they do not merely inhibit us from being responsive to the poem's own historical specificity.

Exercises

1 Read both the passage from Wordsworth's *The Prelude* (1805) and Thomas Hardy's poem 'In a Wood' (1898), and then try to answer the questions.

> Oh there is blessing in this gentle breeze
> That blows from the green fields and from the clouds
> And from the sky: it beats against my cheek,

And seems half conscious of the joy it gives.
O welcome Messenger! O welcome Friend!   5
A captive greets thee, coming from a house
Of bondage, from yon City's walls set free,
A prison where he hath been long immured.
Now I am free, enfranchis'd and at large,
May fix my habitation where I will.   10
What dwelling shall receive me? In what Vale
Shall be my harbour? Underneath what grove
Shall I take up my home, and what sweet stream
Shall with its murmur lull me to my rest?
The earth is all before me: with a heart   15
Joyous, nor scar'd at its own liberty,
I look about, and should the guide I chuse
Be nothing better than a wandering cloud,
I cannot miss my way.
            (Wordsworth, *The Prelude*, 1805, I, 1–19)

In A Wood
See 'The Woodlanders'
Pale beech and pine so blue,
    Set in one clay,
Bough to bough cannot you
    Live out your day?
When the rains skim and skip,
Why mar sweet comradeship,
Blighting with poison-drip
    Neighbourly spray?

Heart-halt and spirit-lame,
    City-opprest,
Unto this wood I came
    As to a nest;
Dreaming that sylvan peace
Offered the harrowed ease –
Nature a soft release
    From men's unrest.

But, having entered in,
    Great growths and small
Show them to men akin –
    Combatants all!
Sycamore shoulders oak,
Bines the slim sapling yoke,

Ivy-spun halters choke
  Elms stout and tall.

Touches from ash, O wych,
  Sting you like scorn!
You, too, brave hollies, twitch
  Sidelong from thorn.
Even the rank poplars bear
Lothly a rival's air,
Cankering in black despair
  If overborne.

Since, then, no grace I find
  Taught me of trees,
Turn I back to my kind,
  Worthy as these.
There at least smiles abound,
There discourse trills around,
There, now and then, are found
  Life-loyalties.
1887: 1896

(a) Before you begin working on these poetic texts, re-read our discussion in Chapter 10 of the differences between the idea of nature which was shared by Pope and his contemporaries and the view of nature expressed by the poetry of the Romantic period.

(b) Now try to discern the expectations and assumptions about nature which cause Wordsworth to turn from the city to the countryside in the first nine-teen lines of *The Prelude*. What is it about these assumptions that identify them as Romantic? Choose evidence to support your decision.

(c) Now examine the expectations and assumptions which cause Hardy's speaker to turn from the city to the wood. Are these expectations Neoclassical or Romantic, or are they different from both?

(d) Analyse as carefully as possible the assumptions about nature which Hardy's speaker develops through actually being in the wood. How does this new view of nature compare with the speaker's expectations?

(e) Would you say that the speaker's new view of nature is an objective one based on the actual experience, or is it simply an *interpretation* of nature? If it is an interpretation of nature, are there any clues in the poem itself which indicate why the speaker might interpret nature in this way?

(f) Is there anything in the poem itself which might lead you to believe that it is expressing a philosophy of nature which had a wider historical context?

(g) Hardy's subtitle to the poem suggests that an immediate context for this poem might be his own novel *The Woodlanders* (1887). Using whatever resources are available to you, try to find out more about Hardy's novel. You might do this by reading the blurb on the back cover (if there is one), by reading an introduction, or – better still – by reading the novel itself. You could also try to discover more about the intellectual and philosophical context in which Hardy's writings participate by scanning library catalogues, book indexes and lists of contents, or the Internet. The following books and articles contain relevant material or discussions:

> Alfred Tennyson, *In Memoriam* (1850), sections 54–56.
> Isobel Armstrong (1993) *Victorian Poetry*, pp. 261–5.
> U.C. Knoepflmacher and G.B. Tennyson, eds (1977) *Nature and the Victorian Imagination*.
> Gillian Beer (1983) *Darwin's Plots: Evolutionary narrative in . . . nineteenth-century fiction*.
> George Levine (1988) *Darwin and the Novelists*.

When you have read as much as you can find that seems useful, make a list of the main points you have discovered concerning the historical and intellectual context for Hardy's poem. In what ways does 'In a Wood' articulate a view of nature which is informed by this context?

(h) Find a copy of Tennyson's 'The Charge of the Light Brigade'. What is the effect of the insistent falling triple rhythm of Tennyson's poem? Does it have any relevance to the historical event which is the poem's subject? Now try to analyse the metre of 'In a Wood'. Do you think J.O. Bailey is right to say 'To some extent the verse resembles that of Tennyson's "The Charge of the Light Brigade" ' (*The Poetry of Thomas Hardy: A Handbook and Commentary*, p. 98)? In the light of what you have discovered about Hardy's view of nature, why might such an allusive echoing of Tennyson's metre be appropriate?

2 Read the following poem by W.H. Auden (published in his 1940 collection *Another Time*) and then try to answer the questions that follow.

September 1, 1939

> I sit in one of the dives
> On Fifty-Second Street
> Uncertain and afraid
> As the clever hopes expire
> Of a low dishonest decade: 5
> Waves of anger and fear
> Circulate over the bright
> And darkened lands of the earth,

Obsessing our private lives;
The unmentionable odour of death   10
Offends the September night.

Accurate scholarship can
Unearth the whole offence
From Luther until now
That has driven a culture mad,   15
Find what occurred at Linz,
What huge imago made
A psychopathic god:
I and the public know
What all schoolchildren learn,   20
Those to whom evil is done
Do evil in return.

Exiled Thucydides knew
All that a speech can say
About Democracy,   25
And what dictators do,
The elderly rubbish they talk
To an apathetic grave;
Analysed all in his book,
The enlightenment driven away,   30
The habit-forming pain,
Mismanagement and grief:
We must suffer them all again.

Into this neutral air
Where blind skyscrapers use   35
Their full height to proclaim
The strength of Collective Man,
Each language pours its vain
Competitive excuse:
But who can live for long   40
In an euphoric dream;
Out of the mirror they stare,
Imperialism's face
And the international wrong.

Faces along the bar   45
Cling to their average day:
The lights must never go out,
The music must always play,

All the conventions conspire
To make this fort assume   50
The furniture of home;
Lest we should see where we are,
Lost in a haunted wood,
Children afraid of the night
Who have never been happy or good.   55

The windiest militant trash
Important Persons shout
Is not so crude as our wish:
What mad Nijinsky wrote
About Diaghilev   60
Is true of the normal heart;
For the error bred in the bone
Of each woman and each man
Craves what it cannot have,
Not universal love   65
But to be loved alone.

From the conservative dark
Into the ethical life
The dense commuters come,
Repeating their morning vow,   70
'I *will* be true to the wife,
I'll concentrate more on my work',
And helpless governors wake
To resume their compulsory game:
Who can release them now,   75
Who can reach the deaf,
Who can speak for the dumb?

All I have is a voice
To undo the folded lie,
The romantic lie in the brain   80
Of the sensual man-in-the-street
And the lie of Authority
Whose buildings grope the sky:
There is no such thing as the State
And no one exists alone;   85
Hunger allows no choice
To the citizen or the police;
We must love one another or die.

> Defenceless under the night
> Our world in stupor lies;   90
> Yet, dotted everywhere,
> Ironic points of light
> Flash out wherever the Just
> Exchange their messages:
> May I, composed like them   95
> Of Eros and of dust,
> Beleaguered by the same
> Negation and despair,
> Show an affirming flame.

(a) To discover this poem's historical context and theme, try to find out what happened on 1 September 1939.

(b) Read the poem carefully in order to locate, as precisely as you can, its setting: where is the speaker?

(c) Read the poem closely in order to discern how it interprets the historical events it is responding to.

(d) The speaker implies that scholarship can explain the historical origins of what is happening by looking at history from Luther to Linz. Try to find out more about Luther and Linz. When you have done this, try to decide whether what you have found helps you to understand the historical events and/or the poem. What is the speaker's attitude towards such explanations? What alternative explanations does he have?

(e) Try to trace the other allusions in the poem: how do they help you understand the poem or what the poem is talking about?

(f) What is the speaker's overall attitude toward/tone regarding the situation in which he finds himself?

(g) In 2002, Pippa Heywood edited a poetry collection called *Poems for Refugees* (London: Vintage, 2002). This collection of poems chosen by well-known figures was put together as a response to the events of 11 September 2001 and the ensuing Afghan war. (The profits from the book were donated to the charity War Child in support of child refugees in Afghanistan.) The second poem in the collection, chosen by Stephen Fry, is Auden's 'September 1, 1939'. In an afterword, Fry explains his choice: 'I was asked if I might think of a poem for this collection just a week or so after the attack on the World Trade Centre in September 2001. Auden's "September 1, 1939" struck me as blisteringly and almost appallingly appropriate' (p. 13). Do you agree?

(h) What are the consequences of the fact that the events of 9/11 seem to change the way we read and respond to 'September 1, 1939'? Should we (i) insist that we must respect the historical context that the poem refers to and so put aside all associations with 9/11? or (ii) recognise that the historical situation in which we read a poem is inescapable and just as important in interpreting or responding to a poem as the historical context in which the poem was written or which the poem refers to?

(i) Would you say that the events of 9/11 have changed the meaning of 'September 1, 1939' or simply changed the way we interpret or respond to it?

Chapter 15

The Locations of Poetry

■ 'L'art pour l'art' (Art for art's sake)

The majority of the poets, readers and critics who were most influential in shaping views about poetry in the twentieth century held that poetry transcends social, historical and political concerns. Many readers report that this is why they are interested in poetry, and many writers of poetry have a similar outlook. Like most assumptions about poetry, however, this particular belief has a history. Tracing the outlines of that history will allow us to suggest that the idea that literature transcends politics and history is itself shaped by specific historical and political conditions.

The theoretical and philosophical basis for the modern form of the idea that art transcends the particularities of time and place may be found in Immanuel Kant's *Critique of Aesthetic Judgment* (1790), in which Kant argues that the authentic aesthetic experience is a 'disinterested' response to an object whose beauty is wholly detached from considerations of use or morality. This understanding of the aesthetic as 'disinterested' – aloof from the pragmatic interests and concerns of everyday life – was highly influential in nineteenth- and twentieth-century beliefs and theories about art. Kant's aesthetics stimulated the theoretical speculations of the German Romantic movement (in writers such as Schelling, Goethe and Schiller) which developed the notion that a work of art is an independent organic form with universal significance. Such ideas influenced the Romantic poetic theories of English-speaking writers such as Coleridge, Emerson and Edgar Allan Poe. The 'aestheticism' of nineteenth-century writers such as Poe, Walter Pater, Algernon Swinburne, Oscar Wilde, Gustave Flaubert and Charles Baudelaire evolved as a reaction, encapsulated in the slogan 'Art for art's sake', against attempts to make art socially utilitarian.[1] But even if we welcome any attempt to resist the reduction of art to a social tool, we still need to recognise that aestheticism itself gains its impulse in response to specific historical and political conditions.[2]

The most influential version of aestheticism in the Anglo-American academy in the twentieth century was the critical theory and practice of New Criticism. New Critics took up the idea that a work of art is a self-sufficient aesthetic object isolated from society and history in order to claim that the central business of literary criticism ought to be the 'close reading' of literary texts. One of the poems they cited in support of this position was Archibald MacLeish's 'Ars Poetica' (1926):[3]

> A poem should be palpable and mute
> As a globed fruit,
>
> Dumb
> As old medallions to the thumb,
>
> Silent as the sleeve-worn stone   5
> Of casement ledges where the moss has grown –
>
> A poem should be wordless
> As the flight of birds.
>
>   *
>
> A poem should be motionless in time
> As the moon climbs,   10
>
> Leaving, as the moon releases
> Twig by twig the night-entangled trees,
>
> Leaving, as the moon behind the winter leaves,
> Memory by memory the mind –
>
> A poem should be motionless in time   15
> As the moon climbs.
>
>   *
>
> A poem should be equal to:
> Not true.
>
> For all the history of grief
> An empty doorway and a maple leaf.   20

[1] For an account of the impact of aestheticism in poetry – especially in Symbolism – see 'Aestheticism' in *Princeton*.

[2] M.H. Abrams examines the social conditions in which aestheticism emerged in 'Art-as-Such: The Sociology of Modern Aesthetics', in Abrams, *Doing things with Texts: Essays in criticism and critical theory* (New York: Norton, 1989).

[3] MacLeish's poem is cited – seemingly with approval – by *Well Wrought Urn*, p. 139.

> For love
> The leaning grasses and two lights above the sea –
>
> A poem should not mean
> But be.

This poem consists of a series of prescriptions about what a poem 'should be' which effectively strive to take poetry out of discourse, history and politics altogether. Yet the poem's premises fall apart under the briefest examination. The most famous of the assertions – 'A poem should not mean / But be' – undermines its own claims, since it evidently has a meaning (even if it could never be true) which MacLeish seems to offer as an article of doctrine. Similar contradictions are revealed in the assertions that a poem should be mute, dumb, silent and wordless – which are all made through words and through a series of similes which, by definition, are a feature of language. The poem's most problematic assertion, however, is that 'An empty doorway and a maple leaf' could stand as a figurative equation 'For all the history of grief'. We need only recall some of the episodes in the history of suffering in the twentieth century to realise that this is an impossible equation. To represent such suffering with 'An empty doorway and a maple leaf' would be an aestheticisation which would erase that suffering and serve conservative versions of history. This suggests that, for all its claims to divorce poetry from politics, 'Ars Poetica' needs to be read as a deeply political poem.[4]

▣ The Politics of Reading and Writing

The fact that the New Critics took 'Ars Poetica' as a serious statement of an aspect of their own theory of poetry suggests that we ought to look at the political and historical context in which New Criticism arose and came to dominate the university teaching of literature in the United States from the 1940s to the 1960s. Terry Eagleton has suggested that the New Critics' ahistorical and apolitical treatment of poetry needs to be seen in terms of their associations with Southern agrarian conservatism in the United States (see Eagleton, 1983, pp. 46–50). John Barrell argues that the claim to rise above history and politics into a position of universal humanity entails the repression

---

[4] We are concerned here with problematising the way MacLeish's poem has been interpreted and used, and are putting aside the question of whether or not its contradictions are intended to be ironic. It is nevertheless interesting to place 'Ars Poetica' within MacLeish's life-work and its relation to literary and political histories. MacLeish (1892–1982) was an American poet who lived in Paris from 1917 to 1928. 'Ars Poetica' was published in this period in a volume of lyrics called *Streets in the Moon* (1926), and its doctrine and form perhaps indicate the influence of Pound, Eliot and the French Symbolists. After this period, however, MacLeish's poems, plays, and essays often focused on political problems – including the Depression, Hitler's rise to power and the Communist scare in the United States.

of history and political differences. Only those who are middle-class, masculine (and, we would add, racially white) can afford to imagine that such differences make no difference. For other kinds of reader, the presupposition that good reading entails assuming a balanced, universal standpoint involves the repression of their own identities. As Barrell puts it,

> In short, the ideology of control, of balance, of unity . . . and the identification of these with the essential and the universal . . . require that working-class writers and readers alike, and female writers and readers, should regard their class and gender as contingent to, as irrelevant to, their identity as writers and readers.
>
> (Barrell, *Poetry, Language and Politics*, p. 6)

The refusal of the idea that there is any single, correct position from which to read literary texts, however, does not mean that reading is reduced to the merely personal – to 'what it means to me'. This would simply be another way of excluding politics and history from reading.

The idea that writing is purely personal expression, and that our inner being is somehow aloof from political, social and historical influences, is one of the basic assumptions of the liberal-humanist viewpoint which is still prominent in Western democracies. Yet it might be that the laudable idea that we are all essentially the same actually obscures the fact that social differences between people do make a difference in societies which discriminate according to those differences. Langston Hughes's 'Theme for English B' (1951) critically explores the assumption that writing is an expression of a self which exists apart from society, history and politics by suggesting that this assumption is blind to differences of ethnicity and race which may 'colour' the writing.

Theme for English B

The instructor said,

> *Go home and write*
> *a page tonight.*
> *And let that page come out of you –*
> *Then, it will be true.*   5

I wonder if it's that simple?
I am twenty-two, colored, born in Winston-Salem.
I went to school there, then Durham, then here
to this college on the hill above Harlem.
I am the only colored student in my class.   10
The steps of the hill lead down into Harlem,
through a park, then I cross St. Nicholas,
Eighth Avenue, Seventh, and I come to the Y,

the Harlem Branch Y, where I take the elevator
up to my room, sit down, and write this page: 15

It's not easy to know what is true for you or me
at twenty-two, my age. But I guess I'm what
I feel and see and hear, Harlem, I hear you:
hear you, hear me – we two – you, me, talk on this page.
(I hear New York, too.) Me – who?   20
Well, I like to eat, sleep, drink, and be in love.
I like to work, read, learn, and understand life.
I like a pipe for a Christmas present,
or records – Bessie, bop, or Bach.
I guess being colored doesn't make me not like   25
the same things other folks like who are other races.
So will my page be colored that I write?
Being me, it will not be white.
But it will be
a part of you, instructor.   30
You are white –
yet a part of me, as I am a part of you.
That's American.
Sometimes perhaps you don't want to be a part of me.
Nor do I often want to be a part of you.   35
But we are, that's true!
I guess you learn from me –
although you're older – and white –
and somewhat more free.

This is my page for English B.   40

Like all the best students, this speaker questions the assumptions of the assign-
ment he is given in class. That leads him to examine his own identity in terms
of his age, race and personal history, and to think about how these factors
affect his relation to the university (he reflects on the fact that he is 'the only
colored student in [his] class' and that his instructor is white). He is also led to
reflect on the racial geography of New York in terms of the gulf between
Columbia University on the hill and Harlem across the park. That geography
is literally written into his page for English B as he begins to realise that his
identity is fundamentally bound up with it:

> I guess I'm what
> I feel and see and hear, Harlem, I hear you:
> hear you, hear me – we two – you, me, talk on this page. (17–19)

Thus the very notion that there is an independent or transcendent identity out of which we write is brought into question by the historical, material and geographical ways in which racial difference shapes experience in the United States. Those differences are as much 'American' as the ideology of common humanity referred to in the third section. The black student becomes the white instructor's teacher precisely because the instructor's 'Theme for English B' had overlooked the possibility that the self is profoundly shaped by the contexts in which it is formed and that racial difference makes a difference in a society in which race influences where you live and your educational opportunities.

In the last few decades, the idea that politics is confined to the process of governing countries or to the various 'radical' groups which resist that process has given way to a more comprehensive and enabling understanding of politics. One of the many contributions of recent feminist thought is encapsulated in the slogan 'The personal is political'. This slogan implies that politics imbues every aspect of our lives and the way our private and communal lives are imaginatively represented and staged in various kinds of text. This extended notion of politics implies that all ways of representing the world and the way human beings live within it and interrelate are potentially political. And since literature is one of the most powerful ways in which we represent the world and construct images of human life, we can anticipate that it plays a significant role in producing and questioning what is called 'ideology'. James H. Kavanagh claims that 'society . . . uses apparatuses of ideology to form members of its classes into social subjects who are unlikely ever to consider rebellion'. Ideology achieves this through offering individual subjects pictures of society and of their place within it:

> One writer on ideology has remarked: 'A society is possible in the last analysis because the individuals within it carry around in their heads some sort of picture of that society'. . . . This observation, with the important addition of 'and their place in it,' might serve as a fair introduction to current ideological theory.[6]

If ideology can be thought of as an internalised set of images about our society and our place within it, it is worth asking where such images come from. Clearly they do not come from propaganda, since we pride ourselves in thinking that we are not swayed by that. Instead, ideology is generated through the endless stream of images and texts which are offered for consumption in the West: advertisements, the Internet, soaps, news programmes, newspapers, comics, films, videos, education, religion, pop music, cartoons, magazines, political speeches, art, literature, philosophy, literary and cultural criticism,

---

[6] James H. Kavanagh, 'Ideology', in Lentricchia and McLaughlin, *Critical Terms for Literary Study*, pp. 306–20 (308–9), quoting Karl Mannheim, *Ideology and Utopia: An introduction to the sociology of knowledge* (New York: Harcourt Brace, 1964), p. xxiii.

and so on. The primary purpose of such cultural products is not, of course, to distribute ideological messages. Instead, ideology (ideas about the way the world is or should be) is generated as a kind of unnoticed by-product or 'side-effect' of such cultural texts. Apart from their primary purposes, such discourses, texts and images tend to produce and reproduce normative images of our society and its values. From such sources we learn our class, race and gender roles; we learn who we are as a nation and how we differ from others; we learn what is 'normal' and what is 'deviant' or 'marginal'.[7]

Since the Renaissance, lyric poetry – with its emphasis on the interior emotions of sexual love and religious reflection – has constituted a discourse of interior experience. The private has become pre-eminently the terrain and prerogative of lyric poetry, and our own training as readers has caused us to focus on lyric poetry at the expense of other genres precisely because of its stress on the personal. A certain reading of lyric poetry, then, has served to reinforce the ideological distinction between the personal and the political. We have been taught that the public 'context' of a poem is a mere backdrop for the more important dramas of interior consciousness. This serves the conservative political establishment all too well, since private emotion has become the most effective and addictive 'opium of the people' (to allude to Marx's famous statement about religion in the nineteenth century). Yet if we hold on to the idea that the personal is political, we can realise that there is always a subtle sexual politics at work in lyric poetry. Although the very individualism affirmed in lyric poetry since the Renaissance can be seen as complicit with bourgeois ideology,[8] the most interesting poetry is never a mere passive vehicle for any ideological position. The realisation that the personal is political is not a defeatist admission that ideology has succeeded in colonising the most sacred recesses of our inner being, leaving us no place to turn. Poetry is often an effective means for exposing and resisting dominant ideologies – not by a retreat into the personal, but by rewriting the personal in other, more enabling terms.

This last point can be understood by re-reading Langston Hughes's 'Theme for English B' or by returning, once again, to our discussion of Adrienne Rich's 'Song' (see Chapter 5). Rich's poem is a lyric concerned with the interior consciousness of a female speaker. The dominant ideological image of a lonely woman in Anglo-American society in the 1970s (and perhaps today) is negative. Our society typically represents (or represented) marriage, home-making

---

[7] For a fascinating analysis of the role popular culture played in generating bourgeois 'myths' in 1950s France, see Barthes, *Mythologies*.

[8] Antony Easthope, in *Poetry as Discourse* (London: Methuen, 1983), argues that the use of iambic pentameter in literary poetry since the Renaissance has contributed to the construction of a bourgeois myth of individual subjectivity. This is unconvincing not only because of the paucity of evidence which he offers but also because literary poetry has used the four-beat form at least as much as iambic pentameter.

and child-rearing as the highest and most 'natural' goals for women, and seeks (or once sought) to reinforce those desires through generating negative images of those women – spinsters, lesbians, and so on – who 'fail' or opt out. In this way, the interior desires and anxieties of women about their 'success' or otherwise with regard to their 'highest calling' are always–already influenced – perhaps constituted – by the ideological representations of society. Rich's poem responds to this not by retreating into a more authentic, less ideologically tainted interior consciousness but by attempting to write another kind of script for women. This script offers a more enabling version of loneliness, a different way of experiencing it which draws on our culture's stock of positive images of self-reliant independence usually reserved for men.

Reading poetry, then, can have political effects for the reader: it can reinforce or challenge our assumptions; it can contribute towards our empowerment or our disempowerment. Poetry can also powerfully articulate the shared feelings of a group, but if it is to achieve anything other than preaching to the converted it has to do more than that. If poetry engages with complex issues in ways which do not overlook those complexities, then poetry itself may have to be 'complex'. Such a complexity is very different from the mystifying complexity celebrated by New Criticism. If readers of poetry are going to be anything other than passive recipients of messages, then poems must exercise our reading skills and imaginative powers. In fact, it might be argued that it is politically more crucial that we develop our powers of deep, careful reading and imaginative intelligence than that we read yet another political message with which we simply agree or disagree. Reading poetry is more difficult and challenging than reading messages: it helps us actively to develop our critical intelligence because it can challenge or complicate our pre-established ways of seeing the world – and that might be more politically urgent than the passive reception and reiteration of messages (radical or conservative).

■ The Locations of Poetry

One of the purposes of this book is to influence the way poetry is taught and studied in academic institutions. But we should not make the mistake of assuming that poetry is primarily written for such institutions. Poetry has been written at different times and places for different audiences and different groups of readers. The academic study of literature does not always acknowledge the importance of recognising the particular social and historical locations in which the texts we study were originally produced. Many of the dominant assumptions about literature since Romanticism have been based on the idea that literature transcends the time and place of its production in order to attain a 'universal' significance. Any sense that a poem ought to be contingent upon its location of production has been seen as a limitation by academic critics. For Adrienne Rich, however, the idea that poetry is always 'located' rather than universal is not a limiting of poetry but, rather, its empowerment. Returning from a trip to Nicaragua in 1983 – a country where, in the Sandinista period, 'everyone [was] a poet' – she is led to reflect on the cost of the dominant belief in the United States (and Britain) that poetry transcends national, racial, class and sexual locations: 'What toll is taken of art when it is separated from the social fabric? How is art curbed, how are we made to feel useless and helpless, in a system which so depends on our alienation?'[9] Rich found inspirational models of poetry's communal role on the margins of mainstream America and in countries marginalised from Euro-American hegemony – in Nicaragua, in the work of contemporary Cuban women poets, in the writing and art of contemporary North American Indian women and black American women (*Blood, Bread, and Poetry*, pp. 184–7). But looking to the margins is not to imagine them as 'pure' places, nor to assume that marginalised groups in the United States are not part of, as well as apart from, mainstream America:

> we were . . . living and writing not only within a women's community. We are trying to build a political and cultural movement in the heart of capitalism, in a country where racism assumes every form of physical, institutional, and psychic violence, and in which more than one person in seven lives below the poverty line. The United States feminist movement is rooted in the United States, a nation with a particular history of hostility both to art and to socialism. . . . As a lesbian-feminist poet and writer, I need to understand how this location affects me, along with the realities of blood and bread within this nation.
>
> . . . As women, I think it essential that we admit and explore our cultural identities, our national identities, even as we reject the patriotism, jingoism, nationalism offered to us as 'the American way of life'.
>
> (*Blood, Bread, and Poetry*, p. 183)

But the fact that Rich needed to go outside the academy to find inspirational models for her own political writing and activity does not mean that departments of literature in universities are hermetically sealed from such developments. Although Rich might be suspicious of the academicisation of Women's Studies (see p. xiii), she was herself teaching at Stanford University at the time *Blood, Bread, and Poetry* was published, while the title essay from which we have been quoting originated as a talk given for the Institute for the Humanities, University of Massachusetts in 1983. The fact is that universities and colleges have themselves become sites where some of the political issues we have been discussing, together with questions about their relation to literature, have been articulated and fought out. Although the academy might not

---

[9] 'Blood, Bread, and Poetry: The Location of the Poet', in Adrienne Rich, *Blood, Bread, and Poetry: Selected prose 1979–1985* (London: Virago, 1987), p. 185.

be wholly representative of society, it is certainly part of it – neither wholly radical nor wholly conservative. Since Rich wrote 'Blood, Bread, and Poetry', the teaching of poetry has become politicised in at least some of the ways her essay seems to call for. Departments of Literature and Cultural Studies have become spaces in which women's literature, feminist criticism and theory, and black literature and criticism are being produced and taught. Of course, such attempts in university departments to draw attention to the links between politics and poetry – and between politics and the teaching and criticism of poetry – have not occurred without resistance. These developments have alarmed some critics and poets – especially those still under the influence of New Criticism.

We have been arguing throughout this book that poetry needs to be seen as a fundamental part of society not only in terms of content, language and form, but also in terms of the relation of poetry and its institutions to society as a whole. Poetry needs readers as well as writers, and hence some means of reproduction and circulation (poetry readings, books, magazines, recordings). In other words, poetry is itself an industry, and this industry varies through history according to the particular society or cultural milieu in which it is produced and consumed. These seemingly extraneous factors all have an impact on the poetry produced. Folk poetry is addressed to a different audience, and has different roles and methods of production and circulation, than 'art' poetry does. And 'art' poetry is written, financed, circulated and consumed differently at different historical moments. In the Renaissance period, writers such as Shakespeare, Ben Jonson or John Donne relied on aristocratic or court patronage, and circulated their poetry to a relatively limited educated élite. Shakespeare's plays, by contrast, were produced for immediate consumption in popular playhouses which were the most successful form of mass entertainment in the period during which he lived (though many of his plays were also produced at court). By the Romantic period, audiences were expanding (owing to the financial revolution we now call capitalism, and to increasing literacy) and the writer could aspire to make an independent living from book sales. Wordsworth and Coleridge published *Lyrical Ballads* in 1798 not only as an experiment in a new kind of poetry but also in order to make money (they failed in the latter aim). The poems of Lord Byron and Walter Scott, by contrast, sold in huge numbers. Today, contemporary poets rarely sell enough copies of their usually slim volumes of poetry to make a living. Instead, they have to supplement their income through poetry readings, Arts Council grants, teaching creative writing, and so on. One of the largest markets for poetry today is created by educational institutions, although only a small fraction of contemporary poetry finds its way on to school or undergraduate curricula. The twentieth century witnessed an enormous explosion of literary studies and the institutionalisation of 'English' as an academic discipline. This has itself transformed the sociology of literature, creating a new relationship between texts and readers which is in many ways unprecedented. This book is itself a product of that historical and cultural shift.

Poetry, then, can be studied as a changing institution or industry. This entails looking at the way the institutions of poetry relate to other social and economic institutions. The role and status of poets differ in different kinds of communities and at different moments in history. Bards and singers played a vital role in pre-print cultures through ritually retelling the histories and myths of the community or by conveying news from district to district. Folk poetry continued to serve such functions in England until the eighteenth century. At the same time, beginning in the Renaissance, an aristocratic or court poetry developed, written by and for the political élite of Elizabethan England. Thus art poetry and folk poetry became divorced from one another along class lines, the first circulating among a classically educated élite, the second serving the uneducated and illiterate majority as a means of entertainment, education and political resistance. Élite or art poetry remained central to the dominant culture through to the end of the eighteenth century. Pope, for example, assumes that he speaks for the cultural élite of his time, and that his poetry can play a role in the shaping of Britain's political life: he is clearly writing a public poetry, and claims a certain representative authority for his views.

By the end of the eighteenth century, however, art poetry itself began to be marginalised. To understand this, we would need to examine political and economic developments in the latter half of that century. The rise of middle-class capitalism did not displace aristocratic power but allied with it against the disenfranchised majority of the population. This emerging political formation became increasingly reactionary after the French Revolution and violently resisted attempts in Britain to imitate the French example. Our image of the poet as an outsider isolated from society originates from this period. Regardless of their class origins, poets such as Burns, Blake and the early Wordsworth felt excluded from and resistant to the dominant political order. These Romantic poets combined criticism of repression within Britain and British imperialism with a new interest in folk poetry. Publications such as Burns's *Poems, Chiefly in the Scottish Dialect* (1786), Blake's *Songs of Innocence and of Experience* (1789/1794), and Wordsworth and Coleridge's *Lyrical Ballads* (1798/1800) attempt to reconnect art poetry with the subject matter, forms and language of folk poetry. The political radicalism of Romantic poets such as Shelley and Blake has been hugely influential in shaping our received notion that poets are figures on the margins of mainstream society whose imaginative insights offer alternatives to the dominant ideology. Yet we need to remember that not all poets have been radicals: some of Wordsworth's best poetry was written after he abandoned the radical cause.

The marginalisation of poets such as Blake and Shelley in the Romantic period should not mislead us into thinking that poetry itself had become marginalised. As we have mentioned, the poetry of writers such as Scott and Byron achieved sales figures that would be astonishing today. In the nineteenth century, poets such as Tennyson, Browning and Arnold were significant public figures whose poems engaged with some of the central political questions of the Victorian period.[10] Nonetheless, poetry's role as a major vehicle of public discourse began to be taken over by the novel. This gradual marginalisation of poetry continued through the twentieth century. Although he was a poet of radical persuasions, W.H. Auden could write in 1939, on the eve of the Second World War, that 'poetry makes nothing happen'.[11] Although the New Critics made poems the central objects of their criticism and classroom teaching, and claimed that poetry was the central discourse of humanist enquiry, they nonetheless divorced poetry from the shaping political issues of the moments in which it was written and read. The range of new literary theories which have displaced New Criticism in the universities are usually more interested in narrative fiction than in poetry and when they do focus on poetry they tend to treat it as if it were prose.[12] And if poetry is therefore relatively neglected at the cutting edge of academic research, there is also evidence to suggest that it presents something of a conundrum to pupils, teachers and curriculum designers in secondary and high schools in Britain and the United States.

Yet despite – or perhaps because of – its marginalisation, poetry and poetic uses of language have always been important to marginalised groups in establishing ways of speaking and thinking which are alternative to the dominant discourse. While literary poetry has been a fairly élitist discourse at least since the Renaissance, there has always been an alternative, popular poetry alongside it. This poetry has often taken the form of protest poetry – as, for example, in the working-class Chartist poetry of the early nineteenth century. As we have already indicated, oral poetry once played a significant role in the lives of the illiterate majority in Britain. The most important oral form was the folk ballad, the earliest extant examples of which date from the later medieval period. Folk ballads typically represent the views of a community rather than an individual. As we saw in Chapter 11, broadside or street ballads were sold in British streets and country fairs from 1500 to 1920. In the USA, broadside ballads flourished after the Civil War and were still used in African-American communities in the early years of the twentieth century (see *Princeton*).

---

[10] For a compelling account of the inter-animation of poetry and politics in nineteenth-century Britain, see Armstrong, *Victorian Poetry*.

[11] See W.H. Auden, 'In Memory of W.B. Yeats'; Auden goes on to say that poetry 'survives, / A Way of happening, a mouth', but the poem remains equivocal about the political effectiveness of poetry.

[12] An exciting exception to this is Hošek and Parker, *Lyric Poetry: Beyond the New Criticism*.

In the twentieth century, poetry and poetic expression became important for groups traditionally excluded from mainstream culture in Britain, the United States and elsewhere, suggesting that literature in general, and poetry in particular, can play a significant part in the establishment and assertion of a sense of individual and group identity through language and culture. Such poetry works both as a means of protesting against the dominant culture and as a medium through which members of the marginalised group may 'speak to' each other. As Rich suggests, 'Every group that lives under the naming and image-making power of a dominant culture is at risk from [the] mental fragmentation' which results from the dissonance between these images and their own experience. Such groups need 'an art which can resist' that dissonance (*Blood, Bread, and Poetry*, pp. 181, 175).

A striking instance of the power of poetic language to speak to and form a sense of alternative community was the remarkable 'poeticisation' of counterculture pop lyrics in the 1960s. Bob Dylan more or less pioneered this development with his early protest songs, which drew on a range of traditions, including folk music and the blues. In albums such as *Highway 61 Revisited* (1965) and *Blonde on Blonde* (1966) he went on to develop his poetic lyrics to extraordinary limits. In doing so he paved the way for the whole countercultural movement, inspiring writers such as John Lennon, Paul McCartney and Jim Morrison to introduce compelling poetic elements into their lyrics. In this way, a whole generation of young people 'turned on and tuned in' to the power of poetic language. As pop music has returned to mainstream commercial culture, the radical and poetic edge of pop lyrics has largely disappeared, although writers such as Joni Mitchell, Patti Smith, Peter Gabriel, Elvis Costello, Nick Cave and others have continued to produce poetic songs outside mainstream pop music.

Poetry – published in small alternative presses – has played a part in the Peace Movement, the Civil Rights Movement, the Women's Movement, the Gay Liberation Campaign, and so on.[13] It is revealing, and moving, that one of the ways in which people have attempted to cope with AIDS has been through the writing of poetry.[14] It is significant that literacy was one of the Sandinista government's immediate priorities after the overthrow of the Somoza regime in

---

[13] The following books of poems are just samples of many others: Pat Arrowsmith, *On the Brink* (London: CND, 1981); Alison Fell *et al.*, *Smile, Smile, Smile, Smile* (London: Sheba Feminist Publishers, 1980); Christian McEwen, ed., *Naming the Waves: Contemporary lesbian poetry* (London: Virago, 1988). For examples of black American poetry written during the period of the Civil Rights movement, see Dudley Randall, ed., *The Black Poets* (New York: Bantam Books, 1971), pp. 181–33.

[14] See, for example, John Harold, ed., *How Can You Write a Poem when You're Dying of AIDS?* (New York: Bantam Books, 1971).

Nicaragua in 1979, and that the writing of poetry in poetry workshops became one of the main vehicles through which the people of Nicaragua explored their experiences of the revolution and hopes for a new society.[15] Rich visited Nicaragua in this period, reporting that 'What was constantly and tellingly manifested was a belief in art, not as a commodity, not as a luxury, not as suspect activity, but as a precious resource to be made available to all' (*Blood, Bread, and Poetry*, p. 185). The struggle against apartheid in South Africa was also voiced in poetry.[16] As we will see in the following chapter, poetry is also an important means by which many former colonialised peoples articulated their resistance to colonial powers and cultures and now articulate their postcolonial identities. Ethnic minorities and marginalised peoples in Britain and the United States have resorted to poetry and poetic uses of language as part of their struggle for recognition or a sense of identity.[17] In the United States, there was a remarkable flourishing of Native American poetry in English in the twentieth century,[18] while rap music is simply the most recent form in which young black people (and increasingly, young white people) produce and consume poetic language.[19] Often, such 'alternative' poetry employs, and hence values, non-standard Englishes, or even different languages – as in the poetry of Caribbean British poets such as Linton Kwesi Johnson or the recent flourishing of poetry in urban Scotland.[20] The following poem by John Agard thematises the implications of using non-standard English (Agard was born in Guyana in 1949 and moved to England in 1977):

[15] See John Lyons and I. Forster, trans., *Poems of Love and Revolution from the Nicaraguan Poetry Workshops* (London: Nicaraguan Solidarity Campaign, 1983).

[16] For an introductory discussion of black and protest poetry in South Africa during the apartheid period, see 'South African Poetry' in *Princeton*. A useful general anthology of South African poetry is Stephen Gray, ed., *The Penguin Book of Southern African Verse* (Harmondsworth: Penguin, 1988); an anthology devoted to black South African poetry is Tim Couzens and E. Patel, eds, *The Return of Amasi Bird: Black South African Poetry (1891–1981)* (Johannesburg: Raven Press, 1982).

[17] See, for example, Grace Nichols, *I is a long memoried woman* (London: Caribbean Cultural International, 1983). A good introductory anthology is Paula Burnett, ed., *The Penguin Book of Caribbean Verse in English* (Harmondsworth: Penguin, 1986).

[18] See Duane Niatum, ed., *Harper's Anthology of 20th Century Native American Poetry* (New York: Harper Collins, 1988).

[19] See Lawrence A. Stanley, ed., *Rap: The lyrics* (Harmondsworth: Penguin, 1992). Of especial interest is the introduction, 'Rap Music as American History', by Jefferson Morley.

[20] Linton Kwesi Johnson's dub poetry, best known on records such as *Making History* (1984), employs the Creole language of the Jamaica of his childhood to comment on black experience in London; for poems which use the Scots language to articulate contemporary Scottish experience, see Daniel O'Rourke, ed., *Dream State: The new Scottish poets* (Edinburgh: Polygon, 1994).

Listen Mr Oxford Don

Me not no Oxford don
me a simple immigrant
from Clapham Common
I didn't graduate
I immigrate   5

But listen Mr Oxford don
I'm a man on de run
and a man on de run
is a dangerous one

I ent have no gun   10
I ent have no knife
but mugging de Queen's English
is the story of my life

I don't need no axe
to split/ up yu syntax   15
I don't need no hammer
to mash/ up yu grammar

I warning you Mr Oxford don
I'm a wanted man
and a wanted man   20
is a dangerous one

Dem accuse me of assault
on de Oxford dictionary/
imagine a concise peaceful man like me/
dem want me serve time   25
for inciting rhyme to riot
but I tekking it quiet
down here in Clapham Common

I'm not a violent man Mr Oxford don
I only armed wit mih human breath   30
but human breath is a dangerous weapon
So mek dem send one big word after me
I ent serving no jail sentence
I slashing suffix in self-defence
I bashing future wit present tense   35
and if necessary

I making de Queen's English accessory/ to my offence

Agard's poem is addressed to 'Mr Oxford Don' – which may refer to a particular academic from Oxford University, to Oxford dons in general, or perhaps to any academic teacher (such as the authors of this book). But that is not quite the same thing as saying that Oxford dons, or academic teachers more generally, are the implied audience for this poem. If we want to locate the poem's target audience, we could do so by finding out where it was first published and who it was written for. 'Listen Mr Oxford Don' first appeared in 1985 in a book of poems called *Mangoes and Bullets*, published by Pluto Press. Such alternative-press poetry books tend to have a small but specialised readership. Agard also performed his poems in London cabaret spots to 'alternative' audiences. But Agard's poem has since been reprinted in an anthology called *The New British Poetry, 1968–88* (1988). This anthology offers an excellent introduction to the range of different poetic voices that were challenging mainstream establishment poetry in Britain in the period, but the market for the anthology may inevitably be significantly different from *Mangoes and Bullets*, and the anthology's very title suggests that it has started the process of assimilating Agard's work to a national corpus – which now necessarily includes British Caribbean writers – even if this 'assimilation' (a loaded term in this context) may also entail *challenging* people's understanding of national identity. Quite apart from any conclusions we might draw from the conditions of the poem's publication, we can also pick up clues from the poem itself that the implied reader of Agard's poem is not the same as its addressee. Try reading the poem again and asking whether it is written (a) for Oxford dons to read or (b) for some other kind of reader. If you decide on (b), try to define that readership. (Then, perhaps, do the same exercise with Langston Hughes's 'Theme for English B'.)

Although both these poems are addressed to people in the same profession as the authors of the book you are now reading, we ourselves do not think either of these poems was written specifically for readers like us. The fact that we have included them in this chapter, however, perhaps suggests that we are contributing to the institutionalisation of poetic texts that were originally written to challenge institutions. Yet we are seeking neither to exclude nor to 'assimilate' this poetry to 'national' canons but, rather, to use it to indicate the way the literature of marginalised groups is beginning to challenge, transform or even explode the very notion of a national canon. A similar point could be made about much of the material we have discussed in the text or cited in the footnotes of this chapter. It would be a wholly relevant exercise if you were now to go through the sources cited in the footnotes to this chapter and ask which of them imply that the material has already been appropriated by the literary academy or establishment, and which of them imply that this is poetry which still remains wholly in the possession of its original readership or market. If a book's title or the publisher's details do not indicate this for you, try finding the book in your library in order to see what context and reader-ship the volume as a whole implies. If the book is not in your academic library, that might also tell you something about the academicisation of particular texts and authors at the expense of others. This is an exercise in market research.

■ National Poetries

One of the reasons why the poetry of marginalised figures such as John Agard can be so disturbing for the poetic establishment (represented by 'Mr Oxford Don') is because that establishment assumes there is a mutually constitutive relationship between a nation and its language and literature. As Agard realises, an attack on Standard English represents an attack on the very notion of Englishness which it sustains. The sense of group solidarity which the pro-duction and circulation of poetry can produce has played a role in the found-ing and perpetuating of nations throughout history. Poetry played an active role in the development of new forms of nationalism and the emergence of new nation-states in eighteenth- and nineteenth-century Europe. Our understanding of the nation-state – based on a confluence of political organisation, race and language – is, in fact, a relatively recent one. Our modern notion of race emerged through problematic racial theories of biological heredity developed in the eighteenth and nineteenth centuries.[21] The wave of European national-ism which followed the French Revolution and led to the founding of nation-states such as Germany and Italy combined such notions of racial heredity with theories of a shared cultural history. The ideological needs of emerging nation-states thus led to attempts to discover or establish national literary tra-ditions. It is no coincidence that the first major theoretical discussion of the idea of a national literature was by a German philosopher, Johann Gottfried Herder, who has been described as 'the first important philosopher of modern nationalism' (Appiah, in Lentricchia and McLaughlin, *Critical Terms for Literary Study*, p. 283). The German nation-state is a relatively modern con-struction or invention, since it was assembled out of a number of principalities whose only connection was that the people spoke dialects of German. In *On the New German Literature* (1767), Herder argues that a shared language is the basis of a shared nationality, and that the essence and high point of a nation's language were to be found in its poetry – from the anonymous folk songs of the past to the work of the great poets. In Italy, nineteenth-century nationalists drew inspiration from the poetry of Dante and Petrarch, especially the latter's 'Italia mia' ('My Italy') from his *Canzoniere* (which Petrarch

---

[21] See Kwame Anthony Appiah, 'Race', in Lentricchia and McLaughlin, *Critical Terms for Literary Study*, pp. 274–87 (276).

467

worked on from the late 1330s until his death in 1374). The invention of national literary traditions, then, was wholly bound up with the process of forging nation-states in eighteenth- and nineteenth-century Europe. Similar processes took place in those European countries which were already organised along national lines. Sir Philip Sidney's *Apology for Poetry* (1595) can be seen as an attempt to found a vernacular literary tradition in English at the end of the sixteenth century. It is only in the eighteenth and nineteenth centuries, however, in the most intense period of Britain's transformation from a feudal nation to a modern, capitalist and imperialist nation-state, that the scholarly creation of an English literary tradition really got under way.

The idea of a national literature – and of a national poetry in particular – played a significant role in the attempt to forge national identity in the United States: 'American poetry – marginalized economically but essential to psychological, moral, and religious life – played a powerful part in [The United States'] act of self-creation and self-expression' (*Princeton*). The poetry of the colonial period – including the nationalistic poetry of the 'Connecticut Wits' – was largely dependent upon European models. The 'real watershed of American poetry' was Ralph Waldo Emerson's Americanised version of Romanticism (*Princeton*). Emerson's *Essays, First Series* (1841) reads as a set of philosophical justifications for a cultural frontier spirit. In the essay 'Self-Reliance', for example, 'manly' independence is recommended not only as the cure for the 'spiritual decline' of the eastern states but also as the founding attitude of American culture. The culture of the 'New World' must go its own way independently of the 'Old World'. In doing this, American individuals will emulate, not merely imitate, the great geniuses of the past:

> A man should learn to detect and watch that gleam of light which flashes across his mind from within, more than the lustre of the firmament of bards and sages . . .
> What have I to do with the sacredness of traditions, if I live wholly from within?[22]

Emerson's essays paved the way for a specifically American poetics based on a Romantic notion of self-reliance and authenticity which supposedly freed the poet from the traditions and forms of European culture. Walt Whitman's 'Song of Myself' (first published in *Leaves of Grass* in 1855) epitomises this new bid for independence in its title, in its use of a 'free verse' which broke the mould of European forms, and in its adoption of a distinctive American idiom. The first section of this epic of the democratic individual's consciousness will give you a sufficient idea:

> I celebrate myself, and sing myself,
> And what I assume you shall assume,

---

[22] 'Self-Reliance', in Emerson, *Emerson's Essays* (London: Dent, 1971), p. 30 and p. 33.

For every atom belonging to me as good belongs to you.
I loaf and invite my soul,
I lean and loaf at my ease observing a spear of summer grass.   5

My tongue, every atom of my blood, formed from this soil,
    this air,
Born here of parents born here from parents the same, and
    their parents the same,
I, now thirty-seven years old in perfect health begin,
Hoping to cease not till death.

Creeds and schools in abeyance,   10
Retiring back a while sufficed at what they are, but
    never forgotten,
I harbor for good or bad, I permit to speak at every hazard,
Nature without check with original energy.

In these lines, Whitman lays the foundations of an American poetic tradition which assumes a cultural independence to match the political independence achieved a century earlier. Whitman's self-expression is based on an assumption of representative individualism which takes it for granted that his reader is the same as himself:

I celebrate myself, and sing myself,
And what I assume you shall assume,
For every atom belonging to me as good belongs to you. (1–3)

With the 'Creeds and schools in abeyance', Whitman claims to be inspired and impelled by nature's 'original energy'. He asserts that his poetry is wholly native to America: his 'tongue' – like his 'blood' – is 'formed from this soil, this air' because he was born of parents whose parents' parents were born on the same soil. This yoking together of language, soil and blood as constituents of native and national authenticity is, however, disturbingly reminiscent of the rhetorical forging of nations and national feeling which we have already examined. By assuming that his reader will be the same as himself, Whitman excludes all readers who are different. (And the implication that Whitman's conception of what it is to be American is a profoundly racial one is supported in another poem, 'Pioneers! O Pioneers!')

■ The Undoing of National Traditions

Whitman's staking of his claim to be a native American on the basis that his family had lived on the soil for three generations cannot help but remind us that such a lineage was pathetically brief compared with the 20,000 years or more that the Native American Indians have inhabited the continent.[23] Each of the groups of native peoples on the American continent had an established tradition of poetry long before white people ever set foot on the soil.[24] Despite the genocide and the drift away from ethnic roots, there is still a significant Native American presence in the United States. There are currently three hundred and fifteen Native American 'nations', each with its distinct tradition. The inherited traditions of these various peoples include a metrical, ritualistic oral poetry used for spiritual purposes. Yet Native American culture has changed through the impact of the European invasion. Today, there is a significant body of American Indian writing in English which has accumulated over the last two hundred years. The fact that these writers are writing in English demonstrates that literary traditions, at least in the modern world, are never 'pure'. In 1975, Duane Niatum edited a collection of contemporary Native American poetry which Brian Swann describes as 'poetry of mingled roots, drawing on Faulkner, Winters, Vallejo, Hugo, Wright, Roethke, Neruda and other sources available to late twentieth-century writers, as well as on the native oral tradition and individual vision' (in Niatum, ed., *Harper's Anthology of 20th Century Native American Poetry*, p. xvi). The accumulated effects of centuries of intermarriage and rape, however, have made the very definition of what it is to be an American Indian problematic. Whereas the Bureau of Indian Affairs states that someone must possess one-quarter Indian blood to be officially regarded as a Native American, Swann suggests that Indian identity is a matter not of blood but of cultural identification with and acceptance by other Native Americans (in Niatum, p. xx). Yet the use of English and the intermingling of blood and traditions raises the question of whether it is legitimate to talk of a contemporary Native American poetic tradition at all. Is poetry by Native Americans 'just poetry with a variety of themes and techniques that happens to be written by Native Americans' (p. xviii)? Native American writers are wary of the category 'Native American Writing' because it risks perpetuating stereotypes, yet Swann ends by claiming that this poetry presents a common critique of modern America which draws on the visionary oral traditions of the poets' ancestors in order to offer alternative visions of life which might alleviate contemporary ills. Thus we can see that the desire to maintain a distinct poetry is bound up with the desire to assert a people's distinction from other peoples and with the belief that such a distinct people and poetry can offer positive alternatives to what is perceived as the dangerous impoverishment of the dominant culture.

[23] See John Gattso, ed., *Native America*, 3rd edn (n.p.: APA Insight Guide, 1992), pp. 31–2.
[24] See A. Grove Day, *The Sky Clears: Poetry of the American Indians* (Lincoln: University of Nebraska Press, 1951); and 'American Indian Poetry' in *Princeton*.

Complicating the ideal of an independent American poetic tradition, then, is the possibility that national traditions are never hermetically sealed from each other and the fact that the peoples of the United States comprise several distinct but overlapping races and nations. If Native Americans are turning more and more to the idea of themselves as constituting separate nations within the USA, then the same pattern can be seen in African-American poetry. Poetic writing has long been one of the survival strategies of blacks in the USA, as is witnessed in early field songs, spirituals and the blues. But as early as the second half of the eighteenth century, black writers began to write literary poetry and sought acceptance into the white literary tradition. Phillis Wheatley (c. 1753–94) imitated Pope, and even the writers of the Harlem Renaissance in the 1920s were influenced by English poets of more than a century earlier.[25] Although the Harlem Renaissance writers and the generation of poets which followed them sought to define a black voice and consciousness, they can, in a sense, be seen as a literary precursor to the integrationist ideals of the early Civil Rights movement of the 1960s.

Gwendolyn Brooks is one of the most important poets of the post-Harlem-Renaissance generation. Her poetry often deals with questions of being a black woman in the United States, but her early poems tend to use fairly conventional poetic forms (such as the sonnet) and Standard American English. The poem 'kitchenette building' (1945), though not quite a sonnet, is a case in point:

kitchenette building
We are things of dry hours and the involuntary plan,
Grayed in, and gray. 'Dream' makes a giddy sound, not strong
Like 'rent,' 'feeding a wife,' 'satisfying a man.'

But could a dream send up through onion fumes
Its white and violet, fight with fried potatoes   5
And yesterday's garbage ripening in the hall,
Flutter, or sing an aria down these rooms

Even if we were willing to let it in,
Had time to warm it, keep it very clean,
Anticipate a message, let it begin?   10
We wonder. But not well! not for a minute!
Since Number Five is out of the bathroom now,
We think of lukewarm water, hope to get in it.

The speaker (who uses 'we') speaks for people living an impoverished existence in which problems of money, food and keeping clean take up all the available

---

[25] See Dudley Randall, *The Black Poets*, pp. xxiii–xxvi (xxv).

time and energy, making it virtually impossible to entertain a 'dream' among the fumes of onions, fried potatoes and yesterday's garbage. Although the poem does not say what the 'dream' is, it seems abstract and ephemeral in contrast with the very material realities which make immediate and unignorable demands in the present. The dream could simply be to escape from such poverty, but the term may also refer to the dream of freedom from racial repression. This is certainly the way Langston Hughes uses it in his slightly later 'Harlem' (1951):

> What happens to a dream deferred?
>
> Does it dry up
> like a raisin in the sun?
> Or fester like a sore –
> And then run?   5
> Does it stink like rotten meat?
> Or crust and sugar over –
> like a syrupy sweet?
>
> Maybe it just sags
> like a heavy load.   10
>
> Or does it explode?

This poem tries to anticipate what happens to a repressed people if their dream of liberation is continually deferred. In some ways, then, it prefigured the 'explosion' of the Civil Rights movement of a decade later. Again, it is worth asking who you think these poems were written for, and who their implied reader is.

The more radical black poets of the 1960s and 1970s rejected integration – perhaps because the violent resistance of some sectors of white society raised the question of why anyone would want to join such a society, but perhaps also because integration turned out to mean wholesale acceptance of white values rather than any creative exchange between the two communities. Integration allowed a few blacks to join the white middle class at the cost of tragically neglecting the black urban poor.[26] In response to this, rather than trying to join the institutions of white poetry, black poets and cultural workers sought to create an identifiably black poetry circulated through black publishing outlets:

> Poets turned to poetry of the folk, of the streets, to jazz musicians, to the language of black people for their models. Their first impulse was no longer to send a poem to *Poetry Magazine* or *Harper's*, but to think of *Black World*, *Journal of Black Poetry*, *Black Dialogue*, *Soulbook*, *Freedomways*, or *Liberator*.
>
> (Randall, *The Black Poets*, pp. xxv–vi)

[26] See Morley, 'Rap Music as American History', in Stanley, *Rap*, pp. xv–xxxi (xx–xxi).

Although the Civil Rights movement was clearly of major importance in gaining basic civil rights for black people, the stress on integration worked to absorb successful blacks into the white middle class while inadvertently creating ghettos of the urban poor. These were the conditions which fuelled the Black Power movement in the mid-1960s, with its stress on black pride and black nationalism; similar conditions in the last decade or so have made contemporary rap a powerful representative force in black America culture. Jefferson Morley argues that the rise of rap music in the United States is a response to the backlash in the late 1970s against the achievements of Civil Rights legislation. The inventors of rap were the children of the urban poor who had been excluded from the benefits of integrationist policies (Morley, pp. xx–xxi).

In the multicultural, multiracial society of the United States, then, culture, language and 'blood' can never be fused into a single entity and made to coincide with the nation-state (Spanish is increasingly a first language alongside English in the United States). Instead, different 'nations' overlap and intermingle, each one forging a sense of identity through poetry and other cultural practices but in doing so revealing the constitutive **hybridity** of all cultural identities in the New World (and indeed throughout the world). In this sense, the United States can be seen as a paradigm of the postmodern, post-colonial condition in which the imaginary coincidence of language, blood and soil is starkly exposed as the fictional construct it always was. The mobility of peoples and cultural forms in our contemporary world radically questions the link between nations and poetic traditions which was forged in the nationalist movements of the eighteenth and nineteenth centuries and perpetuated in the organisation of literature courses in the academy ever since. In Britain, the founding assumptions of Englishness and English poetry are increasingly being brought into question by the cultural productions of post-colonial peoples within the British Isles and in the former colonies throughout the world (as we will see in the following chapter). What *is* English poetry when English has become both a world language and a range of different Englishes in different places? The geographical and political borders of the nation-state can no longer be imagined to coincide with literary production in English.

One of the ways in which a culture may construct a sense of identity is by differentiating itself from that which it is not (its 'other'). Such differences might be national, ethnic, racial, religious, and so on or a combination of these. Nation-states have been fabricated in this way, and dominant cultures within nation-states typically define themselves as 'central' in relation to different kinds of 'margins'. Such processes can be enabling for small nations or groups struggling to establish and maintain a sense of identity under the shadow of more powerful neighbours or colonisers. Yet they have also led to wars, to genocide, and to 'ethnic cleansing'. In the early twenty-first century, however, as a result of complex histories and the increasing mobility of people and peoples, the idea that cultures exist independently of one another is becoming increasingly hard to maintain. In countries such as Britain and the United States, it is no longer clear where the 'centre' might be when the centre itself is internally differentiated by different kinds of 'marginal' groups and cultures, and where a number of different centre–margin relations are in the process of transformation and proliferation. Various kinds of critical theory – such as feminist criticism, gender studies, cultural and post-colonial studies – have all questioned, in specific and not always mutually compatible ways, the means by which certain aspects of a culture are constituted as central through the marginalisation of other cultural forms and practices.

Hesitating on the margins of Europe, Britain is particularly interesting in this respect in terms of the close proximity (in the British Isles) of different nations and the way they comprise different classes, races, ethnic backgrounds, religious affiliations, gender positions and sexual preferences. One of the reasons for this is that Britain continues to be shaped by its colonial past and by the way it has impacted upon a range of different cultures and societies throughout the world. The cultures formally assumed to exist at the margins of the British Empire no longer look to Britain as a centre, and also form presences within British culture itself in a way which leads to reconsiderations of what Britishness actually means. As the T-shirt slogan has it, 'We are over here because you were over there'. The historical interconnection between Britain and its former colonies still has a shaping influence on the politics and culture of those former colonies and of Britain itself. Such processes have resulted in a range of different and vibrant literary cultures that are normally grouped together under the umbrella term 'post-colonial literature' – which necessarily includes a wide range of intriguing national poetic traditions (as we will see in the following chapter).

The term 'diaspora' – originally used to refer to the dispersion of the Jews among various nations after the Babylonian captivity – is increasingly being used by cultural critics to describe other kinds of dispersions and movements of peoples which have shaped and continue to transform the various mixes of peoples which can be found today in most nation-states (European colonialism and the slave trade are only the most stark examples).[27] The consequence of diaspora is that cultural activities, traditions and interactions are no longer – if they ever were – confined within nation states. As Homi Bhabha puts it, 'The very concepts of homogeneous national cultures, . . . of historical traditions, or "organic" ethnic communities – as the grounds for cultural comparativism – are in a profound process of redefinition'.[28] Such redefinitions necessarily affect

[27] Stuart Hall, 'Cultural Identity and Diaspora', in Patrick Williams and Laura Chrisman, eds, *Colonial Discourse and Postcolonial Theory* (New York: Harvester Wheatsheaf, 1993), pp. 392–403.

[28] Homi Bhabha, *The Location of Culture* (London: Routledge, 1994), p. 5.

the way culture is packaged and studied in the education system. Hitherto, literature has been taught in terms of national traditions – English literature, American literature, Scottish literature, and so on. Dividing literature up in these ways has always meant fudging borderline cases: James Thomson (a Scot) is sometimes taught as an English poet; 'English' Modernism typically includes Yeats and Joyce (both Irish), Eliot, Pound and James (Americans) and Conrad (Polish). But Bhabha is describing a more profound problem than this. The long history of colonial, post-colonial and neocolonial diaspora means that culture itself has become a borderline condition. One of the most contentious issues in contemporary politics is the extent to which national borders are simply crossing-points in the migratory journeys of peoples and cultures, semi-porous barriers that enclose disparate cultures that are always interacting with and modifying each other, always on the move. (An author such as Salman Rushdie – born in Bombay, resident in Britain – can be taken as a representative figure for the processes we are describing.)

These arguments do not imply, however, that literature has transcended its relationship to specific locations and histories, but that the locations and histories to which literature responds are no longer those of the nation-state. This does not mean that we should or can abandon attending to 'national traditions', but that we need to be attentive to the way those traditions are invented, and the roles they play in relation to other cultures. Nostalgia for an 'English' or an 'American' tradition is not necessarily the same as attempts to construct, say, a Scottish tradition or a Nicaraguan tradition. Yet there are dangers lurking in any notion of tradition. As Bhabha notes, the African critic Frantz Fanon stresses both the importance and the attendant problems of the defence of cultural traditions:

> Fanon recognizes the crucial importance, for subordinated peoples, of asserting their indigenous cultural traditions and retrieving their repressed histories. But he is far too aware of the dangers of the fixity and fetishism of identities within the calcification of colonial cultures to recommend that 'roots' be struck in the celebratory romance of the past or by homogenizing the history of the present.
>
> (*Location of Culture*, p. 9)[29]

These insights stress both the importance and the problems of celebrating and studying subordinated cultural traditions – whether they be black American poetry, black British poetry, black South African poetry, Scottish women's poetry, lesbian poetry, and so on. The critique of the dominant traditions of English and American literature both helps to draw attention to those traditions which have been marginalised and brings into question the very notion of

---

[29] For Fanon's work on colonial and post-colonial nationalism, see Frantz Fanon, *The Wretched of the Earth*, trans. Constance Farrington (London: Penguin, 1967).

tradition. Cultural traditions overlap and interact with one another; they arise not out of the authentic, organic essence of a people but out of the inter-animating differences between peoples. Communities do not have essential identities but productive differences with other communities and within them-selves. In Scotland, for example, despite the dominant cultural image of Scottish identity, the people are not all Scottish, not all white, not all male, not all heterosexual, not all nationalistic. There is no Scottish 'essence', no stable definition of what it is to be Scottish. This is not unique to Scotland, but descriptive of all 'identities'.

Yet if this is a general cultural condition of the modern world, it is configured differently in each cultural location according to local specificities. The fact that Scotland has not been an independent nation-state since 1707 continues to impact upon Scottish culture. In many instances this leads to an unselfcritical nostalgia for, and dream of, an 'authentic' cultural tradition cor-responding to an 'authentic' political identity.[30] Traces of this may be seen in Daniel O'Rourke's introduction to the first edition of *Dream State: The new Scottish poets*, where he asserts that 'A fully authentic culture requires a fully authentic politics; and a fully authentic politics requires a state'.[31] While there might be compelling arguments for Scotland becoming an independent state, O'Rourke's assertion ignores the fact that neither politics nor culture is confined within the boundaries of nation-states. To assume this is to overlook instances such as black American or post-colonial writing, whose cultural poli-tics expose divisions within and cut across nation-states. This is not to claim that these are 'fully authentic' cultures, but to question the very notion of 'fully authentic' culture.

The high quality of the poetry which O'Rourke includes in his anthology belies his nationalist cultural ideology, since it somehow came to be written despite Scotland's not being an independent nation-state. To explain this, O'Rourke turns to the other side of the coin of his problematic cultural theory: such poetry represents a kind of *avant-garde* celebration of Scottishness despite the political reality. *Dream State* is nonetheless exciting for the way it opens up and transforms established notions of Scottishness – for example, by including the work of poets whose racial identity challenges conventional definitions of Scottishness. Yet when he describes Jackie Kay as 'Black. Lesbian. And a Scot',

---

[30] The confusions to which this leads can be seen in critical responses to the film *Rob Roy* (MGM, 1995): while the Scottish listings magazine *The List* describes it as 'one of the best films about Scotland and the Scottish psyche ever made', other critics condemned the film for perpetuating a misleading and disabling image of Scotland and the Scots based in tartanised fantasies of the past.

[31] Daniel O'Rourke, *Dream State*, Dream State: The New Scottish Poets (Edinburgh: Polygon, 1994), p. xliv.

and suggests that 'her status as an outsider' is thereby 'triply underscored' (*Dream State*, p. xxxv), O'Rourke seems to imply that the power of Kay's poetry, or its particular insight, derives from her status as an 'outsider' (which appears to contradict his claim that an 'authentic poetry' could arise only within an 'authentic state'). Each of these aspects of Kay's identity marks her as an 'outsider' in different and sometimes contradictory ways. As a Scot, what is she 'outside'? And how is this complicated by the fact that she lives in London? It is clear that to be black and lesbian is to be not white, not male, and not heterosexual. What happens, though, when being white forms part of the dominant conception of what it is to be Scottish? Does this mean that Kay – a Scot – may sometimes be seen as an outsider by fellow Scots? Kay herself (1993) foregrounds this possibility:

In My Country

walking by the waters
down where an honest river
shakes hands with the sea,
a woman passed round me
in a slow watchful circle,   5
as if I were a superstition;

or the worst dregs of her imagination,
so when she finally spoke
her words spliced into bars
of an old wheel. A segment of air.   10
Where do you come from?
'Here,' I said, 'Here. These parts.'

O'Rourke's own poetry also belies his nostalgic belief that culture needs to be grounded in a nation-state. His poem 'Great Western Road' (1994) is a marvellous celebration of the inter-animation between the specificities of a local culture and place (here a major street in Glasgow) and the multicultural and international cultural presences which are a part of that place:

Great Western Road

Glasgow, you look beatific in blue
and I've a Saturday before me
for galleries and poems,
a house full of Haydn,
and beneath my kitchen window,   5
tennis stars in saris
lobbing backhands at the bins.

477

French coffee, and who knows maybe
Allen Ginsberg in my bath!
then round to the dairy   10
where scones are cooling on the rack
and Jimmy won't let me leave
till I've tried one there and then,
here, where the new Glasgow started –
an old grey city going blond   15
whose Asian shops are full of fruits
we owe to Cap'n Bligh
and I'm so juiced I could walk clear
to Loch Lomond,
past buses stripping the willow   20
all along Great Western Road
but I just browse bargains in banjos
and pop-art knitted ties,
before checking out the crime section
at Caledonian Books,   25
finding Friesias in the flowershops
and in the second hand record store,
Bruckner's Third,
The Cleveland
under Szell: 30
so sad; like falling for passing students
with that black haired, blue eyed look,
or buying basil and chorizos . . .
In the afternoon I'll look at paintings
in Dougie Thompson's Mayfest show,   35
maybe stroll down to the studio
to view some archive film,
past the motorways and multi-storeys
of Grieve's Ultimate Cowcaddens,
the peeling pawn at George's Cross   40
where, today, everything is redeemable
because tonight there'll be guitar poets
from Russia at the Third Eye Centre.
And later I'll cook zarzuela
for a new and nimble friend.   45
God Glasgow it's glorious
just to gulp you down in heartfuls,
feeling something like love.

Exercises

1 The following exercise on O'Rourke's 'Great Western Road' will, we hope, reveal to you not only something about the way poetry is located both in terms of its subject matter and in terms of the time and place of its production, but also the way your own reading of a poem is positioned by your geographical and cultural location. If you live in Glasgow, some of the following questions ought to be relatively easy to answer. The further you live away from Glasgow or Scotland, the harder the questions may become. You may have to do some research – using maps of Glasgow and Scotland, guidebooks, general reference sources or the Internet. At the same time, you may make guesses based on cultural intuitions.

(a) Make a list of all the references, images or allusions in the poem which seem to you to be specific to Scotland or to Glasgow.

(b) Make a list of all the references, images or allusions in the poem which seem to you not to be specific to Scotland or to Glasgow.

(c) Make a list of all the references, images or allusions in the poem which seem to you to refer to 'high' culture.

(d) Make a list of all the references, images or allusions in the poem which seem to you to refer to 'popular' culture.

(e) Having located these different kinds of cultural material in the poem, try to decide how each group of images relates to one another. Are Scottish and non-Scottish cultural elements held apart from one another? Are the high-cultural elements kept aloof from the popular?

(f) Having carried out these analyses, what do you think it is about Glasgow which makes the poem's speaker feel 'something like love' for the city?

(g) How has this exercise given you a sense of your own place as a reader as well as a sense of Glasgow as a place?

2 The following exercise is designed to help you think about how children's poetry, and poetry in general, shapes what we might call our mental geography – that is, the way we locate ourselves imaginatively in the world and how we imagine other people and parts of the world. The following texts come from two of the most important and successful collections in the history of poetry for children. The first poem comes from Isaac Watts' *Divine and Moral Songs* (1715); the second poem is from Robert Louis Stevenson's *A Child's Garden of Verses* (1885). Read the poems first and then answer the questions that follow.

Praise for Birth and Education in a Christian Land

Great God, to thee my voice I raise,
  To thee my youngest hours belong:
I would begin my life with praise,
  Till growing years improve the song.

'Tis to thy sovereign grace I owe   5
  That I was born on Christian ground;
Where streams of heavenly mercy flow,
  And words of sweet salvation sound.

I would not change my native land
  For rich Peru, with all her gold: 10
A nobler prize lies in my hand
  Than east or western Indies hold.

How do I pity those that dwell
  Where ignorance and darkness reign!
They know no heaven – they fear no hell –   15
  That endless joy – that endless pain.

Thy glorious promises, O Lord,
  Kindle my hopes and my desire:
While all the preachers of thy word
  Warn me t' escape eternal fire.   20

Thy praise shall still employ my breath,
  Since thou hast mark'd my way to heaven,
Nor will I run the road to death,
  And waste the blessings thou hast given.

Foreign Children

Little Indian, Sioux or Crow,
Little frosty Eskimo,
Little Turk or Japanee,
O! don't you wish that you were me?

You have seen the scarlet trees   5
And the lions over seas;
You have eaten ostrich eggs,
And turned the turtles off their legs.

Such a life is very fine,
But it's not so nice as mine: 10
You must often, as you trod,
Have wearied *not* to be abroad.

You have curious things to eat,
I am fed on proper meat;
You must dwell beyond the foam,   15
But I am safe and live at home.

Little Indian, Sioux or Crow,
Little frosty Eskimo,
Little Turk or Japanee,
O! don't you wish that you were me?   20

(a) Identify the speaker in each of the poems. How does each poem define or construct their voices, attitudes and opinions? Do they use similar discourses? – you might find it helpful to think about the different register of the language used by each in answering this question. Who are the addressees in each poem?

(b) Try to sum up the attitude of each speaker towards (i) his own nationality or identity; (ii) the identity or nationality of those he is speaking to or about.

(c) How does each speaker think about or imagine the relationship between (i) self and other, (ii) home and abroad?

(d) Do some research in the library, on the Internet, or elsewhere, to find out more about: (i) each of the two poets, particularly their religious beliefs and/or political opinions; (ii) the growth of the British empire and British relations with the world beyond Europe at the different dates when the two poems were written (what continuities and what differences were there between the early-eighteenth-century attitudes, when Watts was writing, and those of the late-nineteenth, when Stevenson was writing)?

(e) In the context you have identified for the writing and reception of each poem at the time it was written, what effect is either poem likely to have had on its readers, and their opinions and beliefs?

(f) Could you make a case for an ironic reading of Stevenson's poem? You might find it useful to look at what we say about the concept of the 'implied reader' in Chapter 7 before answering this question.

Chapter 16

Post-colonial Poetry

■ Post-colonial Studies

One of the most important developments in literary and cultural studies in British, European and American universities in recent years – roughly parallel with the rise of popular interest in World Music and the academic development of ethnomusicology – has been the emergence of post-colonial studies, a discipline that focuses on the historical, political and cultural impacts of European colonialism on its former colonies. European colonialism, which began in the late fifteenth century and continued up to the second half of the twentieth century, was driven by political and commercial rivalry between the European states, a process which led to the 'discovery' by European explorers of new lands and the 'New World'. Many schoolchildren have memorised the following couplet (the name of the poet, Winifred Sackville Stonier Jr, is generally forgotten):

> In fourteen-hundred and ninety-two
> Columbus sailed the ocean blue.

Columbus was a Genoese explorer who sailed the ocean blue as an agent of Spain in order to discover a westward passage to Asia that would allow Spain to gain an advantage over Portugal, its main trading rival. When Columbus first encountered the islands of the Caribbean he thought he had arrived in India – which is why the collective name for the English-speaking islands of the Caribbean is the West Indies and why the indigenous peoples of the whole American continent have been called 'Indians'.

In the sixteenth century, Spain and Portugal began to set up colonies in the Americas and the Caribbean, along the coasts of Africa, and in the East Indies.

In this period, the Spanish empire was said to be 'the Empire on which the sun never sets' (*el imperio en el que nunca se pone el sol*). Over the next couple of centuries Spain's empire declined in face of the energetic expansion of France, Holland and England as rival empires. By the second half of the eighteenth century a combination of various factors, including war, commercial ambition and Protestant zeal, had established Britain as the dominant world empire. After the Seven Years War (1756–63), in which Britain defeated France in a war for control of the world, Sir George McCartney referred to the British empire as 'this vast empire on which the sun never sets and whose bounds nature has not yet ascertained'.[1] Even though America was lost in 1776, India became the 'jewel in the crown' and Australia began to be colonised at the end of the eighteenth century. By the early nineteenth century, 'Great Britain had acquired the largest empire the world had ever seen, encompassing forty-three colonies in five continents' (Ferguson, *Empire: How Britain Made the Modern World*, p. 51). By 1909, the British Empire had expanded still further: it 'now covered around 25 per cent of the world's land surface . . . and controlled roughly the same proportion of the world's population: some 444 million people in all lived under some form of British rule' (p. 240). The defeat of Germany in the First World War (1914–18) added 'around 1.8 million square miles . . . to the Empire and around 13 million new subjects' (p. 314). Although the British Empire largely unravelled during the rest of the twentieth century (most of its colonies had gained independence by the end of the century), and although we are now supposedly in a post-colonial era, the British Foreign and Commonwealth Office website tells us that Britain still possesses fourteen Overseas Territories that are 'spread throughout the globe', ranging from 'the tiny island of Pitcairn with its 47 inhabitants, set in the middle of the Pacific Ocean, to Bermuda, which has a population of over 62 000' (www.fco.gov.uk). Indeed, the term 'neo-colonialism' is used to refer to the ongoing 'colonial' influence that the developed West has over the so-called 'Third World' or 'developing' countries. Today, the United States – once a group of thirteen English colonies – is the major neo-colonial power in the world.

It cannot therefore be said that we live in a post-colonial world, if by that we mean that colonialism and its impact are over and done with. Even in those countries that have gained independence from the European colonial powers, the legacy and impact of colonialism remain. Because of this, the term 'post-colonial' is controversial and is used differently by different critics. In a new

---

[1] Sir George McCartney, quoted by Niall Ferguson, *Empire: How Britain Made the Modern World* (London: Penguin, 2004), p. 35. Ferguson's popular but controversial book is a lively and insightful introduction to the rise, decline and fall of the British empire.

chapter added to the second edition of *The Empire Writes Back: Theory and Practice in Post-colonial Literatures* (2002), Bill Ashcroft, Gareth Griffiths and Helen Tiffin reflect on the developments in post-colonial studies since their seminal first edition of 1989:

> Most contentious of all has been the term 'post-colonial' itself. *The Empire Writes Back* uses the term 'post-colonial' to refer to 'all the culture affected by the imperial process from the moment of colonization to the present day' . . . Such a broad-reaching definition has been opposed by those who believe it necessary to limit the term either by selecting only certain periods as genuinely post-colonial (most notably the period after independence), or by suggesting that some groups of people affected by the colonizing process are not post-colonial (notably settlers), or, finally, by suggesting that some societies are not yet post-colonial (meaning free of the attitudes of colonization. The case of indigenous people in settler societies is an example of this latter argument).[2]

Despite such critical debates, Ashcroft *et al.* decide that 'post-colonial' 'is still best employed, as it was in the first edition, to refer to post-*colonization* . . . *during* and *after* the actual period of direct colonial rule' (*Empire Writes Back*, p. 195). In this chapter, we use the term 'post-colonial' in the same way since it allows us to examine the different roles that poetry plays in the former colonies during the period of colonial rule, the struggle for independence and the fashioning of post-independence culture. We also use the term to include all groups of people affected by the colonial process – not only the indigenous or former slave peoples who have achieved independence, but also colonisers, settlers and indigenous peoples in settler societies. This is because the culture and poetry of any post-colonial society is contributed to and shaped by the various ethnic groups that colonisation has brought together. Any extensive study of the poetry of a post-colonial society therefore needs to pay attention to the inputs from each ethnic group at each historical moment, starting with the situation at the moment of colonial invasion and continuing up to the present.

While the culture and politics of the former European colonies share what is sometimes called the post-colonial condition, there are also important differences between these countries. Post-colonial theorists distinguish colonies or former colonies into two broad categories – 'colonies of occupation' and 'settler colonies':

> Nigeria and India are examples of colonies of occupation, where indigenous people remained in the majority but were administered by a foreign power. Examples of settler colonies where, over time, the invading Europeans (or their descendants)

---

[2] Bill Ashcroft, Gareth Griffiths and Helen Tiffin, *The Empire Writes Back: Theory and Practice in Post-colonial Literatures*, 2nd edn (London: Routledge, 2002), p. 194.

annihilated, displaced, and/or marginalized the indigenes to become a majority non-indigenous population, include Argentina, Australia, Canada and the United States.[3]

But there are other former European colonies that don't fit neatly into either of these two categories:

> The countries of the Caribbean, for example, are not usually considered 'settler colonies', even though the indigenous Caribs and Arawaks were virtually annihilated one hundred years after Columbus' entry into the area. Here the European 'settlers' comprised a relatively small but powerful group of white planters, while the majority of the 'settlers' were Africans kidnapped as slaves and forcibly 'settled' in the region. Kenya, Ireland, South Africa, Mozambique and Algeria also provide examples of colonies whose patterns of settlement and cultural and racial legacies fall somewhere between the abstract paradigms of settler colony and colony of occupation.
>
> (*Key Concepts*, p. 211)

Each of these different kinds of former colony involves a different political, cultural and ethnic situation that has formative influences on the literature that is produced within it. Thus, although 'post-colonial literature' is a useful term that groups together a number of different literary cultures that have important things in common, any study of the literature of any individual former colony has to take into account the specificities of its history, ethnic profile, geography and contemporary context.

Although post-colonial studies sometimes focuses on the cultural conditions and practices of the former colonies of the various European nations, our present concern with poetry in the English language means that we will concentrate here on the poetic traditions of one group of former British colonies – the West Indies – and examine one poem from the former British colony of South Africa. It should be borne in mind, however, that former colonies of the British Empire also include India, Pakistan, Bangladesh, Malaysia, Singapore, Sri Lanka, Australia, New Zealand, Canada and a number of African countries. To this list of former British colonies one might add Ireland (often said to be Britain's, or England's, oldest colony) and the United States, which gained its independence in 1776 and whose development of a sense of national identity and a national literature can be considered in post-colonial terms. Most of these former British colonies use English as their official language or lingua franca and have developed their own particular Anglophone literary culture, shaped by specific historical, cultural and ethnic conditions and particular engagements with the dominant traditions of writing in English. In many of these countries, Standard English, the imposed language of the colonising

---

[3] Bill Ashcroft, Gareth Griffiths and Helen Tiffin, *Post-Colonial Studies: The Key Concepts* (Abingdon: Routledge, 1998), p. 211. This book – hereafter referred to as *Key Concepts* – is a useful introduction to the key terms and debates in post-colonial studies.

power, has entered into various tense but productive relationships with indigenous non-English languages to produce hybrid languages (vernacular or creole languages – sometimes called 'nation languages'[4]). In such contexts, language, literature and culture in general become highly politicised as speakers, writers and cultural producers face what is often called 'the language question' – i.e., whether to use Standard English (thereby accepting the language of the oppressor but also gaining access to a world-wide audience), local languages where they survive (in order to achieve cultural 'authenticity' or 'purity', though at the cost of limiting the potential audience), or some mixture or hybrid between Standard English and local languages or vernaculars. The various solutions that different writers have come up with in response to this challenge are one source of the creative energy and specificity that characterise post-colonial literature.

Yet such conditions and issues are not confined to writers living in the former colonies. The various influxes of immigrants to Britain from some of these former colonies, especially since the 1950s, mean that we can also think of post-colonial literature being written in Britain: in effect, Britain has itself become a post-colonial country producing a range of post-colonial literatures. John Agard's 'Listen Mr Oxford Don', which we examined in the previous chapter, is just one highly self-conscious example of what we could call post-colonial British Caribbean poetry (given that Guyana was once a British colony that is sometimes included in the 'West Indies'). As we have seen, Agard's poem critically and creatively explores precisely those questions about language that face many writers from Britain's former colonies.

One of the issues faced by writers and intellectuals in post-colonial societies is the extent to which it is possible not only to resist or overthrow the colonial power but also to 'decolonise the mind' or the culture of a people who have been or continue to be subject to that colonial power – that is, is it possible either to return to a pre-colonial state of cultural 'purity' or to create a post-colonial culture and literature that is entirely free of the impact of the colonial period? Such questions were asked by the early pioneers of post-colonial theory, most of whom came from colonised societies themselves. One of these pioneers was Frantz Fanon (1925–1961), a black intellectual who was born and grew up in the French Caribbean colony of Martinique. After studying medicine and psychiatry in France, Fanon worked in a hospital during the Algerian War of 1954–62 in which Algeria achieved independence from France. In *Les damnés de la terre* (1961), first translated into English in 1965 as *The Wretched of the Earth*, Fanon justifies violent resistance against European colonial powers on the basis that colonialism is an ongoing violent

---

[4] The term 'nation language' was coined by Edward Kamau Brathwaite, *History of the Voice: The Development of Nation Language in Anglophone Caribbean Poetry* (London and Port of Spain: New Beacon Books, 1984). This book is the best introduction to the use of language in Caribbean poetry.

repression of colonised peoples. In a chapter 'On National Culture', Fanon examines the role of literature and the literary intellectual in the struggle to achieve independent nationhood. He suggests that a colonial power not only oppresses the colonised people in a political and material sense, but also works to produce their 'cultural estrangement' by distorting or erasing their culture and sense of their own past. The aim of this cultural oppression is to prevent indigenous culture from playing any role in inspiring resistance to the colonial power and to convince the people that they had been rescued by the coloniser from a cultureless state of barbarity: 'the total result looked for by colonial domination was indeed to convince the natives that colonialism came to lighten their darkness. The effect consciously sought by colonialism was to drive into the natives' heads the idea that if the settlers were to leave, they would at once fall back into barbarism, degradation and bestiality'.[5] Thus the representation of black Africans as savages and cannibals was a racist strategy that served to maintain and justify colonial exploitation. One strategic response to this on the part of African intellectuals and poets was to affirm the existence of a general African culture prior to and independent of the European colonisers' culture. One manifestation of this desire to celebrate the supposed distinctiveness of African personality, culture and literature was the concept of *négritude* developed by the black Caribbean poet and politician, Aimé Césaire, in his 1939 poem, *Cahier d'un Retour au Pays Natal* ('Notebook of a Return to my Native Land'). This concept enabled black writers to counter the objectification and othering of black Africans in colonial discourse by providing a means of representing and inscribing an enabling model of black people's subjectivity. Despite its strategic usefulness, however, Fanon had serious reservations about the idea that African writers in post-colonial societies could somehow tap into an essential negritude that had remained pure under the impact of colonialism and that was shared by all Africans despite their pre- and post-colonial differences. For Fanon, both revolutionary action and the fashioning of a genuine culture could only take place within each specific colony and would hence manifest itself as a series of national struggles rather than as a general pan-African struggle.

An alternative strategic response to the colonial misrepresentation of African cultures and peoples, and one that Fanon seems to value more highly than the assertion of Africanness, is the 'passionate search for a national culture which existed before the colonial era [and which] finds its legitimate reason in the anxiety shared by native intellectuals to shrink away from the Western culture in which they all risk being swamped' (*Wretched of the Earth*, p. 168). Fanon suggests that this search was at least partially successful and effective:

[5] Franz Fanon, *The Wretched of the Earth* (1961), trans. Constance Farrington (London: Penguin, 1967), p. 169.

Perhaps this passionate research and this anger are kept up or at least directed by the secret hope of discovering beyond the misery of today, beyond self-contempt, resignation and abjuration, some very beautiful and splendid era whose existence rehabilitates us both in regard to ourselves and in regard to others. . . . and, let us make no mistake, it was with the greatest delight that they discovered that there was nothing to be ashamed of in the past, but rather dignity, glory and solemnity. The claim to a national culture in the past does not only rehabilitate that nation and serve as a justification for the hope of a future national culture. In the sphere of psycho-affective equilibrium it is responsible for an important change in the native. (p. 169)

Fanon's analysis here indicates that the colonial representation of black Africans had a devastating impact on Africans' sense of self-worth and that the discovery of a national culture in the past helps individuals to overcome 'self-contempt, resignation and abjuration'. This claim points to an important double role of post-colonial literature: to create a national tradition that serves to represent a post-colonial people to itself and enable collective resistance to colonialism; and to present modes of subjectivity and self-representation that provide alternatives to the images of 'natives' offered by colonial discourse. For Fanon, although each colonised nation struggles against its particular oppressor in particular conditions, its literary writers typically undergo a three-stage development that can be found in most colonial contexts. In the first phase, the indigenous writer tries to join the literary tradition of the colonial power and rejects all local or indigenous elements.

Writers in the first phase exhibit displacement and an inauthentic hybrid identity: they become 'individuals without an anchor, without a horizon, colourless, stateless, rootless . . . It will . . . be quite normal to hear certain natives declare "I speak as a Senegalese and as a Frenchman"' (p. 175). In the second phase, triggered by the emergence of nationalist movements, the native writer suddenly feels that the wholesale adoption of the coloniser's culture makes 'him a stranger in his own land' and attempts to spurn what he (or she) had so carefully acquired (p. 176). Fanon suggests that this is a psychological necessity, but is not easily accomplished. The writer 'decides to remember what he is' (p. 179), but is alienated from the people and their culture and produces works that interpret native traditions in terms of the aesthetic paradigms of the colonising culture resulting in a hybridisation that renders his or her writing inauthentic and ineffective. In the third phase, the writer leaves behind this obsession with the traditions of the past and seeks a leading role in the people's revolutionary struggle. But even in this revolutionary phase, the indigenous writer's work is in danger of being colonised by the colonial culture: 'At the very moment when the native intellectual is anxiously trying to create a cultural work he fails to realize that he is utilizing techniques and language which are borrowed from the stranger in his country' (p. 180).

Fanon's analysis of indigenous culture and writing in post-colonial societies can be interpreted in different ways. He might be suggesting that literature can play no effective role in the political resistance against the coloniser and that pre-independence indigenous culture cannot purge itself of the coloniser's culture. Yet he does go on to suggest that indigenous writing can become authentically revolutionary and posits the emergence of a national literature that is able to contribute to the political decolonisation of the colonised society. And although he rejects the possibility of returning to a pre-colonial pan-African negritude and mocks the efforts of some intellectuals to recover an authentic pre-colonial national culture, he does affirm the positive benefits of rediscovering national cultures. His identification of the difficulty of casting off the colonial culture at each stage in the development of a post-colonial national literature can be read as suggesting either that post-colonial literature is irredeemably hybridised or that post-colonial writers need to take great care to make sure that their writing has indeed liberated itself from the aesthetic paradigms of the coloniser's culture. Certainly, Fanon's suggestion that a successful revolutionary struggle brings about 'not only the disappearance of colonialism but also the disappearance of the colonized man' (p. 198) implies that the post-colonial subject can recover or achieve an authentic selfhood freed from the impact of colonialism. The logical development of this tendency in Fanon's analysis was carried out by the black Kenyan writer and theorist Ngugi wa Thiong'o, who argued that authentic African literatures could only be written in African languages for African readers and consequently abandoned English in order to write in Gikuyu and Ki-Swahili. Only in this way, he argued in books such as *Decolonising the Mind: The Politics of Language in African Literature* (1986), could African peoples decolonise their minds and hence achieve full independence.[6]

Fanon's analysis of the colonial condition of indigenous peoples, their revolutionary awakening and the role of literature at each stage was deeply informed by Marxism and by his expertise in psychology. In a sense, he produces a psychological-Marxist diagnosis of the post-colonial condition and prescribes a cure. The most prominent later theorists of colonialism often refer to Fanon, yet they tend to focus more on the discourses that sustained colonialism rather than on the condition and responses of colonised peoples, and shape their analyses according to the critical theory of European post-structuralism rather than the theoretical paradigms used by Fanon. The three dominant gurus of colonial discourse theory are Edward Said, Gayatri Spivak and Homi Bhabha. Said's work, in books such as *Orientalism* (1978) and *Culture and Imperialism* (1993), is primarily about western representations of

---

[6] See Ngugi wa Thiong'o, *Decolonising the Mind: The Politics of Language in African Literature* (Oxford: James Currey, 1986).

the 'third world'. Spivak's *In Other Worlds: Essays in Cultural Politics* (1988) maps her transformation from deconstructive literary critic to deconstructive post-colonial critic (though she pays little attention to post-colonial poetry). Bhabha's seminal *The Location of Culture* (1994) draws on Marxism, structuralism and psychoanalysis in order to develop a compelling but difficult set of theoretical arguments.[7] Under the influence of Said, Spivak and Bhabha, the cultural theory that has shaped academic research on colonial discourse and post-colonial studies is largely concerned with questions about the conditions that inform and distort cultural production and identity formation in post-colonial contexts and typically draws on theoretical writings about history, politics, race, language, identity, subjectivity and gender. Such theoretical writings tend to relegate literature to a subordinate role as just another discourse in the mix, literature serving the theory rather than the other way round.[8] And when they do engage with literature, post-colonial theory and criticism tend to marginalise poetry by focusing almost exclusively on narrative fiction. Although Bhabha does 'cite' or invite us to 'listen to' to a number of post-colonial poems, they are quoted and discussed not as poetry but simply as illustrations of the theory.[9]

■ Hybridity

This is not to say that post-colonial theory is not useful for the interpretation of post-colonial poetry. One of the most useful, but controversial, concepts that has been developed in post-colonial theory is that of 'hybridity'. In horticulture, 'hybridity' refers to the cross-breeding of two species to form a new, 'hybrid' species. In post-colonial theory, hybridity refers to a range of different kinds of 'cross-breeding' – ethnic, linguistic, cultural, political, etc. – that can take place in the 'contact zone' between two or more peoples and cultures that colonisation creates. As such, hybridity is often used interchangeably with 'creolisation' – 'The process of intermixing and cultural change that produces a creole society' (*Key Concepts*, p. 58). On one level, then, the notion of hybridity is a descriptive term for the mixing or cross-fertilisation of cultures that is

---

[7] See Edward Said, *Orientalism* (London: Routledge & Kegan Paul, 1978) and *Culture and Imperialism* (London: Chatto & Windus, 1993); Gayatri Chakravorty Spivak, *In Other Worlds: Essays in Cultural Politics* (London: Routledge, 1988); Bhabha, *Location of Culture*.

[8] For representative collections of essays on post-colonial theory, see Williams and Chrisman, *Colonial Discourse and Postcolonial Theory: A Reader*, Bill Ashcroft, Gareth Griffiths and Helen Tiffin, eds, *The Post-Colonial Studies Reader* (London: Routledge, 1995), and Bart Moore-Gilbert, Gareth Stanton and Willy Maley, eds, *Postcolonial Criticism* (London: Longman, 1997). Only a few of the essays in these collections are about literature, and even fewer refer to poetry.

[9] See Bhabha, *Location of Culture*, pp. 7, 11, 45–47, 56, 58–59, 215, 231–35.

an inevitable consequence of colonialism. In literature, for example, hybridity might be found or enacted in a sonnet (a genre/form that originated in the European literary tradition) written in, say, the nation language of Jamaica. Yet 'hybridity' is a problematic term to use in post-colonial studies. As Robert Young points out, hybridity was a concept used by colonisers themselves in the nineteenth century as a racist means of representing and containing the 'threat' of miscegenation that was raised by inter-ethnic sexual relations (typically between white males and indigenous or enslaved females) in the colonial 'contact zone'. The notion of hybridity can also serve to disguise the violent power relations of the colonial situation, implying that both coloniser and colonised happily assimilate elements of each other's culture in a process of benign enrichment and cross-cultural exchange. But Young also points out that there are more useful accounts of hybridity that bring out the political tensions and struggles of the colonial condition. In particular, the Russian literary theorist Mikhail Bakhtin's account of hybridity 'sets different points of view against each other in a conflictual structure, which retains "a certain elemental organic energy and openendedness" '; this gives hybridity, Young suggests, the potential to challenge and reverse 'the structures of domination in the colonial situation'.[10] Young sees a similar potential in Bhabha's account of hybridity. For Bhabha, 'the culture of western modernity' needs to be re-interpreted 'from the postcolonial perspective'; in order to make this possible, Bhabha provides 'a theory of cultural hybridity and the "translation" of social difference which goes beyond the polarities of Self and Other, East and West' (*Location of Culture*, back cover). In other words, he attempts to alert western readers of post-colonial texts to the possibility that hybridity is not only the characteristic mark of post-coloniality, but also the condition of culture in general – a move that challenges the supposed hierarchy between the 'pure' culture of the western coloniser and the 'inferior' because hybrid culture of the colonised people.

Bhabha's claim that western cultures and peoples are always already hybrid can be readily supported by any informed reflection on the ethnic and cultural origins of any western people. Despite the fact that English colonisers tended to look down on the 'hybrid' peoples and cultures of their colonies, the English are themselves one of the most hybridised people in the world. The most prominent ethnic hybridisation that went into the making of Englishness was that between the Anglo-Saxon and French Norman peoples after the Norman

---

[10] See Robert J.C. Young, *Colonial Desire: Hybridity in Theory, Culture and Race* (London: Routledge, 1995), pp. 21–23. This often interesting book pays virtually no attention to poetry. For Mikhail Bakhtin's discussion of hybridisation, see his *The Dialogic Imagination: Four Essays*, ed. Holquist (Austin: University of Texas Press, 1981), pp. 358–62. Although Bakhtin discusses hybridisation as a linguistic technique found in novels, his ideas can be applied to poetry – especially to post-colonial poetry.

Conquest of 1066 – an event which allows us to think of the English as a post-colonial people. But there have been many other inputs as well. In 1701, Daniel Defoe's poem 'The True-Born Englishman' satirically enumerated the wide range of different peoples that had already gone into the mix of Englishness in the early eighteenth century in order to conclude: 'Thus from a mixture of all kinds began / That heterogeneous thing, an Englishman'. Shortly afterwards, the union of the English and Scottish parliaments helped to create the hybrid nation state of Britain. Since then, of course, a variety of other peoples has gone into the mix of Britishness. The English language, too, is a hybrid language: basically, Middle English emerged in the Middle Ages as a fusion between Anglo-Saxon and Norman French, though a number of other languages have also contributed to it (including Greek and Latin and various 'Third World' languages encountered during the colonial period). Thus, as Bhabha suggests, when western intellectuals, critics or students read a text produced by a 'Third World' post-colonial writer, they cannot do so from a position of cultural purity or superiority. For Young, 'Bakhtin's intentional hybrid has been transformed by Bhabha into an active moment of challenge and resistance against a dominant colonial power . . . depriving the imposed imperial culture, not only of the authority that it has for so long imposed politically, often through violence, but even of its own claims to authenticity' (*Colonial Desire*, p. 23).

On the one hand, then, the colonised people's culture is recognised as having been made hybrid by the colonial imposition (e.g., the imposition of English on the indigenous people); on the other hand, that hybridity can be strategically used as a means of appropriating, transforming, making strange and challenging the culture and cultural assumptions that helped sustain colonial oppression. Whereas Fanon implies that hybridisation between indigenous and colonial cultures compromises indigenous writers' attempts to produce a revolutionary national literature, more recent post-colonial theorists seem to suggest that political decolonisation (the achievement of independence) cannot be brought about by, or lead to, cultural decolonisation. For such theorists, hybridisation is an inevitable and irreversible effect of the post-colonial situation and, far from being an impediment, serves to empower colonised peoples and challenges colonial culture. As we will see, hybridity of various kinds is frequently found in post-colonial poetry and often features in the critical discussion of such poetry. This is announced in the title of the first book-length study of 'Third World' post-colonial poetry – Jahan Ramazani's *The Hybrid Muse: Postcolonial Poetry in English* (2001).[11]

---

[11] Jahan Ramazani, *The Hybrid Muse: Postcolonial Poetry in English* (Chicago: University of Chicago Press, 2001).

◼ Post-colonial Literature: Language, History, Place

The study of Commonwealth Literature in British and American universities emerged in the 1960s. But post-colonial studies did not begin to focus on post-colonial literature until the 1980s. One of the ground-breaking books in this shift was Ashcroft, Griffiths and Tiffin's *The Empire Writes Back* (first edition, 1989), whose title was taken from a phrase coined by Salman Rushdie: 'the Empire writes back to the Centre' (itself an allusion to *Star Wars, Episode V: The Empire Strikes Back* (20th Century Fox, 1980)). Ashcroft *et al.* stress that their title doesn't mean that post-colonial writers are writing *for* the metropolitan centre – i.e., the former colonial powers – but writing *against* it (though we will suggest that it can mean both). Ashcroft *et al.* are primarily concerned with mapping the processes and strategies by which post-colonial national literary traditions were created by post-colonial writers in the former British colonies. Given that 'The imperial education system installs a "standard" version of the metropolitan language as the norm, and marginalizes all "Variants" as impurities', the 'most significant feature in the emergence of modern post-colonial literatures' is 'the appropriation of [the English] language and [the means of] writing for new and distinctive usages' (*Empire Writes Back*, pp. 7, 6). The fashioning of a 'post-colonial voice' that can effectively challenge the colonial power or its culture involves developing a range of linguistic and literary strategies that hybridise or make local both the English language and the conventions of English literature (p. 7).

Language, and especially literary language, is shaped by – and helps to shape – intimate relationships between people and the place in which they live. Such relationships have been one of the central preoccupations of English poetry, especially since the poetic revolution of English Romanticism spearheaded by William Wordsworth. Post-colonial literature is also preoccupied with these relationships. Yet the intimate reciprocity between people and place, language and landscape, that characterises English Romanticism is not so readily achieved in the post-colonial context. Colonialism entails the violent insertion of a new people into a geographical place, disempowering, displacing or eradicating indigenous people and sometimes replacing them with imported slaves. As a consequence, post-colonial literature tends to explore thematic concerns such as exile, diaspora, dispossession, alienation, the frontier, the naming of places, nostalgia and homesickness, the attempt to establish a sense of belonging in an alien land, the recovery of ancient relationships to the land, the dream of return, etc. Yet colonialism also imports and imposes a foreign language on the displaced peoples and on the land itself. Thus the task that faces the post-colonial writer is to try to overcome alienation from the colonised place by using a language that is itself alien to that place (and often to the writer as well).

Given that the language and literature of England are so intimately bound up with a particular way of perceiving a particular kind of place and landscape, post-colonial writers need to modify both language and literary conventions in order to explore their own relationship with an alien landscape and ecology or to mourn or recover from the loss of intimate or sacred contact with an ancestral environment. J.M. Coetzee suggests, for example, that for South African writers of European descent the silent emptiness of the South African landscape 'remains alien, impenetrable, until a language is found in which to win it, speak it, represent it'. Standard literary English 'carries echoes of a very different natural world – a world of downs and fells, oaks and daffodils, robins and badgers', and white settler writers need to dampen those echoes if they are to discover 'a natural or Adamic language' adequate to name and articulate their relationship with their own environment.[12]

Standard English and the conventions of the English literary tradition can be manipulated in a number of ways in order to produce texts that are responsive to the specific place and history of a post-colonial society. The writer can foreground geographical features, ecology, weather patterns, seasons, flora and fauna, and so on. Where there are indigenous languages, or remnants of them, the grafting of their words, grammatical forms and rhythms into English links the text to the post-colonial place. (It is revealing that one of the few Carib words to survive the extinction of the Carib people in the West Indies is 'hurricane'.) Where indigenous oral poetic traditions remain intact, allusions to local or indigenous literature or songs can be used to imbue post-colonial literature in English with aspects of the repressed people's culture, history and place. The writer can also reproduce and develop local vernacular uses. References to historical figures and events can give a sense of the specific history of place and serve to recall repressed histories. The inclusion of local place names and people's names also works to ground the text in the particular place and culture.

Each of these techniques works by grafting an aspect of the post-colonial place onto the English language and its literary conventions in order to create hybrid forms that work to make the post-colonial text responsive to local place and history. The texts that employ these techniques have the potential to establish or regenerate local readers' relationship to their own place, culture and history. For the non-local reader, however, such techniques have a potentially defamiliarising effect, forcing him or her to engage with the specific differences of the literature and history of the post-colonial place. Un-glossed or un-translated words and phrases, for example, can either alienate such a reader or coax him or her 'into an active engagement with the horizons of the culture in which these terms have meaning' (*Empire Writes Back*, p. 64). In either case, the reader's world

---

[12] J.M. Coetzee, *White Writing: On the Culture of Letters in South Africa* (New Haven: Yale University Press, 1988), pp. 7, 8.

view is challenged and changed: his or her sense of self and other, centre and periphery, is potentially reconfigured. What this seems to demonstrate (though Ashcroft *et al.* try to reject this possibility in *Empire Writes Back*) is that at least one kind of intended or implied reader of the post-colonial text is the reader who resides in the metropolitan 'centre' – e.g., in Britain. In this sense, the empire is writing back *to* and *for* the centre in order to challenge or educate it.

▣ Post-colonial Poetry: A South African Poem

Although the vast majority of the literary examples and case studies in *The Empire Writes Back* are concerned with prose fiction, most of its theoretical analysis can be applied to poetry. In his introduction to *The Hybrid Muse*, Ramazani makes out a case for poetry as ideally suited to the techniques of hybridisation that Ashcroft *el al.* identify as typical of post-colonial literature. He suggests that the 'clearest example of formal interculturation in postcolonial poetry is the hybridization of Western literary models and non-Western oral traditions' (*Hybrid Muse*, p. 18). Rajeev S. Patke's *Postcolonial Poetry in English* (2006) stresses the ways in which the poetry of a wide variety of post-colonial societies is concerned not only with place but also with the troubled, and often untold, histories that have shaped those post-colonial places. As he announces early on, post-colonial poets 'revisit history as a zone of imaginative recovery and recuperation'.[13] As we will see, hybridisation, the representation of place, and the reclaiming of repressed histories are interrelated strategies in post-colonial poetry.

To illustrate the way the ideas of post-colonial theory apply in practice to poetry produced within a post-colonial context we would like to look briefly at the poetry of South Africa from the second half of the twentieth century. South Africa was a British colony that became a self-governing British dominion in 1910, a sovereign state within the British Empire in 1934, and an independent republic in 1961. But the major political issue in South Africa in the second half of the twentieth century was apartheid – a system of racial repression and classification instituted in 1948 that extended and perpetuated colonial rule over the country's non-white peoples. After a long and violent struggle by black people and by some white, coloured and Indian South Africans, the apartheid system began to be dismantled in 1990 and was finally eradicated by the election of Nelson Mandela as president in 1994. As in most post-colonial societies, the people of South Africa are made up of a rich ethnic mix: it has the largest communities of 'Coloured' (i.e., racially mixed), White and Indian people in Africa; nonetheless, Black South Africans of various ethnic groups account for almost 80% of the population. The peoples of this ethnically

---

[13] Rajeev S. Patke, *Postcolonial Poetry in English* (Oxford and New York: Oxford University Press, 2006), p. 9.

mixed nation speak a wide variety of languages, including English and Afrikaans and the languages of indigenous peoples and immigrant Asians.

One of the most interesting poets of the immediate post-independence period in South Africa was Arthur Nortje (1942–1970), who was classified as 'coloured' under the apartheid system (he was the illegitimate son of a 'coloured' woman and a Jewish father) and emigrated to Canada in 1967 (effectively going into exile). Nortje's poetry is preoccupied with the major themes of the post-colonial/apartheid condition: identity, exile, origins, history and place. As Adam Schwartzman suggests, 'through his engagement with the experience of 1960s South Africa – ravaged by bannings, arrests and forced removals – he had made the language of displacement, estrangement and isolation his own'.[14] In 'Waiting' (a forty-five line poem from Nortje's 1973 collection, *Dead Roots*), the speaker explores the 'isolation of exile' and reflects that 'Origins trouble the voyager much, those roots / that have sipped the waters of another continent' (13–14). Although he tends to use Standard English, Nortje's poetry can nonetheless signal difference of place, history and political milieu through local references and allusions:

> Come back, come back mayibuye
> cried the breakers of stone and cried the crowds
> cried Mr. Kumalo before the withering fire
> mayibuye Afrika. (18–21)

The reference here to 'Mr. Kumalo' is not explained in the poem (nor is it included in Schwartzman's Glossary), and this forces the reader from outside South Africa to realise that he or she may not be the intended or implied reader of this poem (the informed South African reader probably doesn't need the name to be glossed: a Google search suggests that the reference may be to Dumisani Kumalo, who played a leading role in the campaign to isolate apartheid South Africa). The phrase 'mayibuye Africa' ('come back Africa') is perhaps better known to the outside world (it was a rallying cry of the ANC), but its use, again, signals this poem's linguistic, geographical and political difference from the metropolitan 'centre' of Standard English. The fact that this slogan is 'cried' by 'the breakers of stone' and by 'crowds' suggests that the speaker is referring to the people's resistance to the apartheid regime (key events prior to Nortje's poem include the Sharpeville Massacre of 1961 and the Treason Trials of 1964 in which Mandela and others were found guilty of treason). As his autobiography reveals, Mandela and the other political prisoners on Robben Island spent a good deal of their time breaking stones.[15]

---

[14] Adam Schwartzman, ed., Introduction to *Ten South African Poets* (Manchester: Carcanet, 1999), pp. 1–21 (4–5).

[15] See Nelson Mandela, *Long Walk to Freedom* (London: Little, Brown & Co., 1994), pp. 458–59, 479–82.

Distance from England and the English literary tradition is also signalled in the poem's third verse paragraph:

> Now there is the loneliness of lost
> beauties at Cabo de Esperancia, Table Mountain:
> all the dead poets who sang of spring's
> miraculous recrudescence in the sandscapes of Karoo
> sang of thoughts that pierced like arrows, spoke
> through the strangled throat of multi-humanity
> bruised like a python in the maggot-fattening sun. (22–28)

For the South African reader, the references to place names in these lines work to locate the poem in a familiar landscape, but to the outside reader they function as another characteristic means of signalling that this poetry is rooted in a geographical place that is 'other' than the English landscape (they also hint at the politics of the naming of places in a post-colonial country): *Cabo de Esperancia* is Spanish for the Cape of Good Hope (we are not sure why Nortje uses the Spanish name: it was first named *Cabo da Boa Esperança* by the Portuguese), and Table Mountain is a famous Cape Town landmark (from the top of which Robben Island can be seen). Both place names presumably displaced their indigenous names. The speaker's experience of 'the loneliness of lost / beauties' at these places might arise from his sense of exile, but it also suggests that these places have somehow lost their beauties (perhaps because of the ugliness of the political situation). Not knowing anything about 'Karoo', we did a Google search and discovered that it is a semi-desert region of South Africa (north-west of Cape Town) of over 400 000 square kilometers and that its name means the 'Place of Great Dryness' (the name given to it by the Khoisan people who lived there). During the second Anglo-Boer War of 1899–1902 it was the scene of 'a bloody war of attrition' (www.thegreatkaroo.com). These lines also assert that a poetic tradition ('all the dead poets') exists that 'sang of spring's / miraculous recrudescence in the sandscapes of Karoo' – suggesting that South African poets have already set up an intimate relationship between language and this particular landscape. Yet given the fact that 'recrudescence' is a medical term for the reappearance of a disease after it has been quiescent (its original meaning, from the Latin *crudus*, was to become raw or sore again), we are invited to think of spring in this landscape as a returning disease or rawness (rather than being a promise of renewal that it so often is in English poetry). The disturbing violence of this unexpected view of spring is continued in the suggestion that these poets 'sang of thoughts that pierced like arrows' and 'spoke / through the strangled throat of multi-humanity / bruised like a python in the maggot-fattening sun'. These similes and metaphors indicate that this spring and this landscape (and this poetry) are a long way from English

Romanticism and the benevolent English landscape that it celebrated. Indeed, the images suggest not only a harsh landscape but one in which harsh things have been done. (As we have seen, the Karoo was the scene of a bloody war of attrition during the second Anglo-Boer War.) The lines can also be read as an image of apartheid's repression of the various non-white peoples of South Africa. Given South Africa's political history and the de-humanising system of apartheid, the poem seems to suggest, the relationship between language and landscape in South African poetry is inevitably disturbing and disorientating.

Our brief reading of Nortje's 'Waiting' has involved the recognition that this poem – its language, place names, allusions, way of describing the landscape and hints regarding the history of that landscape and the contemporary political situation – leaves us (two white English academics living in Scotland) very much on the outside. By contrast, it may well be that, although a South African reader will recognise the 'unhomely' image of South Africa that this poem creates, he or she may feel 'at home' in the poem at least in the sense that it contains relatively familiar references and allusions. The poem, then, works differently for different audiences. It may or may not have been written for metropolitan critics like ourselves, but its effect on us when we do read it is momentarily to reverse the polarity of our world view and our sense of our place in the world. While we might habitually think that we inhabit 'the centre' (we come from the country that was once the centre of the British Empire and is still the location of the 'original' English literary tradition), reading a poem like 'Waiting' momentarily jolts us out of that habit and rearranges our mental geography – putting us on the margin to its centre, making us 'the other'. This, we suggest, is an inevitable and important effect of reading post-colonial poetry written in a country that is not one's own, whether or not it was written to produce that effect.

Nortje's 'Waiting' is just one poem from one South African poet, but it refers to or imagines a line of South African poets who have sung of the troubled landscape of the Karoo. Schwartzman's *Ten South African Poets* gathers together selections of the poetry of ten very different poets from the apartheid and post-apartheid eras that can be said to form part of an evolving tradition of South African poetry. One of the tasks that face post-colonial writers in general is to help bring into being the literary traditions of their post-colonial societies. The literary traditions that emerge can be seen as hybrids formed by grafting elements of the English literary tradition with local genres, forms, language uses, rhythms, allusions, place names, and so on. One of the effects of these developments is to transform the English literary tradition itself and to dismantle the mental world view that placed English literature at the 'centre' and located other literatures in English at the 'margins'. In what follows, we want to explore this further by presenting an extended analysis of the poetic traditions of the British West Indies.

■ West Indian Poetry: Making National Traditions

The Caribbean consists of about seven thousand islands and islets organised into twenty-eight territories, including sovereign nation states, overseas departments and dependencies, that form an archipelago that arcs for about two thousand miles between the southern tip of Florida and the northern coast of South America. When Columbus first landed in the 'New World' and claimed it for Spain, the Caribbean islands were inhabited by two main indigenous American groups, the Taínos and the Caribs, who had migrated from South America around 2000 BCE.[16] The Spanish established a number of colonies in the Caribbean, using the Amerindians as slaves in gold mines and on sugar plantations. Within fifty years or so, the Amerindians in the Spanish colonies had been virtually wiped out by slaughter, maltreatment and imported diseases. From the 1520s onwards the Spanish began to import large numbers of slaves from western Africa to labour on the plantations. In the Spanish Caribbean, then, a terrible pattern had been set up that would later be followed by other European invaders.

In the seventeenth century, French, English and Dutch colonies were established in the Caribbean, mostly to produce sugar by the use of slave-labour from western Africa. A contemporary account of the population of the English colony of Barbados in 1655 reveals part of its extraordinary ethnic mixture: 'This island is inhabited with all sorts: with English, French, Dutch, Scots, Irish, Spaniards they being Jews, with Indians and miserable Negroes born to perpetual slavery' (Henry Whistler, quoted by Heuman, *The Caribbean*, p. 19). But the 'miserable Negroes' were also ethnically mixed. Between the 'discovery' of the New World and the final eradication of the slave trade, the European colonisers shipped about eleven million slaves from the west coast of Africa to the New World. (This figure does not include the large numbers who died on the 'Middle Passage' across the Atlantic.) These slaves, traded to European merchants by other west African peoples, were taken from a range of different ethno-linguistic groups 'and transported and sold in "mixed lots", as a deliberate means of limiting the possibilities of rebellion' (Ashcroft *et al.*, *Empire Writes Back*, p. 144). In the Caribbean, further ethnic variation was introduced by sexual relations between plantation owners and their slaves, resulting in 'coloured' offspring ('mulattos'). Subsequently, the various permutations of sexual relationships between black, coloured and white people produced further gradations of ethnic mixing. (The term 'Creole' is used confusingly to refer variously to a person of European ancestry born in the West Indies, a native-born black person and a native-born person of mixed European and black ancestry; 'Creole' is also used to refer to a language that develops

---

[16] Most of our potted history of the Caribbean is taken from Gad Heuman, *The Caribbean* (London: Hodder Arnold, 2006).

through extended contact between a European and a non-European language community, as in the Creole languages that emerged in the Caribbean.)

Caribbean slaves struggled against their enslavement throughout the slavery period and this often manifested itself in slave revolts. The slave revolution in the French colony of Saint Dominique in the 1790s, which led in 1804 to the establishment of Haiti as the first independent black republic in the Caribbean, had an electrifying impact on the slave populations of the rest of the Caribbean islands and inspired rebellions throughout the early decades of the nineteenth century.[17] Simultaneously, the abolitionist movement that had begun in Britain in the early 1780s eventually led in 1807 to the abolition of the British slave trade. Subsequently, the British Anti-Slavery Society eventually succeeded in outlawing slavery itself in all of Britain's colonies: 'At midnight on 31 July 1834, three-quarters of a million people in the British West Indies (and slaves elsewhere in the British Empire) celebrated their freedom' (Heuman, *The Caribbean*, p. 84). (Emancipation in the colonies of the other European powers followed later in the century.) As a result, the former slaves of the British West Indies had the right to withdraw their labour from the plantations, which forced the planters to look elsewhere for new sources of labour. Hundreds of thousands of indentured labourers were imported from other parts of the British Empire, especially from India, thus adding new ethnicities to the already complex mix. In the emerging social system of the British Caribbean, blacks and East Indians were generally at the bottom of the pile with whites at the top and 'mixed race people' in the middle.

Perhaps the most important source of resistance to the continued colonial oppression of black people in the Caribbean in the late nineteenth and early twentieth centuries was a series of related political and cultural movements that promoted racial pride and solidarity among black people and re-affirmed their African roots. As mentioned earlier, in the French Caribbean, Aimé Césaire's *Cahier d'un Retour au Pays Natal* (1939) affirmed the value and specificity of African culture and '*négritude*'. In the British Caribbean, the black Jamaican Marcus Garvey was a key intellectual figure in the promotion of black pride and the idea of returning to Africa. In his 'Centenary's Day' (1934), the collective speaker announces (in Standard English and a conventional English poetic form) that 'To Affric's shore we're bound again, / In freedom's glory won at large; / In thoughts we claim a just bargain, / To sail in liberty's fair barge'. The most important political development was the crowning in November 1930 of Prince Ras Tafari Makonnen (Haile Selassie) as emperor of Ethiopia. Selassie presented himself as a Messiah figure and descendent of King Solomon, and some preachers in Jamaica began to promote the

---

[17] The classic account of the revolution in Saint Dominique is C.L.R James, *The Black Jacobins: Toussaint L'Ouverture and the San Domingo Revolution* (1938, repr. London: Penguin, 2001).

ideas of Rastafarianism, a millenarian religious movement that envisaged a future in which black people of African origins would return to live in a free Africa ruled over by Selassie. Such ideas were particularly attractive to the urban poor in Jamaica, many of whom began to wear their hair in dreadlocks and made ganja (marijuana) a key feature of their religious practices. Since the mid-twentieth century, however, the Rastafarians have concentrated more on the Africanisation of Jamaica, although the idea of returning to Africa persists. For most people today, outside the Caribbean, perhaps the most prominent manifestation of Rastafarianism can be heard in the lyrics of Bob Marley.

The principal islands of the British West Indies gained their independence as follows: Jamaica (1962), Trinidad and Tobago (1962), Barbados (1966), Guyana (1966), Grenada (1974), Dominica (1978), St Lucia (1979), St Vincent and the Grenadines (1979), Antigua and Barbuda (1981), Saint Kitts and Nevis (1983). (Some smaller islands remain UK overseas territories.) But independence did not always or immediately realise the aspirations of the black underclass. Although Jamaica prospered, many people of African descent continued to endure poverty, unemployment and illiteracy. In such conditions, left-wing politics, Rastafarianism and the black power movement had an increasing impact from the late 1960s onwards. In the 1970s and 1980s, more left leaning governments emerged in the British Caribbean that were sympathetic towards Fidel Castro's Cuba. Such developments were undermined or crushed by the United States, which from the early twentieth century onwards gradually became the dominant neo-colonial power in the region.

One of the important things to stress about the Caribbean is that 'the entire contemporary population', apart from a few small pockets of surviving Amerindians, 'has suffered a displacement and an "exile" – from Africa, India, China, the "Middle East", and Europe' (Ashcroft *et al.*, *Empire Writes Back*, p. 25). This means that there is no pre-colonial condition that the present population of the Caribbean could imagine returning to. The same is true of the language situation. The policy of dividing African slaves up into 'mixed lots' meant that

> within two or three generations (sometimes within one) the only language available to the Africans for communication either amongst themselves or with the master was the European language of the master. African slaves could not avoid an awareness of the cruel pressure of an imposed language and the loss of their own 'voice', a loss incurred, moreover, in an alien landscape.
>
> (*Empire Writes Back*, p. 145)

In the British West Indies, then, the question of language was and is particularly fraught. On the one hand, 'English had a much more tainted historical role in the Caribbean' than in other British colonies (pp. 25–6); on the other hand, the English language is the only available common language. As a result, the people and poets of the West Indies have developed unique vernacular uses of English that subvert Standard English and the world view it embodies.

Those vernacular uses draw on the remnants of the slaves' African languages. As Paula Burnett points out, although words of African origin in the English-speaking Caribbean 'can be counted in hundreds', the vernaculars 'show strong African influence in their syntax and intonation'.[18] The very fact that there has been a great deal of debate about how to describe and define Caribbean language uses (are they examples of patois, dialect, vernacular, or nation languages?) reveals how politically charged the question of language is in the former colonies.

Burnett's *The Penguin Book of Caribbean Verse in English* (1986), which has a good introduction and collects together oral and written poetry from the eighteenth century to the 1980s, is perhaps the best general introduction to Caribbean poetry in English.[19] The literary poetic tradition of the Anglophone Caribbean has its beginnings almost three hundred years ago in the poetry of early white settlers, as in the anonymous 'A Pindaric Ode on the Arrival of His Excellency Sir Nicholas Lawes, Governor of Jamaica' (1718), the earliest surviving poem published in Jamaica. James Grainger, who was born in Scotland in 1724 and moved to St Kitts in 1759, is 'the only early poet of the Caribbean to have achieved a lasting reputation outside the islands' (Burnett, *The Penguin Book of Caribbean Verse in English*, p. 393). He describes his 'The Sugar-Cane' (1764), which is regularly included in collections of eighteenth-century English poetry, as a 'West India **georgic**' – a poem modelled on Virgil's *Georgics* and designed to be a 'practical guide to the cultivation of sugar' (p. 393). As these two examples reveal, early white Caribbean poetry, like other English poetry of the eighteenth century, was modelled on the classics. But Burnett stresses that she has chosen examples from this early phase 'because they illustrate the creolization of a European literary tradition through the portrayal of a uniquely Caribbean landscape, society or experience, which is the first stage in the establishment of a distinct Caribbean literature' (p. xxiv). The first black poet of the Caribbean literary tradition was Francis Williams (c. 1700–c. 1770), 'A free-born Jamaican black chosen by John, second Duke of Montagu . . . to be the subject of an experiment to prove that a negro was as educable as a white man, and therefore sent to England for education at grammar school and Cambridge University' (p. 392). Williams wrote poetry in English and Latin.

At the other end of the spectrum of early Caribbean poetry are the oral poems and songs of the slaves. According to Marjorie Reeves and Jenyth

---

[18] Burnett, *The Penguin Book of Caribbean Verse in English*, p. xxvi.

[19] Another good collection, with an idiosyncratic introduction, is E.A. Markham, ed., *Hinterland: Caribbean Poetry from the West Indies and Britain* (Northumberland: Bloodaxe, 1989). For useful discussions of Caribbean poetry, see Dennis Walder, *Post-Colonial Literatures in English: History, Language, Theory* (Oxford: Blackwell, 1998), pp. 118–51, and Patke, *Postcolonial Poetry in English*, pp. 80–104, 172–79, 186–95, 207–23.

Worsley, 'Unlike tribal languages, music was an aspect of African culture which the plantation owners did not attempt to suppress'. The slaves brought with them 'songs for digging, for gathering, for mourning and celebrating, and, of course, for storytelling'.[20] In the new conditions of the Caribbean, these songs were reworked, and new songs were created, in the hybrid languages that emerged in the plantations. Another British cultural influence on the slaves' vernacular songs was the English translation of the Bible, especially after emancipation when evangelists sought to constrain the freed slaves in new ways. In fact, biblical language has continued to be a crucial element of the Caribbean oral tradition: 'The Bible is part of the linguistic reservoir of Caribbean people in general, but the language of the Old Testament and Revelation in particular has been formative on the characteristic speech of Rastafarians, giving a sonorous authority to the songs of many **reggae** musicians and dub poets' (p. xxxvi). While the Bible offered oral poets the non-metrical models of Hebrew poetry, evangelical hymns provided a stanza and metrical form known as 'common measure' (see Glossary) that became common in West Indian oral and written poetry. But the black people of the Caribbean were not merely passive recipients of European forms: they reworked the evangelical hymn into hybrid forms called spirituals (such as 'He's got the whole wide world in His hands' and 'Were you there when they crucified my Lord?') that often have a call-and-answer structure. At the end of the nineteenth century, a former slave described the spontaneous group formation of a spiritual as follows: 'I'd sing [a cry to the Lord] to some ole "shout" song I'd heard em sing from Africa, and dey'd all take it up and repeat it, and keep a-adding to it, and den it would be a spiritual'.[21] Such forms and patterns also found their way into the oral poetry of the Caribbean, as in the first stanza of James Martinez's 'Dis Time No Stan' Like Befo' Time' (1920):

> Sometime I sit an wonder long;
> True, true.
> Dere's somet'ing sure is goin wrong;
> True, true.
> De time is sur'ly getting bad –
> It's nough to mek a feller mad –
> I r'ally now am feeling sad;
> True, true.

---

[20] Marjorie Reeves and J. Worsley, eds, *Favourite Hymns: 2000 Years of Magnificat* (London and New York: Continuum, 2001), p. 184.

[21] Reeves and Worsley, *Favourite Hymns*, p. 184, quoting T.E. Fulrop and A.J. Raboteau, *African-American Religions: Interpretive Essays in History and Culture* (London: Routledge, 1977), p. 64.

The oral and literary poetry of the West Indies lived parallel lives until the beginning of the twentieth century. This was in large part due to the fact that Creole vernaculars were seen as a mark of social and cultural inferiority in comparison with Standard English. As Burnett notes, 'The educational establishment had been labouring for years to teach those whose language was the vernacular to speak standard British English, which was the passport to social advancement, and it did not readily succumb to an acknowledgement that the vernacular could be the language of art' (pp. xxxviii–xxxix). Furthermore, as Edward Kamau Brathwaite recalled in 1979, the colonial education system also sought to ensure that the people of the West Indies would be educated in the English literary tradition: 'Shakespeare, George Eliot, Jane Austen – British literature and literary forms, the models which had very little to do, really, with the environment and the reality of non-Europe – were dominant in the Caribbean educational system'. As a consequence, 'in terms of what we write, our perceptual models, we are more conscious (in terms of sensibility) of the falling snow, for instance – the models are all there for the falling of the snow – than of the force of the hurricanes which take place every year' (Brathwaite, *History of the Voice*, p. 8). Such a mismatch between language and landscape, poetry and place, is precisely why Brathwaite promoted the writing of poetry in the 'nation languages' of the Anglophone Caribbean.

The first collections of vernacular literary poetry were Claude McKay's *Songs of Jamaica* and *Constab Ballads* (1912), though McKay soon abandoned vernacular poetry (his most well-known poem, 'If We Must Die', is a sonnet in Standard English) and emigrated to the United States, where he became a leading figure in the Harlem Renaissance. The unapologetic promotion and celebration of poetry in the Jamaican nation language began in the 1940s in the oral and written poems of Louise Bennett (1919–2006), whose poems began to appear in book form and in Jamaican newspapers in the early 1940s; they were immediately popular, though they were also sometimes condemned in the name of 'proper English'.[22] As Brathwaite notes, 'it was not until the post-independence seventies that she was officially – as distinct from popularly – recognized and given the highest honours' (*History of the Voice*, p. 27). Bennett's 'Back to Africa' (1947) is a satirical take on the idea that black Caribbean people could only discover or recover their true identity by returning to their African roots:

---

[22] Louise Bennett's best known books are *Jamaica Labrish* (1966), *Anancy and Miss Lou* (1979), *Selected Poems* (1982) and *Aunty Roachy Seh* (1993). For a useful discussion of Bennett's poetry, see Ramazani, 'Irony and Postcoloniality: Louise Bennett's Anancy Poetics', in *Hybrid Muse*, pp. 103–40.

Back to Africa

Back to Africa, Miss Mattie?
You no know wha you dah seh?   [Do you know what you are saying?]
You haf fe come from somewhe fus   [have to come from somewhere first]
Before you go back deh!   [back there]

Me know say dat you great great great   [I know you say that your]
Granma was African,
But Mattie, doan you great great great   [don't you know your]
Granpa was Englishman?

Den you great granmader fader   [And your great grandmother's father]
By you fader side was Jew?   [on your father's side was a Jew?]
An you granpa by you mader side   [grandfather on your mother's side]
Was Frenchie parlez-vous?

But de balance a you family,   [the majority of your family]
You whole generation,
Oonoo all barn dung a Bun Grung –   [you were all born down Burned
                                               Ground]
Oonoo all is Jamaican!   [you are all]

Den is weh you gwine, Miss Mattie?   [Then why are you going]
Oh, you view de countenance,
An between you and de Africans
Is great resemblance!

Ascorden to dat, all dem blue-yeye   [according to this, all those blue-eyed]
White American
Who-fa great granpa was Englishman   [whose]
Mus go back a Englan!   [must go back to England!]

What a debil of a bumb-an-bore,   [a devil of a lot of pushing and jostling]
Rig-jig an palam-pam   [crowded dancing and confusion]
Ef de whole worl start fe go back   [if the whole world started to go back]
Whe dem great granpa come from!

Ef a hard time you dah run from   [If you're running from a hard time
                                               here]
Tek you chance! But Mattie, do   [take your chance]
Sure a whe you come from so you got   [be sure where]
Somewhe fe come back to!   [somewhere to come back to]

Go a foreign, seek you fortune,   [Go abroad]
But no tell nobody say   [but don't tell anyone that]
You dah go fe seek your homelan,   [you go there to seek your homeland]
For a right deh so you deh!   [for you're there right here]

This poem foregrounds and celebrates Jamaican hybridity in two ways. Bennett's speaker highlights the ethnic hybridity of the people of the West Indies: she tells 'Miss Mattie' that she is mistaken to think that her true home-land is Africa since she has English, French and Jewish forebears as well as African. More striking, perhaps, is the speaker's use of Jamaican Creole. As Ramazani suggests, 'to read a poem of Louise Bennett's is to feel plunged in the oral strategies of Jamaican "labrish" or gossip, the wit, puns and insults of West Indian "broad talk" or performance rhetoric'. But Ramazani also points out that 'in the rumshops and in the yard, Jamaican men and women do not typically frame their utterances in the ballad stanza, as Bennett almost always does' (*Hybrid Muse*, p. 18). Bennett's poems, then, can be seen as hybrids that graft Jamaican Creole speech patterns and oral forms onto a European poetic genre. (One way to approach a post-colonial poem, then, is to examine whether it can be seen as a hybrid between a European poetic genre and a post-colonial 'nation language'.)

But for Brathwaite, the development of authentic nation-language poetry was more than a matter of substituting hurricanes for snow, and more than a matter of using the vernacular. It also involved breaking with the dominant metrical forms of English poetry – particularly iambic pentameter, but also the ballad stanza or common measure employed by Louise Bennett. In arguing this, he takes the idea that New World experiences need new language uses to what looks like an absurd extreme: 'the pentameter . . . carries with it a certain kind of experience, which is not the experience of a hurricane. The hurricane does not roar in pentameters. And that's the problem: how do you get a rhythm which approximates the *natural* experience, the *environmental* experi-ence' (*History of the Voice*, p. 10). In response, we would say that of course the hurricane does not roar in pentameters, but nor does it roar in the rhythms of Caribbean vernacular poetry. And although it is true that iambic pentameter carries certain associations through the way it has been used in the English poetic tradition, it has no intrinsic qualities that make it any more or any less appropriate for particular kinds of voices or experience.

Brathwaite nonetheless provides an indispensable analysis of the way Anglophone poetry in the West Indies in the second half of the twentieth cen-tury broke with regular metrical forms by drawing on indigenous models such as the calypso in order to develop a poetic tradition that embodies the speech forms, sounds and rhythms of black Caribbean people. (In fact, the roots of calypso derive from the songs of the African slaves who were transported to the Caribbean.) Brathwaite's own poetry in the trilogy *The Arrivants* (1967–69) is an intriguing attempt to exemplify his own argument: although it only occasionally reproduces Afro-Caribbean speech sounds, it experiments extensively with rhythm and lineation in order to generate a sense of Afro-Caribbean speech rhythms (it also orientates West Indian poetry very much towards an idealised Africa).[23] Paradoxically, however, one of the models that Brathwaite draws on is the free verse of American modernism on the assumption that pioneers such as Walt Whitman invented poetic forms that broke with the forms associated with the former colonial power and established an authentic American poetics purged of European influences. Thus the attempt to establish a decolonised poetics in the Caribbean actually results in a hybrid between indigenous and Western elements.

But even if Caribbean nation languages and poetics are hybrid forms, those forms are nonetheless specific to Caribbean culture and represent significant divergences from the European tradition. In 1986, Burnett could report that 'there is almost no major poet of the English-speaking Caribbean who does not have the vernacular as one of the languages of his poetry, but it is still to the oral tradition that we have to look for forms independent of the English literary tradition'. She goes on to suggest that the emergence in the 1960s of reggae and later of dub poetry (see Glossary) is a striking instance of how modern technology has facilitated 'a remarkable re-invention of an ancient tradition' – i.e., oral performance poetry in the vernacular (*Penguin Book of Caribbean Verse*, p. xl). The emergence of vernacular oral and literary poetry in the Caribbean, especially in the period immediately before and after independence, reveals the formative relationship between the creation of a vernacular literature and the creation of a nation. (Indeed, similar processes can be seen in the founding of nations and national literatures in Europe, beginning with Dante's argument in *De vulgari eloquentia* (1304) that his own Tuscan vernacular should replace Latin as the nation language of Italy and Italian poetry.) Yet we need to bear in mind that modern West Indian English encompasses a wide variety of linguistic styles and registers, ranging from deep Creole to what might be called West Indian Standard English, and that many speakers can range quite widely along this continuum (just as speakers in any language community shift between registers). The poetic use of West Indian English ranges in a similar way. It is also the case that most poets reserve Caribbean nation languages for the invented voices of dramatic monologues (their other poems and expository prose uses Standard West Indian English).

Many Caribbean dramatic monologues revisit the history of slavery in order to retell it from the slaves' point of view, suggesting that an independent poetry can only be fashioned through reclaiming and reliving the history of hurt. David Dabydeen, whose ancestors went to the Caribbean from India as indentured labourers and who migrated with his parents from Guyana to Britain in 1969, aged fourteen, describes the poems in his *Slave Song* (1984) as 'a jumble

---

[23] See Edward Kamau Brathwaite, *The Arrivants: A New World Trilogy* (Oxford: Oxford University Press, 1967).

of fact and myth, past and present' and as exploring 'the erotic energies of the colonial experience, ranging from a corrosive to a lyrical sexuality'.[24] Some of Dabydeen's poetry is located at the extreme vernacular end of the language spectrum. In 'Slave Song', the speaker – a male slave – endures his maltreatment by taunting his white master (in his imagination), saying that no matter how he is punished he can still have sex with his master's wife/daughter (in his imagination):

> Tie me haan up.
> Juk out me eye.
> Haal me teet out
> So me na go bite.
> Put chain rung me neck.   5
> Lash me foot tight.
> Set yu daag fo gyaad
> Maan till nite –
>
> Bu yu caan stap me cack floodin in de goldmine
> Caan stap me cack splashin in de sunshine!   10

Here, 'goldmine' and 'sunshine' are metaphors that reflect the speaker's assumption that the white (presumably blonde) woman's pubic hair is blonde. In the midst of brutal treatment, the brutalised slave imagines the sexual conquest of the master's woman in a way that is at once an act of crude revenge, a moment of lyrical idealisation and an achievement of a kind of liberty. This effect is produced by a number of contrasts between lines 1–8 and lines 9–10: the turn in grammar ('Bu' = but) is accompanied by a shift in metrical form from the constricted two-beat metre of the first eight lines (many of which are end-stopped) to the four- (or five?) beat lines of the run-on rhyming couplet (whose end-rhymes consist of the two celebratory metaphors for the woman's genitals). Yet our analysis of these poetic techniques does not overcome the 'othering' effect of this poem, whose deep Creole and subject matter remain disconcerting (for these readers, at least). Giving this slave a voice in a dramatic monologue challenges the tendency in colonial discourse of 'othering' slaves, reducing them to objects; yet this speaker's subjectivity suggests that the slave remains caught up in the ambivalent power struggles of colonial desire.

Although Grace Nichols's *I is a long-memoried woman* (1983) is much nearer to the Standard English end of the language continuum, it can nonetheless be seen as a powerful example of the drive in the 1980s towards the

---

[24] David Dabydeen, *Slave Song* (Sydney: Dangaroo Press, 1984), p. 10.

decolonisation and Africanisation of the Caribbean.[25] It consists of a series of first- and third-person poems that focus on the experience of a slave woman who endures the full horrors of the Middle Passage (while giving birth) and of slavery in the plantations. The poems foreground the origins of black Caribbean people in the various cultures and ethnicities of western Africa. The woman is a kind of 'everywoman': although she comes from the Ivory Coast, she dimly recalls previous incarnations in the Congo, Sierra Leone and the Gold Coast, and greets new arrivals in the Caribbean from various ethno-linguistics groups: Ibo, Yoruba, Ashanti, Fanti and Mane. Later, she calls on the aid of various gods from these cultures – including Ala, the Ibo goddess of fertility, Asase Yaa, the Ashanti earth goddess of fertility, Yemanji, the Yoruba goddess of the ocean and motherhood, Ogun, the Yaruba god who represents the motive force of nature, and Anansi, the Ashanti trickster and hero who brings rain to stop fires. In the poetic narrative, the combined power of such gods, invoked by *obeah* (a Caribbean folk magic that originated in central and western Africa), helps to bring about an imagined total overthrow of the European colonisers. These poems can thus be seen as trying to reconstruct a western African mythology in the Caribbean that can counter-balance or even banish the cultural and religious impact of European colonisation. In doing so, they also reclaim black Caribbean people's history and origins and fashion and celebrate a black female Caribbean subjectivity rooted in Africanness. Yet the poetry of *I is a long-memoried woman* is a self-conscious hybrid between African mythology and the English language. The poet/speaker asserts that the language she uses has roots in the lost language of her ancestors:

> I have crossed an ocean
> I have lost my tongue
> from the roots of the old one
> a new one has sprung

Yet the fact that this (like most of the other poems in the collection) is said in Standard English highlights the fact that this new tongue is a hybrid one. While the content of these poems imagines the Africanisation of the Caribbean, their language makes them into an intriguing example of post-colonial hybridity. The fact that Nichols emigrated to Britain in 1977 and publishes her books with British publishers (*I is a long-memoried woman* was first published in London) suggests that she is writing in, for and against the metropolitan centre of the former British Empire at one and the same time.

Not every major West Indian poet is wholly committed to the vernacular or to the tendency, in Brathwaite and others, to imply that it is necessary or even

---

[25] Grace Nichols, *I is a long-memoried woman* (London: Carribean Cultural International, 1983).

possible to decolonise the Caribbean mind and culture – either by a return (literal or metaphorical) to Africa or through the forging of a West Indian literature and culture purged of the effects of colonisation. Born on the island of Saint Lucia in 1930, Derek Walcott's mixed ethnicity (his grandfathers were white, his grandmothers were black) perhaps accounts for the fact that his poetry and prose writings began to explore the idea of hybridity well before post-colonial theory:

> Decades before the academic dissemination of such concepts as hybridity, creolization, cross-culturality, . . . Walcott argued vehemently for an intercultural model of postcolonial literature. Against a 'separatist' black literature that 'belligerently asserts its isolation, its difference,' he counterposes a vision of the Caribbean writer as inevitably 'mixed': New World blacks must use what Walcott ironically calls 'the white man's words' as well as 'his God, his dress, his machinery, his food. And, of course, his literature.'[26]

As Walcott said in an interview in 1983, 'I do not consider English to be the language of my masters. I consider English to be my birthright. I happen to have been born in an English and a Creole place, and love both languages'.[27] As a consequence, Walcott tends to reject the notion of negritude or 'Africanness' as a fantasy of pure origins and criticises the 'back to Africa' tendency, celebrating instead the hybridity of Caribbean culture as a tense but creative mix of African and British-European influences. For Walcott, the fact that all ethnic groups in the Caribbean are relative newcomers with a new hybridised language provides poets with a unique opportunity:

> Walcott advocates appropriation and celebration, arguing that to the Caribbean writer falls the enviable task (unavailable to Europe and Europeans) of 'giving things their names'. . . . [Walcott] proposes an Adamic celebration of language, invoking the poet's excitement in establishing 'original relations' with his 'new' universe, the newness qualified of course by the prior experiences of the old. . . . here too, it is 'the bitter memory' (6) of the old which supplies the energy in the new
> (Ashcroft *et al.*, *Empire Writes Back*, pp. 49–50).[28]

As we will see, the internal energy of Walcott's poetry is generated out of dynamic relationships between the bitter memory of colonial history

---

[26] Ramazani, *Hybrid Muse*, p. 63, quoting Derek Walcott, 'Necessity of Negritude', in Robert D. Hamner, ed., *Critical Perspectives on Derek Walcott* (Washington DC: Three Continents Press, 1993), pp. 20–23 (20).

[27] *Conversations with Derek Walcott*, ed. W. Baer (Jackson: University Press of Mississippi, 1996), p. 82.

[28] Ashcroft *et al.* refer to and quote from Derek Walcott, 'The Muse of History', in Orde Coombes, ed., *Is Massa Day Dead? Black Moods in the Caribbean* (New York: Doubleday, 1974).

(especially slavery), the inspiring traditions of European literature, the vigour of the vernacular, and alluring glimpses of the possibility of being an Adamic poet with the rare privilege of being able to name a new world.

Although Walcott generally writes in a highly inventive Standard English combined with local themes, references and allusions, he sometimes creates local voices marked by a relatively mild West Indian Creole. Walcott's 'first major nation language effort' (Brathwaite, *History of the Voice*, p. 10) was 'The Schooner *Flight*' (1979), a 472-line dramatic monologue in eleven sections whose speaker, Shabine, is a mixed race poet (like his creator):

> I know these islands from Monos to Nassau,
> a rusty head sailor with sea-green eyes
> that they nickname Shabine, the patois for
> any red nigger, and I, Shabine, saw
> when these slums of empire was paradise.
> I'm just a red nigger who love the sea,
> I had a sound colonial education,
> I have Dutch, nigger, and English in me,
> and either I'm nobody, or I'm a nation. (35–43)

These lines indicate that the poem, written in the early independence period, is concerned with questions of individual and national identity (the four islands that Shabine visits or passes – Trinidad, Barbados, Dominica and Saint Lucia – achieved independence in 1962, 1966, 1978 and 1979 respectively). Shabine foregrounds his ethnic hybridity and his 'sound colonial education', claiming that in these respects he represents a 'nation' which is similarly hybrid and similarly educated. Indeed, for part of the poem, Shabine's silent audience appears to be a group of listeners very much like himself – he addresses 'khaki-pants red niggers like you and me' (90). Yet the fact that Shabine's name is not his own but a general nickname – 'the patois for / any red nigger' – suggests that his identity is constructed by others and by his post-colonial condition (we never find out his real name). Furthermore, his claim that his ethnic hybridity makes him a representative figure is rejected by both sides of the racial divide:

> I had no nation now but the imagination.
> After the white man, the niggers didn't want me
> when the power swing to their side.
> The first chain my hands and apologize, 'History';
> the next said I wasn't black enough for their pride. (151–155)

Shabine, then, presents himself as multiply displaced (not black, not white), an oppressed victim within an oppressed and now oppressive society. In Shabine's own terms, if he is not a nation, then he must be 'nobody'. This, together with his mixed feelings about a love triangle between himself, his mistress and his wife and an acute sense of Trinidad's political corruption (which he got caught up in), drives him into exile and a life of wandering on the seas. The poem traces his voyage and shows him discovering or recreating his own identity, and a new relationship to the islands of the Caribbean, through the poetic imagination ('I had no nation now but the imagination').

In the poem's opening lines, Shabine leaves his sleeping mistress (Maria Concepcion) in order to crew on a schooner aptly named *Flight*:

> 1 *Adios, Carenage*
> In idle August, while the sea soft,
> and leaves of brown islands stick to the rim
> of this Caribbean, I blow out the light
> by the dreamless face of Maria Concepcion
> to ship as a seaman on the schooner *Flight*.
> Out in the yard turning grey in the dawn,
> I stood like a stone and nothing else move
> but the cold sea rippling like galvanize
> and the nail holes of stars in the sky roof,
> till a wind start to interfere with the trees.
> I pass me dry neighbour sweeping she yard
> as I went downhill, and I nearly said:
> 'Sweep soft, you witch, 'cause she don't sleep hard,'
> but the bitch look through me like I was dead. (1–14)

A sense of place is constructed throughout the poem by the use of local place names. The name of the first section, 'Adios, Carenage', together with place names later in the section, indicate that Shabine begins his journey in Carenage (which means 'safe anchorage'), five miles west of Port of Spain, the capital of Trinidad. A sense of place is also achieved by the distinctive Caribbean rhythms and syntax in phrases such as 'while the sea soft', 'nothing else move', and, most of all, 'I pass me dry neighbour sweeping she yard'. As Ashcroft *et al.* say of another passage from the poem, the poetry hovers 'in the tension between the vernacular and the standard by alternating one with the other' (*Empire Writes Back*, p. 68). Significantly, too, the poem seems also to hover in the tension between iambic pentameter and four-beat '**dactyls**' (triple falling rhythms) – the rhythm that Brathwaite identifies with calypso and Afro-Caribbean speech (*History of the Voice*, p. 17) (though we will see that there are other influences on the poem's metre as well).

The poem's linguistic modulations are accompanied by modulations between local references and allusions to English and European poetic traditions, as can be seen in the following successive passages from the end of the first section:

> I swear to you all, by my mother's milk,
> by the stars that shall fly from tonight's furnace,
> that I loved them, my children, my wife, my home;
> I loved them as poets love the poetry
> that kills them, as drowned sailors the sea.
> You ever look up from some lonely beach
> and see a far schooner? Well, when I write
> this poem, each phrase go be soaked in salt;
> I go draw and knot every line as tight
> as ropes in this rigging; in simple speech
> my common language go be the wind,
> my pages the sails of the schooner *Flight*. (65–76)

The language of the first passage is elevated, almost bardic, with a use of repetition that is quite appropriate for the vow that Shabine is making. The lines are further enriched and elevated by allusions, perhaps, to Oscar Wilde's 'each man kills the thing he loves' (*The Ballad of Reading Gaol* (1898), I, vii) and to T.S. Eliot's 'drowned Phoenician Sailor' (*The Waste Land* (1922), 47). This high poetic style modulates effortlessly into the 'common language' of the following passage, where the use of 'go' for 'will' signals a Caribbean vernacular, and where the poet-speaker foregrounds his own poetic technique by drawing metaphors from the natural environment and from his own craft as a sailor (thus making his poetic and nautical crafts into equivalents of each other). In shifting back and forth between elevated poetic English and Caribbean nation language, the poem appears to give equal value to both. By using both languages in highly inventive, poetic ways Walcott challenges both the metropolitan centre's elevation of Standard English over the vernacular and those champions of the vernacular who distrust Standard English as a colonial imposition. This also raises questions about the intended readership. The fact that Walcott's use of Caribbean vernacular is so much milder than that in Dabydeen's 'Slave Song' indicates that he might be writing for an international audience as well as for his compatriots (many of whom, like Walcott himself, are able to range from deep Creole to Standard English).

Shabine's voyage on the schooner takes him from Trinidad north-north-east to Barbados, from Barbados north-west to St Lucia (Walcott's place of birth and the home of Shabine's wife and family), and then northwards from St Lucia, passing Dominica and heading for the Bahamas. The poem uses the fictional motif of the sea voyage in order to explore the history and political development of West Indian culture, but also to narrate a voyage of self-discovery. In doing so, the poem draws on and alludes to earlier poems from the European tradition – as Shabine says, in a passage we will look at below, 'my memory revolve / on all sailors before me' (225–26). The archetypal narrative poem in that tradition is Homer's *The Odyssey* (*c.* 6th century BCE), which focuses on the wandering sea voyage of Odysseus and his companions as they sail from island to island in the Ægean Sea trying to reach their island home of Ithaca. (In *Omeros* (1990), a later epic poem, Walcott develops a complex system of correspondences between his characters and Homer's and between the Caribbean and Greek archipelagos.[29]) The link between 'The Schooner *Flight*' and *The Odyssey* is hinted at by a potential allusion in a passage we looked at above. When Shabine says that 'either I'm nobody, or I'm a nation', it is possible, as Maria Fumagalli has argued, that Shabine–Walcott is alluding to the trick that Odysseus plays on the giant Cyclops in book IX of *The Odyssey* (Cyclops has Odysseus and his men trapped in his cave and Odysseus tells him that his name is 'nobody'; when Odysseus and his men drive a burning stake in Cyclops' one eye, his screams of agony bring his neighbours to his aid, but when Cyclops tells them that 'nobody' has attacked him they go away again). As Fumagalli says, 'the pseudonym "nobody" that Shabine claims for himself is the imaginative stratagem that allows Odysseus to save his life'.[30] Furthermore, when Shabine says 'and I, Shabine, saw / when these slums of empire was paradise' (38–39), he or his creator may be alluding, via Eliot's *The Waste Land*, to another figure from Greek mythology and literature – the blind seer Tiresias. As one of the speakers of Eliot's poem, Tiresias uses the following formulae: 'I Tiresias, though blind . . . / . . . can see' (218–19); 'I, Tiresias, . . . / Perceived the scene, and foretold the rest' (228–29); 'And I Tiresias have foresuffered all' (243). As we will see, Shabine is also a visionary figure who occasionally sees through the pain of colonial history to experience the Caribbean as if it was an Edenic new world.

Like most of the West Indian poems we have looked at, 'The Schooner *Flight*' is concerned with re-examining the impact of colonial history in order, perhaps, to revalue and reclaim it. In Section 5, 'Shabine Encounters the Middle Passage', as the *Flight* sails from Trinidad to Barbados on the first leg of its voyage, Shabine has a visionary encounter with a fleet of ghostly ships commanded by some of the 'great admirals' of the colonial era and crewed by dead sailors (who would have been pressed men) with whom Shabine seems to identify:

---

[29] See Derek Walcott, *Omeros* (New York: Farrar, Strauss and Giroux; London: Faber and Faber, 1990). For a revealing discussion of Walcott's epic poem, see Ramazani, 'The Wound of Postcolonial History: Derek Walcott's *Omeros*', *Hybrid Muse*, pp. 49–71.

[30] Maria Fumagalli, *The Flight of the Vernacular: Seamus Heaney, Derek Walcott and the Impress of Dante* (Amsterdam and New York: Rodopi, 2001), p. 113.

> Man, I brisk in the galley first thing next dawn,
> brewing li'l coffee; fog coil from the sea
> like the kettle steaming when I put it down
> slow, slow, 'cause I couldn't believe what I see:
> where the horizon was one silver haze,
> the fog swirl and swell into sails, so close
> that I saw it was sails, my hair grip my skull,
> it was horrors, but it was beautiful.
> We float through a rustling forest of ships
> with sails like dry paper, behind the glass
> I saw men with rusty eyeholes like cannons,
> and wherever their half-naked crews cross the sun,
> right through their tissue, you traced their bones
> like leaves against the sunlight; frigates, barkentines,
> the backward-moving current swept them on,
> and high on their decks I saw great admirals,
> Rodney, Nelson, de Grasse, I heard the hoarse orders
> they gave those Shabines, and the forest
> of masts sail right through the *Flight*,
> and all you could hear was the ghostly sound
> of waves rustling like grass in a low wind
> and the hissing weeds they trailed from the stern;
> slowly they heaved from east to west
> like this round world was some cranked water wheel,
> every ship pouring like a wooden bucket
> dredged from the deep; my memory revolve
> on all sailors before me, then the sun
> heat the horizon's ring and they was mist. (200–227)

Clearly, a lot could be said about this passage, especially concerning the inventive use of figurative language. Here, we want to make just two points. First, the passage revisits key events and figures in the colonial history of the Caribbean. Vice-Admiral Horatio Nelson (1758–1805) is the most famous of British naval commanders but, although he did serve in the West Indies, his most important campaigns were elsewhere. Using Google, we discovered that Admiral Lord George Rodney (1719–1792), by contrast, played a major role in extending and defending Britain's colonisation of the Caribbean. In 1762, as British Commander-in-Chief of the Leeward Islands, Rodney captured Martinique, Grenada, Saint Lucia (Walcott's birthplace) and St Vincent from the French. In 1779, he was again appointed to command the Barbados and Leeward Islands, from where he continued to spearhead Britain's naval struggle against France and Spain for dominance in the Caribbean, culminating in the overwhelming defeat of the French, commanded by Admiral François Joseph Paul de Grasse (1722–1788), at the Battle of Les Saintes on 12 April 1782. A few days later, Rodney saved Jamaica from French invasion and finally shattered French naval strength in the Caribbean. Shabine might therefore be witnessing a ghostly replay of one of the most decisive naval battles for colonial control of the region. In Shabine's vision, however, admirals Rodney and de Grosse appear not to be engaging in battle but to be sailing together in a westward direction towards the Caribbean Sea (implying, perhaps, that from Shabine's point of view the historical colonial rivalry between the British and the French is less important than the fact that they were both colonial oppressors). And although the vision of these ghosts of the past 'was horrors' it was also 'beautiful', which perhaps suggests that the colonial past is now remote enough to be recreated as aesthetic experience. The fact that the vision turns to mist in the morning sun implies that the colonial struggle between Britain and France over the Caribbean is now an insubstantial thing of the past.

The second thing that we want to stress about this passage is that it appears to be an extended composite allusion to some of the most haunting scenes in what is perhaps the most famous English poem about a sea voyage – Samuel Taylor Coleridge's 'The Rime of the Ancient Mariner' (1798). Coleridge's poem is a dialogue between a wedding guest and an ancient mariner who insists on telling the uncanny tale of his experiences at sea. The mariner tells of how, during the course of a voyage from England south to the equator and on towards the South Pole (perhaps on a voyage of colonial business or exploration), he shot an albatross (a fatal deed in sailors' lore) in a random act of violence. His crewmates curse the mariner for killing a lucky omen or spirit and hang the dead albatross round his neck. Having rounded the Cape Horn, the ship heads north into uncharted parts of the Pacific Ocean. As they near the equator, the wind dies down and the ship is becalmed in terrible heat. At this point, the mariner has a vision of an approaching spectral ship emerging out of the mist and silhouetted against the sinking sun (see 'The Ancient Mariner', part 3, 143–223). The ship itself has several features that link it to Shabine's vision: it is described as a 'skeleton ship' and as a 'spectre-bark', and its crew consists solely of a spectre-woman ('The Night-mare Life-in-Death was she') and Death. These two figures throw dice for the mariner and his crew mates. Death wins the crew, all two hundred of whom promptly drop dead on the decks, while the woman wins the mariner and condemns him to live a life-in-death – trapped on his becalmed ship, surrounded by his dead shipmates, suffering a terrible thirst, and looking out on a natural world that he regards as alien and threatening. His release and redemption begins when, in contrast to his wanton killing of the albatross, he feels able to love and bless the water-snakes who play in the sea around the ship (as we will see, Shabine has a similar moment of redemption and recovery):

O happy living things! no tongue
Their beauty might declare:
A spring of love gushed from my heart,
And I blessed them unaware:
Sure my kind saint took pity on me,
And I blessed them unaware.

The selfsame moment I could pray;
And from my neck so free
The Albatross fell off, and sank
Like lead into the sea. (282–91)

After a gentle sleep, rain comes to slake the mariner's thirst, the ship begins to move seemingly of its own accord (there is no breeze), and spirits reanimate his dead shipmates – who become 'a ghastly crew' that helps the mariner to sail the ship homewards (see 'The Ancient Mariner', part 5, 326–44). In other words, Shabine's vision of ghostly ships crewed by the dead fuses two different ships in 'The Ancient Mariner' – the death ship that the mariner himself sees and the mariner's own ship crewed by his dead shipmates. Shabine's vision also draws on a third scene in Coleridge's poem. When the ship eventually reaches the mariner's home port it is approached by a harbour pilot, who takes a hermit along with him in his boat for spiritual support because the ship looks so uncanny. The hermit's horrified exclamations appear to supply some of the imagery that feeds into Shabine's vision of the colonial ships:

The planks look warped! and see those sails,
How thin they are and sere!
I never saw ought like to them,
Unless perchance it were

Brown skeletons of leaves that lag
My forest brook along. (529–34)

Shabine's vision of the colonial ships of the past thus alludes to various scenes in 'The Ancient Mariner' (we will return later to the question of why it does so). But the passing of the colonial ships does not bring Shabine's vision to an end. Immediately afterwards he sees ghostly slave ships heading toward the Caribbean on the Middle Passage:

Next we pass slave ships. Flags of all nations,
our fathers below deck too deep, I suppose,
to hear us shouting. So we stop shouting. Who knows
who his grandfather is, much less his name? (228–231)

These lines suggest that the facts of slavery mean that the descendants of former slaves cannot revisit history to discover their true lineage and names and cannot reconnect with their fathers. This means that there is no point in 'shouting' – no point in trying to bridge the chasm between present and past and/or no point in complaining about the history of slavery. But this does not mean that slavery can be forgiven or forgotten. Shabine's visionary encounters with colonial history allow him to pronounce that attempts to justify colonial barbarity in the name of progress are a 'dirty joke' (310).

In this poem, the possibility of redemption comes not from returning to Africa but out of a near-death experience in a terrible storm that snapped 'the neck / of the *Flight*' (381–82). Shabine represents the storm in biblical terms and tells us that he found the strength to face impending death through memories of his childhood religious faith and the pride it gave him in the way his race survived the horrors of the sea-crossing from western Africa and, by extension, the horrors of slavery:

> Then a strength like it seize me and the strength said:
> 'I from a backward people who still fear God.'
> Let Him, in His might, heave Leviathan upward
> by the winch of His will, the beast pouring lace
> from his sea-bottom bed; and that was the faith
> that had fade from a child in the Methodist chapel
> in Chisel Street, Castries, when the whale-bell
> sang service and, in hard pews ribbed like the whale,
> proud with despair, we sang how our race
> survive the sea's maw, our history, our peril,
> and now I was ready for whatever death will. (400–410)

Shabine, then, asserts both his Methodist and his African heritage, and derives strength from both. But he survives the storm because of his captain's heroism, which he figures in Christ-like terms – which, in turn, allows him to figure his own survival as a kind of religious salvation and rebirth (with allusions to the biblical Jonah).

After the storm, in a passage that perhaps recalls the rain that refreshes the Ancient Mariner after he blesses the sea snakes, Shabine experiences a moment of Edenic purity in which he perceives the Caribbean landscape as if for the first time:

> I wanted nothing after that day.
> Across my own face, like the face of the sun,
> a light rain was falling, with the sea calm.

519

> Fall gently, rain, on the sea's upturned face
> like a girl showering; make these islands fresh
> as Shabine once knew them! Let every trace,
> every hot road, smell like clothes she just press
> and sprinkle with drizzle. I finish dream;
> whatever the rain wash and the sun iron:
> the white clouds, the sea and sky with one seam,
> is clothes enough for my nakedness. (428–38)

Yet Shabine inevitably falls from this Edenic moment back into the realities of history. He recognises that it is not possible to return to a state of purity prior to the history of hurt he has experienced first hand. And although the storm-damage has prevented the *Flight* from passing beyond the Caribbean Sea into the Atlantic, Shabine has come to realise that the islands of the Caribbean offer him infinite possibilities:

> Though my *Flight* never pass the incoming tide
> of this island sea beyond the loud reefs
> of the final Bahamas, I am satisfied
> if my hand gave voice to one people's grief.
> Open the map. More islands there, man,
> than peas on a tin plate, all different size,
> one thousand in the Bahamas alone. (439–45)

In his exalted mood he feels able, in a passage that recalls a similar moment in 'The Ancient Mariner', to bless the towns and islands that he once felt excluded from:

> and from this bowsprit, I bless every town,
> the blue smell of smoke in hills behind them,
> and the one small road winding down them like twine
> to the roofs below (447–50).

Having imaginatively reconnected with the landscape and people of the Caribbean, Shabine re-imagines his maritime exile as a quest for an Edenic island that is at once 'vain' and exalting:

> I have only one theme:
> The bowsprit, the arrow, the longing, the lunging heart –
> the flight to a target whose aim we'll never know,
> vain search for one island that heals with its harbour
> and a guiltless horizon, where the almond's shadow
> doesn't injure the sand. There are so many islands! (450–55)

Poetry, then, does not deliver us from history, but it gives voice to a people's grief and articulates and nourishes our longing to be delivered, even as it recognises that this longing is 'vain' and registers history's indelible impact on nations and individuals. At the poem's conclusion, Shabine does not return to a safe anchorage but continues to sail the Caribbean in ecstatic solitude, at one with and at home in the seascape.

The narrative trajectory of 'The Schooner *Flight*' reveals that it has more interesting things in common with 'The Ancient Mariner' than visions of ghostly ships crewed by dead mariners. The concern in Coleridge's poem with the mariner–narrator's exile, alienation from nature and human society, beatific redemption, reconnection with the natural and social world, homecoming and compulsion to narrate his tale is reworked in 'The Schooner *Flight*' in ways that are specific to Walcott's post-colonial project. The fact that both characters feel compelled to carry on wandering at the end of their poems links 'The Schooner *Flight*' to poems such as Canto XXVI of Dante's *Inferno* (1321) and Tennyson's 'Ulysses' (1833), both of which portray Odysseus as unable to settle at home when he finally reaches it and as eager to continue his life of wandering the seas. Yet although Tennyson's Ulysses (an alternative name for Odysseus) wishes 'to seek a newer world / . . . beyond the sunset, and the baths / Of all the western stars' (57–61), Shabine is already in that newer world in the west and has discovered that the whole Caribbean Sea and all its islands is a kind of home that he can wander in forever. Rather than feeling confined by the rim of the Caribbean Sea and wishing to cross the Atlantic to Africa or Europe, Shabine revels in his multi-cultural paradise.

'The Schooner *Flight*', then, is a poem that asserts and celebrates its hybridity in a number of ways. It foregrounds its speaker's and its addressees' ethnic hybridity; it strategically uses a language that hybridises Standard English with a Caribbean nation language; and it makes a series of connections between its Caribbean odyssey and prominent poems from the European and English poetic traditions. Another strategic hybridity is the way the poem presents its West Indian themes and speech patterns in a poetic genre (a dramatic monologue) that was developed in the English poetic tradition (as we saw in Chapter 7). But there is another allusion to an English poem in 'The Schooner *Flight*' that requires us to revisit the question of its metrical form. As Brathwaite points out in *History of the Voice*, the poem's first line ('In idle August, while the sea soft') is an allusion to the first line of the Prologue to William Langland's *The Vision of Piers Plowman* (*c.* 1362–1387): 'In a somer seson, whan softe was the sonne'. As Brathwaite also points out, Langland's poem uses a metrical form that preceded the reign of iambic pentameter in English poetry. Using the techniques presented in Chapter 2, we expect that you will readily discover that the first line of *Piers Plowman* is in four-beat rising metre that is mostly in triple form – a metrical pattern that is reinforced by alliteration. In fact, *Piers*

Plowman is using and playing with the alliterative metre of old English verse produced by poets prior to and some time after the Norman Conquest of 1066 (see 'alliterative verse' in Glossary). Walcott's poem signals its affiliation with *Piers Plowman* by its own use of four-beat rising triple rhythm that is often reinforced by alliteration – as in the first line, and as in the following line: 'vain search for one island that heals with its harbour' (453). And what's more, Langland was using a rustic dialect of Middle English at about the same time that Geoffrey Chaucer was beginning to write iambic pentameter poems in a south-eastern dialect that would evolve into Standard English. In other words, Langland, like Chaucer, was making the first moves in the creation of a new poetic tradition in the vernacular that broke with the Latin and Norman French that were the languages of state and church in medieval England. Walcott, then, seems to be linking his own attempt to create a hybrid English-vernacular poetic tradition for the newly independent nations of the West Indies with a poem – *Piers Plowman* – that can be seen as trying to do the same thing in medieval England and might have done so were it not for the triumph of Chaucer's language and metre. As a consequence, it might be said that Walcott's metre owes as much to *Piers Plowman* as it does to the rhythms of Caribbean song-forms and vernacular speech. Or rather, that it discovers a kind of equivalence between Langland's metre and rhythmic forms that have become indigenous to the West Indies. In terms of metrical form, too, then, 'The Schooner *Flight*' makes an inventive and politically resonant use of strategic hybridity in order to help found a West Indian poetic tradition based not on the possibility of decolonisation but on the resourceful hybridisation of West Indian and European forms and traditions.

Walcott's poem, then, self-consciously employs the kind of strategic hybridity that characterises the most successful post-colonial poetry. Walcott can be said to be reclaiming and repossessing English and European poetry as crucial elements of his mixed cultural heritage. But the fact that allusions only work for readers who are able to spot them (as we saw in Chapter 13) indicates that Walcott's intended or imagined readership is limited to readers who are familiar with the English and European literary traditions. That readership includes educated readers in the metropolitan centres of Europe and the United States, but it also includes educated readers throughout the world (both in former colonies and elsewhere): as we have indicated, it was Brathwaite who alerted us to the allusion to *Piers Plowman* in the first line of 'The Schooner *Flight*'. As a consequence, we might ask whether Walcott's poetry has transcended its post-colonial condition and become part of an international literature in English that is equally accessible to educated readers throughout the world. We might also ask whether metropolitan critics (like the writers of the present book) value Walcott's poetry because it alludes to the poetic tradition that we have spent our lives studying and employs the kinds of poetic techniques we have presented in this book. In response, we would say no to the first question and yes to the second. Our analysis of 'The Schooner *Flight*' has revealed that Walcott's distinctively West Indian themes and perspectives are an irreducible aspect of his poetry. As a consequence, although his poetry uses techniques and allusions that we can appreciate, it nonetheless challenges our world view as white academics working in the metropolitan centre. Walcott's poetry helps to bring into being a distinctive West Indian English poetry which confidently asserts its right to exist on the world stage alongside the poetry of the metropolitan 'centre'. Walcott's achievement in this respect can be seen in the poems gathered together in his *Collected Poems, 1948–1984* (1986) and was recognised when he received the Nobel Prize for Literature in 1992, shortly after the publication of *Omeros*, the major epic poem of our time.[31]

Exercise

1 Read the following poem several times, then answer the questions that follow. The poem was written by Jean 'Binta' Breeze and published in her recent collection *The Arrival of Brighteye and Other Poems* (Bloodaxe, 2000). Breeze is a Jamaican dub poet who lives in Jamaica and Cambridge (England). About half the poems in *The Arrival of Brighteye* are in Standard English and half in Jamaican Creole. As Rajeev Patke says, she 'moves freely across the continuum from Creole to Standard English, just as she moves fluently from the performance stage to the printed page' (*Postcolonial Poetry in English*, p. 194). The poem uses what has become a relatively standard orthography for presenting West Indian Creole.

The Wife of Bath speaks in Brixton Market

My life is my own bible
wen it comes to all de woes
in married life
fah since I reach twelve,
Tanks to Eternal Gawd,   5
is five husban I have
            (if dat is passible)
but all of dem was wort someting
in dem own way
doah dem say   10
dat troo Jesas only go to one weddin

---

[31] See Derek Walcott, *Collected Poems, 1948–1984* (New York and Toronto: Harper & Collins, 1986).

in Canaan
we no suppose fi married
more dan once
but den again   15
dem say Im tell de Samaritan woman
by de well
dat doah she did have five husban
de laas one never count
       is wat Im mean by dat   20
       why jus de fif one lef out
       ow much she can have den
          four?
Im don't give no precise number
Well,   25
       people can argue it forever
       but me sure of one serious ting
       Im order we to sex an multiply
Im also say dat
       de man mus lef im madda an im fadda   30
       an cling to me
but Im never say
how many
       mi no hear no mention of bigamy
       or polygamy   35
       so why me or anyone
       should tink it is a crime
And wat about de wise king Soloman
look how much wife im tek, Lawd,
ah wish ah did have as much in bed as him!   40
God mus did give him some 'great' gif
No one alive did ever have such fun
But still
I will tank de Lawd
fah doah I have only five   45
I shall welcome de sixt one
wenever im choose to arrive
because I nat lacking up my foot at all
if one husban dead
anadda christian man will surely come   50
fah even de apostle say dat den mi free
to tek anadda man dat can please me
       betta to married dan to bun

Abraham, Joseph,
nuff adda holy man   55
did have nuff wife
Whey God forbid dat?
Yuh see no clear word?
Where Im ever order virginity?
        Dere is no such commandment!   60
is de apostle Paul come talk bout maidenhead
an him never qualify fi talk bout dat.
Im say a man may counsel a woman
but counselling is nat command
wat I do wid my body is my personal business   65
an if God did command virginity
nobady wouldn married
fah married woulda dead
an no more pickney wouldn born
so no new maidenhead.   70

How Paul him want to tek command
wen Jesas wouldn dweet
we all know pum pum is something sweet
an nuff sword will falla it.
Whoever, jus like de apostle,   75
want to do widdouten sex
is free to choose dat,
but wid we, no badda vex
fah if my husban wear out an im dead
you free to marry me   80
dat is nat bigamy
an to enjoy good sex
is nat a frailty
nat unless yuh did decide, like Paul,
fi tek up chastity   85
because a man don't want pure gold pot
in im house
im want some mek wid good wood
as a spouse
an God did give we all a different gif   90
we choose wat we is suited for
everyone don't have to give up everyting fah Christ
Im neva aks we dat
dat is fah who want perfect peace

an you all know already   95
dat is nat me
I gwine mek de bes of all my years
fah dat is de joy an fruit of marriage
an why we have dese private parts so sweet
dem cyan jus mek so an don't put to use   100
except to piss
or tell man apart from woman
das wat you tink?
fram wat me feel already
dat could nat be so   105
a man mus give im wife er tings
Piss yes, an tell we apart
but wat pleasure dese instrument brings!

(a) What is the speech situation in this poem? Who is speaking to whom, and where are they? Where is Brixton Market? What is the significance of the fact that the poem is set in Brixton Market?

(b) What is the poem's genre?

(c) Try to identify as many features of Jamaican Creole as you can in this poem. It would help if you sort these variant features into different linguistic categories: vocabulary; grammar and syntax; rhythm; pronunciation; orthography (i.e., the attempt to render variant speech sounds by variant spelling). If you don't know the meaning of any word or phrase in the poem, or if it is puzzling in this context, look it up in an appropriate dictionary – such as the on-line *Urban Dictionary* or any of the available dictionaries of Caribbean English; we guarantee that it will be worth the effort.

(d) Identify any words, phrases or passages that are in Standard English. Is there any pattern in the use of Standard English or Creole? Are they used, for example, for different kinds of subject matter or register?

(e) Are there grounds for saying that the poem is written in a hybrid language?

(f) The poem makes a number of allusions to biblical figures and incidents: if you are not sure about what is being referred to, look them up in the Bible, in a Concordance to the Bible, or on the Internet.

(g) Try to summarise the Wife of Bath's basic argument: what is she saying? whom or what is she arguing with? whom is she trying to convince? Can the poem be seen as addressing any historical or contemporary debates about Christianity and sex? If so, what is its stance regarding those debates?

(h) What role does the mix of Jamaican Creole, Standard English and biblical language and allusion play in the speaker's argument? Do these languages blend or clash? Do they support or undercut one another? Does their juxta-position produce comedy, or irony, or authenticity, or some other effect?

(i) The poem's most prominent allusion is in the title itself. The Wife of Bath is a memorable character and story-teller in Geoffrey Chaucer's long narrative poem *The Canterbury Tales* (written 1387–1400, first published by Caxton in 1476). *Canterbury Tales* holds an important place in English literary his-tory. It was one of the first poems to be written in the version of Middle English (a hybrid language between Anglo-Saxon and Norman French) that served as the forerunner to modern Standard English. It was also one of the first poems in English to be printed. And by presenting a vivid picture of the people of England to the people of England, Chaucer's poem was a key text in the formation, or re-formation, of a sense of English national identity. For these reasons, it is often thought of as one of the founding texts of the English literary tradition. Breeze's 'The Wife of Bath speaks in Brixton Market' turns out to be a reworking of the first one hundred and thirty-seven lines of 'The Wife of Bath's Prologue' from *Canterbury Tales*. In order to begin to think about the implications of the relationship between Breeze's and Chaucer's poems, you will need to read the first 137 lines of 'The Wife of Bath's Prologue' (ideally in the original Middle English) in any edition of *Canterbury Tales* (there are sites on the Internet that present the poem alongside modern English 'translations').

(j) What are the principle similarities and differences between Chaucer's and Breeze's poems (think about form as well as content)? Does the Wife of Bath argue more or less the same thing in both poems, or are there signifi-cant differences? Would you describe Breeze's poem as a Creole translation or version of Chaucer's poem?

(k) Given the role of Chaucer's *Canterbury Tales* in the evolution of Standard English and the establishment of the English literary tradition, along with the part it played in the formation of English national identity, what are the implications and effects of the way that Breeze has re-worked part of Chaucer's poem into Jamaican Creole and set it in Brixton Market?

(l) Can Breeze's poem be called a hybrid poem (in addition to using a hybrid language)? If so, what is grafted onto what?

(m) What relationship does Breeze's poem set up between the Jamaican poetic tradition and the English poetic tradition?

(n) Is Breeze's poem an example of the 'Empire' writing back to the metropolitan centre? Or is it suggesting that the metropolitan centre has itself become transformed? If Chaucer's poem defined English national identity in the fourteenth and fifteenth century, what might Breeze's poem be suggesting about British national identity in the twenty-first century?

Part Four

AN OPEN-ENDED CONCLUSION

Chapter 17

Closure, Pluralism and Undecidability

■ Poetic Closure

In a weak sense, 'closure' refers simply to the manner in which texts come to a close. Novels and plays, for example, often close with either the death or the marriage of their principal characters (the former in tragedy, the latter in comedy). Yet such events may also work to achieve closure in a strong sense by purporting to resolve the struggles, tensions and loose ends of the whole narrative or dramatic action. Closure is achieved when the text leaves the reader with no further questions or expectations, and with a sense that the conclusion draws together everything that has gone before. Pause for a moment here and think of the way your favourite novel, play or film ends: how does its ending resolve the tensions of the plot in order to achieve a sense of conclusion? (If it does not do this, you may have chosen an example of 'anti-closure' – which we shall discuss later in this chapter.)

Like other kinds of narrative, narrative poems also typically end with some kind of narrative resolution. Our earlier discussion of Herbert's 'Redemption' (see Chapter 9) indicates that there may be narrative elements in lyric poems which are brought to a close in a similar fashion. In addition to narrative closure, however, poetry has a wide range of specifically poetic means of producing closural effects, and it is always rewarding to pay especial interest to the endings of poems in terms of the way they achieve, or try to achieve, closure. As we saw in Chapter 2, the metrical structure of stanzas can allow differing degrees of resolution, and metrical resolution can be reinforced by the completion of a rhyme scheme (as in Browning's 'Meeting at Night' – a poem which uses a range of techniques to produce a sense of closure). Or closure can be indicated through the final return of a repeated refrain, perhaps with a conclusive variation. Or some poems are enclosed, as it were, by a kind of 'frame' in which the first line is repeated, perhaps with a significant change, in the last line.[1]

As we saw in Chapter 12, sonnets are particularly predisposed to produce closure, especially through the convention followed in many of ending with a conclusive rhyming couplet. The effect of this is typically to bring the more complex rhyme scheme of the rest of the sonnet to a stable resting point and to act as a kind of 'punch-line' which resolves the poem's thematic issues. Think back to the way the final couplet of 'In the Children's Hospital' abandons irony in favour of a resounding conclusion:

> But would the sound of your sticks on the floor
> Thundered in her skull for evermore!

Herbert's 'Redemption' also employs this kind of formal resolution to reinforce the thematic resolution:

> . . . there I him espied,
> Who straight, *Your suit is granted*, said, and died.

The sense of finality here is achieved through a combination of narrative, thematic and formal resolution. The word 'died' simultaneously brings the narrative to a climactic end, resolves the irregular syntax, and completes the poem's rhyme scheme.

Closure of this kind is aimed for and valued in the poetry of most nations and all periods. The basic assumption of New Criticism is that poems are to be valued in so far as they demonstrate coherence and organic unity. Barbara Herrnstein Smith echoes this assumption by claiming that a poem is successful to the extent that it achieves closure. Her claim is based on her belief that 'Our most gratifying experiences tend to be not the interminable ones but rather those that conclude' (*Poetic Closure*, p. 1). And because most events in life seem shapeless and inconclusive, we create or seek out framed and highly organised structures within which we can produce and experience closure. Games are one kind of organised structure which allows this; works of art are another. Both games and works of art are designed in order to generate tension and conflict which are eventually resolved. For Smith, a poem is a designed sequence of language whose design entails purpose and whose purpose implies conclusion. Poetic closure, then, produces intellectual and aesthetic pleasure of

---

[1] For a thorough account of the variety of closural devices employed in the way poems end, see Smith, *Poetic Closure*. For a witty and thought-provoking discussion of the openness of textual endings, see Bennett and Royle, *An Introduction to Literature, Criticism and Theory*, pp. 197–205.

a kind which is akin to the delight we derive from the solving of puzzles. And if, as in the case of 'Redemption', such a resolution apparently reaffirms the basis of a religious faith, then we can see the power of and need for closure. Indeed, we can say that this is the theological, spiritual and emotional 'reward' of Herbert's poem.

Yet not all poetry is as strongly committed to closure as Smith implies. She herself points out that some of the most interesting poems in the language are literally unfinished or have been left as 'fragments' (for example, Keats's *Fall of Hyperion*).[2] More importantly, poems frustrate our expectations of closure as often as they fulfil them. The frustration of closure need not be seen as artistic failure but as a design which achieves artistic, intellectual and emotional effects quite different from closure but just as powerful. Sometimes poems ask difficult questions which are not easily resolved; sometimes we like poems to trouble us rather than leave things in a state of harmonious resolution. Keats's 'Ode to a Nightingale' ends with questions rather than conclusions:

> Was it a vision or a waking dream?
> Fled is that music: – Do I wake or sleep?

By ending like this, the final stanza appears to put in doubt the whole delicate structure of imagination which makes the poem so powerful and memorable. The poem thus paradoxically questions its own poetic power in a way which makes it especially fascinating and unsettling.

Although this resistance to closure can be found in poetry of all periods, it became a characteristic mark of a certain strand of twentieth-century poetry. This development can be related to more wide-ranging changes in artistic practices and theories in the twentieth century. As Smith notes, 'anti-closure is a recognisable impulse in all contemporary art, and at its furthest reaches it reflects changing presuppositions concerning the nature of art itself' (pp. 237–8). These changing presuppositions, at the time when Smith was writing in 1968, were most marked in *avant-garde* art such as the music of John Cage and Stockhausen, the painting of artists like Rothko and the work of writers such as Samuel Beckett and Alain Robbe-Grillet. The productions of these *avant-garde* artists were seen as breaking with the teleological presuppositions which have dominated Western thought since its beginnings. 'Teleology' is the assumption that everything was made or happens for a purpose, and contributes in some way towards a final goal (*telos* = end). Teleological assumptions govern quite different understandings of history: in Christianity,

---

[2] In fact, the Romantic poets – so often said to have made organic unity the mark of poetry – virtually elevated the 'fragment' into a new poetic genre; see Curran, *Poetic Form and British Romanticism*.

everything is thought to have been made by God, and history is supposed to be ultimately leading towards God's final plan; in Marxism, history is a process developing according to its own laws towards a classless society in which wealth and the means of production will be in the hands of the people rather than individual capitalists or the state. These kinds of teleological presuppositions are also implicit in the way we think about a work of art: we tend to assume that every detail of a work of art has been included in the design (pattern) because it contributes towards the final design (purpose). In the 'anti-teleological' designs of *avant-garde* art, however, the sense of goal-orientated purpose is abandoned in favour of apparently purposeless connections between random elements. In Beckett's *Waiting for Godot* (1952), for example, the two central characters are waiting for a conclusion which never comes and are depicted as, in effect, killing time in ways which are both comically and tragically inconclusive. Ezra Pound's statement towards the end of the last section of *The Cantos* (1969), 'I cannot make it cohere' (cxvi), can be taken as representative of this strand of modern literature.

Smith links this development in art to the larger-scale uncertainties which trouble the modern world: 'The song of uncertainty in modern poetry expresses the temper (or distemper) of our times thematically; it also reflects it in its very structure' (p. 242). As her parenthesis indicates, Smith tends to see these trends in poetry as symptomatic of a general 'malaise' (p. 254). Indeed, she attempts either to minimise the tendency of modern poetry to resist closure or to interpret lack of closure in particular poems as the inevitable 'conclusion' of a poem which faces up to the modern condition.[3] Smith argues that what she calls 'anti-closure' is 'an impulse, not a reality' (p. 261). Her book is an act of containment or closure in itself, and can be seen as a symptomatic response to the discomfort produced by poetry which resists closure. A good example of this is her analysis of the ending of Robert Lowell's 'The Drinker' (1964). We will quote the last two stanzas, then part of her analysis:

> The cheese wilts in the rat-trap,
> The milk turns to junket in the cornflakes bowl,
> car keys and razor blades
> shine in an ashtray.

> Is he killing time? Out on the street,
> Two cops on horseback clop through
> April rain to check the parking meter violations –
> their oilskins yellow as forsythia.

---

[3] For example, see Smith's attempt to interpret the irresolution of Eliot's Prufrock character as itself the resolution offered by 'The Love Song of J. Alfred Prufrock', *Poetic Closure*, pp. 145–8, 248–50.

This is Smith's discussion of this ending:

> The assertion with which the poem began ('This man is killing time') – ambiguous, ironic, and therefore unstable in any case – now becomes a question, no less ambiguous, ironic, or unstable. Having posed it, or perhaps hearing it posed, the speaker does not answer, but instead turns to glance outside the window – and changes the subject. The concluding observation, however, is perhaps not entirely irrelevant after all; for what he discovers in the scene outside are images of his own concerns. . . . Rain falls, the cops clop, and parking meters click. The answer is unspoken, but the answer may be there; time is being killed, but time, as on the clocks of those parking meters, is running out.
>
> (*Poetic Closure*, pp. 252–3)

Smith recognises that if the poem's ending is really an 'irrelevant' response to its central question, then the poem would be left 'ambiguous, ironic, and therefore unstable'. Her analysis is designed to prevent such instability by interpreting the apparently insignificant events in the street as constituting a 'message' for the speaker. This not only stabilises the poem but also reassures us that – in poetry, if not in life – every detail is coherently meaningful. Even the most arbitrary-looking and apparently inconclusive ending can be seen to achieve closure if we only read carefully enough.

Yet it does not follow that design inevitably entails closure: a work of art may be designed to *resist* closure. And, as we will see, we can never know if the design we detect or produce is the author's design. Because of this, we need to assume that *the poem itself* is a design, and be as responsive as we can to every aspect of the text, whether or not it contributes towards or helps to resist closure. Our desire that poems should close may be more a matter of our inherited reading assumptions than a necessary characteristic of the designs we call poems.

It will be illuminating to investigate why we tend to find artistic resolution rewarding and irresolution disturbing. The assumption that coherence and unity are the marks of successful art is grounded in the very foundations of Western thought and culture. The belief that harmony, unity and coherence are positive, while their opposites are negative, dominates Western philosophy from Plato (*c.* 427–348 BCE) to Hegel (1770–1831). Unity and coherence are also political values: we are led to believe that nations ought to have a sense of identity and purpose which transcends internal differences. Unity is also the founding assumption of the monotheistic religions which have been most influential in the West. In Christianity, the Father, the Son and the Holy Ghost are mysteriously unified in the three-in-one of the Trinity. Multiplicity and division, by contrast, are associated with evil – in the Bible, an 'unclean spirit' possessing a man declares that its 'name is Legion: for we are many' (Mark 5: 8–10). This statement also indicates that the very notion of human identity assumes unity. Wholeness is generally thought to be equivalent to physical and mental health, and this is the basic theoretical claim of the psychological practice called 'Gestalt therapy'. *Gestalt* is a German word meaning figure, shape or form; Gestalt therapy employs the term to mean an 'organised whole' and assumes that psychological illness arises when a person is out of touch with their 'whole self'. The aim of the therapy is to help such people to become whole again by integrating their 'fragmented parts'.[4]

■ Gestalt Reader Response Theory

Gestalt theory entails an account of perception and the way human beings process the data received through the senses. The claim is that the human mind habitually seeks to 'make sense' of sense impressions by trying to organise them into consistent patterns. Faced with apparently incoherent data, the human mind will automatically try to make it cohere. Wolfgang Iser, a pioneer of Reader Response Theory, argues that this 'consistency-building habit . . . underlies all comprehension'.[5] When we encounter puzzling visual images we automatically attempt to resolve them into coherence according to '*Gestalten*' (patterns of expectation) developed through previous experience. As Iser puts it, 'the gestalten of memory extract meaning from and impose order on the natural heterogeneity of life' (*Act of Reading*, p. 125). Scientists try to interpret experimental data by attempting to discover or create a coherent pattern or gestalt. This is what we mean when we say we are trying to 'make sense' of something. For something to 'make sense' it has to be susceptible of being perceived as a gestalt. Consistency-building appears to be an innate reflex of the human mind, but it is also reinforced by the patterning habits of our culture. When we look at a clear night sky we cannot help but perceive the random scattering of stars as a set of patterns or constellations which our culture has inherited from earlier civilisations.

Our response to works of art of all kinds can be seen as a gestalt-forming, consistency-building process.[6] When reading, we tend to assume that there is a coherent pattern to be discovered in the text, and we are constantly on the lookout for connections and correlations in order to be able to discover that pattern, or to create patterns of our own which are consistent with the textual data. Reading, then, is an active process of consistency-building rather than a

---

[4] See Muriel James and D. Jongeward, *Born To Win: Transactional analysis with Gestalt experiments* (New York: Signet, 1978), pp. 6–10.

[5] Wolfgang Iser, *The Act of Reading: A theory of aesthetic response* (Baltimore, MD: Johns Hopkins University Press, 1978), p. 129.

[6] See Gombrich, *Art and Illusion*.

passive recognition of a coherence which is simply there in the text. Ambiguity in everyday language hinders this consistency-building activity. When we are reading for information, we may well wish that the text (say, a newspaper report) will efficiently present a straightforward message in a coherent way. If we encounter ambiguities or inconsistencies, we are likely to consider them as irritating faults of style and to choose the meaning which fits the pattern we are constructing. Creating a pattern in reading thus involves excluding as well as including data. Ambiguities of a different kind can arise when the pattern we are creating is challenged by the text itself. Our probable response is either to make the text fit the pattern or to abandon the pattern in favour of one which more successfully integrates the new information.

In reading literature, this process of continually creating, updating or replacing our interpretative patterns accounts for a significant part of our aesthetic and intellectual pleasure. This is most obvious in reading detective or suspense novels which deliberately present us with textual information which appears to fit into a number of patterns and keeps us guessing till the end. Such genres offer clear-cut examples of the way texts engage what Iser calls our 'gestalt-forming imagination'. Gestalt Reader Response Theory thus attends to the dynamic, temporal nature of reading, and helps us to understand some of the pleasures of reading and textual closure. But in reading literature we are likely to be bored by a poem or story whose gestalt is too 'obvious'. We enjoy the challenge of making sense out of puzzling information, and we like to be kept guessing through unexpected twists and turns. This is one reason why literary texts employ devices such as suspense, contradiction and ambiguity.

The gestalt model of reading can also help to account for our experience of reading Herbert's 'Redemption' (see Chapter 9). The textual information presented in the sonnet's first twelve lines invites us to make sense of it as being about a tenant–lord relationship in the seventeenth century. This is the gestalt which the poem offers to us. Although textual details such as the lord's manor being 'in heaven' jar with this gestalt, our pattern of expectation may be so strong that we can miss or choose to ignore this incompatible detail. The poem's ending, however, cannot be accommodated to this socio-economic gestalt, and this may produce confusion and frustration. Yet if we recognise that the unexpected ending re-enacts in miniature the basic story of Christian belief, we can reinterpret the socio-economic details of the poem as a spiritual allegory and so make them fit with this new gestalt.

But if the sheer complexity of literary texts is the reason why we enjoy attempting to produce coherent interpretations of them, it is also the reason why even the most comprehensive interpretation has to leave out aspects of the text which do not fit the gestalt we have chosen. Iser argues that this is inevitable, and that no coherent reading of a text will ever fully account for all its complexities:

The moment we try to impose a consistent pattern on the text, discrepancies are bound to arise. These are, as it were, the reverse side of the interpretive coin, an involuntary product of the process that creates discrepancies by trying to avoid them.[7]

In contrast with Smith's or New Criticism's attempt to identify a complex consistency which is simply 'there' in the text, Reader Response Theory such as Iser's indicates that reading literary texts is an ongoing, never-ending attempt to *impose* coherence. A New Critical interpretation can thus be seen as a symptomatic *response* to a text rather than a final account of it. Closure becomes not a feature of the text, but a temporary achievement of reading. Reading, then, never stops: it can never finally close a text (in any sense) and have done with it. Brooks's brilliant reading of Wordsworth's 'Immortality Ode' (which we examined in Chapter 9) is simply a temporary stopping place, one of the gestalts which the poem has provoked in a particular reader.

Reading for closure thus unwittingly becomes an open-ended activity which testifies to the dynamic nature of both literature and reading:

> Any 'living event' must, to a greater or lesser degree, remain open. In reading, this obliges the reader to seek continually for consistency, because only then can he close up situations and comprehend the unfamiliar. But consistency-building is itself a living process, in which one is constantly forced to make selective decisions – and these decisions in their turn give a reality to the possibilities they exclude, insofar as they may take effect as a latent disturbance of the consistency established. This is what causes the reader to be entangled in the text 'gestalt' that he himself has produced.
>
> Through this entanglement the reader is bound to open himself up to the workings of the text, and so leave behind his own preconceptions.
>
> (Iser, in Lodge, *Modern Criticism and Theory*, p. 225)

Reading, then, is not just a question of what we do to texts but of what texts do to us. We find texts compelling because their openness lures us into attempting to produce consistent readings which will enable us to 'comprehend the unfamiliar'. Yet that very activity draws attention to the text's unfamiliarity – to those aspects which cannot be accommodated in our familiarising, coherent gestalt. We are thus drawn into a text, opened up to its workings, and compelled to attend to the ways in which the preconceptions we brought to the text may be inadequate to account for its specific complexities.

■ Critical Pluralism: Positions and Perspectives

If an interpretation of a text is a product of the interaction between the text itself and the gestalt-forming habits and strategies which a reader brings to it,

---

[7] Wolfgang Iser, 'The Reading Process: A phenomenological approach', reprinted in Lodge, *Modern Criticism and Theory*, pp. 211–28 (224).

and if no single gestalt can account for everything in a text, then Gestalt Reader Response Theory is suggesting that a poem will be read differently by different readers according to the assumptions they bring to it. Wayne Booth attempts to account for this effect by turning to scientific reflections on the fact that science tends to develop incompatible but equally rigorous and revealing explanatory models of physical phenomena. He cites the analogy of a cone being looked at by different observers from different fixed positions. The observers directly above and below see a circle; observers from the side see triangles; observers from other positions see highly irregular shapes. None of these observers is wrong, but none is wholly right: 'each observer of the cone sees *everything there is to see from his position*, even by the most acute observer; nothing limits his result except perspective'.[8] But these different, apparently incompatible observations could be reconciled with each other – either by the observers abandoning their fixed positions or by correlating all the data from the different angles of vision. The inevitable conclusion would be the recognition that 'it is really a cone'.

Interpreting poems, however, is a much less straightforward process than looking at a cone and comparing notes about it with others. Contrasting the complexities of Auden's 'Surgical Ward' with the 'immense simplicity of our cone', Booth asks: 'If a cone is "really" a cone, what is "Surgical Ward"?' (*Critical Understanding*, p. 32). As Booth points out, most philosophers since Kant have more or less accepted Kant's argument in his *Critique of Pure Reason* (1781) that we never see things in the world as they are in themselves but only in the way in which our perceptual systems (our senses and our minds) enable us to see them. But although the conformity of human perceptual systems might allow us to agree about our perceptions of, say, a cone, a poem presents a much more intractable problem. What is a poem 'in itself'? As Booth suggests,

> Ushenko's analogy fails us here, because in criticism we have nothing comparable to our knowledge that the cone is, after all, a cone. . . . Not only is there in criticism no predetermined authority of views, but the things that criticism deals with – 'Surgical Ward' and its cousins – are so immeasurably complex that no one can easily say how we would recognize an adequate view if we saw one.
>
> (*Critical Understanding*, p. 33)[9]

---

[8] Wayne C. Booth, *Critical Understanding: The powers and limits of pluralism* (Chicago: University of Chicago Press, 1979), p. 31.

[9] Like many literary critics, Booth (and Abrams, below) tends to see science as an empirical discipline which produces coherent descriptions of the 'real facts' of the world (in contrast to literature and literary criticism). For a more accurate and compelling account of science as an activity of generating various models of the universe which are undecidably incompatible with one another, see Stephen Hawking , *A Brief History of Time: From the big bang to black holes* (Toronto: Bantam, 1988).

This problem is reflected in the history of literary criticism. Different historical periods have made very different assumptions about what literature is and have consequently come up with startlingly different accounts of the 'same' texts. One of the best brief introductions to this history is the opening chapter of Abrams's *The Mirror and the Lamp* (1953), which neatly schematises the shifting perspectives of literary criticism and theory from Plato to the New Critics. Abrams himself takes up a 'historical pluralist' position with regard to this history. In other words, he values the very different accounts of literature produced in the last two-and-a-half thousand years because each, in its own way, sheds some light on the problems of literary criticism and enables productive readings of texts. Abrams is a pluralist not only because each different perspective offers its own insights but because there seems little prospect of finally proving one at the expense of the other, or of reconciling these different insights. This is because we cannot perceive the 'text itself' without interpreting it from a theoretical perspective of one kind or another:

> We still need to face up to the full consequences of the realization that criticism is not a physical, nor even a psychological, science. By setting out from and terminating in an appeal to the facts, any good aesthetic theory is, indeed, empirical in its method. . . . [Yet] these facts turn out to have the curious and scientifically reprehensible property of being conspicuously altered by the nature of the very principles which appeal to them for their support. Because many critical statements of fact are thus partially relative to the perspective of the theory within which they occur, they are not 'true,' in the strict scientific sense that they approach the ideal of being verifiable by any intelligent human being, no matter what his point of view. Any hope, therefore, for the kind of basic agreement in criticism that we have in the exact sciences is doomed to disappointment.[10]

It is crucial to realise, however, that Abrams is not opening doors to an 'anything goes' relativism. He says that 'any good aesthetic theory is, indeed, empirical in its method' because it sets out from and terminates in 'an appeal to the facts'. By 'facts', we take Abrams to mean identifiable features of the text being discussed (a rhyme, a metaphor, a syntactical structure, and so on) or the contexts which impinge upon a text (literary conventions, historical context, and so on). In other words, he is saying that any theoretical perspective or reading needs to support its claims by reference to evidence. Yet Abrams is also saying that what one theory counts as evidence might not be admitted by another or might be interpreted differently. The 'facts' themselves are always seen through and interpreted by the perspective of the theory which uses them. If this is the case, we cannot make categorical truth claims for a literary theory

---

[10] Abrams, *The Mirror and the Lamp*, p. 4. (This chapter is reprinted in Lodge, *Twentieth Century Literary Criticism*, pp. 1–26.)

or critical interpretation but can only judge it on the basis of whether it offers a valid insight about literature or a literary text.

Abrams's historical pluralism can be graphically illustrated by the history of critical interpretations of a text such as *Hamlet*. In the four-hundred-year period since it was written, critics and theatre producers have tried to solve the puzzle of *Hamlet* and have come up with a huge range of differing 'solutions'. Each period has viewed the play differently, and critics within each period have disagreed over it. The actual text of the play – the words on the page or the stage – clearly does not change with each interpretation. It is, rather, the meaning of those words, sentences, speeches, actions, reactions, interactions, plots, subplots, and so on which seems to change according to how these elements and their mutual interrelations are interpreted. Of course, there is something about the text itself which allows these various readings. None of these readings would seem valid if they did not tell us something about the play and offer textual evidence to support them. Yet these readings also tell us something about the interests of the period in which the interpretation is made and about the theoretical assumptions of the reader. All reading takes place from a certain position in relation to the text being read. The Romantic poets inevitably interpreted *Hamlet* as a Romantic play and concentrated on those elements in the text which seemed to support their response. To Freud, *Hamlet* seemed the most compelling enactment of the Oedipus complex since Sophocles' *Oedipus Rex* (*c.* 427–26 BCE), from which he took the name of his most famous theory. In other words, *Hamlet* can generate so many different interpretations because different readers are looking for different things in its complex text. Read in different contexts with different expectations, *Hamlet* appears differently. There seems to be no way out of this: the continuing interest in *Hamlet* shows no sign of coming to an end, or of reaching a final interpretation. Interpretation, then, becomes open-ended. This is the source of the ongoing fascination of literature and the basis of the fact that literature can continue to be taught without it becoming a predictable process of teaching by rote.

Pluralism thus indicates that it would be an act of bad faith to teach a literary text as if it had only one meaning which all students simply have to recognise and reproduce. A teacher's interpretation of a text will change during his or her career – partly through the inevitable process of 'getting to know it better', but also because his or her critical interests will change through reading criticism and rethinking approaches. A teacher's interpretation can also change through interaction with students. Students' readings can surprise teachers and change what they think about a text, and this is one of the most rewarding aspects of teaching literature. But to admit or become conscious of this entails a change in traditional teaching practices and assumptions. If we can no longer pretend to teach correct meanings or to teach students *what* to think, we can turn to the more rewarding activity of teaching *ways* of thinking which will facilitate students' own productive readings of texts. This cannot be achieved by returning to the pre-critical stage of encouraging students to be 'subjective' or 'creative'. It can be facilitated, instead, by putting students in touch with critical and theoretical ideas and with the history and conventions of the poetic system – a pedagogical process designed to develop students' and other readers' 'literary competence'. This is what this book has tried to do. Rather than presenting you with a series of readings of poems which you are expected to accept, we are trying to enable you to produce your own informed readings of poems and to be critical of other readings (including our own). In this way, teaching and studying poetry becomes an open-ended process.

■ Critical Differences and 'A slumber did my spirit seal'

Pluralism acknowledges the fact that the history of literary criticism is marked by a series of transformations in literary theory. Each theory produces its own characteristic readings of the 'same' text. Although each reading of a text is likely to claim that it is the true and final interpretation, and that all previous readings were either wrong or inadequate, pluralism will tend to value the new reading to the extent that it sheds 'new light' on a poem which can be added to the insights offered by other perspectives. Yet this progressive model is complicated by Iser's suggestion that one of the effects of a consistent reading will be to expose possibilities in the text which are incompatible with that reading. On Iser's model, the history of interpretations of a poem will reveal not a gradual development towards a single, more and more correct reading but the proliferation of different and sometimes incompatible readings.

Just a glance at the history of critical interpretations of Wordsworth's 'A slumber did my spirit seal' presents a sobering example which seems to confirm Iser's account of the effects of reading. We will quote the poem again before sketching a history of some of its readings:

> A slumber did my spirit seal;
>   I had no human fears:
> She seemed a thing that could not feel
>   The touch of earthly years.
>
> No motion has she now, no force;   5
>   She neither hears nor sees;
> Rolled round in earth's diurnal course,
>   With rocks, and stones, and trees.

When we discussed this poem in Chapter 7, we drew attention to the ambiguity of 'human' in the second line, the ambiguity of 'thing' in the third line, and the overall ambiguity of the tone. The critical debate we will concentrate on here pivots around the question of tone. Since we will be presenting evidence to the effect that the poem's tone is 'undecidable', it will be interesting for you to re-read it in order to develop your own ideas about its tone before you go on to read what follows. The crucial issue of tone here is the question of the speaker's attitude towards and feelings about the death of the person being remembered in the poem.

The number of books and articles which are at least partly devoted to discussing these eight seemingly simple lines is quite astonishing. Despite the poem's apparent simplicity, there have been a number of critical disputes over its meaning and tone.[11] We will focus on just one of these disputes in so far as it will contribute to our present discussion.[12] As Gerald Graff points out, 'Critics who have discussed this poem have divided between those who read it as the tragic lament we would normally expect to hear on its subject – the death of a girl or woman – and those who read the poem as an expression of a pantheistic religious outlook, in which the death of "she" is seen as a return to the living unity of nature and is thus to be regarded cheerfully'.[13] The latter view might seem an odd one, were it not for the fact that biographers interpret Wordsworth's poems and letters of the period in which the poem was written as revealing pantheistic beliefs (pantheism is a religious doctrine which identifies God with the natural world). And it is especially hard to decide if the poem is a lament or a celebration because it contains no explicit signals of emotion. The fact that the dead girl or woman is 'Rolled round in earth's diurnal course, / With rocks, and stones, and trees' is simply stated without any indication of the speaker's feelings. On the one hand, this could be read as a terrible recognition of the way death reduces us to the status of mere things in a godless universe. On the other hand, a pantheistic reading could claim that the speaker is reconciled to her death through his belief that she has returned to an elemental oneness with living nature. The critic E.D. Hirsch staged a debate between these different readings of 'A Slumber' in order to support his thesis that critical differences need to be resolved through reference to probable authorial intention.

[11] For a critical overview of the debate about Wordsworth's poem, see Brian G. Caraher, *Wordsworth's 'Slumber' and the Problematics of Reading* (Pennsylvania: Pennsylvania State University, 1991).

[12] A different critical debate over 'A slumber' was staged in a collection of essays in which M.H. Abrams attempted to refute J. Hillis Miller's 'deconstructive' demonstration of the poem's 'indeterminacy'. See J. Hillis Miller, 'On Edge: The crossways of contemporary criticism', and M.H. Abrams, 'Construing and Deconstructing', in Morris Eaves and M. Fischer, eds, *Romanticism and Contemporary Criticism* (Ithaca, NY: Cornell University Press, 1986), pp. 96–126, 127–82.

[13] Gerard Graff, 'Determinacy/Indeterminacy', in Lentricchia and McLaughlin, *Critical Terms for Literary Study*, pp. 163–76 (168).

The first reading from which Hirsch quotes is by Cleanth Brooks. We will quote from it at more length than Hirsch does in order to give a better sense of Brooks's subtle account of the poem. He begins by suggesting that the slumber which sealed the speaker's spirit was a mysterious inattentiveness to the fact that 'she' was a mortal being who must inevitably die. Thus the 'human fears' which he lacked can be read as both 'the fears normal to human beings' and 'fears *for* the loved one as a mortal human being'.[14] The second stanza records the speaker's 'agonized shock at the loved one's present lack of motion', and indicates 'her utter and horrible inertness',

> not by saying that she lies as quiet as marble or as a lump of clay; on the contrary, he attempts to suggest it by imagining her in violent motion – violent but imposed motion, the same motion indeed which the very stones share, whirled about as they are in earth's diurnal course. . . . Part of the effect [of this resides in] . . . the sense of the girl's falling back into the clutter of things, companioned by things . . . completely inanimate like rocks and stones.
>
> (Brooks, in Zabel, ed., *Literary Opinion in America*, p. 736)

For Brooks, a sense of tragic irony is registered by the way the second stanza undercuts the first. The girl's 'slumber' of death in the second stanza awakens the speaker from his 'slumber' of spirit in the first. Whereas 'the girl once seemed something not subject to earthly limitations at all', she is now completely limited to the mechanical turning of the earth. Having formerly believed that she was immortal, the speaker is forced to recognise the fact that 'she still does not "feel the touch of earthly years", for, like the rocks and stones, she feels nothing at all' (p. 737).

The second reading of 'A slumber' which Hirsch examines is one by F.W. Bateson. Bateson makes the commonplace but problematic assumption, on the basis of the association between 'A slumber' and a number of other poems Wordsworth wrote in the same period, that the 'she' of the poem refers to a person or imaginary character called 'Lucy'. Bateson attends to virtually the same features of the poem as Brooks but arrives at a quite different conclusion:

> The structural basis of the poem is clearly the contrast between the two verses. Verse one deals with the past. . . . Lucy had been such a vital person that the possibility of her growing old or dying had not crossed Wordsworth's mind. Verse two concerns the present. . . . Lucy is dead. . . . Lucy, who had seemed immune from the passage of *earthly years*, must now submit to *earth's diurnal course*. So far from escaping the *touch* of years she is now undergoing a daily contact with the earth. The use of the solemn Latinism *diurnal*, the only three-syllable word in this mainly monosyllabic poem, completes the contrast. But the final impression the poem leaves is not of two

---

[14] Cleanth Brooks, 'Irony as a Principle of Structure', in Zabel, *Literary Opinion in America*, pp. 729–41 (735).

contrasting moods, but of a single mood mounting to a climax in the pantheistic magnificence of the last two lines.[15]

Bateson argues that this pantheistic climax somehow includes the more normal human response to the death of a loved one:

> The typical poem can be thought of . . . as a miniature drama in which two 'sides' meet, come into conflict and are eventually reconciled. In Wordsworth's 'A slumber did my spirit seal' . . . the two 'sides' could perhaps be labelled 'humanism' (Wordsworth *ought* to have had 'human fears') and 'pantheism' (the mysticism of 'rocks, and stones, and trees'). The vague living-Lucy of this poem is opposed to the grander dead-Lucy who has become involved in the sublime processes of nature. We put the poem down satisfied, because its last two lines succeed in effecting a reconciliation between the two philosophies or social attitudes. Lucy is actually more alive now that she is dead, because she is now a part of the life of nature, and not just a human 'thing'.
>
> (*English Poetry*, p. 59)

Bateson's presupposition that the 'typical' poem can be thought of 'as a miniature drama in which two "sides" meet, come into conflict and are eventually reconciled' is a New Critical version of the notion of poetic closure which we examined above. At this theoretical level, Bateson and Brooks would agree with one another: both critics seem committed to the assumption that 'good' or 'typical' poems cohere in this way, and each of their readings makes coherent sense of features which are actually present in the poem. Yet these equally coherent readings are nonetheless incompatible with one another. Brooks maintains that the speaker experiences a great sense of loss and horror at Lucy's reduction to the state of thinghood. Bateson posits that this natural human response is transcended by a recognition of Lucy's continuing spiritual vitality as part of a spiritualised natural world. Inevitably, there have been attempts to reconcile these readings (see Caraher, *Wordsworth's Slumber*, p. 72n), but we would argue that this critical disagreement acts out an undecidable ambiguity which is potentially there within the poem itself. Rather than striving for an interpretation which would unify these readings, we suggest that an attentive discussion of the poem needs instead to show how it allows both.

It is instructive, then, to see what Hirsch makes of this critical disagreement. He recognises that 'both . . . interpretations are permitted by the text' and that they are incompatible with each other.[16] Yet his commitment to the idea that a poem can have only one determinate meaning leads Hirsch to posit that one of the two interpretations must be wrong. He stresses that he is not ruling out the possibility of poetic ambiguity: 'I do not, however, imply that a poem or any other text must be unambiguous. It is perfectly possible . . . that Wordsworth's

---

[15] F.W. Bateson, *English Poetry: A critical introduction* (London: Longman, 1966), p. 29.

[16] E.D. Hirsch, *Validity in Interpretation* (New Haven, CT: Yale University Press, 1967), pp. 228–9.

poem ambiguously implies both bitter irony and positive affirmation' (*Validity in Interpretation*, p. 230). Hirsch's notion of ambiguity, then, involves complexities of meaning which enter into a both/and relationship ('both bitter irony and positive affirmation'). What he is not willing to allow is ambiguity as the simultaneous possibility of incompatible either/or meanings (as we defined it in Chapter 9). This would make ambiguity undecidable.

Hirsch's belief that Brooks's and Bateson's readings constitute an 'either/or' situation (they are equally valid and mutually exclusive) forces him to try to decide between them. He attempts to eliminate one or the other through recourse to probability: 'The best way to show that one reading is more plausible and coherent than another is to show that one context is more *probable* than the other.' On this criterion, he points out that Brooks's reading is justified not only by the text itself but by what we know of general human attitudes and feelings in such cases of bereavement. Yet Hirsch nevertheless sides with Bateson on the basis of conjectures about Wordsworth's probable outlook and intention at the time of writing. Referring to Wordsworth's pantheism, he suggests that 'Instead of regarding rocks and stones and trees merely as inert objects, he *probably* regarded them in 1799 as deeply alive, as part of the immortal life of nature' (p. 239; emphasis added). Rather than arriving at determinate meaning, then, Hirsch recognises that he is left juggling probabilities:

> It is still possible, of course, that Brooks is right and Bateson wrong. A poet's typical attitudes do not always apply to a particular poem. . . . Be that as it may, we shall never be certain what any writer means, and since Bateson grounds his interpretation in a conscious construction of the poet's outlook, his reading must be deemed the more probable one until the uncovering of some presently unknown data makes a different construction of the poet's stance appear more valid. (p. 240)

By refusing the possibility that the poem's ambiguity might be undecidable (or even resolvable) Hirsch has ended up in a rather comic state of indeterminacy. Faced with apparently irresolvable ambiguity in the text, he looks away from the text towards authorial intention about which 'we shall never be certain'.

■ 'American' Deconstruction and Indeterminacy

Our analysis of the critical debate over Wordsworth's 'A slumber did my spirit seal' reveals that many readers assume that the task of criticism is to solve the interpretative 'problem' posed by the poem. For most critics, the poem's enigmatic power presents a challenge which it is criticism's task to overcome in a kind of intellectual combat designed to eliminate ambiguity. There is a subtle violence involved in such readings: the poem is forced to admit its secret, to tell its tale as a coherent, closed story. Ironically, however, each 'solution' seems to add to rather than reduce the poem's mystery, and Hirsch's attempt to solve the problem of the poem by recourse to speculations about Wordsworth's probable intentions leads him into what we called a comic state of indeterminacy. Gerald Graff finds Hirsch's strategy unconvincing, and concludes: 'There seems to be no alternative except to regard this as a poem of indeterminate meaning. It supports the cheerful-pantheist context, but it supports the tragic-lament context equally well – or equally badly' (in Lentricchia and McLaughlin, *Critical Terms for Literary Study*, p. 169).

Although New Criticism remains of value to critics and students of poetry precisely because it teaches us to be closely attentive to poetic language, the example of practitioners such as Brooks and Bateson reveals how its commitment to producing unified interpretations can lead to a closing down of interpretative possibilities. New Criticism's commitment to unified readings is one of the reasons why more recent critics have found it problematic. Contemporary theory tends to favour irresolution rather than resolution in texts and in interpretations of texts. As Timothy Bahti put it in 1986, 'for New Criticism texts were fundamentally ambiguous and interpretations fundamentally were not. Today, texts are ambiguous and interpretations are indeterminate.'[17]

The notion of interpretative indeterminacy being invoked by Graff and Bahti was developed in the United States in the 1970s and 1980s, principally by the so-called 'Yale School' of deconstructive critics. The notion of indeterminacy has provoked a great deal of critical controversy. It is often thought to imply a number of odd things: that there is no such thing as authorial intention; that literary texts are meaningless; that literary texts necessarily fail in their attempt to express 'the truth about the human condition'; that interpretation is impossible or fruitless; that interpretations of a text can be neither right nor wrong; that because no reading can be completely determinate, we cannot determine anything; that all readings are only subjective or relative, and therefore that literary criticism is a free-for-all without limits; and that it leads to or involves a sceptical nihilism which will undermine all human and humanist values. Graff notes that the idea that the meaning of literary texts may be indeterminate 'has alarmed many teachers of literature, who fear that if the possibility of correctness in interpretation is denied, the basis of their classroom and research practices is undermined'. He quotes Hirsch's fear in *Validity in Interpretation* that 'without the stable determinacy of meaning there can be no knowledge in interpretation, nor any knowledge in the many humanistic disciplines based upon textual interpretation' (in Lentricchia and McLaughlin, *Critical Terms for Literary Study*, p. 163).

---

[17] Timothy Bahti, 'Ambiguity and Indeterminacy: The juncture', *Comparative Literature* (1986), pp. 38, 209–23 (213). For a reading of 'A slumber' which attempts to show how its meanings and tone remain indeterminate, see Geoffrey Hartman, 'The Interpreter's Freud', in Lodge, *Modern Criticism and Theory*, pp. 412–24.

The assumptions behind Hirsch's fear can easily be problematised. Although a great deal of our knowledge in the humanistic disciplines (literature, history, philosophy, and so on) is clearly based on interpretation, interpretations do change and humanistic 'knowledge' is not stable for all time. In literary studies, only the most uninteresting 'knowledge' is stable (dates, titles, names of characters, plots). The really interesting facts, as Abrams suggests, are necessarily unstable because they become salient only to the critical perspective which is predisposed to notice them and because different perspectives will see them differently (or not see them at all). But even Abrams, who is otherwise committed to critical and theoretical pluralism and claims to admire and have learned from some of the writings of deconstructive theorists, fears the consequences of introducing deconstruction into the undergraduate curriculum before undergraduates have been trained in more traditional ways of reading. In 1986, he announced his anxiety that students will inevitably convert deconstruction into a 'set of crude dogmas' or that an emphasis on interpretative indeterminacy would leave teachers unable to prevent students from 'falling either into the extreme of a paralysis of interpretative indecision or into the opposite extreme of interpretative abandon, on the principle that . . . my misreading is as good as your misreading' ('Construing and Deconstructing', in Eaves and Fischer, *Romanticism and Contemporary Criticism*, p. 155).

There are a number of points which need to be made in response to Abrams's anxieties. First, although fresh converts to any theory tend to regard its leading thinkers as gurus and their writings as scripture, the notion of indeterminacy itself is anti-dogmatic and ought always to involve a reflection back on itself which would prevent it from becoming a crude dogma. Secondly, we will go on to suggest that 'interpretative indecision' does not lead to 'paralysis' but is a possible result – possible, but not inevitable – of sensitive, slow-motion reading (decisiveness, by contrast, is sometimes achieved through a heavy-handed reading which tries to 'break through' or disregard a text's subtleties). Thirdly, it should be stressed that although the notion of indeterminacy does imply that no reading can be wholly right for all time, it does not mean that readings cannot be wrong. As Jonathan Culler puts it, 'a literary work can have a range of meanings, but not just any meaning'.[18]

The assumption that no interpretation can wholly determine, for all time, the meaning of ambiguous texts does not imply, as some critics apparently believe, that there is no point in continuing with the activities of interpretation and criticism.[19] Instead, what is entailed is a different understanding of what

---

[18] Culler, 'Prolegomena to a Theory of Reading', in Susan Suleiman and I. Crossman, eds, *The Reader in the Text* (Princeton, NJ: Princeton University Press, 1980), pp. 48–61 (52).

[19] For an example of such an interpretation of 'deconstructive' accounts of indeterminacy, see Abrams, 'The Deconstructive Angel', reprinted in Lodge, *Modern Criticism and Theory*, pp. 265–76 (272).

we mean by interpretation. Bahti suggests that the model of interpretation that we work with in intellectual communities in the West derives from the Judaeo-Christian exegetical tradition which assumes that the goal of interpretation, whether by individuals or by communal effort over time, is to achieve a final, coherent reading which will account for the totality of a text's features. Deconstructive criticism questions this tradition by showing that the goal of closure is an impossible one which may lead the interpreter into violently repressing the subtle ways in which texts resist closure. Yet this does not entail any suggestion that a text has no meaning, or that it is open to any meaning we care to suggest. At its best, the assumption of the possibility of indeterminacy leads to a careful, hesitant reading practice which implies that we can never have done with reading a poem. We suggest that this sensitivity to ambiguity and willingness to accept indeterminacy are extraordinarily important attitudes to develop in reading literature.

In 1980, Geoffrey Hartman, a leading figure in the 'Yale School' of deconstruction, attempted to dispel the 'bad vibes' of the word 'indeterminacy' (bad vibes which include the fear that the term involves 'an attack on the communicative or edifying function of literature'). Hartman's account of indeterminacy suggests instead that it involves the most responsible kind of reading:

> indeterminacy, though not an end to be pursued but something disclosed by liberal and thoughtful reading, is more like a traffic sign warning of an impasse. It suggests (1) that where there is a conflict of interpretations or codes, that conflict can be rehearsed or reordered but not always resolved, and (2) that even where there is no such conflict we have no certainty of controlling implications that may not be apparent or articulable at any one point in time.[20]

The crux of Hartman's account of indeterminacy is a lesson in reading. Its guiding concept is that we should resist our drive to convert art into determinate meaning, and collaborate instead with the way texts themselves resist such conversion. This means that we should not be too eager to extract meaning – that we need to dwell within a text for as long as it takes:

> indeterminacy does not merely *delay* the determination of meaning, that is, suspend premature judgments and allow greater thoughtfulness. The delay is not . . . [merely] a device to slow the act of reading till we appreciate . . . its complexity. The delay is intrinsic: from a certain point of view, it is thoughtfulness itself, Keats's 'negative capability,' a labor that aims not to overcome the . . . indeterminate but to stay within it as long as is necessary. (*Criticism in the Wilderness*, p. 270)

In such a process, what is 'gained' is not a meaning to be carried away but the experience of 'thoughtfulness' which a text can provoke – thoughtfulness

---

[20] Geoffrey Hartman, *Criticism in the Wilderness: The study of literature today* (New Haven, CT: Yale University Press, 1980), p. 265.

about how texts work rather than what they mean, about how they work on and within us in order to produce an understanding which can challenge what we think we understand already.

If literary texts have an inbuilt uncertainty principle which is more clearly highlighted rather than overcome by our attempts to achieve interpretative closure (as we have seen Iser argue), then the question is whether we can produce readings of texts which resist our gestalt-seeking drive in order to remain faithful to the nature of the text being read. Hartman's notion of indeterminacy relinquishes the idea that texts have something to 'tell' us (if we only subject them to a rigorous enough interrogation) in favour of being attentive to what they *ask* us. In asking us questions, texts shift the locus of meaning from within themselves to the interface between text and reader. Hartman's examples are the 'rhetorical questions' which often open up the endings of Yeats's poems. Hartman refers to Yeats's 'Leda and the Swan' and to 'The Second Coming', but a nice example for our present discussion is a short poem called 'The Scholars' (1917):

> Bald heads forgetful of their sins,
> Old, learned, respectable bald heads
> Edit and annotate the lines
> That young men, tossing on their beds,
> Rhymed out in love's despair 5
> To flatter beauty's ignorant ear.
>
> All shuffle there; all cough in ink;
> All wear the carpet with their shoes;
> All think what other people think;
> All know the man their neighbour knows. 10
> Lord, what would they say
> Did their Catullus walk that way?

This poem satirises the way pedantic scholars treat poems as objects of learned annotation. Rather than being moved (intellectually or emotionally) by the poems they deal with, these scholars are presented as literally walking in each other's footsteps, treading the same old ground that everyone else treads. The rhetorical question at the end appears to ask us to imagine what would happen if these old scholars were suddenly confronted with Catullus – a Latin love poet whose poems are presumably the object of their learned attentions. Far from closing the poem with a rhetorical flourish, however, this question leaves us with 'a sense of open-endedness'.[21] What *would* these scholars say if they

---

[21] This is Barbara Herrnstein Smith's account of the effect of a number of closing rhetorical questions in Yeats's and Eliot's poems, *Poetic Closure*, pp. 246–50.

met Catullus on their walk? Yet even taking the question in this sense is to suspend attention to the ambiguity of the last line – which could mean: either (1) if Catullus actually walked into their scholarly cloisters; or (2) if Catullus had merely walked in other people's footsteps in the way that these scholars do. Yeats's 'The Scholars', then, is not merely a poem that satirises those literary critics who treat poems as dead things whose meaning is fixed by a conservative scholarly community; it is also a poem whose indeterminate open-endedness actively challenges the models of poetry and criticism held by such a community.

Once we become attentive to this kind of open-endedness, such poems continue to haunt and fascinate us. Although most of us benefit from the work of annotators (telling us, for example, who Catullus was), we cannot treat 'The Scholars' in the way its scholars treat poems. As Hartman puts it,

> To keep a poem in mind is to keep it there, not to resolve it into available meanings. This suspensive discourse is criticism, and it can be distinguished from the [knowledge] of scholarly interpretation as well as from the positivity of applied teacherly interpretation.

> (*Criticism in the Wilderness*, p. 274)

Hartman recognises why, at a historical moment in which many of our certainties have been put in doubt, people might be troubled by 'a mode of thinking that seems to offer no decidability, no resolution'. Yet he suggests that literature, read in a certain way, offers not eternal truths but an insight into our true condition: 'the perplexity that art arouses in careful readers and viewers is hardly licentious. It is the reality; it is only as strange as truth.' (p. 283) It is only the propaganda of both closed and so-called 'open' societies which offers the quick fix of instant messages and 'truths' and which censors and represses dissidence. To be alert to the indeterminacy of art is to participate in a mode of discourse and a way of reading which resist such dogmatic truths and the social formations which rely on them.

■ 'French' Deconstruction and Undecidability

Deconstructive criticism was introduced into Anglo-American critical discourse in the late 1960s through the writings of French theorists such as Jacques Derrida and Roland Barthes. Derrida's essay 'Structure, Sign and Play in the Discourse of the Human Sciences' was first aired in the United States at a conference in 1966. In this essay, Derrida argues that we habitually limit the possibilities of meaning in texts through invoking the notion of a stable centre which is, paradoxically, both inside and outside the text. In literary criticism, for example, this 'centre' is typically the notion of authorial intention which is invoked to control the play of possible meanings – as we saw in Hirsch's attempt to stabilise the interpretation of Wordsworth's 'A slumber'. This 'centre' is thought of as both 'inside' the text (if we read it carefully enough we are bound to see Wordsworth's intention) and outside the text (if some dispute arises over the text itself we could always, in theory, go outside it to get at the author's intention). Other kinds of 'centre' are posited by other kinds of critic: thus the point of stability invoked might be the 'organic unity' and autonomy of the text itself, or it might be some kind of external referent – such as historical context, or 'human nature', or a self-evident 'truth'. Derrida's argument is that none of these imagined points of origin or stability is immune from the play of language which they are supposed to anchor. (We have seen the indeterminacy which results from Hirsch's attempt to stabilise readings of 'A slumber' by recourse to Wordsworth's 'probable' intention or belief.) Without being able to arrest the play of signification through recourse to any 'transcendental signified' which exists outside the play of language, we are said to be left with two alternatives, two interpretations of interpretation: either we read with a constant yearning to discover something which would limit the play of possible meanings, or we read with a 'joyous affirmation of the play . . . of a world of signs . . . which is offered to an active interpretation'.[22]

Because it suggests that a text can no longer be thought of as having a stable meaning which transcends the productive play of language, Derrida's essay has sometimes been taken as implying that we are free to indulge in an unlicensed activity of free play. Whether or not the essay actually implies this, Derrida's subsequent work increasingly stressed the notion of responsibility – to, among other things, the specificities of the text being read and the contexts of its production and interpretation.[23] And this essay should be read alongside an equally influential section of Derrida's *Of Grammatology* (1976) in which he considers 'The Exorbitant Question of Method'. Far from dismissing the notion of authorial intention, Derrida stresses the importance in deconstructive reading of attempting to interpret 'the conscious, voluntary, intentional relationship that the writer institutes in his exchanges with the history to which he belongs thanks to the element of language'. He calls this a 'doubling commentary' which 'should no doubt have its place in a critical reading':

> To recognize and respect all its classical exigencies is not easy and requires all the instruments of traditional criticism. Without this recognition and this respect, critical production would risk developing in any direction at all and authorize itself to say almost anything.[24]

[22] 'Structure, Sign and Play in the Discourse of the Human Sciences', in Jacques Derrida, *Writing and Difference*, trans. Alan Bass (London: Routledge, 1978), p. 292. This essay can also be found in Lodge, *Modern Criticism and Theory*, pp. 108–23.

[23] See, for example, ' "This Strange Institution Called Literature": An interview with Jacques Derrida', in Derek Attridge, *Jacques Derrida, Acts of Literature* (New York: Routledge, 1992), pp. 33–75.

[24] Derrida, *Of Grammatology*, p. 158.

Derrida, then, insists on the necessity of a careful textual commentary which would seek to interpret a text in terms of its author's apparent intentions, the various histories and historical contexts to which it might relate, and the ways it employs the rules of the language in which it is written. What he objects to is the way this discipline of reading pretends to get at the truth of a text and is usually used to limit rather than open up interpretative possibilities: 'this indispensable guardrail has always only *protected*, it has never *opened*, a reading' (*Of Grammatology*, p. 158).

A great deal of the misunderstanding about deconstruction has arisen – as we have seen – over the term 'indeterminacy'. This term has been associated with Derrida's thought by both his supporters and his detractors in Britain and the United States. It would seem crucial, then, to note that Derrida distances himself from the idea of indeterminacy and prefers, instead, the term 'undecidability'. In 1988, in an essay called 'Afterword: Toward an ethic of discussion', Derrida answers a set of questions put to him by Gerald Graff in which Graff voices the negative criticisms of many 'commentators'. In response to Graff's question concerning the controversy in the United States over Derrida's supposed assertion that meaning is always indeterminate, Derrida says:

> I do not believe that I have ever spoken of 'indeterminacy', whether in regard to 'meaning' or anything else. Undecidability is something else again. . . . undecidability is always a *determinate* oscillation between possibilities (for example, of meaning, but also of acts). These possibilities are themselves highly *determined* in strictly *defined* situations (for example, discursive – syntactical or rhetorical – but also political, ethical, etc.). . . . The analyses that I have devoted to undecidability concern just these determinations and these definitions, not at all some vague 'indeterminacy'. . . . Which is to say that from the point of view of semantics, but also of ethics and politics, 'deconstruction' should never lead either to relativism or to any sort of indeterminacy.[25]

Derrida is surely correct in his description of indeterminacy as implying vagueness, relativity and the impossibility of determining possible meanings. It is thus perhaps understandable that the use of the term indeterminacy in American deconstruction has allowed critics hostile to deconstruction to endow it with 'bad vibes' and give it a bad press. Undecidability, however, entails none of the things which 'commentators' ascribe to indeterminacy. It involves instead 'a *determinate* oscillation between possibilities . . . of meaning' which involves '*defined* situations' which may be syntactical, rhetorical, political or ethical. Yet, although Hartman's use of the term indeterminacy is perhaps unfortunate, his description of it as primarily implying 'that where

---

[25] Jacques Derrida, *Limited Inc.*, ed. Gerald Ciraff (Evanston, IL: Northwestern University Press, 1988), p. 148.

there is a conflict of interpretations or codes, that conflict can be rehearsed or reordered but not always resolved' seems quite close to Derrida's description of undecidability. In our reading of 'The Scholars' (influenced by Hartman's description of indeterminacy) we claimed that the final question can be read in one of two determinate ways – as asking what the scholars would say either (1) if Catullus actually walked into their scholarly cloisters; or (2) if Catullus had merely walked in other people's footsteps in the way these scholars do. In other words, Hartman's indeterminacy can be seen as an infelicitous and misleading name for an assumption that is actually quite close to Derrida's notion of undecidability. And undecidability, Derrida insists, has nothing to do with 'either . . . relativism or . . . any sort of indeterminacy'.

■ Undecidability, Poetry and Political Responsibility

Barbara Johnson, another important Yale critic, has responded to attacks on deconstruction from both Left and Right by developing Derrida's many suggestions that undecidability is a deeply ethical and political condition or effect. If the Right has accused deconstruction of undermining Western values, the Left has criticised its emphasis on slow-motion reading and undecidability as avoiding and disabling political intervention. Johnson meditates on these issues in her book *A World of Difference* (1989):

> Nothing could be more convincing than the idea that political radicality requires decisiveness, not indecision. . . . The privileging of ambiguity would always appear to be an avoidance of action. Yet if undecidability is politically suspect, it is so not only to the left, but also to the right. Nothing could be more comforting to the established order than the requirement that everything be assigned a clear meaning or stand. It is precisely because the established order leaves no room for unneutralized . . . ambiguity that it seems urgent to meet decisiveness with decisiveness. But for that same reason it also seems urgent not to. I am reminded of a sentence in Adrienne Rich's *On Lies, Secrets, and Silence*, which runs: 'Much of what is narrowly termed "politics" seems to rest on a longing for certainty even at the cost of honesty, for an analysis which, once given, need not be re-examined'.[26]

This quotation from Rich indicates the way Johnson brings together Yale deconstruction with feminist cultural politics in order to allow each to make a difference to the other. In the last chapter of *A World of Difference* – in which, among other things, she reads poems by women poets about motherhood and abortion alongside documents from the abortion debate in the United States – Johnson argues that both politics and poetry exist *because* there is undecidability in our world:

---

[26] Barbara Johnson, *A World of Difference*, 2nd ed. (Baltimore, MO: Johns Hopkins University Press, 1989), pp. 30–31.

It is often said, in literary-theoretical circles, that to focus on undecidability is to be apolitical. Everything I have read about the abortion controversy in its present form in the United States leads me to suspect that, on the contrary, the undecidable *is* the political. There is politics precisely because there is undecidability. And there is also poetry.

(*A World of Difference*, pp. 193–4)

To determine meanings and attitudes once and for all would bring political debate to a close, and therefore bring politics itself to a close. It would also close down poetry. These things were attempted, in different ways and places, at several points in the twentieth century (the repression of political debate and cultural production went hand in hand in Nazi Germany and the Soviet bloc, and in the McCarthy period in the United States). At the time of writing this second edition of *Reading Poetry* (in 2006) it looks as if the events of 11 September 2001 and after have prompted the revival of various fundamentalist world views that mirror each other in seeking to close down debate and undecidability on the supposition that there are fundamental truths that are beyond discussion: such views are incompatible with politics and with poetry.

Johnson implies that poetry is a discourse in which undecidable questions may be dramatised in a mode which is relatively free from the constraints of other discourses. Perhaps because poetry is thought to have no consequences, undecidability in poems is not overridden by the requirements of clarity or communicative efficacy. This allows poems to 'live with' our ambiguities in a way which makes concrete the entanglement of the personal, the political and the rhetorical. The poems on abortion which Johnson analyses confront the full contradictions of the abortion issue in the 'lived experience' and rhetorical contradictions of their speakers' undecidable dilemmas. The decisions which these female speakers make do not repress the factors which make such decisions impossible but necessary. Such poems become the crucial sites in which large-scale political and moral problems are 'personified'. Since poems are not precious objects encased in books on shelves, but come to life and have their resonances in us through reading, they can cause us to live out the undecidable dilemmas they explore. Thus poems can change us and make things happen.

Let us conclude by looking at just one of the poems Johnson discusses – Anne Sexton's 'The Abortion' (1962):

> *Somebody who should have been born*
> *is gone.*
>
> Just as the earth puckered its mouth,
> each bud puffing out from its knot,
> I changed my shoes, and then drove south.   5
>
> Up past the Blue Mountains, where
> Pennsylvania humps on endlessly,
> wearing, like a crayoned cat, its green hair,

> its roads sunken in like a gray washboard;
> where, in truth, the ground cracks evilly,   10
> a dark socket from which the coal has poured,
>
> *Somebody who should have been born*
> *is gone.*
>
> the grass as bristly and stout as chives,
> and me wondering when the ground would break,   15
> and me wondering how anything fragile survives;
>
> up in Pennsylvania, I met a little man,
> not Rumpelstiltskin, at all, at all . . .
> he took the fullness that love began.
>
> Returning north, even the sky grew thin   20
> like a high window looking nowhere.
> The road was as flat as a sheet of tin.
>
> *Somebody who should have been born*
> *is gone.*
>
> Yes, woman, such logic will lead   25
> to loss without death. Or say what you meant,
> you coward . . . this baby that I bleed.

In many ways, this poem is quite conventional and highly structured. It is divided up into three-line stanzas in which the first and third lines rhyme with each other, and it uses a repeated refrain. The speaker's past-tense account of her journey to have an abortion uses the quite standard technique of figuratively describing the landscape she passed through as if it reflected her own inner feelings. Yet these conventional structures and devices are used and modified in ways which give the poem an unforgettable charge.

As the speaker begins her journey, the signs of coming spring are seen as if the earth were a newborn baby – and thus painfully contrast with what she is about to do:

> Just as the earth puckered its mouth,
> each bud puffing out from its knot,
> I changed my shoes, and then drove south. (3–5)

Even the mundane detail of changing her shoes contrasts the terrible routineness of setting out on such a journey with the rebirth of the spring. The vivid account of the journey implies that its tiniest banal detail has etched itself on her mind. Yet these details can suddenly become painful images of what she cannot put out of her mind:

> where, in truth, the ground cracks evilly,
> a dark socket from which the coal has poured, (10–11)

Here, the devastation of the landscape produced by the mining of coal can suddenly become a disturbing image of abortion or bleeding. And a similar thing happens in the next stanza as she wonders how anything fragile can survive in this devastated landscape:

> the grass as bristly and stout as chives,
> and me wondering when the ground would break,
> and me wondering how anything fragile survives. (14–16)

Only things as bristly and stout as this grass seem able to survive, and the fear for fragile things cannot help but suggest the vulnerability of babies. This woman seems to be undertaking this journey out of a terrible necessity, and has her eyes open to all the consequences. She seems to be mourning even as she is going through with her decision. Rather than rendering her insensitive to what she is doing, or to the fragility of life, her choice seems to have had the reverse effect. In fact, her heightened sensitivity turns her journey into a nightmare which we share as each detail of the landscape looms up and reminds her of what she is doing. Her sense of guilt even causes her to imagine that the ground might break from under her in some terrifying moment of retribution.

In Pennsylvania she met 'a little man' (17) whose name was *not* Rumpelstiltskin (a little man in one of the Grimm Brothers' tales who tries, but fails, to take away the queen's child because she guessed that his name *was* Rumpelstiltskin). If this is a moment of grim humour it is quickly undercut by the fact that this little man *did* take 'the fullness that love began' (19). This is a pregnancy which began in an act of 'love' with a now mysteriously absent man and ends at the hands of a little man she met in Pennsylvania. As she returns north, the formerly budding landscape now seems bereft of its fullness in a way which implicitly mirrors the woman's sense of loss.

If what we have looked at thus far constituted the whole text, it would be a moving but conventional and closed poem expressing the terrible ambivalences of a woman driving to and from an abortion. Yet the details we have not yet looked at are much less susceptible to being read in these ways. First, the poem is broken into and broken up by the repeated refrain: '*Somebody who should have been born / is gone*'. Marked off from the rest of the poem by **typography**, italics and the present tense, this refrain regularly intrudes itself into the speaker's retrospective narrative (its second appearance, for example, breaks into the middle of a sentence). If the past-tense narrative calls the aborted foetus 'the fullness that love began', this refrain refers to that foetus as a 'somebody' even though it was never born. Thus the question is raised about

557

when a foetus becomes a somebody. What is undecidable about this intrusive 'voice' is where it comes from. It could be the general voice of the anti-abortion faction or it could also be a particular representative of that faction who, as it were, keeps interrupting the speaker's narration. Or it could even be an echo of the anti-abortion viewpoint sounding in the speaker's own mind like a Freudian superego or the internalised voice of the moral majority. Whichever way we take it, Johnson notes that it works like 'a voice-over narrator taking superegoistic control of the moral bottom line, [putting] . . . the first-person narrator's authority in question without necessarily constituting the voice of a separate entity' (*A World of Difference*, p. 194). Yet it could also be the speaker's own voice articulating her sense of guilt or loss, or agonising over what she has done and had to do. For, as Johnson says in discussing Gwendolyn Brooks's 'The Mother', we cannot assume 'that a woman who has chosen abortion does not have the right to mourn' (p. 191). The right to choose does not deny the right to life or the agony of having to choose one over the other. This is one of the reasons why the question of abortion is undecidable.

Further undecidable problems open up the poem in the last stanza. The ending itself is curtailed, since instead of the group of three stanzas which constitutes the poem's earlier pattern, we are left with just a single stanza. And this stanza abandons the relative stability of the past-tense narration by offering present-tense statements whose addressee seems undecidable:

> Yes, woman, such logic will lead
> to loss without death. Or say what you meant,
> you coward . . . this baby that I bleed.

The speaker addresses someone as 'woman', but it is not clear whether the addressee is the speaker herself, someone else who is present, woman as a generic term, or any woman who reads the poem. And what is the tone of this last-but-one sentence? Is it rueful self-reflection? Is the speaker arguing with some self-opinionated other woman? Is the speaker ironically commenting on the situation of women in general with regard to abortion? Or is the speaker confiding in a woman reader? And what does 'such logic' refer to? Is it a reference to the insistent, inexorable 'logic' of the refrain which has just been repeated for the third time? And what is 'loss without death'? Is it that the woman, if she goes on thinking of the foetus as 'somebody' who should have been born, will come to experience loss without having experienced the baby's death? Is this possible on the supposition that since the baby was never actually born it could be said never to have died? In opening up this possibility, the poem again links the woman's experience of this impossible dilemma to the legal problems involved in deciding exactly when human life begins. Johnson quotes a judge's comments on this issue in an abortion trial in the USA:

We need not resolve the difficult question of when life begins. When those trained in the respective disciplines of medicine, philosophy, and theology are unable to arrive at any consensus, the judiciary, at this point in the development of man's knowledge, is not in a position to speculate as to the answer.[27]

The last sentence of the poem does not help us to answer any of the questions which have been opened up. In fact, in urging straightforward clarity – 'say what you meant, / you coward' – it simply generates more questions because we still cannot decide who 'you' refers to. The very last phrase offers not closure but perpetual openness (in several senses). If 'this baby that I bleed' is what is really meant by 'loss without death', then it adds new questions. For the first time, the speaker refers to a 'baby' – to '*this* baby'. Are we then to understand this last phrase as indicating that now, at this moment, the speaker is beginning to abort what she now thinks of as a baby? Has she finally overcome her cowardice by confronting the reality of what has happened/is happening? Although the little man in Pennsylvania is said to have taken the 'fullness that love began', that could be understood as meaning that he induced the abortion which is now beginning as the poem ends. If she 'bleeds' the baby, then this indicates that she is losing part of herself. Simultaneously, 'I bleed' could also be a recognition that she has caused/is causing the baby to bleed. Alternatively, 'I bleed' could also be read as 'I bleed for' in both a literal and a figurative sense. The after-effects of the abortion may include internal bleeding and/or an ongoing, open-ended sense of compassionate mourning for the lost baby. Thus the poem ends literally with the continuing present of 'I bleed' – which suggests that this abortion will never be terminated.

Exercises

1 This exercise is concerned primarily with the problem of how we manage to 'make sense of' complex poems, but it also draws upon some of the techniques identified in earlier chapters – allusion, the use of a fixed form, the 'double pattern', parallelism, tone, irony, ambiguity. You may need to refer back to those chapters, or to the Glossary, when you are answering the questions that follow.

Sestina d'Inverno
Here in this bleak city of Rochester,
Where there are twenty-seven words for 'snow',
Not all of them polite, the wayward mind
Basks in some Yucatan of its own making,

[27] Johnson is quoting from Justice Blackmun's comments in the case of Roe v. Wade: see Jay L. Garfield and P. Hennessey, eds, *Abortion: Moral and legal perspectives* (Amherst: University of Massachusetts Press, 1984), p. 27.

Some coppery, sleek lagoon, or cinnamon island 5
Alive with lemon tints and burnished natives,

And O that we were there. But here the natives
Of this gray, sunless city of Rochester
Have sown whole mines of salt about their land
(Bare ruined Carthage that it is) while snow 10
Comes down as if The Flood were in the making.
Yet on that ocean Marvell called his mind

An ark sets forth which is itself the mind,
Bound for some pungent green, some shore whose natives
Blend coriander, cayenne, mint in the making 15
Roasts that would gladden the Earl of Rochester
With sinfulness, and melt a polar snow.
It might be well to remember that an island

Was a blessed haven once, more than an island,
The grand, utopian dream of a noble mind. 20
In that kind climate the mere thought of snow
Was but a wedding cake; the youthful natives,
Unable to conceive of Rochester,
Made love, and were acrobatic in the making.

Dream as we may, there is far more to making 25
Do than some wistful reverie of an island,
Especially now when hope lies with the Rochester
Gas and Electric Co., which doesn't mind
Such profitable weather, while the natives
Sink, like Pompeians, under a world of snow. 30

The one thing indisputable here is snow,
The single verity of heaven's making,
Deeply indifferent to the dreams of the natives
And the torn hoarding-posters of some island.
Under our igloo skies the frozen mind 35
Holds to one truth: it is gray, and is called Rochester.

No island fantasy survives Rochester,
Where to the natives destiny is snow
That is neither to our mind nor of our making.

(Anthony Hecht, 1977)

(a) Spend some time reading and re-reading the poem until you have some
sense of what it is saying and how it is working. We have seen F.W. Bateson

argue that a poem 'can be thought of . . . as a miniature drama in which two "sides" meet, come into conflict and are eventually reconciled'. To what extent does this poem stage a conflict of different visions?

(b) A 'sestina' is a fixed form consisting of six stanzas of six lines with a concluding three-line *envoi*; each line ends, not with a rhyme, but with one of six selected words which are repeated, according to a fixed permutation, in a different order in successive stanzas (see Glossary). On the basis of this formal description, would you describe the sestina as an 'open' or a 'closed' poetic form?

(c) Go through the poem to see how it makes use of the sestina form. Do the poem's repeated end-of-line words have a purely formal function? Or are they also keywords in the sense that they are focal points for its themes and subject matter? Try to identify the poem's major themes in relation to its repeated keywords, then attempt once more to summarise its meaning. Do the words change in meaning as the poem develops? How do any such shifts in meaning relate to the development of the poem as a whole?

(d) Now re-read the concluding *envoi*. How far do each of its lines serve as a summation of the poem's overall meaning? Go through the earlier stanzas to see if you can make sense of them in the light of the *envoi*'s concluding statements. How far does the *envoi* signal not only formal closure but also full semantic and thematic closure?

(e) How close have you now come to discovering or realising an overall gestalt for this poem? Are there any details or features which do not fit in with your gestalt? If there are, how might you account for them?

(f) The poem contains quite a number of references and literary allusions:

The title can be translated as 'Sestina for winter'. Rochester (1) is a city in New York State. Yucatan (4) is in Mexico. 'O that we were there' (7) quotes the refrain of a medieval carol – 'there' is in heaven. 'Bare ruined Carthage' (10) alludes to Shakespeare's 'Bare ruined choirs' in Sonnet 73, line 4; the Romans sowed the land around Carthage with salt after destroying the Carthaginian state in the Third Punic War (151–46 BCE). 'The Flood' (11) alludes to Noah's Flood in Genesis 7–8; 'that ocean Marvell called his mind' (12) alludes to Andrew Marvell, 'The Garden', line 43. 'Earl of Rochester' (16), libertine Restoration courtier and poet, 1621–80. 'Pompeians' (30), inhabitants of the Roman city buried beneath volcanic ash from Mount Vesuvius.

How does this information modify your reading of the poem? Which of the allusions seem worth tracing to their original sources? Find the sources you have selected, and then try to decide if this modifies your reading of 'Sestina d'Inverno'. What is the effect of using so many literary allusions? Does this process have any relationship to the poem's argument or its overall meaning?

(g) Can you find any examples of double syntax in the poem? If so, do they relate in any way to the poem's complexities of meaning?

(h) Anthony Hecht is a British poet, yet this poem is responding to a location in the United States. What are the effects of the 'location' of the speaker in relation to the poem's 'location'? Can you locate the poem's implied reader? Can you identify any conventional assumptions or received ideas about the United States in the poem? If so, where do they come from and how do they work, or what is their effect in this poem?

(i) Having worked your way through these questions, would it be possible to argue that 'Sestina d'Inverno' is a more open text than its form might lead us to expect? Are there, for example, any 'undecidable' moments in the poem which resist closure or unsettle any attempt to fit the poem into a single gestalt? If you decided in your answer to question (a) that there is a conflict of visions in the poem, are they reconciled into a single coherent vision by the end?

2 Read the following poem – Derek Walcott's 'A Far Cry from Africa' (1962) – and then try to answer the questions that follow. The poem reflects on Caribbean black people's connections with black Africans in the context of the violent uprising against British rule in Kenya by the Mau Mau resistance fighters of the Kikuyu tribe (1952–60) that helped to bring about Kenyan independence in 1963. In 1962, the year the poem was published, Jamaica and Trinidad and Tobago opted out of the short-lived West Indies Federation and, with popular support, achieved independence from Britain. The poem thus appeared in a context in which independence movements were very much in the air both in Africa and the West Indies (though Walcott's native St Lucia was not to achieve independence until 1979).

A Far Cry from Africa

A wind is ruffling the tawny pelt
Of Africa. Kikuyu, quick as flies,
Batten upon the bloodstreams of the veldt.
Corpses are scattered through a paradise.
Only the worm, colonel of carrion, cries: 5
'Waste no compassion on these separate dead!'
Statistics justify and scholars seize
The salients of colonial policy.
What is that to the white child hacked in bed?
To savages, expendable as Jews?   10

Threshed out by beaters, the long rushes break
In a white dust of ibises whose cries

Have wheeled since civilization's dawn
From the parched river or beast-teeming plain.
The violence of beast on beast is read   15
As natural law, but upright man
Seeks his divinity by inflicting pain.
Delirious as these worried beasts, his wars
Dance to the tightened carcass of a drum,
While he calls courage still that native dread   20
Of the white peace contracted by the dead.

Again brutish necessity wipes its hands
Upon the napkin of a dirty cause, again
A waste of our compassion, as with Spain,
The gorilla wrestles with the superman.   25
I who am poisoned with the blood of both,
Where shall I turn, divided to the vein?
I who have cursed
The drunken officer of British rule, how choose
Between this Africa and the English tongue I love?   30
Betray them both, or give back what they give?
How can I face such slaughter and be cool?
How can I turn from Africa and live?

(a) Using a good reference book or the Internet, look up information about (i) the Mau Mau uprising in Kenya, (ii) the reference to Spain, (iii) any other reference in the poem that you don't fully understand.

(b) Try to establish the poem's speech situation: who and where is the speaker?

(c) Identify all the poem's significant metaphors and similes and try to describe their implications.

(d) What image of Africa does this poem create? Is that image straightforward or is it complex or ambiguous?

(e) Try to establish the speaker's attitude towards (i) the Mau Mau resistance fighters of the Kikuyu tribe and (ii) British colonial rule in Kenya.

(f) How does the speaker account for the violence in Kenya? What is the speaker's attitude towards others' explanations of the violence?

(g) Try to paraphrase, and work out the implications of, the following: (i) 'The violence of beast on beast is read / As natural law, but upright man / Seeks his divinity by inflicting pain' (15–17); (ii) 'Again brutish necessity wipes its hands / Upon the napkin of a dirty cause' (22–23); (iii) 'The gorilla wrestles with the superman' (25).

(h) Identify as many instances of ambiguity as you can in the poem. For each instance, try to spell out how the ambiguity works and what the alternative meanings are.

(i) In the previous chapter, we suggested that hybridity is a characteristic feature of the post-colonial condition. Identify as many kinds of hybridity in the poem as you can and, for each instance, try to say what the consequences are in the poem.

(j) We saw in the previous chapter that Africa is an important and highly charged idea for black Caribbean people. In this context, try to decide what the speaker's attitude is towards Africa.

(k) What does the poem's title mean?

(l) Try to identify any allusions in the poem. For each one, try to work out its significance (by using information sources or reading the text that is being alluded to).

(m) Identify the poem's metrical form. What are the implications of the fact that the poem is written in this form? Are there any moments where the poem deviates from the metrical pattern? If so, do the deviations have any significance?

(n) The poem includes seven questions; does the poem offer any answers to these questions?

(o) Would you say that the issues and questions that this poem opens up are presented as undecidable (in the sense explored in this chapter) or is the speaker able to come to a resolution or decision? In each case, give evidence in support of your claim.

Glossary

Key: rhet. = rhetorical term (see **rhetoric**).

    Gk. = Greek

    Lat. = Latin

    C20 = twentieth century (and so on).

    Princeton = Preminger and Brogan (eds), *New Princeton Encyclopedia of Poetry and Poetics*, 1993.

    Use of **bold** type signals a technical term defined elsewhere in the Glossary and also, if appropriate, chapters in the present book where we discuss the term more fully.

accent 1. variation of pronunciation according to place, class or period, sometimes of socio-political interest or affects rhyme sounds; 2. relative emphasis on stressed and unstressed syllables in pronunciation that constitutes poetic **rhythm**; see **stress**.

accentual-syllabic metrical system in which both the number of syllables and the number of stresses per line is controlled; the five-beat line is normally accentual-syllabic; see **iambic pentameter**.

addressee term used to describe the fact that a poem's **speaker** is often addressing someone or something that is part of the poem itself; to be distinguished from the poem's reader.

alexandrine twelve-syllable line with six beats, hence also referred to as **hexameters**, the standard metre for ancient Greek and Latin epic; became the general default metre for French poetry of many different kinds following the C12 *Roman d'Alexandre* from which it gets its name. Last line of **Spenserian stanza** is an alexandrine.

allegory type of **figurative** writing in which abstract ideas are represented as actions, objects, places or personifications; normally requires a narrative in which the allegorical characters act out or demonstrate their moral qualities and values, e.g. Spenser's *Faerie Queene* or Bunyan's *Pilgrim's Progress*, though occasionally poets may describe allegorical figures of a more static and pictorial type, whose allegorical attributes (e.g. Justice with her sword and scales) teach a moral lesson; cf. **emblem, symbol, personification**.

alliteration repetition of the same initial consonant sound in adjacent or nearby words, especially at the beginning of stressed syllables; thus a syllable that alliterates takes the form **consonant**-vowel-consonant, and our use of bold here indicates where the same sound occurs, as in 'bulldogs in **b**attle'; beware of making exaggerated claims for the effect of merely random repetitions; cf. **assonance**.

alliterative verse metrical form found in Old English poetry, e.g. *Beowulf*, and some later Middle English verse, in which at least three of the four stressed syllables in each line are linked together by **alliteration**.

> And ay the lorde of the londe is lent on his gamnes,
> To hunt in holtes and hethe at hyndes barayne.
> Such a somme he ther slowe bi that the sunne heldet,
> O dos and other dere, to deme were wonder.
> ('And already the lord of the land has gone to his sports, to hunt the barren hinds in wood and heath. By the time the sun had set he had slain so many does and other deer that it is wonderful to recount', *Sir Gawain and the Green Knight*, late C14, lines 1339–2).

allusion when one text includes deliberate echoes of another; it is wise to distinguish such deliberate echoes from intertextuality, a Structuralist concept which it resembles but which refers to the wider process through which all language reworks received textual materials and which is a universal and involuntary process. Allusion involves intentionality, as when Ernest Hemingway entitles his novel *For Whom the Bell Tolls* (1940), alluding to a meditation in which John Donne reflects that since 'no man is an island' we should, when we hear the funeral bell tolling for someone else's death, think of our own. Although in everyday usage the term can be a synonym for any kind of extra-textual reference (as in 'What are you alluding to?'), literary allusion is essentially from one text to another, nearly always in the form of a quotation or near quotation. This requires the reader to compare both texts and assess the similarities and dissimilarities of the speakers' situations and their use of the same words; there may be some difference or distance, in which case the allusion may be **ironic**. See **Ch.13**.

ambiguity when a poem or passage can be read in more than one way; in most human communication ambiguity is seen as a fault since it makes a writer's meaning or **intention** unclear, but William Empson's influential *Seven Types of Ambiguity* (1930) argues that multiple meanings are characteristic of poetic language, where they enrich the reading experience and are taken as the sign of a good writer's response to the complexity of human experience. Empson's book provided models for close-reading of literary texts ('practical criticism') which remain widely influential, though the theoretical basis of his argument has often been challenged. If you detect ambiguity in a poem you need to do some close analysis and accurate paraphrase, citing dictionary definitions if necessary, and also show how the variant meanings may be accommodated to the surrounding syntax or argument of the poem as a whole: you cannot make a poem mean anything you want it to just because you are keen on 'ambiguity' and have identified some variant meanings of a single word. See **Ch.9**.

anapaest name in classical prosody for a metrical foot consisting of two unstressed syllables followed by one stressed one (or, in Latin, two short syllables plus one long one), corresponding to what the new metrics calls 'rising triple' metre, and scanned: ˘ ˘ / (*tee-tee-tum*, as in 'interrupt'). See **foot**.

anaphora rhet. repetition of the same word or words at the start of successive phrases, sentences or lines of verse, cf. **homoeoteleuton**, **parison**. Anaphora is a device of **parallelism**, and may relate to other parallels set up by the verse in various ways which it may be interesting to analyse. Anaphora is one of the structuring devices of ancient Hebrew poetry in the Bible and is sometimes used in modern **free verse**. Walt Whitman's use of anaphora is insistent, if not obsessive, as in the following passage from a poem entitled 'With Antecedents' (1860). You might ask whether the anaphora here is just an excuse or compensation for the apparent formlessness of the verse in other respects, or whether, on the contrary, it could be justified as an appropriate way of formulating the idea of American inclusiveness.

> With antecedents,
> With my fathers and mothers and the accumulations of past ages,
> With all which, had it not been, I would not now be here, as I am,
> With Egypt, India, Phenicia, Greece and Rome,
> With the Kelt, the Scandinavian, the Alb and the Saxon,
> With antique maritime ventures, laws, artisanship, wars and journeys,
> With the poet, the skald, the saga, the myth, and the oracle,
> With the sale of slaves, with enthusiasts, with the troubadour, the crusader,
>   and the monk,
> With those old continents whence we have come to this new continent,
> With the fading kingdoms and kings over there,
> With the fading religions and priests,
> With the small shores we look back to from our own large and present shores,
> With countless years drawing themselves onward and arrived at these years,
> You and me arrived – America arrived and making this year,
> This year! sending itself ahead countless years to come.

antithesis rhet. bringing together of opposites; e.g. 'In friendship false, implacable in hate: / Resolved to ruine or to rule the state.' (Dryden, *Absalom and Achitophel*, 173–4); note in this case how **alliteration** marks the antitheses; cf. **parallelism**, **chiasmus**.

apostrophe rhet. figure of speech in which the poet addresses an absent person or thing as though it were present, a dead one as though alive, or a non-human as though it could hear and respond; hence Keats's 'Ode to a Nightingale' tells us through its very title that it is an apostrophe, unlike 'Ode on a Grecian Urn' where we have to wait for the opening lines before we realise that the poet is talking to a pot. Because it is so rarely found outside poetry apostrophe carries considerable added value, rhetorical heightening, and elevation of tone, as *Princeton*'s example from Charles Calverley irresistibly demonstrates: 'O Beer, O Hodgson, Guinness, Allsopp, Bass, / Names that should be on every infant's tongue'; cf. **personification** and **invocation**.

assonance rhet. recurrence of the same vowel sounds in nearby stressed syllables; assonance takes the form consonant-**vowel**-consonant, and our use of bold here indicates where the coincidence of sound occurs in the syllable, as in 'bl**a**ck m**a**t'; cf. **alliteration**.

Augustan term traditionally used to describe the period (*c.* 1680–1745) that includes such poets as John Dryden, Alexander Pope, Jonathan Swift, John Gay and their early-C18 contemporaries, who aspired to create, or at least 'improve', English writing, esp. poetry, through the imitation of such classical models as Horace and Virgil, who flourished in the early Roman Empire under Augustus.

ballad genre of popular narrative poetry often recording a startling or sensational story; originally an oral form and usually sung (hence a type of **lyric**) using inherited materials and tunes which make it unnecessary if not impossible to identify the original author: traditional ballads are all 'anon.' In C18 an antiquarian taste developed for collecting and printing such traditional ballads, e.g. Thomas Percy, *Reliques of Ancient English Poetry* (1765). Walter Scott's *Minstrelsy of the Scottish Border* (1802–03) popularised the rich tradition of 'border ballads'. By late C18 and early C19 the Romantics' interest in poetry concerned with the lives and feelings of ordinary people led to literary imitations of the traditional ballad, e.g. Wordsworth and Coleridge, *Lyrical Ballads* (1798), Keats's 'La Belle Dame sans Merci'. Ballads continued as an oral form, however, in folk song of many regions and different countries up to the present day, and versions of 'traditional ballads' have been recorded by collectors within living memory. See **Ch.11**.

ballad metre metrical form used by most, though by no means all, traditional ballads, but also found in other kinds of poems (such as some nursery rhymes); normally printed as a quatrain stanza consisting of alternating four-beat and three-beat lines, with only the second and fourth lines rhyming: *abcb*.

> The King sits in Dunfermling town,
> Drinking the blude-reid wine;
> O whare will I get a guid skipper,
> To sail this schip of mine?
> ('Sir Patrick Spens')

The stanza might equally well be described as a seven-beat rhyming couplet with a caesura after the fourth beat, corresponding to the traditional metre known as **fourteeners**; thus the well-known nursery rhyme could be written out as follows:

> Mary had a little lamb, [caesura] its fleece was white as snow;
> And everywhere that Mary went, [caesura] the lamb was sure to go.

The ballad stanza is also known in hymnology as 'common measure' from its use in metrical psalms, a tradition that informs the finely pointed use that Emily Dickinson (1830–86) regularly makes of it:

> Because I could not stop for Death—
> He kindly stopped for me—
> The Carriage held but just Ourselves—
> And Immortality.

bathos rhet. anticlimax; normally an evaluative term to condemn a poet's failure to scale the poetic heights (i.e. the classical 'sublime'), but turned to mock-heroic advantage by Alexander Pope who wrote a satirical *ars poetica* or *Treatise on the Art of Sinking in Poetry* (1727) entitled *Peri Bathous*, a parody of Longinus's *Peri Hypsous* ('On the Sublime'). Augustan poets perfected the art of bathos as a high-order satiric skill involving the play of contrasting **registers** in **mock epic** verse, where it becomes second nature to set up the high **decorum** of the epic style only to deflate it with a 'low' word, as in the following example: 'Shadwell alone of all my sons is he / Who stands confirm'd in full stupidity' (Dryden, *MacFlecknoe*, 17–18); here, the high style of epic congratulation is reduced to bathos with the word 'stupidity' which has a different **register** unsuitable for the inflated style of epic.

blank verse unrhymed **iambic pentameter**, i.e. five beat rising duple metre. Metre first used by Henry Howard, Earl of Surrey, for his translation (*ca.* 1539–46) of two books of Virgil's *Aeneid*; became in later C16 the major verse form for use in drama (including Shakespeare's plays), but in C17 its epic credentials were restored by Milton in *Paradise Lost*. In C18 **heroic couplets** became the approved metre for (mock-) heroic verse, blank verse not being widely used before C19, although James Thomson uses it in *The Seasons* (1730). In early C19 Wordsworth championed Milton as his revolutionary predecessor and role-model, pioneering a revival of blank verse in such poems as *The Prelude* and *The Excursion*. In blank verse, the absence of end-rhyme and the varied use of **caesura**, **enjambment** and **end-stopped** lines allow the poet to create a subtle interplay between metrical beat and natural speech rhythms; see **Ch.3**. Do not confuse with **free verse**.

blason poetic genre originating in France dedicated to praise or blame, normally erotic and listing the beauties of a woman's body parts; easily turned to parody as with Shakespeare, sonnet 130: 'My mistress' eyes are nothing like the sun'.

caesura mid-line metrical pause or syntactical break often, though not always, signalled by punctuation; in longer lines of six or more beats the caesura is likely to fall regularly in mid-line with the danger of monotony; in **iambic pentameter** and especially **heroic couplets** caesura is likely to occur after the second or the third beat, suggesting the flexibility of the speaking voice despite the regularity of the metre; caesura also offers scope for **parallelism** or **antithesis**: 'Beauties in vain their pretty eyes may roll; / Charms strike the sight, but merit wins the soul' (Pope, *Rape of the Lock*, V: 33–34); here, caesura, signalled by the comma, separates the parallel statements in line 34; there is no parallelism in line 33, though a caesura after 'vain' is possible.

canto very long poems are sometimes divided into books or cantos, traditionally divisions in a long poem consisting of the amount a minstrel might sing at one 'fit'; hence providing the title for Ezra Pound, *The Cantos* (1925–1970).

chiasmus rhet. literally 'crossing over'; a type of inversion in which similar phrases (not necessarily the same words) are repeated in reverse order, e.g. Dryden, 'Success let others teach, learn thou from me / Pangs without birth, and fruitless Industry' (*MacFlecknoe*, 147–8), where, in line 148, 'Pangs' is similar to 'Industry' and 'without birth' means the same as 'fruitless', but the syntax is reversed (noun-adjective becomes adjective-noun) or crossed over in an AB/BA pattern on either side of the **caesura** (a similar chiasmus can be seen in line 147).

closed couplet pair of end-rhymed lines in which the syntax (i.e. phrase or sentence) is complete at the end of the second line. Normally in **iambic pentameter**, it is also known as the 'heroic couplet' from C18 assumption that this was the appropriate metre for epic (i.e. 'heroic') verse; the closed couplet became the staple metre for verse of many kinds, but especially satire, in C18; cf. **closure** and **open couplets**.

closure term used to refer to the way texts achieve a sense of finality at the end (see Herrnstein Smith, *Poetic Closure: A Study of How Poems End*). May refer to content, as when one asks whether all the narrative threads have been tied up at the end of a novel, or it may refer to formal completeness and coherence – a rhyme scheme completed; the return to images, themes or ideas at the end of a poem that have been announced at the beginning; the fulfilment of readers' expectations which may be set up by the poem itself or by received conventions of the genre to which it belongs. Modernist poetics, and certain schools of literary theory (e.g. **deconstruction**), have favoured open-endedness and have valued readings which resist closure by revealing hidden tensions or fractures in apparently closed texts.

conceit an arresting or challenging **metaphor**, of which two kinds are commonly found in English criticism, the Petrarchan and the 'metaphysical'. Petrarchan conceits replay the metaphorical clichés found in the *Canzone* of Francesco Petrarch, typically comparing the lover's ardour to anything very hot and his mistress's disdain to ice; such exaggeration is also found in the 'metaphysical' conceit as practised by Donne and his followers in which, however, more inventive or original analogies are found between very dissimilar things, as when Donne compares two lovers to a pair of compasses in 'A Valediction: Forbidding Mourning'. Improbable and arresting analogies became the sign of a poet's rhetorical invention ('wit') in C17, sometimes identified as typical of the 'baroque', an art-historical term which has won growing acceptance in referring to continental literary traditions that influenced **metaphysical** poetry in England.

concrete poetry term adopted in 1955 by a Swiss poet to describe a type of modernist experimental writing exploiting visual effects achieved by the shape of a poem on the page, sometimes formatting it mimetically to suggest an object, as in Renaissance pattern poetry copying ancient Greek models (cf. Herbert's *Easter Wings*, Ch. 3), or sometimes jumbling letters to suggest random, aleatory patterns of significance. Combining some major preoccupations of European modernism in both literature and the visual arts, concrete poetry's notable exponents in English include John Hollander, M.L. Rosenthal, Ian Hamilton Finlay and Edwin Morgan. The work of e. e. cummings anticipates concrete poetry in its radical rejection of accepted conventions of **typography** and its reformatting of the way the poem appears on the page. See **Ch.3**.

connotation term in linguistics to distinguish those meanings of a word that can be defined in a dictionary – known as 'denotation' – from those more subtle, secondary meanings or associations which are less easy to define but which often make a major contribution to a poem's meaning or effect. The demand for close reading usually requires students to recognise the connotations of particular words or phrases; these may be subtle, more or less subjective, and difficult to prove, so the best way of working is to offer some evidence to show that the words or phrases have such connotations in other uses and to demonstrate how such connotations can be accommodated to the poem's overall syntax or argument; cf. **register**.

consonance a kind of reverse **alliteration** in which there is a repetition of sounds made by the final consonants or consonant groups of nearby words (in alliteration it is the initial consonants that are repeated); the syllable-pattern takes the form consonant-vowel-**consonant**, where our use of bold indicates where the repetition occurs, as in sa**nd**/gri**nd** or defea**t**/narra**t**e; sometimes called half-rhyme; some critics define consonance as the repetition of both initial and final consonant sounds (**consonant**-vowel-**consonant**), as in 'to **c**oo**k** a **c**a**k**e' – in which case it is the same as **pararhyme**.

couplet pair of lines that rhyme, cf. **closed couplet, open couplet, triplet, quatrain**.

dactyl name in classical prosody for a metrical foot consisting of one stressed syllable followed by two unstressed ones or, in Latin, one long syllable plus two short ones, corresponding to what the new metrics calls 'falling triple' metre, and scanned: / ˘ ˘ (*tum-tee-tee*, as in 'company'). See **foot**.

decasyllabic line or lines with ten syllables; in duple metre it will have five stresses, hence normally the same as **pentameter**; cf. **octosyllabic**.

deconstruction theory of literature developed out of Jacques Derrida's 'deconstructive' readings of philosophy and linguistics, and championed by figures such as Paul de Man, Geoffrey Hartman, J. Hillis Miller and Barbara Johnson. Derrida's reading of Saussure's linguistic theory led him to claim that language generates meaning not through its relation to some extra-linguistic reality (the real world, ideas, authorial intention, history, the human condition, nature, God, etc.) but through the play of *différance* that characterises language itself. In other words, language does not embody truth but endlessly differs from and defers it.

According to Derrida, Western philosophy typically tries to evade what we might call the linguistic condition by making recourse to a 'metaphysics of presence' – claiming that philosophy is a special kind of discourse that uses language in order to give us access to extra-linguistic truth (such as ideas, or reason, or being). Derrida's response is to develop close readings of philosophical texts to show how their own language and rhetorical strategies undo and make ironic their own metaphysical claims. Deconstructive literary criticism is similar in that it produces a close reading of a literary text in order to demonstrate how its language and textual strategies simultaneously promise and undercut some metaphysical meaning. Although other kinds of literary criticism (from New Criticism to Marxism) attempt to uncover a text's real meaning, deconstructive literary criticism holds that literature is a special kind of discourse that celebrates (rather than disguising) the way that language generates meaningful effects without ever cohering in a meaning that is total and final. As *Princeton* puts it, for deconstructive literary theory, literature 'distinguishes itself by spotlighting its rhetoricity. It foregounds its metaphors, figures and images to illustrate the oppositions and contradictions that never ultimately reconcile themselves or come to rest' (p. 280). Such criticism contrasts strongly with established reading habits in which the critic aims to have mastered and included all the different elements of a text in a coherent or consistent reading or interpretation. While most authors and critics view a literary text as embodying an extra-linguistic truth (about the human condition, say) the deconstructive critic attempts to show how the text itself undoes such truth claims by rendering its meanings undecidable. While deconstructive criticism can produce extraordinary insightful readings of individual literary texts, its ultimate aim is to extend Derrida's larger claims about philosophy and language on the basis that Western metaphysics (its sense of certainty) has potentially negative political and ethical consequences.

decorum classical term referring to the assumption that some kinds of language or ways of speaking are more appropriate to certain subjects or speech occasions than to others. C18 neoclassical criticism tends to focus on the 'rules' regarding the kind of style appropriate to different genres or different types of subject matter, and normally arranges them in a hierarchy of 'high' and 'low' styles or registers. So a writer who made Queen Dido speak like a fishwife would be guilty of a breach of decorum; cf. **register**.

diction lexical- or word-choice, normally found in the phrase 'poetic diction' which refers to the use by C18 poets of a heightened **register** of poetic language, circumlocution ('finny tribe' for fish), and the avoidance of common or vulgar expressions. Wordsworth led the revolt against such poetic diction with his argument in the 'Preface' to *Lyrical Ballads* (1800) that poetry should be written in 'a selection of the real language of men'. But although C18 poetic diction was killed off and buried, Romantic poetry (including most of Wordsworth's) developed its own heightened diction (e.g. Keats's 'Ode to a Nightingale'). Many post-Romantic poets and poetic movements rejected Romantic diction, but nonetheless replaced it with a poetic diction that generally distinguishes itself from everyday diction. Students are sometimes asked to comment on a poet's 'word-choice', and this may involve commenting on diction (perhaps by showing how a particular word, rather than a close synonym, has specific **connotations** or is part of a particular **register**). In general, though, requiring students to pay attention to 'word choice' is a redundant or woolly question, since a poem consists of nothing but a set of words that the poet has chosen.

dimeter the name in classical prosody for a line of two feet; in English verse the two-beat line, rarely used: 'Give me one kisse, / And no more; / If so be, this / Makes you poore; / To enrich you, / I'le restore / For that one, / Two thousand score.' (Robert Herrick, 'To Dianeme', 1648)

double pattern term invented by Richard Bradford (1993) to analyse the interplay between syntax and metrical form in poetry. See **Ch.3**.

dramatic monologue poem voiced by a single speaker who is not the poet but, normally, a vividly realised character who expresses his or her personality through the strongly dramatised voice and in a specific situation (usually to a silent **addressee**). The genre is most associated with Robert Browning: his *Dramatic Romances and Lyrics* (1845) included such definitive examples as 'My Last Duchess' and 'Porphyria's Lover'; his *Men and Women* (1855) included 'Fra Lippo Lippi' and 'Bishop Blougram's Apology'. Notable successors include T.S. Eliot's 'The Love Song of J. Alfred Prufrock' (1917) and the twenty-nine modern examples in Carol Ann Duffy's *The World's Wife* (1999).

dramatic poetry poetry written in dramatic form with dramatic action and speaking characters, though not intended for the stage (as opposed to the poetic drama, say, of Shakespeare).

dub poetry a form of performance poetry in which the words are spoken over reggae rhythms (either pre-recorded or live). Dub poetry is mostly concerned with politics, social justice and current events seen from a black Caribbean perspective. It originated in Jamaica in the 1970s, but some of its most prominent practitioners are British poets of Caribbean descent (such as Linton Kwesi Johnson and Benjamin Zephaniah). See **reggae**.

duple metre verse form in which the repeated beat-offbeat of the metre is produced by groups of two-syllable units.

eclogue genre of **pastoral** poem imitating the *Eclogues* (aka *Bucolics*) of Virgil (37 BCE), usually in the form of dramatic dialogues between shepherds in an idyllic pastoral setting; revived most notably in C16 by Edmund Spenser in his *Shepheardes Calendar* (1579) and continually adapted for a variety of different didactic and satiric ends in C18.

ekphrasis rhet. strictly poetry which describes a painting or work of art, e.g. Keats, 'Ode on a Grecian Urn', Auden, 'Musée des Beaux Arts'; the term was used in C16 to refer to any writing that offers a vivid description characterised by *enargeia* (vividness of description), capable of bringing the object before the reader's eyes as in a painting, and thus vindicating champions of poetry in the Italian *paragone* debates who claimed that poetry was superior to its sister art of painting; the idea that poetry can present a vivid picture to the mind stems from Horace's theorem *ut pictura poesis* ('as in poetry, so in painting') in his *Ars Poetica* (*c.* 10 BCE).

elegy in modern usage the name for a genre of poetry, which may take many forms, written to commemorate a dead person; famous examples include Milton's 'Lycidas', Gray's 'Elegy Written in a Country Churchyard', Tennyson's *In Memoriam*, Yeats's 'In Memory of Major Robert Gregory'. The elegy functions to lament or commemorate the deceased and to console the bereaved, and it takes its name from the classical meter known as *elegiac* which was used for poems on a variety of subjects, including the very different type of erotic verse typified by the *Amores* and the *Ars Amatoria* of Ovid, which is why in the early modern period the name is also associated with the Ovidian love *Elegies* of John Donne and others (at this period what we call 'elegy' was likely to be called 'obsequy').

emblem combination of a symbolic picture with an enigmatic motto or title and an explanatory verse epigram found in emblem books of the sixteenth and seventeenth centuries, influencing types of imagery in poetry and the visual arts where an 'emblem' or 'emblematic' image is one either derived from the emblem books themselves or functioning in similar ways. Andrew Marvell's 'On a Drop of Dew' (*c.* 1660), for instance, spends twenty lines describing a dew drop in ways that suggest the condition of the soul on earth, and a further twenty describing the soul as if it were a dew drop; Henry Lee's poem on an ageing warrior ('His golden locks time hath to silver turned', 1590) predicts that 'His helmet now shall make an hive for bees', which is a familiar emblem of peace or disarmament; cf. **allegory, topos**.

end-stopped when the unit of sense or syntax (sentence, clause or phrase) is complete at the end of the line, often – though not always – signalled by punctuation; the opposite of **enjambment**.

enjambment when the sense or syntax is carried over the line ending in verse, from a French word meaning to step over (literally 'get your leg over'); enjambment discourages the reader from making the kind of pause at the line ending which **closure** of the metrical pattern at line endings tends to imply; hence enjambment involves what *Princeton* calls 'noncoincidence of the frames of syntax and metre . . . giving the reader mixed messages' (p. 359); these 'frames' are often identified as **rhythm** and **metre** where 'rhythm' refers to the natural syntactical flow of the language as opposed to the regular patterning of the imposed metre. You will often find teachers and examiners prompting you to say something about the relation of rhythm to metre, and enjambment probably offers the quickest way of rising to this challenge. Enjambment is the opposite of **end-stopped** lines, where the syntax of a phrase or sentence is completed at the end of the verse line; punctuation can be a pretty reliable guide to such completion. Though a key characteristic of most blank verse, enjambment is also found over rhymed endings especially in **iambic pentameters**, though **closed couplets** are always, as the name implies, end-stopped at the end of the couplet. See **Ch.3**.

envoi short concluding stanza found at the end of certain medieval French genres, and modern imitations, especially the *ballade*, in which the poet presents his poem to his patron or sends it about its business; normally characterised by a shift of voice as the poet addresses his patron ('Prince'), his reader or his poem.

epic long narrative poem on a mythological, national or historical subject, normally based on a legendary story. In classical epic (especially Homer) the narrative focus shifts from time to time to show us the gods overhead, presiding over, contesting or determining the future course of events below; these heavenly deliberations are known, technically, as 'epic machinery' since they drive the plot. Cf. **romance**, which resembles epic in its treatment of heroic exploits and/or adventurous travellers.

epic simile an extended simile interrupting the narrative to offer a detailed description and comparison of the kind that became conventional after imitations of Homer's extended comparisons in *The Iliad*.

epideictic demonstrative writing that colours things in a certain way, normally **panegyric**; one of three branches of classical **rhetoric**, the others being: deliberative (i.e. political – 'What should be done?') and forensic (i.e. legal – 'What did the accused do?'). Epideictic corresponds to what we might now call 'spin-doctoring' ('How should we present this?'). Rhetoric is the art of persuasion, and students were traditionally taught to practise its techniques in both prose and verse.

epigram originally a term in Greek meaning 'inscription', it came to refer to a brief, concise, moralising or aphoristic composition designed to catch the reader's attention and rest in the memory. Epigrams in the *Greek Anthology* (*c.* 60 BCE) tend to be pictorial and **ekphrastic**; the Latin epigrams of Martial are more pointed and satiric, influencing the modern form, e.g. Jonathan Swift's 'On Carthy's Translation Of Longinus': 'What Midas touch'd became true gold, but then, / Gold becomes lead touch'd lightly by thy pen.'

eye-rhyme two or more words which look like rhymes to the eye, but do not rhyme to the ear, e.g. 'through', 'plough'. Unusual, and not strictly rhymes at all. Beware of describing as eye-rhyme words which, though now pronounced differently, were once pronounced the same, e.g. Pope: 'Fair Nymphs, and well-dressed Youths around her shone, / But ev'ry eye was fix'd on her alone' (*The Rape of the Lock*, II, 5–6); or 'No common weapons in their hands are found, / Like Gods they fight, nor dread a mortal Wound' (ibid., V, 42–43). Whether 'wind' was ever pronounced so as to rhyme with 'find', and if so when the pronunciation changed, is an open question in linguistics, but in poetry it is nearly always allowed as 'poetic licence' rather than described strictly as eye-rhyme.

falling rhythm a poetic rhythm whose units 'fall' in stress from a stressed syllable to an unstressed syllable or syllables; cf. **rising rhythm**.

feminine rhyme name given to disyllabic (or duple) rhymes, e.g. *Shelley/jelly*, *twenty/plenty*, consisting of a stressed followed by an unstressed syllable. Monosyllabic rhymes are called **masculine**; cf. **rhyme**.

field aspect of linguistic **register** that refers to the area of usage in which an expression is normally found; some vocabulary is 'field-specific' – legal terminology, football commentaries, cookery books, scientific discourse, government reports, etc. not only have specialised technical terms but also their own ways of putting things. Poetry can borrow these, though it may also, in particular periods or genres, have its own poetic **diction** or rules of **decorum**. Poets also, however, use language with a variety of different registers and words drawn from many different fields, as when Robin Robertson describes 'The wind off the sea / like a thrown knife; a styptic cold' ('Sea Fret', in *Swithering*, 2006, p. 39), where it is not only the **metaphor** that is poetically effective, but also the unexpected use of the word 'styptic' with its specifically medical register or field.

figurative rhet. language that is highly shaped, stylised or embellished, traditionally including a large number of 'figures of speech' that were taught in classical **rhetoric** and supplied the names we still use for such rhetorical devices as **anaphora, antithesis, apostrophe, chiasmus, homoeoteleuton, hyperbole, litotes, paranomasia, periphrasis, synecdoche**. Classical rhetoric sometimes made a distinction between 'figures', which involve changing the form of expressions ('figures of words'), and 'tropes' which involve a change of meaning or swerve of sense (Gk. *tropein*, 'to turn', 'to swerve'), but the distinction was always difficult to maintain and in modern usage figurative has become virtually synonymous with **metaphorical**.

foot term used in classical **prosody** (metrical analysis) to refer to a repeated unit of stress patterns in the poetic line, but which we do not use in this book and which is becoming supplanted in modern poetics by the 'beat-offbeat' models we explain in **Ch.2**. Since you are likely to find the traditional metrical units used in much criticism, however, we identify here the most common of the traditional metrical feet, though we are not recommending that you should use them. We indicate below how the classical terminology corresponds to the terms we are recommending in this book. Stressed syllable = /, unstressed = ˘

iamb	˘ /	*tee-tum* ('defend') = rising duple
trochee	/ ˘	*tum-tee* ('metre') = falling duple
pyrrhic	˘ ˘	*tee-tee* ('on a') = not required in the new metrics
spondee	/ /	*tum-tum* ('see through') = not required in the new metrics

anapaest ˘ ˘ /   *tee-tee-tum* ('interrupt') = rising triple

dactyll / ˘ ˘   *tum-tee-tee* ('company') = falling triple

fourteener metrical line of fourteen syllables, in duple rhythm; when set out as quatrain stanzas they are the same thing as **ballad metre**; cf. **poulter's measure**.

> Learn freedom and felicity. Hawks flying where they list
> Be kindlier and more sound than hawks best tended on the fist.
> (William Warner, *Albion's England*, 1589)

free verse verse which does not comply with any regular metrical template; not to be confused with **blank verse**.

genre name for any discrete kind of poem. Different genres may be defined according to their various purposes, occasions or subject matter, or by their formal characteristics, some genres (e.g., **haiku, limerick, sonnet, villanelle**) having a fixed form, others having a tendency to use a particular style or metre (**ballad, dramatic monologue, epic, georgic, ode**). Neoclassical theory (in C17 and C18) assumed that poetic genres were universal and could be regulated by strict rules based on the best classical models and ancient examples of each, which is why many poetic genres still have classical names (**epigram, eclogue, satire**). However, genre theory now recognises that all genres emerge, develop (e.g., **concrete poetry**) and eventually die out in a complex and highly interactive literary system and also that many poems mix two or more genres. Often the most 'original' works are those that use established genres in unusual or surprising ways. The idea that any poet writes in a vacuum, or 'off the top of her head' is, however, pretty untenable and there is a strong case for believing that we can neither write intelligibly, nor read poetry accurately, without some sense of the generic models which are in play, which means that the more poetry, of different kinds, that we read, the better readers (and writers) we are likely to become; cf. **stanza forms**, and see **Ch.11**.

georgic genre of didactic (i.e. teaching, instructive) poem which became extremely popular in early C18, imitating the Latin *Georgics* of Virgil (29 BCE) which instruct the reader in, and celebrate the skills of, agriculture. C18 imitations teach any similar skill or art and include James Thomson's *The Seasons* (1726), John Armstrong's *The Art of Preserving Health* (1744), Robert Dodsley's *Agriculture* (1754) and *The Art of Preaching* (1772), William Cowper's *The Task* (1785). John Gay's *Trivia: or the Art of Walking the Streets of London* (1716) offers a satirical take on the georgic and offers a good example of what we mean by 'mixed' genre, being both a georgic and a **satire** (or perhaps we should call it 'mock-georgic' by analogy with 'mock-heroic').

ground term used in analysing **metaphor**, the common property shared by both **tenor** and **vehicle**.

haiku unrhymed single-stanza poem based on Japanese models; haikus in English normally have three lines shaped by syllable count not stress pattern: five syllables + seven syllables + five syllables per line:

> What is a haiku?
> A haiku – a single breath,
> That breathes with the river
> (George Bruce, 2003)

In Japanese, haikus are shaped by counting *onji* – the sound symbols or phonetic characters used in phonetic script: 'haiku' means 'one breath' and haikus use only as many *onji* as can be recited in a single breath.

half-rhyme see **consonance**.

heroic couplet see **closed couplet**.

hexameter verse line consisting of six feet (six beats) also known as **alexandrine**. The classical hexameter was the staple metre for Greek and Latin epic poetry, and consists of five dactyls ($/$ ˘ ˘) followed, usually, by an end-of-line spondee ($/$ $/$), and with a mid-line **caesura**. Although occasionally attempted in English by individual poets from C16 to C19, the classical hexameter is generally felt to be not well suited to extensive use in English, largely because of the insistent triple rhythm which English stress rhythm, unlike Latin quantitative rhythm, imposes on it. However, Longfellow made notable use of it in a 'modern' American poem, *Evangeline* (1847):

> Bent like a laboring oar, that toils in the surf of the ocean,
> Bent, but not broken, by age was the form of the notary public (III, 1–2).

Arthur Hugh Clough (1819–59), however, loosened the rather wooden feel the metre has in Longfellow to capture the flow of the speaking voice in informal conversation in long poems on contemporary life such as *Amours de Voyage* (1858):

> Rome disappoints me much; I hardly as yet understand, but
> *Rubbishy* seems the word that most exactly would suit it. (I, 19–20)

homoeoteleuton pron. 'home-ee-o-til Uton', rhet. repetition of the same word or words at the end of successive phrases, sentences or lines of verse; cf. **anaphora**.

hybridity, hybridisation terms used in post-colonial studies to refer to different kinds of cross-breeding – ethnic, linguistic, cultural, political, etc. – between peoples and cultures that colonisation creates. Often used interchangeably with 'creolisation', cultural intermingling characterised by the linguistic intermixture of languages and dialects known as 'creole'. See **Ch.16**.

hyperbole pron. 'high-PER-bilee', rhet. deliberate exaggeration, e.g. when Burns says he will love his girl 'Till a' the seas gang dry'; Burns's hyperbole is also an example of the specific **topos** known in classical **rhetoric** as *impossibilia*, a list of impossible things: streams will flow back to their source, the cart will pull the horse, the lamb will hunt the wolf, the lion will flee the hare, often – though not here – used satirically to argue that the world is upside down.

iambic name in classical prosody for a metrical foot consisting of an unstressed followed by a stressed syllable or, in Latin, short syllable plus long syllable, corresponding to what the new metrics calls 'rising duple metre, and scanned: ˘ / (*tee-tum*, as in 'defend'). See **foot**.

iambic pentameter traditional name for five-beat lines (pentameter) in rising duple metre (iambic); thus five beats/stresses and ten syllables per line; see **accentual-syllabic, decasyllabic**.

iconography developed in C20 art history to define and classify types of symbolic imagery in the visual arts, particularly the use of inherited symbols, schemes of symbolism and particular iconologies, which may be religious, courtly, political, moral or didactic. Poets, particularly though not exclusively in earlier periods, may draw on such received iconologies; cf. **image, symbol, emblem**.

image term used to refer to any visual (or other sensuous) detail or aspect of a poem, which may be either descriptive and literal or figurative and symbolic. Teachers and examiners often encourage students to comment on the imagery of poems since images are supposed to lend vividness or sensory immediacy to a text and can be a test of a student's 'personal' response. However, the complexity and imprecision of this terminology ought to be accompanied by a health warning about its theoretical and practical dangers, since an image can be a metaphor or simile, a descriptive detail, a religious symbol or icon, an allegorical figure, an imaginary being or object, or an impression in the reader's mind. Historically the different ways in which poetry uses imagery, or relates to the visual world, have changed radically, in parallel with philosophical developments in theories of knowledge or changes in literary taste. Whilst Sidney's *Defence of Poesie* (1595) characterised poetry as 'a speaking picture' which could teach moral truths by delighting the senses, C18 empiricists favoured a plain style which would not lead readers astray by metaphorical shifts; Romantic readers favoured poetry which imagined immaterial realities in what were often unconventional ways; C20 Russian Formalism valued poetry's capacity to make us see familiar things in unfamiliar ways. And so on. In C20 a school of criticism developed which claimed that the value of poetry was its capacity to make abstract ideas 'concrete': poets thus clothe or embody their moral or metaphysical ideas in metaphorical images and it is only by responding fully to the concrete, i.e. sensuous, qualities of its imagery that a reader could realise the poetic 'message'. This theory was closely connected to the literary movement known as **symbolism**. Recent theories have placed the emphasis more on how our images of the world, including those in poetry, are socially and politically constructed; cf. **metaphor, symbol, ekphrasis, Imagism**.

Imagism name of a literary movement that lasted a very short time – 1912–17 – but had a strong influence on 'modern' poetry and literary theory of the 1920s and 1930s; championed by Ezra Pound and applied to his own poetry and that of a few proteges, chiefly Hilda Dolittle, the movement demanded absolute clarity and directness in the use of images that would show, rather than tell, what the poem was saying and use no word that did not contribute directly to the immediate effect.

intention a term that sends out danger signals in literary interpretation largely as a result of an influential essay published in 1946 by W.K. Wimsatt and Monroe Beardsley entitled 'The intentional fallacy', which argues that we shouldn't go outside the poem – to the poet – to discover the intention because, in a good poem, the intention will be clear from the text itself: if it is not, the poet has failed; cf. **ambiguity**. Valid interpretation is therefore to be justified by demonstrating that a critic's reading can be accommodated to the overall structure of meanings within the poem rather than to the author's known or supposed personal feelings or beliefs. Hence 'anti-intentionalism', a critical position which raises issues of some theoretical complexity and controversy in the second half of C20, especially in 'New Criticism'.

internal rhyme a rhyme between words that are within the verse line, or between an end word and a mid-line word, as opposed to 'end-rhyme'; relatively rare and, unlike end-rhyme, seldom required by a traditional verse form or stanza pattern, hence more likely to be used for purely poetic or semantic effect. See **rhyme**.

inversion saying things back to front, or a word out of its normal place in the sentence; common in poetry, e.g. 'the mountains high' = the high mountains, often merely to make a rhyme, though it can be for emphasis.

invocation moment in a poem, usually at the beginning, when the poet or poetic speaker calls on a muse or deity for aid in a kind of **apostrophe**; found most often in **epic** poetry.

irony rhet. two principal types of irony are known as 'verbal irony' and 'dramatic irony' (or situational irony). Verbal irony is when you say one thing but mean something different, often (though not always) the opposite, hence creating a gap between literal meaning and intended meaning (which is why irony is a kind of figure). We may need to know the speaker's situation before we can judge if s/he is being ironic, as when someone has just helped themselves to a large second helping and you say 'I hope you have had enough!' This is ironic, because what you really mean is 'I think you've had too much', and could be classed as sarcasm, when you say the opposite of what you mean; but irony may not always be as extreme as this. Claims that a writer is being ironic are notoriously difficult to prove, hence often need to be validated through analysis of the distance between literal meaning and likely **intention**. This will usually depend – as with 'I hope you've had enough!' – on context and situation. Irony is often signalled by a speaker's **tone**, so we can say the tone is ironic, but it is best to justify your use of this term by showing the distance between what is said and what is meant. 'Dramatic irony' is a plot device, typically in classical tragedy, when the audience knows more than the speaker, who may refer to his/her circumstances in a way that reveals a misunderstanding of them and their potentially tragic outcome; the irony depends on the audience knowing something that the speaker does not, which opens up a distance between their understanding of events and his/hers. Both types of irony, then, involve a distance between what is said and its true significance: in verbal irony, the speaker is aware of and indeed creates that distance; in dramatic or situational irony, the speaker is not aware of that distance. In both cases, readers or audience only get the irony when they see the distance between what is said and its significance. See **Ch.8**.

Italian sonnet see **sonnet**.

litotes rhet. type of understatement when an affirmative is expressed by the negative of its contrary, e.g. 'Mary is no dullard' = bright; 'the Prime Minister was economical with the truth' = he lied; or Philip Larkin making love:

> Nothing shows why
> At this unique distance from isolation
>
> It becomes still more difficult to find
> Words at once true and kind,
> Or not untrue and not unkind.
> (from 'Talking in Bed', 1964)

lyric literally 'song to be sung to the lyre' (Gk.), hence originally any poetic genre written to be sung; one of three broad categories of poetry (the other two being 'narrative' and 'dramatic'). Lyric can itself be described as a **genre**, though it includes so many other distinct genres (**ballad, ode, sonnet, villanelle, sestina, elegy**, etc.) that it might be better to classify it as a 'mode' of writing. Since lyric has come to refer not just to poems that are actually meant to be sung but also to verse designed for silent reading that uses any of the stanza forms, styles or genre conventions periodically associated with song lyrics, it has lost much of its specificity and you are likely find almost any short poem using a complex ('melodic') stanza form described as 'lyric', particularly if the voice or presence of the speaker/singer is foregrounded through the **tone**. See **Ch.7**.

masculine rhyme single-syllable rhyme (or mono rhyme) formed between final stressed syllables, e.g. Robert Herrick, 'The Vine' (1648): 'I dreamed this mortal part of mine / Was metamorphosed to a vine'. Here the rhyme words are both monosyllables, but disyllabic words can form masculine rhymes, as long as it is only their final, stressed syllable that makes the rhyme; thus if we changed Herrick's second line to: 'Had changed in death, and turned divine', it would still be a masculine rhyme, even though 'divine' is disyllabic; cf. **rhyme, feminine rhyme**.

metaphor rhet. literally 'transference'; normally when one thing is described in terms of another on the basis of some similarity, e.g. 'My thoughts are all a case of knives' (Herbert, 'Affliction'). The best tools for analysis of metaphor are those of I.A. Richards: **'tenor'** = the thing spoken of (here 'thoughts'), **'vehicle'** = the thing it is being compared to (here 'case of knives'), and 'ground' = whatever tenor and vehicle have in common (some similarity) that justifies the comparison in the present context (here possibly: sharpness, wounding, affliction). The metaphor transfers its ground (affliction, etc.) from vehicle to tenor. In this example, both tenor and vehicle are stated in the text: this kind of metaphor can thus be described as an explicit metaphor (although the reader still has to find the ground of the metaphor). Implicit metaphors are metaphors in which only the vehicle is present in the text and the reader has to infer both the tenor and the ground. The opening lines of Samuel Daniel's sonnet sequence, *Delia* (1544) announce that 'Unto the boundless Ocean of thy beauty / Runs this poor river, charged with streams of zeal'. It is clear from the context that Daniel is not talking about bodies of water and waterways; instead, 'boundless Ocean', 'poor river' and 'streams of zeal' need to be read as metaphors. But although 'poor river' is clearly a metaphorical vehicle, it is not clear what the tenor is: to interpret it, the reader needs to imagine what literal term could be put in its place. Is it a metaphor for the poet-speaker himself as he approaches his beloved, or is it a metaphor for his sonnet or sonnet sequence? In either case, what is the ground of the metaphor – what is the similarity between the poet and/or his poems and a poor river approaching an ocean? As this example makes clear, implicit metaphors often require more interpretive effort from the reader than explicit metaphors do. Yet all metaphors leave the reader with at least some interpretive work, which is why they are prominent among the features of poetic language that cry out for analysis in any practical criticism exercise or analysis. It is normal to distinguish metaphor from **simile**, though both are types of **figurative** language; the distinction is quite straightforward: metaphor hides the fact that it is making a comparison, whereas **similes** own up to the fact, nearly always by using the words 'as' or 'like' – thus if Herbert had written 'My thoughts are like a case of knives' it would be a simile not a metaphor. The distinction may seem trivial, but it can make a difference to the directness and conviction of the expression, as here. In 'mixed metaphor' the writer switches vehicles in mid-stream; it is generally seen as a fault, though note Shakespeare's 'to take arms against a sea of troubles' (*Hamlet*, V, i, 59). 'Extended metaphor', on the contrary, pursues the same vehicle at some length (as Daniel does with ocean, river and streams), and it can be a good test of your reading skills to identify, where appropriate, the ways a writer keeps a significant theme alive by maintaining a figure (i.e., vehicle) at some length, or reviving it after it seems to have gone to sleep. 'How do I know if a word or phrase is metaphorical?' Answer: If it cannot have its literal meaning in this context: 'knives' are implements used to cut up meat or wound enemies; 'thoughts' cannot literally do this, so it must be a metaphor. Recent theory has recommended use of the terms 'subject' and 'analogue' as replacements for I.A. Richards's 'tenor' and 'vehicle'; it is still too early to say whether these will catch on. See **Chs 5, 6**.

metaphysical poetry name given in C17–C18 poetry written in the style associated with John Donne, George Herbert, Andrew Marvell and Henry Vaughan, characterised by intellectual ingenuity, wit and the use of **conceits**. Samuel Johnson famously described the style as one in which 'the most heterogeneous ideas are yoked by violence together' hence breaching neoclassical rules of clarity and **decorum**; in C20 its practice and practitioners were championed by T.S. Eliot as exemplifying a 'unified sensibility' capable of 'devouring all kinds of experience' in ways that modernist poets could learn from; in 1921, H.J.C. Grierson edited his influential anthology of *Metaphysical Lyrics and Poems* which encouraged the idea that the Metaphysical poets were, historically, a distinctive C17 school or group. More recent histories have cast doubt on the idea that the Metaphysical poets were a coherent group of mutually influencing poets, stressing rather their absorption of wider, continental styles associated with mannerism and the baroque.

metonymy rhet. literally 'change of name', when one word is put in place of another because the two are closely associated; e.g., 'for them the blazing hearth shall burn', where 'hearth' is a metonym for 'fire'; cf. **metaphor**, but note the distinction: metaphor, unlike metonymy, requires a transfer of sense between similar but different things and not just a substitution of names based on association. You don't have to find the **ground** of a metonym in order to understand it.

metre (or measure), the division of poetry into regular lines according to a pre-arranged template of beats and offbeats that are realised by a fixed number of stressed syllables and (sometimes) unstressed syllables per line.

mixed metre the use within a poem of a mixture of different metres, mostly in a set pattern (as in the Romantic ode).

mock epic a prose or poetic text (also called 'mock heroic') that employs the conventions of the **epic** in treating a trivial theme in order to produce comic and/or satiric effects; the most well-known example is Pope's *The Rape of the Lock* (1714).

monometer in classical **prosody** a verse line consisting of just one **foot**, in English verse with one **beat**; very rarely used, though e.g. Robert Herrick, 'I must / Not trust / Here to any; / Bereav'd, / Deceiv'd, / By so many: / As one / Undone / By my losses; / Comply / Will I / With my crosses' ('Anacreontike'), where every third line is a **dimeter** and the rest of the lines are monometer.

narrative poetry poetry that tells a story in ways analogous to the novel (and hence distinguished from **lyric** and **dramatic poetry**); genres include **epic, ballad** and **romance.**

Negative Capability phrase coined by John Keats in a letter of 1817 to describe the quality 'which Shakespeare possessed so enormously . . . that is, when a man is capable of being in uncertainties, mysteries, doubts without any irritable reaching after fact and reason'. Such 'half-knowledge' contrasts with the rigorous logic of philosophy or the sciences, and is seen as peculiar to poetry, where it may also refer to the power of empathy which Keats saw as fundamental to the creative imagination, involving a loss of self-consciousness by the poet and close identification imaginatively with an (often imaginary) object, such as the nightingale in his 'Ode to a Nightingale'.

octave stanza of eight lines; also used to refer to the first eight lines of a **sonnet**, particularly though not exclusively the Italian type where the two opening **quatrains** are rhyme-linked.

octosyllabic line or lines with eight syllables; in duple metre it will have four stresses and thus 'octosyllabic' normally means the same as four-beat duple.

ode genre of formal, ceremonious or celebratory **lyric** derived from the choral odes sung and danced in ancient Greek theatre consisting of three parts, *strophe*, *antistrophe* and *epode*; surviving examples written by Pindar (522–442 BCE) show abrupt shifts of subject matter suggesting inspired incoherence, apparently irregular or complex line- and stanza-lengths and an exalted, intense tone. Latin Odes of Horace (65–08 BCE) celebrate public events in a heightened tone, and establish the **decorum** for most modern imitations of the genre such as Andrew Marvell's 'Horatian Ode upon Cromwell's Return from Ireland' (1650, see **Ch.14**). In the Romantic ode – such as Wordsworth's 'Ode: Intimations of Immortality', Coleridge's 'Dejection', Shelley's 'Ode to the West Wind' or Keats's odes, 'To a Nightingale', 'To Autumn', 'On a Grecian Urn' and 'To Psyche' – it is not public events or religious invocation of a deity that is involved so much as the ode's traditional association with the inspired poet; in such Romantic odes the subject is the nature, struggle or crisis of poetic inspiration.

onomatopoeia a word or sequence of words that supposedly imitates the sounds of the actions or things being described or referred to; examples include 'buzz' or 'crack'; relatively rare in poetry, though inexperienced readers (sometimes encouraged by teachers who ought to know better) often claim that a poem's sound effects (such as **alliteration**) are onomatopoeic or somehow relate to the poem's meaning. Our readers are urged to be extremely cautious about making such claims, which are often nonsensical.

open couplet rhyming couplet in which the sense and syntax overflow the second rhyme ending (in contrast with **closed couplets**).

ottava rima Italian stanza-form, imitated by English poets, consisting of eight lines rhyming *abababcc*; it became the dominant Italian form for verse narrative in C16 following its use in Ariosto's *Orlando Furioso* (1516), with various English Renaissance imitators. C19 revival included Byron (*Beppo*, *Don Juan*), Shelley (*The Witch of Atlas*) and Keats (*Isabella*), with notable C20 successors including W.B. Yeats (e.g. 'Sailing to Byzantium', 'Among School Children'). Byron's use of ottava rima in *Don Juan* exploits the comic possibilities of the closing rhyming **couplet** and **feminine rhyme**:

> Young Juan now was sixteen years of age,
>> Tall, handsome, slender, but well knit: he seem'd

> Active, though not so sprightly as a page;
>   And everybody but his mother deem'd
> Him almost man; but she flew in a rage
>   And bit her lips (for else she might have scream'd)
> If any said so, for to be precocious
> Was in her eyes a thing the most atrocious.
>   (*Don Juan*, I, 54–61)

These techniques and effects are characteristic of Byron but not a necessary feature of ottava rima, though the final *cc* rhyme favours such summary, set-apart conclusions to the stanza.

oxymoron rhet. the conjunction of two mutually contradictory words, describing something in terms of its opposite, e.g. 'darkness visible' (Milton, *Paradise Lost*, I, 64), 'blinding sight' (Dylan Thomas, 'Do not go gentle into that good night'); cf. **antithesis, paradox**.

palinode poem of retraction in which the speaker withdraws an argument or attack made earlier, classically staged in the strophe/antistrophe opposition of the **ode**, though by no means restricted to the ode form:

> Take those iambics which I wrote,
> When anger made me piping hot,
>   And give them to your cook,
> To singe your fowl, or save your paste
> The next time when you have a feast;
>   They'll save you many a book.
> (Jonathan Swift, 'Palinodia', 7–14)

panegyric poem of praise, opposite of **satire**; a type of **epideictic** writing aiming to celebrate famous or admirable people and their achievements and thus to encourage virtue by making it attractive to the reader. Marvell's *Horatian Ode upon Cromwell's Return from Ireland* (see **Ch.14**) is – at least overtly – panegyric. Until the late C18, when poets often required the support of patrons before copyright gave them any immediate financial return from the sale of their work, panegyric was often necessary to win the patron's attention or favour. That does not necessarily make it insincere or self-serving, and the art of praising the good was traditionally seen as one of the essential functions of rhetorical writing in both prose and verse, hence it tends to flourish in periods when satire is also written.

paradox the union of opposites, often to express a hidden or mysterious truth; e.g., 'In the midst of life we are in death'; early-modern writers developed a distinct **genre** of sustained satire known as 'paradoxical encomium' of which the best known example is Erasmus's *In Praise of Folly* in which praise is ironically bestowed on something the opposite of praiseworthy; paradox literally means 'contrary to received opinion'; cf. **oxymoron, antithesis**.

parallelism correspondence of successive clauses or passages, especially in Hebrew poetry. The term was used by Hopkins to cover correspondences and recurrences of many different kinds – **rhythm, rhyme, alliteration, metaphor**, repetition – which he sees as characteristic of poetry. Following Hopkins, Roman Jakobson saw parallelism as a key element in what he defined as the 'poetic function' of language. Parallelism is not exact repetition, but repetition with difference. In rhet. parallelism is normally seen as the opposite of **antithesis**. See **Ch.4**.

paranomasia rhet. when two words are used close together with similar sounds but different meanings, hence often the same as a pun; cf. **ambiguity**.

pararhyme see **rhyme**.

parison rhet. succession of phrases with the same syntactical form; cf. **parallelism, anaphora**.

parody in poetry, the exaggerated imitation of a serious form or **genre** for comic and/or satirical effect.

pastoral a poem (or play or prose fiction) which portrays the lives of shepherds and shepherdesses in idealistic ways and celebrates simple, rural life.

pentameter classical verse line of five feet, or five-beat line in English poetry; normally duple rising rhythm (i.e. iambic pentameter); hence also known as **decasyllabic**; the staple metre of much English verse; cf. **blank verse, heroic couplet, iambic pentameter**.

periphrasis rhet. roundabout way of saying something, using more words than strictly necessary; e.g. 'The undiscover'd country, from whose bourn / No traveller returns' (*Hamlet*, III.i.79–80) = death.

persona Lat. 'mask'; term often used in criticism to signal that the critic recognises the difference between the poet who wrote a poem and the actual **speaker** in the poem; although we recognise the importance of this distinction, we prefer to use the term 'speaker' since, in its strict sense of 'mask', the term 'persona' (from the Latin) has a more specific application to those places, in texts of all kinds, where the author is expressing himself/herself indirectly through a fictitious disguise. Thus if we think the speaker Ulysses is expressing Tennyson's own values or judgements in the poem 'Ulysses' then we can describe him as the author's persona, or spokesman. All poems have speakers, but not all poems use personas (or, if you prefer the Latin plural, *personae*).

personification the presentation of inanimate things or abstractions as if they were living persons or allegorical figures; also known by the rhet. term 'prosopopoeia'. Classical precedent authorised such poetic figures, notably with Aeschylus's personifications of Strength and Force in *Prometheus Bound* (c. 400 BCE). In *Paradise Lost* (1667), Milton personifies the forces of Sin and her daughter Death who guard the gateway to hell. Up until early C18 capitalisation of common nouns, which was a normal typographic practice with printers, can make any abstract noun look like a personification since modern English **typography** (though not German, in which all nouns still have initial capitals) has reserved such capital initials for proper nouns (i.e. personal names). Thomas Gray's 'Ode: On a Distant Prospect of Eton College' (1747) thus signals the personifications through capitalisation:

> These shall the fury Passions tear,
>> The vultures of the mind,
> Disdainful Anger, pallid Fear,
>> And Shame that skulks behind;
> Or pining Love, shall waste their youth,
> Or Jealousy, with rankling tooth,
>> That inly gnaws the secret heart,
> And Envy wan, and faded Care,
> Grim-visag'd comfortless Despair,
>> And Sorrow's piercing dart. (70–79)

Here it is not just the capitalisation, but the descriptive epithets ascribing human qualities to the abstract nouns, that confirm their status as personifications. You might want to consider whether such personifications make Gray's description look like a bit of Baroque sculpture, so that it becomes implicitly **ekphrastic**. However, we should hesitate before claiming that the capitals in C18 editions of Pope's *Essay on Man* (1733–34), for instance, mean that we should read all the following abstract nouns as personifications; like the concluding axiom, this capitalisation may be merely for emphasis (indeed it may have been the printer's decision rather than the poet's):

> All Nature is but Art, unknown to thee;
> All Chance, Direction, which thou canst not see;
> All Discord, Harmony not understood;
> All partial Evil, universal Good:
> And, spite of Pride, in erring Reason's spite,
> One truth is clear, WHATEVER IS, IS RIGHT.
>> (I, 289–94; as printed in *Works*, London, 1751)

cf. **allegory**, **apostrophe**.

Petrarchan sonnet see **sonnet**.

pitch term used to describe an aspect of linguistic **register** that relates to the various levels of formality, politeness or social class in which different expressions are normally used.

poetic diction see **diction**.

poulter's measure verse form not much used since C16; rhyming couplets made up of one twelve-syllable line followed by one of fourteen syllables, or when split into quatrains with lines of 3 + 3 + 4 + 3 stresses known to hymnology as 'short measure'.

> If it were so that God would grant me my request,
> And that I might of earthly thinges have that I liked best,
> I would not wishe to clime to princely high estate,
> Which slipper is and slides so oft, and hath so sickly fate.
>
> (Anon. 1557)

prosody the art of versification and its analysis in terms of metre, rhythm, rhyme and stanza form.

prosopopoeia see **personification**.

quatrain four-line stanza; see **stanza forms**.

refrain phrase or line(s) that recurs at the end of a stanza; often found in songs.

reggae popular music **genre** developed in Jamaica in the 1960s. 'Reggae is founded upon a rhythm style which is characterized by regular chops on the back beat, known as the 'skank', played by a rhythm guitarist, and a bass drum hitting on the third beat of each measure' (*Wikipedia*). The Rastafarian movement influenced reggae musicians in the 1970s and 1980s (especially Bob Marley), but the lyrics also include love songs and social commentary. See **dub poetry**.

register term used in linguistics to refer to the fact that language typically varies according to context; thus the 'register' of a word or expression is characterised by the context in which it is normally used. The register of a piece of language has several different aspects, of which **tone**, **field** and **pitch** are worth distinguishing, and the register of a word or phrase may be the source of a large part of its **connotations**: all these terms might usefully come into play if you are asked to comment on what examiners like to call a poet's 'use of language' (an expression itself heavily overwritten with the register of modern English examiners' jargon). The many different situations in which we speak or write affect the relative formality or informality of the language we use – an aspect of register known as pitch; if we are speaking on a highly specialised subject we may need to use technical terms or expressions which are unlikely to be used outside that specialised field: some words have a narrowly restricted, others a virtually unrestricted field. Our choice of a particular word or phrase may equally be influenced by our attitude to or relationship with the listener: it may be familiar or polite, humorous or serious, personal or impersonal – which are all matters of tone. The register of an expression can often best be judged by imagining the context in which it would normally be used; another strategy is to place it alongside near-synonyms – if we take, for example, the range of nouns that Roget's indispensable *Thesaurus* places under the heading 'Resentment' we get:

> displeasure, animus, animosity, anger, wrath, indignation, pique, miff, huff, soreness, dudgeon, moodiness, acerbity, bitterness, asperity, spleen, gall, heart-burning, heart-swelling, rankling, temper, bad blood, ill blood, ill-humour, bile, choler, ire, fume, dander, passion, fit, tantrum . . .

And there are more . . . Although these words all have much the same meaning or denotation, their connotation, field, pitch and tone vary enormously. If you ask yourself 'Where am I likely to hear or use this particular synonym for anger?' you will be fixing its likely register, i.e. context. And if you check which of these synonyms imply disapproval, and which remain neutral or non-judgmental, you will be distinguishing their **tone**. Or if you ask which words are more likely to be used in conversation and which in, say, a parliamentary report, you will be deciding their field or pitch (Would an official report be likely to speak of the Prime Minister being 'in a dander' about current crime figures? It would be much more likely to refer to his 'displeasure' or his 'indignation'.) And some of these words look dated and old-fashioned now: that is also part of their register, which is archaic. Register is a useful concept to bear in mind when reading poetry whenever you are trying to identify or describe the exact meaning and tone; it becomes most exciting on those occasions (though they are rare) when we find a poem doing a bit of register switching, as when Jonathan Swift in 'The Lady's Dressing Room' sets a polite pastoral **decorum**, full of classical **allusions** as he describes Strephon poking his nose into Celia's affairs, only to register his dismay at the discovery that 'Oh! Celia, Celia, Celia shits' (117) (this is also an example of **bathos**). Or we find register switch undercutting romantic decorum when Dorothy Parker's C20 female speaker in a poem called 'One Perfect Rose' asks: 'why is it no one ever sent me yet / One perfect limousine, do you suppose?' The answer has everything to do with the radically different register of the two words 'rose' and 'limousine'. Such register-switches are uncommon in poetry, though they are striking when you find them.

rhetoric the art of using language to persuade or influence people, traditionally one of the triad of subjects (the 'trivium') which made up the basic curriculum of 'grammar' schools, based on classical texts by authors such as Aristotle (*Rhetorica*), Cicero (*De Oratore*) and Quintilian (*De Oratore*). Traditionally there were thought to be three branches of rhetoric: deliberative, i.e. changing listeners' opinions (what we might think of as the rhetoric of politicians); judicial, i.e. forensic (the rhetoric of lawyers); **epideictic**, i.e. demonstrative, dressing a subject up to make it look good or bad as in **panegyric** or **satire** (the branch of rhetoric traditionally practised by poets). Because classical rhetoric gave names to the various figures of speech used by writers of all kinds, many rhetorical terms have been taken over by criticism for the analysis of poetry, and we therefore have entries for the most important of these, marked 'rhet.', in the present Glossary, e.g. **anaphora, antithesis, apostrophe, chiasmus, homoeoteleuton, hyperbole, litotes, metaphor, paranomasia, periphrasis, synecdoche,** etc. Since virtually all poets before the late-eighteenth century studied rhetoric as part of their schooling, however, rhetorical figures and techniques for the invention (*inventio*) and presentation (*dispositio*) of material tend to influence not just their use of such rhetorical figures, but the whole way they write – from the choice of a subject or argument to its development and arrangement; rhetoric thus covers just about everything that we might mean by 'composition'; indeed rhetoric had always included verse composition as well as prose, and for that reason the traditional arts of rhetoric had a major influence on the writing of poetry right up to the late-eighteenth century. For the Romantic poets, however, poetry was the expression of the higher truths of the imagination and hence the opposite of rhetoric (which, for the Romantics, tries to persuade us that something is true even if it isn't); hence Keats writes 'We hate poetry that has a palpable design upon us' (Letter to John Hamilton Reynolds, 3 February 1818). This distinction between poetry and rhetoric has become enshrined in our culture: as we saw in Chapter 7, John Stuart Mill wrote in 1833 that 'Eloquence is *heard*, poetry is *overheard*. Eloquence supposes an audience; the peculiarity of poetry appears to us to lie in the poet's utter unconsciousness of a listener. Poetry is feeling confessing itself to itself, in moments of solitude'. Rhetoric has had a largely bad press since the Romantics as something essentially antithetical to poetry and to truth (as in 'that's just rhetoric'). Post-structuralist theories of literature (see **Ch.17**) sought to reconnect poetry and rhetoric (though not in the classical sense of rhetoric), and some political approaches to literature inspired by Marxism have affinities with the idea that poetry is engaged in persuasion.

rhyme an acoustic echo in spoken or sung language when the final stressed vowel sound and the sound of the final consonant or consonant group (if present) in nearby words or syllables are repeated, as in *eat/feet/street*, or *greeting/meeting/eating*. Rhyme consists of similarity in difference: the similarity is in the vowel sound, the difference occurs in the initial consonant sound of the stressed syllable or word, as signalled here by our use of bold. Thus rhyme takes the form consonant-**vowel-consonant**, and it is the vowel and final consonant sounds that are the same, while the initial consonants must differ (or the lack of a consonant, as in *eat/feet*, will make the difference). In polysyllabic words, the rhyme effect is normally achieved by the stressed syllables while the unstressed syllables are exactly the same (as in *greeting/eating*). The fact that the rhyme effect takes place between stressed syllables allows words like 'deflating' and 'debating' to rhyme, where the difference occurs in the initial consonants of the stressed syllables, not the initial syllables of the word. Rhyme is normally used at the end of lines and, in oral poetry and song, functions as a mnemonic device (it helps the poem/song to be memorable). It is possible to distinguish different types of rhyme according to the number of syllables involved in the rhyme: monosyllabic rhymes are known as **masculine rhymes** (or mono rhymes), as for example *eat/feet/street*; note that they need not consist of monosyllabic words, though they often do – as long as only the final, stressed syllable of a word is involved in the rhyme it is masculine, hence when Pope rhymes 'song' with 'prolong' (*Epistle to Arbuthnot*, 27–28) this is a masculine rhyme even though 'prolong' is a disyllabic word. When a rhyme is formed between two pairs of successive syllables it is known as a **feminine rhyme**

(or a duple rhyme), as in *greeting/eating*, though it is possible to make feminine rhymes out of successive syllables in different words, as when Pope rhymes 'take it' and 'make it' (*Epistle to Arbuthnot*, 45–46). Triple rhyme consists of a stressed followed by two unstressed syllables, as in *Tennyson/venison*; such polysyllabic rhymes tend to sound comic in English, as Byron recognised: 'They have a number, though they ne'er exhibit 'em / Four wives by law, and concubines ad libitum' (*Beppo* (1818), LXX). Variants on standard rhyme are **pararhyme, half-rhyme** and **consonance**, terms which are seldom clearly differentiated and can refer to various kinds of near-rhyme which may take many different forms, e.g. Owen's *killed/cold* (see **Ch.4**); Emily Dickinson in various places rhymes *port/chart, route/gate, ground/mind*; Swift rhymes *justice/hostess*. At the opposite end of the scale from **half-rhyme** is *rime riche*, when a word is rhymed with itself or with a homonym (a word pronounced the same, but with a different meaning). See **internal rhyme, alliteration, assonance, consonance.**

rhyme royal stanza of seven **iambic pentameter** lines rhymed *ababbcc*; first used by Chaucer and his immediate successors and then in C16 by Spenser (*Foure Hymnes*) and Shakespeare (*Rape of Lucrece*, 1594):

> Even here she sheathed in her harmless breast
> A harmful knife, that thence her soul unsheathed:
> That blow did bail it from the deep unrest
> Of that polluted prison where it breathed.
> Her contrite sighs unto the clouds bequeathed
> Her winged sprite and through her wounds doth fly
> Life's lasting date from cancelled destiny. (lines 1723–29)

rhyme scheme the regular pattern of end-rhymes in the **stanzas** of a poem; it is normally analysed by giving each rhyme a successive letter of the alphabet beginning with *a*; thus a poem in **couplets** is analysed as *aabbcc*, and so on. Some poems, or poetic **genres**, use a traditional rhyme scheme or 'fixed form'; to identify these see **stanza forms.**

rhythm a sequence of regularly recurring functions or events, as in walking, chanting or speech; a fundamental and inescapable term in **prosody**, but problematic in its usage and application because there are different ways of defining its relation to **metre**. Most current theories are keen to maintain a difference between metre and rhythm, at the simplest level because only such a distinction allows us to differentiate between the metrical pattern and the more variable stresses and inflexions of the speaking voice. Sometimes there will be no difference since the poet may have arranged the language so that all the syllables that would normally carry the stress in speaking coincide with the regular beats required by a duple or triple metre but, as we suggest in **Ch.2**, the metrical beat need not be an inflexible grid which forces every syllable into its allotted space by dominating the natural speech patterns, particularly in iambic pentameters. For this reason we often need to indicate or analyse the natural stress patterns of the spoken language separately from the metrical beats and offbeats, as we did with the 'To be or not to be . . .' soliloquy from *Hamlet* (see **Ch.2**). It is therefore important to make a distinction between 'rhythm' (looser and more natural) and 'metre' (more controlled and regular). The new prosody we use in this book makes a distinction between metrical beat and linguistic **stress**. Stressed syllables are a feature of normal usage and are (mostly) determined by the physiology of the human speech organs and by custom, though they may change over time; the metrical beat is a regular and recurrent feature of verse which can be organised into patterns that determine line length and verse form. Where the required beat does not coincide with the normally stressed syllable of a word in received pronunciation, we describe the required adjustments as 'stress promotion' or 'demotion'. Traditional prosody would talk in terms of a 'reversed foot' (i.e. normally **trochee**: ‾ ˘ for an expected iamb: ˘ ‾) or 'spondaic substitution' (**spondee**: ‾ ‾ for an expected iamb: ˘ ‾).

rising rhythm a poetic rhythm whose units 'rise' in stress from an unstressed syllable or syllables to a stressed syllable; cf. **falling rhythm**.

romance narrative **genre** (in verse or prose) featuring stories of chivalry, adventure and love usually involving knightly protagonists engaged in purely fictional rather than strictly historical or legendary exploits (cf. **epic**). Originated in later Middle Ages in France; English examples include Arthurian material, *Sir Gawayne and the Green Knight* (late C14), *Floire et Blancheflor* (*c.* 1150), *King Horn* (*c.* 1225). Italian renaissance successors such as Ariosto, *Orlando Furioso* (1516) were the models for most subsequent examples, including Spenser's *Faerie Queene* (1596–1609). In C19 the romance underwent a revival, especially in Keats's and Tennyson's poetry.

rondeau thirteen-line fixed form, normally divided into three stanzas of 5 + 3 + 5 lines but using only two rhyme sounds, and with the refrain in lines 9 and 15 circling back to the opening words of the poem and known as the *rentrement* (R): *aabba aabR aabbaR*:

> If it be so that I forsake thee
> As banished from thy company,
> Yet my heart, my mind, and mine affection
> Shall still remain in thy perfection,
> And right as thou list so order me.   5
>   But some would say in their opinion
>   Revulsed is my good intention.
>   Then may I well blame thy cruelty
>   If it be so.
> But myself I say on this fashion: 10
> I have her heart in my possession,

> And of itself there cannot, perdie,
> By no means love an heartless body;
> And on my faith good is the reason
>   If it be so.   15
>   (Thomas Wyatt, *c.* 1540)

satire comic writing (in poetry, prose or drama) that sets out to condemn vice or folly; particularly associated with C18 neoclassical poetry, where it is often the subgenre known as **mock epic**.

scansion analysis of patterns of stress and rhyme in poetry.

sestet stanza of six lines, also used to refer to the final six lines of the **sonnet**, particularly Italian sonnet where they are interlinked by different rhymes from those used in the **octave**.

sestina fixed form characterised by end-word repetition, not **rhyme**, each of the six key-words at line endings being repeated in a six-fold permutation over six stanzas, plus a final three-line *envoi* using two of the key-words in each line: *ABCDEF FAEBDC CFDABE ECBFAD DEACFB BDFECA (BE/DC/FA)*. Perhaps the most complicated of fixed forms and most difficult to write, the sestina originated in late C12 troubadour literature. Modern poets continue to rise to the challenge, e.g. Anthony Hecht in his 'Sestina d'Inverno' (see Chapter 17, exercise 1).

Shakespearean sonnet see **sonnet**.

simile rhet. figure in which one thing is explicitly compared to another on the basis of some similarity; simile is akin to **metaphor** but is really a comparison rather than a figure; when Byron's **speaker** says that his beloved 'walks in beauty, like the night / Of cloudless climes and starry skies' (1815) we are invited to imagine what the night and the woman's beauty have in common.

sonnet fourteen-line single **stanza** poem, normally rhymed: *abab cdcd efef gg* ('Shakespearian' or 'English' sonnet) or: *abba abba cde cde* ('Petrarchan' or 'Italian' sonnet). Other **rhyme schemes** are commonly found, of which only 'Spenserian' is generally recognised or widely imitated: *abab bcbc cdcd ee*. Normal to refer to the first two quatrains of a sonnet as the **octave**, and the concluding six lines (however they are rhymed) as the **sestet**. The shift between the octave and the sestet is called the **turn** or **volta**, and is often accompanied by a shift in the poem's mood or argument. See **Ch.12**.

speaker term used to distinguish the often fictional speaker of a poem from the person who wrote it; cf. **persona**, **speech situation**, and see **Ch.7**.

speech situation term used to describe and analyse the way many poems can be understood as speech acts carried out by explicit or implicit fictional **speakers** in particular situations and addressed to fictional **addressees**; often, working out the speech situation (who is speaking to whom and why?) is the most effective way of beginning to understand a poem.

Spenserian stanza stanza first used in Spenser's *The Faerie Queene* (1590); eight iambic **pentameters** plus a final **alexandrine**, rhymed: *ababbcbcc*. Spenser uses this complex **rhyme scheme** and **stanza** form to tell a lengthy narrative; most later poems which use this verse form also use it to tell extended narratives, as in Byron's *Childe Harold's Pilgrimage* (1812) and Shelley's *Revolt of Islam* (1818) and *Adonais* (1821); cf. **ottava rima** and **rhyme royal** on which Spenser is thought to have modelled his new metre.

spondee name in classical **prosody** for a metrical **foot** consisting of two stressed syllables or, in Latin, two long ones, and scanned: / / (*tum-tum*, as in 'see through'). This metrical term (not used in the new metrics), is most likely to be used by traditional critics to describe a moment when, in **duple metre**, what should be an unstressed syllable carries greater weight, and hence what classical metrics would describe as an iamb looks more like a spondee, e.g. the last two syllables of the line from *Paradise Lost* which we quoted in **Ch.2**: 'Silence, ye troubl'd waves, and thou deep, peace' (VII, 217). The first two syllables in this line ('Silence') have a different, but very common, type of stress promotion/demotion which traditional prosody calls a 'reversed foot', **trochee** (/ ˘) for **iamb** (˘ /) which captures the imperative mood. See **foot**.

stanza a poem is written in stanzas when it is divided up into groups of equal numbers of lines arranged according to a fixed scheme depending in nearly all cases on the pattern of end-rhymes (in discussing poetry, 'stanza' is used in preference to **verse**), although also note the difference between stanzas and **verse paragraphs**. A poet may well invent or improvise an original, one-off **rhyme scheme** or **stanza form** for a poem, but many stanza forms have become common or conventional and they have names which you may be expected to know and recognise (see stanza forms). Fixed forms will often, though not always, also specify **metre** and line length; stanzas consisting of lines all the same length are called 'isometric', those with lines of different lengths are 'heterometric'.

stanza forms we offer here a finder's guide to the most common stanza forms in English poetry so that you can tell whether any poem you are reading is using one of them. To identify your stanza form: 1) count the number of lines in each **stanza**; 2) work out the **rhyme scheme**; 3) if necessary work out the **metre**. Then see if these correspond to any of the following stanza forms. Where no metre or line length is specified below that is because it is not conventionally fixed. If once you have identified your verse form you need to know more, look it up under its name elsewhere in this Glossary, where we normally offer examples. One form, the **rondeau**, totalling (usually) thirteen lines divided 5 + 3 + 5 does not fit this scheme, and should be looked up separately in the present Glossary. Two-line units (**couplets**) are not usually divided into stanzas, but rather made up into longer **verse paragraphs** and for this reason are not included here.

3-line stanza (tercet)

triplet three successive lines with the same rhyme: *aaa*.

terza rima successive stanzas linked by rhyme: *aba bcb cdc ded*.

villanelle six three-line stanzas with two alternating **refrains**, plus a concluding four-line stanza using both refrains (refrains marked here as numbered capitals): *A1bA2 abA1 abA2 abA1 abA2 abA1A2*.

haiku unrhymed single-stanza poem based on Japanese models; in English haiku line length is determined by syllable-count not stress pattern – typically 5 + 7 + 5 syllables per line.

4-line stanza (quatrain)

ballad metre four-beat lines alternating with three-beat lines, rhymed: *abcb*

pantoum Malayan poetic form (*pantun*) which came into English poetry through France: consists of variable number of four-line stanzas rhyming *abab* in which the second and fourth lines of the first quatrain become the first and third lines of the next, and so on; in the last quatrain the unrepeated first and third lines are used in reverse as second and fourth lines; a number of contemporary poets have used the form.

5-line stanza

limerick two three-beat lines, plus two two-beat lines, plus one three-beat line, all in triple metre, rhymed *aabba*. See **Ch.11**.

6-line stanza (sestet)

sestina fixed form characterised by end-word repetition, not rhyme, each of the six key-words at line endings being repeated in a six-fold permutation over six stanzas, plus a final three-line *envoi* using two of the key-words in each line: *ABCDEF FAEBDC CFDABE ECBFAD DEACFB BDFECA (BE/DC/FA)*.

7-line stanza

rhyme royal seven iambic pentameter lines rhymed *ababbcc*.

8-line stanzas (octets/octaves)

ballade made up of stanzas of eight four-beat lines with a refrain, with concluding four-line *envoi* (refrain marked with capital): *ababbcbC* and the envoi: *bcbC*.

ottava rima eight **iambic pentameter** lines rhymed *abababcc*.

triolet eight-line single stanza form using only two rhymes and a fixed pattern of repeated lines (indicated here by capital letters): *ABaAabAB*.

9-line stanza

Spenserian stanza eight **iambic pentameters**, plus a final **alexandrine**, rhymed: *ababbcbcc.*

stress relative emphasis on stressed and unstressed syllables in pronunciation that constitutes poetic **rhythm**. See **accent**.

syllable a word or distinct part of a word that is formed by a single effort of the speech organs; a syllable centres on a vowel sound and a single vowel may form a syllable or even a one-syllable word: 'a' and 'I' are words in English; more often, a syllable begins and/or ends with consonant clusters, as in 'ant', 'rant', and so on; multisyllabic words may be broken down into separate syllables: ranting = ran + ting; the ability to see how words are made up of syllables is crucial to the analysis of poetic **rhythm** and **metre**.

symbol in general, any thing that stands for or represents something else, so the term can include virtually any signifier, token or sign in any medium (painting, statuary, road signs, commercial logos, etc.). In poetry, however, the term is best reserved for particular types of imagery or **metaphor**. These include, first, the traditional symbols of inherited belief systems, especially religious ones: in Christian **iconography** such symbols as the cross, fish, dove, rainbow, etc. have well-established theological or doctrinal meanings on which poets can draw. Secular cultural or political practices also develop such iconographies, as when a political regime adopts heraldic devices and **emblems** – the Tudor rose or the Nazi swastika. The religious use of symbols was perhaps the main influence on modern theories of poetic symbolism which, at least since the Romantic movement (late C18–mid C19), have tried to claim a quasi-religious role for poetry through its use of symbols. Although consisting of images drawn from the physical or material world, poetic symbols in Romantic theory and poetry are felt to penetrate some deeper spiritual or metaphysical realities, which may not be conventionally religious nor correspond to any established doctrine. The poetry of William Blake (1757–1827) perhaps offers one of the earliest and most powerful examples of this type of poetic symbolism and justifications of its use. The later C19 **Symbolist Movement** shared much of this epistemology, to which it added the strong conviction that, unlike ordinary signs, poetic symbols are autotelic and unparaphraseable – i.e., what they stand for cannot be abstracted or separated from the poem itself; unlike metaphor, the poetic symbol is thus a **vehicle** without a **tenor**, or which is also its own tenor. Symbolist theory is logically and philosophically problematic, though poetically productive, and influenced many C20 poets, such as W.B. Yeats, together with theories of poetry which were highly influential on the 'New Criticism' of the 1940s–1960s; cf. **image**, **allegory**.

Symbolist Movement poetic movement or style which gives its name to the theory of literature sometimes referred to as 'Symbolism'. Originating in France with poets Charles Baudelaire (1821–67) and Stephane Mallarmé (1842–95), who supplied much of its theory as well as its stylistic models, it influenced English Modernist practitioners such as W.B. Yeats (1865–1939) and T.S. Eliot (1888–1965). A taste for poems developing images with an aura of indefinable suggestibility, in which verbal **tone**, sound, **connotation** and feeling play a large part, led Baudelaire and Mallarmé to distinguish the poetic **symbol** from religious symbols, insofar as the aura of suggestion surrounding the poetic symbol could not be tied down to any reference – natural or supernatural – outside the poem itself. Unlike ordinary symbols, poetic symbols refer to something which only comes into existence within the poem; in this sense, they are self-referential, which means they are not really symbols at all. The fact that they can only be created, or evoked, by poetic language gives poetry a unique epistemological status, which influenced C20 assumptions about 'creativity' (this is what poetry creates, rather than what it is 'about' or what it refers to), and which has been highly influential on poetics and criticism. It is often the subtlest nuances of sound, tone, feeling and connotation that, in a Symbolist poem or a Symbolist reading, create the precise aura of meaning and suggestion surrounding the symbol; for this reason such poems have often attracted teachers intent on developing their students' capacity to respond to such things through close reading or 'practical criticism'. In Yeats's 'The Wild Swans at Coole' (1917), for example, the swans are at once 'real' swans and implicitly symbolic ('Mysterious and beautiful').

synecdoche rhet. substitution of part for whole, e.g. 'lend a hand'.

tenor term used in analysing **metaphor**, q.v.

tercet three-line verse unit or **stanza**, however rhymed, hence including interlinked stanzas of *terza rima* or of **villanelle**; cf. **triplet**.

terza rima fixed form in which successive three-line **stanzas** are linked by **rhyme:** *aba bcb cdc ded*, most famously invented by Dante as the metre for his *Divina Commedia* (early C14).

tetrameter in classical **prosody** the name for verse line of four feet; English verse with four beats, cf. **octosyllabic**, and see **Ch.2**.

tone term used to describe the attitude of a poem's **speaker** towards the **addressee**, the issue being talked about, or sometimes towards himself or herself.

topos Gk. 'place, commonplace' (plural *topoi*); rhet. a commonplace idea or argument, often proverbial, shared by many writers or borrowed as a topic for imitation from one of the ancients by later writers or for composition exercises by students in the schoolroom; e.g. in an **elegy** you could (and many traditional poets did) say, 'May the grass grow greener on this grave'; or in a satire you could argue that the modern world is upside-down; or to praise the achievement of peace after a victory you could declare that bees will now make their hives in the unused helmets; cf. **emblem**. When Pope, in the passage from *An Essay on Criticism* (1709/11) that we cited in **Ch.10**, p. 304, writes 'A vile Conceit in pompous words expressed, / Is like a Clown in regal Purple drest' he is reworking a *topos* which is frequently found in **emblem** books showing an ape dressed like a king, *simius in purpura* ('the ape in purple'). Traditional ('neoclassical') poets often exercise their ingenuity ('invention') in finding new ways of expressing such borrowed topics; see Curtius, *European Literature and the Latin Middle Ages*.

triolet eight-line single **stanza form** using only two **rhymes** and a fixed pattern of repeated lines (indicated here by capital letters): *ABaAabAB*. Not common in English poetry, it was invented by medieval French poets and only used in English by a few late-Victorian and Edwardian versifiers, though its difficulty has some-times rescued it from being dismissed as merely polite, light verse. W.E. Henley offers the most often quoted example:

> Easy is the triolet,
> If you really learn to make it!
> Once a neat refrain you get,
> Easy is the triolet.
> As you see! – I pay my debt
> With another rhyme. Deuce take it,
> Easy is the triolet,
> If you really learn to make it!

triple metre verse form in which the repeated beat-offbeat pattern of the metre is produced by groups of three-syllable units.

triplet three successive lines rhyming *aaa*, not often found as a **stanza form** but occasionally inserted into C18 **heroic couplets** to provide momentary variation or amplification. Do not confuse with **tercet**, which is any three-line verse unit.

trochee name in classical **prosody** for a metrical **foot** consisting of a stressed fol-lowed by an unstressed syllable or, in Latin, long syllable plus short syllable, corre-sponding to what the new metrics calls 'falling duple metre, and scanned: / ˘ (*tum-tee*, as in 'metre'). See **foot**.

turn a distinctive change in the argument or mood of a poem, particularly a **sonnet**; also called a **volta**.

typography the way a poem's words are laid out on the page (including use of capitalisation); it can be significant especially in **free verse** and in **concrete poetry** (or pattern poetry); in other **genres** it may not be wholly under the control of the poet, but have more to do with the printer's house style and thus may vary from one edition to another. The poet seldom has much control over indentation and line-spacing, so beware of ascribing too much significance to accidents of typography. Avoid such comments as: 'The fact that the poet has inserted a space between the octave and sestet of this sonnet emphasises its speaker's change of heart at the volta'; the speaker's change of heart at the volta may be an intrinsic part of the sonnet, while the space might be inserted by the printer. See **personification**.

vehicle term used in analysing **metaphor**.

verse term used in opposition to 'prose'; at its most basic level the distinction between verse and prose is a question of **typography**: verse is set out in lines, whereas prose is not. Thus verse is sometimes used as a synonym for poetry (as in the titles of collections of 'verse'). But we might also say that poetry is written in verse – that is, set out in lines. Although verse is a typographical feature of poetry, it also sometimes carries a value judgement: all poetry is written in verse (in Chapter 2, we rejected the idea of prose poetry), but not all verse (some critics say) is poetry (would you claim that the verses in commercial Valentine cards are poetry?). Whereas songs may be divided into verses, poems are divided either into **stanzas** or into **verse paragraphs**.

verse form see **stanza forms**.

verse paragraph division of verse, especially **blank verse**, into sections of irregular numbers of lines according to the meaning (rather than using a fixed **stanza** pattern) – in much the same way that prose is divided into paragraphs.

vers libre French term for **free verse**.

villanelle six three-line **stanzas** with only two **rhyme sounds** throughout and two alternating **refrains**, plus a concluding four-line stanza using both refrains (refrains marked here as numbered capitals): *A1bA2 abA1 abA2 abA1 abA2 abA1A2*. Verse form originating in C16 France, revived and formalised in C19 with numerous C20 successors of which the best known is probably Dylan Thomas's **elegy** on his father (1952), a poem in a fixed form which forcefully challenges the assumption that sincerity demands simple rather than complex or artificial forms:

> Do not go gentle into that good night,
> Old age should burn and rave at close of day;
> Rage, rage against the dying of the light.
>
> Though wise men at their end know dark is right,
> Because their words had forked no lightning they
> Do not go gentle into that good night.
>
> Good men, the last wave by, crying how bright
> Their frail deeds might have danced in a green bay,
> Rage, rage against the dying of the light.
>
> Wild men who caught and sang the sun in flight,
> And learn, too late, they grieved it on its way,
> Do not go gentle into that good night.
>
> Grave men, near to death, who see with blinding sight
> Blind eyes could blaze like meteors and be gay,
> Rage, rage against the dying of the light.

> And you, my father, there on the sad height,
> Curse, bless, me now with your fierce tears, I pray.
> Do not go gentle into that good night.
> Rage, rage against the dying of the light.

volta a distinctive change in the argument or mood of a **sonnet**, where it normally takes place at the shift between the **octave** and the **sestet** and may be signalled by a change in the **rhyme scheme** and by words such as 'yet' or 'but'; also called a **turn**.

zeugma rhet. Gk. 'yoking together'; normally two words that are grammatically linked to a third but in different ways, e.g. Pope's 'Or stain her honour, or her new brocade' (*Rape of the Lock*, II: 107); the two kinds of staining in this lines are **parallel** but not equivalent.

Key to Poems and Passages Discussed or Used for Exercises

For page nos see Index

Costello, Elvis	'Peace In Our Time' (1984)
Cummings, E.E.	'Me up at does' (1963); 'O sweet spontaneous . . .' (1923); 'somewhere i have never travelled, gladly beyond' (1931)
Dabydeen, David	'Slave Song' (1984)
Daniel, Samuel	'Ulysses and the Siren' (1605)
Dante Alighieri	'The power of love borne in my lady's eyes' (*c.* 1292–1300)
Dickinson, Emily	'I heard a Fly buzz – when I died' (*c.* 1862); 'I think I was Enchanted' (*c.* 1862)
Donne, John	'A Valediction: Forbidding Mourning' (1633); 'At the round earth's imagin'd corners' (1633); 'The Flea' (1633)
Doolittle, Hilda	'Sea Rose' (1916)
Duffy, Carol Ann	'Boy' (1990)
Eliot, T.S.	'The Love Song of J. Alfred Prufrock' (1917)
Gray, Thomas	'Ode: On a Distant Prospect of Eton College' (1747), 70–79
Hardy, Thomas	'In a Wood' (1896); 'The Darkling Thrush' (1901)
Heaney, Seamus	'Punishment' (1975)
Hecht, Anthony	'Sestina d'Inverno' (1977)
Herbert, George	'Easter Wings' (1633); 'Mortification' (1633); 'Redemption' (1633)
Hill, Geoffrey	'September Song' (1968)
Hollander, John	'Swan and Shadow' (1967)
Homer,	*The Iliad* (*c.* 750 BC)
Hopkins, Gerard Manley	'God's Grandeur' (1877); 'Heaven-Haven' (1865–66)
Hughes, Langston	'The Negro Speaks of Rivers' (1926); 'Theme for English B' (1951); 'Harlem' (1951)
Hughes, Ted	'The Thought-Fox' (1957)
Johnson, Samuel	*The Vanity of Human Wishes*, 1–6 (1749)
Jonson, Ben	'To the Memory of my Beloved, the Author Mr William Shakespeare' (1623)
Kay, Jackie	'In My Country' (1993)
Keats, John	'La Belle Dame sans Merci' (1820); 'Ode to a Nightingale' (1819); 'Ode to Psyche' (1820); 'If by dull rhymes our English must be chain'd' (1819)
Koch, Kenneth	'Variations on a Theme by William Carlos Williams' (1962); 'My Olivetti Speaks' (1998)
Lowell, Robert	'The Drinker' (1964)
MacCaig, Norman	'Fetching Cows' (1965)
MacDiarmid Hugh	'In the Children's Hospital' (1935)

MacLeish, Archibald	'Ars Poetica' (1926)
Martinez, James	'Dis Time No Stan' Like Befo' Time' (1920)
Marvell, Andrew	'An Horatian Ode upon Cromwell's Return from Ireland' (1650)
Miles, Josephine	'Reason' (1956)
Millay, Edna St Vincent	'I dreamed I moved among the Elysian fields' (1930); 'Spring' (1920)
Milton, John,	*Paradise Lost* (1667), II, 910–20; III, 37–38; III, 123–26; VII, 210–17; XII, 646–49; V, 856–60; 'When I consider how my light is spent' (*c.* 1652)
Morgan, Edwin	'Glasgow Sonnets, X' (1972)
Morris, William	'The Haystack in the Floods' (1858)
Muir, Edwin	'Childhood' (1925)
Nichols, Grace	'I have crossed an ocean' (1983)
Nortje, Arthur	'Waiting' (1973)
O'Rourke, Daniel	'Great Western Road' (1994)
Owen, Wilfred	'Strange Meeting' (1919)
Petrarch, Francesco	'Lord Love, who holds the chief place in my mind' (*c.* 1350)
Pope, Alexander	*An Essay on Criticism* (1709), 215–18, 297–336, 219–32, 318–19
Pound, Ezra	'In a Station of the Metro' (1916); *Canto I* (1921)
Rich, Adrienne	'Orion' (1965), 'Song' (1973)
Roethke, Theodore	'Elegy for Jane' (1953)
Rossetti, Christina	'Up-Hill' (1858); 'Winter: My Secret' (1866)
Sexton, Anne	'The Abortion' (1962)
Shakespeare, William	Sonnet 18: 'Shall I compare thee to a summer's day?' (1609); Sonnet 29: 'When in disgrace with fortune and men's eyes' (1609); Sonnet 73: 'That time of year thou mayst in me behold' (1609); Sonnet 130: 'My mistress' eyes are nothing like the sun' (1609); Sonnet 138: 'When my love swears that she is made of truth'; *Hamlet* III.i: 'To be, or not to be . . .'; *Rape of Lucrece*, lines 1723–29 (1594)
Shelley, Percy Bysshe	'Ode to the West Wind' (1820); 'Ozymandias' (1818)
Sidney, Sir Philip	'Loving in truth, and fain in verse my love to show' (1591)
Simic, Charles	'The Garden of Earthly Delights' (1974)
Smith, Charlotte	'Sonnet: Composed during a Walk on the Downs, in November 1787'
Smith, Stevie	'Not Waving But Drowning' (1957)
Soutar, William	'He Who Weeps for Beauty Gone' (1930)

Bibliography

Aarsleff, Hans, *From Locke to Saussure: Essays on the study of language and intellectual history* (Minneapolis: University of Minnesota Press, 1982).

Abrams, M.H., *The Mirror and the Lamp: Romantic theory and the critical tradition* (Oxford: Oxford University Press, 1953).

Abrams, M.H., 'The Deconstructive Angel', *Critical Inquiry* 3 (1977), reprinted in Lodge, ed., *Modern Criticism and Theory*, pp. 265–76.

Abrams, M.H. 'Construing and Deconstructing', in Eaves and Fischer, eds, *Romanticism and Contemporary Criticism* (Ithaca, NY: Cornell University Press, 1986), pp. 127–82.

Abrams, M.H., *Doing things with Texts: Essays in criticism and critical theory* (New York: Norton, 1989).

Abrams, M.H., *A Glossary of Literary Terms*, 6th edn (New York: Harcourt Brace Jovanovich, 1993).

Addison, Joseph, *Critical Essays from the Spectator*, ed. Donald F. Bond (Oxford: Oxford University Press 1970).

Adorno, Theodor, *Prisms: Cultural criticism and society*, trans. S. Weber (London: N. Spearman, 1967).

Allison, A.W. *et al.*, eds, *The Norton Anthology of Poetry: Third Edition* (New York: W.W. Norton, 1983).

Allnutt, Gillian, F. D'Aguiar, K. Edwards and E. Mottron, eds, *The New British Poetry, 1968–88* (London: Paladin, 1988).

Allott, Miriam, ed., *The Poems of John Keats* (Harlow: Longman, 1970).

Appiah, Kwame A., 'Race', in Lentricchia and McLaughlin, eds, *Critical Terms for Literary Study*, pp. 274–87.

Aristotle, *The Art of Rhetoric*, trans. H.C. Lawson Tancred (Harmondsworth: Penguin, 1991).

Armstrong, Isobel, *Language as Living Form in Nineteenth-Century Poetry* (Sussex: Harvester, 1982).

Armstrong, Isobel, *Victorian Poetry: Poetry, poetics and politics* (London: Routledge, 1993).

Arrowsmith, Pat, *On the Brink . . .* (London: CND, 1981).

Ashcroft, Bill, Gareth Griffiths and Helen Tiffin, eds, *The Post-Colonial Studies Reader* (London: Routledge, 1995).

Ashcroft, Bill, Gareth Griffiths and Helen Tiffin, *Post-Colonial Studies: The Key Concepts* (Abingdon: Routledge, 1998).

Ashcroft, Bill, Gareth Griffiths and Helen Tiffin, *The Empire Writes Back: Theory and Practice in Post-colonial Literatures*, 2nd edn (London: Routledge, 2002).

Ashfield, Andrew, ed., *Romantic Women Poets, 1770–1838: An anthology* (Manchester: Manchester University Press, 1995).

Attridge, Derek, *The Rhythms of English Poetry* (London: Longman, 1982).

Attridge, Derek, *Peculiar Language: Literature as difference from the Renaissance to James Joyce* (Ithaca, NY: Cornell University Press, 1988).

Attridge, Derek, *Jacques Derrida, Acts of Literature* (New York: Routledge, 1992).

Attridge, Derek, *Poetic Rhythm* (Cambridge: Cambridge University Press, 1995).

Attridge, Derek, 'Performing Metaphors: The Singularity of Literary Figuration', in *Paragraph*, 28, ii (July 2005), 18–34.

Attridge, Derek, A. Durant, N. Fabb and C. McCabe, eds, *The Linguistics of Writing* (Manchester: Manchester University Press, 1987).

Auden, W.H., *Collected Poems*, ed. E. Mendelson (London: Faber & Faber, 1976).

Baer, W., ed., *Conversations with Derek Walcott* (Jackson: University Press of Mississippi, 1996).

Bahti, Timothy, 'Ambiguity and Indeterminacy: The juncture', *Comparative Literature* 38 (1986), pp. 209–23.

Bailey, J.O., *The Poetry of Thomas Hardy: A handbook and commentary* (Chapel Hill, NC: University of North Carolina Press, 1970).

Bakhtin, Mikhail, *The Dialogic Imagination: Four Essays*, ed. Michael Holquist (Austin: University of Texas Press, 1981).

Barrell, John, *Poetry, Language and Politics* (Manchester: Manchester University Press, 1988).

Barrett Browning, Elizabeth, *Aurora Leigh and Other Poems* (London: The Women's Press, 1978).

Barrett Browning, Elizabeth, *Aurora Leigh*, ed. Kerry McSweeney (Oxford: Oxford University Press, 1993).

Barthes, Roland, *Mythologies*, trans. Annette Lavers (London: Granada, 1973).

Barthes, Roland, *Image–Music–Text*, trans. Stephen Heath (London: Fontana, 1977).

Barthes, Roland, *The Semiotic Challenge*, trans. R. Howard (Oxford: Blackwell, 1988).

Bate, Walter Jackson, *The Burden of the Past and the English Poet* (London: Chatto & Windus, 1971).

Bateson, F.W., *English Poetry: A critical introduction* (London: Longman, 1966).

Beer, Gillian, *Darwin's Plots: Evolutionary narrative in Darwin, George Eliot and nineteenth-century fiction* (London: Routledge, 1983).

Bennett, Andrew and N. Royle, *An Introduction to Literature, Criticism and Theory: Key critical concepts* (Hemel Hempstead: Harvester Wheatsheaf, 1995).

Bennett, Tony, *Formalism and Marxism* (London: Methuen, 1979).

Bentley, Richard, ed., *Milton's Paradise Lost: A new edition* (London: 1732).

Bhabha, Homi, *The Location of Culture* (London: Routledge, 1994).

Bloom, Harold, *The Anxiety of Influence* (Oxford: Oxford University Press, 1973).

Bloom, Harold, *A Map of Misreading* (Oxford: Oxford University Press, 1975).

Bloom, Harold, *Poetry and Repression: Revisionism from Blake to Stevens* (New Haven, CT: Yale University Press, 1976).

Bloom, Harold, *Ruin the Sacred Truths: Poetry and belief from the Bible to the present* (Cambridge MA: Harvard University Press, 1989).

Booth, Wayne C., *A Rhetoric of Irony* (Chicago: University of Chicago Press, 1974).

Booth, Wayne C., *Critical Understanding: The powers and limits of pluralism* (Chicago: University of Chicago Press, 1979).

Bradford, Richard, *Silence and Sound: Theories of poetics from the eighteenth century* (London and Toronto: Associated University Presses, 1992).

Bradford, Richard, *A Linguistic History of English Poetry* (London: Routledge, 1993).

Brathwaite, Edward Kamau, *The Arrivants: A New World Trilogy* (Oxford: Oxford University Press, 1967).

Brathwaite, Edward Kamau, *History of the Voice: The Development of Nation Language in Anglophone Caribbean Poetry* (London and Port of Spain: New Beacon Books, 1984).

Breen, Jennifer, ed., *Women Romantic Poets, 1785–1832: An anthology* (London: J.M. Dent, 1992).

Brewer, E.C., *Dictionary of Phrase and Fable* (London, 1870, revised edition London: Cassell, 1981).

Brogan, T.V.F., ed., *The New Princeton Handbook of Poetic Terms* (Princeton, NJ: Princeton University Press, 1994).

Brooks, Cleanth, 'Irony as a Principle of Structure', in Zabel, ed., *Literary Opinion in America*, 3rd edn pp. 729–41.

Brooks, Cleanth, *Modern Poetry and the Tradition* (Chapel Hill: University of North Carolina Press, 1967).

Brooks, Cleanth, *The Well Wrought Urn* (London: Methuen, 1968).

Brooks, Cleanth and R.P. Warren, *Understanding Poetry* (New York: Holt, Rinehart & Winston, 1938).

Brower, Reuben A., *Alexander Pope: The poetry of allusion* (Oxford: Oxford University Press, 1959).

Brown, Eleanor, *Maiden Speech* (Newcastle upon Tyne: Bloodaxe Books, 1996).

Buchbinder, David, *Contemporary Literary Theory and the Reading of Poetry* (London: Macmillan, 1991).

Burnett, Paula, ed., *The Penguin Book of Caribbean Verse in English* (Harmondsworth: Penguin, 1986).

Bush, Douglas, 'Marvell's *Horatian Ode*', in Carey, ed., *Andrew Marvell: A Critical anthology*, pp. 199–210.

Butler, Lance St John, *Registering the Difference: Reading Literature through Register* (Manchester and New York: Manchester University Press, 1999).

Butler, Marilyn, *Romantics, Rebels, and Reactionaries* (Oxford: Oxford University Press, 1981).

Capps, Jack L., *Emily Dickinson's Reading* (Cambridge, MA: Harvard University Press, 1966).

Caraher, Brian G., *Wordsworth's 'Slumber' and the Problematics of Reading* (Pennsylvania: Pennsylvania State University Press, 1991).

Carey, John, ed., *Andrew Marvell: A critical anthology* (Harmondsworth: Penguin, 1969).

Carper, Thomas and Derek Attridge, *Meter and Meaning: An introduction to rhythm in poetry* (London: Routledge, 2003).

Césaire, Aimé, *Cahier dún Retour au Pays Natal / Return to my Native Land*, with a parallel English translation by Emily Snyder and a Preface by André Breton (Paris: Présence Africaine, 1971).

Charles, Amy, ed., *The Williams Manuscript of George Herbert's Poems* (Delmar, NY: Scholars' Facsimiles and Reprints, 1977).

Clayton, Jay and E. Rothstein, eds, *Influence and Intertextuality in Literary History* (Madison: University of Wisconsin Press, 1991).

Coetzee, J.M., *White Writing: On the Culture of Letters in South Africa* (New Haven: Yale University Press, 1988).

Coleridge, Samuel Taylor, *Biographia Literaria: Biographical sketches of my literary life and opinions*, eds James Engell and W. Jackson Bate (Princeton: Princeton University Press, 1983).

Coleridge, Samuel Taylor, *The Oxford Authors: Samuel Taylor Coleridge*, ed. H.J. Jackson (Oxford: Oxford University Press, 1985).

Collins, Billy, *Taking Off Emily Dickinson's Clothes: Selected Poems* (Basingstoke and Oxford: Picador, 2000).

Collier, Peter and Helga Geyer-Ryan, *Literary Theory Today* (London: Polity Press, 1990).

Cook, Jon, ed., *Poetry in Theory: An anthology 1900–2000* (Oxford and Malden, MA: Blackwell, 2004).

Coombes, Orde, ed., *Is Massa Day Dead? Black Moods in the Caribbean* (New York: Doubleday, 1974).

Corcoran, Neil, *A Student's Guide to Seamus Heaney* (London: Faber, 1986).

Corcoran, Neil, *English Poetry Since 1940* (London: Longman, 1993).

Couzens, Tim and E. Patel, eds, *The Return of Amasi Bird: Black South African poetry 1891–1981* (Johannesburg: Raven Press, 1982).

Crabbe, George, *Selected Poems*, ed. Gavin Edwards (London and New York: Penguin, 1991).

Craig, Cairns, ed., *The History of Scottish Literature*, 4 vols (Aberdeen: Aberdeen University Press, 1987–89).

Culler, Jonathan, *Structuralist Poetics: Structuralism, linguistics and the study of literature* (London: Routledge & Kegan Paul, 1975).

Culler, Jonathan, *Saussure* (Glasgow: Fontana, 1976).

Culler, Jonathan, 'Prolegomena to a Theory of Reading', in Suleiman and Crossman, eds, *The Reader in the Text*, pp. 48–61.

Culler, Jonathan, *The Pursuit of Signs: Semiotics, literature, deconstruction* (London: Routledge, 1981).

Culler, Jonathan, ed., *On Puns: The foundation of letters* (Oxford: Blackwell, 1988).

Curran, Stuart, *Poetic Form and British Romanticism* (Oxford: Oxford University Press, 1986).

Curtius, Ernst Robert, *European Literature and the Latin Middle Ages* (Princeton, NJ: Princeton University Press, 1991).

Dabydeen, David, *Slave Song* (Sydney: Dangaroo Press, 1984).

Daiches, David, *A Critical History of English Literature*, 4 vols, 2nd edn (London: Secker & Warburg, 1969).

Dante, *Vita Nuova*, trans. Mark Musa (Oxford and New York: Oxford University Press, 1992).

de Man, Paul, *Allegories of Reading: Figural language in Rousseau, Nietzsche, Rilke, and Proust* (New Haven, CT: Yale University Press, 1979).

de Man, Paul, *Blindness and Insight: Essays in the rhetoric of contemporary criticism*, 2nd edn (London: Routledge, 1983).

Derrida, Jacques, *Of Grammatology*, trans. Gayatri Chakravorty Spivak (Baltimore, MD: Johns Hopkins University Press, 1976).

Derrida, Jacques, *Writing and Difference*, trans. Alan Bass (London: Routledge, 1978).

Derrida, Jacques, *Limited Inc.*, ed. Gerald Graff (Evanston, IL: Northwestern University Press, 1988).

Derrida, Jacques, 'Biodegradables: Seven diary fragments', *Critical Inquiry* 15 (1989), pp. 812–73.

Dickinson, Emily, *The Letters of Emily Dickinson*, ed. Mabel L. Todd (London: Victor Gollancz, 1951).

Dorsch, T. S., trans., *Classical Literary Criticism* (Harmondsworth: Penguin, 1965).

Eagleton, Terry, *Marxism and Literary Criticism* (London: Methuen, 1976).

Eagleton, Terry, *Literary Theory: An introduction* (Oxford: Blackwell, 1983).

Easthope, Antony, *Poetry as Discourse* (London: Methuen, 1983).

Easthope, Antony and J. Thompson, eds, *Contemporary Poetry Meets Modern Theory* (Hemel Hempstead: Harvester Wheatsheaf, 1991).

Eaves, Morris and M. Fischer, eds, *Romanticism and Contemporary Criticism* (Ithaca, NY: Cornell University Press, 1986).

Eliot, T.S., *Selected Prose* (Harmondsworth: Penguin, 1953).

Eliot, T.S., *Selected Prose of T.S. Eliot*, ed. Frank Kermode (London: Faber, 1975).

Elliott, E. *et al.* eds, *Columbia Literary History of the United States* (New York: Columbia University Press, 1988).

Emerson, Ralph Waldo, *Emerson's Essays* (London: Dent, 1971).

Empson, William, *Seven Types of Ambiguity* (London: Penguin, 1961).

Enright, D.J., *The Alluring Problem: An essay on irony* (Oxford: Oxford University Press, 1968).

Erkkila, Betsy, *The Wicked Sisters: Women poets, literary history and discord* (Oxford: Oxford University Press, 1992).

Fanon, Frantz, *The Wretched of the Earth*, trans. Constance Farrington (London: Penguin, 1967).

Fell, Alison *et al. Smile, Smile, Smile, Smile* (London: Sheba Feminist Publishers, 1980).

Fenton, James, *An Introduction to English Poetry* (London and New York: Penguin, 2003).

Ferguson, Margaret, Mary Jo Salter and Jon Stallworthy, eds, *The Norton Anthology of Poetry*, 5th edn (New York and London: Norton, 2004).

Ferguson, Niall, *Empire: How Britain Made the Modern World* (London: Penguin, 2004).

Fish, Stanley, *Surprised by Sin: The reader in Paradise Lost* (New York: St Martin's Press, 1967).

Fish, Stanley 'Interpreting the Variorum', *Critical Inquiry* (1976), reprinted in Lodge, ed., *Modern Criticism and Theory*, pp. 311–29.

Fish, Stanley, *Is There a Text in this Class?* (Cambridge, MA: Harvard University Press, 1980).

Foucault, Michel, *The Order of Things: An archaeology of the human sciences* (London: Tavistock, 1970).

Fowler, Alastair, *Kinds of Literature: An introduction to the theory of genres and modes* (Oxford: Clarendon Press, 1982).

Fowler, Alastair, *A History of English Literature: Forms and kinds from the Middle Ages to the present* (Oxford: Blackwell, 1987).

Freud, Sigmund, *The Interpretation of Dreams*, trans. J. Strachey (Harmondsworth: Penguin, 1976).

Fry, Stephen, *The Ode Less Travelled: Unlocking the poet within* (London: Hutchinson, 2005).

Frye, Northrop, *Anatomy of Criticism* (Princeton, NJ: Princeton University Press, 1957).

Fulrop T.E., and A.J. Raboteau, *African-American Religions: Interpretive Essays in History and Culture* (London: Routledge, 1977).

Fumagalli, Maria, *The Flight of the Vernacular: Seamus Heaney, Derek Walcott and the Impress of Dante* (Amsterdam and New York: Rodophi, 2001).

Furst, Lilian, *Fictions of Romantic Irony in European Narrative, 1760–1857* (London: Macmillan, 1984).

Fussell, Paul, *The Rhetorical World of Augustan Humanism* (Oxford: Oxford University Press, 1965).

Fussell, Paul, *Poetic Meter and Poetic Form* (New York: Random House, 1979).

Gabel, John B., Charles B. Wheeler and Anthony D. York, *The Bible as Literature: An Introduction* (Oxford and New York: Oxford University Press, 2000).

Garber, Frederick, ed., *Romantic Irony* (Budapest: Akademiai Kiado, 1988).

Garfield, Jay L. and P. Hennessey, eds, *Abortion: Moral and legal perspectives* (Amherst: University of Massachusetts Press, 1984).

Gattso, John, ed., *Native America*, 3rd edn (n.p.: APA Insight Guide, 1992).

Gerould, G.H., *The Ballad of Tradition* (Oxford: Oxford University Press, 1957).

Gilbert, Sandra and Susan Gubar, *The Madwoman in the Attic* (New Haven: Yale University Press, 1979).

Gittings, Robert, ed., *The Odes of Keats and Their Earliest Known Manuscripts* (London: Heinemann, 1970).

Gombrich, E.H., *Art and Illusion: A study in the psychology of pictorial representation*, 5th edn (London: Phaidon, 1972).

Gray, Stephen, ed., *The Penguin Book of Southern African Verse* (Harmondsworth: Penguin, 1988).

Greer, G., J. Medoff, M. Sansone and S. Hastings, eds, *Kissing the Rod: An anthology of seventeenth-century women's verse* (London: Virago, 1988).

Grove Day, A., *The Sky Clears: Poetry of the American Indians* (Lincoln: University of Nebraska Press, 1951).

Hamner, Robert D., ed., *Critical Perspectives on Derek Walcott* (Washington DC: Three Continents Press, 1993).

Harold, John, ed., *How Can You Write a Poem when You're Dying of AIDS?* (New York: Bantam Books, 1971).

Hartman, Geoffrey, *Criticism in the Wilderness: The study of literature today* (New Haven, CT: Yale University Press, 1980).

Hawking, Stephen, *A Brief History of Time: From the big bang to black holes* (Toronto: Bantam, 1988).

Healy, Thomas and J. Sawday, eds, *Literature and the English Civil War* (Cambridge: Cambridge University Press, 1990).

Hemans, Felicia, *Records of Woman: With Other Poems*, ed. Paula R. Feldman (Kentucky: University of Kentucky Press, 1999).

Heuman, Gad, *The Caribbean* (London: Hodder Arnold, 2006).

Heywood, Pippa, ed., *Poems for Refugees* (London: Vintage, 2002).

Higginson, W.J. and Penny Harter, *The Haiku Handbook: How to Write, Share, and Teach Haiku* (Tokyo, New York and London: Kodansha, 1985).

Hill, Christopher, *God's Englishman: Oliver Cromwell and the English Revolution* (London: Weidenfeld & Nicolson, 1970).

Hill, Geoffrey, *Collected Poems* (Harmondsworth: Penguin, 1985).

Hirsch, E.D., *Validity in Interpretation* (New Haven, CT: Yale University Press, 1967).

Hobsbawm, Eric, *The Age of Revolution, 1789–1848* (New York: New American Library, 1962).

Hollander, John, *The Figure of Echo: A mode of allusion in Milton and after* (Berkeley: University of California Press, 1981).

Hollander, John, *Rhyme's Reason: A guide to English verse* (New Haven, CT: Yale University Press 1981).

Homer, *The Iliad*, trans. Robert Fitzgerald (Oxford, Oxford University Press, 1984).

Hopkins, Gerard Manley, 'To Robert Bridges' (14 August, 1879), in *Gerard Manley Hopkins: Selected Letters*, ed. Catherine Phillips (Oxford: Clarendon Press, 1990), pp. 126–30.

Hopkins, Gerard Manley, *Poems and Prose*, ed. W.H. Gardner (Harmondsworth: Penguin, 1984).

Hošek, Chaviva and P. Parker, eds, *Lyric Poetry: Beyond the New Criticism* (Ithaca, NY: Cornell University Press, 1985).

Hume, David, *A Treatise of Human Nature*, ed. Ernst C. Mossner (London: Penguin, 1969).

Iser, Wolfgang, 'The Reading Process: A phenomenological approach', *New Literary History* 3 (1972), reprinted in Lodge, ed., *Modern Criticism and Theory*, pp. 211–28.

Iser, Wolfgang, *The Implied Reader: Patterns of Communication in Prose Fiction from Bunyan to Beckett* (Baltimore, MD: Johns Hopkins University Press, 1974).

Iser, Wolfgang, *The Act of Reading: A theory of aesthetic response* (Baltimore, MD: Johns Hopkins University Press, 1978).

Jakobson, Roman, *Language in Literature*, eds K. Pomorska and S. Rudy (Cambridge, MA: Harvard University Press, 1987).

James, C.L.R, *The Black Jacobins: Toussaint L'Ouverture and the San Domingo Revolution* (1938, repr. London: Penguin, 2001).

James, Muriel and D. Jongeward, *Born To Win: Transactional analysis with Gestalt experiments* (New York: Signet, 1978).

Jarvis, Robin, *Wordsworth, Milton and the Theory of Poetic Relations* (London: Macmillan, 1991).

Jefferson, Ann and D. Robey, *Modern Literary Theory: A comparative introduction*, 2nd edn (London: Batsford, 1986).

Jeffries, Lesley, *The Language of Twentieth-Century Poetry* (London: Macmillan, 1993).

Johnson, Barbara, *A World of Difference*, 2nd edn (Baltimore, MD: Johns Hopkins University Press, 1989).

Jones, Edmund D., ed., *English Critical Essays: Nineteenth century* (London: Oxford University Press, 1950).

Jones, Peter, ed., *Imagist Poetry* (Harmondsworth: Penguin, 1972).

Keats, John, *The Poems of John Keats*, ed. Miriam Allott (London: Longman, 1970; New York: Norton, 1972).

Keats, John, *Letters of John Keats, A Selection*, ed. Robert Gittings (Oxford: Oxford University Press, 1975).

Kennedy, X.J. and Dana Gioia, *An Introduction to Poetry*, 11th edn (London and New York: Longman, 2004).

Kermode, Frank, ed., *The Living Milton: Essays by various hands* (London: Routledge & Kegan Paul, 1960).

Kinsley, James, *The Oxford Book of Ballads* (Oxford: Oxford University Press, 1989).

Knoepflmacher, U.C. and G.B. Tennyson, eds, *Nature and the Victorian Imagination* (Berkeley: University of California Press, 1977).

Kolodny, Annette 'A Map for Rereading: Or, gender and the interpretation of literary texts', in *New Literary History: A journal of theory and interpretation* 11 (1990), pp. 451–67, 587–92.

Kristeva, Julia, *Desire in Language: A semiotic approach to literature and art* (New York: Columbia University Press, 1980).

Kuhn, Thomas S., *The Structure of Scientific Revolutions* (Chicago: University of Chicago Press, 1970).

Lakoff, George and M. Johnson, *Metaphors We Live By* (Chicago: University of Chicago Press, 1980).

Langbaum, Robert, *The Poetry of Experience: The dramatic monologue in modern literary tradition* (Chicago: University of Chicago Press, 1957).

Leavis, F.R., *Revaluation: Tradition and development in English poetry* (London: Penguin, 1964).

Leavis, F.R., *New Bearings in English Poetry* (London: Penguin, 1971).

Leech, Geoffrey, *A Linguistic Guide to English Poetry* (London: Longman, 1969).

Leitch, Vincent B. *et al.*, eds, *The Norton Anthology of Theory and Criticism* (New York and London: Norton, 2001).

Lennard, John, *The Poetry Handbook* (Oxford: Oxford University Press, 2005).

Lentricchia, Frank and T. McLaughlin, eds, *Critical Terms for Literary Study* (Chicago: University of Chicago Press, 1990).

Levin, Phillis, ed., *The Penguin Book of the Sonnet: 500 years of a classic tradition in English* (London: Penguin, 2001).

Levine, George, *Darwin and the Novelists: Patterns of science in Victorian fiction* (Cambridge, MA: Harvard University Press, 1988).

Locke, John, *An Essay Concerning Human Understanding*, ed. Peter H. Nidditch (Oxford: Oxford University Press, 1984).

Lodge, David, ed., *Twentieth Century Literary Criticism: A reader* (London: Longman, 1972).

Lodge, David, ed., *Modern Criticism and Theory: A reader* (London: Longman, 1988).

Lyons, John and I. Forster, trans., *Poems of Love and Revolution from the Nicaraguan Poetry Workshops, bilingual edition* (London: Nicaraguan Solidarity Campaign, 1983).

Lyotard, Jean-François, *The Postmodern Condition: A report on knowledge*, trans. Geoff Bennington and Brian Massumi (Manchester: Manchester University Press, 1984).

McEwen, Christian, ed., *Naming the Waves: Contemporary lesbian poetry* (London: Virago, 1988).

Macherey, Pierre, *A Theory of Literary Production* (London: Routledge & Kegan Paul, 1978).

Mahood, M., *Shakespeare's Wordplay* (London: Methuen, 1957).

Mandela, Nelson, *Long Walk to Freedom* (London: Little, Brown & Co., 1994).

Mannheim, Karl, *Ideology and Utopia: An introduction to the sociology of knowledge* (New York: Harcourt Brace, 1964).

Markham, E.A., ed., *Hinterland: Caribbean Poetry from the West Indies and Britain* (Northumberland: Bloodaxe, 1989).

Marks, Elaine and I. de Courtivron, eds, *New French Feminisms* (Sussex: Harvester, 1981).

Matthews, G.M., ed., *Keats: The critical heritage* (London: Routledge, 1971).

Mellor, Anne K., *English Romantic Irony* (Cambridge, MA: Harvard University Press, 1980).

Mercer, Derrik, ed., *Chronicle of the Twentieth Century* (London: Dorling Kindersley, 1995).

Mill, John Stuart, *Essays on Poetry*, ed. F. Parvin Sharpless (Columbia: University of South Carolina Press, 1976).

Miller, J. Hillis, 'On Edge: The crossways of contemporary criticism', in Eaves and Fischer, eds, *Romanticism and Contemporary Criticism*, pp. 96–126.

Moers, Ellen, *Literary Women* (London: The Women's Press, 1978).

Montefiore, Jan, *Feminism and Poetry: Language, experience, identity in women's writing* (London: Pandora, 1987).

Montgomery, M., A. Durant, N. Fabb, T. Furniss and S. Mills, *Ways of Reading: Advanced reading skills for students of English literature*, 3rd edn (London: Routledge, 2007).

Moore-Gilbert, Bart, Ganeth Stanton and Willy Maley, eds, *Postcolonial Criticism* (London: Longman, 1997).

Morley, Jefferson, 'Rap Music as American History', introduction to Lawrence A. Stanley, ed., *Rap: The lyrics* (Harmondsworth: Penguin, 1992).

Muecke, D.C., *The Compass of Irony* (London: Methuen, 1969).

Muecke, D.C., *Irony* (London: Methuen, 1970).

Murray, David, ed., *Literary Theory and Poetry: Extending the canon* (London: Batsford, 1989).

Niatum, Duane, ed., *Harper's Anthology of 20th Century Native American Poetry* (New York: Harper Collins, 1988).

Nichols, Grace, *I is a long memoried woman* (London: Caribbean Cultural International, 1983).

Nietzsche, Friedrich, *The Portable Nietzsche*, ed. Walter Kaufmann (New York: Viking Penguin, 1954).

Nowottny, Winifred, *The Language Poets Use* (London: The Athlone Press, 1962).

Opie, Iona and Peter Opie, eds, *The Oxford Book of Children's Verse* (Oxford and New York: Oxford University Press, 1973).

O'Rourke, Daniel, ed., *Dream State: The new Scottish poets* (Edinburgh: Polygon, 1994).

Owen, Wilfred, *The Poems of Wilfred Owen*, ed. Jon Stallworthy (London: Chatto & Windus, 1990).

Parker, Michael, *Seamus Heaney: The making of the poet* (Basingstoke: Macmillan, 1993).

Parrott, E.O., ed., *The Penguin Book of Limericks* (Harmondsworth: Penguin, 1983).

Parry, Graham, *The Seventeenth Century: The intellectual and cultural context of English literature 1603–1700* (London: Longman, 1989).

Paschen, Elise, ed., *Poetry Speaks to Children* (Naperville, ILL: Sourcebooks, 2005).

Patke, Rajeev S., *Postcolonial Poetry in English* (Oxford and New York: Oxford University Press, 2006).

Peirce, Charles S., 'On the Algebra of Logic: A Contribution to the Philosophy of Notation' (1885), in *Writings of Charles S. Peirce: A Chronological Edition, Volume 5, 1884–1886*, ed. Christian J.W. Kloesel, *et al.* (Bloomington and Indianapolis: Indiana University Press, 1993), pp. 162–90.

Perrine, Laurence, *Sound and Sense*, 2nd edn (New York: Harcourt Brace Jovanovich, 1963).

Petrarch, Francesco, *Canzoniere*, trans. J.G. Nichols (Manchester: Carcanet, 2000).

Pirie, David B., ed., *The Romantic Period* (Harmondsworth: Penguin, 1994).

Philip, Neil, ed., *The New Oxford Book of Children's Verse* (Oxford and New York: Oxford University Press, 1996).

Pocock, J.G.A., *Virtue, Commerce and History: Essays on political thought and history, chiefly in the eighteenth century* (Cambridge: Cambridge University Press, 1985).

Pope, Alexander, *The Poems of Alexander Pope*, ed. John Butt (London: Methuen, 1963).

Preminger, Alex and T.V.F. Brogan, eds, *The New Princeton Encyclopedia of Poetry and Poetics* (Princeton, NJ: Princeton University Press, 1993).

Prickett, Stephen, ed., *The Romantics* (London: Methuen, 1981).

Princeton, see Preminger.

Ramazani, Jahan, *The Hybrid Muse: Postcolonial Poetry in English* (Chicago: University of Chicago Press, 2001).

Randall, Dudley, ed., *The Black Poets* (New York: Bantam Books, 1971).

Reeves, Marjorie and J. Worsley, eds, *Favourite Hymns: 2000 Years of Magnificat* (London and New York: Continuum, 2001).

Rich, Adrienne, *On Lies, Secrets, and Silence* (New York: Norton, 1979).

Rich, Adrienne, *Blood, Bread, and Poetry: Selected prose, 1979–1985* (London: Virago, 1987).

Richards, I.A., *The Philosophy of Rhetoric* (New York: Oxford University Press, 1965).

Richards, I.A., *Principles of Literary Criticism* (London: Routledge, 1967).

Ricks, Christopher, *Milton's Grand Style* (Oxford: Oxford University Press, 1963).

Ricks, Christopher, 'A Pure Organic Pleasure from the Lines', *Essays in Criticism* 21 (1971), 1–32, repr. in Ricks, *The Force of Poetry*, pp. 89–116.

Ricks, Christopher, *The Force of Poetry* (Oxford: Oxford University Press, 1984).

Ricks, Christopher, *Dylan's Visions of Sin* (London: Penguin, 2003).

Ricoeur, Paul, *The Rule of Metaphor: Multi-disciplinary studies of the creation of meaning in language*, trans. Robert Czerny (London: Routledge, 1986).

Røstvig, Maren-Sofie, 'Andrew Marvell and the Caroline Poets', in Christopher Ricks, ed., *Sphere History of Literature in the English Language*, vol. 2: *English Poetry and Prose, 1540–1674* (London: Sphere, 1970), pp. 206–48.

Said, Edward, *Orientalism* (London: Routledge & Kegan Paul, 1978).

Said, Edward, *Culture and Imperialism* (London: Chatto & Windus, 1993).

Saussure, Ferdinand de, *Course in General Linguistics*, trans. Wade Baskin (New York: McGraw-Hill, 1959).

Schmidt, Michael, ed., *A Reader's Guide to Fifty Modern British Poets* (London: Heinemann, 1979).

Scholes, Robert, *Elements of Poetry* (New York: Oxford University Press, 1969).

Schwartzman, Adam, ed., *Ten South African Poets* (Manchester: Carcanet, 1999).

Selden, Raman, *A Reader's Guide to Contemporary Literary Theory* (Sussex: Harvester, 1985).

Selden, Raman, *Practising Theory and Reading Literature: An introduction* (Hemel Hempstead: Harvester Wheatsheaf, 1989).

Seward, Barbara, *The Symbolic Rose* (New York: Columbia University Press, 1960).

Shelley, P.B., *Shelley's Poetry and Prose*, ed. S. Reiman and J. Powers (New York: Norton, 1977).

Showalter, Elaine, *A Literature of Their Own* (Princeton, NJ: Princeton University Press, 1977).

Sidney, Sir Philip, *The Prose Works of Sir Philip Sidney*, vol. III, ed. A. Feuillerat (Cambridge: Cambridge University Press, 1962).

Simpson, David, *Irony and Authority in Romantic Poetry* (London: Macmillan, 1979).

Smith, Barbara Herrnstein, *Poetic Closure: A study of how poems end* (Chicago: University of Chicago Press, 1968).

Smith, Barbara Herrnstein, *On the Margins of Discourse* (Chicago: University of Chicago Press, 1978).

Spiller, Michael, *The Development of the Sonnet* (London: Routledge, 1992).

Spivak, Gayatri Chakravorty, *In Other Worlds: Essays in Cultural Politics* (London: Routledge, 1988).

Stanley, Lawrence A., ed., *Rap: The lyrics* (Harmondsworth: Penguin, 1992).

States, B.O., *Irony and Drama: A poetics* (Ithaca, NY: Cornell University Press, 1971).

Stauffer, Donald, *A Short History of American Poetry* (New York: Dutton, 1974).

Still, Judith and M. Worton, eds, *Intertextuality: Theories and practices* (Manchester: Manchester University Press, 1990).

Stillinger, Jack, ed., *John Keats: Poetry Manuscripts at Harvard* (Cambridge, MA. and London: Belknap Press of Harvard University Press, 1990).

Stone, Brian, *The Poetry of Keats* (Harmondsworth: Penguin, 1992).

Strachan, John and Richard Terry, *Poetry* (Edinburgh: Edinburgh University Press, 2000).

Strand, Mark and Eavan Boland, *The Making of a Poem: A Norton Anthology of Poetic Forms* (New York and London: Norton, 2000).

Su, Soon Peng, *Lexical Ambiguity in Poetry* (London: Longman, 1994).

Suleiman, Susan and I. Crossman, eds, *The Reader in the Text* (Princeton, NJ: Princeton University Press, 1980).

Thiong'o, Ngugi wa, *Decolonising the Mind: The Politics of Language in African Literature* (Oxford: James Currey, 1986).

Todorov, Tzvetan, *Genres in Discourse*, trans. Catherine Porter (Cambridge: Cambridge University Press, 1990).

Urban, W.M., *Language and Reality: the philosophy of language and the principles of symbolism* (New York: G. Allen & Unwin, 1939).

Verdonk, Peter, ed., *Twentieth-Century Poetry: From text to context* (London: Routledge, 1993).

Vinson, James, ed., *Contemporary Poets*, 3rd edn (London: Macmillan, 1980).

Volosinov, V.N., *Marxism and the Philosophy of Language*, trans. L. Matejka and I. R. Titunik (New York: Seminar Press, 1973).

Wainwright, Jeffrey, *Poetry: The Basics* (London: Routledge, 2004).

Walcott, Derek, *Collected Poems, 1948–1984* (New York and Toronto: Harper & Collins, 1986).

Walcott, Derek, *Omeros* (New York: Farrar, Strauss & Giroux; London: Faber & Faber, 1990).

Walder, Dennis, *Post-Colonial Literatures in English: History, Language, Theory* (Oxford: Blackwell, 1998).

Wallace, John M., *Destiny His Choice: The loyalism of Andrew Marvell* (Cambridge: Cambridge University Press, 1968).

Wellek, René and Austin Warren, *Theory of Literature* (Harmondsworth: Penguin, 1949, repr. 1985).

Widdowson, H.G., *Stylistics and the Teaching of Literature* (London: Longman, 1975).

Wilding, Michael, *Dragon's Teeth: Literature in the English Revolution* (Oxford: Clarendon Press, 1987).

Williams, F.N., *Penguin Dictionary of English and European History, 1485–1789* (Harmondsworth: Penguin, 1980).

Williams, Patrick and Laura Chrisman, eds, *Colonial Discourse and Postcolonial Theory: A Reader* (New York: Harvester Wheatsheaf, 1993).

Williams, Raymond, *Keywords: A vocabulary of culture and society* (London: Fontana, 1983).

Williams, Raymond, *Culture and Society: Coleridge to Orwell* (London: Hogarth, 1987).

Wimsatt, W.K., *The Verbal Icon: Studies in the meaning of poetry* (Kentucky: University of Kentucky Press, 1954).

Wimsatt, W.K. and M.C. Beardsley, 'The intentional fallacy', *Sewanee Review* 54 (1946), reprinted in Wimsatt, *The Verbal Icon*, pp. 3–18.

Wimsatt, W.K. and C. Brooks, *Literary Criticism: A short history* (London: Routledge, 1965).

Woolf, Virginia, *A Room of One's Own* (London: Grafton, 1977).

Wordsworth, William, *The Lyrical Ballads*, ed. R.L. Brett and A.R. Jones (London: Methuen, 1968).

Wordsworth, William, *Home at Grasmere*, in *The Cornell Wordsworth*, ed. Beth Darlington (Ithaca, NY: Cornell University Press, 1977).

Wordsworth, William, *Selected Prose*, ed. John O. Hayden (Harmondsworth: Penguin, 1988).

Young, Robert J.C., *Colonial Desire: Hybridity in Theory, Culture and Race* (London: Routledge, 1995).

Zabel, M.D., ed., *Literary Opinion in America*, 3rd edn (New York: Harper, 1962).

Index